# QuickBooks® 2023

# 2023

## ALL-IN-ONE

### by Stephen L. Nelson, MBA, CPA, MS in Taxation

with Christian Block, CPA

for
dummies®

A Wiley Brand

## QuickBooks® 2023 All-in-One For Dummies®

Published by: **John Wiley & Sons, Inc.**, 111 River Street, Hoboken, NJ 07030-5774, www.wiley.com

Copyright © 2023 by John Wiley & Sons, Inc., Hoboken, New Jersey

Published simultaneously in Canada

For general information on our other products and services, please contact our Customer Care Department within the U.S. at 877-762-2974, outside the U.S. at 317-572-3993, or fax 317-572-4002. For technical support, please visit https://hub.wiley.com/community/support/dummies.

Wiley publishes in a variety of print and electronic formats and by print-on-demand. Some material included with standard print versions of this book may not be included in e-books or in print-on-demand. If this book refers to media such as a CD or DVD that is not included in the version you purchased, you may download this material at http://booksupport.wiley.com. For more information about Wiley products, visit www.wiley.com.

Library of Congress Control Number: 2022946385

ISBN: 978-1-119-90613-1 (pbk); 978-1-119-90615-5 (ebk); 978-1-119-90614-8 (ebk)

SKY10036757_101222

# Contents at a Glance

# Table of Contents

# Introduction

Few people read introductions to reference books, so I'll make this brief. I just want to tell you which versions of QuickBooks this book works for, what's in the reference, what it assumes about your existing skills, and what conventions I use.

## About This Book

The desktop version of QuickBooks comes in several flavors, including QuickBooks Pro, QuickBooks Premier, and QuickBooks Enterprise Solutions. This reference talks about QuickBooks 21 Enterprise Solutions, which is a superset of QuickBooks 2023 Premier and QuickBooks 2023 Pro. If you're using QuickBooks Self-Employed or QuickBooks Online, you shouldn't use this book. Instead, you should check out *QuickBooks Online For Dummies, 2023 Edition* by David Ringstrom.

On the other hand, even though this book is written for QuickBooks Enterprise Solutions, if you're using QuickBooks Premier or QuickBooks Pro, don't worry. You're just fine with this book. And don't freak out if you're using some version of QuickBooks that's very similar to QuickBooks 2023, such as QuickBooks 2022 or QuickBooks 2021. Although this reference is about QuickBooks 2023, it also works just fine for the 2021, 2022, and probably 2024 versions of QuickBooks because QuickBooks is a very mature product at this point. The changes from one year to the next are modest. This means that if you're using QuickBooks 2022, stuff may look a little different if you closely compare the images in this book with what you see on your screen, but the information in this reference will still apply to your situation.

Note, too, that specialty versions of QuickBooks, such as QuickBooks Accountant's Edition and QuickBooks Contractor, also work almost identically to QuickBooks Premier.

**TIP**

If you use QuickBooks Pro and see some whistle or bell that you really want to use but that isn't available in your version of QuickBooks, you'll know that you should upgrade to the Premier or Enterprise Solutions version of QuickBooks.

**REMEMBER**

The bottom line? Yes, QuickBooks comes in several flavors. Yes, Intuit publishes new editions of its QuickBooks products every year. But you can use this book for any recent version of QuickBooks Pro, Premier, or Enterprise Solutions.

To make the best use of your time and energy, you should know about the conventions I use in this book:

>> When I want you to type something such as **Jennifer,** it's in bold letters.

>> By the way, except for passwords, you don't have to worry about the case of the stuff you type in QuickBooks. If I tell you to type Jennifer, you can type **JENNIFER**. Or you can follow poet e e cummings's lead and type **jennifer**.

>> Whenever I tell you to choose a command from a menu, I say something like Choose Lists ⇨ Items, which simply means to first choose the Lists menu and then choose Items. The ⇨ separates one part of the command from the next part.

>> You can choose menus and commands and select dialog box elements with the mouse. Just click the thing that you want to select.

>> While I'm on the subject of conventions, let me also mention something about QuickBooks conventions, because it turns out that there's really no good place to point this out: QuickBooks doesn't use document windows the same way that other Windows programs do. Instead, it locks the active window into place and then displays a list of windows in its Navigator pane, which is like another little window. To move to a listed window, you click it.

**TIP**

You can tell QuickBooks to use windows like every other program does, however, by choosing View ⇨ Multiple Windows. You can even remove the Navigator pane by choosing View ⇨ Open Window List.

# Foolish Assumptions

I'm making only three assumptions about your QuickBooks and accounting skills:

>> You have a PC with Windows 7, Windows 8, or Windows 10. (I took pictures of the QuickBooks windows and dialog boxes in Windows 10, in case you're interested.)

>> You know a little bit about how to work with your computer.

» You have, or will buy, a copy of QuickBooks Pro, QuickBooks Premier, or QuickBooks Enterprise Solutions for each computer on which you want to run the program.

In other words, I don't assume that you're a computer genius or an MBA, or that you're super-experienced in the arcane rules of accounting. I assume that QuickBooks and accounting are new subjects to you. But I also assume that you want to understand the subjects because you need to do so for your job or your business.

TIP

Note that I wrote this book in 2022 for the 2023 version of QuickBooks. QuickBooks automatically adds a time stamp of the date on which I enter transactions into the system. Consequently, in some screen shots, you can see that I entered the transactions into QuickBooks in 2022, even though the transaction dates for my examples are in 2023. I hope you don't find this situation too confusing; there's just no way I can work around it.

# Icons Used in This Book

Like many computer books, this book uses icons, or little pictures, to flag things that don't quite fit into the flow of things.

WARNING

The Warning icon tells you to watch out! It marks important information that may save you headaches when using QuickBooks 2023.

REMEMBER

Remember icons mark the information that's especially important to know. To siphon off the most important information in each chapter, skim these icons.

TIP

The Tip icon marks tips (duh!) and shortcuts that you can use to make QuickBooks easier.

TECHNICAL
STUFF

The Technical Stuff icon marks information of a highly technical nature that you normally can skip.

# Beyond the Book

*QuickBooks 2023 All-in-One For Dummies* includes some extra content that you bought with your book but didn't get inside the book. This extra, premium stuff is available online:

>> The Cheat Sheet for this book is at www.dummies.com.

   In the Search field, type **QuickBooks 2023 All-in-One For Dummies Cheat Sheet** to find the Cheat Sheet for this book.

>> Updates to this book, if there are any, are also at www.dummies.com. Search for the book's title to find the associated updates.

# Where to Go from Here

This reference combines eight short books, including a book about accounting, one about setting up the QuickBooks system, one for bookkeepers using QuickBooks, one for accountants and managers using QuickBooks, a book about small-business financial management, a book about business planning, a book about taking care of a QuickBooks accounting system, and a book of appendixes of useful information.

If you have a specific question about what's covered or where some topic is covered, refer to the table of contents in the front of this reference. Also remember that the book provides an index to help you find just the pages that have the information you need.

While I'm on the subject of what's in this book and how to find information, let me make four tangential points:

>> You'll never read this book from cover to cover unless you're someone who has an obsessive-compulsive personality (like me) and many hours to devote to reading. But that's okay. This reference isn't meant to be read from cover to cover like some Val McDermid page-turner. Instead, chapters within the eight books are organized into largely self-contained descriptions of how you do the things that you need to do. You just read the paragraph, page, or chapter that provides the information you want.

>> I haven't discussed in any detail how to use the QuickBooks Premier and QuickBooks Enterprise Solutions features for business planning. The wizard-based approach that QuickBooks Premier and QuickBooks Enterprise

Solutions provide for business planning is not, in my humble opinion, the right way. Instead, I discuss in detail alternative, superior approaches to business planning and budgeting (using spreadsheets) in Book 6. (Just so you know: The approach I describe and recommend here is the same one that any business school teaches its students.)

>> At a few points in the book, you'll find me saying things like "Well, I really don't think you should use this part of the product." I just want to explain here, up front, where I'm coming from. First, know that I think QuickBooks is an outstanding product, but not every feature or command is good. I've mentioned that the new business planning tools aren't ones that I can recommend. And payroll, very frankly, is another pain-in-the-butt feature that most businesses should avoid. (I do briefly discuss payroll in Book 3, Chapter 5.) So if I think that a particular feature is one that you shouldn't use, I don't take up page space (or much page space) describing the feature. I'd rather use that space to describe other stuff that I believe is valuable to you and other readers.

>> I should also mention one final thing: Accounting software programs require you to do a certain amount of preparation before you can use them to get real work done. If you haven't started to use QuickBooks yet, I recommend that you skim Book 1 and then read Book 2 to find out what you need to do first.

# 1

# An Accounting Primer

# Contents at a Glance

» **Taking a look at common financial statements**

» **Understanding the philosophy of accounting**

» **Discovering income tax accounting and reporting**

# Chapter **1**

# Principles of Accounting

Any discussion of how to use QuickBooks to manage your business better begins with a discussion of the basics of accounting. For this reason, in this chapter and the next two, I attempt to provide the same information that you'd receive in an introductory college accounting course. I tailor the entire discussion, of course, to QuickBooks and the small-business environment. What you'll read about here and in the next two chapters of this book pretty much describes how accounting works in a small-business setting when you're using QuickBooks.

If you've had some experience with accounting, if you know how to read an income statement and balance sheet, or if you know how to construct a journal entry, you don't need to read this chapter or the next ones. But if you're new to accounting and business bookkeeping, take the time to read this chapter carefully. I start by giving you a high-level overview of the purpose of accounting. Then I review the common financial statements that any accounting system worth its salt produces. I also discuss some of the important principles of accounting and the philosophy of accounting. Finally, I talk a little bit about income tax law and tax accounting.

# The Purpose of Accounting

In the movie *Creator,* Peter O'Toole plays an eccentric professor. At one point, O'Toole's character attempts to talk a young student into working as an unpaid research assistant. When the student protests, noting that he needs 15 credit hours, O'Toole creates a special 15-credit independent-study course named "Introduction to the Big Picture." In the next section, I describe the "big picture" of accounting. At its core, accounting makes perfect, logical sense.

## The big picture

The most important thing to understand about accounting is that it provides financial information to stakeholders. *Stakeholders* are the people who do business with or interact with a firm; they include managers, employees, investors, banks, vendors, government authorities, and agencies that may tax a firm. Stakeholders and their information requirements deserve a bit more discussion. Why? Because the information needs of these stakeholders determine what an accounting system must do.

## Managers, investors, and entrepreneurs

The first category of stakeholders includes the firm's managers, investors, and entrepreneurs. This group needs financial information to determine whether a business is making money. This group also wants any information that gives insight into whether a business is growing or contracting and how healthy or sick it is. To fulfill its obligations and duties, this group often needs detailed information. A manager or entrepreneur may want to know which customers are particularly profitable — or unprofitable. An active investor may want to know which product lines are growing or contracting.

A related set of information requirements concerns asset and liability record keeping. An *asset* is something that the firm owns, such as cash, inventory, or equipment. A *liability* is some debt or obligation that the firm owes, such as bank loans and accounts payable.

Obviously, someone at a firm — perhaps a manager, bookkeeper, or accountant — needs to have very detailed records of the amount of cash that the firm has in its bank accounts, the inventory that the firm has in its warehouse or on its shelves, and the equipment that the firm owns and uses in its operations.

If you look over the preceding two or three paragraphs, nothing I've said is particularly surprising. It makes sense, right? Someone who works in a business, manages a business, or actively invests in a business needs good general information about the financial affairs of the firm and, in many cases, very detailed information about important assets (such as cash) and liabilities (such as bank loans).

# External creditors

A second category of stakeholders includes outside firms that lend money to a business and credit-reporting agencies that supply information to these lenders. Banks want to know about the financial affairs and financial condition of a firm before lending money, for example. The accounting system needs to produce the financial information that a bank requires to consider a loan request.

What information do lenders want? Lenders want to know that a business is profitable and enjoys a positive cash flow. Profits and positive cash flows allow a business to repay debt easily. A bank or other lender also wants to see assets that could be liquidated, in a worst-case scenario, to pay a loan — and other debts that may represent a claim on the firm's assets.

Vendors also typically require financial information from a firm. A vendor often lends money to a firm by extending trade credit. What's noteworthy about this fact is that vendors sometimes require special accounting. One category of vendors that a company such as John Wiley & Sons, Inc., deals with is its authors. To pay an author the royalty that they're entitled to, Wiley puts in a fair amount of work to calculate royalty-per-unit amounts and then reports and remits these amounts to each author.

Other firms sometimes have similar financial reporting requirements for vendors. Franchisees (such as the person who owns and operates the local McDonald's) pay a franchise fee based on revenue. Retailers may perform special accounting and reporting to enjoy rebates and incentives from the manufacturers of the products that they sell.

# Government agencies

Predictable stakeholders that require financial information from a business also include the federal and state government agencies that have jurisdiction over the firm. Every business in the United States needs to report on its revenue, expenses, and profits so that it can correctly calculate income tax due to the federal government (and often, the state government too) and then pay that tax.

Firms with employees must also report to the federal and state governments on wages paid to those employees and pay payroll taxes based on metrics, such as number of employees, wages paid to employees, and unemployment benefits claimed by past employees.

Providing this sort of financial information to government agencies represents a key duty of a firm's accounting system.

## Business form generation

In addition to the financial reporting described in the preceding paragraphs, accounting systems typically perform a key task for businesses: producing business forms. An accounting system almost always produces the checks needed to pay vendors, for example. In addition, an accounting system prepares the invoices and payroll checks. More sophisticated accounting systems, such as those used by large firms, prepare many other business forms, including purchase orders, monthly customer statements, credit memos to customers, and sales receipts.

TIP

Every accounting function that I've described so far is performed ably by each version of QuickBooks: QuickBooks Simple Start, QuickBooks Pro, QuickBooks Premier, and QuickBooks Enterprise.

# Reviewing the Common Financial Statements

With the background information just provided, I'm ready to talk about some of the common financial statements or accounting reports that an accounting system like QuickBooks produces. If you understand which reports you want your accounting system to produce, you should find it much easier to collect the raw data necessary to prepare these reports.

In the following sections, I describe the three principal financial statements: the income statement, the balance sheet, and the statement of cash flows. I also briefly describe a fourth, catch-all category: accounting reports.

Don't worry — I go through this material slowly. You need to understand what financial statements your accounting systems are supposed to provide and what data these financial statements supply.

# The income statement

Perhaps the most important financial statement that an accounting system produces is the income statement, also known as a profit and loss statement. An *income statement* summarizes a firm's revenue and expenses for a particular period. *Revenue* represents amounts that a business earns by providing goods and services to its customers. *Expenses* represent amounts that a firm spends providing those goods and services. If a business can provide goods or services to customers for revenue that exceeds its expenses, the firm earns a profit. If expenses exceed revenue, obviously, the firm suffers a loss.

To show you how all this works — and it's really pretty simple — take a look at Tables 1-1 and 1-2. Table 1-1 summarizes the sales that an imaginary business enjoys. Table 1-2 summarizes the expenses that the same business incurs for the same period. These two tables provide all the information necessary to construct an income statement.

**TABLE 1-1** **A Sales Journal**

| | |
|---|---|
| Joe | $1,000 |
| Bob | 500 |
| Frank | 1,000 |
| Abdul | 2,000 |
| Yoshio | 2,750 |
| Marie | 2,250 |
| Jeremy | 1,000 |
| Chang | 2,500 |
| *Total Sales* | *$13,000* |

Using the information from Tables 1-1 and 1-2, you can construct the simple income statement shown in Table 1-3. Understanding the details of an income statement is key to understanding how accounting works and what accounting tries to do. Therefore, I want to go into some detail in discussing this income statement.

The first thing to note about the income statement shown in Table 1-3 is the sales revenue figure of $13,000. This figure shows the sales generated for a particular period. The $13,000 figure shown in Table 1-3 comes directly from the sales journal shown in Table 1-1.

**TABLE 1-2**

## An Expenses Journal

| | |
|---|---|
| Purchases of hot dogs and buns | $3,000 |
| Rent | 1,000 |
| Wages | 4,000 |
| Supplies | 1,000 |
| **Total Expenses** | **$9,000** |

**TABLE 1-3**

## Simple Income Statement

| | |
|---|---|
| Sales revenue | $13,000 |
| Less: Cost of goods sold | 3,000 |
| **Gross Margin** | **$10,000** |
| **Operating Expenses** | |
| Rent | $1,000 |
| Wages | 4,000 |
| Supplies | 1,000 |
| **Total Operating Expenses** | **6,000** |
| **Operating Profit** | **$4,000** |

One important thing to recognize about accounting for sales revenue is that revenue gets counted when goods or services are provided, not when a customer pays for the goods or services. If you look at the list of sales shown in Table 1-1, for example, Joe (the first customer listed) may have paid $1,000 in cash, but Bob, Frank, and Abdul (the second, third, and fourth customers) may have paid for their purchases with a credit card. Yoshio, Marie, Jeremy, and Chang (the fifth through eighth customers listed) may not have even paid for their purchases at the time the goods or services were provided. These customers may simply have promised to pay for the purchases at some later date. The timing of payment for goods or services doesn't matter, however. Accountants have figured out that you count revenue when goods or services are provided. Information about when customers pay for those goods or services, if you want that information, can come from lists of customer payments.

*Cost of goods sold* and *gross margins* are two other values that you commonly see in income statements. Before I discuss cost of goods sold and gross margins, however, let me add a little more detail to this example. Suppose that the financial information in Tables 1-1, 1-2, and 1-3 shows the financial results from your business: the hot dog stand that you operate for one day at the major sporting event in the city where you live. Table 1-1 describes sales to hungry customers. Table 1-2 summarizes the one-day expenses of operating your super-duper hot dog stand.

In this case, the actual items that you sell — hot dogs and buns — are shown separately in the income statement as cost of goods sold. By separately showing the cost of the goods sold, the income statement can show what is called a gross margin. The *gross margin* is the amount of revenue left over after paying for the cost of goods. In Table 1-3, the cost of goods sold equals $3,000 for purchases of dogs and buns. The difference between the $13,000 of sales revenue and the $3,000 of cost of goods sold equals $10,000, which is the gross margin.

TIP

Knowing how to calculate gross margin allows you to estimate firm break-even points and to perform profit, volume, and cost analyses. All these techniques are extremely useful for thinking about the financial affairs of your business. In fact, Book 6, Chapter 1 describes how you can perform these analyses.

The *operating expenses* portion of the simple income statement shown in Table 1-3 repeats the other information listed in the expenses journal. The $1,000 of rent, the $4,000 of wages, and the $1,000 of supplies get totaled. Then these operating expenses are subtracted from the gross.

Do you see, then, what an income statement does? An income statement reports on the revenue that a firm has generated. It shows the cost of goods sold and calculates the gross margin. It identifies and shows operating expenses, and finally shows the profits of the business.

One other important point: Income statements summarize revenue, expenses, and profits for a particular period. Some managers and entrepreneurs, for example, may want to prepare income statements on a daily basis. Public companies are required to prepare income statements on a quarterly and annual basis. And taxing authorities, such as the Internal Revenue Service (IRS), require tax return preparation both quarterly and annually.

TIP

Technically speaking, the quarterly statements required by the IRS don't need to report revenue. The IRS requires quarterly statements only of wages paid to employees. Only the annual income statements required by the IRS report both revenue and expenses. These income statements are produced to prepare an annual income tax return.

# Balance sheet

The second-most-important financial statement that an accounting system produces is a balance sheet. A *balance sheet* reports on a business's assets, liabilities, and owner contributions of capital at a particular point in time:

>> **The *assets*** shown in a balance sheet are items that are owned by the business, which have value and for which money was paid.

>> **The *liabilities*** shown in a balance sheet are amounts that a business owes to other people, businesses, and government agencies.

>> **The *owner contributions of capital*** are the amounts that owners, partners, or shareholders have paid into the business in the form of investment or have reinvested in the business by leaving profits inside the company.

As long as you understand what assets and liabilities are, a balance sheet is easy to understand and interpret. Table 1-4, for example, shows a simple balance sheet. Pretend that this balance sheet shows the condition of the hot dog stand at the beginning of the day, before any hot dogs have been sold. The first portion of the balance sheet shows and totals the two assets of the business: the $1,000 cash in the cash register in a box under the counter and the $3,000 worth of hot dogs and buns that you've purchased to sell during the day.

**TABLE 1-4**

## A Simple Balance Sheet

| Assets | |
| --- | --- |
| Cash | $1,000 |
| Inventory | 3,000 |
| Total assets | $4,000 |
| **Liabilities** | |
| Accounts payable | $2,000 |
| Loan payable | 1,000 |
| **Owner's Equity** | |
| S. Nelson, capital | $1,000 |
| *Total Liabilities and Owner's Equity* | $4,000 |

TIP

Balance sheets can use several other categories to report assets: accounts receivable (amounts that customers owe), investments, fixtures, equipment, and long-term investments. In the case of a small owner-operated business, not all these asset categories show up. But if you look at the balance sheet of a very large business — say, one of the 100 largest businesses in the United States — you see these other categories.

The liabilities section of the balance sheet shows the amounts that the firm owes to other people and businesses. The balance sheet in Table 1-4 shows $2,000 of accounts payable and a $1,000 loan payable. Presumably, the $2,000 of accounts payable is the money that you owe to the vendors who supplied your hot dogs and buns. The $1,000 loan payable represents some loan you've taken out — perhaps from some well-meaning and naive relative.

The owner's equity section shows the amount that the owner, the partners, or shareholders have contributed to the business in the form of original funds invested or profits reinvested. One important point about the balance sheet shown in Table 1-4: This balance sheet shows how owner's equity looks when the business is a sole proprietorship. In the case of a sole proprietor, only one line is reported in the owner's equity section of the balance sheet. This line combines all contributions made by the proprietor — both amounts originally invested and amounts reinvested.

I talk a bit more about owner's equity accounting later in this chapter because the owner's equity sections look different for partnerships and corporations. Before I get into that discussion, however, let me make two important observations about the balance sheet shown in Table 1-4:

>> **A balance sheet needs to *balance*.** This means that the total assets must equal the total liabilities and owner's equity. In the balance sheet shown in Table 1-4, for example, total assets show as $4,000. Total liabilities and owner's equity also show as $4,000. This equality is no coincidence. If an accounting system works right, and the accountants and bookkeepers entering information into this system do their jobs right, the balance sheet balances.

>> **A balance sheet provides a snapshot of a business's financial condition at a particular point in time.** I mention in the introductory remarks related to Table 1-4 that the balance sheet in this table shows the financial condition of the business immediately before the day's business activities begin.

REMEMBER

You can prepare a balance sheet for any point in time. It's key that you understand that a balance sheet is prepared for a particular point in time.

By convention, businesses prepare balance sheets to show the financial condition at the end of the period of time for which an income statement is prepared. A business typically prepares an income statement on an annual basis. In this orthodox situation, a firm also prepares a balance sheet at the very end of the year.

At this point, I return to something that I allude to earlier in the chapter: the fact that the owner's equity section of a balance sheet looks different for different types of businesses.

Table 1-5 shows how the owner's equity section of a balance sheet looks for a partnership. In Table 1-5, I show how the owner's equity section of the business appears if, instead of having a sole proprietor named S. Nelson running the hot dog stand, the business is actually owned and operated by three partners named Tom, Maria, and Amani. In this case, the partners' equity section shows the amounts originally invested and any amounts reinvested by the partners. As is the case with sole proprietorships, each partner's contributions and reinvested profits appear on a single line.

**TABLE 1-5**      **Owner's Equity for a Partnership**

| Partners' Equity | |
| --- | --- |
| Tom, capital | $500 |
| Maria, capital | 250 |
| Amani, capital | 250 |
| **Total Partner Capital** | **$1,000** |

Take a look at Table 1-6, which shows how the owner's equity section looks for a corporation.

**TABLE 1-6**      **Owner's Equity for a Corporation**

| Shareholders' Equity | |
| --- | --- |
| Capital stock, 100 shares at $1 par | $100 |
| Contributed capital in excess of par | 400 |
| Retained earnings | 500 |
| **Total Shareholders' Equity** | **$1,000** |

This next part is a little bit weird. For a corporation, the amounts that appear in the owner's equity or shareholders' equity section actually fall into two major categories: retained earnings and contributed capital. *Retained earnings* represent profits that the shareholders have left in the business. *Contributed capital* is the money originally contributed by the shareholders to the corporation.

The retained-earnings thing makes sense, right? That's just the money — the profits — that investors have reinvested in the business.

The contributed-capital thing is more complicated. Here's how it works. If you buy a share of stock in some new corporation — for, say, $5 — typically, some portion of that price per share is for par value. Now, don't ask me to justify par value. It stems from business practices that were common a century or more ago. Just trust that typically, if you pay some amount — again, say $5 — for a share, some portion of the amount that you pay — maybe 10 cents a share or $1 a share — is for par value.

In the owner's equity section of a corporation's balance sheet, capital that's contributed by original investors is broken down into the amounts paid for this mysterious par value and the amounts paid in excess of this par value. In Table 1-6, you can see that $100 of shareholders' equity or owner's equity represents amounts paid for par value. Another $400 of the amounts contributed by the original investors represents amounts paid in excess of par value. The total shareholders' equity, or total corporate owner's equity, equals the sum of the capital stock par value, the contributed capital and excess of par value, and any retained earnings. So in Table 1-6, total shareholders' equity equals $1,000.

## Statement of cash flows

Now I come to the one tricky financial statement: the statement of cash flows.

**WARNING**

Before I begin, I have one comment to make about the statement of cash flows. As an accountant, I've worked with many bright managers and businesspeople. No matter how much hand-holding and explanation I (or other accountants) provide, some of these smart people never quite get some of the numbers on the statement of cash flows. In fact, many of the students who major in accounting never (in my opinion, at least) quite understand how a statement of cash flows really works.

For this reason, don't spend *too* much time spinning your wheels on this statement or trying to understand what it does. QuickBooks does supply a statement of cash flows, but you don't need to use it. In fact, QuickBooks produces cash-basis income statements, which give you almost the same information — and in a format that's easier to understand.

I think the best way to explain what a statement of cash flows does is to ask you to look again at the balance sheet shown in Table 1-4 earlier in this chapter. This table is the balance sheet for the imaginary hot dog stand at the beginning of the day.

Now take a look at Table 1-7, which shows the balance sheet at the end of the day, after operations for the hot dog stand have ended. Notice that at the start of the day (see Table 1-4), cash equals $1,000, and at the end of the day (see Table 1-7), cash equals $5,000. The statement of cash flows explains why cash changes from the one number to the other number over a period of time. In other words, a statement of cash flows explains how cash goes from $1,000 at the start of the day to $5,000 at the end of the day.

**TABLE 1-7**     ## Another Simple Balance Sheet

| Assets | |
| --- | --- |
| Cash | $5,000 |
| Inventory | 0 |
| Total assets | $5,000 |
| **Liabilities** | |
| Accounts payable | $0 |
| Loan payable | 0 |
| **Owner's Equity** | |
| S. Nelson, capital | $5,000 |
| *Total Liabilities and Owner's Equity* | *$5,000* |

Table 1-8, not coincidentally, shows a statement of cash flows that explains how cash flowed for your imaginary business. If you're reading this book, presumably you need to understand this statement. I start at the bottom of the statement and work up.

**REMEMBER**

By convention, accountants show negative numbers inside parentheses. These parentheses flag negative values more clearly than a simple minus sign can.

The last three lines of the statement of cash flows are all easy to understand. The cash balance at the end of the period, $5,000, shows what cash the business holds at the end of the day. The cash balance at the start of the period, $1,000, shows the cash that the business holds at the beginning of the day. Both the cash balance at the start of the period and the cash balance at the end of the period tie to the cash-balance values reported in the two balance sheets. (Look at Table 1-4 and Table 1-7 to corroborate this assertion.) Clearly, if you start the period with $1,000 and end the period with $5,000, cash has increased by $4,000. That's an arithmetical certainty. No question there, right?

**TABLE 1-8**

## A Simple Statement of Cash Flows

| Operating Activities | |
|---|---|
| Net income | $4,000 |
| Decrease in accounts payable | (2,000) |
| Adjustment: Decrease in inventory | 3,000 |
| Net cash provided by operating activities | $5,000 |
| Financing Activities | |
| Decrease in notes payable | (1,000) |
| Net cash provided (used) by financing activities | (1,000) |
| Increase in cash | $4,000 |
| Cash balance at start of period | 1,000 |
| Cash balance at end of period | $5,000 |

The financing activities of the statement of cash flows show how firm borrowing and firm debt repayment affect the firm cash flow. If the business uses its profits to repay the $1,000 loan payable — which is what happened — this $1,000 cash outflow shows up in the financing activities portion of the statement of cash flows as a negative $1,000.

The top portion of the statement of cash flows is often the trickiest to understand. Note, however, that I've talked about everything else in this statement. So with a strong push, you can fight your way through to understanding what's going on here. The operating activities portion of the statement of cash flows essentially shows the cash that comes from the profit. If you look at Table 1-8, for example, you see that the first line in the operating activities portion of the statement of cash flows is net income of $4,000. This is the net income amount reported on the income statement for the period. The net income or operating profit reported in the business's income statement, however, isn't necessarily the same thing as cash income or cash profit. A variety of factors must be adjusted to convert this net income amount to what's essentially a cash amount of operating profit.

In the case of the hot dog stand business, if you use some of the profits to pay off all the accounts payable, this payoff uses up some of your cash profit. This is exactly what Table 1-8 shows. You can see that the decrease in the accounts payable from $2,000 to $0 over the day required, quite logically, $2,000 of the net income. Another way to think about this is that essentially, you used up $2,000 of your cash profits to pay off accounts payable. Remember that the accounts payable is the amount that you owed your vendors for hot dogs and buns.

Another adjustment is required for the decrease in inventory. The decrease in inventory from the start of the period to the end of the period produces cash. Basically, you're liquidating inventory. Another way to think about this is that although this inventory — the hot dogs and buns, in this example — shows up as an expense for the day's income statement, it isn't purchased during the day. It doesn't consume cash during the day; it was purchased at some point in the past.

When you combine the net income, the accounts payable adjustment, and the inventory adjustment, you get the net cash provided by the operating activities. In Table 1-8, these three amounts combine for $5,000 of cash provided by the operations.

After you understand the details of the financing and operating activities areas of the statement of cash flows, the statement makes sense. Net cash provided by the operating activities equals $5,000. Financing activities reduce cash by $1,000. This means that cash actually increased over the period by $4,000, which explains why cash starts the period at $1,000 and ends the period at $5,000.

## Other accounting statements

You can probably come up with examples of several other popular or useful accounting reports. Not surprisingly, a good accounting system such as Quick-Books produces most of these reports. One very common report or financial statement, for example, is a list of the amounts that your customers owe you. It's a good idea to prepare and review such reports on a regular basis to make sure that you don't have customers turning into collection problems.

Table 1-9 shows how the simplest sort of accounts receivable report may look. Each customer is named along with the amount owed.

Table 1-10 shows another common accounting report: an inventory report that the hot dog stand may have at the start of the day. An inventory report like the one shown in Table 1-10 probably would name the various items held for resale, the quantity held, and the amount or value of the inventory item. A report such as this one is useful for making sure that you have the appropriate quantities of inventory in stock. (Think of how useful such a report would be if you really *were* planning to sell thousands of hot dogs at major sporting events in your hometown.)

**TABLE 1-9**

## An Accounts Receivable Report at End of Day

| Customer | Amount |
|---|---|
| W. Churchill | $45.12 |
| G. Patton | 34.32 |
| B. Montgomery | 12.34 |
| H. Petain | 65.87 |
| C. de Gaulle | 43.21 |
| *Total Receivables* | *$200.86* |

**TABLE 1-10**

## An Inventory Report at Start of Day

| Item | Quantity | Amount |
|---|---|---|
| Kielbasa | 2,000 | $900.00 |
| Bratwurst | 2,000 | 1,000.00 |
| Plain buns | 2,000 | 500.00 |
| Sesame buns | 2,000 | 600.00 |
| *Total Inventory* | | *$3,000.00* |

## Putting it all together

By now, you should understand what an accounting system does. When you boil everything down to its essence, it's straightforward, isn't it? Really, an accounting system just provides you the financial information that you need to run your business.

Let me add a tangential but important point: QuickBooks supplies all this accounting information. For the most part, preparing these sorts of financial statements in QuickBooks is pretty darn easy. But first, you'll find it helpful to know a bit more about accounting and bookkeeping. I go over that information in the coming chapters. Also, note that the big-picture stuff covered in this chapter is the most important knowledge that you need. If you understand the ideas described in this chapter, the battle is more than half won.

# CURIOUS ABOUT DIFFERENT BUSINESS FORMS?

Are you curious about the differences among a sole proprietorship, a partnership, and a corporation? A *sole proprietorship* is formed automatically in most states and in most industries when an individual decides to go into business. In many jurisdictions, the sole proprietor needs to acquire or apply for a business license from the state or local city government. Other than clearing that modest hurdle, sole proprietorship requires no special prerequisites.

A *partnership* is formed automatically when two or more people enter into a joint business or investment activity for the purpose of making a profit. As is the case with a sole proprietorship, partnerships typically need to acquire a business license from the state and perhaps the federal government. Partnership formation doesn't necessarily require any additional paperwork or legal maneuvering. If you do enter into a partnership, however, most attorneys (probably all attorneys) will tell you that you do so at a certain amount of risk if you don't have an attorney draw up a partnership agreement that outlines the duties, rights, and responsibilities of the partners. Also be aware that you can form a partnership simply by collaborating in business with someone. The law books are full of stories of people who inadvertently created partnerships merely by collaborating on some project, sharing office space, or working together on some activity.

By comparison, most states allow several other business forms, including *corporations, limited liability companies,* and *limited liability partnerships.* These other business forms sometimes require considerably more work to set up, sometimes the assistance of a good attorney or accountant, and sometimes payment of several hundred — possibly several thousand — dollars in legal and licensing fees. The unique feature of most of these other business forms is that the corporation, limited liability company, or limited liability partnership becomes a separate legal entity. In many cases, this separate legal entity protects investors from creditors that have a claim on the assets of the business. By comparison, in a sole proprietorship or a partnership, the sole proprietor and the partners are liable for the debts and obligations of the proprietorship or the partnership.

If you have questions about the correct business form in which to operate, talk with a good local attorney or accountant. They can assist you in choosing the appropriate business form and in considering both the legal and tax aspects of choosing a particular form. As a general rule, more-sophisticated business forms such as corporations, limited liability companies, and limited liability partnerships deliver significant legal and tax benefits to investors and managers. Unfortunately, these more-sophisticated business forms also require considerably more legal and accounting fiddle-faddling.

# The Philosophy of Accounting

Maybe the phrase *philosophy of accounting* is too strong, but accounting does rest on a rather small set of fundamental assumptions and principles. People often refer to these fundamentals as *generally accepted accounting principles.*

I want to quickly summarize what these principles are. I find — and I bet you'll find the same thing — that understanding the principles provides context and makes accounting practices more understandable. With this in mind, let me go through the half dozen or so key accounting principles and assumptions.

These basic accounting principles underlie business accounting. These principles and assumptions are implicit in all the discussions in this entire book. It's no exaggeration to say that they permeate almost everything related to business accounting.

## Revenue principle

The *revenue principle,* also known as the *realization principle,* states that revenue is earned when the sale is made. Typically, the sale is made when goods or services are provided. A key component of the revenue principle, when it comes to the sale of goods, is that revenue is earned when legal ownership of the goods passes from seller to buyer.

Note that revenue isn't earned when you collect cash for something. It turns out, perhaps counterintuitively, that counting revenue when cash is collected doesn't give the business owner a good idea of what sales really are. Some customers may pay deposits early, before actually receiving the goods or services. Often, customers want to use trade credit, paying a firm at some point in the future for goods or services. Because cash flows can fluctuate wildly — even something like a delay in the mail can affect cash flow — you don't want to use cash collection from customers as a measure of sales. Besides, you can easily track cash collections from customers. So why not have the extra information about when sales actually occur?

## Expense principle

The *expense principle* states that an expense occurs when the business uses goods or receives services. In other words, the expense principle is the flip side of the revenue principle. As is the case with the revenue principle, if you receive some goods, simply receiving the goods means that you've incurred the expense of the goods. Similarly, if you've received some service — services from your lawyer, for example — you've incurred the expense. It doesn't matter that your lawyer takes a few days or a few weeks to send you the bill. You incur an expense when goods or services are received.

## Matching principle

The *matching principle* is related to the revenue and expense principles. The matching principle states that when you recognize revenue, you should match related expenses with the revenue. The best example of the matching principle concerns the case of businesses that resell inventory. In the example of the hot dog stand, you should count the expense of a hot dog and the expense of a bun on the day when you sell that hot dog and that bun. Don't count the expense when you buy the buns and the dogs; count the expense when you sell them. In other words, match the expense of the item with the revenue of the item.

TIP

*Accrual-based accounting*, which is a term you've probably heard, is what you get when you apply the revenue principle, the expense principle, and the matching principle. In a nutshell, accrual-based accounting means that you record revenue when a sale is made and record expenses when goods are used or services are received.

## Cost principle

The *cost principle* states that amounts in your accounting system should be quantified, or measured, by using historical cost. If you have a business, and the business owns a building, that building — according to the cost principle — shows up on your balance sheet at its historical cost. You don't adjust the values in an accounting system for changes in a fair market value. You use the original historical costs.

TIP

I should admit that the cost principle is occasionally violated in a couple of ways. The cost principle is adjusted through the application of depreciation, which I discuss in Book 1, Chapter 3. Also, fair market values are sometimes used to value assets, but only when assets are worth less than they cost.

## Objectivity principle

The *objectivity principle* states that accounting measurements and accounting reports should use objective, factual, and verifiable data. In other words, accountants, accounting systems, and accounting reports should rely on subjectivity as little as possible.

An accountant always wants to use objective data (even if it's bad) rather than subjective data (even if the subjective data is arguably better). The idea is that objectivity provides protection from the corrupting influence that subjectivity can introduce into a firm's accounting records.

## Continuity assumption

The *continuity assumption* — accountants call it an *assumption* rather than a *principle* for reasons unknown to me — states that accounting systems assume that a business will continue to operate. The importance of the continuity assumption becomes clear if you consider the ramifications of assuming that a business won't continue. If a business won't continue, it becomes very unclear how one should value assets if the assets have no resale value. This sounds like gobbledygook, but think about the implicit continuity assumption built in to the balance sheet for the hot dog stand at the beginning of the day. (This is the balance sheet that shows up in Table 1-4 earlier in this chapter.)

Implicit in that balance sheet is the assumption that hot dogs and hot dog buns have some value because they can be sold. If a business won't continue operations, no assurance exists that any of the inventory can be sold. If the inventory can't be sold, what does that say about the owner's equity value shown in the balance sheet?

You can see, I hope, the sorts of accounting problems that you get into without the assumption that the business will continue to operate.

## Unit-of-measure assumption

The *unit-of-measure assumption* assumes that a business's domestic currency is the appropriate unit of measure for the business to use in its accounting. In other words, the unit-of-measure assumption states that it's okay for U.S. businesses to use U.S. dollars in their accounting, and it's okay for UK businesses to use pounds sterling as the unit of measure in their accounting system. The unit-of-measure assumption also states, implicitly, that even though inflation and occasionally deflation change the purchasing power of the unit of measure used in the accounting system, that's still okay. Sure, inflation and deflation foul up some of the numbers in a firm's financial statements. But the unit-of-measure assumption says that's usually okay — especially in light of the fact that no better alternatives exist.

## Separate-entity assumption

The *separate-entity assumption* states that a business entity, like a sole proprietorship, is a separate entity — a separate thing from its business owner. Also, the separate-entity assumption says that a partnership is a separate thing from the partners who own part of the business. This assumption, therefore, enables one to prepare financial statements just for the sole proprietorship or just for the partnership. As a result, the separate-entity assumption also relies on a business to be separate, distinct, and definable compared with its business owners.

# A Few Words about Tax Accounting

I'm not going to talk much about tax accounting or tax preparation in this book, but one key reason why you do accounting and use a program such as QuickBooks is to make your tax accounting easier. That's obvious. So a fair question is this: How does what I've said so far relate to income tax return preparation?

This question is a tough one to answer. Tax laws typically don't map to generally accepted accounting principles. Generally accepted accounting principles aren't the same things as income tax laws. If you use good basic accounting practices as you operate QuickBooks, however, you get financial information that you can use to easily prepare your tax returns, especially if you get some help from your certified public accountant (CPA).

If you want, you can also use income tax rules to fine-tune your accounting and bookkeeping. This practice, which is technically known as an *other comprehensive basis of accounting (OCBOA)*, is generally considered to be an appropriate way to perform accounting for small and medium-size enterprises.

» Grasping how double-entry bookkeeping works

» Looking at an (almost) real-life example

» Figuring out how QuickBooks helps

# Chapter **2**

# Double-Entry Bookkeeping

The preceding chapter describes why businesses create financial statements and how these financial statements can be used. If you've read Book 1, Chapter 1, or if you've spent much time managing a business, you probably know what you need to know about financial statements. In truth, financial statements are pretty straightforward. An income statement, for example, shows a firm's revenue, expenses, and profits. A balance sheet itemizes a firm's assets, liabilities, and owner's equity. So far, so good.

Unfortunately, preparing traditional financial statements is more complicated and tedious. The work of preparing financial statements — called *accounting* or *bookkeeping* — requires either a whole bunch of fiddle-faddling with numbers or learning how to use double-entry bookkeeping.

In this chapter, I start by describing the fiddle-faddle method. This isn't because I think you should use that method. In fact, I assume that you eventually want to use QuickBooks for your accounting and, by extension, for double-entry bookkeeping. But if you understand the fiddle-faddle method, you'll clearly see why double-entry bookkeeping is so much better.

After I describe the fiddle-faddle method, I walk you through the steps to using and understanding double-entry bookkeeping. After you see all the anguish and grief that the fiddle-faddle method causes, you should have no trouble appreciating why double-entry bookkeeping works so much better. And I hope you'll also commit to the 30 or 40 minutes necessary to learn the basics of double-entry bookkeeping.

# The Fiddle-Faddle Method of Accounting

Most small businesses — or at least those small businesses whose owners aren't already trained in accounting — have used the fiddle-faddle method. Take a peek at the financial statements shown in Tables 2-1 and 2-2. If you've read or reviewed Book 1, Chapter 1, you may recognize that these financial statements stem from the imaginary hot dog stand. Table 2-1 shows the income statement for the one day a year that the imaginary business operates. Table 2-2 shows the balance sheet at the start of the first day of operation.

**TABLE 2-1**  **A Simple Income Statement for the Hot Dog Stand**

| Sales Revenue | $13,000 |
|---|---|
| Less: Cost of goods sold | 3,000 |
| Gross margin | $10,000 |
| Operating Expenses | |
| Rent | $1,000 |
| Wages | 4,000 |
| Supplies | 1,000 |
| *Total Operating Expenses* | *6,000* |
| *Operating Profit* | *$4,000* |

With the fiddle-faddle method of accounting, you individually calculate each number shown in the financial statement. The sales revenue figure shown in Table 2-1, for example, equals $13,000. The fiddle-faddle method of accounting requires you to somehow come up with this sales revenue number manually. You may be able to come up with this number by remembering each of the sales that you made during the day. Or, if you prepare invoices or sales receipts, you may be able to come up with this number by adding all the individual sales. If you have a cash register, you may be able to come up with this number by looking at the cash register tape.

**TABLE 2-2**

## A Simple Balance Sheet for the Hot Dog Stand

| Assets | |
|---|---|
| Cash | $1,000 |
| Inventory | 3,000 |
| Total assets | $4,000 |
| **Liabilities** | |
| Accounts payable | $2,000 |
| Loan payable | 1,000 |
| **Owner's Equity** | |
| S. Nelson, capital | $1,000 |
| *Total Liabilities and Owner's Equity* | *$4,000* |

Other revenue and expense numbers get calculated in the same crude manner. The $1,000 of rent expense, for example, gets calculated by remembering what amount you paid for rent or by looking in your checkbook register and finding the check that you wrote for rent.

The balance sheet values get produced in roughly the same way. You can deduce the cash balance of $1,000, for example, by looking at the checkbook or, in a worst-case scenario, the bank statement. You can deduce the inventory balance of $3,000 by adding the individual inventory item values. You can calculate the liability and owner's equity amounts in similar fashion.

Some of the values shown in an income statement or on a balance sheet get *plugged* — meaning that they're calculated by using other numbers from the financial statement. You don't look up the profit amount in any particular place; instead, you calculate profit by subtracting expenses from revenue. You can also calculate balance sheet values such as total assets, owner's equity, and total liabilities, of course.

Okay, I admit it: The fiddle-faddle method of accounting works reasonably well for a very small business as long as you have a good checkbook. So for a very small business, you may be able to get away with this crude, piecemeal approach to accounting.

Unfortunately, the fiddle–faddle method suffers the three horrible weaknesses for a firm that doesn't have super–simple finances:

>> **It's not systematic enough to be automated.** Now, admittedly, you may not care that the fiddle-faddle approach isn't systematic enough for automation. But this point is an important one: A systematic approach like double-entry bookkeeping can be automated, as you can do with QuickBooks. This automation means that the task of preparing financial statements requires — oh, I don't know — maybe five mouse clicks. Because the fiddle-faddle approach can't be automated, every time you want to produce financial statements, you or some poor co-worker must do an enormous amount of work to collect the numbers and all the raw data necessary to produce information like that shown in Table 2-1 and Table 2-2. In reality, of course, with more complicated financial statements, someone does much, much more work.

>> **It's very easy to lose details.** This sounds abstract, but let me give you a good, concrete example. If you look at Table 2-1, you see that the hot dog stand incurs only three operating expenses: rent, wages, and supplies. If you know the operating expense categories that the business incurs, it's fairly easy to look through the check register and find the check or checks that pay rent, for example. You can use a similar approach with the wages and supplies expenses. But what if you also have an advertising expense category, a business license expense, or some other easy-to-forget category? If you forget a category, you miss expenses. If you forget that you spent money advertising and, thereby, forget to tally your advertising expenses, that whole category of operating expense gets omitted from your income statement.

>> **It doesn't allow rigorous error checking.** This business about error checking may seem to be nitpicky, but error checking is important with accounting and bookkeeping systems. With all the numbers and transactions floating around, errors easily creep into the system. I discuss error checking more later in this chapter, but let me give you an example of the sort of error checking an accounting system can (and should) perform. Take a look at the example of the sales transaction. If you sell an item for $1,000, you can check that amount by comparing it with your record of what the customer paid. This makes sense, right? If you sell me an item for $1,000, you should be able to compare that $1,000 sale with the amount of cash that I pay you. A $1,000 sale to me should correspond to a $1,000 cash payment from me. The fiddle-faddle method can't make these comparisons, but double-entry bookkeeping can.

You see where I am now, right? I've admitted that you can construct financial statements by using the fiddle-faddle method. But I hope I've also convinced you that the fiddle-faddle method suffers some really debilitating weaknesses. I'm talking about something as important as how you can best manage the financial affairs of your business. These weaknesses indicate that you need a better tool. Specifically, you need double-entry bookkeeping, which I discuss next.

# How Double-Entry Bookkeeping Works

After you conclude that the fiddle-faddle method is for the birds, you're ready to absorb the necessary accounting theory and learn the bookkeeping tricks required to employ double-entry bookkeeping. Essentially, you need two things to work with double-entry bookkeeping: an understanding of the accounting model and a grasp of the mechanics of debits and credits. Neither of these things is difficult. If you flip ahead a few pages, you can see that I'm going to spend only a few pages talking about this material. How difficult can anything be that can be described in just a few pages? Not very, right?

## The accounting model

Here's the first thing to understand and internalize to use double-entry book-keeping: Modern accounting uses an accounting model that says assets equal liabilities plus owner's equity. The following formula expresses this in a more conventional, algebraic form:

```
assets = liabilities + owner's equity
```

If you think about this for a moment and flip back to Table 2-2, you see that this formula summarizes the organization of a business's balance sheet. Conceptually, the formula says that a business owns stuff and that the money or the funds for that stuff comes either from creditors (such as the bank or some vendor) or the owners (either in the form of original contributed capital or perhaps in reinvested profits). If you understand the balance sheet shown in Table 2-2 and discussed here, you understand the first core principle of double-entry bookkeeping. This isn't that tough so far, is it?

Here's the second thing to understand about the basic accounting model: Revenue increases owner's equity, and expenses decrease owner's equity. Think about that for a minute. That makes intuitive sense. If you receive $1,000 in cash from a customer, you have $1,000 more in the business. If you write a $1,000 check to pay a bill, you have $1,000 less in the business.

Another way to say the same thing is that profits clearly add to owner's equity. Profits get reinvested in the business and boost owner's equity. Profits are calculated as the difference between revenue and expenses. If revenue exceeds expenses, profits exist.

Let me review where I am so far in this discussion about the basic accounting model. The basic model says that assets equal liabilities plus owner's equity. In other words, the total assets of a firm equal the total of its liabilities and owner's equity. Furthermore, revenue increases owner's equity, and expenses decrease owner's equity.

At this point, you don't have to intuitively understand the logic of the accounting model and the way that revenue and expenses plug into the owner's equity of the model. If you do get it, that's great but not necessary. But you do need to memorize or remember (for at least the next few paragraphs) the manner in which the basic model works.

REMEMBER

This point may seem to be redundant, but note that a balance sheet is constructed by using information about a firm's assets, liabilities, and owner's equity. Similarly, note that a firm's income statement is constructed by using information about its revenue and its expenses. All this discussion — all this tediousness — is really about how you collect the information necessary to produce an income statement and a balance sheet.

Now I come to perhaps the most important point to understand to get double-entry bookkeeping. Every transaction and every economic event that occurs in the life of a firm produces two effects: an increase in some account shown in the balance sheet or income statement and a decrease in some account shown in the balance sheet or income statement. When something happens, economically speaking, that something affects at least two types of information shown in the financial statement. In the next few paragraphs, I give you some examples so that you can really understand this concept.

Suppose that in your business, you sell $1,000 worth of an item for $1,000 in cash. In the case of this transaction or economic event, two things occur from the perspective of your financial statements:

>> Your cash increases by $1,000.

>> Your sales revenue increases by $1,000.

Another way to say this same thing is that your $1,000 cash sale affects both your balance sheet (because cash increases) and your income statement (because sales revenue is earned).

See the duality? And just a paragraph ago, you were thinking that this topic might be too complicated for you, weren't you?

Here's another common example. Suppose that you buy $1,000 worth of inventory for cash. In this case, you decrease your cash balance by $1,000, but you increase your inventory balance by $1,000. Note that in this case, both effects of the transaction appear in sort of the same area of your financial statement: the list of assets. Nevertheless, this transaction also affects two accounts.

TIP

When I use the word *account,* I simply mean some value that appears in your income statement or on your balance sheet. If you look at Tables 2-1 and 2-2, for example, any value that appears in those financial statements that isn't simply a calculation represents an account. In essence, an account tracks some group of assets, liabilities, owner's equity, contributions, revenue, or expenses. I talk more about accounts in the next section, where I get to the actual mechanics of double-entry bookkeeping.

Here's another example that shows this duality of effects in an economic event. Suppose that you spend $1,000 in cash on advertising. In this case, this economic event reduces cash by $1,000 and increases the advertising expense amount by $1,000. This economic event affects both the assets portion of the balance sheet and the operating expenses portion of the income statement.

And now — believe it or not — you're ready to see how the mechanics of double-entry bookkeeping work.

## Talking mechanics

Roughly 500 years ago, an Italian monk named Luca Pacioli devised a systematic approach to keeping track of the increases and decreases in account balances. He said that increases in asset and expense accounts should be called *debits,* whereas decreases in asset and expense accounts should be called *credits.* He also said that increases in liabilities, owner's equity, and revenue accounts should be called credits, whereas decreases in liabilities, owner's equity, and revenue accounts should be called debits.

Table 2-3 summarizes the information that I just shared. Unfortunately — and you can't get around this fact — you need to memorize this table or dog-ear the page so that you can refer to it easily.

In Pacioli's debits-and-credits system, any transaction can be described as a set of balancing debits and credits. This system not only works as financial shorthand, but also provides error checking. To get a better idea of how it works, look at some simple examples.

TABLE 2-3

## You Must Remember This

| Account | Debit | Credit |
|---|---|---|
| Assets | Increase | Decrease |
| Expenses | Increase | Decrease |
| Liabilities | Decrease | Increase |
| Owner's equity | Decrease | Increase |
| Revenue | Decrease | Increase |

Take the case of a $1,000 cash sale. By using Pacioli's system or by using double-entry bookkeeping, you can record this transaction as shown here:

| Cash | $1,000 | Debit |
|---|---|---|
| Sales revenue | $1,000 | Credit |

See how that works? The $1,000 cash sale appears as both a debit to cash (which means an increase in cash) and a $1,000 credit to sales (which means a $1,000 increase in sales revenue). Debits equal credits, and that's no accident. The accounting model and Pacioli's assignment of debits and credits mean that any correctly recorded transaction balances. For a correctly recorded transaction, the transaction's debits equal the transaction's credits.

Although you can show transactions as I've just shown the $1,000 cash sale, you and I may just as well use the more orthodox nomenclature. By convention, accountants and bookkeepers show transactions, or what accountants and bookkeepers call journal entries, like the one shown in Table 2-4.

TABLE 2-4

## Journal Entry 1: Recording the Cash Sale

| Account | Debit | Credit |
|---|---|---|
| Cash | $1,000 | |
| Sales revenue | | $1,000 |

See how that works? Each account that's affected by a transaction appears on a separate line. Debits appear in the left column. Credits appear in the right column.

TIP

You actually already understand how this account business works if you have a checkbook. You use it to keep track of both the balance in your checking account and the transactions that change the checking account balance. The rules of double-entry bookkeeping essentially say that you're going to use a similar record-keeping system not only for your cash account, but also for every other account you need to prepare your financial statements.

Here are a couple of other examples of how this transaction recording works. In the first part of this discussion of how double-entry bookkeeping works, I describe two other transactions: purchasing $1,000 of inventory for cash and spending $1,000 in cash on advertising. Table 2-5 shows how the purchase of $1,000 of inventory for cash appears. Table 2-6 shows how spending $1,000 of cash on advertising appears.

## THAT DARN BANK

When I learned about double-entry bookkeeping, I stumbled over the terms *debit* and *credit*. The way I'd heard the terms used before didn't agree with the way that double-entry bookkeeping seemed to describe them. This conflict caused a certain amount of confusion for me. Because I don't want you to suffer the same fate, let me quickly describe my initial confusion.

If you look at Table 2-3, you see that an increase in an asset account is a debit, and a decrease in an asset account is a credit. This means that in the case of your cash account, increases to cash are debits and decreases to cash are credits.

At some time, however, you've undoubtedly talked to the bank and heard someone refer to crediting your bank account — which meant increasing the account balance. And perhaps that someone talked about debiting your account — which meant decreasing the account balance. So what's up with that? Am I wrong, and is the bank right?

Actually, both the bank and I are right. Here's why. The bank is talking about debiting and crediting — not a cash account and not an asset account, but a *liability account*. To the bank, the money that you've placed in the account isn't cash (an asset) but a liability (money that the bank owes you). If you look at Table 2-3, you see that increases in a liability are credit amounts and decreases in a liability are debit amounts. Therefore, from the bank's perspective, when the bank increases the balance in your account, that increase is a credit.

Your assets may represent another firm's liabilities. Your liabilities will represent another firm's assets. Therefore, whenever you hear some other business talking about crediting or debiting your account, what you do is exactly the opposite. If the business credits, you debit. If the business debits, you credit.

TABLE 2-5

## Journal Entry 2: Recording the Inventory Purchase

| Account | Debit | Credit |
|---------|-------|--------|
| Inventory | $1,000 | |
| Cash | | $1,000 |

TABLE 2-6

## Journal Entry 3: Recording the Advertising Expense

| Account | Debit | Credit |
|---------|-------|--------|
| Advertising | $1,000 | |
| Cash | | $1,000 |

By tallying the debits and credits to an account, you can calculate the account balance. Suppose that before Journal Entries 1, 2, and 3, the cash balance equals $2,000. Journal Entry 1 increases cash by $1,000 (the debit). Journal Entries 2 and 3 decrease cash by $1,000 each (the $2,000 credits). If you combine all these entries, you get the new account balance. The following formula shows the calculation:

| | |
|---|---|
| **Beginning Cash Balance** | **$2,000** |
| Plus cash debit from Journal Entry 1 | $1,000 |
| Minus cash credit from Journal Entry 2 | –$1,000 |
| Minus cash credit from Journal Entry 3 | –$1,000 |
| *Ending Cash Balance* | *$1,000* |

Do you see how that works? You start with $2,000 as the cash account balance. The first cash debit of $1,000 increases the cash balance to $3,000, and then the cash credit of $1,000 in Journal Entry 2 decreases the cash balance to $2,000. Finally, the cash credit of $1,000 in Journal Entry 3 decreases the cash balance to $1,000.

You can calculate the account balance for any account by taking the starting account balance and then adding the debits and credits that have occurred since then. By hand, this arithmetic is a little unwieldy. Your computer (with the help of QuickBooks) does this math easily.

# Almost a Real-Life Example

To cement the concepts that I talk about in the preceding paragraphs of this chapter, I want to quickly step through the journal entries, or bookkeeping transactions, that you'd record in the case of the hot dog stand discussed in Book 1, Chapter 1. To start, you need to know that the balance sheet shown in Table 2-2 is the balance sheet at the start of the day, which means that the account balances in all the accounts appear as shown in Table 2-7. This list of account balances is called a *trial balance.* It shows the debit or credit balance for each account.

**TABLE 2-7**

### A Trial Balance at the Start of the Day

| Account | Debit | Credit |
|---|---|---|
| Cash | $1,000 | |
| Inventory | 3,000 | |
| Accounts payable | | $2,000 |
| Loan payable | | 1,000 |
| S. Nelson, capital | ___ | 1,000 |
| *Totals* | *$4,000* | *$4,000* |

I'm assuming that no year-to-date revenue or expenses exist yet for the hot dog stand. In other words, the operation is at a starting period.

**REMEMBER**

You may want to take a quick peek at Table 2-1, shown earlier. It summarizes the business activities of the hot dog stand. The journal entries that follow show how the information necessary for this statement would be recorded.

**TIP**

## Recording rent expense

Suppose that the first transaction to record is a $1,000 check written to pay rent. In this case, the journal entry appears as shown in Table 2-8. In this example, $1,000 is debited to rent expense, and $1,000 is credited to cash.

## Recording wages expense

If you need to record $4,000 of wages expense, you use the journal entry shown in Table 2-9. This journal entry debits wages expense for $4,000 and credits cash for $4,000. In other words, you use $4,000 of cash to pay wages for the business.

TABLE 2-8

## Journal Entry 4: Recording the Rent Expense

| Account | Debit | Credit |
|---------|-------|--------|
| Rent | $1,000 | |
| Cash | | $1,000 |

TABLE 2-9

## Journal Entry 5: Recording the Wages Expense

| Account | Debit | Credit |
|---------|-------|--------|
| Wages expense | $4,000 | |
| Cash | | $4,000 |

## Recording supplies expense

To record $1,000 of supplies expense paid for by writing a check, you record the journal entry shown in Table 2-10. This transaction debits supplies expense for $1,000 and credits cash for $1,000.

TABLE 2-10

## Journal Entry 6: Recording the Supplies Expense

| Account | Debit | Credit |
|---------|-------|--------|
| Supplies | $1,000 | |
| Cash | | $1,000 |

TIP

Note that for each of the preceding transactions, debits equal credits. As long as debits equal credits, you know that the transaction is in balance. This balance is one of the ways that double-entry bookkeeping prevents errors.

## Recording sales revenue

Suppose that you sell $13,000 worth of hot dogs. To record this transaction in a journal entry, you debit cash for $13,000 and credit sales revenue for $13,000, as shown in Table 2-11. I should tell you, however, that in the case of the hot dog stand selling hot dogs for a dollar or two apiece, you wouldn't necessarily use a single journal entry to record sales revenue amounts. Though you could use a single journal entry that tallied the entire day's sales, if you're selling hot dogs at a dollar a dog, you could also record 13,000 $1 transactions. Each of these $1 transactions debits cash for $1 and credits sales revenue for $1.

**TABLE 2-11**

## Journal Entry 7: Recording the Sales Revenue

| Account | Debit | Credit |
|---|---|---|
| Cash | $13,000 | |
| Sales revenue | | $13,000 |

# Recording cost of goods sold

You must record the expense of the hot dogs and buns that you sell. You must also record the fact that if you use up your inventory of hot dogs and buns, your inventory balance has decreased. Table 2-12 shows how you record these items. Cost of goods sold gets debited for $3,000, and inventory gets credited for $3,000.

**TABLE 2-12**

## Journal Entry 8: Recording the Cost of Goods Sold

| Account | Debit | Credit |
|---|---|---|
| Cost of goods sold | $3,000 | |
| Inventory | | $3,000 |

If you're confused about this cost-of-goods-sold transaction — it represents the first transaction that doesn't use cash — read Book 1, Chapter 1, where I describe the two accounting principles. In short, these two principles are as follows:

>> **Expense principle:** Expense is counted when the item gets sold. This means that the inventory isn't counted as cost of goods sold or as an expense when it's purchased. Rather, the expense of each hot dog and bun you sell gets counted when the item is actually sold to somebody.

>> **Matching principle:** Expense or cost of a sale is matched with the revenue of the sale. This means that you recognize the cost of goods sold at the same time that you recognize the sale. Typically, in fact, you can combine Journal Entries 7 and 8.

TIP

Another way to think about the information recorded in Journal Entry 8 is this: Rather than spend cash to provide customers hot dogs and buns, you spend inventory.

# Recording the payoff of accounts payable

Suppose that one thing you do at the end of the day is write a check to pay off the accounts payable. The *accounts payable* are the amounts that you owe vendors — probably the suppliers from which you purchased the hot dogs and buns. To record the payoff of accounts payable, you debit accounts payable for $2,000 and credit cash for $2,000, as shown in Table 2-13.

TABLE 2-13

**Journal Entry 9: Recording the Payoff of Accounts Payable**

| Account | Debit | Credit |
|---|---|---|
| Accounts payable | $2,000 | |
| Cash | | $2,000 |

## Recording the payoff of a loan

Suppose also that you use cash profits from the day to pay off the $1,000 loan that the balance sheet shows (refer to Table 2-2 earlier in this chapter). To record this transaction, you debit loan payable for $1,000 and credit cash for $1,000, as shown in Table 2-14.

TABLE 2-14

**Journal Entry 10: Recording the Payoff of the Loan**

| Account | Debit | Credit |
|---|---|---|
| Loan payable | $1,000 | |
| Cash | | $1,000 |

## Calculating account balance

You may already be able to guess that if you know an account's starting balance and have a way to add up the debits and the credits to the account, you can easily calculate the ending account balance.

Take the case of the cash account balance of the hot dog stand. If you look at the balance sheet shown in Table 2-2, you see that the beginning balance for cash is $1,000. You can easily construct a little schedule of how the account balance changes — this schedule is called a *T-account* — that calculates the ending balance. (In case you're wondering, a T-account is a visual aid to help in accounting. You start by drawing a big capital *T*, with debits on the left side and credits on the right side.) In fact, Table 2-15 does just this. If you look closely at Table 2-15, you see that the cash beginning balance is $1,000. Then, on the following lines of the

T-account, you see the effects of Journal Entries 4, 5, 6, 7, 9, and 10. Some of these journal entries credit cash. Some of them debit cash. You can calculate the ending cash balance by combining the debit and credit amounts.

The information shown in Table 2-15 should make sense to you. But in case you're still trying to memorize what debits and credits mean, I'm going to give you a bit more detail. To calculate the ending balance shown in Table 2-15, you add up the debits, add up the credits, and combine the two sums. The net amount in the cash account equals the $5,000 debit. If you recall from the preceding paragraphs, a debit balance in an asset account, such as cash, represents a positive amount. A $5,000 debit balance in the cash account, therefore, indicates that you have $5,000 of cash in the account.

**TABLE 2-15**

## A T-Account of the Cash Account

| | Debit | Credit |
|---|---|---|
| Beginning balance | $1,000 | |
| Journal Entry 4 | | $1,000 |
| Journal Entry 5 | | 4,000 |
| Journal Entry 6 | | 1,000 |
| Journal Entry 7 | 13,000 | |
| Journal Entry 9 | | 2,000 |
| Journal Entry 10 | ____ | $1,000 |
| Ending balance | $5,000 | |

Cash is usually the trickiest account to analyze with a T-account because so many journal entries affect cash. In many cases, however, a T-account analysis of an account balance is much more straightforward. If you look at Table 2-16, you see a T-account analysis of the inventory account. This T-account analysis shows that the beginning inventory account balance equals $3,000. But when Journal Entry 8 credits inventory for $3,000 — this is the journal entry that records the cost of goods sold — the inventory balance is wiped out.

Paying off the accounts payable and loan payable accounts is similarly straightforward. Table 2-17 shows the T-account analysis of the accounts payable account. Table 2-18 shows the T-account analysis of the loan payable account. In both cases, the T-account analysis shows that the liability accounts start with a credit beginning balance. (Remember that a liability account would have a credit balance if the firm really owed money.) Then, when the payments are recorded to pay off the accounts payable and loan payable in Journal Entries 9 and 10, the liability account is debited. The result, in the case of both accounts, is that the liability account balance is reduced to zero.

TABLE 2-16

### A T-Account of the Inventory Account

| | Debit | Credit |
|---|---|---|
| Beginning balance | $3,000 | |
| Journal Entry 8 | _____ | $3,000 |
| Ending balance | $0 | |

TABLE 2-17

### A T-Account of Accounts Payable

| | Debit | Credit |
|---|---|---|
| Beginning balance | | $2,000 |
| Journal Entry 9 | $2,000 | |
| Ending balance | $0 | |

TABLE 2-18

### A T-Account of the Loan Payable Account

| | Debit | Credit |
|---|---|---|
| Beginning balance | | $1,000 |
| Journal Entry 10 | $1,000 | |
| Ending balance | $0 | |

I'm not going to show T-account analyses of the other accounts that the preceding journal entries use. In every other case, the only debit or credit to the account comes from the journal entry, which means that the journal entry amount is the account balance. Only one journal entry affects the sales revenue account: Journal Entry 7, which credits sales revenue for $13,000. Because the sales revenue account has no beginning balance, that $13,000 credit equals the sales revenue account balance. The expense accounts work the same way.

## Using T-account analysis results

If you construct (or your accounting program constructs) T-accounts for each balance sheet and income statement account, you can easily calculate account balances at a particular point in time by using the T-account analysis results. Table 2-19 shows a trial balance at the end of the day for the hot dog stand. You can calculate each of these account balances by using T-account analysis.

**TABLE 2-19**

## A Trial Balance at End of Day

| Account | Debit | Credit |
|---|---|---|
| Cash | $5,000 | |
| Inventory | 0 | |
| Accounts payable | | $0 |
| Loan payable | | 0 |
| S. Nelson, capital | | $1,000 |
| Sales revenue | | 13,000 |
| Cost of goods sold | 3,000 | |
| Rent | 1,000 | |
| Wages expense | 4,000 | |
| Supplies | 1,000 | |
| **Totals** | **$14,000** | **$14,000** |

The first line shown in the trial balance in Table 2-19 is the cash account, with a debit balance of $5,000. This debit account balance comes from the T-account analysis shown in Table 2-15. The account balances for inventory, accounts payable, and loan payable also come from the T-account analyses shown previously in this chapter (Tables 2-16, 2-17, and 2-18).

**REMEMBER**

As I note in the preceding section, you don't need to perform T-account analyses for the other accounts shown in the trial balance provided in Table 2-19. These other accounts show a single debit or credit.

I need to make one final and perhaps already-obvious point: The information provided in Table 2-19 is the information necessary to construct an income statement for the day and a balance sheet as of the end of the day. If you take sales revenue, cost of goods sold, rent, wages expense, and supplies expense from the trial balance, you have all the information that you need to construct an income statement for the day. In fact, the information shown in Table 2-19 is the information used to construct the income statement shown in Table 2-1.

Similarly, the asset, liability, and owner's equity balance information shown in the trial balance provided in Table 2-19 supplies the information necessary to construct a balance sheet as of the end of the day.

**TIP**

The end-of-day balance sheet won't balance unless you also include the profits of the day. These profits, called *retained earnings*, are lumped into the owner's capital account and equal $4,000. You can see what this end-of-day balance sheet looks like by reading Book 1, Chapter 1. In that chapter, Table 1-9 shows the end-of-day balance sheet for the hot-dog-stand business.

# A Few Words about How QuickBooks Works

Before I end this chapter, I want to make a few comments about how QuickBooks helps you. First — and this point may be the most important one — QuickBooks makes most of these journal entries for you. In Journal Entry 6, for example, I show you how to record a $1,000 check written to pay supplies, but you'd never have to make this journal entry in QuickBooks. When you use QuickBooks to record a $1,000 check that pays Acme Supplies for some paper products that you purchased, QuickBooks automatically debits supplies expense (as long as you indicate that the check is for supplies) and then credits cash.

Similarly, in the case of Journal Entries 7 and 8, when you produce an invoice that records a sale, QuickBooks makes these journal entries for you. If you sold $13,000 worth of hot dogs and buns, and those hot dogs and buns actually cost you $3,000, QuickBooks debits cash for $13,000, credits sales revenue for $13,000, debits cost of goods sold for $3,000, and credits inventory for $3,000. In other words, for most of your routine transactions, QuickBooks handles the journal entries for you behind the scenes.

This doesn't mean, however, that you can always avoid working with journal entries. Any transaction that can't be handled through a standard QuickBooks form — such as the Invoice form or the Write Checks form — must be recorded by using a journal entry. If you purchase some fixed asset by writing a check, for example, the purchase of the fixed asset gets recorded automatically by QuickBooks. But the depreciation that will be used to expense the asset over its estimated economic life — something I talk a bit about in the next chapter — must be recorded with journal entries that you construct yourself and enter a different way.

One other really important point: I note in the preceding paragraphs that the trial balance information shown in Table 2-19 provides the raw data that you need to prepare your financial statement. I don't want to leave you with a misunderstanding, however: You don't have to use this sort of raw data to prepare your financial statements. Predictably, QuickBooks easily, quickly, and effortlessly builds your financial statements by using this trial balance information.

Just to put these comments together, then, QuickBooks automatically creates most journal entries for you, builds a trial balance by using journal entry information, and — when asked — produces financial statements. Most of the work of double-entry bookkeeping, then, goes on behind the scenes. You don't worry about many journal entries on a day-to-day basis. And if you don't want to ever see a trial balance, you don't have to. In fact, if you use QuickBooks only to produce invoices and to write checks that pay the bills, almost all the information that you need to prepare your financial statements gets collected automatically. So that's really neat.

**REMEMBER**

Not all the information that's necessary for producing good, accurate financial statements gets collected automatically. You'll encounter a handful of important cases that should be handled on a special basis through journal entries that you or your CPA must construct and enter.

**IN THIS CHAPTER**

» **Sorting out accounts receivable and accounts payable**

» **Keeping track of inventory**

» **Figuring out fixed assets**

» **Finding out about asset write-downs**

» **Recognizing liabilities**

» **Handling revenue and expense account closings**

# Chapter **3**

# Special Accounting Problems

E ven if you understand the principles of accounting (which I describe in Book 1, Chapter 1) and the basics of double-entry bookkeeping (which I describe in Book 1, Chapter 2), you still may not have all the information that you need to keep good records. Tracking the amounts that customers owe you and the amounts that you owe vendors can be a bit tricky, for example. Inventory can also present challenging record-keeping problems — a fact that's not surprising to you as a retailer. And things like fixed assets . . . oh, don't even get me started.

For these reasons, this chapter describes the most common complexities that business owners confront. You don't need to be an accountant or an experienced bookkeeper to understand the material in this chapter. You do need to proceed carefully, take your time, and think a bit about how the material I describe here applies to your specific business situation.

# Working with Accounts Receivable

If you read Book 1, Chapter 1, you already know that accounting principles state that sales revenue needs to be recognized when a sale is made and that the sale is made when a business provides goods or services to a customer.

In other words — and this point is really important — sales revenue doesn't get recorded when you receive payment from a customer. Sales revenue gets recorded when a customer has a legal obligation to pay you because you have (or your business has) provided the customer the goods or services.

## Recording a sale

This requirement to record sales revenue at the time that goods or services are provided means that accounting for sales revenue is slightly more complicated than you may have first guessed. The first transaction — the transaction that records a sale — is shown in Table 3-1.

**TABLE 3-1**

### Journal Entry 1: Recording a Credit Sale

| Account | Debit | Credit |
|---------|-------|--------|
| Accounts receivable | $1,000 | |
| Sales revenue | | $1,000 |

Journal Entry 1 shows how a $1,000 sale may be recorded. The journal entry shows a $1,000 debit to accounts receivable (sometimes abbreviated *A/R*) and a $1,000 credit to sales revenue. To record a $1,000 sale — a credit sale — the journal entry needs to show *both* the $1,000 increase in accounts receivable and the $1,000 increase in sales revenue.

## Recording a payment

When the business receives payment from the customer for the $1,000 receivable, the business records a journal entry like that shown in Table 3-2.

Journal Entry 2 shows a $1,000 debit to cash, which is the $1,000 increase in the cash account that occurs because the customer has just paid you $1,000. Journal Entry 2 also shows a $1,000 credit to accounts receivable. This credit to the accounts receivable asset account reduces the accounts receivable balance.

**TABLE 3-2**

## Journal Entry 2: Recording the Customer Payment

| Account | Debit | Credit |
|---|---|---|
| Cash | $1,000 | |
| Accounts receivable | | $1,000 |

At the point when you record Journal Entries 1 and 2, the net effect is a $1,000 debit to cash (showing that cash has increased by $1,000) and a $1,000 credit to sales revenue (showing that sales revenue has increased by $1,000). The $1,000 debit to accounts receivable and the $1,000 credit to accounts receivable net to zero.

If you think about this accounts receivable business a bit, you should realize that it makes sense. Although the accounts receivable account includes a $1,000 receivable balance, this just means that the customer owes you $1,000. But when the customer finally pays off the $1,000 bill, you need to zero out that receivable.

QuickBooks, by the way, automatically records Journal Entries 1 and 2 for you. Journal Entry 1 gets recorded whenever you issue or create a customer invoice. Therefore, you don't need to worry about the debits and credits shown in Journal Entry 1 except on one special occasion: When you set up QuickBooks and QuickBooks items, you do specify which account should be credited to track sales revenue. So although you may not need to worry much about the mechanics of Journal Entry 1, you should understand how this journal entry works so that you can set up QuickBooks correctly. (Book 2, Chapter 1 describes the mechanics of setting up QuickBooks.)

*Items* are things that get included in the invoices.

**REMEMBER** Journal Entry 2 also gets recorded automatically by QuickBooks. QuickBooks records Journal Entry 2 for you whenever you record a cash payment from a customer. You don't need to worry, then, about the debits and credits necessary for recording customer payments. I find that it's helpful, however, to understand how this journal entry works and how QuickBooks records this customer payment transaction.

## Estimating bad-debt expense

One other important journal entry to understand is shown in Table 3-3.

Journal Entry 3 records an estimate of the uncollectible portion of accounts receivable. (Businesses that don't want to keep accrual-based accounting statements may not need to worry about Journal Entry 3.) Unfortunately, some of the money you bill customers may be uncollectible. Yet Journal Entry 1 records every dollar that you bill your customers as revenue. Therefore, you need a way to offset, or reduce, some of the sales revenue by the amount that ultimately turns out to be uncollectible.

**TABLE 3-3**     **Journal Entry 3: Recording an Allowance for Uncollectible Accounts**

| Account | Debit | Credit |
|---|---|---|
| Bad-debt expense | $100 | |
| Allowance for uncollectible A/R | | $100 |

Journal Entry 3 shows a common way of doing this. This entry debits bad-debt expense — which is an expense account that you may use to record uncollectible customer receivables. Journal Entry 3 also credits another account shown as allowance for uncollectible A/R. This allowance account is called a *contra-asset* account, which means that it basically reduces the balance reported on the balance sheet of an asset account. In the case of the allowance for uncollectible A/R accounts, for example, this $100 credit reduces the accounts receivable balance shown in the balance sheet by $100.

Where the bad-debt expense shown in Journal Entry 3 appears varies from business to business. Some businesses report the bad-debt expense with the other sales revenue, thereby allowing the income statement to show net sales revenue; other businesses report it with the other operating expenses. You should report bad-debt expense wherever it makes most sense in terms of managing your business.

**REMEMBER**

QuickBooks doesn't automatically record the transaction in Journal Entry 3. You record estimates of bad-debt expense yourself by using the QuickBooks Make General Journal Entries command. You can find out more about these types of entries in Book 4, Chapter 1.

## Removing uncollectible accounts receivable

If you do set up an allowance for uncollectible accounts, you also need to remove the uncollectible accounts periodically from both the accounts receivable balance and the allowance for uncollectible accounts. You don't want to do this while any chance to collect on the accounts exists. But at some point, obviously, you may as well clean out the bad receivables from your records. It makes no sense, for example, to have uncollectible receivables from 17 years ago still appearing in your balance sheet. Table 3-4 illustrates how to clean out bad receivables.

**TABLE 3-4**

## Journal Entry 4: Writing Off an Uncollectible Receivable

| Account | Debit | Credit |
| --- | --- | --- |
| Allowance for uncollectible | $100 | |
| Accounts receivable | | $100 |

This journal entry debits the allowance from the uncollectible A/R account for $100. The journal entry also credits the accounts receivable account for $100. In combination, these two entries zero out the allowance for the uncollectible A/R account and remove the uncollectible amount from the accounts receivable account.

**TIP**

Writing off an actual, specific uncollectible receivable for invoice should be done on a case-by-case basis, which is what Journal Entry 4 shows.

None of these entries is particularly tricky as long as you understand the logic — something that I hope I've illuminated for you in this discussion. If you do have trouble with these journal entries or with recording the economic events that they attempt to summarize, you may want to consult your CPA. Most likely, you'd record these same transactions (with different customers and amounts, of course) many, many times over the year. If you can get a bit of help or a template that shows you how to record these transactions, you should be able to record them yourself without any outside help.

**TIP**

To write off an uncollectible account receivable, you record a credit memo and then apply the credit memo to the uncollectible account. The item shown in your credit memo should cause the allowance for uncollectible accounts to be debited.

# Recording Accounts Payable Transactions

Within QuickBooks, you have the option of working with or without an accounts payable account. If you want to, you can record expenses when you write checks. This means that to have a complete list of all your expenses, you must have recorded checks that pay all your expenses. This approach works fine — and, in fact, is the approach that I've always used in my businesses.

QuickBooks also supports a more precise approach of recording expenses. By answering a few questions during the QuickBooks setup process, you can set up an accounts payable account, which is an account that tracks the amounts that you owe your vendors and other suppliers.

# Recording a bill

When you use an accounts payable account, you enter the bills that you get from vendors when you receive them.

Table 3-5 shows the way this transaction is recorded. Journal Entry 5 automatically debits office-supplies expense for $1,000 and credits accounts payable for $1,000. QuickBooks would record this journal entry if you purchased $1,000 of office supplies and then entered that bill into the QuickBooks system.

**TABLE 3-5**

## Journal Entry 5: Recording a Credit Purchase

| Account | Debit | Credit |
|---|---|---|
| Office supplies | $1,000 | |
| Accounts payable | | $1,000 |

# Paying a bill

When you later pay that bill, QuickBooks records Journal Entry 6, shown in Table 3-6. In Journal Entry 6, QuickBooks debits accounts payable for $1,000 and credits cash for $1,000. The net effect on accounts payable combining both the purchase and the payment is zero. That makes sense, right? The approach shown in Journal Entries 5 and 6 counts the amount that you owe some vendor or supplier as a liability — accounts payable — only while you owe the money.

**TABLE 3-6**

## Journal Entry 6: Recording the Payment to Vendor

| Account | Debit | Credit |
|---|---|---|
| Accounts payable | $1,000 | |
| Cash | | $1,000 |

When you record Journal Entry 6 in QuickBooks, you must supply the name of the account that gets debited. QuickBooks obviously knows which account to credit: the accounts payable account. But QuickBooks also has to know the expense or asset account to debit.

QuickBooks does need to know which cash account to credit when you pay an accounts payable amount. You identify this account when you write the check to pay the bill.

## Taking some other accounts payable pointers

Let me make a couple of additional points about Journal Entries 5 and 6:

>> **The accounts payable method is more accurate.** The accounts payable method, which Journal Entries 5 and 6 show, is the best way to record your bills. The accounts payable method means that you record expenses when the expenses actually occur. As you may have already figured out, the accounts payable method is the mirror image of the accounts receivable approach described in the early paragraphs of this chapter. The accounts payable method, as you may intuit, delivers two big benefits: It keeps track of the amounts that you owe vendors and suppliers, and it recognizes expenses as they occur rather than when you pay them (which may be some time later).

>> **Not every debit is for an expense.** Journal Entry 5 shows the debit going to an office-supplies expense account. Many of the accounts payable that you record are amounts owed for expenses. Not every accounts payable transaction stems from incurring some expense, however. You may also need to record the purchase of an asset, such as a piece of equipment. In this case, the debit goes not to an expense account, but to an asset account. Except for this minor change, however, the transaction works the same way. I describe how fixed-asset accounting works later in this chapter, in the "Accounting for Fixed Assets" section.

TIP

Can you guess how an expense or fixed-asset purchase gets recorded if you don't use an accounts payable account? In the case in which you paid $1,000 for office supplies, QuickBooks debits office-supplies expense for $1,000 and credits cash for $1,000 when you write a $1,000 check. As part of writing the check, you identify which expense account to debit.

If you're purchasing a $1,000 piece of equipment, the journal entry looks and works roughly the same way. When you record the purchase, QuickBooks debits the asset account for $1,000 and credits cash for $1,000. Again, this transaction gets recorded when you write the check to pay for the asset.

# Inventory Accounting

Fortunately, most of the inventory accounting that goes on in a business gets handled automatically by QuickBooks. When you purchase an inventory item by writing a check or recording an accounts payable bill, for example, QuickBooks automatically adjusts your inventory accounts for both the dollar value of the inventory and the quantity of the items. When you sell an inventory item to a customer, QuickBooks again automatically adjusts the dollar value of your inventory and adjusts the quantity counts of the items you sell.

Basically, all this means is that QuickBooks maintains a *perpetual inventory system* — an inventory system that lets you know at any time what quantity of items you have in inventory and what value your inventory amounts to. (In the past, smaller firms often used a *periodic inventory* system, which meant that business owners never really knew with any precision the dollar value of their inventory or the quantity counts for the inventory items that they held.)

Although everything in the preceding paragraph represents good news, several inventory-related headaches do require a bit of accounting magic. Specifically, if your firm carries inventory, you need to know how to deal with obsolete inventory, disposal of obsolete inventory, and inventory shrinkage. I discuss all three accounting gambits in the following sections.

## Dealing with obsolete inventory

*Obsolete inventory* refers to items that you've purchased for sale but turn out not to be saleable. Perhaps customers no longer want it. Perhaps you have too much of the inventory item and will never be able to sell everything that you hold.

In either case, you record the fact that your inventory value is actually less than what you purchased it for. And you want to record the fact that really, the money you spent on the obsolete item is an expense. Suppose that you purchased some $100 item and now realize that it's obsolete. How do you record this obsolescence? Table 3-7 shows the conventional approach.

**TABLE 3-7**

### Journal Entry 7: Recording an Allowance for Obsolete Inventory

| Account | Debit | Credit |
| --- | --- | --- |
| Inventory obsolescence | $100 | |
| Allowance for obsolete inventory | | $100 |

As Journal Entry 7 shows, to record the obsolescence of a $100 inventory item, you first debit an expense account called something like "Inventory obsolescence" for $100. Then you credit a contra-asset account named something like "Allowance for obsolete inventory" for $100. As I mention in the discussion of accounts receivable, a contra-asset account gets reported on the balance sheet immediately below the asset account to which it relates. The contra-asset account, with its negative credit balance, reduces the net reported value of the asset account. If the inventory account balance is $3,100, and you have an allowance for an obsolete inventory contra-asset account of $100, the net inventory balance shows up as $3,000. In other words, the contra-asset account gets subtracted from the related asset account.

QuickBooks requires you to record Journal Entry 7 yourself by using the Make General Journal Entries command. You can find out more about these types of entries in Book 4, Chapter 1.

## Disposing of obsolete inventory

When you ultimately do dispose of obsolete inventory, you record a journal entry like the one shown in Table 3-8. This journal entry debits the contra-asset account for $100 and credits inventory for $100. In other words, this journal entry removes the value of the obsolete inventory from both the allowance for obsolete inventory account and the inventory account itself. You record this journal entry when you actually, physically dispose of the inventory — when you pay the junk hauler to haul away the inventory, for example, or when you toss the inventory into the large trash bin behind your office or factory.

Special Accounting Problems

**TABLE 3-8**

### Journal Entry 8: Recording Disposal of Inventory

| Account | Debit | Credit |
|---|---|---|
| Allowance for obsolete inventory | $100 | |
| Inventory | | $100 |

In general, one thing you should do every year for tax accounting reasons is deal with your obsolete inventory. The tax rules generally state that you can't write off obsolete inventory unless you actually dispose of it for income purposes. Typically, however, you can write down inventory to its liquidation value. Such a write-down works the same way as a write-down for obsolete inventory. A write-down can be a little tricky if you've never done it before, however, so you may want to confer with your tax adviser.

One more really important point about recording disposal of obsolete inventory: Within QuickBooks, you record inventory disposal by adjusting the physical item count of the inventory items. I describe how adjusting the physical inventory accounts works in Book 3, Chapter 3. So even though I won't go down that path here, you should know that you don't actually enter a journal entry like the one shown in Journal Entry 8. You adjust the inventory accounts for the obsolete inventory. This adjustment automatically reduces the inventory account balance. When QuickBooks asks you which account to debit, you specify the allowance for obsolete inventory account.

## Dealing with inventory shrinkage

The other chronic inventory headache that many business owners and business managers have to deal with is inventory shrinkage. It's very likely, sometimes for the most innocent reasons, that your inventory records overstate the quantity counts of items. When this happens, you must adjust your records. Essentially, you want to reduce both the dollar value of your inventory and the quantity counts of your inventory items.

### WHY NOT JUST CREDIT THE ASSET ACCOUNT?

If you're really getting into this double-entry bookkeeping, you may wonder why you don't just credit the inventory account in the case of something like obsolete inventory. Wouldn't that save you time and trouble? Well, yes and no.

Simply crediting the inventory account does make sense. Such an approach saves you the task of having to set up a goofy contra-asset account. Accountants, however, have concluded over the centuries that it makes sense to keep a record of your obsolete inventory as long as you own it. There are a bunch of reasons for this approach, but one reason is that you want to know what inventory you need to get rid of or dispose of.

It's not necessary to set up some sort of separate system for keeping track of obsolete inventory. By using the contra-asset account, you can continue to store information about your inventory in the accounting system without making the balance sheet information and income statement information incorrect.

This logic applies to other contra-asset accounts too. Earlier in this chapter, I describe how to set up a contra-asset account for uncollectible accounts receivable. The business about wanting to have some record of your uncollectible accounts receivable — perhaps so that you know you don't want to deal with those customers again — means that you may as well keep this information in the accounting system. A contra-asset account allows you to do so and at the same time not have uncollectible receivables present to overstate your accounts receivable balance.

Table 3-9 shows the journal entry that QuickBooks makes for you to record this event. This journal entry debits an appropriate expense account — in Journal Entry 9, I call the expense account "Shrinkage expense" — for $100. A journal entry also needs to credit the inventory account for $100.

TABLE 3-9

### Journal Entry 9: Recording Inventory Shrinkage

| Account | Debit | Credit |
|---|---|---|
| Shrinkage expense | $100 | |
| Inventory | | $100 |

Within QuickBooks, as I've mentioned, you don't actually record a formal journal entry like the one shown here. You use something called a *physical count worksheet* to adjust the quantities of your inventory item counts to whatever they actually are. When you make this adjustment, QuickBooks automatically credits the inventory account balance and adjusts the quantity counts. QuickBooks also requires you to supply the expense account that it should debit for the shrinkage.

TIP

In the old days (by *the old days,* I mean a few decades ago), businesses compared their accounting records with the physical counts of inventory items only once a year. In fact, the annual inventory physical count was a painful ritual that many distributors and retailers went through. These days, I think, most businesses have found that it works much better to stage physical inventory counts throughout the year. This approach, called *cycle counting,* means that you're probably comparing your accounting records with physical counts for your most valuable items several times a year. For your moderately valuable items, you're probably comparing your inventory accounting records with physical counts once or twice a year. With your least valuable inventory items, you probably compare inventory records with physical counts only irregularly, and you may accept a degree of imprecision. Rather than count screws in some bin, for example, you may weigh the bin and then make an estimate of the screw count. In any case, you want some system that allows you to compare your accounting records with your physical counts. Inventory shrinkage and inventory obsolescence represent real costs of doing business that won't get recorded in your accounting records in any other way.

# Accounting for Fixed Assets

*Fixed assets* are those items that you can't immediately count as expenses when purchased. Fixed assets include such things as vehicles, furniture, equipment, and so forth. These assets are tricky for two reasons: Typically, you must depreciate them (more on that in a bit), and you need to record their disposal at some point in the future for either a gain or a loss.

## Purchasing a fixed asset

Accounting for the purchase of a fixed asset is pretty straightforward. Table 3-10 shows how a fixed-asset purchase typically looks.

**TABLE 3-10**

### Journal Entry 10: Recording Fixed-Asset Purchase

| Account | Debit | Credit |
|---------|-------|--------|
| Delivery truck | $12,000 | |
| Cash | | $12,000 |

If you purchase a $12,000 delivery truck with cash, for example, the journal entry that you use to record this purchase debits "Delivery truck" for $12,000 and credits "Cash" for $12,000.

Within QuickBooks, this journal entry gets made when you write the check to pay for the purchase. The one thing that you absolutely must do is set up a fixed-asset account for the specific asset. In other words, you don't want to debit a general catch-all fixed-asset account. If you buy a delivery truck, you set up a fixed-asset account for that specific delivery truck. If you buy a computer system, you set up a fixed-asset account for that particular computer system. In fact, the general rule is that any fixed asset that you buy individually or dispose of later individually needs its own asset account. The reason is that if you don't have individual fixed-asset accounts, the job of calculating gains and losses on the disposal of the fixed asset turns into a Herculean task later.

## Dealing with depreciation

*Depreciation* is an accounting gimmick to recognize the expense of using a fixed asset over a period of time. Although you may not be all that familiar with the mechanics of depreciation, you probably do understand the logic. For the sake of illustration, suppose that you bought a $12,000 delivery truck. Also suppose that because you know how to do your own repair work and take excellent care of your vehicles, you'll be able to use this truck for ten years. Further suppose that at the end of the ten years, the truck will have a $2,000 salvage value (your best guess). Depreciation says that if you buy something for $12,000 and later sell it for $2,000, that decrease in value can be apportioned to expense. In this case, the

$10,000 decrease in value is counted as expense over ten years. That expense is depreciation.

Accountants and tax accounting laws use a variety of methods to apportion the cost of using an asset over the years in which it's used. A common method is called *straight-line depreciation*; it divides the decrease in value by the number of years that an asset is used. An asset that decreases $10,000 over ten years, for example, produces $1,000 a year of depreciation expense.

To record depreciation, you use a journal entry like the one shown in Table 3-11.

**TABLE 3-11**

## Journal Entry 11: Recording Fixed-Asset Depreciation

| Account | Debit | Credit |
|---|---|---|
| Depreciation expense | $1,000 | |
| Acc. dep. — delivery truck | | $1,000 |

Journal Entry 11 debits an expense account called "Depreciation expense" for $1,000. Journal Entry 11 also credits a contra-asset account called "Acc. dep. — delivery truck" for $1,000. (By convention, because the phrase *accumulated depreciation* is so long, accountants and bookkeepers usually abbreviate it as *acc. dep.*) Note also that you need specific individual accumulated depreciation contra-asset accounts for each specific individual fixed-asset account. You don't want to lump all your accumulated depreciation together into a single catch-all account. Down that way lie madness and ruin.

## CHOOSING A DEPRECIATION METHOD

Straight-line depreciation, which I illustrate here, makes for a good example in a book. It's easy to understand and to illustrate. Most accountants and business owners use more-complicated depreciation methods, however, for a variety of reasons. One of the most important reasons is that tax accounting laws generally allow for depreciation methods that accelerate tax deductions.

You can figure out the annual depreciation according to one of these tax-based depreciation methods with your tax adviser's help. Different rules apply to different types of assets. The rules that you use for a particular asset depend on when you originally purchased the asset. I recommend that you use the same asset depreciation

*(continued)*

*(continued)*

method in QuickBooks that you use for your tax accounting. Depreciation is complicated enough as it is. You don't want to be using one method of depreciation within QuickBooks for your own internal financial management and another method for your tax returns.

While I'm on the subject of depreciation, I should also mention that many small firms have the option of using something called a Section 179 election. (Section 179 is a chunk of law in the Internal Revenue Code.) A Section 179 election allows many businesses to immediately depreciate 100 percent of the cost of many of their fixed assets at the time of purchase. Despite the fact that a Section 179 election means that you can immediately write off the purchase of, for example, a $24,000 delivery truck at the time of purchase, you still want to treat fixed assets expensed via a Section 179 election the way I describe here. The difference is that you'll immediately show the asset as fully depreciated — which means depreciated down to its salvage value or down to zero.

## Disposing of a fixed asset

The final wrinkle of fixed-asset accounting concerns disposal of a fixed asset for a gain or for a loss. When you ultimately sell a fixed asset or trade it in or discard it because it's now junk, you record any gain or loss on the disposal of the asset. You also remove the fixed asset from your accounting records.

To show you how this works, consider again the example of the $12,000 delivery truck. Suppose that you've owned and operated this truck for two years. Over that time, you've depreciated $2,000 of the truck's original purchase price. Further suppose that you're going to sell the truck for $11,000 in cash. Table 3-12 shows the journal entry that you'd make to record this disposal.

**TABLE 3-12**

### Journal Entry 12: Recording Fixed-Asset Sale for Gain

| Account | Debit | Credit |
|---|---|---|
| Delivery truck | | $12,000 |
| Cash | $11,000 | |
| Acc. dep. — delivery truck | $2,000 | |
| Gain on sale | | $1,000 |

The first component of Journal Entry 12 shows the $12,000 credit of the delivery truck asset. This makes sense, right? You remove the delivery truck from your fixed-asset amounts by crediting the account for the same amount that you originally debited the account when you purchased the asset.

The next component of the journal entry shows the $11,000 debit to cash. This component, again, is pretty straightforward. It shows the cash that you receive by selling the asset.

The third component of the journal entry backs out the accumulated depreciation. If you depreciated the truck $1,000 a year for two years, the accumulated depreciation contra-asset account for the truck should equal $2,000. To remove this accumulated depreciation from your balance sheet, you debit the accumulated depreciation account for $2,000.

The final piece of the disposal journal entry is a *plug* — a calculated amount. You know the amount and whether that amount is a debit or credit by looking at the other accounts affected. In the case of Journal Entry 12, you know that a $1,000 credit is necessary to balance the journal entry. Debits must equal credits.

**REMEMBER**

A credit is a gain. A credit is essentially revenue, as you may remember from the discussion of double-entry bookkeeping in Book 1, Chapter 2.

If the plug was a debit amount, the disposal produces a loss. This makes sense; a loss is like an expense, and expenses are debits.

If you're confused about the gain component of Journal Entry 12, let me make this observation. Over the two years of use, the business depreciated the truck by $2,000. In other words, the business, through the depreciation expense, said that the truck lost $2,000 of value. If, however, the $12,000 delivery truck is sold two years later for $11,000, the loss in value doesn't equal $2,000; it equals $1,000. The $1,000 gain essentially recaptures the unnecessary extra depreciation that was charged incorrectly.

You can enter Journal Entries 11 and 12 as journal entries in QuickBooks by using the Make General Journal Entries command.

# Recognizing Liabilities

*Liabilities* are amounts that a business owes to other parties. If a business owes a bank money because of a loan, that's a liability. If a business owes an employee wages or benefits, that's a liability. If a business owes the federal, state, or local government taxes, those are liabilities.

## Borrowing money

Liabilities, fortunately, aren't too tricky to record after you've seen how the journal entries look. Table 3-13, for example, shows how you record money borrowed on a loan. In the case of a $10,000 loan, you would debit cash for $10,000 and credit a loan payable liability account for $10,000.

TABLE 3-13

### Journal Entry 13: Borrowing Money via a Loan

| Account | Debit | Credit |
|---|---|---|
| Cash | $10,000 | |
| Loan payable | | $10,000 |

Sometimes, you may purchase an asset with a loan. Suppose that you purchased $10,000 worth of furniture by using a note payable or a loan. Even though there's no immediate cash effect, you still record the transaction. Table 3-14 shows how you record this transaction. A furniture account gets debited for $10,000, and a loan payable account gets credited for $10,000.

TABLE 3-14

### Journal Entry 14: Buying an Asset with a Loan

| Account | Debit | Credit |
|---|---|---|
| Furniture | $10,000 | |
| Loan payable | | $10,000 |

TIP

You can record Journal Entry 13 directly in your checkbook when you record the $10,000 cash deposit. You can also record Journal Entry 13, as well as Journal Entry 14, by using the Make General Journal Entries command that QuickBooks provides. By the way, you can record Journal Entry 14 only by using the Make General Journal Entries command.

## Making a loan payment

To record the payment on a loan, you or QuickBooks makes a journal entry like the one shown in Table 3-15. Suppose that in connection with the loan shown in Journal Entry 13, you need to pay $2,200. Further suppose that this amount is for $1,200 of loan interest and $1,000 of principal. In this case, you debit loan payable for $1,000, debit loan interest expense for $1,200, and credit cash for $2,200.

TABLE 3-15

## Journal Entry 15: Paying a Loan Payment

| Account | Debit | Credit |
|---|---|---|
| Loan payable | $1,000 | |
| Loan interest expense | 1,200 | |
| Cash | | $2,200 |

Sometimes, the tricky thing about loan payments is breaking the payment amount into its principal and interest components. Ideally, the lender will provide you an amortization schedule that breaks payments into principal and interest.

If a lender doesn't provide such an amortization schedule, you can calculate the interest expense yourself by using either a spreadsheet or a calculator. In Microsoft Excel, right-click any worksheet tab, choose Insert from the shortcut menu, and double-click the Amortization Table on the Spreadsheet Solutions tab of the result dialog box. Then, after you've calculated the interest expense, you can deduce the principal component by subtracting the interest from the payment amount.

# Accruing liabilities

I want to show you one other liability-related journal entry. Very commonly, a business owes money for some goods or services or taxes that must be recorded in the accounting system. If, at the end of an accounting period — say, at the end of the year — you owe $1,200 of interest on some loan, you really need to record that interest expense in your accounting system. You want to record the fact that although the loan balance may show as $10,000 in your accounting records, you probably really owe $11,200, because you owe both the $10,000 of principal and $1,200 of accrued interest.

To accrue a liability, you use a journal entry like the one shown in Table 3-16. This journal entry shows the accrual of $1,200 of interest expense on a loan payable.

TABLE 3-16

## Journal Entry 16: Accruing a Liability

| Account | Debit | Credit |
|---|---|---|
| Loan interest expense | $1,200 | |
| Loan interest payable | | $1,200 |

The journal entry shows a $1,200 debit to loan interest expense and a $1,200 credit to loan interest payable. This journal entry records amounts that you owe as of the end of the accounting period that don't get recorded in some other way.

You need to be careful about using journal entries like the one shown in Table 3-16. Typically, you want to use such journal entries when it's very important to count all your expenses and to measure all your liabilities accurately.

One common situation in which you want to be especially careful about making such accruals occurs if you sell your firm. Any prospective purchaser wants to have not only a very good estimate of your true expenses for the accounting period, but also a very accurate estimate of liabilities at the time the business is being evaluated.

Liability accruals like the one shown in Journal Entry 16 present a problem to the accountant or bookkeeper, however. To return to the example of the accrued interest shown in Journal Entry 16, suppose that at a later time, the business makes a $3,000 payment, which includes the interest accrued in Journal Entry 16. When the accountant or bookkeeper later records this loan payment, they must remember or recognize the earlier journal entry. You don't want the accountant or bookkeeper to double-count interest expense by recording the same interest again. This makes sense, right?

Because accountants and bookkeepers can't reliably remember these sorts of accrual entries — they may need to recall them months later — they typically back out the effect of the accrual from the first day of the new accounting period.

If Journal Entry 16 were recorded at the end of year 1 to accurately estimate interest expense and liability balances, an accountant or bookkeeper could, on the first day of year 2, enter a reversing journal entry. This reversing journal entry would credit loan interest expense for $1,200 and debit loan interest payable for $1,200. In other words, this reversing journal entry reverses the earlier accrual. Because the accrual entry is still in year 1, however, year 1's estimates of interest expense and liability account balances are still correct.

Table 3-17 shows how a reversing entry looks. Again, notice that it's simply the mirror image of Journal Entry 16. The debits and credits are flip-flopped.

When the actual loan interest payment is made, the journal entry appears as though no accrual or reversal ever existed, as Table 3-18 shows. Suppose that at some time in year 2, the business pays $1,800 in interest by making a cash payment. Journal Entry 18 shows how this transaction gets recorded.

| | | |
|---|---|---|
| **TABLE 3-17** | **Journal Entry 17: Reversing an Accrual** | |

| Account | Debit | Credit |
|---|---|---|
| Loan interest expense | | $1,200 |
| Loan interest payable | $1,200 | |

| | | |
|---|---|---|
| **TABLE 3-18** | **Journal Entry 18: The "Real" Loan Interest Payment** | |

| Account | Debit | Credit |
|---|---|---|
| Loan interest expense | $1,800 | |
| Cash | | $1,800 |

Let me quickly summarize what happens with Journal Entries 16, 17, and 18:

>> **Journal Entry 16** enables you to show that at the end of year 1, the business owes $1,200 of interest on a loan — even though that interest hasn't yet been paid. Journal Entry 16 also shows that even though the money wasn't paid, loan interest expense of $1,200 was incurred.

>> **Journal Entries 17 and 18** need to be combined to be understood. Journal Entry 17, for example, reduces the loan interest payable to zero. Remember that the loan interest payable would be a balance sheet liability account. The combination of the $1,200 debit and credit zero this account out. The $1,200 credit to loan interest expense in Journal Entry 17 must be combined with the $1,800 debit to loan interest expense in Journal Entry 18. This seems funny, because after all, aren't you really paying $1,800 of interest? That's true. But looking back at Journal Entry 16, you can see that you've already recorded $1,200 of loan interest expense. That interest expense has been recorded for year 1 in this example. If you have $1,800 of loan interest in total, what's left over for year 2 is the remaining $600. The combination of the $1,200 credit to loan interest expense and the $1,800 debit to loan interest expense produces this $600 of loan interest expense. The only other component of these two journal entries is the $1,800 credit to cash. This credit to cash represents just the actual cash payment that's made to pay the loan interest amount.

You need to be careful when working with accrual entries, reversing entries, and then the real entries that follow and correct everything in the end. These tools can be enormously helpful when it's important to measure expenses and liabilities accurately. You must remember to complete the entire sequence of transactions, however; you can't stop halfway.

One last important point: In Journal Entries 16, 17, and 18, I talk about how to accrue loan interest expense. You can use this accrual technique to recognize any liability — a fact that I want to emphasize. You can use the technique demonstrated in these journal entries to deal with liabilities for things such as wages owed to employees, taxes owed to the government, and so forth.

Some firms, particularly those with sophisticated accounting systems, can even use this technique to record hard-to-quantify liabilities, such as warranty liabilities. (A *warranty* is a promise that you make to a customer. You might promise that your product won't break, for example.) These promises create liabilities and expenses. An accurate accounting system requires that you record these expenses as they occur and recognize these liabilities as they come into existence.

# Closing Out Revenue and Expense Accounts

You're about to enter the twilight zone of accounting. In this section, I talk about what happens to revenue and expense accounts at the end of the year in traditional manual accounting systems. Then I explain why QuickBooks doesn't quite work that way and what you need to do about it.

If you want to skip anything in this chapter, this section may be that material. On the other hand, if you (like me) have a compulsive personality and deem it essential to read everything in this chapter (even stuff that's not particularly exciting), read on.

Book 1, Chapter 1 and Book 1, Chapter 2 describe an imaginary hot dog stand, a one-day business that (in my imagination) you operate. (If you've been reading this chapter and have no questions, you don't even need to worry about the two preceding chapters.) Table 3-19 shows the trial balance for this business at the end of the day of operation.

## The traditional close

As I hope you already know, revenue and expense accounts count revenue and expenses for a particular period of time. Revenue and expense accounts may count for the month, the quarter, or the year, for example.

One thing that accounting systems traditionally do is zero out the revenue and expense accounts at the end of the year. This makes sense if you think about it a bit. You want your counters reset at the beginning of the year so that counting the new year's revenue and the new year's expenses is easy. In the case of a trial balance like the one shown in Table 3-19, for example, you'd typically make the journal entry shown in Table 3-20.

TABLE 3-19

## A Trial Balance at the End of the Period

| Account | Debit | Credit |
|---|---|---|
| Cash | $5,000 | |
| Inventory | 0 | |
| Accounts payable | | $0 |
| Loan payable | | 0 |
| S. Nelson, capital | | 1,000 |
| Sales revenue | | 13,000 |
| Cost of goods sold | 3,000 | |
| Rent | 1,000 | |
| Wages expense | 4,000 | |
| Supplies | 1,000 | |
| **Totals** | **$14,000** | **$14,000** |

TABLE 3-20

## Journal Entry 19: Closing the Period

| Account | Debit | Credit |
|---|---|---|
| Sales revenue | $13,000 | |
| Cost of goods sold | | $3,000 |
| Rent | | 1,000 |
| Wages expense | | 4,000 |
| Supplies | | 1,000 |
| Owner's equity | | 4,000 |

If you look at Journal Entry 19 (Table 3-20), for example, you see that the first line in the journal entry is a $13,000 debit for sales revenue. If you look back at the trial balance shown in Table 3-19, you see that sales revenue has a $13,000 credit balance. The combination of the account balance shown in Table 3-19 and the closing entry shown in Journal Entry 19 (Table 3-20) effectively zeros out the sales revenue account.

The same sort of accounting magic occurs for each of the other expense accounts shown in the trial balance. The cost-of-goods-sold balance is equal to a $3,000 debit in Table 3-19 and is zeroed out in Journal Entry 19 with a $3,000 credit. And so it goes.

## The QuickBooks close

The sort of accounting taught at local community colleges makes just the sort of closing entry shown in Journal Entry 19, but you don't need or even want to make such a closing entry within QuickBooks.

The closing entry shown in Journal Entry 19 gets made in a manual system so that the revenue and expense accounts can be reset to zero. By comparison, QuickBooks, relying on the power of the computer, doesn't need to have these accounts reset to zero to calculate the revenue and expense for the new accounting period correctly. QuickBooks, as you discover throughout this book, can calculate revenue or sales for any period and for any interval of time, using its report generation tool to summarize the revenue and expenses that occur within a particular time interval.

This seemingly missed step doesn't cause any idiosyncratic behavior on the part of QuickBooks. QuickBooks lumps the revenue and expenses from all the previous years into a retained earnings amount reported on the balance sheet. Net income for the current year is also reported in the equity portion of the balance sheet. In addition, if you have a corporation, QuickBooks typically includes a dividends paid account in the equity portion of the balance sheet. I'm getting ahead of myself, however.

The main thing that I want you to know is that this seemingly critical textbook journal entry for closing out revenue and expense accounts isn't made within QuickBooks. This is okay, because QuickBooks doesn't *need* to make the traditional closing entry.

You may want to ask your accountant about this entry. Typically, however, any dividends paid by a corporation are zeroed out or combined with retained earnings at the end of the year. If you want to combine dividends paid for the current year with accumulative retained earnings, you do this with a journal entry. The journal entry credits the dividends paid account and debits retained earnings for the amount of dividends paid for the year. I hesitate to encourage you to make this journal entry willy-nilly, however. I think it's okay to skip making the entry. And before you make it, consult your tax adviser.

# One More Thing . . .

In this chapter, I try to address some of the common, complicated journal entries and accounting transactions that business owners encounter. I know that I can't answer every question here, but I do want to provide as thorough a set of instructions as possible. All this is leading up to a special request: If you've read this chapter and didn't find a discussion of the sort of journal entry or accounting transaction that you need to record, send me an email or write me a letter that tells me what help you hoped to find here but didn't. (You can get contact information at https://stephenlnelson.com.)

I can't promise you that I'll be able to supply an answer. But if you describe a journal entry that I should have included, I'll try to respond to your email with instructions on how to make the journal entry. I'll also include a description of the journal entry in the next edition of this book.

# 2

# Getting Ready to Use QuickBooks

# Contents at a Glance

IN THIS CHAPTER

» **Planning how you'll use QuickBooks**

» **Installing the QuickBooks program**

» **Preparing for setup**

» **Setting up QuickBooks**

» **Figuring out your starting trial balance**

Chapter **1**

# Setting Up QuickBooks

To use QuickBooks, you need to do two things: Install the QuickBooks software and run the QuickBooks Setup process. This chapter gives you a bird's-eye view of both these tasks. I also want to spend just a few paragraphs talking about some of the planning that you should do before you set up QuickBooks and some of the missing steps in the QuickBooks Setup process — things it should do but doesn't. (Don't worry. I tell you how to complete the missing steps, partly at the end of this chapter and in the next chapter.)

## Planning Your New QuickBooks System

I start with a couple of big-picture discussions: what accounting does and what accounting systems do. If you understand this big-picture stuff from the very start, you'll find that the QuickBooks Setup process makes a whole lot more sense.

### What accounting does

Think about what accounting does. People may argue about the little details, but most would agree that accounting does the following four important things:

» Measures profits and losses

>> Reports on the financial condition of a firm (its assets, liabilities, and net worth)

>> Provides detailed records of the assets, liabilities, and owner's equity accounts

>> Supplies financial information to stakeholders, especially to management

## What accounting systems do

Now take a brief look at what accounting systems, or at least small-business accounting systems, typically do:

>> Produce financial statements, including income statements, balance sheets, and other accounting reports

>> Generate business forms, including checks, paychecks, invoices, customer statements, and so forth

>> Keep detailed records of key accounts, including cash, *accounts receivable* (amounts that customers owe a firm), *accounts payable* (amounts that a firm owes its vendors), inventory items, fixed assets, and so on

>> Perform specialized information management functions

In the publishing industry, for example, book publishers often pay authors royalties. So royalty accounting is a task that book publishers' accounting systems typically must do.

## What QuickBooks does

After you understand what accounting does and what accounting systems typically do, you can see with some perspective what QuickBooks does:

>> Produces financial statements

>> Generates many common business forms, including checks, paychecks, customer invoices, customer statements, credit memos, and purchase orders

>> Keeps detailed records of a few key accounts in simple settings: cash, accounts receivable, accounts payable, and inventory

Allow me to make an important observation here: QuickBooks does three of the four things that you expect an accounting system to do. Compare the list that I just provided with the preceding list ("What accounting systems do"). I'll save you the time of finding the fourth thing: QuickBooks doesn't supply the specialized accounting stuff. It doesn't do royalty accounting, for example, as discussed in the earlier example.

## And now for the bad news

So QuickBooks does three of the four things that accounting systems do, but it doesn't do everything. QuickBooks is often an incomplete accounting solution. Be careful, therefore, about setting your expectations. Typically, you also need to figure out work-arounds for some of your special accounting requirements.

QuickBooks gives users and businesses a lot of flexibility. To return to an earlier example, a book publisher can do much of what it needs to do for royalty accounting in QuickBooks. This royalty-accounting work simply requires a certain amount of fiddling as the business is setting up QuickBooks.

But QuickBooks (or at least the most popular versions) does suffer a couple of significant weaknesses:

>> **QuickBooks Pro doesn't supply a good way to handle the manufacturing of inventory.** QuickBooks Premier and QuickBooks Enterprise Solutions do support simple manufacturing accounting, however, and QuickBooks Enterprise Solutions provides some additional inventory management capability (multiple inventory sites, lot and serial number tracking, and FIFO [first-in, first-out] costing) as part of its Advance Inventory feature. These versions of QuickBooks help you account for the process of turning raw materials into finished goods and also deal with some real-life inventory complexities.

>> **Only QuickBooks Enterprise Solutions handles the situation of storing inventory in multiple locations.** In other words, QuickBooks Pro and QuickBooks Premier simply show, for example, that you have 3,000 widgets. They don't let you keep track of the fact that you have 1,000 widgets at the warehouse, 500 widgets at store A, and 1,500 widgets at store B.

In spite of the fact that QuickBooks may be an incomplete solution and may not handle inventory the way you want or need it to, QuickBooks is still a very good solution. No, wait — that's not really strong enough. What QuickBooks does, it does *very well*.

As with a lot of things in life, finding the right accounting solution is all about balance. Some of the factors that you may consider when choosing your accounting software would be ease of use, portability, price, data security, customer service, and integration with other business tools. The desktop version of QuickBooks has been a good balance of the things I need, which is why I use it for my business.

**TIP**

The desktop version of QuickBooks provides considerably more horsepower than the online version of QuickBooks (or other cloud-based systems). That said, the online version makes it far easier to work with an outside accountant or bookkeeper. Accordingly, for those clients who really need outside professional help but don't need advanced desktop features (such as job costing), the online version of QuickBooks is a very reasonable choice too.

# Installing QuickBooks

You install QuickBooks the same way that you install most applications or programs: by download or via a disc containing the software. I'd begin at https://quickbooks.intuit.com/desktop, where you can compare some product options, chat with a sales agent, or (if you're ready) purchase the version of your choosing. After purchase, you should be able to download the product; definitely reach out to Intuit if you can't. If you purchase a copy of QuickBooks from a bricks-and-mortar store, you just need to insert the disc into the proper drive.

After downloading the program (or inserting the disc containing the software), you don't need to do anything special to install QuickBooks. Simply follow the onscreen instructions. Typically, you're prompted to enter the installation key or installation code. This code and key are available within the QuickBooks packaging — usually, on the back of the envelope that the disc comes in — if you purchase the software in a local store. Otherwise, Intuit provides these items during the online purchase process.

The QuickBooks installation process may ask you to answer questions about how you want QuickBooks to be installed. Almost always, you want to accept the default suggestions. In other words, QuickBooks may ask you whether it can create a new folder in which to install the program files. In this case, choose yes.

## TROUBLESHOOTING CD/DVD INSTALLATION

If your version of Microsoft Windows doesn't recognize that you've stuffed the QuickBooks CD into the machine's CD or DVD drive, you have a couple of choices:

- **You can wait.** If you wait, Windows probably will recognize that you've placed the QuickBooks CD in the CD or DVD drive, and after a short wait (even though it may seem like an eternity), Windows starts the process of installing the QuickBooks program.

- **You can manually force the installation of the QuickBooks program.** Windows includes a tool that you can use to add or remove new programs (unsurprisingly named the Add/Remove Programs tool). I don't describe how this Control Panel tool works here, but you can refer to a book such as *Windows 11 For Dummies*, by Andy Rathbone (John Wiley & Sons, Inc.), or Windows online Help to get this information. In a nutshell, you simply open the Control Panel window, click the Add/Remove Programs tool, and follow the onscreen instructions to tell Windows to install a program stored on the CD or DVD in the computer's CD or DVD drive.

**REMEMBER**

QuickBooks can work as a multiuser accounting system, which means that several people can use QuickBooks. The QuickBooks data file — the repository of all the QuickBooks information — typically resides on a centrally available computer or server. People who want to work with the QuickBooks data file simply install the QuickBooks program on their computers and then use the program to access centrally located QuickBooks data files. This multiuser system isn't complicated to run; in fact, I talk about it quite a bit in Book 7, Chapter 1.

**WARNING**

You need to own a separate copy of QuickBooks for each computer on which you install QuickBooks. You can also buy multiuser copies of QuickBooks that let you install the QuickBooks program on up to 5 computers (or on up to 40 computers if you're running QuickBooks Enterprise Solutions). I mention this because you don't want to get involved in software piracy — which is a felony — as part of inadvertently setting up QuickBooks the wrong way. The bottom line: You need a legal copy of QuickBooks for every machine on which you install QuickBooks.

# Dealing with the Presetup Jitters

After you install QuickBooks, you run an onscreen wizard to set up QuickBooks for your firm's accounting. Cleverly, this onscreen wizard is called QuickBooks Setup. In the following sections, I explain what you need to do before you use QuickBooks Setup so that you work in an efficient manner. I also give you an overview of what you'll do as you go through QuickBooks Setup.

## Preparing for setup

In running QuickBooks Setup, you provide quite a bit of information to QuickBooks. As a practical matter, setup and post–setup cleanup (which I describe in this chapter and the next one) require that you have the following:

>> Accurate financial statements as of the conversion-to-QuickBooks date

>> Detailed records of your accounts payable, accounts receivable, inventory, and fixed assets

>> A complete or nearly complete list of employees, customers, vendors, and inventory items (if you buy and sell inventory)

You want to get all this stuff together before you start QuickBooks Setup, because (depending on how you go about setting up QuickBooks) you may be asked about this stuff as part of the process. Don't try to scurry around looking for a particular piece of data while you're running the Setup Wizard; collect this data up front. Then stack all the necessary paperwork on your desk next to your computer.

Let me also note that you're going to make several accounting decisions as you go through QuickBooks Setup. You may be asked to decide whether you want to use an accounts payable system, for example. You may choose to use the Setup Wizard to tell QuickBooks whether you want to send customers monthly statements. You may also be asked whether you want to prepare estimates for customers or whether you want to use classes to further track your income and spending.

**WARNING**

In general, when you're asked any of the accounting questions, you can simply accept the default answer. You're required by law to be consistent in your accounting for tax purposes, however. If you want to change your accounting — technically called a *change of accounting method* by the Internal Revenue Service — you must request permission from the IRS to make that change. How to do this and the ramifications of doing it are beyond the scope of this book, but be forewarned: The IRS insists that you be consistent in your accounting. If you've been treating particular items of income or expense in a certain way, the IRS says, "Hey, taxpayer, you must continue to treat them that way unless you get permission from us to change."

**TIP**

I should make a clarification: You can use one accounting method for your tax return and then, within QuickBooks, use a different accounting method. You may be locked into using accrual-basis accounting on your tax return, for example, but that doesn't mean you can't use cash-basis accounting in QuickBooks and in managing your business. Accordingly, what I say in the preceding paragraphs is a little bit inaccurate. Technically. But you probably don't want to use one accounting approach on your tax return and a different approach in QuickBooks. Too complicated.

One final note: You should have your tax return from last year handy because it supplies information that you need for running QuickBooks Setup. Last year's tax return, for example, supplies your taxpayer ID number, your legal business name, and your method of accounting.

## Seeing what happens during setup

As you walk through the setup process, you work with QuickBooks to set preferences (which determine how QuickBooks works and which features are initially available) and to set up a chart of accounts and your bank accounts.

The *chart of accounts*, just so you know, identifies those income, expense, asset, liability, and owner's equity accounts that appear in your financial statements.

When you complete QuickBooks Setup, you're almost ready to begin using QuickBooks. In fact, in a pinch, you could (after QuickBooks Setup) limp along with QuickBooks.

WARNING

An important point of clarification: You may think that you should be ready to rock and roll after installing QuickBooks and running through the setup process. But you have two other tasks to complete: identifying your starting trial balance (which I describe at the end of this chapter) and loading your key master files (which I describe mostly in the next chapter). The *trial balance* identifies your year-to-date income and expense numbers, as well as your asset, liability, and owner's equity numbers as of the conversion date. The *master files* store information about customers, vendors, employees, and inventory items that you use repeatedly. The customer master file, for example, stores a customer's name and address, phone number, and the contact person's name (if different).

# Running the QuickBooks Setup Wizard

After you install the QuickBooks program, the installation program may start QuickBooks automatically and then start QuickBooks Setup. You can also start QuickBooks Setup by starting the QuickBooks program the same way that you start any program and then choosing File ➪ New Company.

## Getting the big welcome

The QuickBooks Desktop Setup screen of QuickBooks Setup (see Figure 1-1) appears when you choose File ➪ New Company. The screen gets you started creating a new company file within QuickBooks. The screen has two radio buttons to choose between. The For Myself (I'm the Admin) button enables you to set up the new file as the admin, in which case you use your email address to create the file. The For Someone Else button enables you to set up the file on behalf of the admin, in which case you use that person's email address to set up the file.

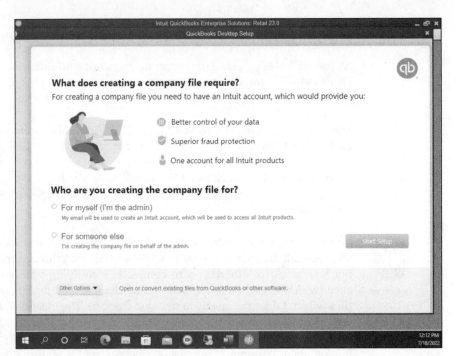

**FIGURE 1-1:**
The QuickBooks
Desktop Setup
window.

The Other Options drop-down list (refer to Figure 1-1) allows you to choose the advanced setup option, which walks you through a bunch of screens full of information that let you rather tightly specify how the company file that QuickBooks sets up should look.

## Supplying company information

The first few screens of the EasyStep Interview collect several important pieces of general information about your business, including your company name and the firm's legal name, your company address, the industry in which you operate, your federal tax ID number, the first month of the fiscal year (typically, January), the type of income tax form that your firm uses to report to the IRS, and the industry or type of company that you're operating (retail, service, and so forth). The first screen of the EasyStep Interview is shown in Figure 1-2.

**WARNING**

QuickBooks isn't very smart about the tax accounting rules for limited liability companies (LLCs). An LLC can be treated as a sole proprietorship if it has one owner and as a partnership if it has more than one owner. But LLCs may also elect to be treated as S corporations or C corporations. If you've made such an election for your LLC, be sure to indicate that the LLC is an S corporation or C corporation.

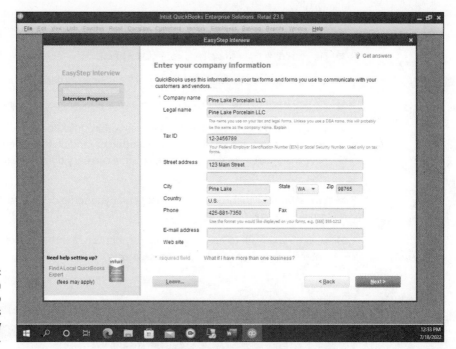

**FIGURE 1-2:**
The first screen
of the EasyStep
Interview collects
general company
information.

**TIP**

To move to the next screen in the EasyStep Interview, click the Next button. To move to the previous screen, click the Back button. If you get discouraged and want to give up, click the Leave button. But try not to get discouraged.

After collecting this general company information, QuickBooks creates the company data file that stores your firm's financial information. QuickBooks suggests a default name or a QuickBooks data file based on the company name (see Figure 1-3). All you need to do is accept the suggested name and the suggested folder location (unless you want to save the data file in the Documents folder, which isn't a bad idea).

## Customizing QuickBooks

After QuickBooks collects the general company information mentioned in the preceding paragraphs, the EasyStep Interview asks you some very specific questions about how you run your business so that it can set the QuickBooks preferences. Preferences in effect turn various accounting features of QuickBooks on or off, thereby controlling how the program works and looks. Here are the sorts of questions that the EasyStep Interview asks to set the QuickBooks preferences:

» Does your firm maintain inventory?

Setting Up QuickBooks

>> Do you want to track the inventory that you buy and sell?

>> Do you collect sales tax from your customers?

>> Do you want to use sales orders to track customer orders and back orders?

>> Do you want to use QuickBooks to help with your employee payroll?

>> Do you need to track multiple currencies within QuickBooks because you deal with customers and vendors in other countries, and do these people regularly have the audacity to pay or invoice you in a currency different from the one your country uses?

>> Would you like to track the time that you or your employees spend on jobs or projects for customers?

>> How do you want to handle bills and payments (enter the checks directly, or enter the bills first and the payments later)?

**FIGURE 1-3:**
The Filename for New Company dialog box.

# Setting your start date

Perhaps the key decision that you make in setting up any accounting system is the day on which you begin using your new system. This day is called the *conversion date.* Typically, you want to begin using an accounting system on the first day of the year or the first day of a new month. Accordingly, one other big question you're asked is about the conversion date. You're prompted to identify the start date by using the dialog box shown in Figure 1-4.

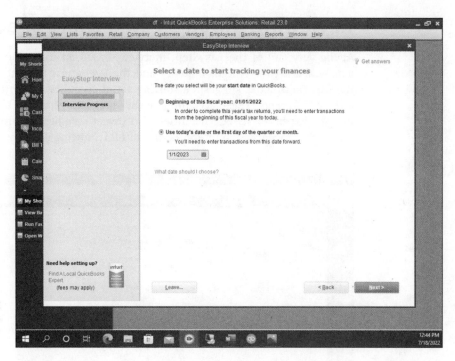

**FIGURE 1-4:**
The EasyStep
Interview dialog
box that lets
you select the
start date.

TIP

The easiest time to start using a new accounting system is the beginning of the year. The reason? You get to enter a simpler trial balance. At the start of the year, for example, you enter only asset, liability, and owner's equity account balances.

At any other time, you also enter year-to-date income and year-to-date expense account balances. Typically, you have this year-to-date income and expense information available only at the start of the month. For this reason, the only other feasible start date that you can pick is the start of a month.

In this case, you get year-to-date income amounts through the end of the previous month from your previous accounting system. If you've been using Sage 50 Accounting, for example, get year-to-date income and expense amounts from Sage.

After you've provided the start date, supplied the basic company information, identified most of your accounting preferences, and identified the date on which you want to start using QuickBooks, you're almost done.

Setting Up QuickBooks

**TIP**

If you click the Leave button, QuickBooks leaves you in the QuickBooks program, ready to get to work. The EasyStep Interview process isn't lost forever, however. To get back into the interview, just open the file you were in the process of setting up. When you do, the EasyStep Interview restarts.

# Reviewing the suggested chart of accounts

At the very end of the EasyStep Interview, based on the information that you supply about your type of industry and the tax return form that you file with the IRS, QuickBooks suggests a starting set of accounts, which accountants call a *chart of accounts*. These accounts are the categories that you use to track your income, expenses, assets, liabilities, and owner's equity. Figure 1-5 shows the screen that the EasyStep Interview displays for showing you these accounts.

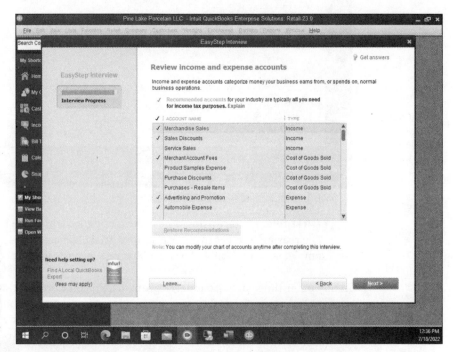

**FIGURE 1-5:**
The EasyStep Interview screen shows you its recommended income and expense accounts.

The accounts that QuickBooks marks with a check, as the screen explains, are the recommended accounts. If you don't do anything else, these checked accounts are the ones you'll use (at least to start) within QuickBooks. You can remove a suggested account by clicking the check mark. QuickBooks removes the check mark, which means that the account won't be part of the final chart of accounts. You can also click an account to add a check mark and have the account included in the starting chart of accounts.

**TIP**

You can click the Restore Recommendations button at the bottom of the list to return to the initial recommended chart of accounts (if you made changes that you later decide you don't want).

When the suggested chart of accounts looks okay to you, click Next. It's fine to accept what QuickBooks suggests because you can change the chart of accounts later.

## Adding your information to the company file

After you and QuickBooks set up the company file, QuickBooks prompts you to enter your own information in the company file (see Figure 1-6).

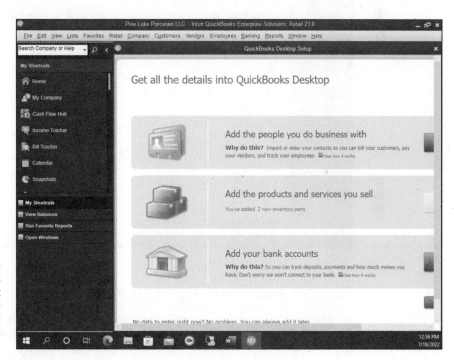

**FIGURE 1-6:**
The QuickBooks Setup screen that prompts you to enter your own information in the company file.

### Customers, vendors, and employees

To describe customers, vendors, and employees, click the first Add button. Quick-Books asks whether it's possible to get this data from someplace else, such as an email program or email service (Outlook, Gmail, and so forth), or whether you want to enter the information into a worksheet manually. You're probably going to enter the information manually, so click the appropriate button and then click Continue. When QuickBooks displays a worksheet window (see Figure 1-7), enter each customer, vendor, or employee in its own row and be sure to include both the name and address information. Click Continue (not shown in Figure 1-7) when you finish. Then QuickBooks asks (using a screen I don't show here) whether you want to enter opening balances — amounts you owe or are owed — for customers and vendors. Indicate that you do by clicking the Enter Opening Balances link and then enter the opening balances in the screen that QuickBooks provides.

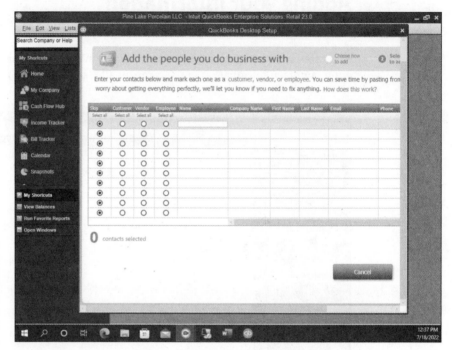

**FIGURE 1-7:** The QuickBooks Setup screen that collects information about the people you do business with.

## Services and inventory items you sell

To describe the stuff you sell, click the second Add button in the second box shown in Figure 1-6. QuickBooks asks about the stuff you sell — whether you sell services, whether you sell inventory items, and whether you want to track any such inventory items you sell, for example. Answer these questions by clicking the button that conforms to your situation and then click Continue. When QuickBooks displays a worksheet window (not shown), describe each item you sell on a separate worksheet row. Also be sure to describe any inventory items you're holding at the time you convert to QuickBooks. Click Continue when you finish. If you sell more than one type of item, you need to repeat this process for each type of item.

### Business bank accounts

To describe your business bank account (or bank accounts), click the Add button in the third box shown in Figure 1-6. When QuickBooks displays the Add Your Bank Accounts worksheet window (not shown), provide each bank account's name, account number, and balance on the conversion date. When you finish entering this information, click Continue.

# Identifying the Starting Trial Balance

Whether you use the default Start version or the Detailed Start/EasyStep Interview version of the QuickBooks Setup process, you don't get a complete trial balance in the QuickBooks company file simply by setting up. Assuming that you follow the instructions and tips provided in the preceding paragraphs, you get only your bank account, accounts receivable, inventory, and accounts payable balances in QuickBooks. Yet you need to enter all the missing trial balance information in QuickBooks, too, to begin getting good reports out of QuickBooks and to use the software for supplying financial data to your tax returns. I end this chapter by talking about how you get the rest of the trial balance data into the QuickBooks company file.

## A simple example to start

To record the rest of your starting trial balance, you record a journal entry. The journal entry records the remaining trial balance amounts for all your other accounts at the conversion or start date: accounts other than your bank accounts, accounts receivable, accounts payable, and inventory.

To see how this process works, suppose that you have the trial balance shown in Table 1-1. Note that these trial balances are used in the discussion in Book 1, Chapter 2 and shown in that chapter's Table 2-19. Notice that no balance is recorded for a bank account, no balance is recorded for accounts receivable (because this account doesn't even show up in the trial balance), and no balances are recorded for inventory or accounts payable (because these accounts have zero balances at the conversion date). For purposes of this example (but not the next example), the cash balance isn't a bank account but is actually cash: a desk drawer full of low-denomination, used bills with nonsequential serial numbers.

Figure 1-8 shows how the Make General Journal Entries window looks when it records the missing trial balance information from Table 1-1. After this journal entry is recorded, the trial balance is correct as of the start date.

**TABLE 1-1**

## A Trial Balance

| Account | Debit | Credit |
|---------|-------|--------|
| Cash | $5,000 | |
| Inventory | 0 | |
| Accounts payable | | $0 |
| S. Nelson, Capital | | 1,000 |
| Sales Revenue | | 13,000 |
| Cost of Goods Sold | 3,000 | |
| Rent Expense | 1,000 | |
| Wages | 4,000 | |
| Supplies | 1,000 | |
| **Totals** | **$14,000** | **$14,000** |

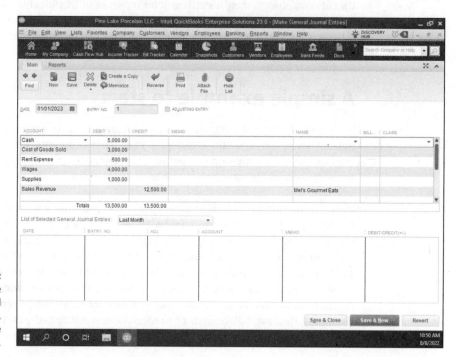

**FIGURE 1-8:**
The Make General Journal Entries window, showing a simple trial balance.

For more information about how to record a journal entry by using the Make General Journal Entries window, see Book 4, Chapter 1. If you want to try this on your own with no further instruction from me, choose the Company ⇨ Make

General Journal Entries command. When QuickBooks displays the Make General Journal Entries window, shown in Figure 1-8, use the Account, Debit, and Credit columns to record your journal entry.

If the idea of making a journal entry terrifies the heck out of you, you may find yourself in a bit of a pickle. You need to become comfortable working with double-entry bookkeeping to set up QuickBooks at a time other than at the beginning of the year. This means, unfortunately, that if you're setting up QuickBooks sometime during the middle of the year, you must enter a general journal entry to fix the weirdness that the QuickBooks Setup creates. If you don't know how double-entry bookkeeping works — if debits and credits aren't your friends — you probably need to get somebody's help. I suggest that you call your CPA or some other friend who truly understands accounting. Get them to come over and enter the last part of the trial balance for you by using the Make General Journal Entries window.

*Note:* This project shouldn't be a big one if you decide to call your CPA. If they come over to your office, and if you have the trial balance ready, it should take them only a few minutes to enter the necessary general journal entry. Perhaps you can buy them a nice lunch, and that will settle the score.

## A real-life example to finish

Okay, true confessions. The example I give in the preceding section? You probably won't be lucky enough that your starting trial balance journal entry will be so simple. You probably *will* have to deal with a bank account and with account balances in your accounts receivable, accounts payable, or inventory accounts. Now I show you how this process works.

Suppose that you have the trial balances shown in Table 1-2. Note that in this example (unlike the preceding example), the first account shown — the one with $5,000 — is a bank account.

Here's the tricky part of recording this trial balance. You don't need — I repeat, don't need — to record all this trial-balance information through a journal entry. Because the bank account, accounts receivable, accounts payable, and inventory portions have already been recorded if you added customer, vendor, item, and bank account information during the QuickBooks Setup process, you just need to enter the rest of the trial balance.

Because you won't be recording all the trial balance, however, your journal entry not only won't match your actual trial balance, but also won't balance. To make it balance, therefore, you plug the difference into an account that QuickBooks supplies for just this sort of bookkeeping madness: the *Opening Balance Equity* account. Figure 1-9 shows this journal entry.

TABLE 1-2

## A Trial Balance

| Account | Debit | Credit |
|---|---|---|
| Checking | $5,000 | |
| Accounts Receivable | 4,000 | |
| Inventory | 2,000 | |
| Loan Payable | | 5,000 |
| S. Nelson, Capital | | 2,000 |
| Sales Revenue | | 13,000 |
| Cost of Goods Sold | 3,000 | |
| Rent Expense | 1,000 | |
| Wages | 4,000 | |
| Supplies | 1,000 | |
| *Totals* | *$20,000* | *$20,000* |

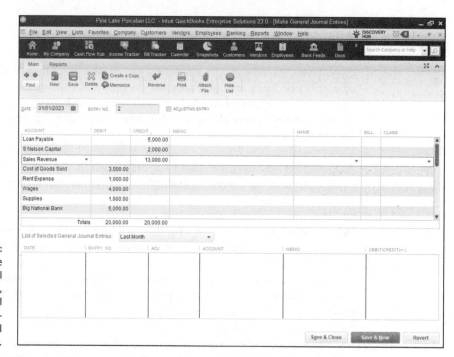

**FIGURE 1-9:**
The Make General Journal Entries window, showing the final part of a more-complicated trial balance.

# Chapter **2**

# Loading the Master File Lists

When you set up QuickBooks 2023, as a practical matter, you not only create a company file that you'll use to store financial information about your business, but also set up master file lists. These master file lists store information that you can use and reuse. One of the master file lists describes each of your customers; this master file of customer information includes the customer's name and address, contact information, account numbers, and so on.

In this chapter, I walk you through the process of adding information to each of the master files — or *lists*, as QuickBooks calls them — that you need to fill (or mostly fill) before you begin using QuickBooks on a day-to-day basis.

One important note: You don't need to *completely* fill your master files before you start doing anything. If you enter your active customers into the customer master file, your active vendors into the vendor master file, and so forth, that amount of information may be all you need to get started. With the information you entered through the QuickBooks Setup process (as described in Book 2, Chapter 1) and the addition of a few more entries in key master files, you may be able to add everything else on the fly. QuickBooks enables you to add entries to the various master files as you work with windows and dialog boxes that reference master-file information.

# Setting Up the Chart of Accounts List

The *Chart of Accounts list* is a list of accounts that you use to categorize your income, expenses, assets, liabilities, and owner's equity amounts. If you want to see a particular line item of financial data on a report, you need an account for that line item. If you want to budget by a particular line item, you need an account for that budget amount. If you want to report some bit of financial information on your tax returns, you need an account to collect that specific data.

Fortunately, the steps for creating new accounts are quite straightforward. To set up a new account within your Chart of Accounts list, follow these steps:

**1.** **Choose the Lists ⇨ Chart of Accounts command.**

QuickBooks displays the Chart of Accounts window, shown in Figure 2-1.

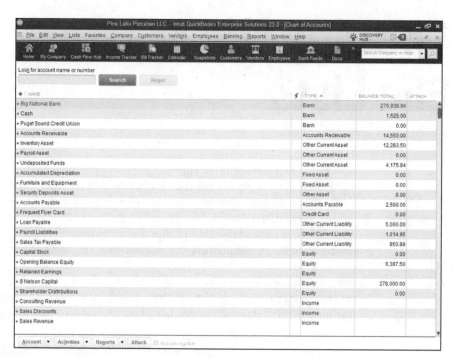

**FIGURE 2-1:**
The Chart of
Accounts window.

**2.** **Click the Account button at the bottom of the window.**

QuickBooks displays the Account menu. One of the Account menu options is New, which is the command that you use to add a new account.

3. **Add an account by choosing Account ⇨ New.**

QuickBooks displays the Add New Account: Choose Account Type window, as shown in Figure 2-2.

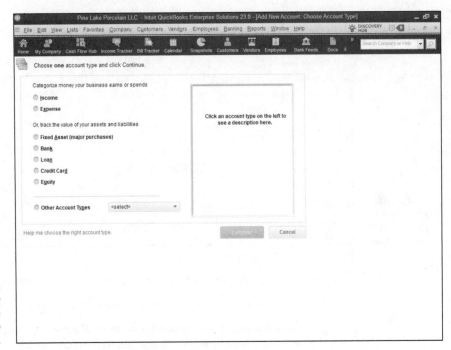

4. **Use the account-type buttons to identify the type of account that you're adding.**

QuickBooks supplies the following account types: Income, Expense, Fixed Asset, Bank, Loan, Credit Card, and Equity, as well as (if you select Other Account Types and open the Other Accounts Types drop-down list) Accounts Receivable, Other Current Asset, Other Asset, Accounts Payable, Other Current Liability, Long Term Liability, Cost of Goods Sold, Other Income, and Other Expense. If you have a question about which account type your new account fits into, you should review Book 1, Chapter 1, which describes how financial statements work. These account groups essentially tell QuickBooks the area of a financial statement account in which data gets reported. Note, too, that the first Add New Account window shows examples of the selected account type in the box above the Continue and Cancel command buttons.

5. **Click Continue.**

QuickBooks displays the second Add New Account window, as shown in Figure 2-3.

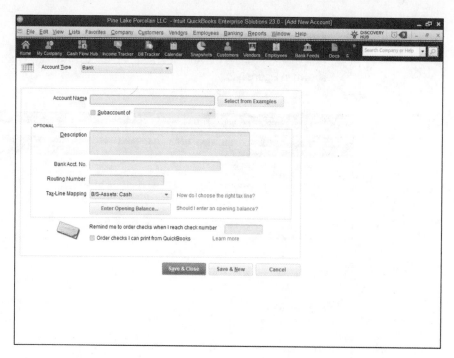

FIGURE 2-3:
The second Add
New Account
window.

**6.** **Use the Account Name box to give your new account a unique name.**

The name that you give the account will appear on your financial statements.

**7.** **If the account you're adding is a subaccount of a parent account, identify the parent account by selecting the Subaccount Of check box.**

After you select the Subaccount Of check box, name the parent account by using the Subaccount Of drop-down list.

**8.** **(Optional) If you're setting up a bank account that uses a currency other than your home-country currency, choose the bank account currency from the Currency drop-down list.**

In Book 2, Chapter 3, I talk a bit more about working with multiple currencies. But let me say this here: If you told QuickBooks that you work in multiple currencies (you would have done this during the QuickBooks EasyStep Interview setup process, discussed in Book 2, Chapter 1), QuickBooks wants you to identify those bank accounts, customers, and vendors that use a currency different from your home currency.

***Note:*** The Currency drop-down list doesn't appear in Figure 2-3 because within the example QuickBooks file I used for this book, the multiple-currency tracking feature isn't turned on. To turn on the multiple-currency feature, choose the Edit ⇨ Preferences command, select the Multiple Currencies preferences settings, click the Company Preferences tab, and then select the Yes I Use More Than One Currency radio button.

**9.** **(Optional) Provide a description for the new account.**

You don't need to provide a description. Without a description, QuickBooks can still use the account name in financial statements. If you want a more-descriptive label placed in accounting reports, however, use the Description box for this purpose.

**10.** **Provide other account information.**

The Add New Account window shown in Figure 2-3 includes a Bank Acct. No. box that lets you record the bank account number for a particular bank account. Other account types may have similar boxes for storing related account information. The credit card account type version of the Add New Account window lets you store the card number, for example. If you do have another box or two in which to store account information, use that space, if necessary, to collect the bits and pieces of data that you want to save.

**11.** **Identify the tax line on which the account information is to be reported by choosing a tax form and tax line from the Tax-Line Mapping drop-down list.**

You may not need to assign a particular account to a tax line if that account data isn't reported on the business's tax return. Cash account balances aren't reported on a sole proprietor's tax return, for example, so a bank account for a sole proprietor doesn't have any required tax line data. Cash account balances are recorded on a corporation's tax return, however. So if you're adding a bank account for a corporation, you use the Tax-Line Mapping drop-down list to identify the tax line on which the bank account information gets reported.

**WARNING**

**12.** **(Optional but dangerous) Consider recording an opening balance for the account.**

Typically, you shouldn't supply an opening account balance for an account, but the second Add New Account window does let you do so. In the window shown in Figure 2-3, you can click the Enter Opening Balance command button. When you click this button, QuickBooks displays a dialog box that you can use to set a starting account balance. All this sounds rather innocuous, but seriously, this is something you rarely do. (You should set starting balances for accounts by using a journal entry, as discussed at the end of Book 2, Chapter 1.) If you know something I don't, though, you can use this capability to set the starting balance for the account as of some date. One last caution, however. My accounting professors taught me two things that suggest that this approach to setting account balances is crazy:

- *Debits are supposed to equal credits.* If you're setting the opening balance for an account as part of setting up the new account, you're recording only half of the accounting transaction.

- *Entering the opening balance as part of setting up a new account means that no audit trail exists for the transaction.* Rather than having an invoice associated with a transaction or a check, or even a general journal entry, you're setting balances on the fly. But hey, maybe you *do* know something I don't.

**13.** After you describe the new account that you want to set up, click either Save & Close or Save & New to save the new account to the Chart of Accounts list.

**14.** (Optional) Click the Next button to save the account information and then redisplay the Add New Account window so that you can add another account.

TIP

If you look closely at Figure 2-3, you'll note some boxes, buttons, and even some hyperlinks that I haven't talked about. QuickBooks does supply other fields for collecting account information. And occasionally, QuickBooks also provides clickable hyperlinks and buttons that you can use to perform special tasks associated with the particular type of account. In the case of a bank account, for example, QuickBooks supplies an Order Checks hyperlink that you can use to learn more about this process.

And that's almost everything you need to know about adding accounts. The one other thing I should mention is the fact that the Account menu — the menu of commands that QuickBooks displays when you click the Account button in the Chart of Accounts window (refer to Figure 2-1) — provides several other useful commands for working with accounts. These commands include Delete, which you use to delete the selected account (as long as you haven't already used the account). The menu also provides an Edit button that you can use to make any changes in the selected account information (by using a window that looks very much like the New Account window shown in Figure 2-3). The Account menu also provides other commands that you can use to work with the Chart of Accounts list. Fortunately, most commands have self-descriptive names: Print List, Make Inactive, and so on.

TIP

The Activities button, which appears at the bottom of the Chart of Accounts window (refer to Figure 2-1), displays a menu of commands that you can use to write checks, make deposits, enter credit card charges, transfer funds, make journal entries, reconcile a bank account, use a register, and produce a working trial balance report. The Reports button displays a menu of commands that you can use to print reports containing account information. The Attach button lets you upload files — a PDF receipt for an equipment purchase, for example — from your computer to save into QuickBooks.

# Setting Up the Item List

If you choose the Lists ➪ Item List command, QuickBooks displays the Item List window, as shown in Figure 2-4. This window lists all the items that you've set up as part of running QuickBooks Setup and items that you've added manually since running the Setup Wizard.

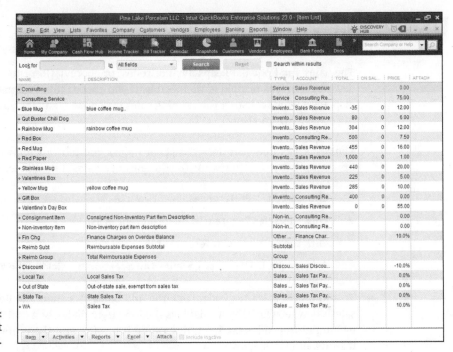

**FIGURE 2-4:**
The Item List window.

I don't talk about how you add items to the Item List window here, because Book 3, Chapter 3 details that process.

**REMEMBER**

Note, however, that the Item list is very important! It lets you keep track of what you buy, hold, and sell to your customers.

# Working with the Price Level List

The Price Level list lets you create price adjustments that you can use on the fly as you invoice customers, issue credit memos, and so forth. Because the Price Level list relates directly to how you work with and bill for inventory items, I describe how you work with that list in Book 3, Chapter 3. Rather than repeat information that's of interest to only a few people and isn't essential for getting started with QuickBooks, I refer you instead to Book 3, Chapter 3.

# Using Sales Tax Codes

The Sales Tax Code list keeps a list of codes, or abbreviations, that you can use to describe items as taxable or nontaxable. If you choose this command, QuickBooks displays a window listing the existing sales tax codes. (Usually, you see two existing codes: Tax and Non.)

The Sales Tax Code list doesn't appear unless you tell QuickBooks to track sales tax during setup or afterward. To add sales tax codes, take the following steps:

1. **Choose Edit ⇨ Preferences.**

2. **Click the Sales Tax item in the preferences list.**

3. **Click the Company Preferences tab.**

4. **Answer the Do You Charge Sales Tax question by clicking the Yes box.**

To add a new sales tax code, click the Add Sales Tax Item and describe the new sales tax when QuickBooks displays the New Item dialog box (not shown). Do this by naming the sales tax item, describing it briefly, and then providing the sales tax rate and tax agency.

# Setting Up a Payroll Item List

The Payroll Item list identifies items that appear on employee payroll check stubs. If you're using an outside payroll service bureau to handle your payroll — and this isn't a bad idea — you don't even need to worry about the Payroll Item list. If you're using the QuickBooks Enhanced Payroll Service, again, don't worry about the Payroll Item list. (In either case, the QuickBooks folks set up the payroll items that you use for recording payroll.) And in the case of Intuit's full-blown "we-do-everything" Payroll Service, you don't even need to track payroll inside QuickBooks, because the QuickBooks people do it at their office location on their computers.

If you do need to add payroll items, follow these steps:

1. **Choose the Lists ⇨ Payroll Item List command.**

   QuickBooks displays the Payroll Item list window (not shown).

2. **To add a new Payroll Item, click the Payroll Item button and then choose Payroll Item ⇨ New.**

   QuickBooks displays the Add New Payroll Item dialog box (not shown). You can choose to set up a new payroll item by using either the EZ Set Up method or the Custom Set Up method:

- *EZ Set Up:* If you want QuickBooks to help you, and you're setting up a common payroll item, click the EZ Set Up button, click Next, and simply follow the onscreen instructions.

- *Custom Set Up:* If you want to perform a custom setup of a payroll item, click the Custom Set Up button and then click Next. QuickBooks walks you through a multiple-screen interview — like the EasyStep Interview discussed in Book 2, Chapter 1 — that asks you about the payroll item to set up. The first dialog box that QuickBooks displays, for example, asks you to identify the type of payroll item that you want to create. You answer this question by selecting one of the radio buttons and then clicking Next.

**3. Name the payroll item.**

After you identify the type of payroll item, you name it. QuickBooks provides another version of the Add New Payroll Item dialog box that includes a field you fill in to give the new item a name.

**4. To finish the payroll item setup, click the Next button to move through the remaining payroll item setup questions.**

You identify the name of the government agency to which the liability is paid, the taxpayer identification number that uniquely identifies you to the taxing agency, the liability account that you use to track the items, the tax-form line that you use to report the item, the rules that QuickBooks should use for calculating the item (such as whether the item is subject to taxes), and a couple of other miscellaneous pieces of data. After you supply all this information and click the Finish button (which appears in the last Add New Payroll Item window), QuickBooks adds the new payroll item to the Payroll Item list.

TIP

The Payroll Item menu supplies commands that are useful for working with the Payroll Item list. In addition to the commands that you use to add an item to the list, the menu supplies commands for deleting payroll items, renaming payroll items, making payroll items active, and printing the list of payroll items.

# Setting Up Classes

QuickBooks lets you use classes to segregate or track financial data in ways that aren't possible when you use other bits of accounting information, such as the account number, the customer, the sales rep, the item, and so forth. A firm can use classes, for example, to segregate financial information by stores, business units, or geographical territories.

To set up classes, follow these steps:

1. **Choose the Lists ⇨ Class List command.**

   QuickBooks displays the Class List window, as shown in Figure 2-5.

   **TIP**

   If you don't see the Class List command, choose Edit ⇨ Preferences, click the Accounting icon, click the Company Preferences tab, and select the Use Class Tracking for Transaction check box.

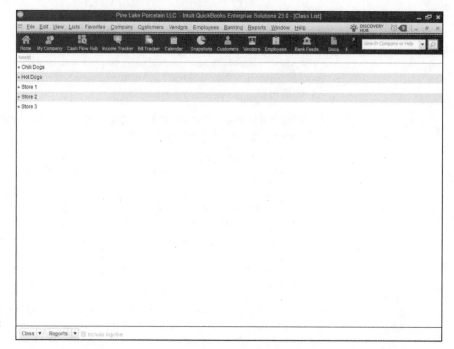

**FIGURE 2-5:**
The Class List window.

2. **To create a new class, choose Class ⇨ New at the bottom of the window.**

   QuickBooks displays the New Class dialog box, as shown in Figure 2-6.

3. **To name the new class, enter a name or abbreviation in the Class Name box.**

   Note that you enter the class name whenever you record a transaction that falls into the class. For this reason, you don't want to create lengthy or easy-to-mistype class names. Keep things short, simple, and easy.

4. **If the class that you're setting up is actually a subclass of a parent class, select the Subclass Of check box and then choose the parent class from the Subclass Of drop-down list.**

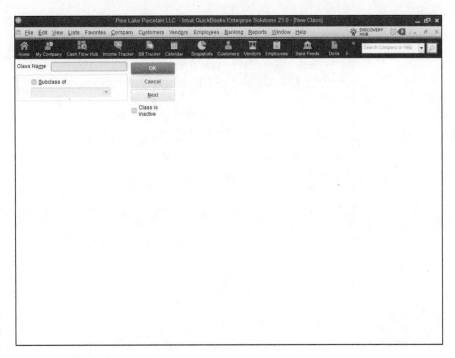

**FIGURE 2-6:**
The New Class
dialog box.

5. **Click OK to save the class.**

   Alternatively, click Cancel to not save the class or click the Next button to save the class and redisplay the New Class dialog box.

   If you don't want the class to be used anymore, you can select the Class Is Inactive check box.

**TIP**

The Class menu, which appears when you click the Class button, also supplies commands for editing the information of the selected class, for deleting the selected class, for making the selected class inactive, and for printing a list of classes, as well as several other useful commands. All these commands are pretty straightforward. Experiment with them to find out how they work.

# Setting Up a Customer List

A Customer list keeps track of all your customers and customer information, such as billing and shipping addresses.

Follow these steps to add a customer to the Customer list:

1. **Choose the Customers ➪ Customer Center command.**

   QuickBooks displays the Customer Information window, as shown in Figure 2-7.

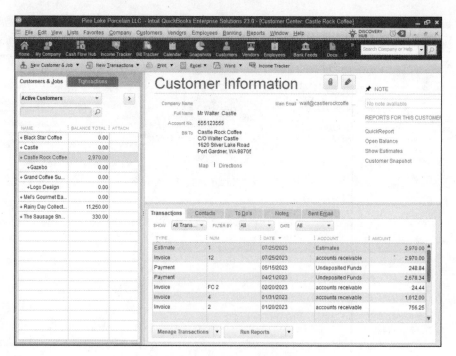

**FIGURE 2-7:**
The Customer
Information
window.

2. **To add a new customer, click the New Customer & Job drop-down list on the toolbar and then choose the New Customer command.**

   QuickBooks displays the New Customer window, as shown in Figure 2-8.

3. **Use the Customer Name box to give the customer a short name.**

   You don't need to enter the customer's full name in the Customer Name box. That information can go in the Company Name box, shown on the Address Info tab. You just want some abbreviated version of the customer name that you can use to refer to the customer within the QuickBooks accounting system.

4. **(Optional) If you bill your customer in a currency different from your usual home currency, choose that currency from the Currency drop-down list.**

   If you told QuickBooks that you work in multiple currencies — you would have done this during the EasyStep Interview setup process — QuickBooks wants you to identify when you invoice a customer and collect payments from a customer in a currency different from your home currency. (**Note:** The Currency drop-down list doesn't appear in Figure 2-8 because the multiple-currency tracking feature isn't turned on. If you want more information, see Book 2, Chapter 3.)

5. **(Usual rule) Ignore the Opening Balance and As Of boxes.**

   You typically don't want to set the customer's opening balance by using the Opening Balance and As Of boxes. That's not the right way to set your new customer accounts receivable balance. If you do this, you're essentially setting up the debit part of an entry without the corresponding credit part. Later, you'll have to enter crazy, wacky journal entries to fix your incomplete bookkeeping. But an exception to the usual rule exists, as discussed in the tip that follows.

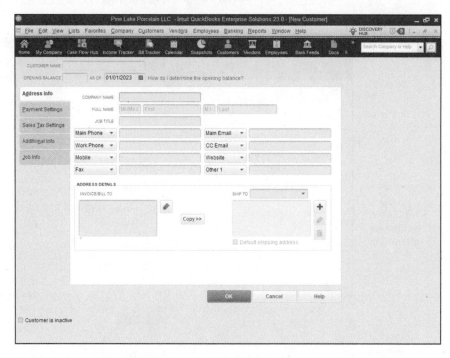

FIGURE 2-8:
The New
Customer
window.

**TIP**

Although the usual rule is that you don't want to set an opening balance for a customer, this rule has an important exception. As discussed at the end of Book 2, Chapter 1, you record your accounts receivable balance on the conversion date by setting an opening balance for each customer as of the conversion date. The sum of these opening balances is what QuickBooks uses to determine your total accounts receivable on the conversion date.

**6.** **Use the boxes of the Address Info tab to supply the company name and contact information, including contact name, phone numbers, fax numbers, email addresses, billing and shipping addresses, and so on.**

I'm not going to tell you that you should enter somebody's first and last name in the Full Name boxes or that the phone numbers of your customer go in the boxes labeled Main Phone and Work Phone. I figure that you don't need that kind of help.

**7.** **Click the Payment Settings tab to display the set of boxes shown in Figure 2-9.**

You can record the customer's account number, credit limit, payment terms, preferred payment and delivery methods, and even credit card information. Note that the Online Payments check boxes let you indicate that a customer

**TIP**

can pay you by using a credit card or bank transfer — but you need to have set up these services already. If you haven't set up the services, QuickBooks prompts you to set them up when you check one of these boxes.

I discuss the Price Level list and how it works in Book 3, Chapter 3.

**FIGURE 2-9:**
The Payment
Settings tab.

8. **(Optional) If you're tracking sales taxes, click the Sales Tax Settings tab to display the boxes you'll use to identify this customer's sales tax rate.**

   The Sales Tax Settings tab (not shown) includes a Tax Code drop-down list that you use to indicate which sales tax code applies to this particular customer. You can also identify the actual sales tax item and, if relevant, the resale number.

9. **Supply a bit of additional information about the customer.**

   If you click the Additional Info tab, shown in Figure 2-10, QuickBooks displays several other boxes that you can use to collect and store customer information. You can use the Customer Type drop-down list, for example, to categorize a customer as fitting into a particular customer type. (I talk about setting up a Customer Type list later in this chapter.) And you can use the Rep drop-down list to identify the customer's default sales rep. Finally, you can click the Define Fields button to specify additional fields that you want to collect and report for the customer.

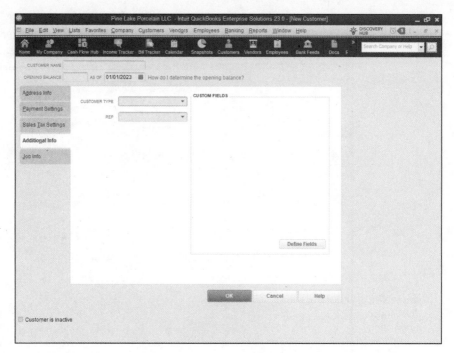

FIGURE 2-10:
The Additional
Info tab.

**10.** **(Optional) Click the Job Info tab to describe the customer job.**

The Job Info tab (not shown) lets you describe information associated with a particular job being performed for a customer. You use the Job Info tab if you not only set up a customer, but also set up a job for that customer. See Book 4, Chapter 5 for more information on how job costing works.

**11.** **When you finish describing the customer, click the Save & Close or Save & New button to save your description.**

# Setting Up the Vendor List

Just as you use a Customer list to keep records of all your customers, you use a Vendor list to keep records of your vendors. Like a Customer list, a Vendor list lets you collect and record information, such as the vendor's address, the contact person, and so on.

To add a vendor to your Vendor list, follow these steps:

**1.** **Choose the Vendors ⇨ Vendor Center command.**

When you do, QuickBooks displays the Vendor Information window, as shown in Figure 2-11.

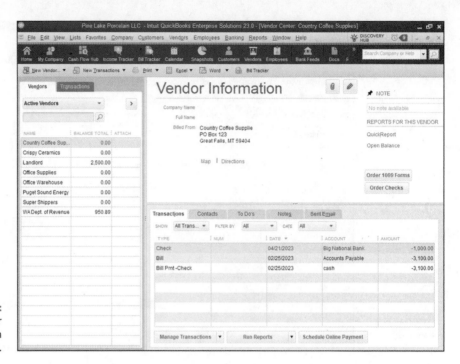

FIGURE 2-11:
The Vendor
Information
window.

2. **To add a new vendor, click the New Vendor drop-down list on the toolbar and then choose New Vendor.**

   QuickBooks displays the New Vendor window, as shown in Figure 2-12.

3. **Give the vendor a name in the Vendor Name box.**

   As is the case with the Customer list, you use this name to refer to the vendor within QuickBooks. For this reason, an abbreviation is fine. You just want something easy to enter and easy to remember.

4. **(Optional) If you pay your vendor in a currency different from your usual home currency, choose that currency from the Currency drop-down list.**

   If you told QuickBooks that you work in multiple currencies — you would have done this during the EasyStep Interview setup process — QuickBooks wants you to identify when you receive bills from or pay a vendor in a currency different from your home currency. (*Note:* Figure 2-12 doesn't show the Currency drop-down list because the multiple-currency tracking feature isn't turned on.)

5. **(Usual rule) Ignore the Opening Balance and As Of fields.**

   Don't do anything with the Opening Balance and As Of boxes. People who don't know better use those boxes to enter the opening balance owed a vendor and the date the amount is owed, but these entries only create problems later. At some point in the future, this poor soul's accountant will need to find and correct this error. As when you add new customers, however, an exception to the usual rule exists, as discussed in the tip that follows.

**TIP**

Although the usual rule is that you don't want to set an opening balance for a vendor, this rule has an important exception. As discussed at the end of Book 2, Chapter 1, you record your accounts payable balance on the conversion date by setting an opening balance for each vendor as of the conversion date. The sum of these opening balances is what QuickBooks uses to determine your total accounts payable on the conversion date.

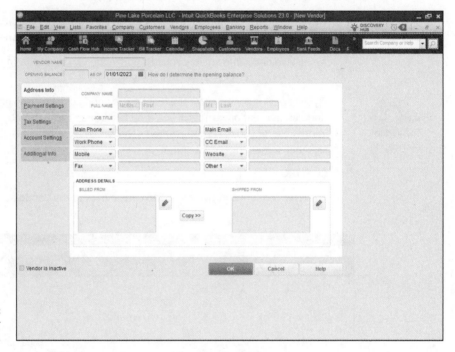

**FIGURE 2-12:**
The New Vendor
window.

**6.** **Supply the vendor address information.**

The Address Info tab supplies a bunch of easy-to-understand boxes that you use to collect vendor name and address information. You enter, predictably, the vendor's full name in the Company Name box.

You can click the Edit buttons on the Address Info tab to display another dialog box called the Edit Address Information dialog box, which lets you enter the address in typical street address, city, state, and zip-code format. The Edit buttons appear to the right of the Billed From and Shipped From address blocks.

### 7. Supply any additional information necessary.

The Payment Settings tab (see Figure 2-13) collects the most relevant vendor information, including account number, credit limit, and payment terms, but if you click the Tax Settings tab, the Account Settings tab, or the Additional Info tab, QuickBooks displays a handful of other boxes that you can use to collect and store information:

- *The Tax Settings tab* lets you collect the vendor's tax identification number so that you can (as sometimes required by federal tax laws) send the vendor a Form 1099 at the end of the year.

- *The Account Settings tab* lets you specify which accounts QuickBooks should use to prefill account fields when entering a transaction for the vendor.

- *The Additional Info tab* lets you categorize the vendor according to type and also lets you create other custom fields.

**TIP**

If you're paying a vendor for the first time, a good guideline is to get their tax ID number. If a vendor won't give you their tax ID number — thereby making it impossible for you to report payments that you make to them — it's probably a sign that something is a bit amiss.

### 8. Click OK.

The New Vendor window closes, and you go back to the Vendor Center.

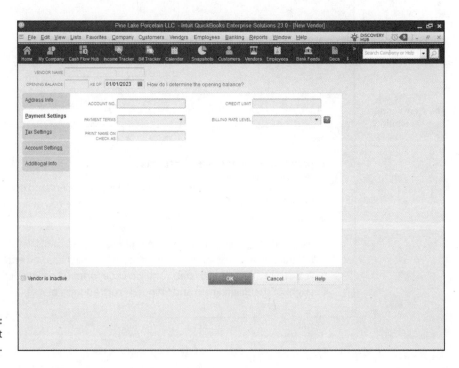

**TIP**

If you click the Account Settings tab (the fourth tab available in the New Vendor window), QuickBooks displays boxes you can use to list the accounts that you want QuickBooks to fill in for you automatically when you record a check to some vendor or when you record a bill from some vendor. If the check to the phone company pays telephone expenses, for example, you could tell QuickBooks to prefill that expense category the next time you enter a bill or record a check to pay that vendor. It won't enter an amount, as (obviously) the amount can change, but you won't have to search all your accounts to find telephone expenses if you use this option.

# Setting Up a Fixed Assets List

If you choose the Lists ⇨ Fixed Asset Item List command, QuickBooks displays the Fixed Asset Item list window. You can use this window to see a list of the fixed assets — furniture, equipment, machinery, vehicles, and so forth — that you've purchased. That is, you can see this list after you click the Item drop-down list, choose New, and fill in the New Item window for each fixed asset. Figure 2-14 shows the New Item window you use to describe each fixed asset.

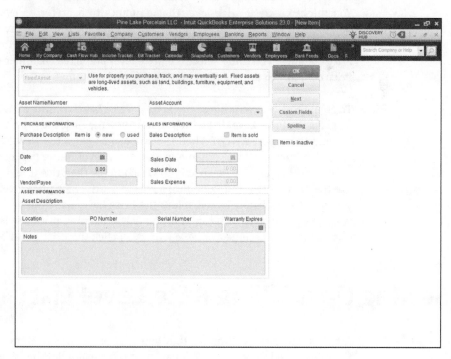

**FIGURE 2-14:** You describe each fixed asset by using the New Item window.

Let me make a couple of comments about the QuickBooks Fixed Asset Item list. The Fixed Asset Item list doesn't really integrate with the QuickBooks general ledger. You record the purchase or disposal of fixed assets by using regular old QuickBooks transactions. You might record the purchase of a particular fixed asset simply by entering a check in the usual fashion. And you might record the disposal of a fixed asset by entering a general ledger journal entry.

The Fixed Assets Item list, then, just acts as a stand-alone list that lets you track the fixed assets you purchased. Because the list is so stand-alone-ish, I'm not going to spend much time talking about it in this book. Let me also say that your CPA probably — no, surely — maintains a list of your fixed assets because they need that list to correctly include depreciation on your tax return and in your financial statements (if you get a CPA to help prepare them). For this reason, some people — including me — see the Fixed Asset Item list as being a little bit redundant.

# Setting Up a Price Level List

A *price level* changes the sales price up or down when you do things like invoice. You might create a price level that amounts to a preferred customer discount on specified items. When you create an invoice for those items, rather than use the standard price for the item (which appears in the Create Invoice window's Price column), you could select the price level preferred customer discount (in the Price column) to use the discounted preferred customer.

To create a price level, choose the Lists ⇨ Price Level command. When QuickBooks displays the Price Level list window (not shown), click the Price Level drop-down list and then choose New. When QuickBooks displays the New Price Level dialog box, give the price level a name in the Price Level Name text box, use the Price Level Type box and list to specify to which items the price level applies, and then use the Adjust Price and Rounding boxes to set the new price level's prices. When you click OK, QuickBooks redisplays the Price Level list window — this time with your new price level. You can edit and delete existing price levels by using other commands that become available when you click the Price Level button.

# Setting Up a Billing Rate Level List

A *billing rate* sets the amount that you charge for service items. Whereas a law firm might sell only hours of legal advice, for example, the item "legal advice" would be billed at different rates for different attorneys. An attorney just out of law school might have their time billed at one rate, whereas a senior partner in the firm might bill at another, probably much higher rate.

To set up a billing rate, you choose the Lists ⇨ Billing Rate Levels List command. When QuickBooks displays the Billing Rate Level window (not shown), click the Billing Rate Level drop-down list and then choose New to display the New Billing Rate Level dialog box. You use the New Billing Rate Level dialog box to define a billing rate, giving the billing rate level a name, and then set a fixed hourly rate for the billing-rate level or different hourly rates for different service items.

After you create billing-rate levels with the Billing Rate Levels List command, by the way, you need to connect those levels with specific employees so that the correct rate gets used when an employee's time is billed. To do this, display the Employee Center window by choosing the Employees ⇨ Employee Center command. Then right-click the employee, choose Edit Employee from the shortcut menu, click the Additional Info tab when QuickBooks displays the Edit Employee dialog box, and select the appropriate billing rate in the Billing Rate Level list box.

# Setting Up Your Employees

If you choose the Employees ⇨ Employee Center command, QuickBooks displays the Employee Center window (not shown). You can use this window to see a list of the employees — active or inactive — whom you've identified to QuickBooks. You can also use this window's New Employee button to add employees to the list.

Because I discuss how to add employees to the Employee list in Book 3, Chapter 5, I won't repeat that information here.

# Setting Up an Other Names List

If you choose the Lists ⇨ Other Names List command, QuickBooks displays the Other Names list window (not shown). The Other Names list identifies those businesses or people that you pay but that don't fall into one of these other standard categories: customers, vendors, and employees. You might use the Other Names list to identify government agencies that you pay, for example.

To add a name to the Other Names list, click the Other Names button, which appears at the bottom of the Other Names window. When QuickBooks displays the Other Names menu, choose New. The New Name window that QuickBooks displays after you choose the New command provides boxes for entering a name, identifying the entity, recording an address, and so on. I don't show this window here because it's a simplified version of the window that you use to identify and describe a customer, vendor, or employee.

# Setting Up the Profile Lists

If you choose the Lists ⇨ Customer & Vendor Profile List command, QuickBooks displays a submenu of commands that you use to create some of the mini-lists that QuickBooks uses to ease your bookkeeping and accounting. The Profile lists include lists of sales reps, customer types, vendor types, job types, payment terms, customer messages, payment methods, shipping methods, and vehicles. Most of the Profile lists are pretty darn simple to use. If you choose the Sales Rep list command, for example, QuickBooks displays the Sales Rep list window. Then you click the Sales Rep drop-down list and choose New. QuickBooks displays the New Sales Rep dialog box, as shown in Figure 2-15. I bet you can figure out how to use this dialog box.

**FIGURE 2-15:**
The New Sales Rep dialog box.

In case you're still experiencing a certain amount of accounting anxiety, let me just point out that you enter the name of the sales representative in the Sales Rep

Name box. Then, throwing caution to the wind, you enter the sales rep's initials in the Sales Rep Initials box. When you click OK, QuickBooks adds the sales rep to your Sales Rep list.

The other Profile lists work in the same simple, scaled-down fashion. You choose the Profile list from the submenu, click the Profile List button, and choose New. When QuickBooks displays a window, you use one or two boxes to describe the new Profile list.

Just to prove to you that this process really is as easy as I say, take a look at the New Customer Message dialog box (accessible from the Customer Message list), shown in Figure 2-16. This dialog box is the one you use to create a new customer message for placement at the bottom of customer invoices and credit memos.

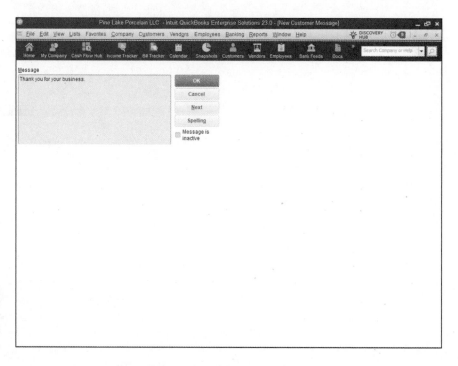

**FIGURE 2-16:**
The New
Customer
Message
dialog box.

**TIP**

If you want to track vehicle mileage within QuickBooks — and note that you usually must track business vehicle mileage to claim business vehicle expenses as a tax deduction — you can maintain a list of business vehicles by using the Vehicle list. This list makes it easy to track your business vehicles — something you do by choosing the Company ⇨ Enter Vehicle Mileage command.

**TIP**

QuickBooks may provide access to other lists via the Lists menu. You can access templates you create for invoicing and other forms by choosing the Lists ⇨ Templates command. (I discuss form templates in Book 3, Chapter 1.) And depending on how you've installed the software, QuickBooks may add lists I haven't mentioned here. Depending on your installation and the state where you operate, QuickBooks may display a list of Workers Compensation items, for example.

Chapter **3**

# Fine-Tuning QuickBooks

You can fine-tune how QuickBooks works for you by setting preferences. In fact, just so you know, much of what you do when you run QuickBooks Setup via the Detailed Start route (also known as the QuickBooks EasyStep Interview) is provide information that QuickBooks uses to fine-tune. If you indicate that you charge customers sales tax, for example, the EasyStep Interview describes how sales tax should work for your business by using the sales tax preferences.

Because these preferences have so much effect on how QuickBooks works and on how a particular user works with QuickBooks, I devote this chapter to describing how you change the preferences. None of this material is particularly complicated, but because QuickBooks provides a rich set of preferences options, I cover quite a bit of material. Don't worry: You don't have to read this chapter from beginning to end. Simply use it as a reference when you have a question about how to change the way QuickBooks works in a particular area.

# Accessing the Preferences Settings

You can set preferences within QuickBooks in two ways:

>> **During the Detailed Start/EasyStep Interview:** You actually set all the preferences, or at least all the starting preferences for QuickBooks, when you run the EasyStep Interview. Most of the time, the preferences that the Detailed Start/EasyStep Interview sets are correct. QuickBooks is very smart about the way it asks questions and translates your answers into preferences settings. But if your business changes, if you make a mistake during the setup interview, or if someone in your office ran the Detailed Start/EasyStep Interview for you, you may still need to check and fiddle-faddle with these preferences.

>> **By changing the preferences manually:** You can change the preferences manually by choosing the Edit ⇨ Preferences command. QuickBooks displays the Preferences dialog box, as shown in Figure 3-1. QuickBooks groups categories of preferences. All the accounting preferences, for example, are grouped into an accounting preference set, and all the checking account preferences are grouped into a checking preference set. If you look closely at Figure 3-1, you see that along the left edge of the Preferences dialog box, QuickBooks displays a list of icons. The first icon is Accounting. The second icon is Benefits & HR. To see the preferences within one of these groups, you click that preference's icon.

One other item to note about the Preferences dialog box is that it supplies, in general, two tabs of preferences for each preference set. Preferences that are specific to an individual user appear on the My Preferences tab, shown in Figure 3-1. Preferences that are tied to the company data file appear on the Company Preferences tab, shown in Figure 3-2.

Not every My Preferences tab gives you options for changing the way that QuickBooks works. Sometimes, a particular set of preferences gives personal options; sometimes, it doesn't.

The My Preferences tab of the Bills set of preferences, for example, provides no personalized options. In other words, you can't tell QuickBooks that in your firm, billing works differently for different users. This makes sense, right? Billing needs to work the same way for every user within a firm. With other preferences settings, QuickBooks may allow different options for different users. You see this as I discuss the various sets of preferences in the remainder of this chapter.

Now I'm going to walk you through a discussion of each of these preferences sets. I talk both about the My Preferences option (if available) and the Company Preferences option.

**FIGURE 3-1:**
The My Preferences tab of the Accounting Preferences dialog box.

**FIGURE 3-2:**
The Company Preferences tab of the General Preferences dialog box.

# Setting the Accounting Preferences

The My Preferences tab of the Accounting Preferences dialog box (refer to Figure 3-1) provides a single option: You can tell QuickBooks that you want it to autofill information when recording a general journal entry.

Don't get irritated with the lack of personalization, however. This almost total lack of individually personalized preferences makes sense, if you think about it. Accounting for a business needs to work the same way for Jane as it does for Joe and for Susan.

You do have the option to set several company preferences for accounting, however. Again, this makes sense if you think about it. Different companies run their accounting systems in different ways.

Figure 3-3 shows the Company Preferences tab of the Accounting Preferences dialog box.

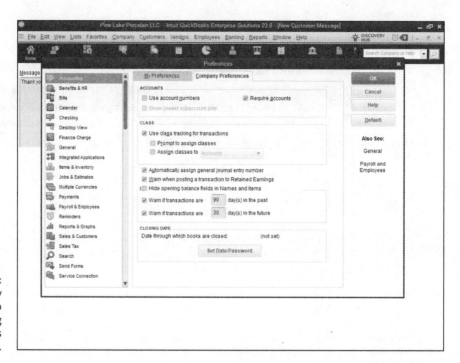

**FIGURE 3-3:**
The Company Preferences tab of the Accounting Preferences dialog box.

## Using account numbers

By default, QuickBooks lets you use names to identify accounts in the Chart of Accounts list or in the accounts list. The account that you use to track wages expense may be known as "wages," for example, but you can select the Use Account Numbers check box to tell QuickBooks that you want to use account numbers rather than account names for identifying accounts. Larger businesses and businesses with very lengthy lists of accounts often use account numbers. When you use numbers, you can more easily control both the ordering of accounts on a financial statement and the insertion of new accounts into the Chart of Accounts list.

The Show Lowest Subaccount Only check box (refer to Figure 3-3) lets you tell QuickBooks that it should display the lowest subaccount rather than the higher parent account in financial statements. QuickBooks allows you to create subaccounts, which are accounts within accounts (discussed further in Book 2, Chapter 2). You can also create sub-subaccounts, which are accounts within subaccounts. You use subaccounts to track assets more finely, liabilities, equity amounts, revenue, and expenses.

## Setting general accounting options

The Company Preferences tab (not shown) provides the following six general accounting check boxes, as well as date warnings and closing date settings. (The check boxes are probably self-explanatory to anybody who has done a bit of accounting with QuickBooks, but for new QuickBooks users, I provide a brief description of what each one does.)

>> **Use Account Numbers:** The Use Account Numbers check box, if selected, enables you to enter an account number for a transaction. The associated check box, Show Lowest Subaccount Only, tells QuickBooks to display only the name and account number of a subaccount (if you're using one) instead of the full heritage of the account. If you use a lot of levels of subaccounts, this option can really clean up views, making it easier to tell what account you're looking at.

>> **Require Accounts:** The Require Accounts check box, if selected, tells QuickBooks that you must specify an account for a transaction. This makes sense. If you aren't using accounts to track the amounts that flow into and out of the business, you aren't really doing accounting. It would never make sense, in my humble opinion, to deselect the Require Accounts check box.

- **Use Class Tracking for Transactions:** The Use Class Tracking for Transactions check box lets you tell QuickBooks that you want to use not only accounts to track your financial information, but also *classes*. Classes let you split account-level information in another way. This sounds complicated, but it's really quite simple. The account list, for example, lets you track revenue and expenses by categories of revenue and expense. You may track expenses by using categories such as wages, rent, and supplies. Classes, therefore, provide you a way to track this information in another dimension. You can split wages expense into those wages spent for two locations of your business, for example. A restaurateur with two restaurants may want to do this. Note that QuickBooks also provides boxes you can check to indicate that QuickBooks should prompt you to assign classes and to assign classes to accounts, items, or names.

- **Automatically Assign General Journal Entry Number:** This check box tells QuickBooks to assign numbers to the general journal entries that you enter by using the Make General Journal Entries command. You want to leave this check box selected. General journal entries, by the way, are typically entered by your CPA or your professional on-staff accountant.

- **Warn When Posting a Transaction to Retained Earnings:** This check box tells QuickBooks to display a warning message whenever you attempt (or someone else attempts) to directly debit or credit its retained earnings account. (Normally, you don't want to directly debit or credit the retained earnings account, and only skilled accountants would enter transactions directly into retained earnings in any case.)

- **Hide Opening Balance Fields in Names and Items:** Check this box to tell QuickBooks to hide opening balance information for customers, vendors, and other names and for items.

- **Date Warnings:** The Date Warnings boxes tell QuickBooks to warn you when you enter (or someone else enters) a transaction with a date too far in the past or too far into the future. If you check either of the Date Warnings boxes, you also want to specify how many days are too far into the past or too far into the future.

- **Closing Date setting:** The Closing Date box lets you identify a date before which your QuickBooks data file can't be changed. In other words, if you set the closing date to December 31, 2023, you're telling QuickBooks that you don't want any changes made to the QuickBooks data file *before* this date. This means that someone can't modify a transaction that's dated before your closing date without getting a scary warning message. It also means that someone can't enter a transaction by using a date before this closing date. You can click the Set Date/Password button to display a dialog box that lets you specify a closing date and create the password required when someone wants to add an old transaction or modify an old transaction.

**TIP**

Long ago, past versions of QuickBooks let you turn an Audit Trail feature on and off by using the Company Preferences tab of the Accounting Preferences dialog box. All recent versions of QuickBooks provide an *always-on audit trail,* however, so you don't see an Audit Trail check-box accounting preference anymore. An audit trail, by the way, simply keeps a list of who makes which changes to transactions. Accountants, predictably, love audit trails. Audit trails enable someone, such as your CPA or an Internal Revenue Service auditor, to come in after the fact and figure out why an account balance is what it is.

# Setting the Bills Preferences

If you display the Preferences dialog box and click the Bills icon, you can set company-level preferences for handling vendor bills. You can specify, for example, that bills are considered to be due a certain number of days after their receipt by entering a value in the appropriate text box. You can also use these company-level preferences to specify that early-payment discounts should be used and to choose an account for recording the value of these discounts. (I don't show you a figure of the Company Preferences tab of the Bills Preferences dialog box. It's really not worth your time.)

# Setting the Calendar Preferences

If you display the Preferences dialog box and click the Calendar icon, you can set your personal preferences for showing calendar information within QuickBooks, including a preference to remember previous calendar settings, the view used to show weeks, which transactions you want to appear on the calendar, and how you want calendar reminders to show. (As with the Bills Preferences, I don't show you a figure of the My Preferences tab of the Calendar Preferences dialog box because the boxes are straightforward.)

# Setting the Checking Preferences

If you display the Preferences dialog box and click the Checking icon, QuickBooks displays either the My Preferences tab, shown in Figure 3-4, or the Company Preferences tab, shown in Figure 3-5.

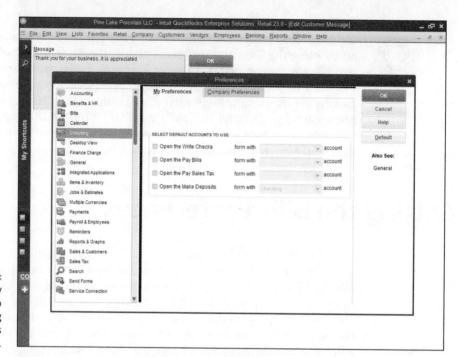

**FIGURE 3-4:**
The My Preferences tab of the Checking Preferences dialog box.

**FIGURE 3-5:**
The Company Preferences tab of the Checking Preferences dialog box.

The My Preferences tab of the Checking Preferences dialog box lets you tell QuickBooks which account it should suggest as a default account when you open particular types of windows within QuickBooks. If you look closely at Figure 3-4, you see the Open the Write Checks box, which is the first check box on the tab. To the right of the Open the Write Checks box, you see the Form with X Account drop-down list. If you select the Open the Write Checks check box, you can choose an account from the Form with X Account drop-down list. This setting tells QuickBooks to use or suggest the specified account every time you open the Write Checks window.

The My Preferences tab also includes check boxes that you can use to specify the default account for the Pay Bills window, the Pay Sales Tax window, and the Make Deposits window. If you have multiple checking accounts set up, setting the default accounts by using the My Preferences tab is a good idea. Setting these preferences makes it less likely that you'll erroneously write checks on or pay bills from the wrong account.

The Company Preferences tab, shown in Figure 3-5, provides options that you can use to describe how checks work within QuickBooks:

>> **Print Account Names on Voucher:** This check box lets you indicate to QuickBooks that it should print account names on the voucher portion of the check.

>> **Change Check Date When Non-Cleared Check Is Printed:** Select this check box to tell QuickBooks to use the current system date as the printed check date.

>> **Start with Payee Field on Check:** Select this check box to tell QuickBooks to place the insertion point, or text cursor, in the Payee field when you open the Write Checks window.

>> **Warn about Duplicate Check Numbers:** Selecting this check box tells QuickBooks to alert you to duplicate check numbers. (You want to leave this check box selected, obviously, so that you don't use duplicate or erroneous check numbers.)

>> **Autofill Payee Account Number in Check Memo:** Select this check box to tell QuickBooks to fill in the payee account number automatically when you write a check. QuickBooks retrieves the account number for a payee from the Vendor list or from the Other Names list.

» **Select Default Accounts to Use:** These check boxes let you specify which account QuickBooks suggests when you open the Create Paychecks window or open the Pay Payroll Liabilities window. Essentially, then, these boxes let you tell QuickBooks which checking account you use to write payroll checks and to pay payroll liabilities, such as federal income tax withholding amounts.

» **Bank Feeds:** If you've turned on online banking for QuickBooks, QuickBooks provides option buttons you can use to change the way that online transaction information appears in the online banking window. Book 3, Chapter 4 discusses the QuickBooks online banking tool set.

# Changing the Desktop View

Figure 3-6 shows the My Preferences tab of the Desktop View Preferences dialog box. The My Preferences tab provides View radio buttons — One Window and Multiple Windows — that let you indicate whether QuickBooks should use one window or multiple windows for displaying all its information. The Multiple Windows option looks like older versions of Microsoft Windows. When this option is selected, an application such as QuickBooks displays multiple floating document windows within the application program window. If you have a question about how this feature works, your best bet is simply to try both view settings.

The Desktop radio buttons let you specify whether and when QuickBooks should save the current appearance, or *view,* of the desktop. You can select the Save When Closing Company radio button to tell QuickBooks that it should save the view of the desktop when you close a company. When you reopen a company, QuickBooks reuses this desktop view. You can also select the Save Current Desktop radio button to tell QuickBooks to save the current view and then reuse this view when QuickBooks later opens. If you don't want to make changes to the default desktop view, select the Don't Save the Desktop radio button.

The Desktop check boxes let you specify whether QuickBooks should display the QuickBooks home page and use colored icons and a light background for the top icon bar. If you select a check box, QuickBooks adds the home page or tweaks the icon-bar coloring.

**FIGURE 3-6:**
The My
Preferences tab
of the Desktop
View Preferences
dialog box.

The Windows Settings buttons let you access the Windows Display Properties and Windows Sounds Properties settings. Typically, you'd make changes to Windows Display Properties and Windows Sounds Properties by using the Control Panel tools, but you can make changes from within QuickBooks by clicking these two buttons. (In actuality, when you click these buttons, QuickBooks starts the Control Panel tools.)

**TIP**

If you have questions about how Windows Display Properties or Sounds Properties work, refer to the Windows Help file or to a good book such as *Windows 11 For Dummies,* by Andy Rathbone (John Wiley & Sons, Inc.).

The Company Preferences available for the Desktop View Preferences let you specify what icons appear on the QuickBooks home page, as shown in Figure 3-7. The Customers set of check boxes, for example, lets you specify which customer-related accounting tasks are available via icons on the home page. The Vendors check box lets you specify whether you want to enter and pay bills using the Enter Bills and Pay Bills command. Near the bottom of the Company Preferences tab of the Desktop View Preferences dialog box, QuickBooks supplies hyperlinks you can click to turn on and off the display of other accounting task icons.

**FIGURE 3-7:**
The Company
Preferences tab
of the Desktop
View Preferences
dialog box.

# Setting Finance Charge Calculation Rules

The Finance Charge Preferences settings let you specify how QuickBooks should calculate finance charges on overdue invoices to customers. None of the My Preferences options is available for finance charges — only Company Preferences options. Because I describe how the Company Preferences tab of the Finance Charge Preferences dialog box works in Book 3, Chapter 1, I won't repeat that information here.

# Setting General Preferences

Figure 3-8 shows the My Preferences tab of the General Preferences dialog box. This tab provides check boxes that you can select to tell QuickBooks to do the following:

>> To move the selection cursor from one field on the window to the next field when you press Enter

>> To open drop-down lists automatically when you're typing

» To beep when you record a transaction

» To place a decimal point two digits from the right end of the number automatically

» To warn you when you're editing an existing transaction

» To bring back all the one-time Help messages that you may have suppressed

» To turn off pop-up messages for products and services

» To show tooltips for clipped text

» To warn you when you're deleting an existing transaction or some unused items on a list

» To run QuickBooks in the background even when you're not using QuickBooks (to make QuickBooks start faster)

» To recall account or transaction information automatically — telling QuickBooks, for example, to automatically recall the last transaction for a particular customer, vendor, or employee

» To use either today's date or the last entered date as the default date

» To keep custom item information changed as part of entering a transaction

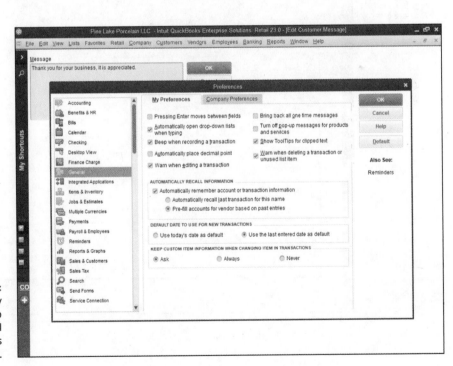

**FIGURE 3-8:**
The My Preferences tab of the General Preferences dialog box.

**TIP**

If you have specific questions about the My Preferences check boxes that are available for the General Preferences options, click the Help button that appears along the right edge of the Preferences dialog box. QuickBooks provides brief but useful descriptions of how the Preferences options work and what they do.

Figure 3-9 shows the Company Preferences tab of the General Preferences dialog box. The Time Format radio buttons let you specify whether QuickBooks should show the minutes in an hour as a decimal value or as minutes. The Time Format radio button descriptions include examples of how these two approaches vary, so look closely at the dialog box if you have questions. The Company Preferences tab includes a check box that lets you specify that QuickBooks should always show years using four digits. The tab also includes a check box that you can select to tell QuickBooks not to update the name information for a particular customer, vendor, employee, or other name when you're saving a new transaction for that customer, vendor, employee, or other name. The Manage Login Settings section allows users to open the company file or switch to another company file without having to re-enter login credentials for a specified period of time. Enabling this feature is probably not a good idea if multiple users are accessing the same company file on the same computer.

**FIGURE 3-9:**
The Company Preferences tab of the General Preferences dialog box.

# Controlling Integrated Applications

The Integrated Applications Preferences aren't personal, so no options are available on the My Preferences tab. The Company Preferences tab of the Integrated Applications Preferences dialog box, however, does control and track other applications or computer programs that open the QuickBooks company data files. Figure 3-10 shows the Company Preferences tab of the Integrated Applications Preferences dialog box.

**FIGURE 3-10:** The Company Preferences tab of the Integrated Applications Preferences dialog box.

The check box titled Don't Allow Any Applications to Access This Company File check box, if selected, tells QuickBooks that it shouldn't allow other applications to access this company data file. The check box titled Notify the User Before Running Any Application Whose Certificate Has Expired, if selected, tells Quick-Books that it shouldn't allow any program whose security certificate is out of date to open the QuickBooks company data file without first notifying the user (that's you).

The list box shows the names of the applications that previously requested access to the QuickBooks company data file. You can remove an application from this list by selecting the application and then clicking the Remove button. You can change the rules or properties that the QuickBooks program applies to access this other application by selecting the application and then clicking the Properties button.

# Controlling Inventory

No personal preferences are available for inventory tracking and control, but QuickBooks provides several Company Preferences features regarding inventory and items, as shown in Figure 3-11. You can turn the QuickBooks inventory and purchase order features on and off. You can specify that you want to be warned if you enter a purchase order number you've previously used. And you can specify how QuickBooks determines whether you have or don't have enough inventory to sell. (In the Enterprise Solutions version of QuickBooks, you can also indicate whether negative inventory balances are allowed.)

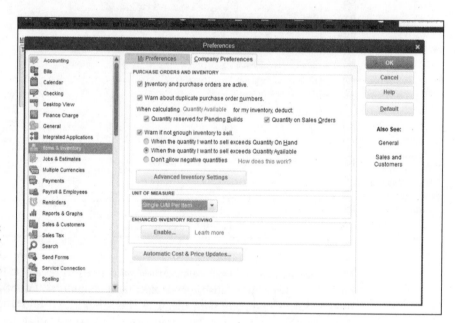

**FIGURE 3-11:**
The Company Preferences tab of the Items & Inventory Preferences dialog box.

If you buy or sell an item using more than one unit of measure — say, you sell fabric both by the yard and by the bolt (the rolled-up fabric) — QuickBooks lets you quantify your inventory items by using more than a single unit of measure. If you're interested in doing this, select Multiple U/M Per Item from the Unit of Measure drop-down list.

If your business operation processes multiple inventory receipts for a single vendor bill, multiple vendor bills for a single item receipt, or prepayments for inventory, you may want to consider enabling QuickBooks's Enhanced Inventory Receiving (EIR) feature if you're using QuickBooks Enterprise Solutions. By turning on this feature, you probably can improve your inventory item counts and avoid the sorts of item count and QuickBooks errors that often occur in these more complicated inventory situations. You can't turn off enhanced inventory receiving after you turn it on, however. Accordingly, research the details of the QuickBooks EIR feature (by clicking the Learn More hyperlink) or consult your accountant before you click the Enable button in the Enhanced Inventory Receiving section.

# Controlling How Jobs and Estimates Work

Because no personal preferences are available for Jobs & Estimates preferences, the My Preferences tab of this Preferences dialog box shows no options. You have several company preferences available regarding jobs and estimates, however, as shown in Figure 3-12. The Pending text box lets you describe what term or word should be used for jobs that have been submitted but haven't been accepted or rejected. The Awarded text box lets you provide a term or description that you want to use within QuickBooks to identify those jobs that customers or clients have accepted. The default description of an awarded job is, cleverly, *Awarded*. The In Progress, Closed, and Not Awarded text boxes similarly let you describe what term you want to use for jobs that fit into these categories.

The Do You Create Estimates? radio buttons let you indicate to QuickBooks whether you want to create job estimates for customers. You select the radio button — Yes or No — that answers the question. The Do You Do Progress Invoicing? radio buttons let you indicate whether you do progress billing for jobs. The Warn about Duplicate Estimate Numbers check box, if selected, tells QuickBooks to warn you about using duplicate estimate numbers. The Don't Print Items That Have Zero Amount check box, if selected, tells QuickBooks not to print estimates that have zero balances.

TIP

Book 4, Chapter 5 talks more about setting up jobs and estimates. You may want to refer to it if you have questions about how project costing and job costing work within QuickBooks.

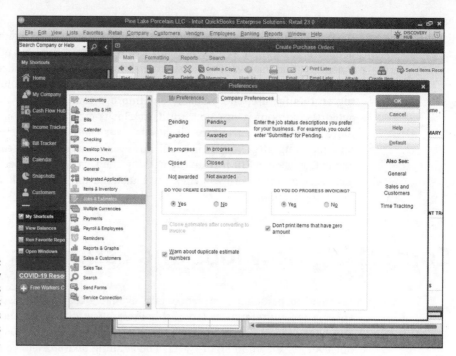

FIGURE 3-12:
The Company
Preferences
tab of the Jobs
& Estimates
Preferences
dialog box.

# Dealing with Multiple Currencies

QuickBooks supports multiple currencies. To turn on QuickBooks's multiple-currencies feature, choose the Edit ⇨ Preferences command, select the Multiple Currencies option in the list box, and click the Company Preferences tab. Then select the Yes I Use More Than One Currency button, and choose your home currency from the drop-down list.

After you tell QuickBooks that you'll be working with multiple currencies, you need to set up a bank account for each extra currency in which you want to work (currencies in addition to your home currency). After that, you can indicate which currency a vendor or customer uses when you set up a new vendor or customer. You can also select a transaction currency for vendors or customers with which you haven't yet transacted any business. You can't change the currency for a vendor or customer with which you've already transacted business in your home currency, however.

After you've performed this setup work, you can work with foreign-currency units (euros rather than dollars, or vice versa) as you pay the foreign currency to vendors, collect the foreign currency from customers, and move money in and out of your foreign-currency bank account.

Furthermore, using the currency exchange information available in the Currency list (available when you choose Lists ➪ Currency List), QuickBooks converts foreign-currency amounts to home-currency amounts so you can prepare reports that use your home currency. QuickBooks, of course, updates its records concerning foreign exchange rates if you display the Currency List window, click the Activities button, and choose Download Latest Exchange Rates.

**TIP**

One final multiple-currency factoid: If you turn on the Multiple Currency feature within QuickBooks, QuickBooks sprinkles little currency reminders throughout its windows and dialog boxes. Amount boxes, for example, show a little abbreviation for the currency that goes into a particular box, thereby reminding you that in this particular text box, you're supposed to enter (for example) British pounds.

# Starting Integrated Payment Processing

The Payments preferences provide several check boxes and links you can use to control the way QuickBooks handles payments.

The Receive Payments check boxes, for example, let you indicate that you want to automatically apply and automatically calculate payments, as well as use the Undeposited Funds account as a temporary holding account for customer payments. (For more information about the Undeposited Funds account and customer payments, see Book 3, Chapter 1.)

The Payments preferences also let you indicate that you'll allow customers to pay you using credit cards and bank transfers via the Automated Clearinghouse (ACH) system. If you set this preference, QuickBooks adds a link on invoices that customers can use to make credit card payments or bank transfers.

Not surprisingly, Intuit charges a modest fee for this service, so if you're interested, pay close attention to current pricing — information that's available when you check the boxes that turn on this feature. (At the time I'm writing this chapter, the fee runs 2 to 3 percent for credit card payments and 50 cents for an ACH payment, and may require a modest monthly fee.)

# Controlling How Payroll Works

The Payroll & Employees Preferences set includes only the Company Preferences tab, shown in Figure 3-13. The QuickBooks Payroll Features radio buttons let you tell QuickBooks how you want to handle payroll: Enhanced Payroll, Payroll, or

Payroll Premium. Note that QuickBooks displays only radio buttons that make sense given the version of QuickBooks you've selected.

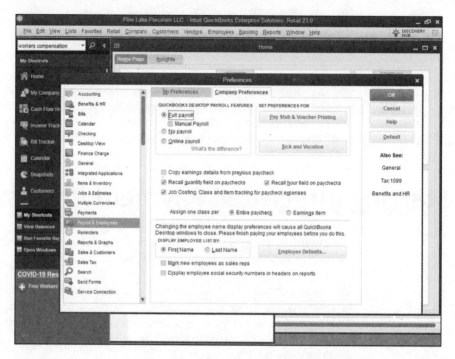

**FIGURE 3-13:**
The Company Preferences tab of the Payroll & Employees Preferences dialog box.

The Pay Stub & Voucher Printing button lets you tell QuickBooks what employee information to print on the payroll check: employee address, company address, sick-pay information, vacation-pay information, and pay-period information. You can figure out how this works by clicking the button and looking at the dialog box that QuickBooks displays.

The Sick and Vacation button lets you fine-tune how QuickBooks monitors employee sick- and vacation-pay accrual and use. Again, click either of these buttons to see a screen that provides more information about how the button works.

In roughly the middle of the Company Preferences tab of the Payroll & Employees Preferences dialog box, QuickBooks supplies several other check boxes and radio buttons:

>> **Copy Earnings Details from Previous Paycheck:** Another duh.

>> **Recall Quantity Field on Paychecks:** QuickBooks recalls or reuses paycheck quantity information from the last pay period's paychecks. (The QuickBooks

Help file suggests that you use this option when you have a "fixed quantity that occurs from paycheck to paycheck." The Help file uses the example of tiered sales commissions where the commission amount is set for each tier.)

>> **Recall Hour Field on Paychecks:** QuickBooks recalls or reuses hours-worked information from the last pay period's paychecks. You use this option when you have a fixed number of hours that occurs from paycheck to paycheck.

>> **Job Costing, Class, and Item Tracking for Paycheck Expenses:** QuickBooks lets you track payroll expenses not just by account, but also by job, class, or item.

>> **Assign One Class Per:** The Entire Paycheck and Earnings Item options enable you to break wage expenses into classes more finely. You can indicate, for example, that you want to use a different class for each item that appears on an employee's paycheck. (***Note:*** These options appear only if classes are enabled.)

The Display Employee List By radio buttons let you choose how employee lists are sorted on reports: by first name or by last name.

If you click the Employee Defaults button, QuickBooks displays a dialog box that you can use to set employee payroll default information, such as deductions for taxes or health insurance.

Finally, at the bottom of the dialog box, QuickBooks provides two other options for handling payroll. The Mark New Employees As Sales Reps check box, if selected, does what you'd expect: It marks new employees that you add to the Employee list as sales reps. And the check box titled Display Employee Social Security Numbers in Headers on Reports, if selected, also does what you'd expect: It adds employee Social Security numbers to reports.

# Telling QuickBooks How Reminders Should Work

The My Preferences tab of the Reminders Preferences dialog box consists of just one check box, which you can use to tell QuickBooks that you want to see the Reminders list when you open a company file. Because the My Preferences tab includes only a single check box, I don't show it here as a figure.

The Company Preferences tab, shown in Figure 3-14, provides a bunch of radio buttons that you can use to specify how QuickBooks should remind you of accounting and bookkeeping tasks that you need to complete: Checks to Print, Paychecks to Print, Invoices/Credit Memos to Print, Overdue Invoices, Almost Due Invoices, Sales Receipts to Print, Sales Orders to Print, Inventory to Reorder, Assembly Items to Build, Bills to Pay, Memorized Transactions Due, Money to Deposit, Purchase Orders to Print, To Do Notes, and Open Authorizations to Capture.

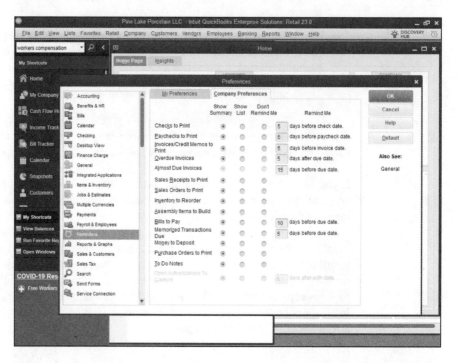

**FIGURE 3-14:**
The Company Preferences tab of the Reminders Preferences dialog box.

For each of these accounting or bookkeeping tasks, you indicate whether you want to see a reminder for the item in the Show Summary list that appears in the QuickBooks Company Preferences Reminders list. You can also choose to actually see the list of tasks — such as the list of checks to print — or you can indicate that you don't want to be reminded of some particular category of accounting or bookkeeping. For some of the reminder notes, you indicate how many workdays in advance you want to be reminded. If you indicate that you want to be reminded to print checks, for example, you must indicate how many days before the check date that you want the reminder to appear. You do this by entering a numeral in one of the Remind Me text boxes.

# Specifying Reports and Graphs Preferences

The My Preferences tab of the Reports & Graphs Preferences dialog box is shown in Figure 3-15. This tab provides radio buttons that you can use to indicate how QuickBooks should refresh reports when the information upon which the report is based changes. The default refresh option is Refresh Automatically. You can also select the Prompt Me to Refresh radio button to have QuickBooks (politely) suggest that you refresh a report only whenever the data changes. (You may not want to refresh automatically if you have a large data set and many reports. Refreshing a report can be rather time-consuming.) You can also select the Don't Refresh radio button if you don't want or don't need to be reminded about refreshing a report.

**FIGURE 3-15:**
The My Preferences tab of the Reports & Graphs Preferences dialog box.

The check box titled Prompt Me to Modify Report Options Before Opening a Report, if selected, tells QuickBooks to open the Modify Report window whenever you create a report. You can use the Modify Report window to control what information is included in a report (such as what date range the report is based on) and other reporting options as well. If this check box isn't selected, QuickBooks creates a report by using the default reporting options.

The Graphs Only check boxes let you control the way QuickBooks graphs report information. You can select the Draw Graphs in 2D check box to tell QuickBooks to draw 2D rather than 3D graphs. (QuickBooks draws 2D graphs much more quickly, so you may want to use that kind.) Note that 2D graphs are visually more precise than 3D graphs. You can also select the Use Patterns check box to tell QuickBooks to draw a graph that uses crosshatching patterns rather than colors for the different pieces of a chart.

TIP

For a complete discussion of the Modify Reports window, take a look at the discussion in Book 4, Chapter 2.

Figure 3-16 shows the Company Preferences tab of the Reports & Graphs Preferences dialog box. This tab provides several useful options for default report generation rules. The Summary Reports Basis radio buttons, for example, let you indicate whether the default accounting method used to create a report should be accrual-basis accounting or cash-basis accounting. The Aging Reports radio buttons let you specify how the age of an invoice or bill should be calculated: from the due date or from the transaction date. The Reports - Show Accounts By radio buttons let you specify how account information appears in reports: account name only, description only, or both name and description.

**FIGURE 3-16:**
The Company Preferences tab of the Reports & Graphs Preferences dialog box.

Two other options are especially noteworthy. The Classify Cash button displays a dialog box that lets you indicate whether changes in a particular account balance should appear in the operating, investing, or financing portion of the statement of cash flows.

**WARNING**

If you're not a professional accountant, you want to get your CPA's help with making changes in this area of QuickBooks. The rules for presenting a statement of cash flows are quite involved.

If you clear the Default Formatting for Reports check box and click the Format button, QuickBooks displays the Reports & Graphs Preferences dialog box, which lets you customize the report header and footer information. Figure 3-17 shows the Header/Footer tab of the Reports & Graphs Preferences dialog box. The Show Header Information check boxes let you specify what information should appear in the report header area. The Show Footer Information check boxes let you make the same specifications for the report footer. The Alignment drop-down list in the Page Layout section lets you specify how information should be aligned on the report page.

**FIGURE 3-17:**
The Header/Footer tab of the Reports & Graphs Preferences dialog box.

Figure 3-18 shows the Fonts & Numbers tab of the Reports & Graphs Preferences dialog box. On this tab, you specify what font and formatting you want to use for bits of report information. If you want to change the font for the report's column labels, for example, click the Column Labels entry in the Change Font For list box; then click the Change Font button. QuickBooks displays a Font Formatting dialog box (not shown) that lets you specify the font, font style, point size, and other special effects.

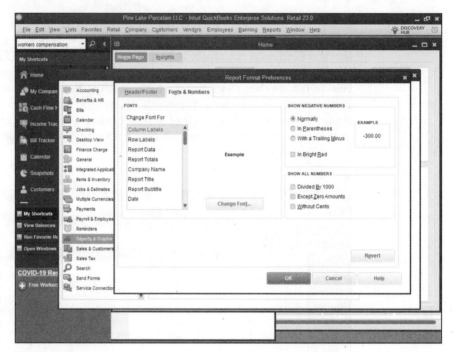

FIGURE 3-18:
The Fonts &
Numbers tab
of the Reports
& Graphs
Preferences
dialog box.

**TIP**

If you're confused about changing report formatting, check out Book 4, Chapter 2, which talks about all this stuff.

# Setting Sales and Customers Preferences

I won't show you the My Preferences tab. The personalized preferences for dealing with sales and customers are pretty basic. The tab lets you specify whether QuickBooks should prompt you to invoice a customer for time or costs you've previously said are billable to that customer.

The company preferences deserve more explanation. Figure 3-19 shows the Company Preferences tab of the Sales & Customers Preferences dialog box. The Sales Forms options relate to the invoice information you supply to customers. The Usual Shipping Method drop-down list lets you specify the default shipping method. The Usual FOB text box lets you set the default free on board (FOB) point. You can select a check box to tell QuickBooks whether it should warn you when you use duplicate invoice numbers.

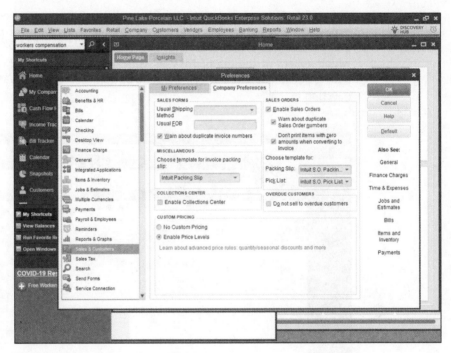

**FIGURE 3-19:**
The Company Preferences tab of the Sales & Customers Preferences dialog box.

The Choose Template for Invoice Packing Slip drop-down list in the Miscellaneous section lets you specify how packing slips should look.

The Collections Center radio button allows you to enable a list of all overdue and almost-due invoices in a single screen.

The Custom Pricing radio buttons — No Custom Pricing and Enable Price Levels — let you turn on QuickBooks' price-levels features. I won't say more about these features here. Price levels are discussed in detail in Book 3, Chapter 3.

The Sales Orders check boxes let you control how the QuickBooks sales orders work, including whether you even want to use sales orders, how numbering should work, and how they should look when they print. The Sales Orders options also include drop-down list boxes you can use to specify how sales orders should look and a check box you can select to tell QuickBooks not to sell more stuff to customers with overdue balances.

# Specifying How Sales Are Taxed

Although no personal preferences are available for sales tax, company preferences do exist. Figure 3-20 shows the Company Preferences tab of the Sales Tax Preferences dialog box. The Do You Charge Sales Tax? radio buttons, which appear at the top of the tab, control whether you can charge sales tax within QuickBooks. You select the radio button — Yes or No — that answers the question.

**FIGURE 3-20:** The Company Preferences tab of the Sales Tax Preferences dialog box.

The Taxable Item Code and Non-Taxable Item Code drop-down lists let you define what code QuickBooks should use to identify taxable and nontaxable sales. By default, QuickBooks uses the clever "tax" code for taxable sales and the equally clever "non" code for nontaxable sales. You can choose the Add New entry from either drop-down list, however, and use the dialog box that QuickBooks displays to create your own taxable and nontaxable codes.

The Add Sales Tax item under the Set Up Sales Tax Item section allows you to set up an item for the sales tax you charge on invoices. You can indicate the default (or most common) sales tax item that you want to include by entering this sales tax item name in the Your Most Common Sales Tax Item drop-down list. To add the sales tax item, choose Add New from this list and complete the dialog box that QuickBooks displays. The New Item dialog box lets you name the sales tax item and identify the sales tax rate.

**TIP**

You can also add a new sales tax item by clicking the Add Sales Tax Item button.

The Taxable Item Code and Non-Taxable Item Code drop-down lists let you select the code words to designate invoice items as subject to sales tax. The check box titled Identify Taxable Amounts as "T" for "Taxable" When Printing, if selected, tells QuickBooks to flag taxable amounts on an invoice with the code *T*.

The When Do You Owe Sales Tax? radio buttons let you indicate when the taxing authority says you owe sales tax: as of the invoice date (which means that the taxing authority requires accrual-basis accounting) or upon receipt of payment (which means that the taxing authority allows cash-basis accounting).

The When Do You Pay Sales Tax? radio buttons (Monthly, Quarterly, and Annually) let you tell QuickBooks how frequently you must remit sales tax amounts. You select the radio button that corresponds to your sales tax payment frequency.

**TIP**

Book 2, Chapter 2 describes how to set up sales tax items.

# Setting the Search Preferences

The My Preferences tab of the Search Preferences dialog box provides a check box you can use to indicate that you want the Search box to appear on the QuickBooks icon toolbar. (This seems pretty self-explanatory, but if you're confused, check the box, click OK, and then look at the way that QuickBooks has modified your icon toolbar.)

The Company Preferences tab of the Search Preferences dialog box (not shown) lets you specify how frequently QuickBooks updates the index of company data file and menu items that are used when you search for data within the Quick-Books program. By default, QuickBooks does its update every hour, but you can request more frequent or less frequent updates. An update of the index takes a few minutes, and during the update, QuickBooks runs more slowly. The Search Company Preferences tab also includes a button you can click to demand an immediate update of the index.

# Setting the Send Forms Preferences

The My Preferences tab of the Send Forms Preferences dialog box lets you check a box to specify whether the To Be E-Mailed check box is selected for customer invoices; click an option button to specify when emailed forms should be processed with web mail (such as Gmail or QuickBooks email); and provides buttons you can click to build a list of email accounts to use for web mail.

The Company Preferences tab of the Send Forms Preferences dialog box is shown in Figure 3-21. This tab lets you specify the default message text, message subject, and salutation for emailed invoices, estimates, and statements. To use the Company Preferences tab, you use the Show drop-down list to specify which type of message text you want to change. Next, click the message you want to change; then click the Edit button. When QuickBooks displays the Edit Email Template dialog box (not shown), change the default message however you want.

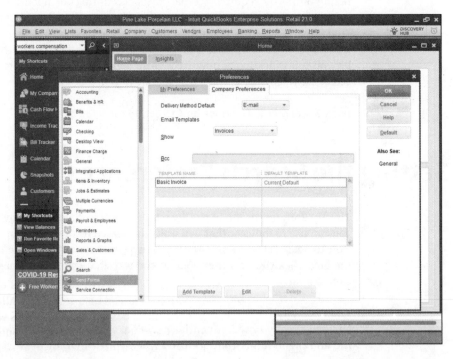

**FIGURE 3-21:**
The Company Preferences tab of the Send Forms Preferences dialog box.

**TIP**

Book 3, Chapter 1 talks about invoicing customers and emailing customer invoices.

# Fine-Tuning the Service Connection

The My Preferences tab of the Service Connection Preferences dialog box provides two check boxes you can select to control how QuickBooks works when you're making web connections, as shown in Figure 3-22. One check box gives you the option of saving downloaded files. The other tells QuickBooks not to close your web browser when it finishes using the web.

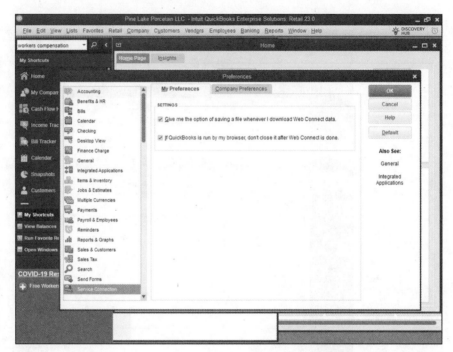

**FIGURE 3-22:**
The My Preferences tab of the Service Connection Preferences dialog box.

The Service Connection Preferences dialog box offers two Company Preferences options (not shown). You can indicate, for example, whether QuickBooks should automatically connect to QuickBooks Services without asking for a password or whether it should always ask for a password. To make this decision, simply select the appropriate radio button. You can also select the Allow Background Downloading of Service Messages check box to tell QuickBooks that background collection of messages is okay. (If you select this check box, QuickBooks downloads new messages during idle times so that it doesn't slow your other Internet activities.)

# Controlling Spell Checking

No company preferences exist for the Spelling Preferences dialog box, but the My Preferences tab (shown in Figure 3-23) provides several options for controlling how spell checking works for you within QuickBooks. Select the check box titled Always Check Spelling Before Printing, Saving, or Sending Supported Forms if you want to have automatic spell checking performed before you distribute a document to an outside party, such as a customer or vendor.

**FIGURE 3-23:**
The My Preferences tab of the Spelling Preferences dialog box.

You can use the Ignore Words With check boxes to tell QuickBooks not to spell-check words or phrases that aren't going to appear correctly spelled because they aren't real words. Select the Internet Addresses check box, for example, to tell QuickBooks that it shouldn't check Internet URL addresses. And select the All UPPERCASE Letters check box to tell QuickBooks that it shouldn't attempt to spell-check words that are acronyms and abbreviations, such as OK and ASAP.

QuickBooks also lets you remove custom-spelled words from your spell-checking dictionary. (You add custom-spelled words during spell checking by telling QuickBooks that a word flagged as possibly misspelled is in fact spelled correctly. To do this, click the Add button when the Check Spelling dialog box appears.)

# Controlling How 1099 Tax Reporting Works

No personal preferences exist for 1099 tax reporting. Company preferences exist, however, as indicated by the Company Preferences tab, shown in Figure 3-24. This tab lets you tell QuickBooks when you're required to file 1099-MISC forms. (Answer the Do You File 1099 Forms? question in the affirmative by selecting the Yes radio button.) The tab also lets you map QuickBooks accounts to the different boxes on the 1099 form you use to report payments to independent contractors. (To do this, click the You Can Do It Here hyperlink.) Confer with your tax adviser if you have questions about these boxes or the 1099 reporting threshold amounts or visit the IRS website at www.irs.gov.

**FIGURE 3-24:** The Company Preferences tab of the Tax: 1099 Preferences dialog box.

# Setting Time and Expenses Preferences

Figure 3-25 shows the Company Preferences tab of the Time & Expenses Preferences dialog box. To turn on time tracking within QuickBooks, enable Do You Track Time? by selecting the Yes radio button. You can also use the First Day of Work Week drop-down list to indicate which day should appear first on the Weekly Time Sheet window. (This setting is what you use to describe billable time for the week.) Book 3, Chapter 1 talks about billing for time in more detail. You may want to look there if you have questions about tracking time and billing for that time.

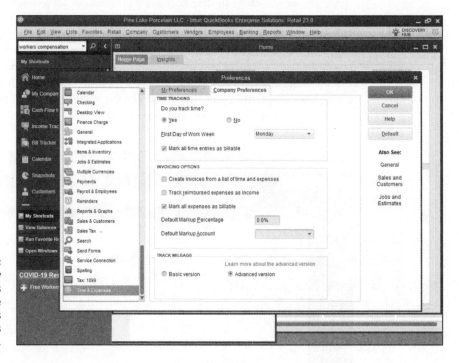

FIGURE 3-25:
The Company
Preferences
tab of the Time
& Expenses
Preferences
dialog box.

**TIP**

You may need to scroll down the list of Preferences to see the Time & Expenses preference settings.

Use the Invoicing Options check boxes to indicate how you want to track reimbursed expenses. To indicate that you sometimes want to base invoices on accumulated time and expenses, select the Create Invoices from a List of Time and Expenses check box. Furthermore, to indicate that you want to track reimbursed expenses that you bill and then later collect from customers or clients as income, select the Track Reimbursed Expenses As Income check box. The Default Markup Percentage text box lets you specify a default retail markup percentage to use in your pricing (although you should double-check that it's showing up properly in estimates before you count on it). The Default Markup Account drop-down list lets you specify which account QuickBooks should use for tracking your markups. If you check the Mark All Expenses as Billable box, you can choose expenses that should be reimbursed when entering bills and code them to a specific customer job.

# 3

# Bookkeeping Chores

# Contents at a Glance

Chapter **1**

# Invoicing Customers

QuickBooks provides several tools for invoicing your customers. This chapter describes these tools, as well as a handful of related tools for recording customer payments and for issuing credit memos.

If you've already been invoicing customers by using some manual method — perhaps you've been preparing invoices with a word processor — you'll find QuickBooks to be a godsend. QuickBooks not only makes invoicing and related tasks easier, but also collects invoice information, recording this information in the QuickBooks data file. Happily, this means that you get the extra benefit of recording accounting transactions simply by using QuickBooks for invoicing.

## Choosing an Invoice Form

QuickBooks allows you to use an invoice form that matches the requirements of your business. Businesses that sell products — such as retailers and wholesalers — need an invoice that includes descriptions of the product items that are sold. Businesses that sell services — such as law, architectural, engineering, and consulting firms — need an invoice that appropriately describes these services. Businesses that sell both products and services need a blend of attributes.

Fortunately, QuickBooks lets you choose the invoice form that best matches your business. To choose an invoice form, display the Create Invoices window by choosing the Customers ⇨ Create Invoices command. When QuickBooks displays the Create Invoices window, use the Template drop-down list, which appears in the top-right portion of the window, to choose the invoice form that you want. This drop-down list provides choices such as an attorney's invoice, a finance-charge invoice, a fixed-fee invoice, a product invoice, a service invoice, and a professional invoice. Choose the invoice template that seems to best match your business. QuickBooks redraws the Create Invoices window when you choose a new invoice form template. This means that you can see what an invoice form template looks like simply by choosing an option from the Template drop-down list.

# Customizing an Invoice Form

Although you can choose a predefined invoice form template for your invoices, QuickBooks gives you more flexibility than that. You can also create custom invoice form templates to design an invoice that looks just the way you want. To do this, you can start with one of the basic invoice form templates and then customize it so that it perfectly matches your requirements.

## Choosing a template to customize

To choose a template to customize, display the Create Invoices window by choosing the Customers ⇨ Create Invoices command. Then, from the Template drop-down list, choose the template that most closely matches what you want your ultimate invoice to look like.

## Reviewing the Additional Customization options

QuickBooks's form customization tools easily confuse new QuickBooks users. But typically, the way to start any customization is to fiddle with what QuickBooks calls its Additional Customization options.

To perform this fiddling, click the Create Invoice window's Formatting tab and then click the Customize Data Layout button. You can't use the Additional Customization dialog box if you're working with one of the default invoice templates — only if you're working with a copy. Accordingly, QuickBooks may prompt you to make a copy of an invoice template when you click the Additional Customization button. In any event, QuickBooks displays the Additional Customization dialog box, as shown in Figure 1-1. This dialog box gives you control of both the information that appears on your invoices and the way that invoices print.

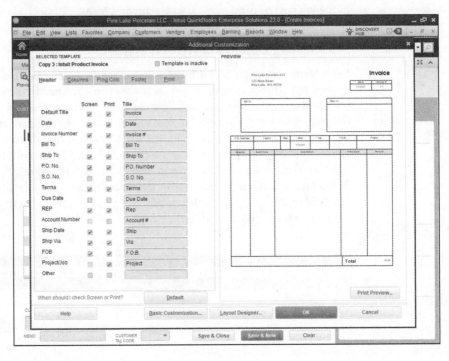

**FIGURE 1-1:**
The Header tab
of the Additional
Customization
dialog box.

## Specifying header information

The Header tab of the Additional Customization dialog box (refer to Figure 1-1) lets you specify what information goes in the top portion of the Create Invoices window and the top area of an actual printed invoice form. This information, called the *header*, provides the invoice number, the invoice date, and the billing and shipping information. You can also choose how information is labeled by filling in or editing the contents of the text boxes. The Default Title check boxes, for example, let you specify whether the form title should appear in the screen version of the invoice (inside the Create Invoices window) and in the printed version of the invoice. The Default Title text box lets you specify what the form title should be. In a similar fashion, the Date check boxes let you specify whether the date should appear in both the screen and print versions of the invoice, as well as what label should be used to describe the invoice date. Figure 1-1 uses the clever descriptive text *Invoice* as the invoice form's title.

TIP

As you make these customizations, QuickBooks updates the Preview box, shown on the right side of the Additional Customization dialog box, so you can see what your changes look like.

Invoicing Customers

If you don't need a particular piece of information in an invoice, don't select the Screen and Print check boxes for that bit of data. Leaving these check boxes deselected tells QuickBooks that it shouldn't include that piece of header information in the window or print version of the invoice form.

## Specifying columns information

The columns portion of an invoice describes in detail the items for which an invoice bills. Product invoice columns describe the specific products, including price and quantity; they also describe the items being invoiced. A service invoice's columns describe the specific services being billed. As you may guess from looking closely at Figure 1-2, the Columns tab of the Additional Customization dialog box looks like the Header tab. You use the Screen and Print check boxes to indicate whether a particular piece of column-level information should appear as a column in the Create Invoices window or in the actual created invoice. Similarly, you use the Title text boxes to provide the descriptive labels that QuickBooks uses in the Create Invoices window and in the printed invoice form.

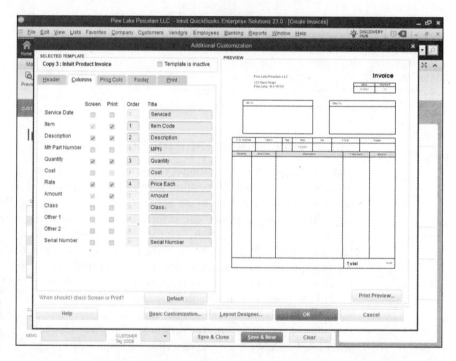

**FIGURE 1-2:**
The Columns tab of the Additional Customization dialog box.

The only unusual options shown on the Columns tab are the Order text boxes. These boxes let you indicate the order (from left to right) in which the columns should appear. If the item number or code should appear in the first column on the left, for example, enter the value **1** in the Item row's Order box.

## Specifying prog columns information

The "prog columns" portion of an invoice provides information relevant to situations in which you're using progress billings. You can click the Prog Cols tab of the Additional Customization dialog box to add and remove such information as the ordered amount, the previously invoiced amount, and any back-ordered amounts.

**TIP**

The Header, Columns, and Prog Cols tabs let you make changes in your invoice forms, but don't get too nervous about making perfect changes the first time. You can easily see exactly how your changes look by using the Preview box (if your eyesight is better than mine) or by clicking OK and then carefully reviewing the new version of the Create Invoices window. If you realize that you've made an error — perhaps you've used the wrong bit of descriptive text, or you've incorrectly ordered the columns — you can customize your invoice again and thereby fix your earlier mistakes.

## Specifying footer information

The Footer tab of the Additional Customization dialog box lets you specify what information appears in the Create Invoices window below the columns area and in the actual printed invoice below the columns area. As Figure 1-3 indicates, the footer information includes a customer message, the invoice total, payments and credit information, a balance-due field, and (optionally) a longer text box. You work with the Footer tab in the same manner that you work with other tabs. If you want some bit of information to appear, select the Screen check box and the Print check box. To change the bit of text that QuickBooks uses, edit the contents of the Title text box.

## Specifying print information

The Print tab of the Additional Customization dialog box, shown in Figure 1-4, lets you exercise a bit of control over how QuickBooks prints invoices that use the template you've customized. The radio buttons at the top of the tab let you specify that when printing this particular invoice template, QuickBooks should use the regular old invoice printer settings or other, special print settings. The Print settings also let you tell QuickBooks how it should number the pages of a multiple-page invoice.

**TIP**

You can return all the customized invoice settings to their default condition by clicking the Default button. When you do, however, you remove any changes or customizations that you've made.

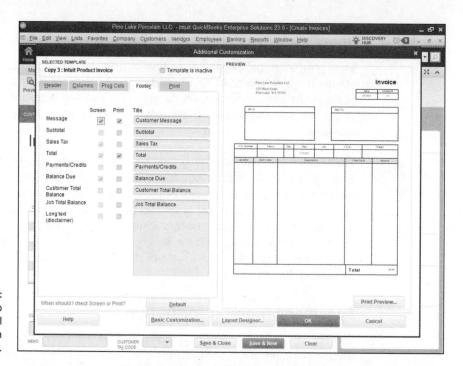

**FIGURE 1-3:**
The Footer tab of the Additional Customization dialog box.

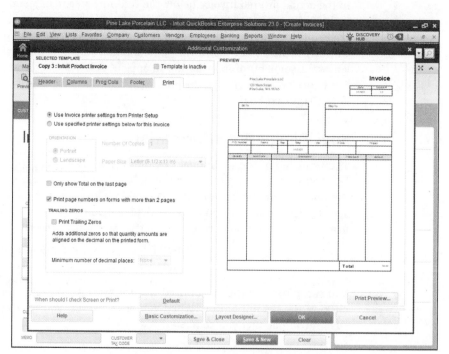

**FIGURE 1-4:**
The Print tab of the Additional Customization dialog box.

# Moving on to basic customization

The Additional Customization dialog box (refer to Figure 1-4, for example) provides a Basic Customization button. If you click this button, QuickBooks displays the Basic Customization dialog box, shown in Figure 1-5, which provides several easy-to-make customization choices.

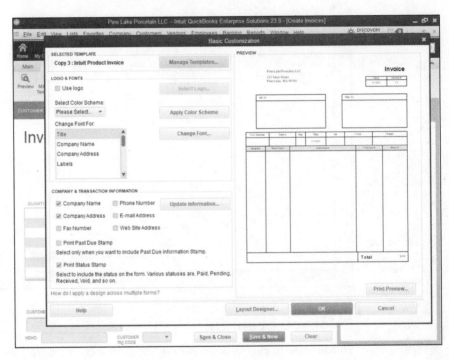

**FIGURE 1-5:**
The Basic Customization dialog box.

To identify which invoice form template you want to customize, click the Manage Templates button; then, when QuickBooks displays the Manage Templates dialog box (see Figure 1-6), choose the invoice template you want to customize. QuickBooks initially supplies a custom invoice template and a finance-charge template that you can customize.

Alternatively, you can select one of these existing templates and click Copy to create and then customize it. When you click OK, QuickBooks closes the Manage Templates dialog box and returns you to the Basic Customization dialog box.

## Logo, please

To add a logo to your invoices, select the Use Logo check box (shown in Figure 1-5). Then, when QuickBooks displays the Select Image dialog box (not shown), use it to select the graphic-image file that shows your logo. The Select Image dialog box works like a standard Windows open-file dialog box.

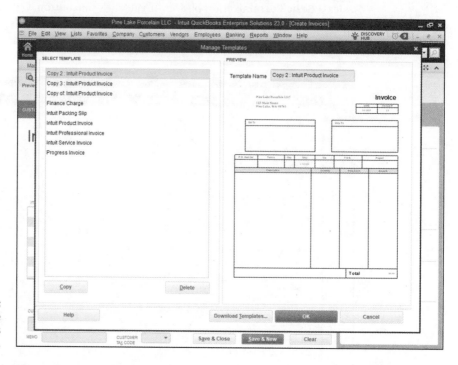

FIGURE 1-6:
The Manage
Templates
dialog box.

## Color you beautiful

To add color to your invoices — say you have a color printer, and you don't care whether you spend a small fortune on colored ink — choose the color scheme you want to use from the Select Color Scheme drop-down list. Then click the Apply Color Scheme button.

## Fiddle with invoice fonts

You can choose the font that QuickBooks uses for the bits of text that go into an invoice. Just select the bit of text you want in the Change Font For list box and then click the Change Font button. QuickBooks displays the Example dialog box, shown in Figure 1-7. Use its Font, Font Style, and Size boxes to specify what the selected bit of text should look like. The Example dialog box includes a Sample box that shows how your font changes look. When you complete your specification of the font, click OK.

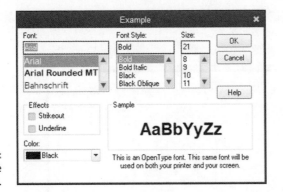

**FIGURE 1-7:**
The Example
dialog box.

## Specifying company and transaction information

The Company & Transaction Information options, also shown in Figure 1-5, let you indicate what information should appear on the form template. You select the check box that corresponds to the bit of information. If you want the company name to appear in the invoice form, for example — which means that you aren't using letterhead or preprinted invoice forms — select the Company Name check box.

**TIP**

If you need to change some bit of company information, click the Update Information button. QuickBooks displays the Company Information dialog box (not shown), which you can use to edit or update your company name, address, telephone number, and so on.

# Working with the Layout Designer tool

Okay. Perhaps you've used the Basic Customization dialog box to make some changes in your invoice's appearance, and you haven't been satisfied. Maybe you've gone the extra mile and noodled around with the Additional Customization dialog box to make further changes, and maybe even that hasn't left you happy with the appearance of your invoice.

Do you have any additional recourse? Are you stuck with an invoice that doesn't look right or that doesn't work for your organization? Heck, no!

If you click the Layout Designer button, which is available in both the Basic Customization and Additional Customization dialog boxes, QuickBooks displays the Layout Designer, as shown in Figure 1-8. The Layout Designer lets you move invoice information around in the actual printed invoice. Your best bet for finding out how to work with the Layout Designer is experimenting with it. My recommendation is that you create an example invoice form template — something you don't really care about — and then use this new invoice form template for some goofing around.

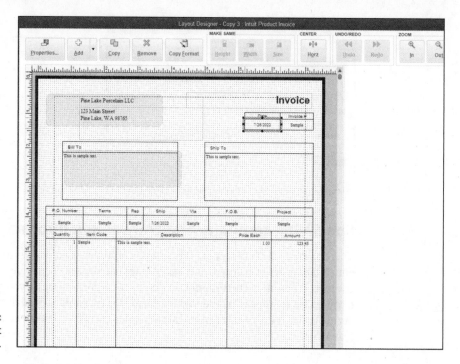

**FIGURE 1-8:**
The Layout
Designer.

Here are some of the things that you may want to try:

>> **Moving and resizing objects:** You can move and resize objects in the form pretty easily. To move some bit of the form, select the bit by clicking it; then use the arrow keys or drag the mouse to move the selected bit. You can resize the selected bit in a similar way. Resize the selected object by dragging the black squares (called *resizing handles)*, which show that the object is selected.

When moving and resizing invoice form objects, keep two points in mind:

- You can select the Show Envelope Window check box to have QuickBooks draw envelope windows in the invoice form to show you where these elements appear. You want to have envelope windows shown to make sure that your customized invoice still has its address information showing through.

- You can click the Grid button to display the Grid and Snap Settings dialog box (not shown). This dialog box provides two check boxes where you can indicate whether QuickBooks should use a grid (the dots you see in Figure 1-8) to line up invoice objects more accurately in the form. The Grid and Snap Settings dialog box also includes a Snap to Grid box so that you can tell QuickBooks that it should make gridlines sticky. *Sticky* gridlines automatically attract invoice objects so that you can more easily line up the objects against the gridlines. Further, the Grid and Snap Settings dialog box includes a Grid Spacing box that you can use to specify how wide or narrow the gridlines should be.

>> **Selecting objects:** You can select multiple objects in the invoice by dragging the mouse. To do so, click at a point above the top-leftmost object that you want to select, and drag the mouse to a point just below the bottom-rightmost object that you want to select. As you drag the mouse from one corner to the other, QuickBooks draws a rectangle. Any object that's inside this rectangle when you release the mouse gets selected.

>> **Resizing multiple objects:** You can change the height, width, and size of multiple selected objects by clicking the Make Same Width, Make Same Height, and Make Same Size buttons. To use these Make Same buttons, you first select the objects that you want to make the same.

>> **Positioning text within fields:** If you click an invoice object and then click the Properties button, QuickBooks displays the Properties dialog box, shown in Figure 1-9. The Properties dialog box includes a Text tab that lets you specify how text should appear within an invoice object area. The dialog box also includes a Border tab that lets you specify whether QuickBooks should draw a border along the edges of the invoice object. What's more, you have the option to add a solid background color to any box by using the Background tab.

**FIGURE 1-9:**
The Properties dialog box.

» **Changing fonts:** You can change the font used for the selected object by clicking the Properties button, clicking the Text tab of the Properties dialog box, and then clicking the Font button that appears on this tab. QuickBooks displays the Example dialog box (refer to Figure 1-7). The Example dialog box lets you choose a font; font style; a point size; and special effects, such as strikeout, underlining, and color.

» **Adjusting margins:** If you click the Margins button, QuickBooks displays the Margins dialog box (not shown), which includes Top, Bottom, Left, and Right text boxes that you use to specify the margin around the invoice. The default or initial margin settings equal half an inch.

TIP

Center a selected object in an invoice form by clicking the Center button to activate the Layout Designer. You can click the Zoom In and Zoom Out buttons to see more or less detail. If you want to undo your most recent change, click Undo, or click the Redo button to undo your last undo option.

After you use the Layout Designer to make whatever changes are appropriate in your new invoice form template, click OK to save your changes.

## Working with the web-based Forms Customization tool

QuickBooks provides one other form design tool that you can tap to create invoice forms (and other QuickBooks forms) that more closely match your requirements: the web-based QuickBooks Forms Customization tool.

You access this tool from the Create Invoices window by clicking the Customize Design button on the Formatting tab. When you do this, QuickBooks displays a web page that steps you through a full-fledged graphic design session for the invoice form. To use this approach, simply follow the web page's instructions.

# Invoicing a Customer

To invoice a customer, use the Create Invoices window to identify the customer and specify the amount that the customer owes. To display the Create Invoices window, choose the Customers ➪ Create Invoices command. When you do, Quick-Books displays a Create Invoices window like the one shown in Figure 1-10. Note, however, that the Create Invoices window you see may not look *exactly* like the one shown in Figure 1-10.

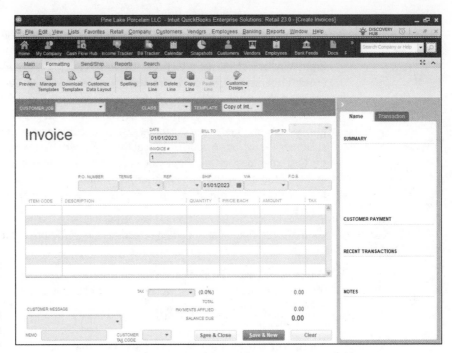

**FIGURE 1-10:**
The Create
Invoices window.

As previously described, you can use more than one type of invoice form. You can also choose to customize an invoice form so that it perfectly matches your business requirements. In the following steps, I describe generally how to invoice a customer. The specific steps that you take may be ever-so-slightly different if you're working with a different invoice form template.

**TIP**

If you want to declutter your Create Invoices window, you may want to close the Open Window List along the left edge (not pictured in figure) of the QuickBooks window to provide more room. You can close your Open Window List by clicking its close box (the small box marked with an X that appears in the top-right corner of the list). To redisplay the Open Window List after you've closed it, choose View ⇨ Open Window List. You can also collapse the History panel on the right edge of the QuickBooks window to provide more room for invoice information.

You can also move or hide the icon bar, shown at the top of Figure 1-10. You can change the location of the icon bar by choosing View and then choosing Top, Left, or Hidden.

After you display the Create Invoices window, take the following steps to invoice a customer:

**1.** **Identify the customer and, if appropriate, the job.**

To do this, choose the customer or customer and job combination from the Customer:Job drop-down list. (Don't worry about this "job" business if you aren't familiar with it; I describe how jobs work in Book 4, Chapter 5. You should understand how customers work, however. You must identify the specific customer you're invoicing by choosing that customer from the Customer:Job list.) If the customer is a new customer that you haven't yet invoiced or described in the Customer List, enter a brief name for the customer — such as an abbreviation of the customer's business name — in the Customer:Job list. QuickBooks indicates that the customer doesn't yet exist in the Customer List and asks whether you want to add the customer; indicate that you do. When prompted, supply the customer information that QuickBooks requests.

**TIP**

For more information about adding customers in QuickBooks, refer to Book 2, Chapter 2.

You can also classify an invoice as fitting into a particular category by using the Class drop-down list. Don't worry at this point about using class tracking. Book 4, Chapter 4 describes how you can use classes to get a better handle on your business's finances.

2. **Confirm or provide new invoice header information.**

   After you identify the customer, QuickBooks fills out the Bill To field and possibly the Ship To field. You probably don't need to change any of this information. You should review the information shown in these boxes to make sure that it's correct, however. Typically, for example, you wouldn't invoice someone unless you've already shipped the product or provided the service. Therefore, you probably should confirm that the invoice date follows the product shipment date or the provision-of-service date. You may also want to confirm that the Ship To address is correct.

3. **Provide or confirm the invoice field information.**

   Invoices include field information that records items such as purchase order numbers, payment terms, ship date, and shipping method. You should make sure that whatever QuickBooks shows in these text boxes is correct. If a customer has provided a purchase-order number, for example, enter that number in the P.O. Number box. Confirm that the payment terms shown in the Terms box are correct. If your invoice includes the Ship Date Field, confirm that the date shown is correct. These boxes are all in a single line above the detailed description of the item(s) you're selling. If the billing and shipping addresses are different, make sure that the Ship To box in the top-right portion of the invoice is filled in properly. Not all these fields need to be filled for every invoice, but you want to supply any information that makes it easier for a customer to pay an invoice, tie an invoice to their purchasing records, and figure out how and when an item is being shipped.

## 4. Describe the items sold.

How the columns area of your invoice looks really depends on whether you're selling products or services. Figure 1-11 shows the columns area for products. The columns area for a service looks simpler because you don't provide much information when describing service items. In the columns area, you want to describe each item — each product or service — for which an invoice bills. To do this, you use a single row for each item. The first item that you want to bill for, then, goes in row 1 of the columns area. For each item, you enter the quantity ordered, the code for the item, and a price or rate. QuickBooks retrieves an item description from your Item list and places this data in the Description column. QuickBooks also calculates the amount billed for the item by multiplying the quantity by the price or rate. You can edit both the Description and Amount fields, however. If you edit the Amount field, QuickBooks recalculates the Price Each field by dividing the amount by the quantity.

To enter additional items in the invoice, enter additional rows. Each item that you want to bill for — each item that should appear as a separate charge in the invoice — appears as a row in the columns area. If you want to invoice a customer for some product, one line in the columns area of the invoice is used for that product. If you want to charge a customer for freight, one line of the invoice area describes that freight charge. If you want to bill a customer for sales tax, again, one line or row of the columns area shows that sales tax charge.

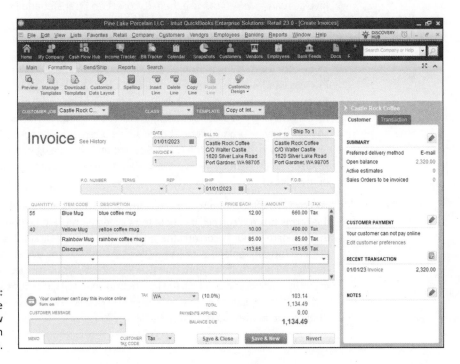

**FIGURE 1-11:** How a Create Invoices window may look when complete.

Discounts represent tricky line items to include in an invoice. For this reason, I provide an example of how a discount item appears in an invoice. Assume that you want to grant some customer a 10 percent discount. To do this, as you now know (or should be able to guess), you include a discount line item in your invoice. But although QuickBooks includes a discount item in its Item list, a discount percentage can be applied only to the previous line item in the invoice. For this reason, QuickBooks also supplies a subtotal line item. You use a subtotal line item to total all the previous items shown in the invoice. By subtotaling all the product items shown in the invoice in Figure 1-11, for example, the business can grant the customer a 10 percent discount on these products.

**TIP**

You need to include the percentage symbol to tell QuickBooks to calculate a discount equal to a percentage of the subtotal. If you omit the percentage symbol, QuickBooks assumes that you want a dollar discount, not a percentage discount. In Figure 1-11, for example, omitting the percentage symbol would turn the 10 percent discount into a $10 discount.

5. **Use the Customer Message box at the bottom of the Create Invoices window to supply a customer message that appears at the bottom of the invoice.**

   If you've created a custom invoice form template that includes other footer information, these footer boxes also appear at the bottom of the Create Invoices window. You can use them to collect and transfer additional footer information.

6. **(Optional) Check your spelling.**

   If you click the Spelling button, which appears along the top edge of the Create Invoices window's Formatting tab, QuickBooks checks the spelling of the words that you use in the invoice. If QuickBooks finds no spelling errors, it displays a message telling you that the spelling check is complete. If QuickBooks finds a spelling error — product code abbreviations often produce spelling errors in QuickBooks — it displays the Check Spelling on Form dialog box, shown in Figure 1-12. (In Figure 1-12, I've misspelled the word *Yellow,* much to the horror of my editor.)

   You can use the Change To box to correct your spelling error — if it actually *is* a spelling error. You can select one of the suggested replacements from the Suggestions list box by clicking the suggestion and then clicking the Replace button. You can replace all occurrences of the misspelling by clicking the Replace All button. If the word that QuickBooks says is misspelled is actually correctly spelled, you can click the Ignore button to tell QuickBooks to ignore this word or the Ignore All button to tell QuickBooks to ignore all occurrences of this word in the invoice form.

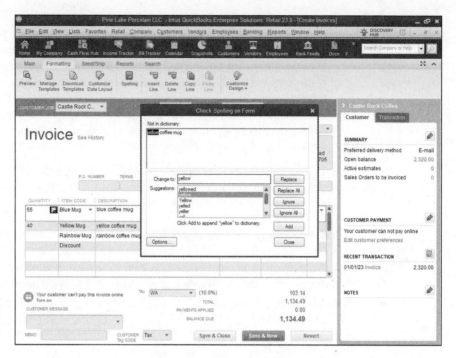

**FIGURE 1-12:**
The Check Spelling on Form dialog box.

If you use terms that are always popping up as misspelled words, at least in QuickBooks, you can click the Add button that appears on the Check Spelling on Form dialog box. Clicking the Add button tells QuickBooks to add the word to its spelling dictionary. After you've added a word to the QuickBooks spelling dictionary, QuickBooks doesn't see the word as being misspelled.

Also note that you can click the Options button to display the Spelling Options dialog box (not shown). The Spelling Options dialog box includes check boxes that you can use to turn certain types of spell-checking logic on or off. You can select a check box to tell QuickBooks to always check the spelling of forms before printing, saving, or sending the form, for example. The dialog box also includes check boxes that tell QuickBooks to ignore certain sorts of words, such as those that use numbers, those that are all uppercase, and those that are mixed case.

**7.** **Click either the Save & Close button or the Save & New button to save your invoice.**

Click the Save & Close button if you want to save the invoice and close the Create Invoices window. Click the Save & New button if you want to save the invoice and then enter another invoice in the blank version of the Create Invoices window.

**TIP**

Click the Send/Ship tab (shown near the top-left corner of Figure 1-10 earlier in this chapter, located directly above the Customize Data Layout icon and between the Formatting and Reports drop-down menus) and then click the FedEx, UPS, or USPS button to start the QuickBooks Shipping Manager window, which lets you automate some of the steps in shipping packages via Federal Express (FedEx), United Parcel Service (UPS), or the U.S. Postal Service (USPS). The first time you start the Shipping Manager, you need to do a bit of setup work.

To page through invoices that you've already created, click the Previous and Next buttons. Or click the Find button and use the Find Invoices dialog box to describe the invoice that you want to locate.

**TIP**

QuickBooks lets you add historical information about a customer to — and remove that information from — the Create Invoices window, the Create Credit Memos/ Refunds window, and most other customer information windows. To add historical information about a customer to a window, click the Show History button that appears in the top-right corner of the window, a bit to the right of the Template drop-down lists; it looks like an arrowhead. You can click links in the historical information panel to drill down and get more information about, for example, a listed transaction.

# Billing for Time

Most of the time, line items that appear in an invoice are items that you describe in the Item list and then quantify directly in the invoice. In some service businesses, however, you may actually sell many units of the same item. A lawyer may sell hours or partial hours of legal advice, and that time may be all that they sell. A CPA may sell hours of consulting, accounting, or tax preparation work.

In these circumstances, you don't want to have an invoice go out to the customer with one line in it that says, for example, "Legal services, 100 hours, $20,000" — unless you don't want to stay in business. Instead, you want an invoice that details each of the tasks that the lawyer performed: estate planning for 1.5 hours, review of a contract for 4 hours, preparation of a new real estate lease for 2 hours, and so forth. To provide this level of detail — detail that's really beneath the item — you use the QuickBooks Time Tracking feature.

QuickBooks supplies two methods for tracking the time spent that will be billed in an invoice as an item. You can use the weekly time sheet, or you can time or record individual activities. I briefly describe how both time-tracking methods work; neither is difficult. Professional service providers — accountants, attorneys, consultants, architects, and so on — who bill based on the time spent should consider using one of these features to make sure that they keep accurate records of the time spent working for a client or customer.

## Using a weekly time sheet

To use the weekly time-sheet method, choose Customers ⇨ Enter Time ⇨ Use Weekly Timesheet. QuickBooks displays the Weekly Timesheet window, shown in Figure 1-13. To use the Weekly Timesheet window, first use the Name box to identify the employee, vendor, or other person performing the service. You should be able to choose this person's name from the Name drop-down list. If you can't choose the person's name from the Name drop-down list, enter it in the box; then, when prompted, tell QuickBooks to which list (employee, vendor, or other names) the name should be added.

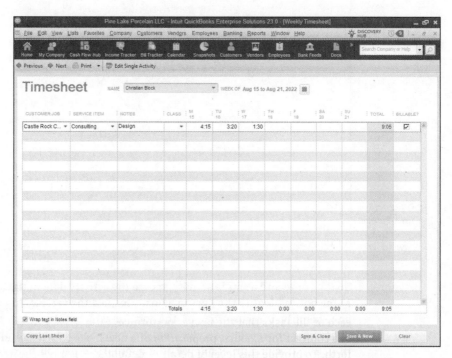

**FIGURE 1-13:** The Weekly Timesheet window.

After you've added the name of the person who performed the work, use the columns of the Weekly Timesheet window to describe the customer or job for which the work was performed, the service code, a brief description or note, the payroll item (if you're using QuickBooks for payroll), the class (if you're tracking classes), and then the hours spent per day. You can enter as many lines in the Weekly Timesheet window as you want. Each line appears separately in an invoice. The notes information appears in the description area of the invoice. For this reason, you want to use appropriate and descriptive notes.

## Timing single activities

If you want to record service activities as they occur, choose Customers ➪ Enter Time ➪ Time/Enter Single Activity. QuickBooks displays the Time/Enter Single Activity window, as shown in Figure 1-14.

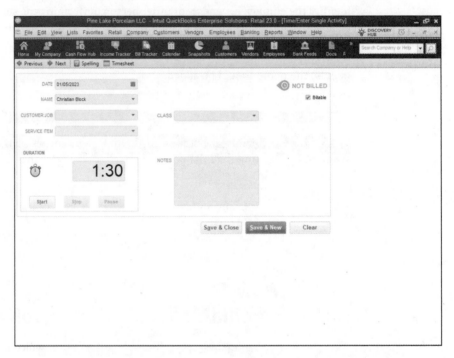

**FIGURE 1-14:**
The Time/Enter Single Activity window.

To time or record a single activity, record the activity date in the Date box. Use the Name box to identify the person who performed the service. In the Customer:Job box, identify the customer or the job for which the service was performed. Choose the appropriate service item from the Service Item drop-down list and (if you're tracking an employee) the appropriate payroll item from the Payroll Item drop-down list. If you're tracking classes, predictably, you can also use the Class drop-down list to classify the activity. Use the Notes box to record a brief, appropriate description of the service. This description appears in the invoice, so be thoughtful about what you write.

After describing or providing this general information about the service, you have two ways to record the time spent on the service:

>> **Record time manually.** You can manually record the time spent on an activity by using the Duration box to enter the time. If you spent 10 minutes, for example, enter **0:10** in the Duration box. If you spent 3 hours and 40 minutes, enter **3:40** in the Duration box.

>> **Have QuickBooks record the time.** You can also have QuickBooks record the time that you spent on the activity. Just click the Start button in the Duration box when you start the activity, and click the Stop button when you stop the activity. If you want to pause the timer (while you take a phone call, for example), click the Pause button.

After you use the Time/Enter Single Activity dialog box to describe the activity that you're performing, click the Save & New or Save & Close button to save the activity information.

TIP

Verify that the Billable check box (in the top-right corner of the dialog box) is selected. By selecting the Billable box, you tell QuickBooks that it should keep this record of a billable activity for later inclusion in an invoice.

You can use the Previous and Next buttons, which appear at the top of the dialog box, to page back and forth through your records of activity timing. Note, too, that a Spelling button is available. Click that button to spell-check the notes description that you enter — which is a good idea, because this information will appear in an invoice later.

## Including billable time on an invoice

To add billable time and cost to an invoice, create the invoice in the usual way, as I describe previously. After you identify the customer (if you've entered time for the customer), and if you've been tracking costs for the customer, QuickBooks displays a message box asking whether you want to bill for any of the time or costs. If you answer yes, QuickBooks displays the Choose Billable Time and Costs dialog box, shown in Figure 1-15.

The Time tab of this dialog box shows each of the times that you've recorded for a customer. To add these times to the invoice, click the Use column for the time. (The Use column is the leftmost column, displaying a check mark.) Or, if you want to select all the times, click the Select All button. Then click OK. QuickBooks adds each of these billable times to the invoice as separate lines. Figure 1-16 shows how billable time information appears in the Create Invoices window.

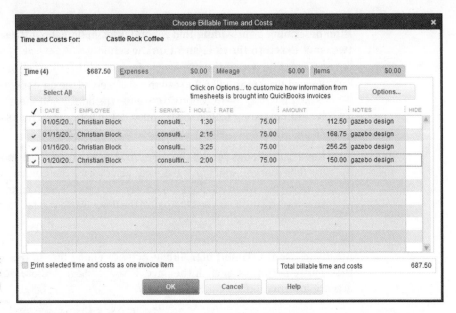

**FIGURE 1-15:**
The Choose Billable Time and Costs dialog box.

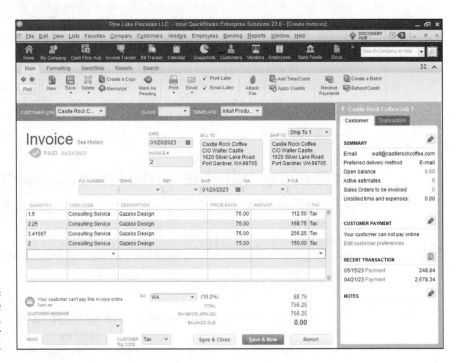

**FIGURE 1-16:**
The Create Invoices window, billing for billable time.

**TIP**

If you leave the check box titled Print Selected Time and Costs As One Invoice Item unselected (refer to Figure 1-15), QuickBooks puts each time recording you log on a separate line of the invoice, as shown in Figure 1-16. If you check the box, however, QuickBooks lets you combine individual time recordings into a single invoice line item. (You may want to experiment with this feature a bit if you're interested.)

**TIP**

As Figure 1-15 suggests, you can click the Items, Expenses, or Mileage tab to see lists of the items, out-of-pocket expenses, or business miles incurred on behalf of a customer. You add charges to an invoice for these sorts of things in the same way that you add charges for time. You can even apply a markup to your out-of-pocket expenses. In Book 2, Chapter 3, I talk about how to record reimbursed expenses (out-of-pocket expenses that you want to charge to customers). And you can record and then bill for miles you incur on behalf of customers by choosing the Company ⇨ Enter Vehicle Mileage command. (When you choose the Enter Vehicle Mileage command, use the dialog box that QuickBooks displays to log the miles covered and identify the customer.) By the way, if you want to return to the Choose Billable Time and Costs dialog box, and you're viewing the Create Invoices window, click the Add Time/Costs button, which appears at the top of the Create Invoices window.

# Printing Invoices

You can print invoices and then mail the printed invoices in a couple of ways:

» You can print individual invoices by clicking the Print button at the top of the Create Invoices window.

» You can also print a batch of invoices by clicking the arrow button below the Print button, choosing Batch from the menu that QuickBooks displays, and then using the Select Invoices to Print dialog box (which QuickBooks displays) to select the To Be Printed Invoices for printing. After you select the invoices that you want to print by clicking them, click OK.

**TIP**

The menu that QuickBooks displays when you click the Print button includes a Preview command. You can choose the Preview command to see a preview version of the printed invoice.

Invoicing Customers

# Emailing Invoices

You can email an invoice from QuickBooks. To do this, click the Email button, which appears at the top of the Create Invoice window, on the Main tab. If you haven't already set up email preferences, indicate which email account you want to use (web mail, an email application such as Microsoft Outlook, or the QuickBooks emailing system), and provide the email address and (optionally) a new email message. Then, not coincidentally, click the Send Now button to send the invoice.

You can set up email preferences by choosing the Edit ⇨ Preferences command and selecting the Send Forms section of the Preferences dialog box. Figure 1-17 shows what an emailed invoice would look like after you set up your business email address and using the default invoice text. You can play around with these options to speed your invoicing process.

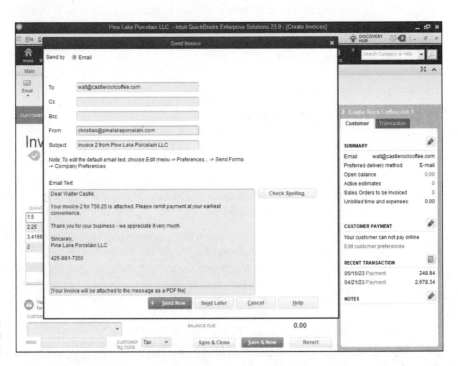

**FIGURE 1-17:**
The Send Invoice
dialog box.

**TIP**

The first time you click the Email button, QuickBooks may ask you to describe your email account or accounts, which you do by following the onscreen prompts. QuickBooks may also suggest that you use its mailing service, which means that you email the invoice to Intuit and then Intuit snail-mails the paper invoice to your client. If you're interested in Intuit's invoice mailing service, follow the onscreen prompts.

**WARNING**

Much to the consternation of many users, recent versions of the QuickBooks program added a message and clickable link to the bottom of your printed and emailed invoices that prompted those users' customers or clients to use a free (for them) online payment system to pay your invoice. This service, called the Intuit Payment Network, costs you a few dollars a month and a 2 to 3 percent service charge for credit card payments. For more information, see the last section of this chapter, "Using Odds and Ends on the Customers Menu."

# Recording Sales Receipts

To bill a customer, you create an invoice, as I describe earlier in this chapter. To record the fact that you sold the customer some item — presumably because the customer simultaneously purchases and pays for the item or service — you don't invoice the customer. Rather, you create a sales receipt. A sales receipt looks very, very similar to an invoice. It doesn't include shipping information, however (because that's irrelevant), and it lets you record the amount that the customer pays.

To record a sales receipt when appropriate, choose the Customers ⇨ Enter Sales Receipts command and then follow these steps:

**1.** **In the Enter Sales Receipts window (shown in Figure 1-18), use the Customer:Job drop-down list to describe the customer or, optionally, the customer and job.**

**2.** **Use the Class drop-down list to identify the class, if you're performing class tracking.**

**TIP**

If you have questions about how the Customer:Job or Class list works, refer to "Invoicing a Customer" earlier in this chapter. The invoice shown in Figure 1-18 displays the class tracking between the Customer Job and Template drop-down columns.

**TIP**

You can customize a sales receipt in the same basic way that you customize an invoice form. Go back to "Customizing an Invoice Form" at the beginning of this chapter.

**3.** **Provide the sales receipt header info.**

A sales receipt, like an invoice, includes some header information. Specifically, the sales receipt includes a sales receipt date and a sales number. The sales receipt also includes a Sold To box, which shows the customer name and address. You should confirm that this information is correct — as it should be if you're recording timely sales receipts and have an up-to-date customer list.

4. **Use the Item column to describe the items that you're selling.**

The Item column of a sales receipt works exactly the same way as the Item column of an invoice. Therefore, rather than repeat myself, I'll direct you to go back to the earlier discussion of how this column works.

5. **(Optional) If you want, enter a customer message in the footer area of the Enter Sales Receipts window.**

This option is available directly above the Memo and Customer Tax Code fields. If you've added other footer information to the Enter Sales Receipts window — because you've customized the sales receipt form template — you can include that information, too.

6. **Describe where the sales proceeds go.**

If the Use Deposited Funds option is disabled, a drop-down list to the right of the Class field will be visible (not visible in Figure 1-18). Use this drop-down list to indicate what to do with the money that you receive from this sale. If you immediately deposit the amount in a bank account, choose the account into which you want to deposit the check. If you want to batch this receipt with a bunch of other receipts — maybe you're going to deposit the day's receipts together in one lump sum — choose Group with Undeposited Funds.

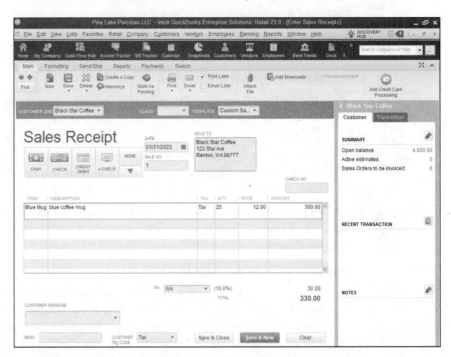

**FIGURE 1-18:**
The Enter Sales
Receipts window.

TIP

If you don't see the Deposit To drop-down list, you may have indicated (perhaps even inadvertently) during setup that you want QuickBooks to assume that funds are deposited in an undeposited-funds account. This probably works just fine. If you do want to specify an account where sales proceeds go when you record the sales receipt, choose the Edit ⇨ Preferences command, click the Payments icon, click the Company Preferences tab, and then deselect Use Undeposited Funds As a Default Deposit to Account.

TIP

Book 3, Chapter 4 talks about making deposits of undeposited funds.

7. **(Optional) To print a copy of the receipt, click the Print button.**

When you've printed the receipt, you can hand it to your customer.

TIP

The Previous, Next, Find, Spelling, Show/Hide History, and Time/Cost functions (found within the Main, Formatting, Send/Ship, Reports, Payments, and Search tabs at the top) in the Enter Sales Receipts window work identically to the same buttons in the Create Invoices window.

8. **Click the Save & Close or Save & New button to save the sales receipt.**

These buttons work the same way in the Enter Sales Receipts window as they do in the Create Invoices window.

TIP

Both the Create Invoices window (described earlier in the chapter) and the Enter Sales Receipts window (just described) include a Print Later check box on the toolbar of the Main tab. If you select this check box, QuickBooks adds the invoice or sales receipt to its list of unprinted invoices or sales receipts. You can print invoices and sales receipts that appear on either side of these lists by choosing File ⇨ Print Forms and then choosing either the Invoices or the Sales Receipt command. There's also an Email Later check box that you can select if you want to email a receipt later. (See the earlier section "Emailing Invoices.")

# Recording Credit Memos

Credit memos show when a customer no longer owes you money or when you owe a customer money. Credit memos may occur because your customer returns items that you previously sold to them. Credit memos may also occur because you issue a customer a refund for some other good reason; perhaps the product wasn't of the quality that you usually sell, or a service wasn't provided in the manner in which it should have been.

To record a credit memo, follow these steps:

1. **Choose the Customers ⇨ Create Credit Memos/Refunds command to display the Create Credit Memos/Refunds window.**

2. **Identify the customer, or the customer and the job, in the Customer: Job drop-down list, shown in Figure 1-19.**

   Use the Class drop-down list for class tracking if you've decided to do that. If you have questions about how either of these lists works, refer to the earlier discussions of these lists, which work the same way for credit memos as they do for invoices.

**TIP**

   The Create Credit Memos/Refunds window supplies a bunch of buttons on the various tabs that work the same way here as they do in the Create Invoices window: Previous, Next, and so on. For information about how to use these buttons if you have questions, refer to the earlier section on this topic.

**TIP**

   As is the case with invoices, you can create custom credit memo forms. To do this, you click the Formatting tab's Customize Data Layout button. Customizing a credit memo works the same way as customizing an invoice form. Refer to the earlier section on this topic if you have questions about how to customize a credit memo.

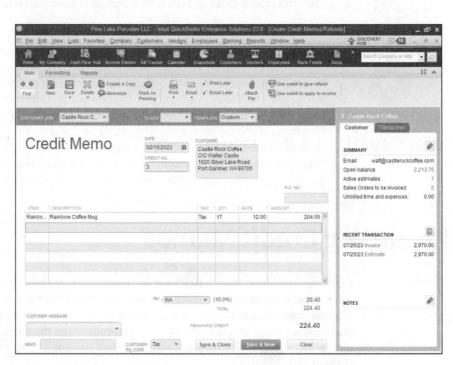

**FIGURE 1-19:**
The Create Credit Memos/Refunds window.

3. **Provide the credit memo date and number and confirm customer information.**

   Credit memos, like invoices and sales receipts, include a header. This header includes the transaction date, number, and the customer information. You should confirm that the credit memo header information is correct in the Create Credit Memos/Refunds window. If it isn't, edit the default information that QuickBooks uses to fill the Create Credit Memos/Refunds window.

**4.** **In the columns area, describe the reason for the credit memo.**

If the customer returned items, for example, use the columns to describe these items and the original price that you're refunding.

**5.** **Click the Print button to print the credit memo.**

Note, too, that you can print credit memos in a batch. Obviously, after you print credit memos, you need to distribute them.

TIP

You can email a copy of the credit memo directly from QuickBooks, too. The steps for emailing a credit memo mirror those for emailing an invoice, which is described earlier in "Emailing Invoices."

**6.** **Click either Save & Close or Save & New to save the credit memo.**

TIP

At the time you save your credit memo, QuickBooks allows you to indicate what you want to do with it: retain it for later application to a customer invoice, immediately apply it to a customer invoice, or issue a refund check. You apply credit memos to invoices as described in the next section of this chapter. You write a refund check the same way that you write other checks. Book 3, Chapter 4 describes writing checks.

# Receiving Customer Payments

When a customer pays an invoice that you've sent, you choose a command from the Customers menu to record the payment. To record a customer payment, follow these steps:

**1.** **Choose the Customers ⇨ Receive Payments command.**

QuickBooks displays the Customer Payment window, shown in Figure 1-20.

**2.** **Use the Received From drop-down list to identify the customer who's paying you.**

**3.** **Record the payment information in the Payment Amount, Date, and Reference # fields on the left side of the window, below the heading Customer Payment.**

You can also choose a payment method by clicking the Cash, Check, Credit Debit, or e-Check button to the right of these fields.

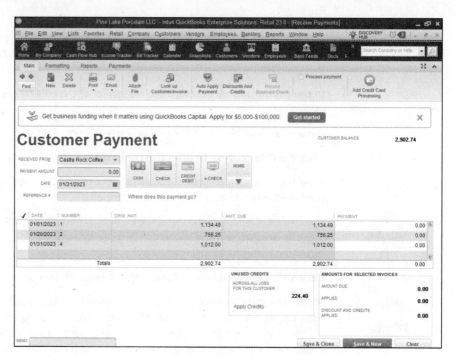

**FIGURE 1-20:**
The Customer
Payment window.

4. **Identify the invoice or invoices paid.**

   QuickBooks lists the open invoices for the customer in the columns area of the Receive Payments window. You can identify which invoices a customer payment pays by clicking the invoices that you see listed.

5. **To apply any credit memos to open invoices as you apply the payment, follow these steps:**

   a. *Click the Discounts and Credits button.*

      QuickBooks displays the Discount and Credits dialog box, shown in Figure 1-21.

   b. *To apply a credit to the selected invoices, click the Credits tab and then select the credit that you want to apply.*

   c. *Apply any discounts to the open invoices, and click Done.*

      Discounts work like credits. In fact, you use the same dialog box (refer to Figure 1-21). When you click Done, QuickBooks closes the Discount and Credits dialog box.

6. **Use the Deposit To box to select the account into which you want to deposit the check, or select the Undeposited Funds option if you want to batch the payments for later deposit.**

**FIGURE 1-21:**
The Discount
and Credits
dialog box.

The Deposit To drop-down list appears in the Receive Payments window when, during the QuickBooks Setup interview, you indicate that you may want to bunch the payments that you later deposit.

If you have a question about how these buttons work, refer to the discussion of these buttons in "Recording Sales Receipts" earlier in this chapter.

**TIP**

Click the Get Online Pmts button to receive online payment information for a customer. (The Get Online Pmts button appears only if you're using online billing or online banking.) Book 3, Chapter 4 provides more information about how online banking works.

7. **Click the Save & Close or Save & New button to save the customer payment information.**

# Assessing Finance Charges

You can tell QuickBooks to assess finance charges on overdue customer invoices. To do this, you first set up the finance-charge calculation rules. Then you can easily assess finance charges on overdue amounts by choosing the QuickBooks command Customers ➪ Assess Finance Charges.

# Setting up finance-charge rules

To set up the finance-charge rules, choose the Edit ⇨ Preferences command. When QuickBooks displays the Preferences dialog box, click the Finance Charge icon and then click the Company Preferences tab. The Preferences dialog box at this point should look like the one shown in Figure 1-22.

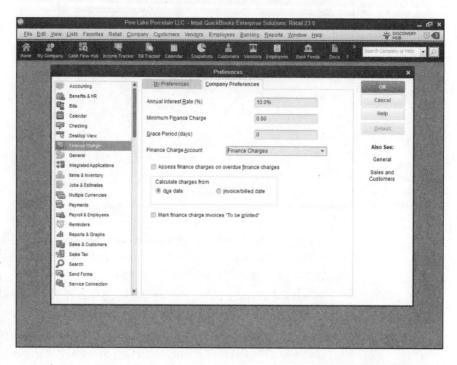

**FIGURE 1-22:** The Company Preferences tab of the Preferences dialog box, displaying the Finance Charge options.

To tell QuickBooks how it should calculate the finance charges, enter the annual interest rate that you'll use for calculating charges in the Annual Interest Rate (%) box. Enter the minimum finance charge amount that you assess in the Minimum Finance Charge box. If you want to create a grace period, enter the number of grace-period days in the Grace Period (Days) box. Use the Finance Charge Account drop-down list to specify the QuickBooks income account to which finance charge revenue should be credited. Select the check box titled Assess Finance Charges on Overdue Finance Charges if you want to charge finance charges on finance charges. Finally, use the Calculate Charges From radio buttons — Due Date and Invoice/Billed Date — to specify the date from which finance charges should be calculated. After you've provided this information, you can click OK to save your finance-charge calculation rules.

**TIP**

QuickBooks assumes that you don't want to print finance-charge invoices. For this reason, the Mark Finance Charge Invoices "To Be Printed" check box isn't selected. Finance charges typically appear only in customer statements.

## Calculating finance charges

After you set up the finance-charge rules, you can easily assess finance charges on overdue invoices. To do this, choose Customers ⇨ Assess Finance Charges. Quick-Books displays the Assess Finance Charges dialog box, as shown in Figure 1-23. This dialog box lists all the overdue invoices that customers owe you and, based on your finance-charge calculation rules, calculates a finance charge.

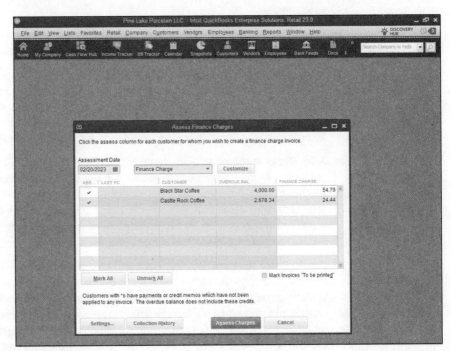

**FIGURE 1-23:**
The Assess
Finance Charges
dialog box.

To assess the finance charge to a particular customer, click the Assess (Ass.) field for the customer. (By default, QuickBooks assumes that you want to assess finance charges whenever a customer's account is past due.) If you don't want to assess finance charges to a particular customer, remove the check mark from the Assess field by clicking it. After you've identified which customers should be assessed finance charges, click the Assess Charges button. QuickBooks essentially creates a new invoice for each of these customers. These new invoices charge the customers a finance fee.

# Using Odds and Ends on the Customers Menu

In this chapter, I discuss most of the important commands on the Customers menu. This menu, however, supplies several other commands that are noteworthy — perhaps even useful — and deserve discussion somewhere in this book. For this reason, I want to briefly describe the other commands that may be available on your Customers menu:

>> **Customer Center:** Displays the Customer Center window, which includes information about your customer list, including the amounts that your customers owe.

>> **Create Estimates:** Displays a window you can use to create an estimate for a customer to show, for example, what a product or service will cost if you sell it to that customer.

>> **Create Sales Orders:** Displays a window you can use to create a sales order. Essentially, a *sales order* is an invoice for something you haven't yet really sold or for services you haven't yet provided. You prepare a sales order to record an order from a customer or client and document the order details.

>> **Sales Order Fulfillment Worksheet:** Displays the Sales Order Fulfillment worksheet window, which lists all your unfulfilled sales orders. You can print batches of sales orders by using this worksheet, too. (**Note:** If you've created sales orders for a particular customer or client, QuickBooks asks whether you want to turn a sales order into an invoice whenever you start working on an invoice for that customer.)

>> **Create Batch Invoices:** Displays the Batch Invoice dialog box, which lets you identify a group of customers you want to bill for some specified item. After you've grouped, or *batched,* the customers in this manner, you can tell QuickBooks to create a bunch (a batch) of invoices. If you charge customers a monthly retainer fee, for example, you could batch the customers on retainer and then create an invoice for each of them that billed for the "monthly retainer fee" item.

>> **Enter Statement Charges:** Displays the Accounts Receivable Register. You shouldn't need to use this command, but you can use it to add amounts to the accounts receivable for a particular customer. The amounts appear in the customer's next statement.

>> **Create Statements:** Displays a window that you can use to create a set of monthly statements for customers. Such statements show the amounts that a customer owes, invoices created for the month, credit memos issued for the month, and payments made during the month.

>> **Income Tracker:** Displays the Income Tracker window, which graphically organizes your estimates, orders, and invoices to show the flow of sales revenue you'll (ideally) receive and also graphically organizes your vendor bills and payments data to show you the flow of expenses you have or will experience.

>> **Lead Center:** Displays the Lead Center window, which lets you store and monitor customer leads. The window lets you name names, collect notes, and keep a to-do list of lead-generation activities.

>> **Add Credit Card Processing:** Displays a web page that explains and tries to talk you into buying Intuit's credit card processing service.

>> **Link Payment Services to Company File:** Makes the connection between your QuickBooks data file and the Intuit servers — something that's necessary if you sign up for credit card or electronic check processing.

>> **Add Marketing and Customer Tools** (available in the Enterprise Solutions version of QuickBooks): Displays a list of web pages you can visit to get information about a work-order management feature and an electronic data interchange feature that work with QuickBooks.

>> **Learn about Point of Sale:** Provides more information about setting up a point-of-sale system. You can also request a 30-day free trial.

>> **Item List:** Displays the Item list, which shows the items that may be included in the invoice or credit memo.

>> **Change Item Prices:** Lets you change the prices of a bunch of items at one time — increasing every price by 5 percent, for example.

# Chapter **2**

# Paying Vendors

You can make the process of tracking vendor information as simple or as sophisticated as you like. In this chapter, I assume that you're going for sophisticated. You can make vendor management simpler, however, by not using purchase orders or an accounts payable system.

**TIP**

You decide whether to use purchase orders and whether to track accounts payable (amounts that you owe vendors) as part of setting up QuickBooks. You can change your decision about using purchase orders or accounts payable later. To do this, you choose the Edit ⇨ Preferences command. For more information, refer to Book 2, Chapter 3.

## Creating a Purchase Order

A purchase order serves a simple purpose: It tells a vendor that you want to purchase some item. In fact, a *purchase order* is a contract to purchase.

Many small businesses don't use purchase orders. But when they grow to a certain size, many businesses decide to use them because purchase orders become permanent records of items that they've ordered. What's more, using purchase orders often formalizes the purchasing process in a company. You may decide, for example, that nobody in your firm can purchase anything that costs more than $100 unless they get a purchase order. If only you can issue purchase orders, you've effectively controlled purchasing activities through this procedure.

# Creating a real purchase order

To use QuickBooks to create purchase orders, follow these steps:

1. **Tell QuickBooks that you want to create a purchase order by choosing Vendors ⇨ Create Purchase Orders.**

   QuickBooks displays the window shown in Figure 2-1.

   **TIP**

   If the Vendors menu doesn't supply a Create Purchase Orders command, QuickBooks doesn't know that you want to create purchase orders. Follow the instructions described in Book 2, Chapter 3 to turn on the purchase order feature.

2. **Use the Vendor drop-down list to identify the vendor from which you want to purchase the item.**

   The Vendor drop-down list lists each of the vendors in your vendor list.

3. **(Optional) Classify the purchase using the Class drop-down list.**

   For more information about how you can use classes, read Book 4, Chapter 4. Note that you don't see a Class drop-down list unless you've turned on class tracking.

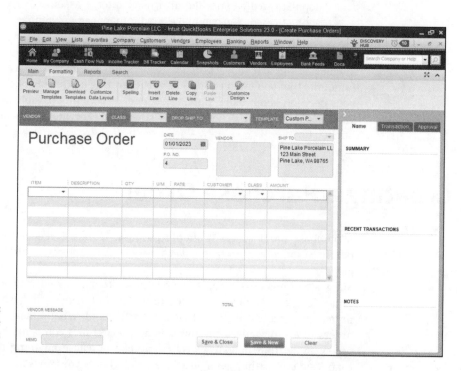

**FIGURE 2-1:**
The Create Purchase Orders window.

**4.** **(Optional) Choose a different Ship To address from the Drop Ship To drop-down list in the top-right corner.**

The Drop Ship To drop-down list displays a list of all your customers, vendors, and employees. You change the Ship To address by choosing one of these other names. After you choose an entry from the Ship To list, QuickBooks fills in the Ship To address box with the appropriate information.

**TIP**

The Create Purchase Orders window's Main, Formatting, and Reports tabs supply some standard and, I hope, familiar buttons and boxes: Previous, Next, New, and so on. Because I spend quite a bit of time talking about these buttons and boxes in Book 3, Chapter 1, I don't provide a redundant discussion of these buttons and boxes here. If you have questions about what the Previous and Next buttons do, refer to Book 3, Chapter 1.

**5.** **Confirm the purchase order date.**

Initially, QuickBooks puts the current system date in the Date box. You should, however, confirm that the date that QuickBooks enters as the purchase order date is correct. This date is the *contract date.* Often, the date sets contractual terms, such as the number of days within which the item is to be shipped.

**6.** **Confirm the purchase order number.**

The purchase order number, or *P.O. number,* uniquely identifies the purchase order document. QuickBooks sequentially numbers purchase orders for you and places the appropriate number in the P.O. No. box. The guess that QuickBooks makes about the right purchase order number is usually correct. If it isn't correct, you can enter a replacement number.

**7.** **Confirm the Vendor and Ship To information.**

The Vendor block and the Ship To block identify the vendor from which you're purchasing the item and the address to which you want the vendor to send the shipment. This information should be correct if your vendor list is up to date and you've correctly used the Ship To drop-down list to identify, if necessary, an alternative Ship To address. Nevertheless, confirm that the information shown in these two address blocks is correct. If the information isn't correct, of course, fix it. You can edit address-block information by selecting the incorrect information and then retyping whatever should be shown.

**8.** **Describe each item that you want to order.**

You use the columns of the Create Purchase Orders window to describe in detail each item that you want to order as part of the purchase. Each item goes in its own row. To describe an item that you want to purchase from the vendor, you provide the following bits of information:

- *Item:* The Item column is where you record the unique item number for the item that you want to buy. Remember that items need to be entered, or described, in the Item list. Book 2, Chapter 2 discusses briefly how you go about setting up the Item list. Book 3, Chapter 3 talks in more detail about the Item list. The main thing to know about the Item list is that anything that you want to show in the invoice — or, for that matter, in a purchase order — must be described in the item file.

- *Description:* In the Description column, you describe the item that you select. You can also edit the Description field so that it makes sense to customers or vendors.

- *Qty:* The Qty column specifies the quantity of the item that you want. Obviously, you enter the number of items that you want in this column.

- *U/M:* The U/M column allows you to show quantities, prices, rates, and costs for an item. A unit of measurement can be set up as a single unit or multiple units.

- *Rate:* The Rate column specifies the price per unit or rate per unit for the item. Note that QuickBooks uses different labels for this column depending on the type of business that you've set up.

- *Customer:* The Customer column identifies the customer for which the item is being purchased.

- *Class:* In the Class column, you classify purchase order items at the item level rather than at the purchase order level. Note that you won't see this column unless you've turned on class tracking.

- *Amount:* The Amount column shows the total expended for the item. QuickBooks calculates the amount for you by multiplying the quantity by the rate (or price). You can edit the column amount. In this case, QuickBooks adjusts the rate (or price) so that quantity times rate always equals the amount.

You enter a description of each item that should be included in the purchase order. This means, for example, that if you want to order six items from a vendor, your purchase order should include six lines of information.

9. **Print the purchase order.**

The purpose of recording a purchase order in QuickBooks is to create a formal record of a purchase. You almost always want to transmit this purchase order to the vendor. The purchase order tells the vendor exactly what you want to purchase and the price that you're willing to pay. To print the purchase order, you can click the Print button. You can also print purchase orders in a batch later if you select the Print Later check box (available on the Main tab) when you're creating purchase orders, save all the purchase orders that you want to print later and then choose File ➪ Print Forms ➪ Purchase Orders.

**10.** **Save the purchase order.**

To save your purchase order, click either the Save & Close button or the Save & New button. If you click the Save & New button, QuickBooks saves that purchase order and redisplays an empty version of the Create Purchase Orders window so that you can record another purchase order.

## Using some purchase order tips and tricks

Even though the preceding section details all you need to know to create a purchase order, I want to make a few more important observations:

>> **Not every purchase deserves a purchase order.** If you're not used to working with purchase orders, it's easy to go overboard when you start using this handy tool. Nevertheless, keep in mind that not all purchases warrant purchase orders (see the next item).

>> **Use purchase orders to manage buying.** Typically, businesses use purchase orders as a way to control and document purchases. In fact, many purchases don't really require a purchase order. Amounts that you've agreed to purchase that are documented through standard contracts — such as bills from the telephone company, the gas company, and your landlord — don't need purchase orders, obviously. In addition, modest purchases, such as office supplies, often don't need purchase orders. You definitely need a way to control these expenditures, but purchase orders probably aren't the way to go.

>> **Consider other, complementary control tools.** Other budgetary controls, such as "approval from the supervisor" or a simple budget, often work just as well.

# Recording the Receipt of Items

When you receive items from a vendor, you can record the receipt. You typically do this when you want to record the receipt of an item even before you receive a bill for the item. In any business with inventory, for example, you want to know exactly how much inventory you have in your warehouse or on your store floor. You don't want to wait to adjust your inventory records for these purchases until you receive the invoice from the vendor. In this scenario, you record when you receive items.

To record item receipts, follow these steps:

**1. Choose the Vendors ➪ Receive Items command.**

QuickBooks displays the Create Item Receipts window, as shown in Figure 2-2.

**2. From the Vendor drop-down list, choose the vendor from which you're receiving items.**

**3. Select any purchase orders that you're receiving items from.**

If open purchase orders exist for the vendor, QuickBooks displays a message box, asking whether you want to receive items against one of the open purchase orders. If the items that you receive are items that you set up in a purchase order, click Yes. When QuickBooks displays the Open Purchase Orders dialog box — the dialog box lists only open purchase orders — select the one that ordered the items you're now receiving and then click OK. QuickBooks fills out the Items tab of the Create Item Receipts window by using the information from the purchase order. This automatic data entry of purchase order information should save you time if the items that you're receiving match items in the purchase order.

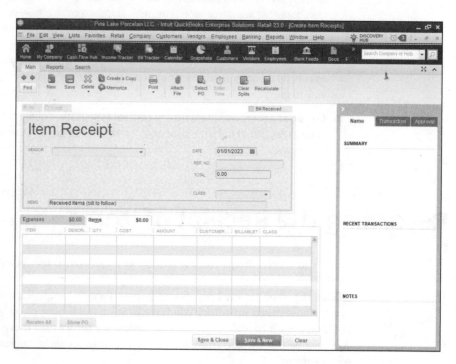

**FIGURE 2-2:**
The Create Item Receipts window.

**4.** **Confirm the receipt date.**

Use the Date field to confirm the date of receipt. As with the Date field in other places in QuickBooks, enter the date in mm/dd/yyyy format. Or click the Calendar button that appears to the right of the Date field and choose the date from the pop-up calendar that QuickBooks displays.

**5.** **(Optional) Enter a reference number.**

You can use the Ref. No. field to provide a reference number. You may want to reference the vendor's order number, for example.

**6.** **Use the Total box to identify the total value of the order received, if available.**

QuickBooks calculates this total for you by adding the individual item costs, so you can wait until later.

**7.** **(Optional) Provide a description in the Memo text box.**

**8.** **Describe the items received.**

Use the Items tab to identify the items that you've received. The Items tab of the Create Item Receipts window resembles and works like the Items tab of the Create Purchase Order window, as described (briefly) earlier in the chapter and (in some detail) in the preceding chapter. For this reason, I don't discuss how you enter, for example, item codes in the Item column. If you have questions about how the Items tab works, refer to one of the other appropriate chapters in this book.

**9.** **Describe any related expenses.**

The Expenses tab of the Create Item Receipts window works like the Expenses tab of the Write Checks window. If you have questions about how the Expenses tab works, see the discussion of writing checks in Book 3, Chapter 4.

**10.** **Click either the Save & Close or Save & New button to save the receipt item.**

If you click the Save & Close button, QuickBooks saves your item receipt information and closes the Create Item Receipts window. If you click the Save & New button, QuickBooks saves the item receipt information and redisplays a fresh, clean version of the Create Item Receipts window. You can use the window to describe the receipts of some other set of items.

That's about all you need to know to work with the Create Item Receipts window. Nevertheless, let me quickly describe a few command buttons that I don't reference in the earlier discussions:

>> **Select PO:** This toolbar button displays the Open Purchase Orders dialog box, which lists the purchase orders open for the selected vendor. By selecting a listed purchase order, you tell QuickBooks to fill out the Items tab with the information from that purchase order or orders.

>> **Receive All/Clear Qtys:** This button is located in the bottom-left corner of the Item Receipt window; it can change depending on whether you have quantities entered. When it's labeled Receive All, this command button says you've received all the items you ordered in some purchase order; when it's labeled Clear Qtys, the button clears the received quantities shown on the Items tab if you've specified a purchase order. When you click this button, it changes from Receive All to Clear Qtys to Receive All, and so on.

>> **Show PO:** This command button shows the selected purchase order and is located next to the Receive All/Clear Qtys button.

>> **Clear Splits:** This toolbar button erases any expense or item information that you've entered on the Expenses or Items tab and moves the total to the Expenses tab.

>> **Recalculate:** This toolbar button recalculates the total amount by using the information that you've entered on the Expenses and Items tabs.

>> **Clear:** This button (which appears in the bottom-right corner of the window) clears all the information that you've entered in the Create Item Receipts window, including Expenses-tab information, Items-tab information, and the vendor information shown at the top of the window. In effect, the Clear button lets you start over.

>> **Enter Time:** This toolbar button opens the Select Time Period dialog box, shown in Figure 2-3, which you use to specify the date range of the work for which you're paying.

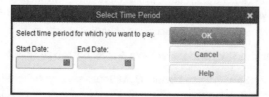

**FIGURE 2-3:**
The Select Time
Period dialog box.

# Simultaneously Recording the Receipt and the Bill

You can record a bill for items that you receive at the same time that you record the receipt of the items. You can do this simply by selecting the Bill Received check box that appears near the top of the Create Item Receipts window (refer to Figure 2-2).

If you know that you're going to record a bill at the same time that you record the receipt of items, you can also choose the Vendors ⇨ Receive Items and Enter Bill command. In other words, rather than choose the Receive Items command from the Vendors menu, you choose the Receive Items and Enter Bill command. When you do this, QuickBooks displays the Enter Bills window, shown in Figure 2-4. Essentially, the Enter Bills window is another version of the Create Item Receipts window except that the Bill Received check box is already selected. To simultaneously record items that you've received and enter a bill, you follow the same steps that you do to record the receipt of the items.

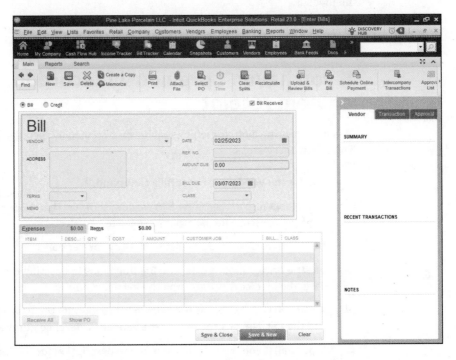

**FIGURE 2-4:**
The Enter Bills window.

One item worth noting about simultaneously recording bills and the receipt of items, however, is this: When you enter a bill, you need to be very precise about the charges of the vendor. In all probability, you won't pay just for the ordered items, for example; you may also pay certain shipping and handling fees. These amounts won't necessarily get recorded on the Items tab. They'll probably be recorded on the Expenses tab.

# Entering a Bill

If you told QuickBooks during the setup process that you want to track unpaid bills, also known as *accounts payable*, you can enter bills as you receive them. As you do this, QuickBooks keeps track of the unpaid bills.

**TIP**

Good, accurate record keeping of unpaid bills, or accounts payable, is essential if you want to do good accrual-basis accounting. As I discuss in Book 1, Chapter 1, accrual-basis accounting produces more accurate financial statements than other methods do.

To enter a bill, you follow either of two sequences of steps.

## If you haven't previously recorded an item receipt

If you're entering a bill for which you haven't previously recorded an item receipt, you follow these steps:

1. **Choose the Vendors ➪ Enter Bills command.**

   QuickBooks displays the Enter Bills window, shown in Figure 2-5. You use this window to describe the bills that you need to pay later.

2. **Use the Vendor drop-down list to identify the vendor.**

3. **Use the Date, Amount Due, and Bill Due fields to describe the invoice date, the invoice due date, and the invoice amount.**

4. **(Optional) Use the Terms drop-down list to identify the payment terms and the Ref. No. box to identify the vendor's reference number.**

5. **(Optional) If you want to, enter a memo description for the bill in the Memo box.**

6. **Identify the expenses billed.**

   Use the Expenses tab of the Enter Bills window to identify the expenses that the bill represents. To identify expenses, you supply the account number that should be debited; the amount; and (optionally) the Memo, Customer:Job, and Class information. If you have questions about how the Expenses tab works, see the discussion of writing checks in Book 3, Chapter 4. The Expenses tab of the Write Checks window works the same way as the Expenses tab of the Enter Bills window.

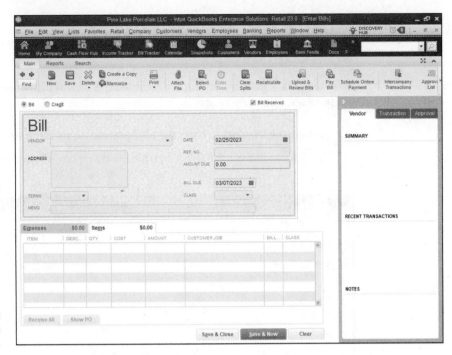

FIGURE 2-5:
The Enter Bills
window again.

**7.** **Identify the items billed on the Items tab.**

Use the Items tab of the Enter Bills window to describe any items for which the vendor bills you. Use the Item column to identify the thing that you purchased, for example; then use the Qty, Cost, and Amount columns to identify what the item cost. You can also use the Customer:Job column if you're tracking bills by customers. If you have questions about how to work with the Items tab, be aware that the Items tab of the Enter Bills window works the same way that the Items tabs of other QuickBooks windows work. You can, for example, refer to the discussion of the Create Invoices window in Book 3, Chapter 1.

**TIP**

The buttons available in the Enter Bills window — Select PO, Receive All, Show PO, Clear Splits, Recalculate, and Clear — work the same way as the similarly titled command buttons scattered around the edges of the Create Item Receipts window, discussed in "Recording the Receipt of Items" earlier in this chapter.

**8.** **Click either the Save & Close or Save & New button to save the bill.**

# If you have previously recorded an item receipt

To enter a bill when you've already recorded the receipt of the item for which the bill invoices, follow these steps:

1. **Choose the Vendors ⇨ Enter Bill for Received Items command.**

   QuickBooks displays the Select Item Receipt dialog box, shown in Figure 2-6.

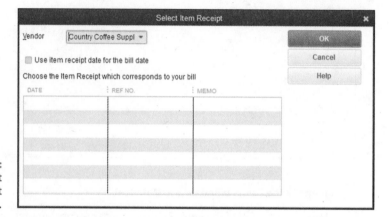

**FIGURE 2-6:**
The Select
Item Receipt
dialog box.

2. **To identify the item receipt for which you're now recording a bill, choose the vendor from the Vendor drop-down list.**

3. **When QuickBooks displays a list of item receipts for the vendor, select the item receipt that corresponds to your bill and click OK.**

   QuickBooks displays the Enter Bills window for the item. QuickBooks fills out much of the Enter Bills window by using the information from the item receipt, as shown in Figure 2-7.

   **TIP**

   You may be able to skip Steps 4–8 if your item receipt information correctly and completely fills the Enter Bills window.

4. **Use the Date, Amount Due, and Bill Due fields to describe the invoice date, the invoice due date, and the invoice amount.**

5. **(Optional) Use the Terms drop-down list to identify the payment terms and the Ref. No. box to identify the vendor's reference number.**

6. **(Optional) If you want to, enter a memo description for the bill in the Memo box.**

7. **Use the Expenses tab of the Enter Bills window to identify the expenses that the bill represents.**

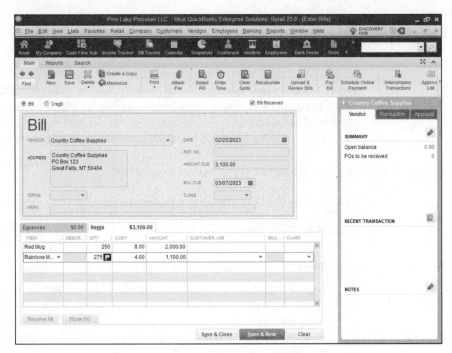

**FIGURE 2-7:**
The Enter Bills window yet again.

To identify expenses, you supply the account number that should be debited, the amount, and (optionally) the Memo, Customer:Job, and Class information. If you have questions about how the Expenses tab works, see the discussion of writing checks in Book 3, Chapter 4. The Expenses tab of the Write Checks window works the same way as the Expenses tab of the Enter Bills window.

**8.** **Use the Items tab of the Enter Bills window to describe any items for which the vendor bills you.**

Use the Item column to identify the thing that you purchased, for example; then use the Qty, Cost, and Amount columns to identify what the item cost. You can also use the Customer:Job column if you're tracking bills by customers. If you have questions about how to work with the Items tab, be aware that the Items tab of the Enter Bills window works the same way that Items tabs of other QuickBooks windows work. You can, for example, refer to the discussion of the Create Invoices window in Book 3, Chapter 1.

**9.** **Click either the Save & Close or Save & New button to save the bill and item receipt information.**

**REMEMBER**

You record credit memos from vendors by using the Enter Bills window too. The only difference in recording a credit memo is that you select the Credit radio button.

Paying Vendors

# Paying Bills

If you use QuickBooks to keep track of the bills that you owe, you don't use the Write Checks window (described in Book 3, Chapter 4) to record the bills that you want to pay. Rather, you tell QuickBooks to display a list of these unpaid bills that you've already recorded — and then you choose which bills QuickBooks should pay and the bank account on which QuickBooks should write the check.

Follow these steps to pay bills in this manner:

## 1. Choose the Vendors ⇨ Pay Bills command.

QuickBooks displays the Pay Bills window, shown in Figure 2-8. You use this window to describe the payment that you want to make.

## 2. Describe which bills you want to pay.

Use the Show Bills radio buttons at the top of the Pay Bills window to identify what you want to see. Select the Due On or Before radio button to show only those bills that are due on or before the specified date. To specify the date, enter the date in the Due On or Before box. To see a list of all the bills that you have to pay, select the Show All Bills radio button.

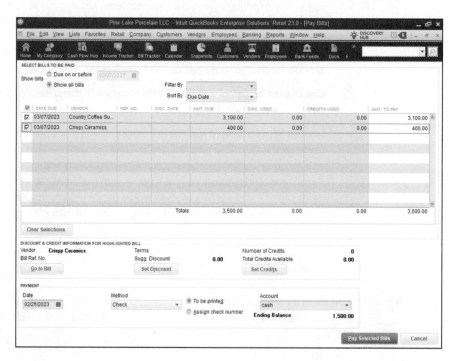

**FIGURE 2-8:**
The Pay Bills window.

**TIP**

You can use the Sort By drop-down list to select the order that QuickBooks uses for listing your bills. You can sort bills by due date, discount date, vendor, and amount due.

**3.** **Select the bills that you want to pay.**

To select bills that you want to pay, click the check column. (The check column is the leftmost column in the list of unpaid bills; it's headed by a check mark.) When you click the check column, QuickBooks marks the bill with a check mark. The check mark tells QuickBooks that you want to pay that bill. To deselect a bill, click the check column again. QuickBooks removes the check mark.

**4.** **(Optional) Review a specific bill.**

You can review detailed information about a specific bill by first clicking the bill to highlight it in the list and then clicking the Go to Bill button. When you do this, QuickBooks opens the Enter Bills window, displaying the bill information. To close the Enter Bills window, click the Close button.

**5.** **Set the discount and credit and then click Done.**

If you click the Set Discount button, QuickBooks displays the Discount tab of the Discount and Credits dialog box, as shown in Figure 2-9. You can use the Discount tab to enter a discount amount for the bill. If you enter a discount amount for the bill, you also enter the discount account. This account is the one that gets credited for the reduction — the discount — in the correct amount.

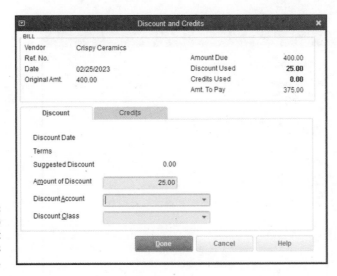

**FIGURE 2-9:**
The Discount tab of the Discount and Credits dialog box.

If you click the Pay Bills window's Set Credits button, QuickBooks displays the Credits tab of the Discount and Credits dialog box, shown in Figure 2-10. The Credits tab lists any credit memos from this vendor. To apply a credit memo to the amount due to a vendor, click the check mark next to the credit and click done. QuickBooks marks applied credits by placing a check in the marked column.

When you complete your work with the Discount and Credits dialog box, click the Done button to close the dialog box and return to the Pay Bills window.

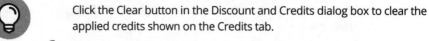

**TIP**

Click the Clear button in the Discount and Credits dialog box to clear the applied credits shown on the Credits tab.

6. **Use the Account drop-down list in the bottom-right corner to select the bank account to be used for making payments.**

    You can double-check to make sure you have enough money in the bank account, because the ending balance is displayed in the account you selected after you complete this payment (refer to Figure 2-8).

7. **Use the Method drop-down list in the Payment section to select the payment method.**

    If you want to pay your bills by check, for example, choose Check. Assuming that you'll print the checks in QuickBooks, select the To Be Printed radio button; otherwise, select the Assign Check Number radio button to have QuickBooks assign the next consecutive check number. You can also pay bills by other methods, such as by credit card and by online payment (if you're set up for online payment or online banking).

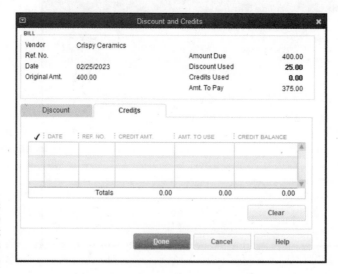

**FIGURE 2-10:**
The Credits tab of the Discount and Credits dialog box.

8. **Use the Date box in the Payment section to record the payment date.**

   This entry interacts with the entry in Step 7. The payment date that you set, for example, affects when an online payment gets made. The payment date also corresponds to the date that's shown on printed checks.

9. **After you select the bills that you want to pay and describe how you want to pay them, click Pay Selected Bills.**

   QuickBooks records the payment transactions in the bank account to pay the selected bills and closes the Pay Bills window.

10. **Complete your task.**

    You still need to print any unprinted checks necessary to pay bills if you're using checks to pay the bills. You also need to transmit any online payment instructions necessary to pay the bills, if that's how you've chosen to pay the bills. If you're going to handwrite checks, you (obviously) need to handwrite the checks and then mail them. In other words, all QuickBooks does at this point is record the payment transactions in the QuickBooks data file. You need to print the checks, send the online payment instructions, or handwrite the checks!

# Reviewing the Other Vendor Menu Commands

In the preceding paragraphs of this chapter, I talk about the most important commands on the Vendor menu. Nevertheless, before I wrap up this little dog-and-pony show, I quickly review for you the other commands and what they do.

## Vendor Center window

The Vendor Center window, shown in Figure 2-11, displays a list of vendors and detailed vendor information for the selected vendor. To use it, choose from the Active Vendors drop-down list the vendor for which you want to see detailed information. The Vendor Center shows a bunch of information for a vendor. All this information comes from the Vendor list, by the way, which is discussed in Book 2, Chapter 2.

TIP

If you keep records of your vendors, including information such as their telephone numbers, just about the best place to store that information, in my humble opinion, is the Vendor list. You have to maintain the Vendor list for QuickBooks to work. Why not also go to a little bit of extra effort and keep all your vendor information there? If you adopt this approach, the Vendor Center window is the window that you can use to quickly look up things such as the vendor's phone or fax number.

The Bill Tracker toolbar button, shown in Figure 2-11, is very useful for keeping track of unbilled purchase orders, open bills, overdue bills, and bills that have been paid within 30 days. The information is neatly presented to make this information visible at a quick glance.

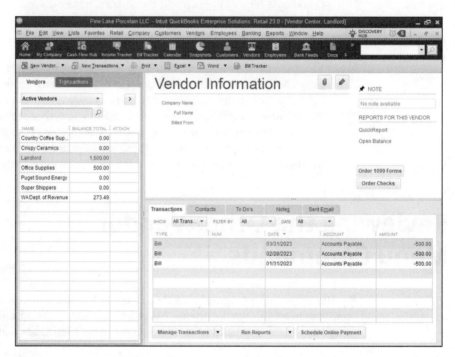

**FIGURE 2-11:**
The Vendor
Center window.

## Sales Tax menu commands

The Sales Tax command displays a submenu of commands that pay sales tax amounts you've collected to the appropriate tax agency; adjust the sales tax liability due; and produce reports on the sales tax liability you owe, the sales tax revenue you've generated, and the sales tax codes you've set up.

*Note:* To see this menu, you need to tell QuickBooks that you collect sales tax. You may tell QuickBooks that you collect sales tax during the QuickBooks setup process. You can also choose Edit ⇨ Preferences and set your Sales Tax preferences for the company.

To pay the sales taxes you owe, simply choose Vendors ⇨ Sales Tax ⇨ Pay Sales Tax. When QuickBooks displays the Pay Sales Tax dialog box (which lists the amounts you owe various sales tax collection agencies), you select the agencies you want to pay or click the Pay All Tax button. QuickBooks records checks in the bank account register (see Book 3, Chapter 4 for details about how to work with the bank register), and you print the checks in the usual way.

To adjust the amount that QuickBooks thinks you owe a sales tax collection agency, you can choose Vendors ⇨ Sales Tax ⇨ Adjust Sales Tax Due. When Quick-Books displays the Sales Tax Adjustment dialog box, select a sales tax agency in the Sales Tax Vendor box and an appropriate expense or income account in the Adjustment Account box. Next, select the appropriate button (Increase Sales Tax By or Decrease Sales Tax By) and enter the adjustment amount in the Amount box.

To print one of the sales tax reports, simply select the command that corresponds with the report. To print the Sales Tax Liability report, for example, choose Vendors ⇨ Sales Tax ⇨ Sales Tax Liability.

The Manage Sales Tax command displays a window with buttons and clickable hyperlinks that you can use to get sales tax information and perform some of the tasks described in the preceding paragraphs.

Visiting the Sales Tax Code List enables you to add, delete or edit codes. It also provides drop-down lists that give you options to do things described earlier, such as pay sales tax liability or view reports that show transactions on which sales tax was charged.

## Inventory Activities menu commands

The Inventory Activities command displays a submenu of commands that you use to work with QuickBooks inventory features and with the related Item list. I'm not going to discuss this stuff here — not because I'm lazy, but because I discuss inventory and the Item list in Book 3, Chapter 3.

## Print/E-file 1099s commands

The Print/E-file 1099s command displays a submenu of commands that let you print 1099-MISC forms for a selected calendar year. You can see the vendors for which you probably need to print 1099s, for example, by choosing the Print/E-file 1099s ⇨ Review 1099 Vendors command. (When you choose this command, Quick-Books displays the Vendor 1099 Review report, which lists vendors and indicates the vendors that are, per your descriptions, eligible for a 1099.)

The reporting threshold may change in the future due to inflation, but the general rule is that if you operate a business or own rental property, you need to send a 1099-MISC to pretty much any unincorporated vendor you pay $600 or more during the year for services. And before you decide not to follow this rule, you should know two other facts.

>> Your business tax return actually needs to disclose whether you followed this rule. Yikes.

>> If you don't send 1099s, you'll pay a penalty from $30 to $100 per late 1099 if you're merely late (with a maximum penalty total set to $500,000). If you simply blow off this requirement, the penalty equals $250 per 1099 — with no maximum penalty.

You can use the Print/E-file 1099s ⇨ 1099 Wizard command to start an online wizard that helps you identify the vendors that require 1099s and then prepare to print or e-file those 1099s.

Finally, you can choose the Print/E-file 1099s menu's 1099 Summary Report and 1099 Detail Report commands to produce reports you can use to identify which vendors need 1099s and what detailed information goes in those 1099s. For information about how to set 1099 preferences, refer to Book 2, Chapter 3.

## Item List command

The Vendors ⇨ Item List command displays the Item List window. You can read more about the Item List window in Book 3, Chapter 3 (the next chapter).

IN THIS CHAPTER

» Viewing your Item list

» Expanding your Item list

» Changing items

» Modifying physical counts and inventory values

» Modifying prices and price levels

» Dealing with a manufacturing firm's inventory

# Chapter **3**

# Tracking Inventory and Items

I f you've worked with QuickBooks, you won't be surprised to hear that the Item list is a key piece of your QuickBooks accounting system. The Item list identifies each of the things that you sell. The Item list also identifies other things that appear in your invoices and — if you use them — purchase orders.

In this chapter, I talk about how you work with the QuickBooks Item list — more specifically, how you look at and use the information in the Item list to track and tally what you sell. I explain how to add information to the list and how to edit information that's already in the list. What's more, I talk about three accounting tasks that are related to your Item list: adjusting physical inventory accounts for inventory shrinkage or spoilage, adjusting price levels of your inventory items, and (if you manufacture inventory) using QuickBooks to handle inventories of manufactured goods.

# Looking at Your Item List

QuickBooks provides a bunch of ways to see the information that you've stored in your Item list. You may already know some of this stuff if you've worked with QuickBooks a bit; some of it may be new to you. In any case, the next sections reviews several ways that you can see the items in your Item list.

## Using the Item Code column

One important point to consider as you look at the Item Code column and Item Code drop-down list in the Create Invoices window (see Figure 3-1) is space. Note that the Item Code column is pretty narrow. Note also that the Item Code drop-down list in Figure 3-1 provides the item code (the left column), the item type, and a lengthier item description. Though you do have quite a bit of space for a description, you can't go hog-wild.

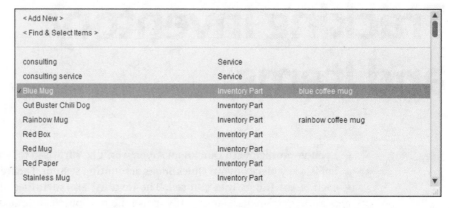

FIGURE 3-1:
The Item Code column and drop-down list in the Create Invoices window.

TIP

I'm using self-explanatory item codes in this reference, as you can see in Figure 3-1. In real life, your codes may be far more cryptic.

## Using the Item List window

If you choose the Lists ➪ Item List command, QuickBooks displays the Item List window, as shown in Figure 3-2. The Item List window identifies the item code or name, the description, the type of item (I talk more about this in the next section of the chapter), the account that gets credited when you sell some of the items, and the inventory stocking and pricing information (if you supply that).

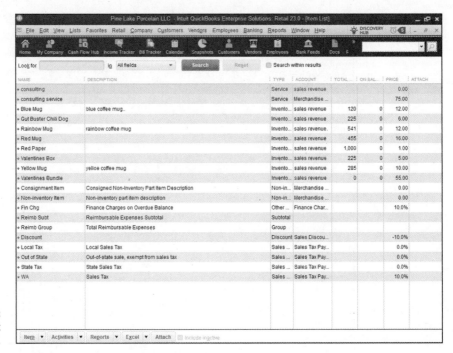

**FIGURE 3-2:**
The Item List window.

The Item list provides a good way to see quickly what items you can put in invoices and purchase orders. The Item list also provides a quick and convenient way to see stocking levels and prices.

If you want more information about an item shown in the Item List window, you can double-click the item. When you double-click the item, QuickBooks displays the Edit Item window, as shown in Figure 3-3. Essentially, the Edit Item window displays all the information available about a particular item. You can use this window to change bits of item information. Later in this chapter, in "Editing Items," I describe how to do this.

## Using inventory reports

I mention one other thing because it's so darn useful. As you'd expect, QuickBooks supplies several interesting, useful inventory reports. If you choose the Report ⇨ Inventory command, for example, QuickBooks displays a submenu of inventory reports. The submenu provides reports that give inventory valuations, inventory stock levels, and a worksheet that you can use to physically count the inventory on store shelves or in the warehouse.

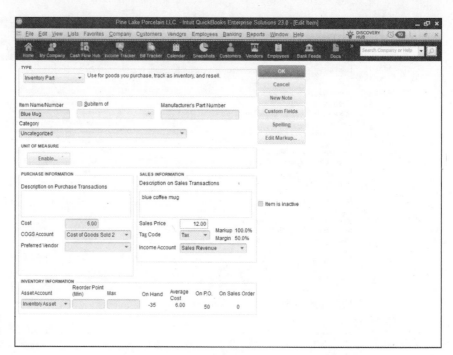

**FIGURE 3-3:**
The Edit Item
window.

**TIP**

Book 4, Chapter 2 describes how you produce reports in QuickBooks and how you customize those reports. If you want to find out more about reports and report customization, see that chapter.

# Adding Items to the Item List

You can add a bunch of types of items to the Item list. Remember that as noted in the early paragraphs of this chapter, the Item list stores descriptions of anything that you stick in an invoice or purchase order.

When you think about this for a minute, you realize that you have different types of items. If you're a retailer, for example, the inventory that you sell may appear in an invoice. If you provide discounts to different sorts of customers, discounts may appear in an invoice as a line item. If you're in a state that taxes sales, sales tax appears as a line item in an invoice.

You describe different items in different ways. You describe an inventory item that may appear in an invoice differently from the way you describe a sales tax that you're required to charge.

Given this disparity, I first describe the general process for adding an item to the Item list. After you know the big-picture stuff, I talk about the items that appear in the Item list individually. Sound okay? I'll get started.

## Adding an item: Basic steps

To add an item to your Item list, follow these steps:

**1. Choose the Lists ⇨ Item List command.**

QuickBooks displays the Item List window (an example of which appears in Figure 3-2, earlier in this chapter).

**2. To display the Item menu, click the Item button, which appears in the bottom-left corner of the Item List window.**

QuickBooks displays the Item menu.

**3. Choose the New command.**

This command tells QuickBooks to display the New Item window, as shown in Figure 3-4.

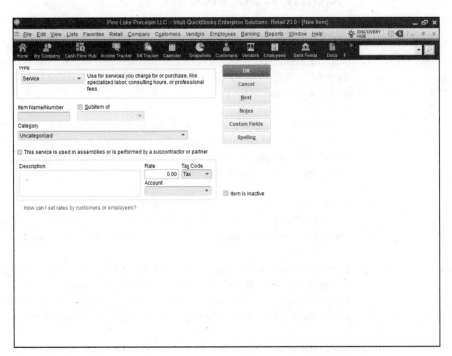

**FIGURE 3-4:**
The New Item window.

4. **Use the boxes of the New Item window to describe the item that you want to add.**

   Your first step is to identify the type of item that you want to add. Based on the type of item, QuickBooks supplies other boxes that you use to describe the item. (I go into more detail about this in the following paragraphs, so don't get freaked out — yet.)

5. **Save the item.**

   After you use the boxes in the New Item window to describe the item that you want to add, click OK. QuickBooks adds the item that you just described in the Item list.

**TIP**

The step-by-step approach described in the preceding paragraphs is the conventional way to add an item, but you can also add items on the fly. If you're using the Create Invoices window or the Create Purchase Orders window, you can open the Item drop-down list and choose Add New Entry. When you do this, QuickBooks displays the New Item window (refer to Figure 3-4). Then you use the New Item window to add the item in the manner discussed here.

## Adding a service item

You use service items to purchase or bill for items that represent service. Take my example. I'm a CPA in Redmond, Washington. One of the things that I do is prepare tax returns for individuals and businesses. When I bill a client for preparing their tax return, the line item that appears in the invoice for Tax Return Preparation is a service item.

In your business, you probably have service items too. A health-care provider, such as a dentist or doctor, provides treatment or performs procedures. Dentists might fill cavities. Doctors might perform physicals or give vaccinations. These activities represent services.

Even retailers and contractors — businesses that you typically think of as selling tangible physical goods — often sell services. A retailer may gift-wrap a purchase, which is a service. A contractor may provide services such as painting and cleanup.

To add a service item, display the New Item window (refer to Figure 3-4, earlier in this chapter) and choose Service from the Type drop-down list. In the Item Name/ Number box, give the service a brief code or name. If the service is a subitem, select the Subitem Of check box and identify the parent item.

Select the check box titled This Service Is Used in Assemblies or Is Performed by a Subcontractor or Partner if the service is provided by (as the window suggests) a subcontractor, owner, or partner. You indicate which services are performed by subcontractors, owners, and partners because these parties are subject to different tax accounting rules.

Next, use the Description box to describe the service. Your description appears in invoices and purchase orders, so you want to be thoughtful here. Use the Rate box to describe the price or rate per unit of service. Use the Tax Code drop-down list to indicate whether the service is taxable. Finally, use the Account drop-down list to identify which income account should be credited when the item is sold to some customer, client, or patient.

## Adding an inventory part

*Inventory parts* are those items in invoices and purchase orders that represent physical goods that you buy, hold, and sell. If you're a retailer, all that stuff that's sitting out on the shelves of your store represents inventory. If you're a manufacturer, the raw materials that you buy and then use to assemble your products represent inventory.

To set up an inventory part, display the New Item window and choose Inventory Part from the Type drop-down list. QuickBooks displays the Inventory Part version of the New Item window, as shown in Figure 3-5.

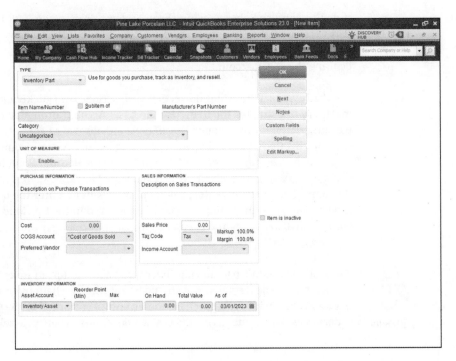

**FIGURE 3-5:**
The Inventory Part version of the New Item window.

Use the Item Name/Number box to provide a descriptive but brief code or name for the item. If the item is a subitem of some other parent item, select the Subitem Of check box and then identify the parent item by using the Subitem Of text box.

The Purchase Information and Sales Information sections let you determine the information that appears in purchase orders and invoices. The Description on Purchase Transactions box in the Purchase Information section, for example, lets you provide the text that QuickBooks displays in purchase orders. You can also guess at the purchase cost by using the Cost text box. Specify the cost of goods sold (COGS) account that should be debited when this item is sold by choosing it from the COGS Account drop-down list, and identify the preferred vendor for purchases of this item by choosing that vendor from the Preferred Vendor drop-down list.

The Sales Information section provides the information that QuickBooks needs to correctly include the item in an invoice. The Description on Sales Transactions box provides a space that you can use to supply the description QuickBooks should use for this item on your invoice. The Sales Price box enables you to provide your price for the item. If you're subject to sales tax, you see (and should use!) the Tax Code drop-down list to specify whether the item is taxable or nontaxable for sales tax purposes. Finally, the Income Account drop-down list lets you specify which income account should be credited when this item is sold.

**TIP**

If you're confused about seeing three Account drop-down lists in the Inventory Part version of the New Item window, keep in mind that when you sell an item, you track the income by crediting an income account and the cost of goods sold by debiting the COGS account.

Use the Inventory Information section to describe how QuickBooks should handle inventory tracking for the item. Use the Asset Account drop-down list, for example, to specify which account QuickBooks should use to track the dollar investment in this item. (Typically, you use the Inventory Asset account, but you could conceivably use some other asset account.) Use the Reorder Point boxes to identify the inventory stocking level at which you want QuickBooks to alert you to reorder the item. If you have inventory on hand for this item, enter the quantity that you have on hand and the value that you have on hand in the On Hand and Total Value boxes. You also specify the date as of which your quantity and value information is correct by using the As Of box.

**WARNING**

You really shouldn't be entering inventory balances for an inventory item when you set it up in the Item list. You should be entering or changing inventory quantities and values when you purchase the inventory (recorded in the Create Purchase Orders window or the Write Checks window) and when you sell the inventory (typically recorded in the Create Invoices window or the Sales Receipts window). If you enter a quantity other than zero or a total value other than zero in the New Item window, you also need to make a journal entry to record the other half of the transaction. If this "other half" business sounds complicated, just trust me: You shouldn't be entering quantity or value information in this window. If you *do* understand this "other half" business that I'm referring to, you should know better than to enter quantity or value information in the New Item window!

You can click the Spelling button to check the spelling of words and phrases that you've entered in the New Item window. You can also click the Next button to save the information that you've entered for an item and redisplay the New Item window so that you can add another item.

## Adding a noninventory part

To add a noninventory part — which is a tangible good that you sell but for which you don't track inventory — display the New Item window and choose Non-Inventory Part from the Type drop-down list. When QuickBooks displays the Non-Inventory Part version of the New Item window (see Figure 3-6), give the noninventory part a name or code by using the Item Name/Number box. If the new item is a subitem, select the Subitem Of check box and then identify the parent item by using the Subitem Of text box. Use the Description box to provide the description that should go in invoices that bill for this noninventory part. Obviously, you enter the price in the Price box. Use the Tax Code drop-down list to identify whether the item is subject to sales tax. Finally, use the Account drop-down list to identify the income account that should be credited for sales of this noninventory part.

Note the check box labeled This Item Is Used in Assemblies or Is Purchased for a Specific Customer:Job. If you select that check box, QuickBooks displays a slightly different version of the Non-Inventory Part window, as shown in Figure 3-7. This version of the window includes Purchase Information and Sales Information sections that work the same way as the Purchase Information and Sales Information sections supplied by the regular Inventory Part version of the New Item window. (Refer to "Adding an inventory part" earlier in the chapter.)

## Adding an other-charge item

An *other-charge item* is an item that you use to purchase or bill for things such as miscellaneous labor or services; materials that you aren't tracking as inventory; and special charges, such as for delivery or setup or rush jobs.

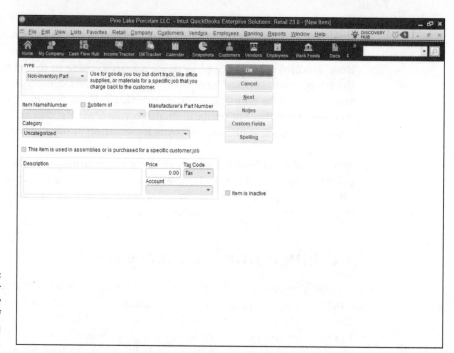

FIGURE 3-6:
The regular
Non-Inventory
Part version of
the New Item
window.

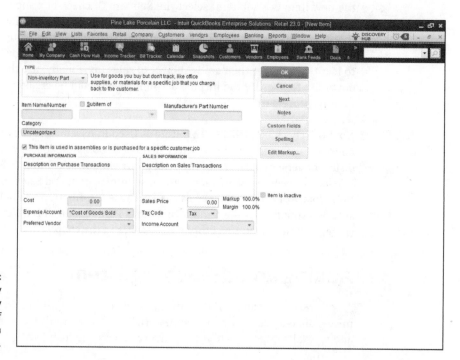

FIGURE 3-7:
The kooky
Non-Inventory
Part version of
the New Item
window.

To set up an other-charge item, display the New Item window and choose Other Charge from the Type drop-down list. When you do, QuickBooks displays the Other Charge version of the New Item window, as shown in Figure 3-8. To finish setting up your other charge item, give the charge a name or code or abbreviation by using the Item Name/Number box. If the other charge item is a subitem, select the Subitem Of check box and then identify the parent item by using the Subitem Of text box. Obviously, you use the Description box to provide a description of the charge. (Remember that this description appears in your invoices.) Use the Amount or % box to identify how the charge gets calculated or billed. Use the Tax Code drop-down list to identify the charge as subject to sales tax — or not subject to sales tax. Use the Account drop-down list to identify the income account that should be credited when you bill for this other charge.

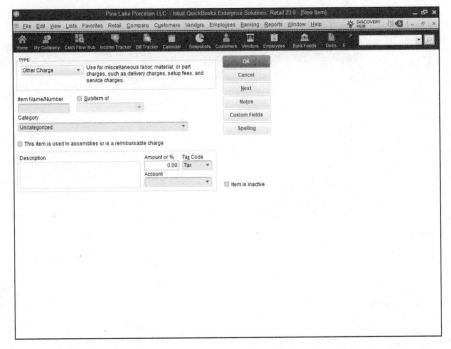

**FIGURE 3-8:**
The Other
Charge version
of the New Item
window.

**TIP**

If you select the check box titled This Item Is Used in Assemblies or Is a Reimbursable Charge, QuickBooks adds a second set of boxes to the New Item window. One set of boxes, labeled Purchase Information, provides information that goes in purchase orders or is used to record purchases and purchase orders. The other set of boxes, labeled Sales Information, goes in invoices and sales receipts to record the actual sale or billing for the other charge.

**TIP**

If you want to enter another charge that should be calculated as a percentage, you must enter the % symbol in the Amount or % box. To include an other-charge item in invoices that equals 25 percent of the previous item in the invoice, for example, enter **25%** in the Amount or % box.

## Adding a subtotal item

If your purchase order, sales receipt, or invoice includes a subtotal line item, you create a subtotal item in your Item list. To do this, display the New Item window and choose Subtotal from the drop-down list. Next, give the subtotal item a name or abbreviation and use the Description box to describe the subtotal. Figure 3-9 shows the Subtotal version of the New Item window.

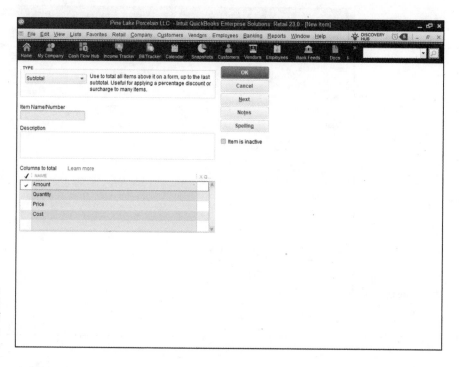

**FIGURE 3-9:**
The Subtotal version of the New Item window.

If you're using other-charge items that are calculated as a percentage or discount items that are calculated as a percentage, you almost certainly need a subtotal item. Another charge that's calculated as a percentage typically would be calculated as a percentage of a subtotal item. Similarly, a discount item that's calculated as a percentage is calculated as a percentage of a subtotal item.

# Adding a group item

A *group item* makes it easier to invoice customers when, from the customer's perspective, they're buying a single item, but from your perspective, you're actually selling several items. This definition sounds curious at first, but let me give you a quick example. Suppose that you're a florist who does booming business on Valentine's Day. Your best-selling items may be red roses and pretty crystal vases. But you probably don't sell individual roses and individual vases. You actually sell a dozen roses with a single vase. Although you want to individually track purchases of dozens of red roses and individual crystal vases in your purchase orders, in your invoices to customers, you want to bill for a dozen red roses in a crystal vase.

TIP

At the end of the chapter, I describe another item type: inventory assembly, which works similarly to the group item type. The inventory assembly item type is for manufacturers.

If that example doesn't make sense, imagine a more complex floral arrangement including a dozen red roses, a crystal vase, baby's breath, flower preservative, tissue-paper wrapping, ribbon, a box, and so forth. In this case, do you really want an invoice that shows perhaps 20 items? Or do you want an invoice that shows a single item: a dozen red roses in a crystal vase? This scenario is why you create group items. A group item lets you create a single item that you use in invoices, but this group item actually combines a bunch of individual items that you're probably using in your purchase orders.

To create a group item, display the New Item window and choose Group from the Type drop-down list. When QuickBooks displays the group version of the New Item window (see Figure 3-10), use the Group Name/Number box to give the group item a name or code. Use the Description box to give the group item an appropriate description. Use the Item, Description, Qty (Quantity), and U/M (Unit of Measurement) columns at the bottom of the window to identify the individual items and item quantities that combine to make a group.

# Adding a discount item

A *discount item* subtracts a fixed amount or a percentage from a subtotal. To set up a discount item, display the New Item window and choose the Discount entry from the Type drop-down list. When you do, QuickBooks displays the Discount version of the New Item window, as shown in Figure 3-11.

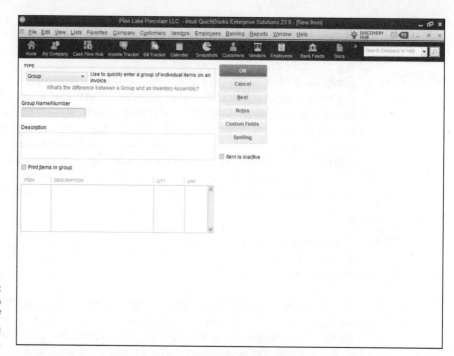

**FIGURE 3-10:**
The Group version of the New Item window.

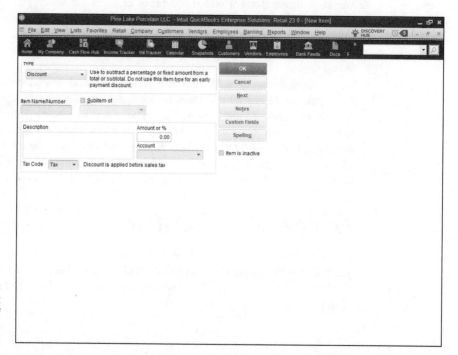

**FIGURE 3-11:**
The Discount version of the New Item window.

To set up your discount item, enter a name or abbreviation for the discount in the Item Name/Number box. If the discount item is a subitem, select the Subitem Of check box and then identify the parent item by using the Subitem Of text box. Typically, you describe the discount by using the Description box. Enter the amount of the discount in the Amount or % box as a dollar amount or as a percentage. (If you enter the discount as a percentage, be sure to include the percentage symbol.) Use the Account drop-down list to specify which account gets debited for the discount. Finally, use the Tax Code drop-down list to indicate whether the discount is applied before sales tax. (In other words, indicate whether the discount is subject to sales tax.)

TIP

If you set up a discount item that calculates the discount as a percentage, you probably need a subtotal item too. Then, in your invoices, follow the subtotal item with the discount item. In this manner, you can easily calculate the discount percentage by looking at the subtotal amount.

## Adding a payment item

If you sometimes accept payments at or before the point you invoice a customer, you can create a payment item and then add the payment item to the bottom of the invoice. If you do this, the invoice, the payment amount, and the net amount due all appear in the same document. That's pretty cool.

To set up a payment item, display the New Item window and choose Payment from the drop-down list. QuickBooks displays the Payment version of the New Item window, shown in Figure 3-12. Use the Item Name/Number box to give the payment item a code or name such as "payment." Use the Description box to provide a nice description of the payment. (No kidding, you may want to include the phrase *Thank you!* as part of the payment description, such as *Payment . . . Thank you!*) Use the Payment Method drop-down list to identify the method of payment: American Express, check, cash, Discover, MasterCard, or Visa, as appropriate. Finally, use the radio buttons — Group with Other Undeposited Funds and Deposit To — to identify what happens to the money received as part of the payment. If you indicate that the money is deposited, you also choose the correct bank account from the Deposit To drop-down list.

## Adding a sales tax item

If you sell items that are subject to sales tax, you also include line items in your invoices that charge for and track these sales taxes. To do this, you create sales tax items. To create a sales tax item, display the New Item window and choose Sales Tax Item from the Type drop-down list. When you do, QuickBooks displays the Sales Tax Item version of the New Item window, as shown in Figure 3-13. Use the

Sales Tax Name box to identify or provide an abbreviation for the sales tax. Use the Description box to give the sales tax a description. Finally, use the Tax Rate (%) box to identify the sales tax rate and the Tax Agency (Vendor That You Collect For) drop-down list to identify the tax agency that you'll pay.

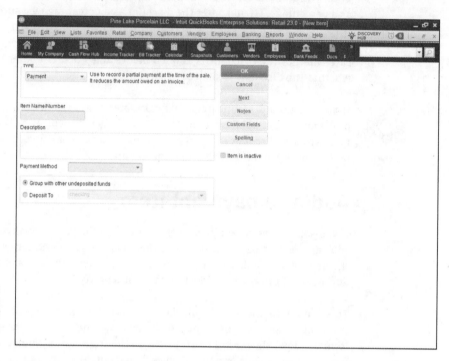

**FIGURE 3-12:** The Payment version of the New Item window.

## Setting up a sales tax group

In many jurisdictions, although businesses may charge a single sales tax on sales, the sales tax is distributed to several tax agencies. A firm may be required to charge a 9 percent sales tax, for example, but perhaps 1 percent goes to the city government, another 2 percent goes to the county government, and the remaining 6 percent goes to the state government. In this case, you can set up a sales tax group, which appears as a single line item invoice. The sales tax group is made up of individual tax items, however.

To add a sales tax group, display the New Item window and choose Sales Tax Group from the Type drop-down list. QuickBooks displays the Sales Tax Group version of the New Item window, as shown in Figure 3-14. Enter a name or an abbreviation for the sales tax in the Group Name/Number box. Provide an appropriate description in the Description box. Then use the Tax Item column to identify the individual tax items that comprise the sales tax group. Note that you should already have set up the tax items that you want to add to the sales tax group.

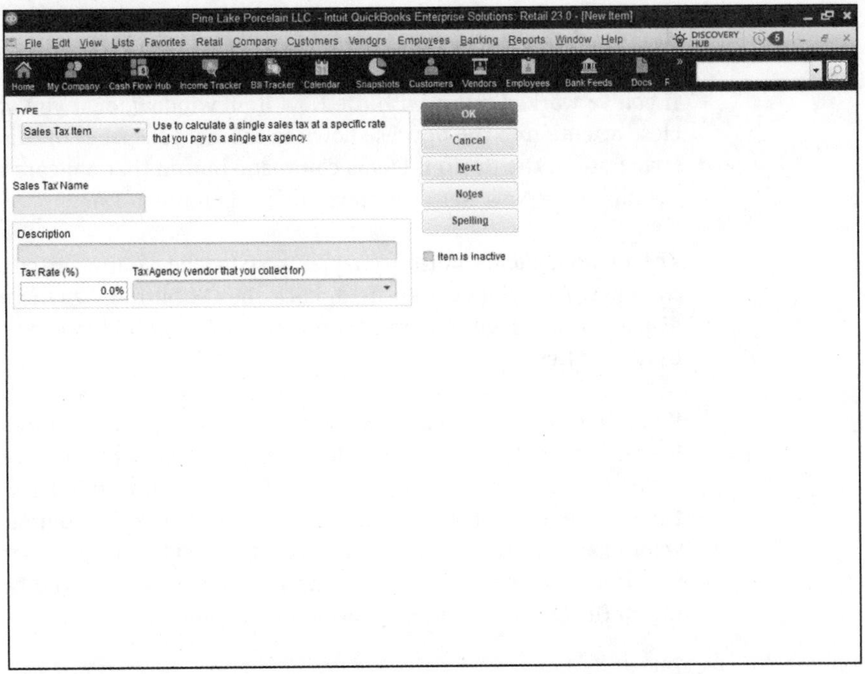

FIGURE 3-13:
The Sales Tax
Item version of
the New Item
window.

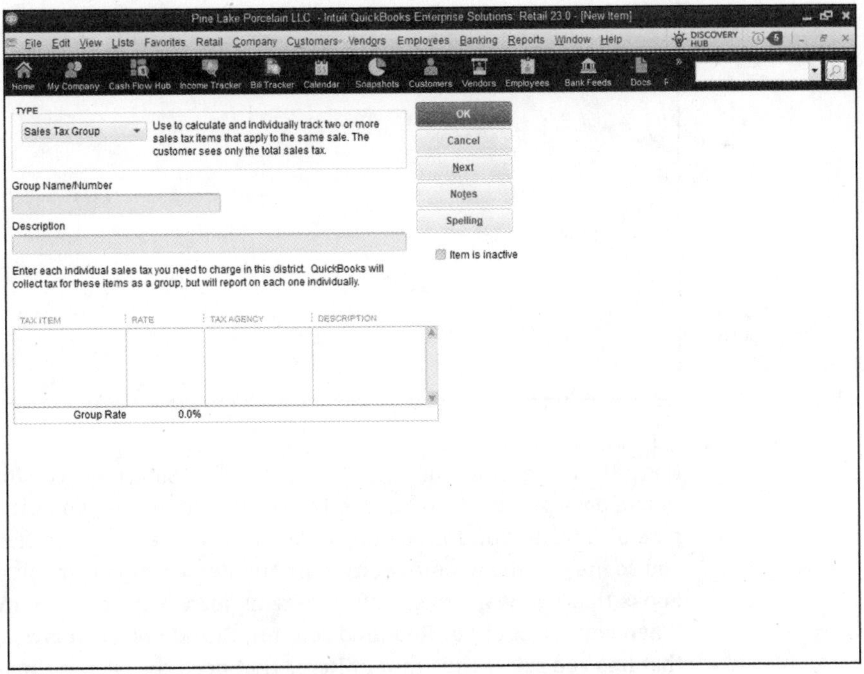

FIGURE 3-14:
The Sales Tax
Group version
of the New Item
window.

# Adding custom fields to items

If you've worked much with the New Item window, or if you've paid particularly close attention to the figures shown in the last few pages of this chapter, you may have noticed the Custom Fields command button that appears in many, although not all, of the New Item windows (refer to Figure 3-12).

The Custom Fields button enables you to add your own custom fields to the Item list. To add a custom field, click the OK button. When you do, QuickBooks displays a message box and then a small dialog box labeled Custom Fields for Unnamed Item.

When QuickBooks displays the Custom Fields for Unnamed Item dialog box, click the Define Fields button. QuickBooks displays the Set Up Custom Fields for Items dialog box, as shown in Figure 3-15. To add custom fields for the item, use the Label column to name the fields and then check the Use column for each field you want to appear. If you want to add a custom field Serial Number for a product you sell or hold in inventory, for example, enter the label **Serial Number** in the first row of the Label column and check the Use column.

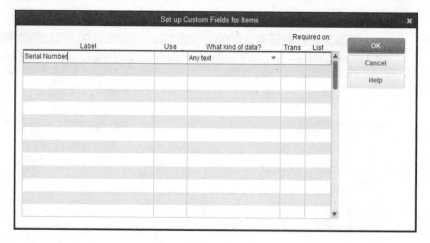

**FIGURE 3-15:**
The Set Up
Custom Fields for
Items dialog box.

*Note:* If you're working with the Enterprise Solutions version of QuickBooks, QuickBooks provides a What Kind of Data? column that you can use to specify the type of information that can be entered in the new custom field: text, numbers, and so on. Use the Required on Trans and Required on List columns to tell Quick-Books that you want to specify the items for which the custom field is required. When you select either Required column, QuickBooks displays another dialog box that lets you select the types of items that need the custom field.

When you click OK, QuickBooks redisplays the Custom Fields for *Item* dialog box; in the example shown in Figure 3-16, the item is a red mug. Now the dialog box shows the new custom field — in this example, Serial Number.

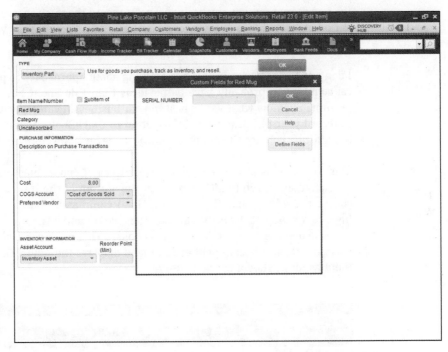

Note that custom fields are available for all items. Also note that you see custom fields for items by displaying the item's information in the New Item window or the Edit Item window and then clicking the Custom Fields button.

# Editing Items

You can change item information. To do so, display the Item List window and then double-click the item. When you do this, QuickBooks displays the Edit Item window, which resembles the New Item window. The difference is that the Edit Item window is already filled in with the item information. To change some bit of item information, edit the contents of the field with the information to be updated. Click OK to save your changes.

# Adjusting physical counts and inventory values

Inventory shrinkage, spoilage, and (unfortunately) theft all combine to reduce the inventory that you physically have. To record these inventory reductions, you periodically count your inventory physically and then update your QuickBooks records with the results of your physical counts.

I don't spend any time in this book talking about approaches to providing physical counts; you probably have better ideas than I do about how to do that. You presumably know what works best in your business. I can tell you, however, that to record your physical count information in QuickBooks, you use a special tool. Specifically, you use the Adjust Quantity/Value on Hand command.

This command is available to you in two places. If you display the Item list, click the Activities button (which appears at the bottom of the Item List window) and choose the Adjust Quantity/Value on Hand command. You can also choose the Inventory ➪ Adjust Quantity/Value on Hand command. (The Inventory menu item was added to the 2018 version of QuickBooks, so it's more convenient than in previous versions.) Choosing either command displays the Adjust Quantity/Value on Hand window, shown in Figure 3-17.

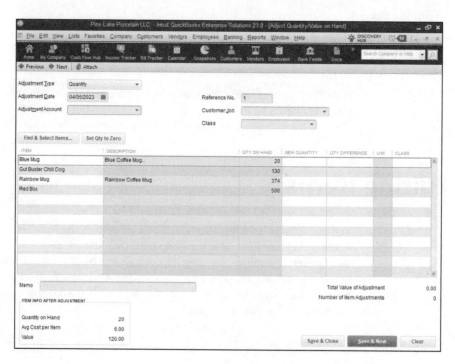

**FIGURE 3-17:** The Adjust Quantity/Value on Hand window.

To use the Adjust Quantity/Value on Hand window, follow these steps:

**1.** **Use the Adjustment Type drop-down list to indicate what you're adjusting.**

You can adjust the quantity or the value, or both the quantity and the value of the items you're holding in inventory. Just choose the appropriate entry from the Adjustment Type drop-down list: Quantity, Total Value, or Quantity and Total Value.

**2.** **Use the Adjustment Date box to record the date of your physical count.**

In other words, you want to adjust your quantities as of the day you took or completed the physical inventory count.

**3.** **Use the Adjustment Account drop-down list to identify the expense account that you want to use to track your inventory shrinkage expense.**

**4.** **(Optional) Provide a reference number (if you use numbers) to uniquely and meaningfully identify or cross-reference the transaction.**

**5.** **(Optional) Identify the Customer:Job and class.**

If it's appropriate (in many cases, it won't be), use the Customer:Job drop-down list to identify the customer and job associated with this inventory shrinkage. In a similar fashion, if appropriate, use the Class drop-down list to identify the class that you want to use for tracking this inventory shrinkage.

**6.** **Supply the correct inventory quantities.**

The Item, Description, and Qty on Hand columns of the Adjust Quantity/Value on Hand window identify the inventory items that you're holding and the current quantity counts. Use the New Quantity column to provide the correct physical count quantity of the item. After you've entered the new quantity, QuickBooks calculates the quantity difference and shows this value in the Qty Difference column.

**TIP**

You can actually enter a value in the New Quantity column or the Qty Difference column. QuickBooks calculates the other quantity by using the current quantity information that you supply. If you enter the new quantity, QuickBooks calculates the quantity difference by subtracting the new quantity from the current quantity. If you enter the quantity difference, QuickBooks calculates the new quantity by adjusting the current quantity for the quantity difference.

**7.** **Adjust the value.**

If you chose Total Value or Quantity and Total Value from the Adjustment Type drop-down list in Step 1, QuickBooks displays an expanded version of the Adjust Quantity/Value on Hand window, as shown in Figure 3-18. This window lets you enter both the correct physical count quantity and the updated value for the inventory item. You enter the physical count quantity, obviously, in the

New Quantity column. You enter the new updated value in the New Value column. You probably use this version of the Adjust Quantity/Value on Hand window only if you're using a lower-of-cost or market inventory valuation method. Both financial accounting standards and tax accounting rules allow you to mark down your inventory to the lower of its original cost or its fair market value. If you're doing this — and how you do this is beyond the scope of this book — you enter the new inventory value in the New Value column.

**TECHNICAL STUFF**

Essentially, using the lower-of-cost or market inventory evaluation method just means that you do what it says: You keep your inventory valued at its original cost or, if its value is less than its original cost, at its new value. Obviously, assessing the value of your inventory is a little tricky. But if you have questions, you can ask your CPA for help. One thing to keep in mind, however, is that you can't go changing your accounting methods willy-nilly without permission from the Internal Revenue Service. And changing your inventory valuation method from cost, say, to lower-of-cost or market is a change in accounting method.

**8.** **Provide a memo description.**

If you want to further describe the quantity or value adjustment, use the Memo box for this purpose. You may want to reference the physical count worksheets, the people performing the physical count, or the documentation that explains the valuation adjustment.

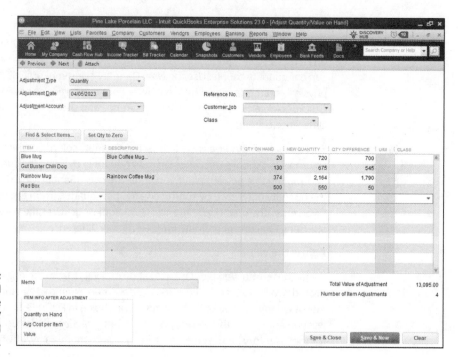

**FIGURE 3-18:** The expanded version of the Adjust Quantity/ Value on Hand window.

9. **Save the adjustment.**

   After you've used the Adjust Quantity/Value on Hand window to describe the quantity changes or value changes in your inventory, click either the Save & Close button or the Save & New button to save the adjustment transaction. As you probably know at this point in your life, Save & Close saves the transaction and closes the window. Save & New saves the transaction but leaves the window open in case you want to make additional changes.

## Adjusting prices and price levels

QuickBooks provides a couple of handy commands and tools that you can use to change the prices that you charge customers for your products and services. In the following sections, I describe both of these handy aids.

## Using the Change Item Prices command

The Change Item Prices command, which appears on the Customers menu, displays the Change Item Prices window, shown in Figure 3-19. This window lets you change prices of a bunch of items at one time by an amount or percentage. To use the Change Item Prices window, first select the items whose prices you want to change by clicking the check-mark column. Next, use the Adjust Price of Marked Items by (Amount or %) box to specify the dollar amount or the percentage amount by which you want to change the price. If you want to change the price of selected items by $2, for example, enter $2 in the box. If you want to change the price of selected items by 5 percent, enter 5% in the box. Use the Based On dropdown list to indicate the base to which you want to add the amount of percentage. After you identify the items that you want to reprice and the way that you want to reprice them, click the Adjust button. QuickBooks recalculates the prices and displays this information in the New Price column. If you want to change the prices for the items selected, click OK.

If you don't like the prices listed in the New Price column, you can keep tinkering with the value in the Adjust Price of Marked Items by (Amount or %) box, clicking the Adjust button to refresh the numbers in the New Price column, and clicking OK only when you're satisfied.

## Using price levels

Price levels are kind of weird; they let you individually adjust the prices of items up or down. If you've agreed to discount items by 10 percent for a certain customer, for example, you can easily do this by using a price level to knock the price down by 10 percent whenever you're invoicing that customer.

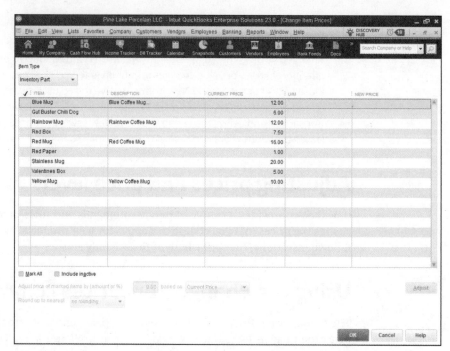

**FIGURE 3-19:**
The Change Item
Prices window.

To use price levels, you first have to set up the price levels by using the Price Level List command. After you set up your price levels, you adjust prices by using price levels when you create an invoice. I describe how both tasks work.

## Creating a price level

To create a price level, choose the Lists ⇨ Price Level List command. When you do, QuickBooks displays the Price Level List window (not shown). To create a price level, click the Price Level button and then choose Price Level ⇨ New. QuickBooks displays the New Price Level window, as shown in Figure 3-20. Name the price level change by using the Price Level Name box. Select the items to which you want to apply the price level by clicking them. (QuickBooks marks selected items with a check mark.) Then use the Adjust Price of Marked Items to Be boxes to indicate that this price level increases or decreases the sales price some percentage higher or lower than the standard price. Finally, use the Round Up to Nearest drop-down list to specify whether and how QuickBooks should round off its calculations. Figure 3-20, for example, shows a price level change that decreases the sales price by 10 percent. After you select the items that the price level should affect, click the Adjust button to see the new price for each item in the custom price column.

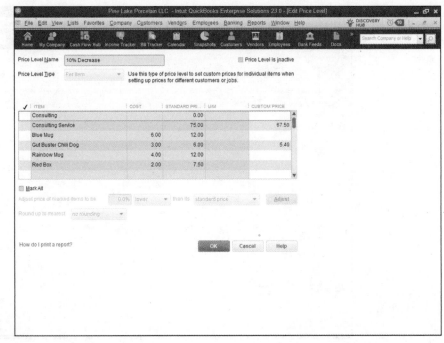

FIGURE 3-20:
The New Price
Level window.

## Using a price level

To use a price level, you create an invoice in the usual way. Click the Price Each column for the item that you want to reprice by using the price level. When you do, QuickBooks turns the Price Each column into a drop-down list. If you click the arrow button that opens the drop-down list, QuickBooks displays both the base rate price and any price levels. If you choose a price level, QuickBooks adjusts the price for the price level change. In Figure 3-21, selecting the 10 percent price level change bumps the price from $6.00 to $5.40. In other words, the 10% Decrease price level change decreases the default price by 10 percent, or 60 cents.

**TIP**

QuickBooks also lets you set a default price level for a customer. When such a default price level is set, QuickBooks automatically uses the appropriate price level when you choose that customer. The Price Level box appears on the Additional Info tabs of the New Customer and Edit Customer windows.

## Enabling advanced pricing

Users of QuickBooks Enterprise 2023 should know one more thing about setting prices. QuickBooks also provides an advanced pricing function, which you turn on by choosing the Edit ➪ Preferences command, selecting the Sales & Customers option, clicking the Company Preferences tab, and then clicking the Enable Advanced Pricing button.

**FIGURE 3-21:** Choosing a price level with the Create Invoices window.

When you enable advanced pricing, you convert any price levels you've previously defined (see the preceding paragraphs) to price rules that you can tell QuickBooks to apply to items, item types, particular vendors, customers, customer types, and job types.

After you turn on advanced pricing, you can choose the Lists ⇨ Price Rule List command to display the Price Rule List window (not shown). To convert a price level to a working price rule, double-click the new price rule and then use the Edit Price Rule dialog box (not shown) to describe the rules QuickBooks should follow to reprice some item automatically.

# Managing Inventory in a Manufacturing Firm

Tracking inventory in a manufacturing firm is more difficult than in other types of businesses. When you boil down everything to its essence, the problem stems from a couple of tricky accounting requirements:

>> **In a manufacturing environment, the manufacturer combines raw materials items into finished-goods items.** This means — and this is the challenging part — that the manufacturing process reduces the inventory count and value for some items (the raw materials or the components) and at the same time increases the count and value of the other, finished-goods items.

>> **In a manufacturing environment, the rules say that you don't count just the value of items in the finished-goods-item inventory values.** You also count the cost of labor and factory overhead used in manufacturing the items.

QuickBooks solves the first problem related to manufacturing inventory, but it doesn't solve or address the second problem. Fortunately, as long as you're a small manufacturer, you probably don't need to worry too much about the second problem. You should ask your CPA about it. But don't worry — Congress and the IRS have provided a bunch of loopholes that make the accounting easier for the small guys.

## Handling manufactured inventory the simple way

If you're using QuickBooks Pro or some earlier versions of QuickBooks Premier, you don't have the ability to account for the manufacture of inventory in Quick-Books. The best you can do is group items to combine into individual items in a customer's invoice. This approach sounds sloppy, but it isn't quite as bad as you may think at first blush. You can choose to show only the group item in a customer invoice. This means — getting back to the example of the florist selling red roses and vases — that the florist can "manufacture" a crystal vase of a dozen red roses and then show the manufactured item as a group item in the customer's invoice.

The one thing that's problematic about the "just use a group item" approach is that it doesn't give you a way to track the finished goods' inventory values.

## Performing inventory accounting in QuickBooks

To account for the manufacture of inventory in QuickBooks Premier or Quick-Books Enterprise Solutions, you add inventory assembly items to the Item list for those items that you manufacture. You also record the manufacture of items as you . . . well, *manufacture* them.

Suppose that Pine Lake Porcelain mostly buys and resells coffee mugs and other porcelain doodads. But also suppose that once a year, Pine Lake Porcelain assembles a collection of red coffee mugs into a boxed St. Valentine's Day gift set. In this case, QuickBooks can record the assembly of a boxed gift set that combines, for example, four red coffee mugs, a cardboard box, and some tissue-paper wrapping.

## Adding inventory assembly items

To describe manufactured items, follow these steps:

1. **Choose Lists ⇨ Item List.**

   QuickBooks displays the Item List window.

2. **Click the Item button in the Item List window and choose New from the drop-down list.**

   QuickBooks displays the New Item window.

3. **Choose the Inventory Assembly item from the Type drop-down list.**

   QuickBooks displays the Inventory Assembly version of the New Item window, as shown in Figure 3-22.

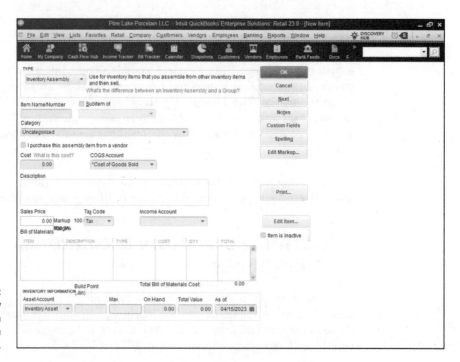

**FIGURE 3-22:** The Inventory Assembly version of the New Item window.

**4. Specify the account to use for tracking this item's cost when you sell it.**

QuickBooks suggests the cost of goods sold account. If you've created other accounts for your COGS, however, choose the other appropriate account.

**5. Describe the manufactured item.**

Type a description of the item that you want to appear in documents that your customers see, such as invoices. (QuickBooks suggests the same description that you used in the Description on Purchase Transactions text box as a default.)

**6. Enter the amount that you charge for the item in the Sales Price box.**

**7. Indicate whether the manufactured item is subject to sales tax by using the Tax Code drop-down list.**

**8. Use the Income Account drop-down list to specify the account that you want QuickBooks to use for tracking the income from the sale of the item.**

**9. Identify the components that go into the finished item.**

Use the Bill of Materials list to identify the individual component items and the quantities needed to make the inventory assembly. Each component item goes on a separate line in the list. Not to be too redundant, but do note that you identify both the component item and the number of component items needed.

**10. Identify the asset account.**

Specify the other current asset account that you want QuickBooks to use for tracking this inventory item's value.

**11. Select a build point.**

Use the Build Point boxes to specify the lowest inventory quantity of this item that can remain before you manufacture more. When the inventory level drops to this quantity, QuickBooks adds a reminder to the Reminders list, notifying you that you need to make more of the item.

**12. Ignore the On Hand and the Total Value boxes.**

See that On Hand box? Leave it set to zero. To enter a number now is to record an uncategorized transaction, which you don't want to do. Leave the Total Value field set to zero too.

**13. Leave the As Of box empty or enter the current date.**

What you do here doesn't matter.

## Recording manufacture or assembly of items

To build some assembly, choose the Retail ⇨ Inventory Activities ⇨ Build Assemblies command. QuickBooks displays the Build Assemblies window, as shown in Figure 3-23. All you do is choose the thing that you want to build from the Assembly Item drop-down list and then enter the quantity that you (or some hapless co-worker) built in the Quantity to Build box in the bottom-right corner. (In Figure 3-23, I've created an assembly — Valentine's Day Box — that consists of some colorful mugs, an attractive gift box, and some scented tissue paper.) Then you click either the Build & Close or Build & New button. (Click the Build & New button if you want to record the assembly of some other items.)

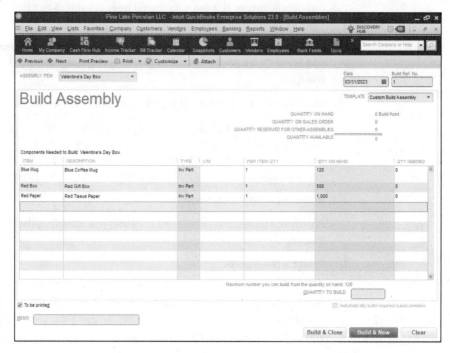

**FIGURE 3-23:**
The Build Assemblies window.

While I'm on the subject, let me make a handful of observations about the Build Assemblies window and the Build Assemblies command:

>> In the top-right corner of the window, QuickBooks shows the quantity of the assembly that you have on hand and the number of customers who have placed orders. That's pretty useful information to have, so remember that it's there.

>> A table in the Build Assemblies window shows you what goes into your product. Not that you care, but this table is a *bill of materials*.

>> At the bottom of the bill of materials list, QuickBooks shows you the maximum number of assemblies that you can make, given your current inventory holdings.

>> When you build an item, QuickBooks adjusts the inventory item counts. If you make boxed gift sets — each with four red mugs, one wrapping tissue, and one box — QuickBooks reduces the item counts of red mugs, wrapping tissues, and boxes, and increases the item counts of the boxed gift sets when you record building the assembly.

**REMEMBER**

Some of the components used in an assembly may not be inventory items. You can use noninventory parts in an assembly.

## Managing multiple inventory locations

QuickBooks Enterprise Solutions lets you deal with the record-keeping challenge of storing inventory in multiple locations. To turn on this capability, called Advanced Inventory Tracking, choose the Edit ➪ Preferences command, click Items and Inventory, click the Company Preferences tab, and then click the Advanced Inventory Settings button. If you're using the Enterprise Solutions version of QuickBooks, QuickBooks displays dialog boxes that allow you to build a list of inventory sites and adds fields to appropriate windows and dialog boxes so that you can track inventory items by site. If you're not using the Enterprise Solutions version of QuickBooks, QuickBooks displays information about how you can upgrade to Enterprise Solutions.

# Chapter **4**

# Managing Cash and Bank Accounts

QuickBooks provides several tools that make working with your bank accounts easier, such as a special window for recording the checks you've written. QuickBooks also lets you easily record deposits into accounts. Additionally, QuickBooks includes tools for easily recording transfers between accounts, for reconciling bank accounts, and for performing online banking transactions. This chapter talks about all these features.

**TIP**

If you've used QuickBooks's little-brother product, Quicken, much of the information that you see here will be familiar. The QuickBooks banking tools look like the popular Quicken checkbook program — good news for the 10 million or so Quicken users.

# Writing Checks

Obviously, any business writes checks to pay bills and to pay employees. Quick-Books includes a command and a window specifically for the purpose of recording and possibly printing checks.

## Recording and printing a check

To record or print checks, choose the Banking ⇨ Write Checks command. Quick-Books displays the Write Checks window, as shown in Figure 4-1.

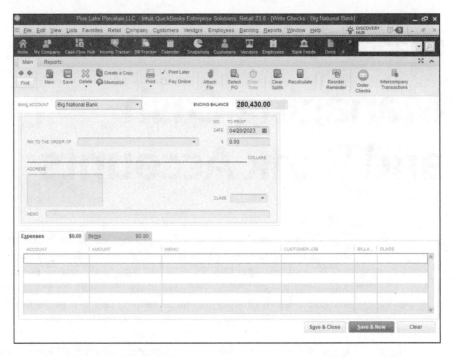

**FIGURE 4-1:**
The Write Checks
window.

Take the following steps to write a check:

1. **Use the Bank Account drop-down list to choose the account on which to write a check.**

2. **Use the No. (check number) field to identify the check number.**

   If you don't know the check number yet because you haven't printed the check, leave the No. field blank. Then select the Print Later check box, which appears on the Main tab of the Write Checks window.

**TIP**

When you select the Print Later check box, QuickBooks displays the phrase *To Print* in the No. field.

3. **Use the Date field to record the date when the check was or will be written.**

   You can enter the check date in mm/dd/yyyy format. You can also enter dates as simply mmdd or m/dd, and QuickBooks transforms them to mm/dd/yyyy. Thus, 8/12, 0812, and 0812/2023 are all valid ways to enter the same date if the current year is 2023.

   Alternatively, you can click the small calendar button that appears to the right of the Date field. When you click the calendar button, QuickBooks displays a pop-up calendar. To select a day shown on the calendar, click the day. The pop-up calendar also includes a pair of buttons that you can click to scroll back and forth through the months.

4. **Use the Pay to the Order Of field to identify the individual or business that you're paying with the check.**

   If the check that you're recording is the first check that you've ever made out to the payee, you must type the payee's name in the Pay to the Order Of field. If you've previously paid the payee, you can click the arrow button at the right end of the Pay to the Order Of field. When you do, QuickBooks displays a list of previous payees. You can choose a payee from this list by clicking the name.

5. **Move the selection cursor to the Dollars (amount) field and type the check amount.**

   QuickBooks writes out the check amount on the line below the Pay to the Order Of field.

6. **(Optional) Provide an address.**

   If you want, you can use the address block to provide the payee's address. Note that QuickBooks writes the payee's name on the first line of the address block when you fill in the Pay to the Order Of field. You can add the other lines to the address block manually. Note, though, that if you've previously entered an address for a payee (such as when you last recorded a check to the payee), QuickBooks reuses this address information for subsequent checks.

   You can edit the address information shown in the Write Checks window.

**TIP**

   You need to record the address only if you're going to print the check and the address will show through the address window or if you're creating an online payment — something that I talk about later in this chapter.

7. **(Optional) Provide a memo description.**

   You can use the Memo field to provide or record additional information. If you're going to print the check, for example, you can use the Memo field to identify your account number or the invoice number that the check pays. If you're simply recording checks and won't be printing them, you can use the Memo field to record more proprietary or confidential information.

**8.** **(Optional) Select the Pay Online check box.**

So here's the deal: If you've told your bank that you want to do the online banking thing and have followed its instructions for setup, you can select the Pay Online check box, which appears after you've set up online banking. This setting tells QuickBooks to transmit this check information to your bank, along with instructions to the bank to make the payment.

More information on setting up online banking is available later in this chapter.

TIP

To transmit the payment instructions to the bank later, choose Banking ⇨ Bank Feeds ⇨ Bank Feeds Center, click Send Items and enter your personal identification number (PIN) when QuickBooks asks for it. Note that QuickBooks doesn't display the Bank Feeds command until you set up an account for online banking.

**9.** **Distribute the check amount to the appropriate expense or asset accounts.**

If the check pays for a particular expense or purchases a particular asset, click the Expenses tab; then use the lines or rows of the Expenses tab to identify the account and the amount that the check pays. To record a $50 check that pays supplies expense, for example, use the Account column of the Expenses tab to select the office-supplies expense account; then use the Amount column to identify the amount of the office supplies. Optionally, use the Memo column to provide a memo description of that line of expense detail. Equally optionally, use the Customer:Job column and the Class column to further describe and categorize the line of account detail information. If you categorize the expense as one incurred for a particular customer or job, you can use the Billable? column to indicate whether this item should be billed to the customer later (see Figure 4-2).

TIP

If a check pays for several types of expenses, the Expenses tab should show several lines.

If you write a check to purchase an asset, the Expenses tab doesn't show an expense account; instead, its tab shows an asset account. If you buy a $5,000 piece of machinery, you may distribute, or categorize, that $5,000 check to an asset account. In this case, the Account column of the Expenses tab shows the asset account name and the Amount column shows the amount of the asset purchased.

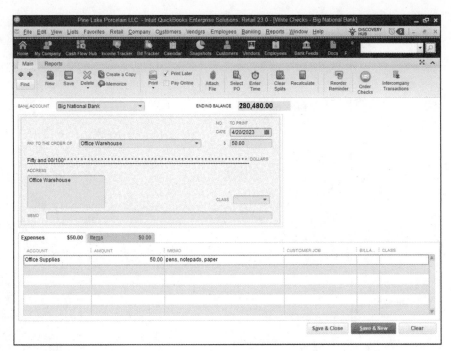

**FIGURE 4-2:**
The Write Checks
window, filled
out to record an
expense.

## 10. Describe the items that the check purchases.

Figure 4-3 shows the Items tab of the Write Checks window. You use the Items tab when you write a check to purchase items shown and described in your Item list. If you write a $1,000 check to buy 400 $2.50 items for inventory, you use the Items tab. To use the Items tab, identify the item being purchased by entering the item code or name in the Item column. Optionally, edit the item description shown in the Description column. Then use the Qty, Cost, and Amount columns to describe the number of items and the total cost of the items purchased. As with the Expenses tab, QuickBooks gives you the option of further classifying an item by using the Customer:Job, Billable?, and Class columns (if you have class tracking enabled).

TIP

Book 3, Chapter 3 describes how items and the Item list work in QuickBooks. If you're unsure how to work with items, refer to that chapter.

## 11. To print a check, click the Print button.

The Print option is on the top menu above the bank account you've selected to pay from. Alternatively, if you want to print checks in a batch, after you've recorded the last check that you want to print, click the down arrow below the Print button. When QuickBooks displays the Print menu, choose its Batch command. QuickBooks displays the Select Checks to Print dialog box, as shown in Figure 4-4. Select the checks that you want to print by clicking them. Use the First Check Number box to identify the number of the first check form to use for printing. Then click OK.

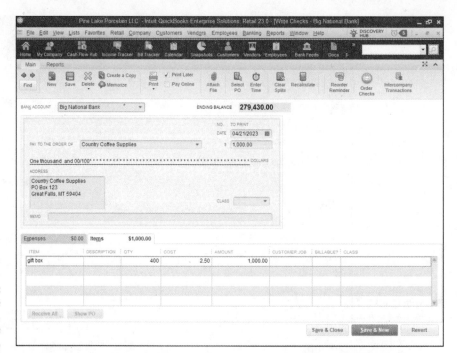

FIGURE 4-3:
The Write
Checks window,
displaying the
Items tab.

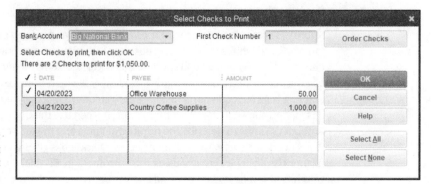

FIGURE 4-4:
The Select
Checks to Print
dialog box.

When QuickBooks displays the Print Checks dialog box, as shown in Figure 4-5, use the Check Style section to identify the type of check forms on which you're printing. If you're using standard or wallet-style checks, you also need to indicate the number of checks. Then click the Print button.

TIP

You can also print check forms in a batch by choosing File ⇨ Print Forms ⇨ Checks. When you choose this command, QuickBooks displays the Select Checks to Print dialog box. Identify which checks you want to print, click OK, and use the Print Checks dialog box to finish printing your checks.

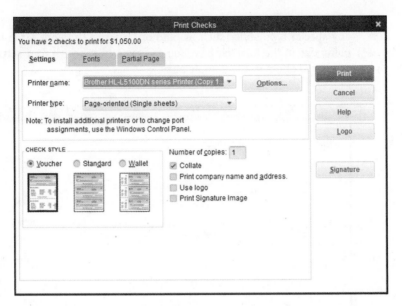

**FIGURE 4-5:**
The Print Checks
dialog box.

**12.** **After you describe the check and the reasons for writing the check, click either the Save & Close or the Save & New button in the Write Checks window.**

The Save & Close button saves the check and also closes the Write Checks window. Click the Save & New button to save the check and then redisplay the Write Checks window so that you can record another check. If you don't want to save the check, click the Clear button.

**TIP**

The Write Checks window provides several buttons on the Main tab, including Previous, Next, Print, and Find. I describe the Print button in an earlier step, but let me note here that the Previous and Next buttons page back and forth to the checks that you've already written. The Find button displays the Find Checks dialog box, which you can use to describe a check similar to the one you're looking for. After you describe the check you're looking for, click the Find button in the Find Checks dialog box.

## Customizing the check form

While I'm on the subject of printing check forms, I'll quickly make a couple of observations. If you click the Fonts tab of the Print Checks dialog box, QuickBooks displays a couple of buttons you can click to specify what fonts QuickBooks should use for printing check forms (see Figure 4-6).

If you click the Font button, for example, QuickBooks displays the Select Font dialog box, shown in Figure 4-7. You select the font you want in the Font list box, any special type style (such as bold or italic) in the Font Style list box, and the point size in the Size list box. You can experiment with font settings and see the combined effect in the Sample box.

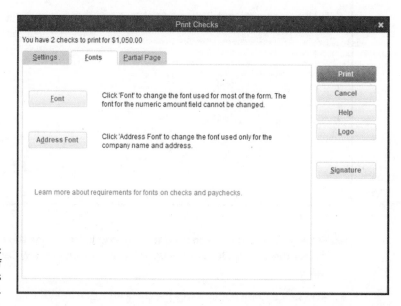

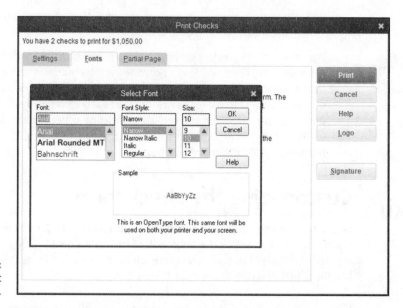

If you click the Partial Page tab, QuickBooks displays the dialog box shown in Figure 4-8. Use this tab's buttons to tell QuickBooks how you feed a partial page of check forms through your printer.

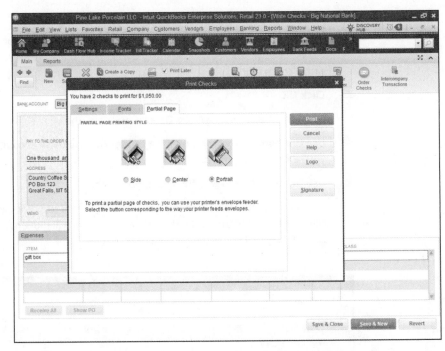

**FIGURE 4-8:**
The Partial Page tab of the Print Checks dialog box.

One final tidbit about customizing check forms: If you click the Logo button of the Print Checks dialog box (refer to Figure 4-8), QuickBooks displays a little dialog box that lets you tell QuickBooks to print a logo on your checks. To print a logo, you need an image file for the logo (perhaps something you've created in Microsoft Paint 3D or another image-editing program). This little dialog box lets you tell QuickBooks where the logo image file is located.

# Making Bank Deposits

QuickBooks also supplies a command and window for recording bank deposits. To record bank deposits, follow these steps:

1. **Choose the Banking ⇨ Make Deposits command.**

   QuickBooks displays the Payments to Deposit dialog box, shown in Figure 4-9. The dialog box shows any payments previously recorded by means of the

Receive Payments and Enter Sales Receipts commands, which appear on the Customers menu. (Note that QuickBooks goes right to the Make Deposits window, shown in Figure 4-10, and skips the Payments to Deposit dialog box if there are no pending deposits to make.)

2. **Select the payments you want to deposit.**

   You can select all the payments listed by clicking the Select All button or select individual payments by clicking them. QuickBooks marks selected payments with a check mark.

3. **Click OK.**

   QuickBooks displays the Make Deposits window, shown in Figure 4-10.

4. **Use the Deposit To drop-down list to identify the bank account into which you're depositing the funds.**

5. **Use the Date box to identify the deposit date.**

   You can enter the date in mm/dd/yyyy fashion, or you can click the small calendar button to the right of the Date field. On the calendar that appears, click the day that you want the Date field to show.

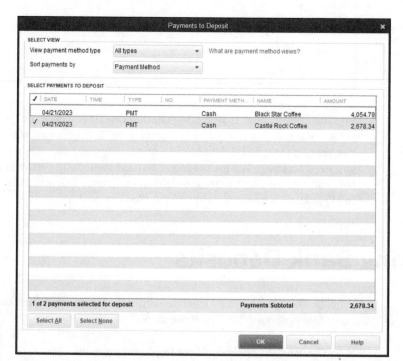

**FIGURE 4-9:**
The Payments to Deposit dialog box.

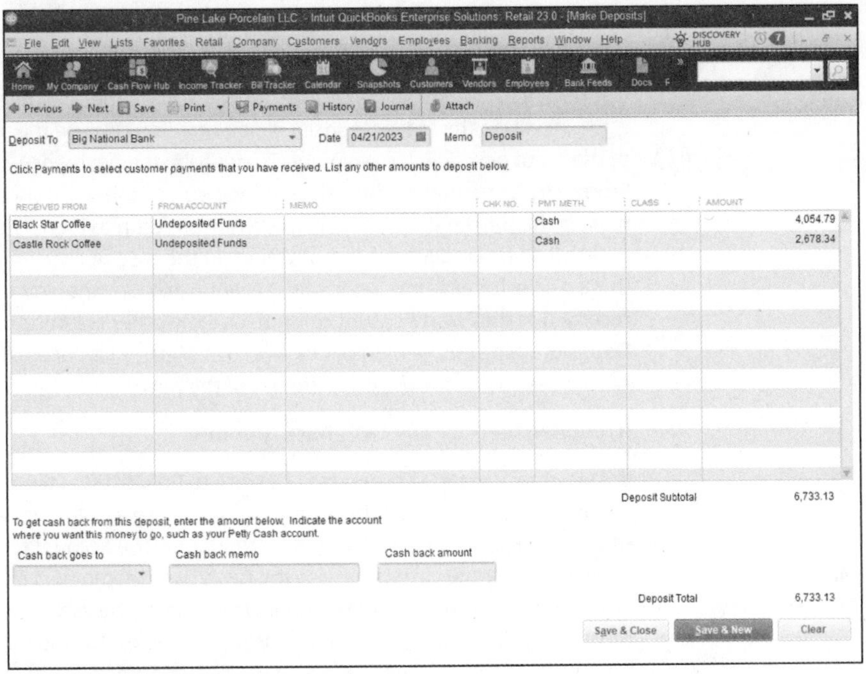

FIGURE 4-10:
The Make
Deposits window.

## 6. (Optional) Provide a memo description.

Initially, QuickBooks uses the Memo field to describe the transaction as a deposit. This is, obviously, a pretty good description of a deposit transaction. If you want to change the memo description to something else even more useful, such as *daily cash sales,* replace the contents of the Memo box.

TIP

Perhaps the best use for the box was suggested by the accountant who reviewed this manuscript: You can use this field to further describe any unusual transactions, such as refunds of expenses, rebates, or asset-sale proceeds.

As you may know either from working with QuickBooks or from the discussion of making sales in Book 3, Chapter 1, you have the option of telling QuickBooks (whenever you receive a payment) that the payment should be deposited directly into the bank account or lumped with other payments in an undeposited-funds bucket.

TIP

Not all customer payments appear in the Make Deposits dialog box. As discussed in Book 3, Chapter 1, you can also indicate that a customer payment should be deposited in a bank account directly from two windows: Receive Payments and Enter Sales Receipts. These direct-into-the-account payments don't appear in the Make Payments dialog box. You record these bank account deposits at the same time that you record the customer payment or the sales receipt.

### 7. (Optional) Record any additional deposit amounts.

If you want to include as part of the deposit some other payment that's not listed initially in the Make Deposits dialog box, you can use the next empty row of the list to describe this payment. To describe the payment, use the Received From column to identify the customer, vendor, or other individual or business making the payment. Use the From Account column to identify the account that should be credited for this payment. In the case of a customer payment that's a sale, for example, your sales revenue account should be the one recorded in the From Account column. Use the other columns of the Make Deposits dialog box — Memo, Chk No., Pmt Meth., Class (if applicable), and Amount — to provide the other details of the payment.

### 8. (Optional) Identify any cash-back amount.

If you're making a $1,000 deposit but want to hold $100 of the deposit back as cash, you record a cash-back amount. To record a cash-back amount, use the Cash Back Goes To drop-down list to identify the account that should be adjusted for the cash back. Use the Cash Back Memo field to describe the reason for the cash-back transaction. Finally, enter the cash-back amount in the cleverly titled Cash Back Amount box. If you want to hold $100 of cash back for an owner draw, for example, you may enter **owner draws** (suppose that this is an account) in the Cash Back Goes To box. Then use the Cash Back Memo field to further describe the reason for the draw. Or not. Finally, enter the cash-back amount, **$100**, in the Cash Back Amount box.

### 9. Save the deposit transaction.

As is the case with other QuickBooks transaction-entry dialog boxes, click either the Save & Close or the Save & New button to save your deposit transaction. Note that after you've saved the deposit transaction, QuickBooks records the deposit in the appropriate bank account. This deposit transaction total — which appears in the Deposit Total field at the bottom of the dialog box — is the amount that appears in your bank statement. It's also the amount that appears in the bank account register. (I talk about bank account registers a little later in the chapter.)

**TIP**

The Make Deposits window also provides Previous and Next buttons that enable you to page back and forth through your deposit transactions. The Print button lets you print a deposit list. The Payments button lets you redisplay the Payments to Deposit dialog box. The History button lets you display a transaction history for the selected payment. The Journal button takes you to the Transaction Journal ledger. Finally, the Attach button opens a dialog box that you can use to attach a document (such as a PDF image of a check) to the deposit.

# Transferring Money between Bank Accounts

The Banking menu supplies a useful command for transferring money between bank accounts. To transfer money between accounts, you can choose Banking ⇨ Transfer Funds. When you do so, QuickBooks displays the Transfer Funds between Accounts window, shown in Figure 4-11.

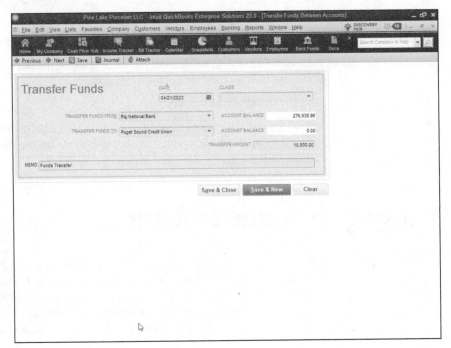

**FIGURE 4-11:**
The Transfer Funds between Accounts window.

To use this window, follow these steps:

1. **Use the Date field to identify the transfer date.**

   You can enter the date in mm/dd/yyyy format, or you can click the small calendar button that appears to the right of the Date field. When QuickBooks displays the calendar, click the day that corresponds to the date you want to enter in the Date field.

2. **Use the Transfer Funds From drop-down list to select the bank account from which you're moving funds.**

You can enter the bank account name in the box, or you can click the arrow at the right end of the box and choose a bank account from the list that QuickBooks supplies.

3. **Use the Transfer Funds To drop-down list to identify the bank account that receives the transferred funds.**

   The Transfer Funds To list works like the Transfer Funds From list.

4. **Use the Transfer Amount box to identify the amount of the transfer.**

   If you transfer $10,000 from one bank account to another, for example, the transfer amount is $10,000. (This is what Figure 4-11 shows.)

5. **(Optional) Provide a memo description for the transfer transaction.**

   If you want (and this is no big deal), you can use the Memo box to provide some brief memo description of the funds transfer.

6. **Save the transfer transaction.**

   To save your transfer transaction, click either the Save & Close or the Save & New button. Alternatively, if you don't want to save the transfer transaction, click the Clear button.

# Working with the Register

You can record checks, deposits, and account transfers by using the commands described in the preceding paragraphs of this chapter, but another method is available: You can use the Register window. The Register window looks like the regular paper register that you use to keep track of transactions for a bank account. QuickBooks allows you to enter transactions directly into an account register.

## Recording register transactions

To enter a bank account transaction directly into an account register, follow these steps:

1. **To display an account register, choose the Banking ⇨ Use Register command.**

   Sometimes, when you choose Banking ⇨ Use Register, QuickBooks displays the Use Register dialog box (see Figure 4-12). If you have only one bank account set up, QuickBooks displays the actual register.

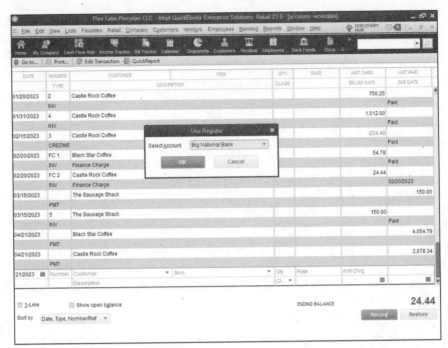

FIGURE 4-12:
The Use Register
dialog box.

The Use Register dialog box asks you to select the bank account that you want to display in a register. Open the Select Account drop-down list, choose the bank account, and then click OK. QuickBooks displays the Register window, shown in Figure 4-13.

TIP

If QuickBooks shows the register of an account other than the one you want to see, choose Banking ⇨ Use Register again. The Use Register dialog box (refer to Figure 4-12) should appear.

The Use Register dialog box lets you select any balance sheet account. You can select a nonbank account, too.

2. **Use the Date column of the register to record the date of the deposit, payment, or transfer.**

   You can enter a date by using mm/dd/yyyy date format. Or you can click the small calendar button to the right of the Date field to display the month that shows the date and then click the day button that corresponds to the date you want to enter.

3. **(Optional) Assign a transaction number.**

   Use the Number column to uniquely identify the transaction. In the case of check transactions, for example, use the Number field to record the check number. For transfers and deposits, you may not need to record a number.

CHAPTER 4 **Managing Cash and Bank Accounts** 255

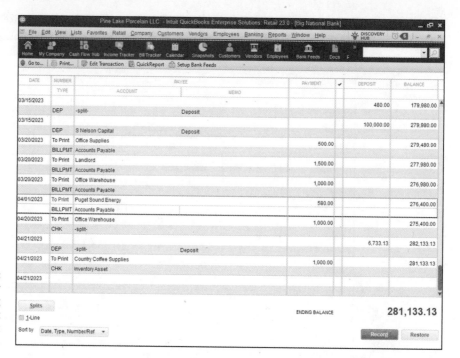

**FIGURE 4-13:**
The Register window, showing transactions that affect the bank account.

4. **Use the Payee field to record the payee for a check, the customer paying a deposit, or some other bit of information in the case of a transfer transaction.**

   Note that you can choose an existing customer, vendor, or a name from one of the QuickBooks lists by clicking the down-arrow button at the right end of the Payee field. When you do this, QuickBooks displays a list of names. Click one to choose it.

5. **Provide the transaction amount.**

   Use the Payment column if you're describing a check transaction or a transfer that moves money from the account. Use the Deposit column if you're describing a deposit into the account or transfer into the account. Enter the amount of the transaction in the appropriate column — Payment or Deposit — by using dollars and cents.

   Note that a check mark will appear between the payment and deposit column when a transaction has been reconciled in the bank reconciliation.

6. **Identify the account.**

   For check transactions, you use the Account field to identify the expense that a check pays or the asset that a check purchases. For deposit transactions, you use the Account field to identify the sales revenue account that the deposit represents. For Transfer transactions, use the Account field to identify the other bank account involved in the transaction. You can enter the Account name in the Account box, or you can open the Account drop-down list and select the account that you want.

7. **(Optional) Provide a memo description.**

If you want, use the Memo field to provide a brief description of the payment, deposit, or transfer transaction.

8. **(Optional) Split the transaction.**

If a transaction needs to be assigned to more than one account, click the Splits button (refer to Figure 4-13). QuickBooks displays the Splits area of the register window, as shown in Figure 4-14. The Splits area lets you split a transaction among several accounts. A check that pays both office supplies and rent expenses, for example, can be split between these two expense accounts. Similarly, a deposit transaction that represents both product revenue and service revenue can be split between these two accounts. When you finish with the Splits area, click its Close button.

**TIP**

You can erase the Splits detail by clicking the Clear button. You can also tell QuickBooks to recalculate the payment or deposit amount by using the split transaction data simply by clicking the Recalc button.

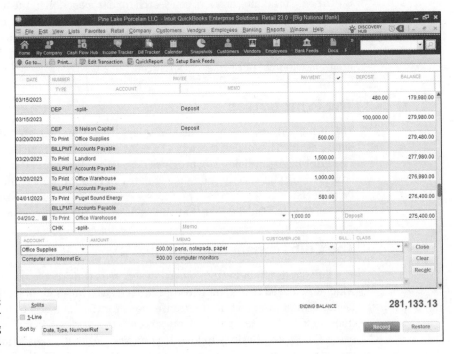

**FIGURE 4-14:** The Register window, showing the Splits area.

The Splits area also lets you do something that isn't possible inside the regular register: record customer and job information, class information, and billing information. To do this, use the Customer:Job column, the Billable column, and the Class column.

9. **To record a transaction in the register, click the Record button.**

   QuickBooks recalculates the account balance and adjusts the ending balance for the new transaction. After you record the transaction, you can see a running tally on the right side with the bank account balance in it after each transaction.

# Using Register window commands and buttons

The Register window provides several buttons and boxes that enable you to work with the Register window more easily and control the way it looks.

## The Go To button

Clicking the Go To button, shown in Figure 4-15 (top-left corner), displays the Go To box. This dialog box lets you search for a transaction in the Register window, such as a transaction in which the Payee/Name uses some name. You can click the Back and Next buttons to move to the previous or next transactions that also match the search criteria. To remove the Go To dialog box from the QuickBooks program window, of course, click Cancel.

## The Print button

The Print button, when clicked, displays the Print Register dialog box (see Figure 4-16). This dialog box lets you print a copy of the register for the account. The Print Register dialog box provides Date Range From and Date Range Through boxes, where you specify the range of dates you want on the printed register. The Print Register dialog box also provides a Print Splits Detail check box, which you can select to tell QuickBooks that you want to see the split transaction detail.

## The Edit Transaction button

The Edit Transaction button, when clicked, tells QuickBooks to display whatever window you used to originally record the selected transaction. Remember that the Register window shows all the transactions for the bank account. These transactions include, for example, checking account transactions that you recorded when using the Write Checks window. If you click the Edit Transaction button when the selected transaction is one that you originally recorded in the Write Checks window, QuickBooks displays that transaction again in the Write Checks window. Edit the transaction in the Write Checks window and click either Save & Close or Save & New to save your changes.

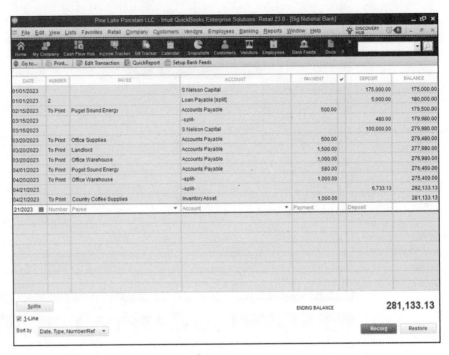

**FIGURE 4-15:**
The Go To dialog box.

## The QuickReport button

Click the QuickReport button to display a report that summarizes register information for the payee or name in the selected transaction. If the selected transaction is a check written to Puget Sound Energy, clicking QuickReport builds a quick-and-dirty report that shows the transactions you've paid to Puget Sound Energy (see Figure 4-17).

## The Download Bank Statement button

Click the Download Bank Statement button to tell QuickBooks that you want to use the Internet to connect to your bank's computer and download recent transactions. Note that you need to prearrange this service with your bank and that this button is called Setup Bank Feeds until you set up an online account. (For more information about QuickBooks's online banking features, see "Bank Feeds command" later in this chapter.)

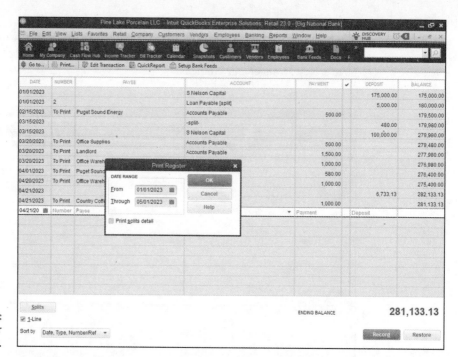

FIGURE 4-16:
The Print Register
dialog box.

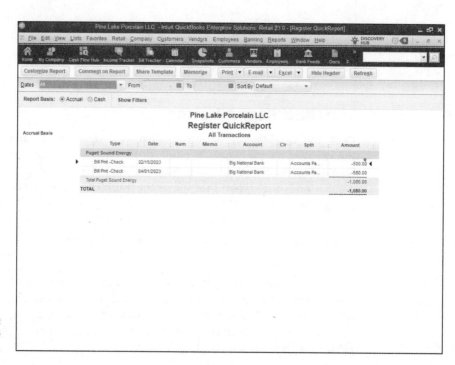

FIGURE 4-17:
A sample
QuickReport.

## The 1-Line check box

QuickBooks lets you display a one- or two-line version of the register (see Figure 4-18). By default, QuickBooks assumes that you want the two-line version of the register, but you can display a more compact, one-line version of the register by selecting the 1-Line check box.

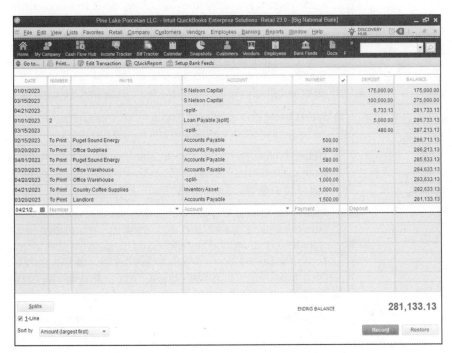

## The Sort By list

The Sort By drop-down list lets you choose how QuickBooks arranges register information. QuickBooks lets you arrange register information by date, by amount, by order entry date, and by several other sorting methods as well. To change the way that QuickBooks orders or organizes the information in the register, open the Sort By drop-down list and choose the ordering sequence that you want.

# Using the Edit Menu Commands

In the preceding paragraphs of this chapter, I describe how to record check transactions, deposit transactions, and transfers between accounts, as well as how to use the register. You often don't need to know any more than I've already described to use the windows discussed and record the transactions described. Know, however, that when you're working with a register, the Edit menu provides several other useful commands for entering new transactions, editing existing transactions, and reusing transaction information:

TIP

>> **Edit Check/Deposit:** This command is equivalent to the Edit Transaction button (which appears in the Register window). If you choose the Edit Check/ Deposit command, QuickBooks displays the Write Checks window so that you can edit the transaction with that tool.

The command name changes depending on the selected transaction. You see the Edit Check command if the selected transaction is a check. You see the Edit Deposit command if the selected transaction is a deposit.

>> **New Check:** This command displays the Write Checks window so that you can record a new check transaction and record it in the register.

>> **Delete Check:** The Delete Check command deletes the selected transaction from the register. (The name of this command changes depending on the transaction selected in the register.)

>> **Memorize Check:** This command, which appears when appropriate, memorizes the selected transaction, adds the check information to the memorized transaction list, and thereby allows you to reuse the check information at some point in the future. (If you have a transaction that you record frequently, such as every month, memorizing the transaction and then reusing it often saves you data entry time.)

>> **Void Check:** This command, which also appears when appropriate, lets you void the selected check transaction.

>> **Copy/Paste:** The Copy command copies the selected check. If you choose the Paste command, QuickBooks pastes the just-copied check into the next empty row of the register.

>> **Go to Transfer:** This command goes to the other side of a transfer transaction. The Go to Transfer command, obviously, makes sense and works only if the selected transaction is a transfer.

>> **Transaction History:** This command displays a window that lists all the transactions related to the current selected transaction. Typically, you use this command when the selected transaction is a customer payment. In this case, the Transaction History window lists all the transactions related to the customer payment transaction. You can use the Transaction History window to go quickly to one of the related transactions. Simply click the transaction listed. You can also edit transactions shown in the Transaction History window by clicking the transaction and then clicking the Edit Payment button.

» **Change Account Color:** This command displays the Change Account Color
dialog box, which lets you choose another color for the striping shown in the
Register window. To select another color, click the color square that shows the
color that you want and then click OK.

» **Use Register:** This command displays the Use Register dialog box, which lets
you select the account that you want to display in a register.

» **Use Calculator:** This command, predictably, displays the Windows Calculator.
If you have questions about how to work with the Windows Calculator, refer
to the Windows documentation, the Windows Help file, or a book such as
the latest edition of *Windows For Dummies,* by Andy Rathbone (John Wiley &
Sons, Inc.).

» **Find:** The Find command displays either the Simple tab of the Find window,
shown in Figure 4-19, or the Advanced tab of the Find window, shown later
in this section. Both tabs allow you to search your register and find
transactions.

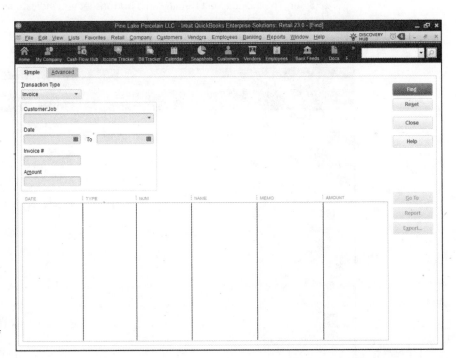

**FIGURE 4-19:**
The Simple tab of
the Find window.

To use the Simple tab, use the Transaction Type, Customer:Job, Date, Invoice #, and Amount controls to describe the transaction you want. Enter as much information as you can, but note that if you enter incorrect information, QuickBooks (obviously) won't be able to find the transaction you're looking for. After you describe the transaction in as much detail as you can, click the Find button. QuickBooks displays a list of transactions that match your search criteria (see Figure 4-20). To go to a particular transaction, click the transaction in the list and then click the Go To button.

The Advanced tab, shown in Figure 4-21, lets you describe a much more precise and complex set of search criteria. Essentially, you can describe in painful detail a filter that QuickBooks should apply to each field that's recorded for a transaction. If you want to filter based on the account, for example, select the account entry in the Filter list. Then open the Account drop-down list and choose one of the account groupings that QuickBooks displays. In Figure 4-21, the All Accounts entry is selected, so all accounts appear, but you can choose the Select Accounts entry instead to display a dialog box that you can use to individually select the accounts you want to look for. The Include Split Detail? radio buttons let you indicate whether you want to use split detail information.

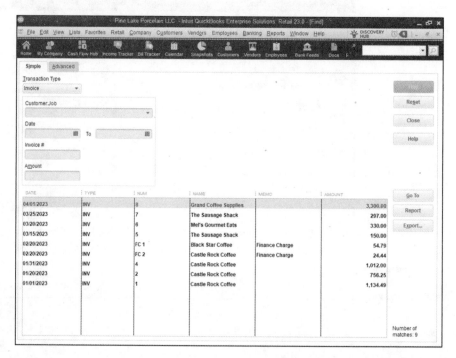

**FIGURE 4-20:**
Result of a simple search in the Find window.

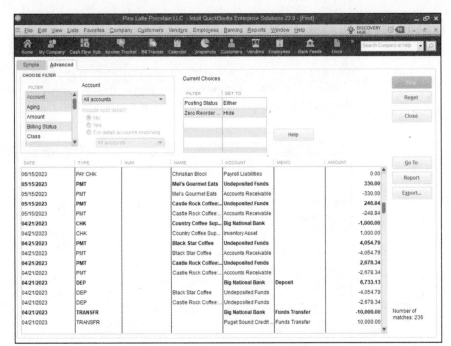

FIGURE 4-21:
The Advanced
tab of the
Find window.

After you describe the filter or filters you want to use, click the Find button. As with the Simple tab of the Find window, QuickBooks displays a list of all the transactions that match your filter. To go to one of the transactions listed, click it and then click the Go To button.

TIP

The Report button, which appears on both on the Simple tab and the Advanced tab, creates a report of all the transactions that the Find command has found. You can print this report — QuickBooks displays it in a regular report window — by choosing the File ⇨ Print Report command or by clicking the Print button that appears at the top of the Report window. The Simple and Advanced tabs of the Find window also include a Reset button. I should say that if you want to start your search over by using a new set of search criteria or filtering criteria, simply click the Reset button.

>> **Search:** This command opens a search window that you can use to search for specific information within your company file.

>> **Preferences:** This command enables you to change the way that QuickBooks works so that it best matches your firm's accounting requirements. Book 2, Chapter 3 discusses the Preferences command in detail.

# Reconciling the Bank Account

You can reconcile a bank account with surprising speed in QuickBooks. To reconcile the bank account, choose the Banking ⇨ Reconcile command. QuickBooks displays the Begin Reconciliation dialog box, shown in Figure 4-22.

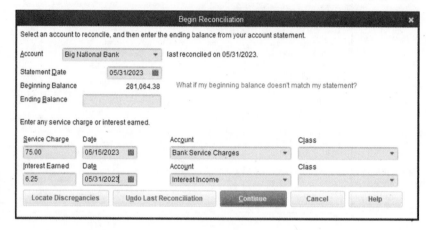

**FIGURE 4-22:** The Begin Reconciliation dialog box.

To begin reconciling your account, follow these steps:

1. **Choose the account that you want to reconcile from the Account drop-down list.**

2. **Use the Statement Date box to identify the ending date of the bank statement that you're using in your reconciliation.**

   As is always the case with date fields in QuickBooks, you enter the date in mm/dd/yyyy date format or click the calendar button and use it to select the correct date.

3. **Enter the ending balance shown on your bank account statement in the Ending Balance box.**

4. **Use the Service Charge and Interest Earned boxes to identify the amount of any service charge or of any interest, the date of any such transaction, and the account that you use to track those charges.**

   If your bank statement shows a service charge, enter the service charge amount in the first Service Charge box. Enter the date of the service charge transaction in the Service Charge Date box. Finally, choose an appropriate expense account for tracking service charges from the Service Charge Account drop-down list. (Bank charges, for example, is a good account to track service charges.)

In a similar fashion, use the Interest Earned boxes to describe any interest earned on a business account.

5. **Review the statement information.**

After you enter information about the bank account, the statement date, the ending balance, and any service charge or interest earned information, take a moment to review the information and confirm that it's correct. You'll have a whale of a time reconciling an account if the amount that you're trying to reconcile to is incorrect.

6. **After you make sure that everything is hunky-dory, click the Continue button.**

QuickBooks displays the Reconcile window, as shown in Figure 4-23.

7. **To identify checks and payment transactions that have cleared your bank account, click the transactions that have cleared.**

The Reconcile window displays two lists of transactions: a list of checks and payments, which appears on the left, and a list of deposits and other credits, which appears on the right. When you click a transaction, QuickBooks marks the transaction with a check mark, indicating that a transaction has cleared. You can mark all the transactions in a list as cleared by clicking the Mark All button. To mark all the transactions in a list as uncleared, click the Unmark All button.

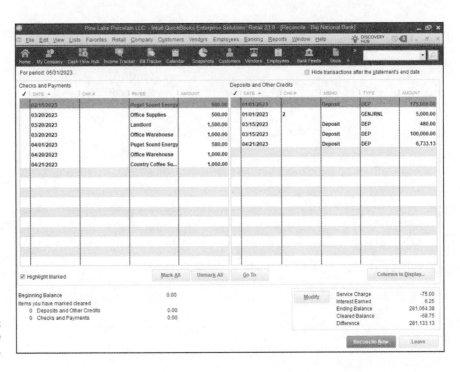

FIGURE 4-23:
The Reconcile
window.

Use the Deposits and Other Credits list to identify those deposit transactions that have cleared the bank account. You identify a cleared deposit transaction in the same way that you identify a cleared check or payment transaction. You can click a transaction, which causes QuickBooks to mark the transaction as cleared. You can also use the Mark All and Unmark All buttons to mark or unmark all the deposits and other credit transactions at one time.

**TIP**

If you realize that as part of the reconciliation, you've incorrectly entered the service charge, interest earned, ending balance, or any other information, click the Modify button. QuickBooks redisplays the Begin Reconciliation dialog box (refer to Figure 4-22). Make the necessary changes and click Continue to return to the Reconcile window.

8. **Verify that the cleared balance equals the ending balance.**

   If you provided correct information in the Begin Reconciliation dialog box (refer to Figure 4-22) and you correctly identified all the transactions that have cleared your account, the ending balance should equal the cleared balance, as shown in Figure 4-24.

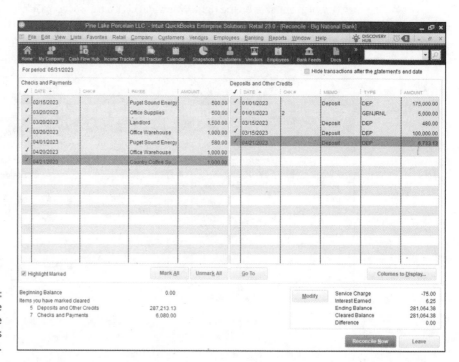

**FIGURE 4-24:**
The Reconcile window when the reconciliation is complete.

**9.** **When the ending balance equals the cleared balance, click the Reconcile Now button.**

QuickBooks permanently records your cleared transactions as cleared and redisplays the Register window. If you can't reconcile an account, you can click the Leave button. QuickBooks saves your half-completed reconciliation so that you can come back later to finish it.

**TIP** Can I interject a couple of tangential comments here? Good. If you want, you can print a little report that summarizes your reconciliation after you click the Reconcile Now button. (QuickBooks gives you this option in a dialog box that it displays.) You can also click the Previous Reports button to display a dialog box that lets you print other old reconciliation reports. You can click the Discrepancy Report button to produce a report that lists transactions that have been edited since you last reconciled the account. Finally, you can click the column headings used in the Reconciliation window to sort and re-sort the bank account information.

## WHEN YOUR ACCOUNT WON'T BALANCE

If your account won't reconcile, the problem stems from one of several conditions. None of the conditions is hard to describe, but all of them can be pretty hard to fix. Here's a quick overview of what may be causing you trouble and what may be preventing you from reconciling your account:

- **Are you working with the right account?** That sounds pretty dumb, doesn't it? But if you have several bank accounts, you may be trying to reconcile the wrong account or using the wrong statement to reconcile your account.

- **Are you missing any transactions?** If the bank has recorded transactions that you haven't, this fact causes your ending balance to not equal your cleared balance. Look on your statement for any transactions that you're missing or forgot to record; then record these transactions and mark them as cleared.

- **Have you recorded transactions correctly?** This may sound silly too, but if you recorded the transaction, and you're a few pennies or a few dollars off — perhaps you've transposed a couple of numbers — you won't be able to reconcile your account. I commonly find that I've entered a transaction or two wrong per month. (Maybe this is because my fingers are too arthritic to record amounts correctly.) But it's probably very common when you're entering dozens and dozens of transactions to occasionally record a transaction wrong. The occasional errors need to be fixed before you can reconcile an account.

*(continued)*

*(continued)*

Note that it's quite likely — especially when you're getting started — that you won't be able to reconcile an account because of multiple errors. If you do something like record a transaction erroneously and then forget to record a couple of transactions, you'll need to fix each error to reconcile your account.

One final tip: Reconciling an account is much easier when you're using online banking. I talk about how online banking works a little later in this chapter.

# Reviewing the Other Banking Commands

Earlier in this chapter, I describe the most common and useful banking commands. You may not need to use the other commands provided on the Banking menu. Nevertheless, my compulsive personality requires that I describe these other commands.

## Order Checks & Envelopes command

The Order Checks & Envelopes command displays a submenu of commands you use to order QuickBooks checks and envelopes or to get information about ordering QuickBooks checks and envelopes.

## Enter Credit Card Charges command

If you set up a credit card account — this is a credit card account that you or your business would use to charge transactions — you can choose the Banking ⇨ Enter Credit Card Charges command to display a window that you can use to enter credit card charges.

When you choose the Enter Credit Card Charges command, the Enter Credit Card Charges window appears (see Figure 4-25). You can figure out how this window works without my help, I'm sure. You identify the credit card account for which you want to record transactions and describe the credit card purchase by using the field at the top of the screen. Then you use the Expenses and Items tabs — these tabs work the same way as the similar tabs in the Write Checks window — to detail the reasons and the accounts affected by your charge.

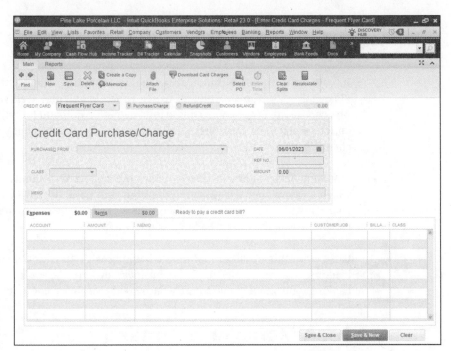

FIGURE 4-25:
The Enter Credit
Card Charges
window.

Managing Cash and
Bank Accounts

If you click the Download Card Charges button (which appears at the top of the Enter Credit Card Charges window), assuming that you've set up credit card accounts that allow for online services, QuickBooks downloads recent credit card transactions directly into the credit card register. Perhaps obviously, for this command to work, several prerequisites must be met:

>> You need a credit card account set up.

>> You need to have set up the credit card account for online services.

>> You need an Internet connection so that QuickBooks can grab the credit card transactions from the credit card company.

## Bank Feeds command

The Bank Feeds command displays a submenu of commands that you use to conduct online banking and to see which financial institutions (banks, savings and loans, and credit unions) let you do online banking. If you want to do online banking — which can save businesses a ton of time — call your existing bank to ask whether it provides the service. If it does, ask for a sign-up packet and for specific instructions on how to get going with online banking. If you don't like the idea of calling your bank directly, choose the Set Up Bank Feed for Account command from the Bank Feeds submenu. This command walks you through the process of applying for and setting up online financial services.

If you want to learn more about online banking, choose the Participating Financial Institutions command to see which banks play well with QuickBooks. And choose the Learn about Online Bill Payment command for online bill payment options when your bank doesn't play well with QuickBooks but you don't want to change banks.

The Bank Feeds submenu also provides the Import Web Connect File command, which lets you open a transaction file from your bank (if that's the way your bank does online banking), and the Change Bank Feeds Mode command, which lets you tweak the way the online banking window looks.

REMEMBER

Can I close this discussion of online banking with an editorial comment? Online banking is a real time-saver for business owners. If you're not using online banking, you should have a pretty darn good reason for not doing so.

## Loan Manager command

The Loan Manager command displays a window that lists loan accounts you've set up. This listing of loan accounts by itself isn't all that special, but the Loan Manager window does something else that *is* special: If you click the Add a Loan button, QuickBooks collects loan information from you so that it can break loan payments into principal and interest.

## Other Names list

The Other Names list displays a window that lists all the other names you've used to record transactions. People and businesses that appear in your Other Names list aren't customers, vendors, or employees. In other words, the Other Names list includes names that don't neatly fit into one of the standard categories.

# Chapter 5

# Paying Employees

Quickbooks provides a do-it-yourself option for paying employees: Enhanced Payroll, which means that QuickBooks helps you with the payroll tax forms. A second payroll option would be QuickBooks Assisted Payroll. With this option, you handle paying your employees within QuickBooks; then Intuit handles making the tax payments and filing the necessary payroll tax forms.

**TIP**

Yet another option to consider in case you're not an accountant and are in need of payroll: Consider splurging a bit and going with one of the full-service payroll providers, such as ADP, Paychex, and Gusto. Having one of them process your payroll greatly simplifies the accounting work and — in my experience — saves you money over time.

If you go with a payroll provider, you can stop reading this chapter right now. Seriously. All you need to do is telephone the payroll service company and say, "Help!"

## Setting Up Payroll

To set up do-it-yourself payroll, you step through a web-based interview. To start this interview, choose Employees ⇨ Payroll ⇨ Turn on Payroll in QuickBooks. QuickBooks displays the page shown in Figure 5-1.

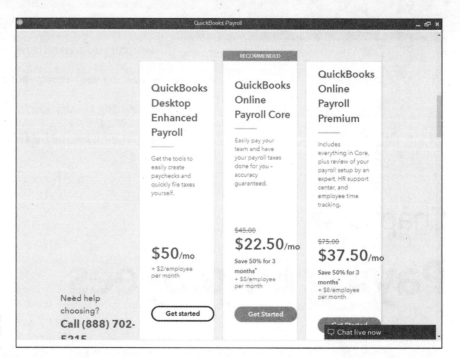

**FIGURE 5-1:**
The first payroll
setup web page.

**TIP**

You have three payroll options: Enhanced Payroll, Payroll Core, and Payroll Premium. If you choose the Enhanced option, QuickBooks will help you remit the payroll tax deposits and then prepare (or mostly prepare) the payroll tax returns for you. The Payroll Core and Payroll Premium options are full-service; Quick-Books prepares the paychecks, direct deposits, and payroll tax forms, and remits payroll tax deposits on your behalf.

You can choose any option by clicking the appropriate Get Started button. If you know you do not want to mess around with payroll tax filings, paying a bit more for the Core or Premium options probably makes sense.

**TIP**

Intuit's pricing for its payroll services changes from time to time; at the time I'm writing (summer 2022), Enhanced service costs approximately $600 per year, and the full-service options are about $550 to $900 per year. The cost of each plan increases as the number of employees and the number of checks you issue increases.

Even though you have three QuickBooks payroll options, in this chapter I assume that you want to use the Enhanced option, which requires a more hands-on approach than the others. You do some of the work. You need to understand federal and state payroll tax rules, but the benefit is lower cost, which adds up if you are paying for the service year after year.

To choose the Enhanced option, click the Get Started button. QuickBooks gives you the option to pay for a full year, which saves you $100, or pay in monthly installments. Then QuickBooks collects your credit card information (so that it can bill you for the service).

## Signing up for a payroll service

To sign up for the payroll service after you've selected a particular option, you fill in a series of web-page forms. Along the way, you enter your business name and address and give your firm's employer identification number (EIN). To move through the web-page forms, click the Continue and Back buttons. QuickBooks steps you through the sign-up process very efficiently. Simply follow the onscreen instructions to describe how your company processes payroll.

**WARNING**

But let me issue a warning: When you *do* set up your company information for payroll, QuickBooks asks for a bunch of information. I won't repeat the instructions that the web pages provide, but you do need to fully describe how you pay your employees, to whom you remit deductions, and other stuff like that. Carefully read the instructions that QuickBooks provides, which takes some time. If you get into trouble, you may want to get an outside accountant's help to set up the Enhanced service or consider the Assisted option.

## Setting up employees

After you set up your company information for payroll, you're ready to set up employees for payroll. As part of the Enhanced setup process, QuickBooks displays a web page where you can add your employees. You can also add employees by displaying the Employee Center. (Choose Employees ➪ Employee Center and click the New Employee button.) When you click the New Employee button, QuickBooks displays the Personal tab of the New Employee window, as shown in Figure 5-2.

To describe an employee, you complete the fields supplied on the Personal tab. All this stuff is self-explanatory. You enter the person's name in the Legal Name boxes. The employee's first name goes in the First box, the middle initial goes in the M.I. box, and so forth.

You click the Address & Contact tab (not shown) to collect and store the employee's mailing address and other contact information, such as their telephone number.

If you want to collect and store additional information for an employee (such as their bank account number for direct deposit), you click the Additional Info tab (also not shown). This tab provides a Define Field button that you can use to collect custom bits of information about an employee. To use the Custom Field option, click the Define Field button and then use the Define Field dialog box to define the fields that you want to add.

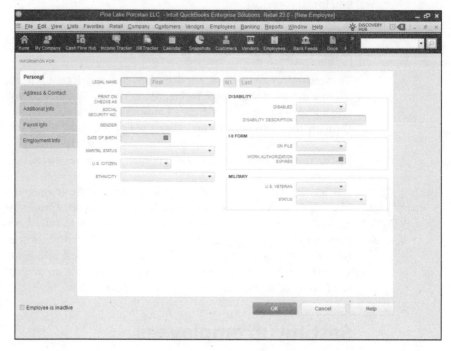

**FIGURE 5-2:**
The Personal tab of the New Employee window.

## Providing payroll and tax information

Use the Payroll Info tab to describe how an employee's salary or wages are calculated, as shown in Figure 5-3. Use the Payroll Schedule drop-down list to set up a regular payroll schedule (such as weekly or semimonthly) and to assign the employee to the payroll schedule. Use the Pay Frequency drop-down list to identify the pay period. Optionally, if you've turned on QuickBooks's class tracking feature, use the Class drop-down list to classify payments to this employee. You enter the payroll item in the Earnings area. If an employee earns an annual salary of $30,000, for example, you enter the salary payroll item in the Item Name column. Then you enter the annual salary of $30,000 in the Hourly/Annual Rate column. If you've set up QuickBooks to handle other additions or deductions on a payroll check (expense reimbursements or pension deductions), use the Additions, Deductions and Company Contributions area to describe these items and the item amounts.

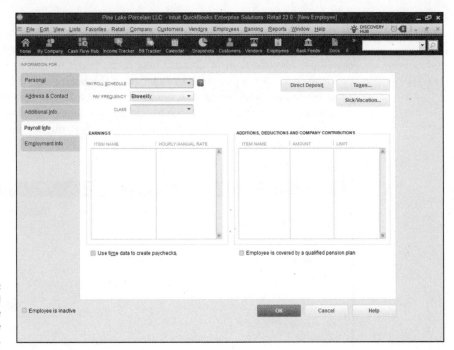

FIGURE 5-3:
The Payroll
Info tab of the
New Employee
window.

To describe which taxes an employee pays, click the Taxes button. QuickBooks displays the Taxes dialog box. Use the Federal tab (shown in Figure 5-4) to identify the year of the W4 on file, employee's filing status, number of dependents claimed, other income, deductions, and any extra withholding specified. In addition, use the Subject To check boxes to indicate whether this employee is subject to Medicare, Social Security, or federal unemployment tax, or whether the employee is eligible for an earned income credit. Note that not all employees are subject to Medicare and Social Security taxes. Consult your tax adviser for more information.

The State tab supplies boxes that you can use to describe state taxes, obviously. I don't show the State tax tab here because this tab varies depending on the state you're in.

The Other tab lets you describe and store any local tax information, such as a city income tax. Again, what you see on the Other tab depends on your locality. For this reason, I don't show it here.

If you click the Sick/Vacation button on the Payroll Info tab of the New Employee dialog box, you see the Sick and Vacation dialog box, shown in Figure 5-5. This dialog box lets you specify how sick or vacation pay and personal leave time are accrued payroll period by payroll period. You can specify the number of sick or vacation leave hours in the Hours Available As Of field at the time you're setting

Paying Employees

up payroll. You can use the Accrual Period drop-down list to specify how often sick or vacation pay should be accrued. If sick or vacation pay is accrued, use the Hours Accrued field to identify how many hours of sick or vacation time an employee earns each paycheck or hour, or at the beginning of the year. If you've set a maximum number of sick hours or vacation hours that an employee can accumulate, enter this value in the Maximum Number of Hours field. If you want to reset the sick hours and vacation hours to zero at the beginning of each year, select the Reset Hours Each New Year? check box.

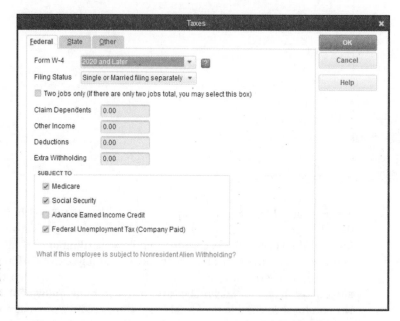

The Vacation area of the Sick and Vacation dialog box works the same way as the Sick area. Enter the number of vacation hours available in the Hours Available As Of field. Use the Accrual Period drop-down list to specify how often employees earn vacation time. Use the Hours Accrued and Maximum Number of Hours fields to control how vacation-time accrual calculations work. Finally, select the Reset Hours Each New Year? check box to zero out vacation time at the beginning of each new year.

TIP

If you've chosen to use the direct-deposit option, click the Direct Deposit button on the Payroll Info tab of the New Employee dialog box (refer to Figure 5-3). QuickBooks prompts you to supply the information necessary to directly deposit checks for employees.

**FIGURE 5-5:**
The Sick and
Vacation
dialog box.

### Providing other employment-related information

If you select the Employment Info tab of the New Employee dialog box, Quick-Books displays the tab you use to store the hire date, fire date, and similar bits of employment data.

## Setting up year-to-date amounts

If you're setting up the Enhanced payroll service at the very beginning of the business's operation or at the beginning of the year, you don't have to set up any year-to-date amounts (because all the year-to-date amounts equal zero). If you're switching to the service sometime in midyear, however, you *do* need to set up year-to-date amounts. For this reason, a QuickBooks wizard walks you through the process of recording year-to-date amounts.

**TIP**

If an outside service bureau such as ADP or Paychex has been doing your payroll processing, the final payroll report from this outside service bureau probably supplies all the information you need to set up the Enhanced payroll service. If you've been working with a bookkeeper or accountant to get payroll done, you should be able to get this person's help to describe year-to-date payroll amounts.

## Checking your payroll setup data

As part of the Enhanced payroll setup process, QuickBooks (or you) may identify payroll data that doesn't seem right. Perhaps an employee whom you know you've paid shows no year-to-date wages. In this case, you correct the incorrect data by following the onscreen instructions. Note, however, that the Enhanced setup process may also identify suspicious payroll data that is in fact correct. In the state of Washington (where I live), for example, officers aren't subject to state unemployment insurance if they so elect. QuickBooks doesn't know this, however, so it flags officers who aren't marked as being subject to state unemployment insurance as possible errors.

Again, if you don't feel comfortable answering some of these payroll setup questions, get an accountant's help. Quite frankly, when you have an outside service bureau prepare your payroll checks, you're really paying for that firm's expertise and knowledge about how all this payroll processing stuff works. You're not really paying for the computer time and the paper on which the checks are written.

# Scheduling Payroll Runs

The Enhanced payroll setup process also steps you through the work of scheduling your payroll runs. In other words, if you'll run your payroll every week, twice a month, or at whatever interval, the setup process asks you to describe the schedule. Again, as with the other tasks that the Enhanced setup process helps you with, all you need to do is provide a few bits and pieces of information.

# Paying Employees

After you go through the steps required to set up the QuickBooks payroll processing capability, paying employees — thank goodness — is pretty easy. To pay employees, follow these steps:

1. **Choose Employees ⇨ Pay Employees ⇨ Scheduled Payroll.**

   QuickBooks displays the Employee Center: Payroll Center window (see Figure 5-6).

2. **Click the Start Scheduled Payroll button.**

3. **Supply the payroll check date and use the Check Date box to supply the date that you want to appear on payroll checks.**

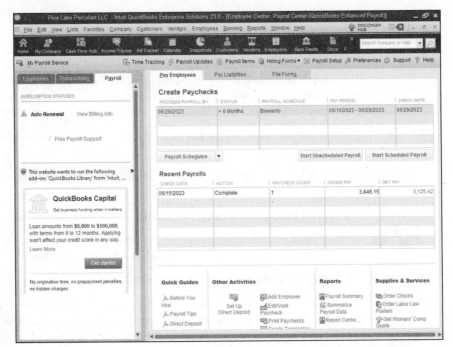

**FIGURE 5-6:**
The Employee
Center: Payroll
Center window.

4. **Identify the date on which the payroll period ends in the Pay Period Ends box.**

5. **Use the Bank Account drop-down list to identify the bank account on which you want to write checks.**

6. **Verify the employees whom you want to pay.**

   QuickBooks lists the active employees included in the scheduled payroll. You want to make sure that the list of selected employees is right. You can click listed employees to select and unselect them.

7. **Click Continue.**

   QuickBooks calculates the payroll checks and payroll deduction amounts for each of the selected employees.

8. **To accept a previewed paycheck described or shown in the dialog box, click its Create Paychecks button.**

   QuickBooks displays a dialog box that lets you print paychecks or pay stubs for direct deposit.

9. **Click the Print Paychecks or Print Pay Stubs button and follow the onscreen instructions.**

When you click either button, QuickBooks displays the Select Paychecks/Pay Stubs to Print dialog box. You should confirm the bank account on which you want to write the checks. If you're printing checks, you should also use the First Check Number box to supply the preprinted form number shown on the first payroll check that you'll print. You should also confirm that the employee paychecks listed in the dialog box are those that you want to print.

**10.** **After you confirm that the paycheck printing information is correct, click OK.**

QuickBooks displays the Print Checks dialog box (the same one that you use to print any check).

**11.** **Print checks in the usual fashion.**

If you want to deselect a paycheck for printing, click the check column to remove the check mark and, thereby, deselect the paycheck.

TIP

**12.** **Distribute the paychecks or pay stubs.**

Obviously, after you print the checks, you sign and then distribute them. I'll leave you to your own devices here. I'm sure that you know how to find employees whom you need to pay and, furthermore, how to hand them their paychecks. Heck, they're probably standing beside your desk right now, waiting for you to finish the payroll checks anyway.

# Editing and Voiding Paychecks

Be careful when you want to change payroll check information. Payroll checks are a little trickier than regular checks because the information from the payroll checks affects a bunch of payroll counters. Payroll checks bump up someone's gross wages for the year, for example, and affect the deduction amounts. For this reason, when you want to make a change or void a paycheck that you previously created, you choose the Employees ➪ Edit/Void Paychecks command. When you do this, QuickBooks displays the Edit/Void Paychecks window (not shown). This window lists paychecks that you've previously created and printed. To change one of the paychecks listed, double-click the paycheck. When QuickBooks displays the Paychecks window, click the Paycheck Detail button. When QuickBooks displays the Review Paychecks window, use it to make the appropriate change to the paycheck. Note that you can change other details, such as the name or address, by using the Paycheck window.

To void the paycheck shown in the Paycheck window, choose the Edit ➪ Void Paycheck command.

TIP

After you edit or void a check, click the Save & Close or the Save & New button to save your changes to the paycheck.

# Paying Payroll Liabilities

Amounts that you withhold from employees' paychecks become liabilities that you later need to pay. If you withhold federal income tax deductions, you need to remit those payments to the Internal Revenue Service.

To pay payroll tax liabilities, choose Employees ⇨ Payroll Taxes and Liabilities ⇨ Pay Scheduled Liabilities. QuickBooks displays the Employee Center window, which lets you select the payroll liabilities you want to pay. Click the liability you want to pay and then click the View/Pay button. QuickBooks writes a check to pay the selected liability. You print this check in the usual way.

TIP

How quickly you need to remit any payroll taxes triggered by payroll depends on a variety of factors, including the size of the deposit. But a good practice is to immediately remit any amounts you owe. Typically, the government agency in question allows you to easily and electronically make tax deposits by using a website. The U.S. Treasury's www.eftps.gov/eftps website, for example, lets you make federal tax deposits easily in this manner. In fact, you're required to use this system if you pay more than $2,500 in payroll taxes a quarter.

# 4

# Accounting Chores

# Contents at a Glance

IN THIS CHAPTER

» **Managing QuickBooks journal entries**

» **Keeping company information up to date**

» **Handling memorized transactions**

» **Working with Accountant and Taxes reports**

» **Making an accountant's copy of the QuickBooks data file**

» **Issuing client data review commands**

Chapter **1**

# For Accountants Only

I n this chapter, I quickly cover stuff that accountants need or want to know. Because I assume that you're an accountant, I go a little faster here than I do in other chapters of this book. Also, I don't provide blow-by-blow instructions for working with the windows and dialog boxes that this chapter discusses.

If you find yourself just a wee bit frustrated with me at this point, go ahead and peruse the paragraphs of this chapter — keeping in mind that what I discuss in this chapter is pretty advanced accounting stuff. You don't want to do the things that this chapter talks about unless you really know your debits and credits. And if you *do* know your debits and credits, you should find the information I provide here to be all that you need.

## Working with QuickBooks Journal Entries

QuickBooks makes it easy for you — an accountant — to record journal entries. If you've spent any time working with QuickBooks, you may know that most of the journal entries that get recorded in the QuickBooks data file are recorded automatically. If somebody writes a check, for example, QuickBooks records the journal entry for that. When somebody creates an invoice, again, QuickBooks records the journal entry for that.

In some cases, however, somebody — probably you — needs to record a journal entry to get some transaction into the QuickBooks data file. You use journal entries to record depreciation, to accrue liabilities, and to record the disposal of assets, for example.

## Recording a journal entry

To record a journal entry, choose Company ⇨ Make General Journal Entries. QuickBooks displays the Make General Journal Entries window, as shown in Figure 1-1.

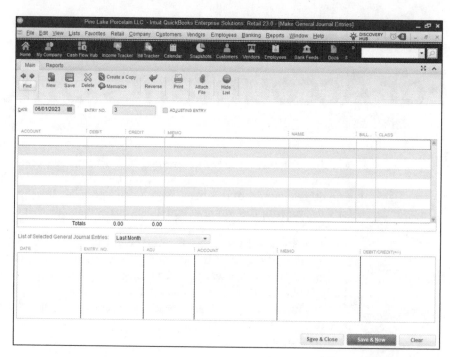

You can probably figure out how to use the Make General Journal Entries window yourself. You enter the general journal entry date in the Date box. You use the Entry No. box to number journal entries or to assign them some meaningful code. After you provide this basic information, you use the columns of the Make General Journal Entries window to record the journal entry. You don't need me to tell you that the general ledger account number or name goes in the Account column, the debit amount in the Debit column, and the credit amount in the Credit column. You may find it useful, though, to be reminded that you can use the Memo column to enter some description of the debit or credit; you can use the Name column to identify the customer, vendor, employee, or other name associated with the credit or debit; you can use the Billable? column to indicate that the debit or credit should be listed as an amount to be billed to the named customer; and you can use the Class column (if you've turned on class tracking) to classify the debit or credit.

**WARNING**

My technical editor, who's also a CPA, reminds me that you should never put a name in the first row of the journal entry. If you do, that name will be associated with every line of that journal entry when you view reports in QuickBooks, even if the name relates only to the first line.

**TIP**

If you do want to associate names with lines of a journal entry, one way to do so cleanly is to leave the first line of the journal entry blank so that no stray entries become inadvertently associated with reports.

## Reversing a journal entry

To reverse a journal entry, first display the Make General Journal Entries window by choosing the Company ➪ Make General Journal Entries command. QuickBooks displays the Make General Journal Entries window (refer to Figure 1-1). Use the left and right arrows in the upper-left side of the screen to page through general journal entries that you've already entered. Found the entry? Good.

An update to this year's version means that all general journal entries can be reversed the same way: When you find the journal entry that you want to reverse, click the Reverse button. (The Reverse button appears along the top edge of the Main tab of the Make General Journal Entries window.) QuickBooks reverses the general journal entry by entering a transaction in the next accounting month with the debits and credits flip-flopped.

**TIP**

The Adjusting Entry check box, available in the Make General Journal Entries window in some versions of QuickBooks, indicates that the journal entry is a special entry made after the fact by the accountant. You can print a report of only special adjusting entries.

**TIP**

Book 1, Chapter 1 discusses the basics of accounting. Book 1, Chapter 2 describes basic bookkeeping, including how debits and credits work. Book 1, Chapter 3 describes how to do special accounting magic tricks, including how and why to enter reversing journal entries. If you find yourself in this chapter even though you're not a degreed accountant, you may want to peruse the information in those chapters to understand what journal entries are and why in the world one would want to reverse one.

### Editing journal entries

Typically, you won't want to fool around and change the journal entries later. If you do feel the need to make changes, however, QuickBooks provides an Edit menu with commands that you can use for just this purpose. For one, QuickBooks supplies a Delete General Journal command that you can use to delete the journal entry shown in the Make General Journal Entries window. QuickBooks also supplies a Void General Journal command that you can use to void the general journal entry shown in the window. Typically — and again, you already know this — you don't want to delete general journal entries. Instead, you want to *void* them. Enough said.

## Updating Company Information

The Company menu supplies a bunch of commands in addition to Make General Journal Entries. Accountants may have occasion to use the Company Information command, for example. This command enables you to update company name and address information, fiscal and tax year settings, the tax form used to report profits, and taxpayer identification numbers.

## Working with Memorized Transactions

A quick tip: Most of the transactions that you enter in QuickBooks, you can have QuickBooks memorize by choosing Edit ➪ Memorize when the transaction appears in the open window. You (or someone else) can reuse a memorized transaction later. You choose the Lists ➪ Memorized Transaction List command, and when QuickBooks displays the list of memorized transactions (shown in Figure 1-2), you double-click the transaction that you want to enter again.

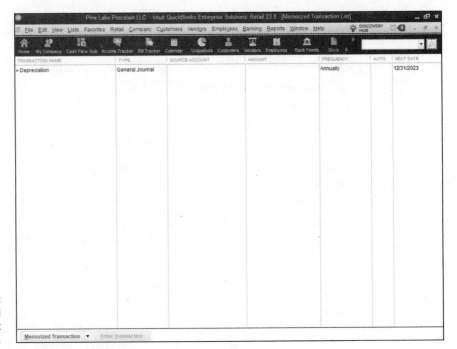

**FIGURE 1-2:**
The Memorized
Transaction List
window.

# Reviewing the Accountant and Taxes Reports

The Accountant & Taxes menu appears when you choose the Reports ⇨ Accountant & Taxes command. Although I don't show pictures of each report that gets displayed when you choose a command from the Accountant & Taxes menu (I do show the Trial Balance report in this section), I want to point out that hidden on this submenu are nearly 20 commands and reports that are particularly interesting and useful to accountants. The following list identifies these reports:

>> **Adjusted Trial Balance:** The Adjusted Trial Balance menu command produces, of course, a Trial Balance report as of a particular date. What's unique about this version of the Trial Balance report (compared with the one described next) is that adjusting journal entries are clearly highlighted. (Adjusting journal entries are those that were marked as such.) Some versions of QuickBooks (like the version you probably use) provide an Adjusting Journal Entry check box. You can check that box to indicate an adjusting journal entry.

>> **Trial Balance:** The Trial Balance menu command produces, of course, a Trial Balance report as of a particular date (see Figure 1-3).

- **General Ledger:** The General Ledger menu command produces a report that simply lists the accounts in your Chart of Accounts list and then changes the account for the month, year, or whatever accounting period you specify.

- **Transaction Detail by Account:** This menu command produces the report that you'd expect: a list of the transactions that affect a particular account.

- **Adjusting Journal Entries:** The Adjusting Journal Entries command produces a list of the journal entries that you or someone else marked as being adjusting journal entries.

- **Journal:** The Journal menu command produces a report that lists transactions by transaction type and number.

- **Audit Trail:** The Audit Trail report is pretty important for accountants — particularly for accountants who are concerned or worried that transactions have changed when they shouldn't have changed. The Audit Trail report lists transactions by the person entering the transactions. The Audit Trail report also lists changes to transactions and identifies who made the changes.

- **Closing Date Exception Report:** If you finalize the accounting data for the year (referred to as *closing the books*) — and you should — the Closing Date Exception Report command identifies changes in closed transactions. (Closing the QuickBooks data file is described in Book 7, Chapter 2.)

- **Customer Credit Card Audit Trail:** A Customer Credit Card Audit Trail report lists only credit card transactions — perfect for people with heavy credit card transaction volumes that they can't make heads or tails of.

- **Voided/Deleted Transactions Summary:** The Voided/Deleted Transactions Summary command produces a summary report of voided transactions and deleted transactions.

- **Voided/Deleted Transactions Detail:** The Voided/Deleted Transactions Detail command produces a detailed listing of all voided transactions and all deleted transactions.

- **Transaction List by Date:** The Transaction List by Date report lists transactions in order of date of entry.

- **Account Listing:** The Account Listing report lists all the accounts in your Chart of Accounts list. The report also gives the account balance and indicates the line on the tax return where the account is reported.

- **Fixed Asset Listing:** The Fixed Asset Listing report lists all the fixed assets in your Fixed Assets list.

- **Income Tax Preparation:** The Income Tax Preparation report shows on which lines of which tax forms account balances are reported.

- **Income Tax Summary:** The Income Tax Summary report uses your income tax preparation data to show what amounts should be reported on what lines of your tax forms. If you're a sole proprietor filing a Schedule C tax form, for example, QuickBooks looks at all the accounts that you use to track gross receipts or sales. Then it totals the balances in those accounts and shows the actual value that should be reported on the gross receipts or sales line of your Schedule C tax form.

>> **Income Tax Detail:** The Income Tax Detail report gives the same information as the Income Tax Summary report, except that this report shows the individual accounts that get bunched together to produce the tax line total.

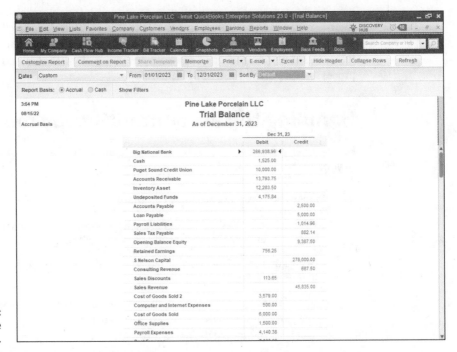

**FIGURE 1-3:**
The Trial Balance report.

# Creating an Accountant's Copy of the QuickBooks Data File

QuickBooks makes it easier for accountants to work with client data files. Consider this scenario: You have a client who needs help finishing the year's accounting period. You have two choices:

>> You can drive over to their shop, probably getting stuck in traffic along the way, and find yourself wondering whether you can bill the client $150 for your travel time.

>> You can have the client use the Accountant's Copy feature of QuickBooks to send you a copy of the QuickBooks data file. You can review this copy of the data file, make whatever fixes or changes are appropriate, and then send the changes to be made back to the client. The client can easily import these changes into their existing QuickBooks file and go on their merry way. Pretty neat, right?

## Creating an accountant's copy

Your client creates the accountant's copy of the QuickBooks data file by using their version of QuickBooks and the real data file. Then your client creates and sends you a file (through postal mail, email, or some other secure electronic format), or Intuit, the maker of QuickBooks, sends the file to you. Fortunately, the process is very straightforward either way.

## Handling the accountant's copy manually

Here's what your client needs to do if the client will take care of sending the file to you:

1. **Choose the File ➪ Create Copy command.**

   QuickBooks displays the Save Copy or Backup dialog box (see Figure 1-4), asking the client whether they want one of the following:

   - A backup copy of the file, which is a duplicate second copy of the QuickBooks file

   - A portable copy of the file, which is a real live copy of the QuickBooks data file that's been slightly scrunched in size so that it's easier to move around (such as by emailing the file as an attachment)

   - An accountant's copy of the file, which is what I talk about in the opening paragraph of this discussion about the accountant's copy, so I won't repeat myself here

2. **Select Accountant's Copy and then click Next to continue.**

3. **Confirm the choice of Accountant's Copy and click Next.**

   QuickBooks displays another dialog box to insist that your poor stressed-out client confirm that they really want an accountant's copy (see Figure 1-5) rather than simply a portable copy of the file.

4. **Specify a dividing date.**

   When a client clicks the Next button to continue with the creation of an accountant's copy, QuickBooks asks them for the dividing date. Transactions falling before this date can be edited *only* inside the accountant's copy. Transactions falling after this date can be edited inside both the accountant's copy *and* the client's copy.

**5. Click Next to continue.**

Another message appears, telling the client that QuickBooks must close all the windows to create an accountant's copy.

**6. Click OK.**

QuickBooks displays an updated Save Accountant's Copy dialog box, shown in Figure 1-6.

**7. Name the accountant's copy.**

Use the File Name box of the Save Accountant's Copy dialog box to name the accountant's copy of the QuickBooks data file. If necessary, the client can also use the Save In drop-down list to specify where the accountant's copy of the QuickBooks data file should be saved.

TIP

The client needs to remember where the accountant's copy of the file gets saved. This file is given to the accountant — via email or snail mail, or on a flash drive — so they can use it.

**8. Create the file.**

After the client names the accountant's copy of the data file and indicates, if necessary, where the accountant's copy should be saved, they click Save. QuickBooks saves an accountant's copy of the QuickBooks data file.

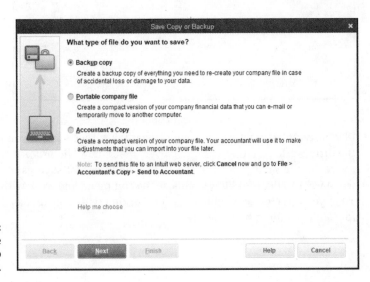

**FIGURE 1-4:**
The first Save Copy or Backup dialog box.

Then this data file is transmitted to the accountant *by the client*. In other words, the client needs to snail-mail or email the file.

Email providers may limit the size of attachments (including QuickBooks files) that can be sent via email. If the size thing fouls up the email, the client can upload the QuickBooks file to the Intuit website by choosing File ⇨ Send Company File ⇨ Accountant's Copy ⇨ Client Activities ⇨ Send to Accountant. Intuit sends the accountant a message with a clickable link that they can use to grab the file.

**TECHNICAL STUFF**

Accountant's copies use three file types. The Accountant Transfer File (with the .qbx file extension) is what a client creates and gives to the accountant. The actual accountant's copy (with the .qba file extension) is what the accountant works with after they open the Accountant Transfer File. Finally, there's the Accountant Export File (with the .qby file extension), which holds the changes that go back to the client.

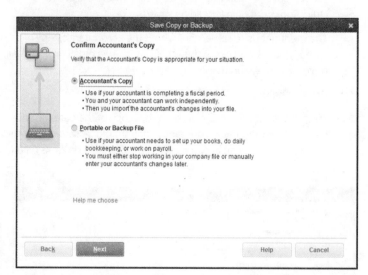

**FIGURE 1-5:**
The second Save Copy or Backup dialog box.

Obviously, it may not be your client who takes these steps; you may have to do the dirty work. In either case, however, that's how the process works. Note that the real-time savings for the accountant and the cost savings to the client occur when you can get the client to choose the command and work with the dialog box. Then you can charge billable time for working with QuickBooks data rather than for fiddle-faddling with the file.

**FIGURE 1-6:**
The final Save
Accountant's
Copy dialog box.

## Sending the accountant's copy electronically

Your client can also send a copy of the QuickBooks accountant's copy electronically by using Intuit's file transfer service. To do this, the client chooses File ⇨ Send Company File ⇨ Accountant's Copy ⇨ Client Activities ⇨ Send to Accountant. QuickBooks provides onscreen instructions for sending, or uploading, the accountant's copy to the Intuit server, including the steps for adding a password to secure the uploaded file.

After the accountant's copy is uploaded, the Intuit server sends the accountant an email message with a link that they can use to download the accountant's copy file. As noted, the client provides a password to restrict access to the downloaded file, so the accountant needs this password from the client before the download. The accountant also needs any QuickBooks password to open the downloaded file.

**TIP**

You want to use the Send Company File command or have your clients use the Send Company File command if you can. The Send Company File command saves you much wailing and gnashing of teeth. It also provides a highly secure way to share accountant's copies. The only problem that I've encountered with the process, in fact, is that the link in the email message you get from Intuit expires after a few days. Accordingly, if your client sends you the file on the first day of your two-week vacation, the link won't work when you get back to the office. The link will have expired.

**TIP**

Because the links Intuit sends you do expire after a few days, in our CPA office, we try to avoid having clients send us their QuickBooks files via the Send Company File command. Instead, we ask clients to upload their QuickBooks files to our www.sharefile.com portal. You may want to provide the same alternative to your clients.

## Using an accountant's copy

Whether the client transmits an accountant's copy manually, emails an accountant's copy, or sends an accountant's copy via the Intuit file transfer service, you use the accountant's copy by choosing File ⇨ Send Company File ⇨ Accountant's Copy ⇨ Open & Convert Transfer File. When you choose this command, QuickBooks displays a series of message boxes explaining how you work with the accountant's copy. To move back and forth through the message boxes, click Next and Back. After you click Next in the last message box, QuickBooks displays the Open Accountant's Copy Transfer File dialog box (not shown).

Use the Look In drop-down list to identify the location of the accountant's copy. If necessary, enter the filename of the accountant's copy in the File Name box. When you click Open, QuickBooks prompts you to name the accountant's copy and then opens the accountant's copy. Note that you won't be able to make the same changes in an accountant's copy that you can make in a regular QuickBooks data file. QuickBooks limits the sorts of changes that you can make in an accountant's copy.

## Reusing an accountant's copy

If you've already opened an accountant's copy file, you can reuse the file by choosing File ⇨ Open Previous Company. When you do, QuickBooks displays a list of the company files (including accountant's copy files) that you've worked with previously. When you click the accountant's copy you want to work with, QuickBooks opens the data file so that you can continue performing your magic.

## Exporting client changes

After you've used an accountant's copy to correct transactions or to enter new transactions, you export the changes so that they can be imported into the client's data file later. To do this, choose File ⇨ Send Company File ⇨ Accountant's Copy ⇨ View/Export Changes for Client. QuickBooks first displays a window that lists the changes you made to the accountant's copy (not shown). Note that you can print this list or create a .pdf file of it by clicking the Print or Save As PDF button.

If you click the Create Change File for Client button, QuickBooks displays the Save Accountant's Export to dialog box (not shown). This dialog box works like a standard Windows dialog box for saving a file or document. You use the Save In drop-down list to identify the location of the changes file. Then use the File Name box to give the file a unique name. When you click Save, QuickBooks saves the changes that you've made to a file. Later, you import this file, or have the client import this file, into the QuickBooks data file.

If you click the Send Changes to Client button, QuickBooks displays the Save Accountant's Changes dialog box (also not shown). This dialog box collects the information necessary to send the client an email with instructions about how to import the accountant changes and a link the client can use to retrieve the actual accountant's changes. One neat thing about this option is that QuickBooks tells the accountant when the client grabs the changes.

**WARNING**

You don't keep your accountant's copy of the data file. In other words, the accountant's copy is a temporary copy of the data file that you use to identify and create a set of changes necessary to update or correct the client's records. After you make the changes, you export the changes to a changes file. Then the client imports those changes (as discussed in the next section). If you make changes again sometime in the near future, you have the client create a new — a *brand-new* — accountant's copy.

**TIP**

To identify when you're working with an accountant's copy, QuickBooks displays the parenthetical phrase *(Accountant's Copy)* along the top of the QuickBooks program window. QuickBooks also identifies regular QuickBooks data files for which accountant's copies have been created by adding the parenthetical phrase *(Accountant's Copy Exists)*. This phrase appears only on the QuickBooks program window title bar from the point when the client creates the accountant's copy to the point when the client imports changes from the accountant's copy.

## Importing accountant's changes

Your client imports the changes that you've made in the accountant's copy of the data file into their working copy of the data file. To do this, the client chooses File ⇨ Send Company File ⇨ Accountant's Copy ⇨ Client Activities ⇨ Import Accountant's Changes.

QuickBooks displays the Import Accountant's Changes dialog box, shown in Figure 1-7. To use the Import Accountant's Changes dialog box, the client uses the Look In drop-down list to identify the location of the changes file. After the client identifies the location — this may be a disc with the changes file on it — they should be able to see the change file in the middle of the Import Accountant's Changes dialog box. The client can double-click the change file to import the changes into their QuickBooks data file. QuickBooks, by the way, displays a window that highlights the accountant's changes to the file for the client.

FIGURE 1-7:
The Import
Accountant's
Changes
dialog box.

QuickBooks prompts the client to back up the QuickBooks data file. I don't describe that process here, but I go into a lot of detail about how to back up a data file in Book 7, Chapter 2.

TIP

After the client imports the changes, QuickBooks removes the parenthetical phrase *(Accountant's Copy Exists)* from the QuickBooks program window title bar.

## Canceling accountant's changes

Here's a little question for you: What happens if the client gives you an accountant's copy of the QuickBooks data file and then realizes that you won't be making changes or that they don't want to accept the changes? Bummer, right? Well, not really.

When a client creates an accountant's copy of the QuickBooks data file, Quick-Books marks the client's data file as one that can be modified through the accountant's changes. QuickBooks does this to allow the accountant's changes later. But if those changes won't be made, the client unmarks the data file as available for changes. To do this, the client chooses File ⇨ Send Company File ⇨ Accountant's Copy ⇨ Client Activities ⇨ Remove Restrictions. When the client chooses this command, QuickBooks displays a message indicating that the client is choosing to cancel out of accountant's-copy mode. After the client chooses this command, they won't be able to import any changes created by using the canceled accountant's copy.

## Troubleshooting accountant's copy transfers

Let me leave you with one last comment concerning accountant's copies. Quite honestly, we've sometimes found the accountant's copy system to be a little . . . er, impractical. Yes, yes, if all goes well, your client gets your journal entries into their QuickBooks with just a few clicks. But obtaining and then opening accountant's transfer files sometimes doesn't work smoothly. (Usually, the lack of smoothness stems from someone sending us an accountant's copy created with the version of QuickBooks released while *Seinfeld* was still running in prime time.)

**TIP**

Our work-around? If we can't easily get an accountant's copy to work, we ask for a backup copy of the client's QuickBooks data file. That backup copy is nearly always easy to get open. Then we print out the journal entries that the clients need to enter on their own into their data file.

# Using the Client Data Review Commands

Before this chapter ends, let me mention the Client Data Review command, which is available in the Accountant Edition versions of QuickBooks Premier and Quick-Books Enterprise Solutions.

Choose Accountant ➪ Client Data Review ➪ Client Data Review to display the Client Data Review – Start Review dialog box. This dialog box starts you on a multiple-step process that walks you through the cleanup of a client's Quick-Books data file, including utilities for finding and fixing unapplied customer and vendor payments and credits (a bane of bookkeepers everywhere), for performing wholesale reclassifications of transactions (useful for undoing wholesale errors), for cleaning up undeposited funds accounts and bad payroll liability account balances (common problems), and for writing off uncollectible invoices.

If you're using an Accountant Edition of QuickBooks and want some tools that clean up some poor client's bookkeeping mess quickly, check out these self-explanatory tools.

**TIP**

If you're not using an Accountant Edition of QuickBooks, you may want to consider signing up as a QuickBooks Certified ProAdvisor just to get an Accountants Edition copy of QuickBooks. Note that the QuickBooks Certified ProAdvisor training covers the Client Data Review tools in detail.

IN THIS CHAPTER

» **Working with good information**

» **Creating a report**

» **Navigating the Report window**

» **Changing a report**

» **Processing multiple reports**

» **Retaining documents**

# Chapter **2**

# Preparing Financial Statements and Reports

QuickBooks produces — oh, I don't know — about 100 different financial statements and reports. I tried to count them for purposes of writing this chapter but lost track after I'd counted 90-some reports. I figured that was close enough for my purposes here.

Because QuickBooks contains so many reports, I don't provide individualized descriptions of each report in this chapter. Rather, I talk about some of the stuff that you need to do before you prepare financial statements. After covering those basics, I talk about how you produce and modify reports, and about some of the useful tools that QuickBooks supplies for working with reports.

# Some Wise Words Up Front

This point is an obvious one, but you should note that the reports you produce in QuickBooks are only as good as the data file. If you have good rich information in your QuickBooks data file, if the file doesn't contain too many mistakes, and if all the transactions are entered, your reports should be pretty darn good.

This simple observation has one important ramification: Often, the first step in preparing good financial statements and useful reports is collecting all the data. In other words, you want to make sure that you've entered all the invoices, purchase orders, checks, and so forth. You also want to make sure that any special accounting transactions, such as for depreciation or asset sales or accruals, have been entered. (Perhaps you need your accountant's help for this task.)

The other chapters in Book 4 talk about how to collect and record all sorts of information, so there's no need to talk more about that here. But to beat this thing to death, the first step in producing a good financial statement or a good report is collecting the right information.

# Producing a Report

As I mention at the beginning of this chapter, QuickBooks provides more than 100 financial statements and accounting reports. You get to these reports by opening the Reports menu. The Reports menu arranges reports in roughly a dozen categories, including Company & Financial, Customers & Receivables, Sales, Jobs, and Time & Mileage.

To produce just about any of the reports available through the Reports menu, select the Report category. If you want to produce a standard financial statement, such as a profit and loss statement, you choose the Reports ⇨ Company & Financial command. QuickBooks displays the Company & Financial submenu, which lists the various types of financial statements available.

You pick the submenu command that describes the financial statement you want. If you want a standard profit and loss financial statement, choose Reports ⇨ Company & Financial ⇨ Profit & Loss Standard. After you choose that command, QuickBooks displays the Report window for the report that you selected, as shown in Figure 2-1.

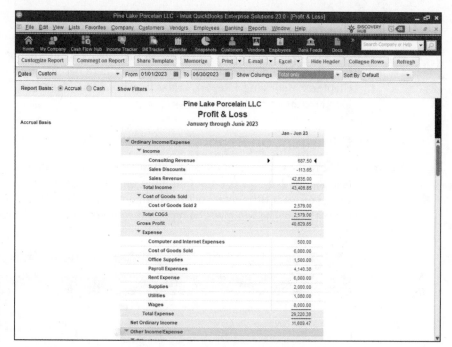

**FIGURE 2-1:**
The Report
window, showing
a profit and loss
statement.

# Working with the Report Window

If you're comfortable working with Microsoft Windows, working with the Quick-
Books Report window should be a snap. Typically, a report won't fit within a
window because it contains too much data. In this case, however, QuickBooks
adds scroll bars, both vertical and horizontal, that you can use to scroll the window around. Pretty straightforward, right?

Along the top edge of the window, QuickBooks displays buttons and boxes. You use
these buttons and boxes to change the display of the Report window and to control
the information shown in the Report window. In the next section, I describe each
of these buttons and boxes.

## Working with Report window buttons

The Report window typically provides ten buttons: Customize Report, Comment
on Report, Share Template, Memorize, Print, E-mail, Excel, Hide Header, Collapse, and Refresh. You can find out what these command buttons do by experi-
mentation. If you don't have time for that, read the following sections.

## Customize Report

The Customize Report button displays the Modify Report dialog box. I won't go into any detail about this command button here because a later section of this chapter, "Modifying a Report," talks in gritty detail about how you use this command button to customize a report.

## Comment on Report

Clicking the Comment on Report button displays the Comment on Report window (see Figure 2-2). To use the Comment on Report dialog box, you click a report value you want to annotate with a comment. QuickBooks opens a comment box at the bottom of the window. You type your comment and then click the Save button.

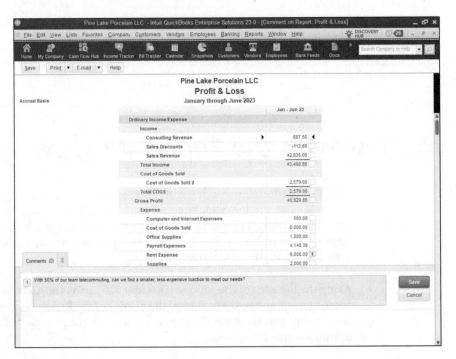

**FIGURE 2-2:**
The Comment on Report window.

When you're done commenting on the report, you need to save the annotated report. Do so by clicking the Save button in the upper-left corner of the screen. QuickBooks asks you to save the report using a unique report name. Later, when you print the report, you can include your comments. (This tool is great for accountants and bookkeepers who want to explain what numbers mean to other readers of the financial statements.) You print a saved commented report by choosing the report from the Reports ➪ Commented Reports submenu.

## Share Template

The Share Template button, which QuickBooks enables after you've customized a report in some way, lets you share your customized report settings (not the data) with other QuickBooks users. When you click this button, QuickBooks displays the Share Template dialog box (not shown). Use the dialog box to give your report template a name (ideally a *clever* name, please), describe your customized report with a few choice words, provide your name and email address and use the option buttons provided to indicate whether you want to remain anonymous. When you click Share, QuickBooks uploads your report template to an Intuit website, where other people can grab the template and use it.

## Memorize

The Memorize button displays the Memorize Report dialog box, shown in Figure 2-3. This dialog box lets you memorize, or save, a particular set of report creation settings. After you memorize these settings, you can produce exactly the same report by choosing the memorized report from the Reports ⇨ Memorized Reports submenu.

**FIGURE 2-3:**
The Memorize
Report
dialog box.

TIP

You can save a memorized report in the Memorized Report Group. To do this, select the Save in Memorized Report Group check box. Then use the Save in Memorized Report Group drop-down list to select the report group in which the memorized report should be saved.

## Print

The Print command button on the top menu bar displays a drop-down list with two options: Report and Save As PDF. If you choose Report, QuickBooks (sometimes after a bit of annoyance) displays the Print Reports dialog box, shown in Figure 2-4, which lets you choose how the report should print and where it should print. The Settings tab, for example, lets you choose the printer, select a page orientation (either portrait or landscape), specify whether you want to print only a range of the report's pages, control page breaking, and adjust the dimensions (width and height) of the report. If you choose Save As PDF by clicking the drop-down arrow to the right of the Print button, QuickBooks displays the Save Document As PDF dialog box, which lets you create a PDF of report document.

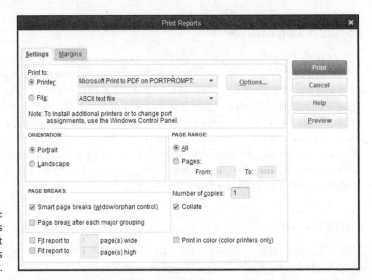

FIGURE 2-4:
The Settings
tab of the Print
Reports
dialog box.

The Margins tab of the Print Reports dialog box, shown in Figure 2-5, lets you specify the margins that QuickBooks should use on the printed report pages. You specify the top, right, bottom, and left margins in inches.

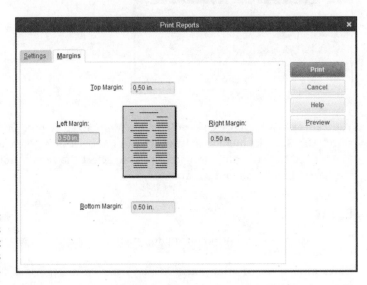

FIGURE 2-5:
The Margins
tab of the Print
Reports
dialog box.

TIP

Click the Preview button to display the Preview window, which shows what your printed report pages look like. The window also includes buttons that let you page to the previous and next pages of the report, zoom in and out on the report, and print the report.

After you've used the Settings tab and the Margins tab to specify how QuickBooks should print a report, click Print. QuickBooks sends the report to your printer.

## E-mail

The E-mail command button lets you email a Microsoft Excel workbook version of a report or a PDF version of a report to someone else as an email attachment.

## Excel

If you click the Excel button, QuickBooks displays a submenu from which you can choose Create New Worksheet or Update Existing Worksheet. Choose Create New Worksheet to display the Send Report to Excel dialog box, shown in Figure 2-6. This dialog box lets you take the information in a report and copy it to a file that a spreadsheet program, such as Excel, can easily open. You can send the copy to a new Excel spreadsheet, to an existing Excel spreadsheet, or to a .csv (comma-separated values) file, which can be opened by just about any spreadsheet or database program.

**FIGURE 2-6:**
The Send
Report to Excel
dialog box.

To copy the report to a new workbook, select the Create New Worksheet radio button. From there, you have the option to create a new Excel spreadsheet (click the In New Workbook option) or a new sheet in an existing file by using the In Existing Workbook radio button; then enter the path and name of the workbook in the text box that QuickBooks opens after you select the radio button. (If you don't know the path and name of the workbook, click the Browse button and then use the dialog box that QuickBooks displays to locate the workbook file.)

If you want to copy the report to an existing Excel spreadsheet, select the Update an Existing Worksheet radio button. QuickBooks causes Excel to refresh the previously exported workbook.

If you want to replace an existing Excel spreadsheet with the new report you're sending to Excel, select the Replace an Existing Worksheet radio button. Then, when QuickBooks opens a text box and adds the Browse button, either enter the path and name of the workbook in the text box or click the Browse button, navigate to the workbook, and select it.

**TECHNICAL STUFF**

Finally, if you want to copy the report information to a .csv file (a file format that can be opened by any spreadsheet or database program), select the Create a Comma Separated Values (.csv) File radio button.

If you click the Advanced command button on the Send Report to Excel dialog box, QuickBooks displays the Advanced Excel Options dialog box, shown in Figure 2-7. This dialog box allows you to control what formatting QuickBooks copies to Excel (do this with the QuickBooks Options check boxes), turn certain Excel formatting features on or off (do this with the Excel Options check boxes), and set up some preliminary workbook printing information in Excel (do this with the Printing Options radio buttons). All this stuff relates to how Excel works. If you're comfortable working with Excel, make the changes that you want. If you aren't comfortable working with Excel, accept QuickBooks's default suggestions. You can change all this stuff later, and rather easily, in Excel.

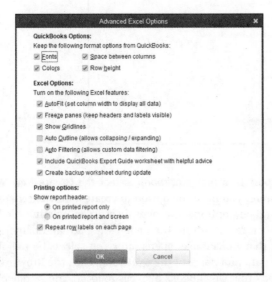

**FIGURE 2-7:**
The Advanced Excel Options dialog box.

TIP

If you're working with QuickBooks, know that Excel is a wonderful tool for digging deeper into your data. In fact, in several chapters of this book, I assume that you're going to exchange information between Excel and QuickBooks. If you've never done this, or if you haven't read those chapters yet, consider acquiring Excel and then taking the time to learn that powerful spreadsheet product. Also note that next time you buy a PC, you may have the option of getting Microsoft Office as part of the purchase price. Excel comes with Office.

## Hide Header

The Hide Header button and the Collapse button change the way that the report appears in the Report window and, if printed, on the page.

You click the Hide Header button to remove the header information, such as the company name. If you hide the header, you can click the Hide Header button again to replace the header.

## Collapse

The Collapse button collapses detail in a report. QuickBooks doesn't show subaccounts in a collapsed report — only accounts.

To uncollapse a report that you previously collapsed, click the Expand button. QuickBooks replaces the Collapse button with the Expand button when the Report window shows a collapsed report.

TIP

Don't spend any time trying to figure out what the Hide Header and Collapse/ Expand buttons do. If you have a question, simply display a report in the Report window and click the command button about which you have a question. The changes in the Report window show you what the command button does.

## Refresh

The Refresh button tells QuickBooks to update a report's information for changes in the QuickBooks data file. This sounds crazy at first, but you can actually leave report windows open. Suppose that a report window shows a profit and loss statement from a week ago. If you've entered several transactions in the past week, the report data may no longer be correct. When you click the Refresh button, QuickBooks knows that it should update the report with the most recent changes.

TIP

QuickBooks typically prompts you to update a report for changes to the QuickBooks data file. If you don't follow QuickBooks's suggestion to update, however, you can click Refresh later to update.

# Using the Report window controls

The Report window provides five controls: Dates, From, To, Columns, and Sort By. These boxes also enable you to control the information shown in the Report window and the appearance of the information. The Report Basis radio button allows you to show the report on an accrual basis or a cash basis. Next to the Report Basis radio button is a Show Filters link in blue text; click this link to see what information the report is filtering.

## Dates, From, and To

The Dates, From, and To controls let you tell QuickBooks what reporting interval you want to show in the report. In other words, you use these boxes to tell QuickBooks the month, quarter, year, or whatever period for which you want to prepare a report.

## Show Columns

The Show Columns drop-down list displays a set of column choices. By default, QuickBooks displays a single total column for a report based on the time period you select. If you produce a report that summarizes annual income and expense data, for example, you can use the Columns drop-down list to tell QuickBooks that you want to see monthly columns. In this situation, QuickBooks shows an annual income statement, but it also shows columns for January, February, March, and so forth, providing some more detail on a certain time period, customer, or vendor. To see how this works, take a look at Figure 2-8. The profit and loss statement in the window is composed of the first quarter, showing months January, February, and March.

Now take a look at Figure 2-9, which shows the same profit and loss statement, except this time, the Show Columns drop-down list shows Customer:Job. In this case, QuickBooks shows you a breakdown of your income and expenses by Customer and Job, as well as the total. The Show Columns drop-down list gives you a bunch of column options. Typically, some options make sense for the report that you're working on; others won't. Nevertheless, you should experiment with this tool occasionally. The Show Columns drop-down list often gives you a neat way to further segregate and refine your data.

## Sort By

The Sort By drop-down list enables you to choose how information should be ordered in a report. For many types of reports, the Sort By drop-down list doesn't provide any meaningful options. For other types of reports, however, the Sort By drop-down list provides handy ways to organize report information.

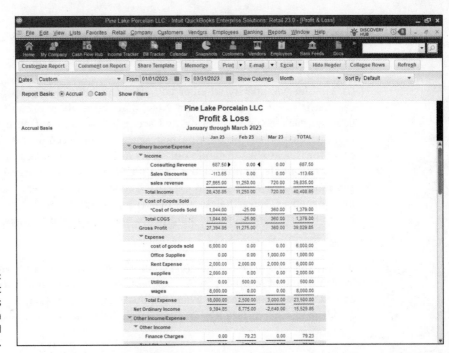

**FIGURE 2-8:**
A simple profit
and loss
statement with
a single Total
column.

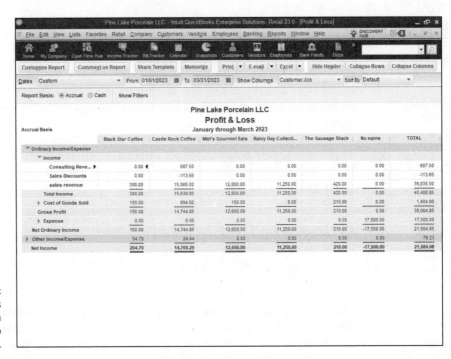

**FIGURE 2-9:**
A profit and loss
statement with
Customer:Job
columns.

### Report Basis

A new feature this year allows you to toggle directly between accrual basis and cash basis on the report. The Report Basis option buttons — Accrual and Cash — let you specify whether you want QuickBooks to prepare a report on a cash basis or on an accrual basis. Now, quite honestly, you can't simply convert between cash-basis accounting and accrual-basis accounting by clicking these buttons. Cash-basis accounting and accrual-basis accounting are too complicated for QuickBooks to figure out on its own. If you use accrual-basis accounting, for example, you must use the QuickBooks Accounts Payable feature, and you must record revenue and expense transactions when you earn revenue and incur expenses. Nevertheless, the Report Basis buttons enable you to flip quickly between cash-centric profit statements and accrual-like financial statements, and that's pretty handy.

TIP

In a nutshell, *cash-basis accounting* counts income and expense when cash moves into and out of a business. *Accrual-basis accounting* counts income when it's earned and counts expense when it's incurred. Book 1, Chapter 1 talks in more detail about the differences between cash-basis accounting and accrual-basis accounting.

# Modifying a Report

If you click the Customize Report button, QuickBooks displays the Modify Report dialog box, which you can use to customize a report. When you customize a report, you change the report's appearance, its layout, and the information that it summarizes.

TIP

The Modify Report dialog box looks different for different report types. Nevertheless, if you look past the cosmetic differences, all the dialog boxes look and work pretty much the same way.

## Using the Display tab

The Display tab of the Modify Report dialog box lets you control the report interval date, the report basis, the columns, and some other formatting.

The Report Date Range controls — Dates, From, and To — do the same thing as the Dates, From, and To boxes in the Report window. These boxes let you control the reporting interval or accounting period. You can choose one of the date descriptions from the Dates drop-down list, or you can use the From and To boxes to specify a particular range of dates. The From and To boxes, shown in Figure 2-10, accept dates in mm/dd/yyyy format.

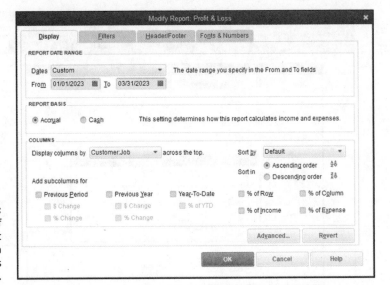

**FIGURE 2-10:**
The Display tab of
the Modify Report
dialog box for a
profit and loss
statement.

The Columns area enables you to control or specify how many columns a report should display. The Display Columns By drop-down list is analogous to the Columns drop-down list in the Report window. The Columns area also lets you choose a Sort By option. Again, this is analogous to the Sort By drop-down list in the Report window.

In addition, the Columns area allows you to add subcolumns (by using the Previous Period, Previous Year, and Year-to-Date check boxes) and add percentages. The neat thing about these percentages is that you're actually adding financial ratios to your financial statement. I don't talk about financial ratios in this chapter, but I do go into great detail in Book 5, Chapter 1 about what financial ratios are and how powerful they can be for assessing and monitoring your financial condition and your financial performance.

TIP

To show each line item of an income statement as a percentage of total income, select the % of Income check box.

For more report formatting options, click the Advanced button. QuickBooks displays the Advanced Options dialog box, shown in Figure 2-11. Use the Display Rows radio buttons to tell QuickBooks when it should or shouldn't display rows of information in a report. Similarly, use the Display Columns radio buttons to tell QuickBooks when it should or shouldn't display columns in a report. You can use the Reporting Calendar radio buttons to select the default annual reporting period. The default year can be a fiscal year (you set this option when setting up QuickBooks), a calendar year, or an income tax year. Click OK to activate these selections.

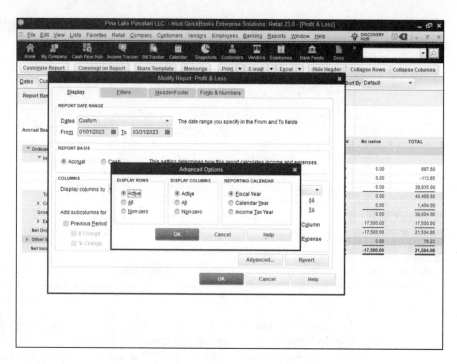

**FIGURE 2-11:**
The Advanced
Options
dialog box.

TIP

To revert to the default display settings, click the Revert button on the Display tab (refer to Figure 2-10).

## Using the Filters tab

The Filters tab, shown in Figure 2-12, is probably the most interesting and useful tab provided by the Modify Report dialog box. This tab enables you to set up filters that you can use to specify what information gets summarized in the report. To use the Filters tab, first select the field on which you want to base a filter from the Filter list box. If you want to filter information based on the account, for example, select Account in the Filter list box.

After you identify the piece of data on which you want to base your filter, open the drop-down list next to the filter. If you selected an account filter, for example, QuickBooks names this drop-down list Account. When you open the drop-down list, QuickBooks displays a set of filtering choices. Figure 2-13 shows common filtering choices available when you're creating an account filter: All Income/Expense Accounts, All Ordinary Income/Expense, All Ordinary Income/COGS, and so forth. You can pick a standard account filter from this list.

Alternatively, you can choose, for example, the multiple-accounts entry from the drop-down list. In this case, QuickBooks displays the Select Account dialog box, shown in Figure 2-14. This dialog box lets you select, on an individual basis, the accounts you want to appear in the report. If you want to create a report based purely on a checking account, an accounts receivable account, and an inventory asset account, you use the Select Account dialog box to select these accounts. To select the accounts that you want, click them. QuickBooks identifies selected accounts with a check mark.

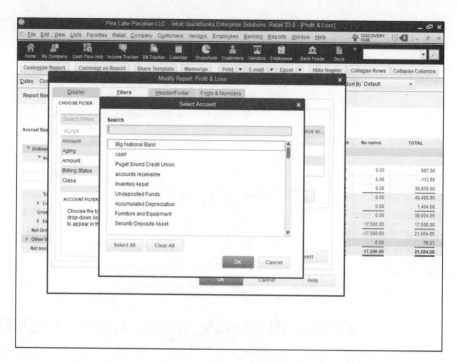

FIGURE 2-14:
The Select
Account
dialog box.

Other fields and boxes on the Filters tab are pretty self-explanatory. The Include Split Detail? option buttons, available for account-based filters, let you tell Quick-Books whether it should include split transaction information. The Current Filter Choices list identifies what report filters are used for the report. You can remove a filter by selecting it from the Current Filter Choices list and then clicking the Remove Selected Filter button. You can also revert to the default filter by clicking the Revert button. Note that different boxes appear on the Filters tab for different filters.

## Using the Header/Footer tab

The Header/Footer tab, shown in Figure 2-15, controls what header and footer information appears on your report. You use the Show Header Information check boxes to control the report header. If you want your company name to appear at the top of the report, for example, select the Company Name check box. And if you want to change the company name that appears at the top of the report, edit the contents of the Company Name text box. The other Show Header Information check boxes work the same way. To remove the report title from the report, deselect the Report Title check box. To use a different report title, edit the contents of the Report Title text box.

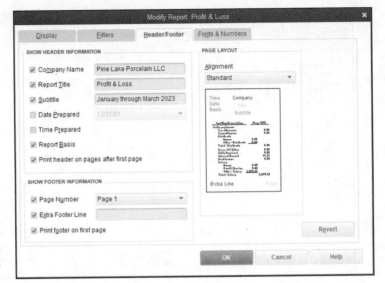

FIGURE 2-15:
The Header/
Footer tab of the
Modify Report
dialog box.

Use the Page Layout area — it provides a single Alignment drop-down list — to choose a layout for your report. By default, QuickBooks uses standard alignment. You can also choose left alignment, right alignment, or centered alignment. QuickBooks shows you how the report layout changes depending on the selected alignment.

**TIP**

As is the case with the other tabs of the Modify Report dialog box, you can click the Revert button to change back to the default header/footer settings.

## Formatting fonts and numbers

The Fonts & Numbers tab, shown in Figure 2-16, lets you change the font for selected pieces of report information. Use the Change Font For list box to select the bit of report information that you want to change. After this selection, click the Change Font button to display a dialog box like the one shown in Figure 2-17. The Column Labels dialog box appears, for example, when you indicate that you want to change the font for column labels. Use the Font combo box to select the font for the column labels. Use the Font Style combo box to select the font style for the column labels. Use the Size combo box to select the point size for the column labels. Optionally, use the Effects check boxes to add or remove special effects. Or get really crazy and use the Color drop-down list to select the color for the piece of report data. When you're finished, verify that your font formatting choices look right by checking out the Sample box; then click OK.

**FIGURE 2-16:**
The Fonts & Numbers tab of the Modify Report dialog box.

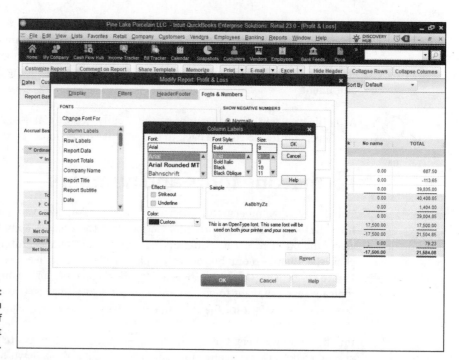

**FIGURE 2-17:**
The Column Labels version of the Change Font dialog box.

**TIP**

When you click OK to close the dialog box used to change a font (refer to Figure 2-16), QuickBooks displays a message box asking whether you want to change all the related fonts. If you do want to change the fonts — and you probably do — click Yes. Note that if you make some change that later turns out to be wrong, you can click the Revert button, which also appears on the Fonts & Numbers tab, to return to the default formatting for fonts and numbers.

The Show Negative Numbers area (refer to Figure 2-16) provides radio buttons and a check box that you can use to instruct QuickBooks to provide special formatting for negative values. Typically, QuickBooks shows negative values with a minus sign in front of the value. Alternatively, you can tell QuickBooks to place parentheses around the negative values (select the In Parentheses radio button) or to display them with a trailing minus sign (select the With a Trailing Minus radio button). You can also use color to flag negative numbers (select the In Bright Red check box).

The Show All Numbers area provides three check boxes that you can use to clean up and simplify your report. If your business is large enough that your report values are very large, select the Divided by 1000 check box. In that case, QuickBooks divides all the report values by 1,000 to make them easier to read. If you select the Except Zero Amounts check box, QuickBooks simplifies your report by not showing zero values. Finally, if you select the Without Cents check box, QuickBooks shows only dollars, not cents.

TIP

If you find yourself becoming overwhelmed by the amount of data being presented in a report, the Show All Numbers check boxes provide a handy way to get a somewhat-clearer view of the big picture.

# Processing Multiple Reports

If you choose the Reports ➪ Process Multiple Reports command, QuickBooks displays the Process Multiple Reports dialog box, shown in Figure 2-18. This dialog box enables you to request a bunch of previously memorized or commented on reports at one time. To use this dialog box, first choose a report group from the drop-down list. Next, select the reports within the report group that you want and check them off the list. If QuickBooks shows a report as selected (indicated with a check mark) that you don't want, click the check mark to remove it. Then, for those reports that you've selected, verify that the From and To boxes show the correct report interval.

After you've selected the reports and provided the report interval dates, you can click the Display button to have QuickBooks display the report windows for each of the reports that you've selected. Alternatively, you can click the Print button to have QuickBooks print paper versions of each of the reports that you selected.

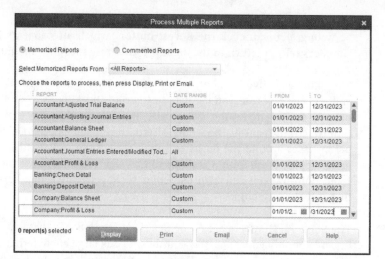

**FIGURE 2-18:**
The Process
Multiple Reports
dialog box.

# A Few Words about Document Retention

People sometimes ask me how long they should keep old reports, copies of invoices, and other bits of accounting information. Unfortunately, I don't really have a one-size-fits-all answer to these questions. I can give you some things to think about, however:

» **Consider whether the other party to a transaction is ever going to want the information.** If you're chronically arguing with a vendor about whether you've paid some bill, for example, it makes sense to hang on to those vendor bills and any records of your payment for as long as the argument may go on. This means that any paperwork that documents vendor bills and payments doesn't necessarily have to be retained if you don't have a problem.

» **Consider tax accounting requirements.** A business is required by law (as a lot of people don't realize) to maintain accounting records to report its profits, losses, income, and deductions to the Internal Revenue Service, so you should maintain anything that you need to calculate your profits or substantiate elements of your calculations. A statute of limitations exists, however, typically running three years from the date you last filed the return. This means that in most cases, you don't need to keep paperwork that's older than three years past the return that it relates to. In other words, if you have data from the year 2019, and you filed the year 2019 tax return on March 15, 2020, by March 16, 2023, you shouldn't (in most cases) need to keep all that old paperwork. The statute of limitations dictates that you should be able to discard the old stuff. A word of caution is in order, however, because a handful of exceptions exist to this three-year statute of limitations:

- If you've been really sloppy and, through your sloppiness, omitted gross income in excess of 25 percent of what your return shows, the statute of limitations equals six years.

- If no return is filed or a fraudulent return is filed, no statute of limitations exists.

- States without income taxes (such as Washington state, where I live and work) use a different set of rules and may use a longer statute of limitations. Washington state, for example, says the statute of limitations runs four years, not three.

>> **Consider the old records that you may need in the future to calculate an item for your tax return.** These records need to be retained. If you bought a factory 30 years ago, for example, keep those purchase records until 3 (or 6) years after you sell the factory.

>> **Consider that in some industries, other document-retention rules or regulations exist.** If you're a physician, you keep your old patient records — and this may include patient accounting information — for longer than three years. These other document-retention rules vary by industry. Find out what the rules are for your industry.

>> **Consider the risk of retaining confidential information too long.** Finally, though you might ponder all the forgoing points and conclude that you should keep your financial records in perpetuity, note that this approach creates risks too. The more financial documentation you archive, the easier in some cases it may be for this information to get lost or stolen. You wouldn't want, for example, to keep so many years' worth of data that you have to rent a warehouse in a bad part of town just to store the stuff.

Summing up, how do you make sense of these vague suggestions? Come up with a rough guess as to how long you think you should hang on to stuff. In my business, subject to the qualifications listed previously, I hang on to stuff for five years. I'm not doing anything criminal, fraudulent, or sloppy, so anything that's over five years old, I toss. By the way, I'm also careful to segregate documents I can throw out by year into boxes. I label the boxes with the year number. I also label the boxes with a note like "Discard in 2024" just so I know when I can toss that stuff out.

**WARNING**

You may want to think twice about simply tossing out financial records. (I'm a little anal about this because I'm a CPA.) I don't actually *toss out* my personal records or any client records, of course: I shred the documents first. You may want to do the same thing.

TIP

By the way, some big-box office-supply stores offer in-store shredding services at reasonable prices. Also, some local governments provide free shredding. Pierce County, in my home state of Washington, for example, no longer accepts shredded paper in its recycling program; instead, it offers free shredding events multiple times throughout the year. Check with your local government to find out whether a similar service is available in your area.

# Chapter **3**

# Preparing a Budget

B udgets provide business owners and managers powerful tools for managing a firm's operation. A budget can give the business owner or manager a way to easily and quantifiably manage the people who work for the business. A budget can often identify problems or opportunities early. Finally, a budget truly gives the owner or manager a way to plan the year's operation, think about what's most important and quantify what the firm should achieve over the year.

For these reasons, this chapter discusses some practical, common-sense approaches to budgeting within QuickBooks. I think you'll be surprised by how straightforward this process is.

## Reviewing Common Budgeting Tactics

Before I get into a detailed discussion of how you create a budget and use that budget within QuickBooks, I want to briefly identify and describe three very useful and common budgeting tactics: top-line budgeting, zero-based budgeting, and benchmarking. None of these three tactics is complicated. You probably know of and understand at least two of them already. You should consider all these tactics, however, as you construct formal or informal budgets for your business.

# Top-line budgeting

A *top-line budget,* which is the simplest budget technique available, takes last year's numbers or last month's numbers and uses them for this year's budget. If inflation has occurred, of course, a top-line budget may inflate last year's or last month's numbers by using an inflation factor. Conversely, if the business has slowed a bit or fallen on hard times, the previous year's or month's numbers may be decreased by some amount.

Although top-line budgeting often receives a bad rap from people who don't like the way it perpetuates the past, top-line budgeting has at least a couple of arguments in its favor:

>> **Top-line budgeting is easy.** Being easy is a big thing in its favor. Other budgeting techniques can be much more work.

>> **Top-line budgeting is based on reality.** The numbers from last year or last month are real. This fact is a unique benefit of top-line budgeting that other budgeting tactics (which I describe in the following paragraphs) don't offer. If you know, for example, that you spent $2,000 on rent last month, the reality of that true, actual number is a very useful starting point for thinking about what you'll spend this month.

Top-line budgeting, however, possesses a well-known weakness: It tends to perpetuate previous bad budgeting decisions. If someone long ago decided to spend $10,000 on an advertisement in some special industry magazine, for example, top-line budgeting may continue to budget that $10,000 annual expense even though it no longer makes sense (or never made sense).

# Zero-based budgeting

*Zero-based budgeting,* which is the opposite of top-line budgeting, works from the bottom up. A zero-based budget starts with individual revenue, expense, asset, liability, and owner's equity accounts. It examines a specific account — postage expense, for example — and then tries to apply common sense and logic in coming up with a good postage-expense budget amount. The budgeter may guess, for example, that the firm will send out 1,000 letters during the year and that the average postage per letter will equal 50 cents. In this case, the zero-based-budgeting approach determines that postage expense for the coming year probably will equal $500. The zero-based budgeter calculates this amount by taking 1,000 letters and multiplying this amount by 50 cents postage cost per letter.

The advantage of zero-based budgeting is that it tends to fix poorly figured, previously budgeted amounts; it doesn't simply perpetuate bad budgeting decisions of the past. New budgeted amounts are based on the application of common sense and simple arithmetic, a combination that often produces pretty good numbers. That's really cool.

Another neat feature of zero-based budgeting is that it makes people who benefit from or use some budgeted amount responsible for that budgeted amount. If some manager spent $50,000 on travel expense last year, top-line budgeting states that they get to spend $50,000 this year. Zero-line budgeting, by contrast, makes the manager prove through the application of common sense and simple arithmetic that $50,000 of travel expense is reasonable for this year.

Zero-based budgeting isn't perfect, however; it possesses a weakness in that it's easy for budgeters to forget numbers or make calculation errors. Previously, I used the example of a budgeter guessing that postage expense for the coming year will be $500. That estimate comes from a guess about the number of letters sent in a year (1,000) and an estimate of the average postage expense for each letter (50 cents). If either of those numbers is wrong, or if (heaven forbid) the budgeter incorrectly multiplies one number by the other, the postage-expense budget number is wrong. If the budgeter is budgeting hundreds or even thousands of budgeted amounts, they'll undoubtedly make a few errors in the process. And they probably won't be able to fix or find those errors because of the volume of budgeted amounts.

# Benchmarking

One very powerful, but unfortunately infrequently used, technique is *benchmarking*, which compares your actual or preliminary budgeted numbers with the numbers of similar-size businesses in your industry. CPA firms spend money on a tax library, for example. Annual fees for a tax library can run from as little as $100 or $200 a year to more than $10,000 a year. (These amounts are fees for a sole proprietor, by the way.) How do you know what number is an appropriate budgeted amount? Well, if you know what other CPA firms or other sole-proprietor CPAs are spending on their tax libraries, that information can probably help you budget what you should or can spend. The challenge, of course, is getting that comparable information.

Fortunately, getting this information is easier than most people realize. You can get information about the financial statistics of comparable firms from two sources:

>> **Your local library:** Usually, you can find several good sources of general financial statistical information about businesses of varying sizes and in varying industries. Dun & Bradstreet, the Risk Management Association,

Robert Morris & Associates, and a fellow named Leo Troy all publish annual summaries of financial ratios and financial statistics based on several sources. If you trot down to the library and visit the reference desk, you can get the librarian's help in locating one or more of these reference sources. Suddenly, you have a wealth of information at your fingertips. You can see how much the average tavern spends on beer and peanuts, for example. You can see how much the average restaurant spends on advertising. In other words, you can see detailed financial information on a business exactly like yours.

» **Industry associations:** In addition to the general information available from reference sources commonly stocked at your local library, many industry associations and professional groups collect and publish industry-specific financial information. One of the first jobs I had early in my career was working as the controller of an electronics manufacturing firm. Our firm was a member of the American Electronics Association. That membership meant that we participated in a survey of financial information of member firms in the association. That survey gave us (and other AEA members) good statistics about average salaries spent for different positions, inventory investment, certain administrative expenses, and so forth.

Continuing with my example of CPAs buying tax libraries, I should mention that two industry associations — the Texas Society of Certified Public Accountants and the American Institute of Certified Public Accountants — publish statistics for CPA firms. These publications identify what the average sole proprietor spends on their tax library. I'll bet you a dill pickle that your industry association — whatever it is — has similar information available. (One other thing about the CPA benchmarking studies: They're online and dynamic, so people who are benchmarking can compare their practices with similar-size firms.)

## Putting it all together

Just for the record — and you've probably already guessed this — you shouldn't use just one approach to build your budget. You may use top-line budgeting for some of your numbers and zero-based budgeting for other numbers. For really important or key numbers in your budget, you may take the time and effort to benchmark your numbers against those of similar-size firms in your industry. Good budgeting, then, involves combining the budgeting tactics described in this chapter to come up with a budget that makes sense and lets you plan your firm's finances for the year.

# Taking a Practical Approach to Budgeting

Business budgeting, unfortunately, isn't simply a matter of listing expected revenue and expense amounts. Typically, you also create a balance sheet. Balance-sheet budgeting is too complicated to do on the back of a cocktail napkin or at the breakfast table in the morning before the kids get up.

Therefore, to create budgeted numbers for a balance sheet, you use a tool and an approach like the one described (in some detail) in Book 6, Chapter 2.

**TIP**

If all you want to budget are revenue amounts and expense amounts, you can do that in a very simple, crude fashion. You *can* list expected revenue amounts by account on the back of a cocktail napkin, for example.

# Using the Set Up Budgets Window

After you've come up with a budget — presumably by using a tool like the one described in Book 6, Chapter 2 and by employing the sorts of budgeting tactics described previously in this chapter — you record your budget in QuickBooks.

## Creating a new budget

To create a new budget in QuickBooks, follow these steps:

1. **Choose Company ⇨ Planning and Budgeting ⇨ Set Up Budgets.**

   QuickBooks opens the Create New Budget dialog box, shown in Figure 3-1, which you use to create a new budget. (Bet you wouldn't have guessed that.)

   *Note:* If you've previously set up a budget, QuickBooks displays the Set Up Budgets window rather than the Create New Budget dialog box. If QuickBooks displays the Set Up Budgets window, you need to click its Create New Budget button to display the Create New Budget dialog box, as discussed in "Working with an existing budget" later in this chapter.

2. **Select the fiscal-year period.**

   Identify the fiscal year you're budgeting for. To do that, enter the fiscal year in the provided text box (refer to Figure 3-1). If you're budgeting for fiscal year 2024, for example, use the buttons to change the year to 2024.

3. **Choose whether to create a profit and loss or balance sheet budget.**

To create a profit and loss budget, select the Profit and Loss radio button, click Next, and proceed to Step 4. To create a balance sheet budget, select the Balance Sheet radio button, click Finish, and skip to Step 5.

Note that you use a different approach for profit and loss budgets and balance sheet budgets. For profit and loss budgets, you budget the amount of revenue or expense expected for the account for the month. For balance sheet budgets, you budget the ending account balance: the ending account balance expected for the asset, liability, or owner's equity account at month's end.

4. **In the Additional Profit and Loss Budget Criteria dialog box (see Figure 3-2), specify additional profit and loss budget criteria and click Next.**

If you chose to create a profit and loss budget in Step 3, select the Customer:Job radio button to further extend your budget to include Job details; select the Class radio button to include classes in your budget; or simply select the No Additional Criteria radio button.

*Note:* To budget by class, you must first turn on class tracking. For more information about class tracking, refer to Book 2, Chapter 3.

5. **In the Create New Budget dialog box (see Figure 3-3), choose whether to create the budget from scratch or previous data.**

To create a budget from scratch and start with a clean slate, select the Create Budget from Scratch radio button. To create a budget based on your actual data from last year, select the radio button titled Create Budget from Previous Year's Actual Data.

6. **Click Finish when you're done.**

QuickBooks displays the Set Up Budgets window (see Figure 3-4).

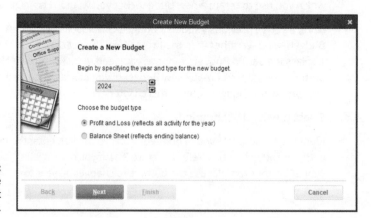

**FIGURE 3-1:** The Create New Budget dialog box.

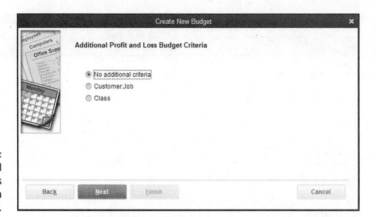

**FIGURE 3-2:**
The Additional
Profit and Loss
Budget Criteria
selections.

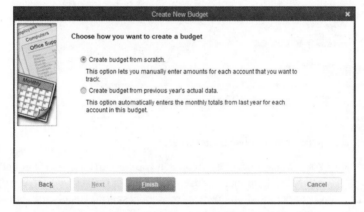

**FIGURE 3-3:**
Choosing
whether to create
a budget from
scratch.

# Working with an existing budget

To edit an existing budget in QuickBooks, follow these steps:

**1.** **Choose Company ⇨ Planning & Budgeting ⇨ Set Up Budgets.**

QuickBooks displays the Set Up Budgets window — the one shown in Figure 3-4. You use this window to record the amount that you expect for each revenue and expense for each month during the year in which you're budgeting.

**2.** **Select a budget or create a new one.**

Choose the budget you want to work with from the Budget drop-down list at the top of the window. To create a new budget (you can have as many budgets as you want), click the Create New Budget button. For help with creating a new budget, see the preceding section.

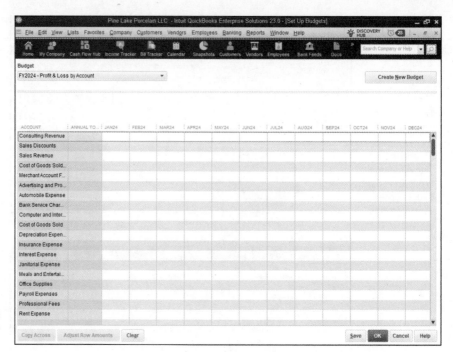

FIGURE 3-4:
The Set Up
Budgets window.

### 3. (Optional) Choose a customer.

You typically budget by account. If you want to budget in finer detail by also estimating amounts for customers, jobs, or classes, you can use the Current Customer:Job drop-down list to identify specific customers from whom you expect revenue or for whom you expend costs.

*Note:* The Customer:Job drop-down list box doesn't appear unless, when you created the budget you're now working with, you indicated that you wanted to budget by customer.

### 4. Record the budgeted amounts for each month of the fiscal year.

Type the amounts you want to budget for each account in the appropriate month columns. Again, remember that revenue and expense accounts are budgeted as the amount expected for the month. Asset, liability, and owner's equity amounts are budgeted as the ending account balance expected for the month.

To copy the budgeted amount for one month into the text boxes for the succeeding months, click the Copy Across button.

### 5. (Optional) Adjust row amounts.

If you find that the yearly total for an account isn't what you want it to be, you can go back and change the amounts for each month so that they add up to the correct total, or you can click the Adjust Row Amounts button. Clicking this button displays the Adjust Row Amounts dialog box, shown in Figure 3-5. Use the Start At drop-down list to choose the month you want to start with (either the first month or the currently selected month). Then choose whether you want to increase or decrease the amounts budgeted and by how much (by entering a dollar amount or a percentage). Click OK when you finish; QuickBooks closes the dialog box.

6. **Repeat as necessary.**

   Repeat Steps 3 through 5 for each account for which you want to record budgeted amounts.

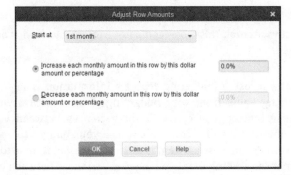

**FIGURE 3-5:**
The Adjust
Row Amounts
dialog box.

Yes, I know, this is a lot of work. Just so you know, in large companies with hundreds or thousands of employees, two or three people spend much of or even all of their year working with the budgeted data.

# Managing with a Budget

After you record your budget in QuickBooks (as described in the earlier section "Using the Set Up Budgets Window"), you can compare your actual financial results with budgeted amounts by choosing commands from the Budgets & Forecasts submenu that QuickBooks displays. When you choose the Reports ⇨ Budgets & Forecasts command, QuickBooks provides several budgeting reports, described in the following list:

» **Budget Overview:** This report summarizes your budgeted amounts. You can use it to look at and error-check your budget.

- » **Budget vs. Actual:** This report lets you compare budgeted income statement information with actual income statement information. The report, therefore, lets you compare your expected revenue and expenses with actual revenue and expenses.

- » **Profit & Loss Budget Performance:** This report lets you compare your actual income, expenses, and profits with your budgeted income, expenses, and profits.

- » **Budget vs. Actual Graph:** This graph isn't a report, but a chart that shows budgeted and actual information.

- » **Forecast Overview:** This report summarizes a QuickBooks forecast. A *forecast* is basically a prediction about your future revenue and cash flow. You use forecasts to do "what if" planning.

- » **Forecast vs. Actual:** This report compares a forecast with what actually happened.

The way that you use a budgeting report's information is key — and also the secret to getting value from your budgeting efforts. With a well-constructed, common-sense budget, you can look for variances between your budget and your actual financial results. You want to use your budget to spot situations in which, for example, an expense item is too low, an asset item is too high, or some revenue number is trailing what you expect. Variances between expected results and actual results indicate unexpected results. Unexpected results often suggest problems . . . or opportunities. Think about the following examples of variance and what the variances may indicate:

- » **Monthly revenue is $40,000 instead of $50,000.** Monthly revenue that's 20 percent less than expected may indicate problems with your product, problems with your sales force, or problems with your customers. In any case, if sales represent only 80 percent of what you expect, you probably need to implement immediate corrective action.

- » **Inventory balances are averaging $50,000 at month's end rather than $100,000 at month's end.** Having a lower-than-expected inventory balance may be good or bad. The ending inventory balance that's half what you expect may indicate that you're selling products much faster than you expected (and that, therefore, you should increase your inventory investment and purchasing of inventory). But having a low inventory investment may also mean that you're simply not getting materials from your vendors as fast as you need them, and as a result, you're at great risk of losing sales because of inadequate stock levels.

>> **Research and development expenses equal $50,000 a year instead of $25,000 a year.** Research and development expenses that are twice what you expect seem to be bad. How can it be good to spend twice as much on an expense as you expect? Doubling your research and development expenditures may be good, however, if you're unexpectedly investing in some promising new product, idea, or technology.

>> **Sales to a particular class of customer are 50 percent higher.** Suppose that you used classes to track sales to customers inside the country and outside the country. If you see that, quite unexpectedly, sales to customers outside the country are 50 percent above what you expect, that variance may indicate an opportunity to sell even more outside the country. Maybe with more effort and energy, outside-the-country customers can become an even larger part of your business. Sometimes, variances identify opportunities that you'd otherwise miss.

# Some Wrap-Up Comments on Budgeting

Before I leave the subject of budgeting, I want to share a handful of final comments:

>> **Budgeting is an example of the old phrase "Plan your work and then work your plan."** Budgets aren't handcuffs. Budgets aren't straitjackets. Budgets are simply planning tools that you use to make thoughtful decisions about your firm's financial affairs for the coming year.

>> **If you aren't getting value from the budgeting process, you shouldn't do it.** Or at the very least, you should change the way you're doing it. No kidding — I won't argue that you should budget if you don't get value from the process. I think, however, that most businesses do get value. If you can manage your business without a budget — and I mention an approach that works for this purpose in a tip at the end of the chapter — I don't think you should budget. You use those tools that deliver the most value to you in managing your firm. For many people, budgeting does just that. If it doesn't for you, skip the work. Time is often the scarcest resource for business owners and managers.

>> **Budgets can be essential tools for managing people with financially quantifiable responsibilities.** Okay, I know budgets have a bad rap, and they aren't perfect, but you know what? If you have people working for you who have responsibilities that you can quantify financially, you can use a budget to manage those people. Suppose that you have salespeople who should

individually sell $25,000 worth of stuff each month. If you budget by salesperson (you probably need to set up a class for each salesperson or a revenue account for each salesperson), you can use a budget to compare actual sales generated by each person with the budgeted sales expected for them. If you look at Joe every month and see that he has $30,000 in sales predictably, you can use that information in your management of Joe. Joe's overproducing probably means that he's doing a good job. If you look at Joe's sister, Julia, and see that she's doing $20,000 in sales every month when you expect her to do $25,000 in sales, you probably see a problem and an opportunity for improvement. All this makes sense, right?

>> **People who like to budget tend (in my experience) to focus on unfavorable variances.** I mention this example because although unfavorable variances often identify problems that need to be corrected, favorable variances sometimes are more interesting and more useful to dissect. Suppose that you have a business in which you expect salespeople to generate $25,000 in sales a month. If Monique is generating $75,000 a month in sales, that's pretty darn interesting. Monique probably knows something or has skills or an approach that the other salespeople don't have. Perhaps, with just a little bit of luck, you can figure out why Monique does so well — and then use this new knowledge to get your other salespeople to sell more stuff each month.

>> **The key budgeting numbers to watch are often a pretty small set.** Although a budget according to QuickBooks (and, I guess, Steve Nelson) may have hundreds of numbers, you may be able to manage your business just fine by looking at just a handful of numbers. Maybe in your business, everything comes down to sales. If sales drive everything else — your expenses and, of course, all your profits — you may not have much reason to track the amount that you're spending each month on your telephone bill or postage expense. If you can distill your financial plan to a few numbers that you need to watch, you can make your budgeting and financial analyses much simpler. All you do is identify the key financial statistics to watch — and then watch them regularly.

**TIP**

Financial ratios are often very useful tools for monitoring a firm's financial performance. I know several business owners who successfully manage their businesses without a formal budget by looking at two or three items, including cost of goods sold and gross margin percentages. *Cost of goods sold* includes the cost of the products or items being sold. *Gross margin percentage* is the percentage of sales left over after paying for the cost of goods sold. To dig into these terms and find out about working with financial ratios, see Book 5, Chapter 1.

# Chapter **4**

# Using Activity-Based Costing

A *ctivity-based costing* (ABC for short) may be the best new accounting idea in the past three decades. No, I must amend that: Activity-based costing *is* the best new idea in accounting in the past three decades.

ABC gives businesses a better way to estimate the profits of products and services, which is more important than you may think. The problem in many businesses is that overhead expenses or operating expenses don't cleanly tie to products or services. Without good allocation of overhead or operating expenses, businesses can't accurately determine which products make money and which don't.

ABC addresses this problem by using the power of the computer (QuickBooks, in this example) to trace overhead costs directly to products and services. Surprisingly, ABC accomplishes this task in a pretty straightforward, simple fashion. In this chapter, I show you what I mean.

# Reviewing Traditional Overhead Allocation

To really understand the contribution that ABC makes, you need to understand how overhead allocation traditionally works. To give you an example, take a look at Table 4-1, which is the same simple income statement that I show in several chapters throughout the book.

TABLE 4-1

## A Simple Income Statement

| | |
|---|---|
| Sales Revenue | $13,000 |
| Less: Cost of goods sold | 3,000 |
| Gross margin | $10,000 |
| Operating expenses | |
| Rent | $1,000 |
| Wages | 4,000 |
| Supplies | 1,000 |
| Total operating expenses | 6,000 |
| *Operating Profit* | *$4,000* |

As you may recall, this simple income statement shows the profit for an imaginary hot-dog-stand business that you operate on the opening day of baseball season in your city.

Suppose that in this imaginary business, you sell two products: a regular hot dog for $2.50 and a super-duper chili dog for $4. Suppose also that you sell 2,000 of both of these products. Therefore, the $13,000 of revenue shown in Table 4-1 actually represents $5,000 in sales of regular hot dogs and $8,000 in sales of chili dogs.

Further suppose that you can break down the cost of goods sold as follows:

>> **Buns:** Each bun cost you 15 cents. This means that you spent $300 on buns for regular dogs and $300 on buns for the chili dogs.

>> **Dogs:** Each hot dog cost you 40 cents. This means that you spent $800 on hot dogs for the regular hot dog product line and another $800 on hot dogs for the chili dog product line.

>> **Chili:** Each serving of chili for the chili dogs cost you 40 cents. (A serving is three heaping tablespoons of chili, as you enjoy telling customers.) This means that you spent another $800 on chili for the chili dog product line.

Given this information, you can create an income statement that shows revenue, cost of goods sold, and gross margin by product line, as shown in Table 4-2. Furthermore, note that Table 4-2 does something very traditional: It allocates operating expenses by using a simple rule. In Table 4-2, I've simply split the operating expenses right down the middle, allocating $3,000 of operating expenses to the regular hot dog product line and $3,000 of operating expenses to the chili dog product line.

**TABLE 4-2**

## Traditional Income Statement by Product Line

| | $2.50 Hot Dogs | $4 Chili Dogs | Total |
|---|---|---|---|
| **Sales Revenue** | | | |
| (2,000 sold in each product line) | $5,000 | $8,000 | $13,000 |
| **Cost of goods sold** | | | |
| $0.15 buns | $300 | $300 | $600 |
| $0.40 hot dogs | 800 | 800 | 1,600 |
| $0.40 of chili for each chili dog | — | 800 | 800 |
| Total cost of goods sold | 1,100 | 1,900 | 3,000 |
| Gross margin | 3,900 | 6,100 | 10,000 |
| **Operating expenses** | | | |
| Rent | $500 | $500 | $1,000 |
| Wages | 2,000 | 2,000 | 4,000 |
| Supplies | 500 | 500 | 1,000 |
| Total operating expenses | 3,000 | 3,000 | 6,000 |
| ***Net Profit*** | ***$900*** | ***$3,100*** | ***$4,000*** |

Stop for a minute to look at the information shown in Table 4-2. When you consider and make decisions based on this information, it becomes much easier to understand traditional overhead allocations.

If you examine the income statement shown in Table 4-2, several pieces of data suggest that there's money in them there chili dogs. Look at the sales revenue, for example. The income statement shows that chili dogs generate $8,000 of sales revenue, whereas regular hot dogs generate only $5,000 of sales revenue. Now look at the gross margin. The income statement shows that chili dogs generate $6,100 of gross margin, whereas regular hot dogs generate only $3,900 of gross margin. Finally, look at the net profit. Based on a simple split of overhead or operating expenses, the net profit from the regular hot dog line equals a measly $900, whereas the net profit from the chili dog product line equals a whopping $3,100.

After reviewing the information shown in Table 4-2, what is your conclusion? It seems pretty clear that you should sell more chili dogs and fewer hot dogs. In fact, you may want to give up on selling regular hot dogs and concentrate on chili dogs. You may also decide that your chili dogs are priced too high; perhaps you could shave the cost a bit on these. You may further decide that the regular hot dogs are priced too low; perhaps the price of these should be bumped up a bit.

Indeed, you can make all sorts of decisions from the collective set of data shown in Table 4-2. You may not realize that the overhead allocation plays an important part in all this. Unfortunately, the overhead allocation shown in Table 4-2 and any of the conclusions I suggest in the preceding paragraphs are wrong. This error, however, doesn't show up until you use activity-based costing, and that's why ABC is cool.

# Understanding How ABC Works

In this section, I tell you how, with ABC, you can create an equivalent income statement for product-line profitability. After that, I generalize about the ABC process and define the buzzwords that people usually use to talk about ABC.

## The ABC product-line income statement

To create an ABC product-line income statement, you attempt to trace the overhead cost directly to products or services. Suppose that in the case of the imaginary hot-dog-stand business, the rent expense is necessary because you need an electrical hookup to keep the pot of chili heated. Perhaps you also need an electrical hookup to run the can opener that you use (surreptitiously) to open the cans of chili needed to refill the pot. This means, then, that the rent expense really can't be split between regular hot dogs and chili dogs. It needs to be allocated to chili dogs.

You can treat the supplies expense in a very similar way. Suppose that the $1,000 of supplies is really just napkins. Also suppose that based on your observations, a regular hot dog customer grabs two napkins for their hot dog, whereas a chili dog customer grabs eight napkins for their chili dog (you know, to clean up the mess on the front of their shirt when the chili spills). In this case, you can use this information to better allocate the $1,000 of supplies expense. Consider that this information means that regular hot dog customers use roughly 4,000 napkins. (I calculated this by multiplying the 2,000 hot dogs you've sold by the 2 napkins used for each regular hot dog customer.) And chili dog customers use 16,000 napkins. (I calculated this by multiplying the 2,000 chili dogs that you've sold by the 8 napkins used by each chili dog customer.)

Using this napkin-use information, you can calculate which percentage of the supplies expense is used by regular hot dog customers and which percentage is used by chili dog customers. If regular hot dog customers use 4,000 of a total 20,000 napkins, 20 percent of the napkins are going to regular hot dog customers (20 percent of the $1,000 of supplies expense equals $200). Therefore, the correct allocation of supplies expense to the regular hot dog line is $200.

You can allocate a portion of the supplies expense for chili dogs by using similar math. If 16,000 of the 20,000 napkins go to chili dog customers, that's 80 percent of the napkins, and 80 percent of the $1,000 of supplies expense equals $800. Therefore, logically, $800 out of $1,000 of supplies expense should be allocated, or traced, to the chili dog product line.

All this makes sense, right? All you're trying to do is trace overhead costs, or operating expenses, to product lines.

The wages expense of $4,000 probably works in a very similar fashion. Before going further, though, I have to delve into some of the ABC buzzwords. Suppose that all the $4,000 of wages expense goes to serving customers hot dogs. Furthermore, suppose that the process of serving a regular hot dog to a customer requires two steps:

1. Grab a hot dog bun.

2. Slide a hot-off-the-grill frankfurter into the bun.

By comparison, the process of serving a chili dog requires five steps:

1. Grab a hot dog bun.

2. Slide a hot-off-the-grill frankfurter into the bun.

3. Ladle a heaping tablespoon of chili into the bun.

**4.** Ladle another heaping tablespoon of chili into the bun.

**5.** Ladle a third heaping tablespoon of chili into the bun.

(Yes, you read that correctly.)

You may see where I'm going with this. I've actually done something very special — something that business-school professors would dress up with a bunch of fancy words in academic business journals. In this example, I state that the wages expense actually gets used in an activity called *serving* or *serving customers.* I also note in this example that the process of serving a regular hot dog customer requires two steps, but the process of serving a chili dog customer requires five steps.

These steps are known as *cost drivers.* That concept may be something you don't understand right away, but in fact, the notion of cost drivers is simple common sense. The term *cost drivers* simply suggests that the number of steps an employee takes to serve a customer is a good base on which to allocate the wages expense that comprises the activity of serving.

You may have already guessed how to do this, but I'll tell you anyway: By looking at the total number of steps required to serve regular hot dogs and the total number of steps required to serve chili dogs, you can trace the wages expense to the regular hot dog and chili dog product lines.

If you sell 2,000 regular hot dogs, and each hot dog requires 2 steps, regular hot dogs require 4,000 steps in total. If you sell 2,000 chili dogs, and each chili dog requires 5 steps, the chili dog product line requires 10,000 steps.

You can use these two values — the number of steps for the regular hot dog line and the number of steps for the chili dog line — to allocate the wages expense. To calculate the percentage of the wages expense that goes into preparing regular hot dogs, you make the following calculation:

```
4,000 (steps for regular hot dogs) / 14,000 (total steps) x $4,000
```

This calculation returns the value $1,143.

In a similar fashion, you can use the steps information to allocate wages expense to the chili dog product line. Here's how that calculation may work:

```
10,000 (steps for chili dogs) / 14,000 (total steps) x $4,000
```

This calculation returns the value $2,857.

Now take a look at Table 4-3, which summarizes all this ABC analysis that I've discussed over the past few paragraphs. The most noteworthy item — and the first item to observe about ABC analysis — is that an ABC approach to product-line profitability often produces surprising results.

TABLE 4-3

## ABC Income Statement by Product Line

|  | $2.50 Hot Dogs | $4 Chili Dogs | Total |
|---|---|---|---|
| **Sales Revenue** | | | |
| (2,000 sold in each product line) | $5,000 | $8,000 | $13,000 |
| **Cost of goods sold** | | | |
| $.15 buns | $300 | $300 | $600 |
| $.40 hot dogs | 800 | 800 | 1,600 |
| $.40 of chili for each chili dog | 0 | 800 | 800 |
| Total cost of goods sold | 1,100 | 1,900 | 3,000 |
| Gross margin | 3,900 | 6,100 | 10,000 |
| **Operating expenses** | | | |
| Rent | $0 | $1,000 | $1,000 |
| Wages | 1,143 | 2,857 | 4,000 |
| Supplies | 200 | 800 | 1,000 |
| Total operating expenses | 1,343 | 4,657 | 6,000 |
| ***Net Profit*** | ***$2,557*** | ***$1,443*** | ***$4,000*** |

If you think back to the impressions you had after looking at the income statement shown in Table 4-2, you may have concluded that chili dogs are really a much better product to sell. As Table 4-3 shows when you look at the net profit number, however, regular hot dogs make twice as much profit as chili dogs — even though they sell for less money and even though they produce much less gross margin. Only a fair and accurate tracing of overhead expenses shows this fact. Wow. Pass the mustard.

All this is pretty neat, isn't it? If you step away from your imaginary hot-dog-stand business and look at your real business, you may find yourself asking new and awkward questions, such as "That product generates all that revenue? Maybe a fair accounting of overhead would show that it actually loses money."

Remember that cheapo product or cheapo service that you never spend much money on — you know the one — and that doesn't generate much gross margin? Well, you may be making a lot more money on it than you thought. Scary, isn't it?

## ABC in a small firm

I want to make three important observations about ABC in a small firm. Some of this stuff is obvious and some of it is redundant, but I think it's important enough for you hear it at least one more time:

>> **ABC is most useful when you have lots of overhead and a bunch of products.** In any environment that doesn't have a lot of overhead, ABC isn't worth the work and won't deliver insights. Likewise, ABC doesn't make sense in any business that sells a single product or that provides a single service, which may be the case in a small firm. (Keep reading, though, because analysis of cost drivers can provide one unique insight.)

>> **ABC may not make sense for custom manufacturing environments.** In a custom manufacturing environment — this is any business in which you make specific things for specific customers — you can often use job costing to provide good product or service profitability measures. In the case of a single-family-home builder, for example, the builder can use job costing to track revenue and expenses by job (single-family home), and that job costing may provide the detailed profitability-by-product-line information that's the big benefit of ABC.

**REMEMBER**

ABC is first and foremost a tool for better allocating overhead costs.

>> **Cost drivers "drive" costs.** In the discussion of the hot-dog-stand business and the activity labeled *serving a customer,* the serving steps are the cost drivers. The number of steps required to serve a customer drive the costs of serving the customer. That may sound really dumb, but sometimes, one of the benefits that ABC provides is insight into how changing the number of cost drivers changes your costs. Suppose that instead of spooning three heaping tablespoons of chili onto a chili dog, you purchase one spoon equivalent to three tablespoons; this change would reduce the number of steps from five to three. Recall the original five-step approach to serving the chili dog customer:

1. Grab a hot dog bun.

2. Slide a hot-off-the-grill frankfurter into the bun.

3. Ladle a heaping tablespoon of chili into the bun.

4. Ladle another heaping tablespoon of chili into the bun.

5. Ladle a third heaping tablespoon of chili into the bun.

This sounds so obvious as to be unworthy of inclusion in this book. But if you get a three-tablespoon spoon, you can simplify the serving of a chili dog into three steps:

1. Grab a bun.

2. Slide a hot dog into the bun.

3. Heap a three-tablespoon serving of chili into the bun.

Changing the number of steps required to serve a customer a chili dog changes the cost of the serving activity for a chili dog. And changing the cost of serving a chili dog changes the profitability (potentially) of serving a chili dog. I say *potentially* because you may not actually reduce your wages expense by buying a three-tablespoon spoon for lathering up your chili dogs with chili, but you get the idea. **Note:** To really save money by reducing the number of steps, you need to be able to cut your wages expense.

The bottom line concerning ABC is this: ABC lets you better allocate overhead costs, and as a bonus, ABC often gives you unique insights into what drives your overhead costs. With this information in hand, you can make better decisions about your product and service lines, and sometimes, you can even change your business operations in a way that reduces your costs.

# Implementing a Simple ABC System

I'll admit this right up front: You can make ABC very complicated. Furthermore, if you go out and hire an outside consultant — somebody who wants to charge you thousands or even tens of thousands of dollars to set up one of these systems — you may end up with something that is very, very powerful and very, very complicated.

That being said, however, ABC systems don't have to be that complicated, particularly if you just want better allocation of your overhead costs rather than a system to look at the cost drivers or the activities that comprise your overhead costs. ABC can be pretty straightforward, especially in a small or medium-size firm. In fact, I think you can implement a good, first-rate ABC system by taking the following four steps:

**1. Look at your overhead costs.**

Verify that you have enough overhead to be worrying about. If you're in a business with big fat margins and very low overhead, ABC may not make any sense for you. The incremental value that you achieve by allocating overhead more precisely may be simply a manifestation of an obsessive-compulsive personality disorder rather than good accounting.

2. **Identify the big overhead cost.**

   You must do this if you decide that you want to allocate some or a bunch of your overhead via an ABC approach. Don't spend time trying to accurately allocate some penny-ante amounts (unless they're simple-to-allocate ones that can be done at the same time as the bigger project). Go for the biggest bang you can get for your buck. Create an ABC system that allocates, with a minimal amount of effort, a large chunk of your overhead. Don't get too pedantic.

3. **Identify the principal activities that use up the overhead costs.**

   In the simple example of the imaginary hot-dog-stand business, you have a single activity: serving a customer. You're certainly going to have more activities than that. But you don't need to create a list of 80 activities. Identify the big activities that enable you to allocate your overhead. The fewer activities you can use to do this, the easier your accounting will be. Find a handful of activities that let you fairly and accurately allocate overhead to product lines. That's the big picture.

4. **Trace the activities to products by using the appropriate measures.**

   After you've identified the handful of activities that let you connect overhead expenses to products, be sure to use the appropriate measure — also known as a cost driver — to tie the overhead expenses to the product lines or service lines.

   In the example of the hot-dog-stand business, one overhead cost — rent — didn't even need a cost driver. The supplies expense also didn't need a cost driver because you were able to allocate that cost through simple observation. The wages expense required a more sophisticated textbook approach to allocation. To allocate the wages expense, you created an activity called *serving the customer* and then allocated that activity's cost based on the number of steps that each product line required.

**REMEMBER**

An ABC system is a tool you can use to manage your overhead costs and the profitability of the products or services that you sell. Practically, you want to focus on the big overhead costs, and in the end, all you really want is an ABC system that produces useful numbers — numbers that help you think about your business more clearly and creatively.

# Seeing How QuickBooks Supports ABC

Okay, you're probably saying to yourself, "Steve, all this sounds pretty good. But you're a little short on specifics and a little long on theory. Where's the beef, buddy?"

Oh, that's right. I do need to tell you how an ABC system works in QuickBooks, don't I? No problem — the approach is really straightforward if you've already been using QuickBooks. In short, all you do to implement a simple ABC system in QuickBooks is what you're doing right now. In other words, just keep on tracking your operating expenses by using a good, decent chart of accounts. That's 90 percent of the battle.

You also need to take care of one or two minor additional items:

>> **Turn on the QuickBooks Class Tracking feature.** Class tracking lets you categorize income and expense transactions as falling not just into income and expense accounts, but also into particular classes.

>> **When you record an expense, identify the class into which the expense falls.** Using classes that correspond to your activities — well, you can see that this is all it takes, right?

# Turning On Class Tracking

To turn on class tracking in QuickBooks, follow these steps:

**1. Choose Edit ⇨ Preferences.**

QuickBooks displays the Preferences dialog box.

**2. Tell QuickBooks you want to work with the accounting preferences.**

To tell QuickBooks that you want to change one of its accounting preferences — Class Tracking, in this case — click the Accounting icon, which appears in the list box along the left edge of the Preferences dialog box. Figure 4-1 shows the Company Preferences tab for the accounting preferences. (If the Company Preferences tab doesn't appear on your screen, simply click the tab name.)

**3. Select the Use Class Tracking for Transactions check box to turn on class tracking.**

**4. You may as well also select the Prompt to Assign Classes box so that QuickBooks reminds you to use the classes.**

**5. Click OK.**

From this point forward, QuickBooks adds a Class drop-down list or field to the windows that you use to record revenue and expenses (the Create Invoices window, the Write Checks window, the Enter Bills window, and so on). All you do is tag transactions as they fit into a particular class.

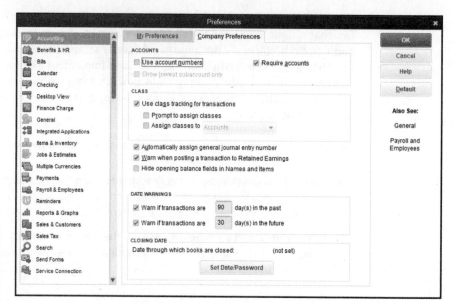

# Using Classes for ABC

After you turn on class tracking, using classes is straightforward. You set up classes for the product lines or service lines for which you want to measure profitability. You classify transactions as fitting into a particular class either as they're recorded (if you can) or after the fact (if you need to fiddle with the activity and cost driver math).

## Setting up your classes

You set up a class for each product or service for which you want to measure profitability. In the imaginary hot-dog-stand business, for example, you set up two classes: one for regular hot dogs and one for chili dogs.

To set up a class, you can just enter the class name in the class box that appears in the window that you use to record invoices, write checks, and make journal entries. (These windows are shown later in this section.) Alternatively, you can choose Lists ⇨ Class List. When QuickBooks displays the Class List window, click the Class button shown at the bottom of the window and choose New from the menu that QuickBooks displays. Use the New Class dialog box that appears, shown in Figure 4-2, to describe the new class.

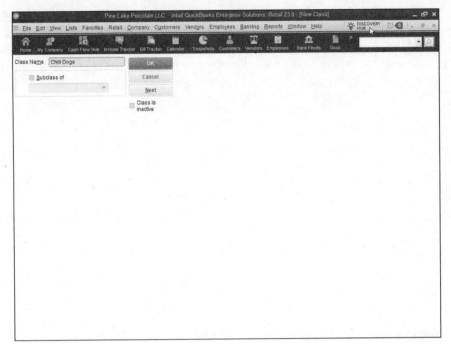

FIGURE 4-2:
The New Class
dialog box.

## Classifying revenue amounts

To classify revenue as fitting into a particular class, use the Class box that appears in the Create Invoices window and in the Enter Sales Receipt window. (These are the two windows that you use to record sales.) If an invoice records sales of a hot dog, for example, you may record the class as Regular Dog. If a sales receipt records sales of a chili dog, you may record the class as Chili Dog. Figure 4-3 shows the Create Invoices window filled out to record the day's chili dog sales.

**TIP**

The Class drop-down list is near the top of the window, next to the Customer:Job drop-down list. It's also in the fifth column in the description of item(s) being invoiced.

## Classifying expense amounts

To record a check that pays some expense that fits into a particular activity, you also use the Class column (which appears on the Expenses tab, as shown in Figure 4-4) to identify the product line or service into which the expense fits. Figure 4-4 shows how the Write Checks window may appear to record $1,000 of rent expense allocated to the chili dog product line.

**TIP**

The Class column is located along the right edge of the Expenses tab.

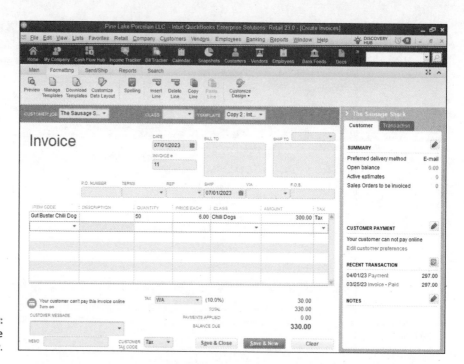

**FIGURE 4-3:**
The Create Invoices window.

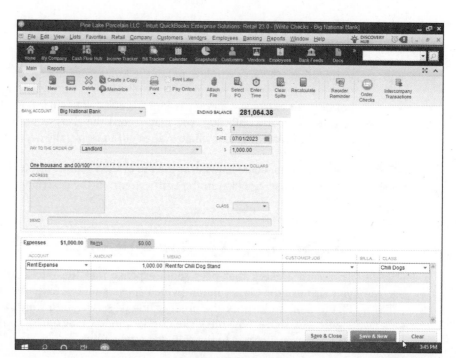

**FIGURE 4-4:**
The Write Checks window.

# Making after-the-fact classifications

In some cases, you won't be able to classify an expense or revenue amount when the initial transaction is recorded. In the hot-dog-stand example, you probably won't be able to figure out how to split the wages expense between regular hot dogs and chili dogs until after you pay the employees. The same thing is true of the supplies expense. In both cases, you need to know how many regular hot dogs and how many chili dogs you sold before you can allocate, or trace, supplies and wages.

In these sorts of cases, you use the Make General Journal Entries window to classify previously unclassified expenses. Figure 4-5 shows you how to take $4,000 of previously unclassified wages expense and allocate the amount to the regular and chili dog product lines.

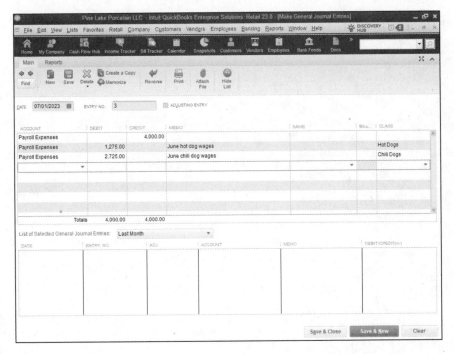

Using Activity-Based Costing

**FIGURE 4-5:**
The Make General Journal Entries window.

**TIP**

The Class column is located along the right edge of the Make General Journal Entries window.

## Producing ABC reports

After you allocate as much overhead as you can to the product or service lines, you can prepare a profit and loss statement by class that shows the profitability-by-product-line data. Book 4, Chapter 2 explains and discusses QuickBooks reports. Note that if you used the example data discussed in this chapter, you could produce a QuickBooks report that looks almost identical to the income statement shown in Table 4-3, earlier in this chapter.

TIP

To produce a profit and loss statement by class, choose Reports ⇨ Company & Financial ⇨ Profit & Loss by Class.

IN THIS CHAPTER

» **Setting up jobs and projects**

» **Accounting for job and project costs**

» **Finding alternative ways to do job costing**

» **Using estimates**

» **Figuring out progress billing**

Chapter **5**

# Setting Up Project and Job Costing Systems

M any businesses work on projects or jobs. One way to look at a home builder's business, for example, is as a series of home construction projects. A manufacturer, such as a commercial printer, may print books, brochures, or posters for its customers. Each of those items represents jobs that are performed for specific customers.

Accounting may work a bit differently when a firm organizes its work into projects or jobs. In some situations, a firm needs to track revenue and expenses — not just by a standard chart of accounts, but also by jobs or projects. Fortunately, QuickBooks makes job costing, or project costing, pretty darn easy. In this chapter, I talk about the tools that QuickBooks provides.

## Setting Up a QuickBooks Job

To set up a QuickBooks job, choose the Customers ⇨ Customer Center command. QuickBooks displays the Customer Center window, shown in Figure 5-1.

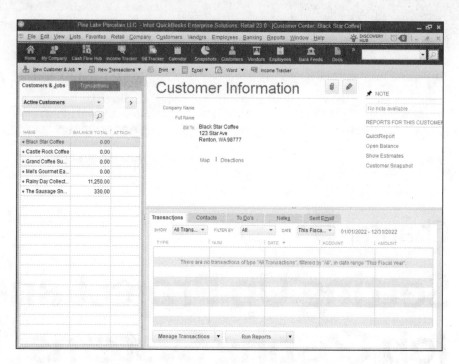

FIGURE 5-1:
The Customer
Center window.

To set up a job for a particular customer, right-click the customer and choose the Add Job menu command from the shortcut menu. When you do so, QuickBooks displays the New Job window, shown in Figure 5-2.

To set up a job for a customer, use the Job Name box to give the job or project a name. A home builder, for example, may use the address of the home as the job. (Perhaps the street address would suffice.)

Optionally, you can use the Address Info, Payment Settings (shown in Figure 5-3), Additional Info, and Job Info tabs to provide additional information about the job. Figure 5-4 shows the Job Info tab of the New Job window. This tab provides drop-down lists that you can use to identify the job status and the job type. The tab also provides text boxes that you can use to enter the job start date, projected end date, and actual end date. If a job is inactive, and you no longer want it to appear in the Customer Center window's list, you can also select the Job Is Inactive check box.

And that, my friend, is that. Essentially, all you do to begin tracking jobs is add jobs to the QuickBooks Customer:Job list. Sweet, right?

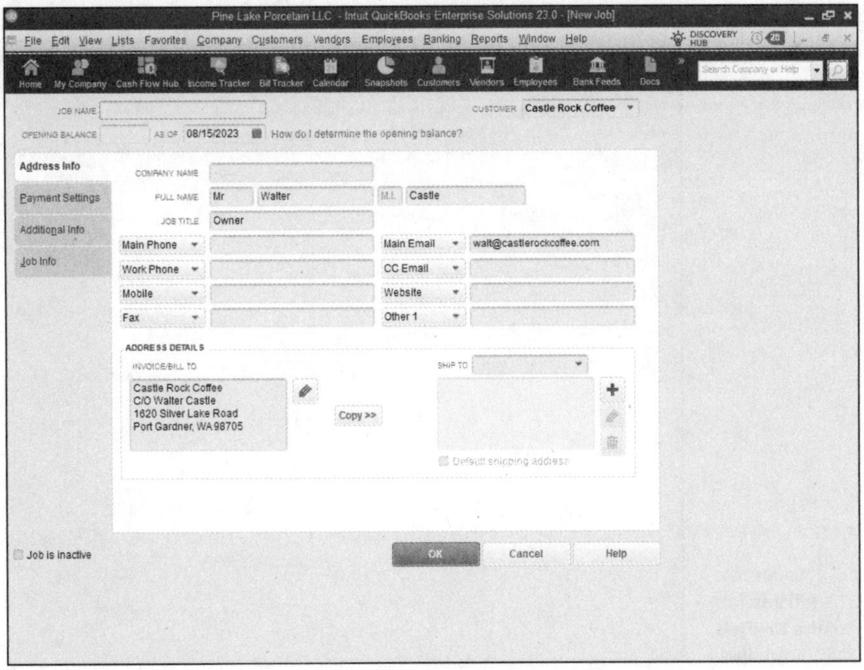

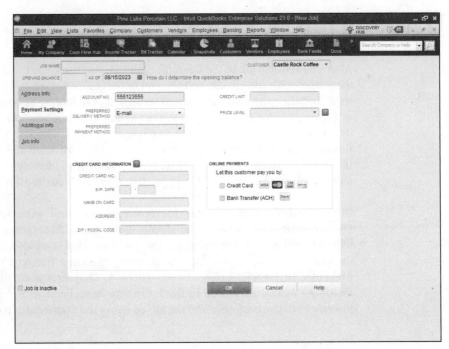

**FIGURE 5-2:**
The Address Info tab of the New Job window.

**FIGURE 5-3:**
The Payment Settings tab of the New Job window.

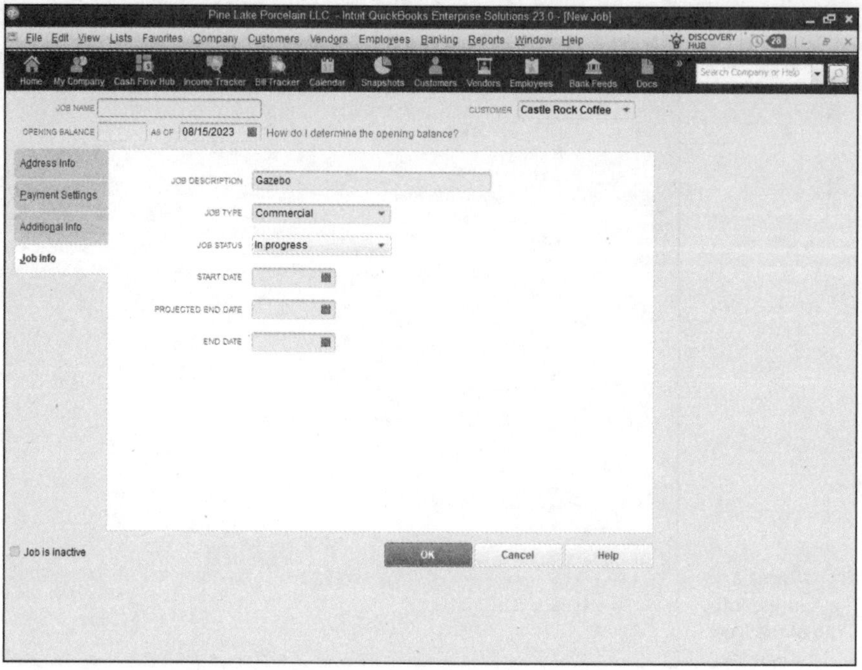

**FIGURE 5-4:**
The Job Info tab of the New Job window.

# Tracking Job or Project Costs

After you set up a job in the Customer:Job list, you track the income and expenses associated with the job. To do this, you enter the customer and job name (rather than just the customer) in the Customer:Job text box. If you take a quick look at Figure 5-5, for example, you see the Create Invoices window. (I go into more detail about the Create Invoices window in Book 3, Chapter 1.) Note that the Customer:Job drop-down list can show both the customer and job name. If an invoice is associated with a particular job, you want to identify both the customer and the job by using the Customer:Job list. And that's really all it takes.

Other windows that you use to record income and expenses also provide Customer:Job drop-down lists. If you look at the Time/Enter Single Activity window, shown in Figure 5-6, you can see that QuickBooks supplies the Customer:Job drop-down list for recording the time that you've worked on a particular customer's project or job. (Book 3, Chapter 1 also talks about billing for time.) Again, all you do to track the time associated with a particular job is identify both the customer and the job by using the Customer:Job drop-down list.

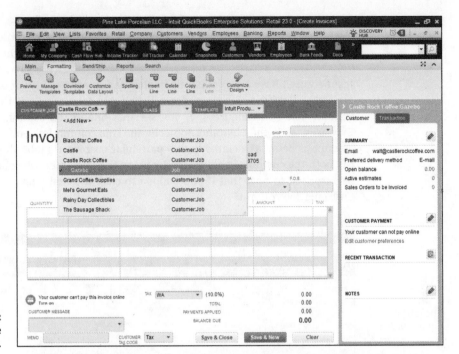

**FIGURE 5-5:**
The Create
Invoices window.

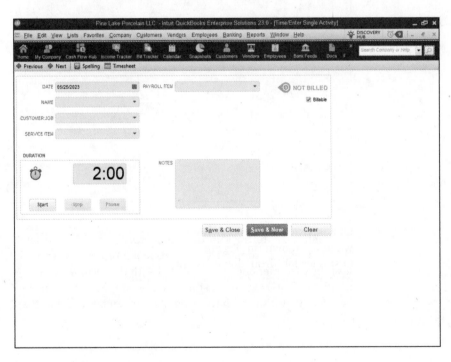

**FIGURE 5-6:**
The Time/Enter
Single Activity
window.

Next time you invoice this client, a pop-up box prompts you to choose whether you want to include any outstanding billable time and costs to the invoice.

Just because I have a compulsive personality, I need to point out one more example of the Customer:Job drop-down list. If you take a look at the Write Checks window, shown in Figure 5-7, you see that one of the columns shown on the Expenses tab is the Customer:Job column. This column lets you tag any expense amount as being associated with a particular customer's job. All you do is identify both the customer and the job by using the Customer:Job column. You won't be surprised to hear that if you happen to click the Items tab, it also supplies a Customer:Job column.

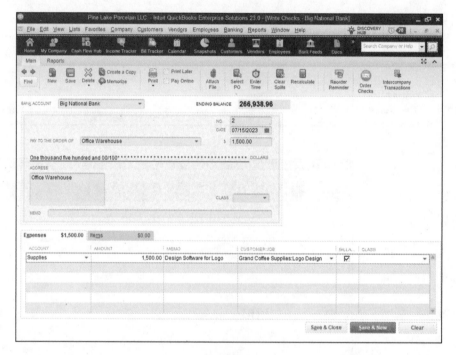

**FIGURE 5-7:**
The Write Checks window.

To summarize, to track income and expense by job, you must identify not only the account that some income transaction or expense transaction falls into, but also the customer and job associated with the income or expense transaction. You do this by entering the customer name and job name in the Customer:Job text box. And that's all you have to do. Just remember to fill in that box.

# ALTERNATIVES TO TRADITIONAL JOB COSTING

Because QuickBooks's job costing approach may not work for everybody — and may even be more than some users need — let me point out that you can do some simple job costing or project costing without using the Customer:Job drop-down list. Here are two options:

- **You can use classes to segregate costs.** Classes work as very reasonable ways to track income and expense transactions for particular jobs if they're associated. I think that the traditional Customer:Job drop-down list provides a more convenient way to do the same thing. But if you have your heart set on using it, you can also use the Class drop-down list. The Class drop-down list or Class column typically appears next to the Customer:Job drop-down list or the Customer:Job column. You work with the Class drop-down list the same way that you work with the Customer:Job drop-down list. Note that the Class drop-down list or column appears only if you enable class tracking by using the Preferences dialog box.

- **You can construct a very detailed chart of accounts, including accounts, subaccounts, and sub-subaccounts.** With a very detailed chart of accounts, you can use collections of accounts to track expenses that are associated with particular projects or jobs. If jobs take a long time to complete, and you're working on only a few jobs, for example, the chart-of-accounts approach works just fine.

If you use an alternative job costing approach with QuickBooks, unfortunately, you won't be able to rely on QuickBooks's job costing reports. QuickBooks provides (as I discuss in the "Job Cost Reporting" section later in this chapter) a bunch of handy job costing reports. QuickBooks expects that you'll use the Customer:Job drop-down list to collect job cost information. If you don't use that list, make sure that you have a good way to track the costs associated with a particular job or customer.

Another problem with both alternative approaches to job costing — classes and lots of subaccounts — is that you may later want to use classes and subaccounts in some way that's incompatible with using them for job costing. Jobs are, very frankly, best accounted for by using the QuickBooks job feature.

# Job Cost Reporting

Other chapters in this reference talk about QuickBooks reports. Book 4, Chapter 2, for example, talks about how you can easily prepare QuickBooks financial statements and reports. Because I've already talked about QuickBooks reports in some detail, including how you print and customize reports, I don't talk about that stuff here. I do want to point out, however, that if you choose the Reports ➪ Jobs, Time & Mileage command, QuickBooks displays a submenu of almost two dozen reports that supply job costing information. The report titles are pretty self-explanatory. Some reports give job profitability, and some reports identify the estimates associated with a particular job. Other reports compare job estimates with actual job costs. You get the picture.

Obviously, you want to experiment with these reports if you do begin to use job costing. These reports let you slice and dice your job accounting data in a bunch of ways. You should be able to use these reports (albeit with some modifications) to supply most of the information that you need to make good job costing decisions and to manage job costs.

# Using Job Estimates

If you've told QuickBooks that you want to create estimates — and you may have done this during QuickBooks setup — you can create job estimates of amounts that you later invoice.

To create a job estimate, choose the Customers ➪ Create Estimates command. QuickBooks displays the Create Estimates window, as shown in Figure 5-8. I don't describe how to fill in the fields of this window, because this window mirrors the Create Invoices window, which is described in detail in Book 3, Chapter 1. In a nutshell, you fill out the Create Estimates window the same way that you fill out the Create Invoices window. This makes sense. An estimate is just an example or guess of the future invoice for a job. Predictably, you collect and supply the same information and you fill in the fields the same way.

If you have questions about how to work with a particular field or box in the Create Estimates window, refer to Book 3, Chapter 1. Find the description of the related field in the Create Invoices window. Whatever you do with that field in the Create Invoices window is the same thing that you do in the Create Estimates window.

TIP

When you invoice a customer for which you've previously prepared an estimate, QuickBooks displays a list of the previously prepared estimates and lets you select one of these estimates as the starting point for an invoice. (This shortcut can be a real time-saver.)

If you didn't turn on Estimates when you set up QuickBooks, you can do so after the fact. Choose the Edit ➪ Preferences command; click the Jobs & Estimates icon in the Preferences dialog box; click the Company Preferences tab, shown in Figure 5-9; and then select the Yes radio button below Do You Create Estimates? You may also want to select the Yes radio button below Do You Do Progress Invoicing? if you do progress invoicing. (I talk about progress invoicing or progress billing in the next section of this chapter.)

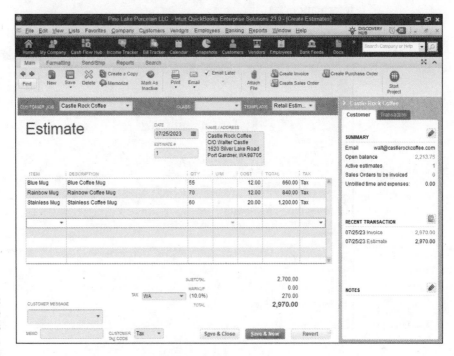

**FIGURE 5-8:**
The Create Estimates window.

TIP

If you use estimates to create invoices, you create another way to track job costs: You can ask QuickBooks to prepare reports that compare, item by item, the estimated amounts for a job with the invoiced amounts for the job. To produce this report, choose Reports ➪ Jobs, Time & Mileage ➪ Item Estimates vs. Actuals.

# Progress Billing

*Progress billing* occurs when you invoice, or bill, a customer for a portion of an amount that you've previously estimated. Take a peek at the Create Estimates window, shown in Figure 5-8 earlier in this chapter. Suppose that this window records an estimate that a client asked you to supply. Further suppose, just for purposes of this discussion, that the estimate is for a consulting job that you're doing.

If you want to later bill the consulting client for the actual work, you click the Create Invoice button that appears along the top edge of the Create Estimates window. If you've previously chosen to do progress billing (refer to Figure 5-9), QuickBooks displays the Create Progress Invoice Based on Estimate dialog box (see Figure 5-10). This dialog box lets you create an invoice by using the estimate information.

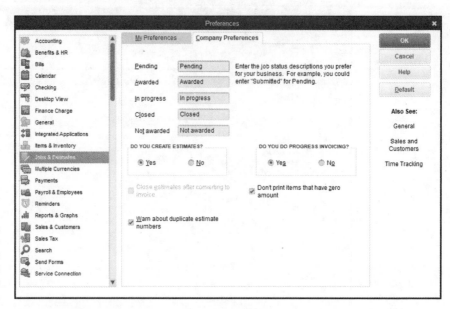

**FIGURE 5-9:**
The Company
Preferences
tab for Jobs &
Estimates
preferences.

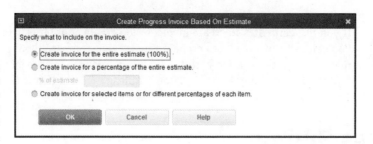

**FIGURE 5-10:**
The Create
Progress Invoice
Based on
Estimate
dialog box.

If you select Create Invoice for the Entire Estimate (100%), QuickBooks creates one invoice that uses all the information from the Create Estimates window. Or you can select one of the other options to bill only a portion of the estimate. You can select the Create Invoice for a Percentage of the Entire Estimate radio button, for example, and then enter the percentage in the % of Estimate box. In this case, QuickBooks bills the customer for some specified percentage of the estimate. Alternatively, you can select the radio button titled Create Invoice for Selected

Items or for Different Percentages of Each Item. In this case, QuickBooks lets you specify that different percentages of the items shown on the estimate should be billed.

When you click OK, QuickBooks either creates the invoice by using the estimate information or (if you indicated that you wanted to specify different percentages for different items on the invoice) displays the Specify Invoice Amounts for Items on Estimate dialog box, shown in Figure 5-11. You use the Amount column to specify a portion of the estimated amount that you want to bill on the progress invoice.

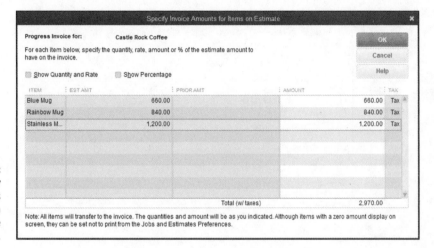

**FIGURE 5-11:**
The Specify
Invoice Amounts
for Items on
Estimate
dialog box.

**TIP**

If you select the Show Quantity and Rate check box on the Specify Invoice Amounts for Items on Estimate dialog box, QuickBooks adds columns to the dialog box that let you see quantity and rate information. Similarly, if you select the Show Percentage check box, QuickBooks adds columns to the dialog box that show percentages. You probably don't need this extra information, but if it's important to be very precise in your invoice, you may want to experiment with these additional columns of information.

# 5

# Financial Management

# Contents at a Glance

IN THIS CHAPTER

» **Introducing examples of and caveats about ratio analysis**

» **Analyzing liquidity ratios**

» **Analyzing leverage ratios**

» **Analyzing activity ratios**

» **Analyzing profitability ratios**

# Chapter **1**

# Ratio Analysis

N umbers from your financial statements make more sense when you can compare them with other numbers and external benchmarks. In this chapter, I talk about how you can perform this sort of analysis, which is called *ratio analysis.* Even if you're not a numbers person, you can use ratio analysis to your benefit. Ratio analysis is easy to apply, and it enables even the nonquantitative type of person who uses it to better understand the information in financial statements.

Let me give you a quick example of ratio analysis. One particularly useful ratio is the *gross margin percentage,* which is your gross margin divided by your total sales. Although this ratio may not seem useful at first blush, it can be very valuable.

If you compare your gross margin percentage for this year with last year's and see a decline, for example, you know that this isn't good. Less gross margin means less money for operating expenses, interest expenses, and profits. On the other hand, if you compare your declining gross margin percentage with a competitor's and see that your competitor's gross margin percentage is declining even more rapidly than yours . . . well, you know that's good. This comparison shows that you may actually be in pretty good shape. At least you aren't hurting, like your competitor.

These are the sorts of insights that ratio analysis can provide. They enable you to put numbers from your income statement and balance sheet in context.

This chapter steps through the formulas, provides examples, and gives useful guidelines for 16 common financial ratios. I group the ratios into four categories: liquidity, leverage (or debt), activity, and profitability.

# Some Caveats about Ratio Analysis

Before you go any further in using ratio analysis to draw conclusions, consider these two warnings about it:

>> **The ratios are only as good as your inputs.** Obviously, the more accurate your QuickBooks accounting records are, the more accurate any ratios that you calculate by using the numbers from your QuickBooks financial statements will be. This makes sense, right? Garbage in, garbage out. Even if your financial records are garbage-free, if they contain something just slightly wacky, such as an unusually large transaction that skews all the numbers, your financial ratios aren't as good as they might be.

>> **Ratios become relevant through comparison.** Your financial ratios become most relevant — I've already hinted at this — when they compare your numbers with those of your competitors, the numbers that you had a year ago, and the numbers that a bank loan agreement specifies are necessary for you to continue achieving to be in the bank's good graces. A comparison with other ratios is crucial because often, your numbers are just numbers if they can't be compared with external benchmarks.

TIP

Industries commonly prepare reports that summarize financial ratio information for other firms in the industry. Early in my career, I was the controller of an electronics manufacturing firm. Our industry group, the American Electronics Association, prepared a financial ratio survey. With this financial ratio survey, I was able to easily compare the financial ratios of the firm I worked at with the financial ratios of other firms. Currently, as a CPA, I find it very useful that the Texas Society of CPAs and American Institute of Certified Public Accountants prepare an annual financial study that shows financial ratios for CPA firms around the United States. You probably also operate in an industry that has a professional association. Keep your eyes and ears open to the possibility that this group or association prepares and distributes reports that include financial ratios. Such reports can be useful tools for you as you manage your firm.

*Note:* When you compare your firm with other firms by using financial ratios, you compare it with firms of a similar size. It usually doesn't make sense to compare, for example, a million-dollar business with a billion-dollar business.

Some of the QuickBooks financial statements provide simple financial ratios automatically. You can add the gross margin percentage (and other percentage measures) to the standard income statement and to the standard balance sheet, for example.

# Liquidity Ratios

*Liquidity ratios* measure how easily and comfortably a firm can pay its immediate financial obligations and exploit immediate short-term financial opportunities. Everything else being equal, the firm that's sitting on a large hoard of cash can more easily pay its bills and take advantage of great opportunities that pop up. (If a competitor gets into trouble and wants to sell valuable assets at fire-sale prices, for example, a very liquid firm with great gobs of cash can more easily exploit such an opportunity.)

## Current ratio

The *current ratio liquidity* measure compares a firm's current assets with its current liabilities. A firm's current assets include cash, inventory, accounts receivable, and any other assets that can (or will be) quickly turned into cash. Most small businesses don't have much in the way of other current assets, although they may have some, such as short-term investments. Current liabilities include bills that must be paid in the coming year, such as accounts payable, wages payable, taxes payable, and — if you're borrowing money on a long-term basis, such as through bank loans — the principal portions of the coming year's payment on a loan.

Following is the exact formula used to calculate the current ratio:

```
current assets/current liabilities
```

The simple balance sheet shown in Table 1-1 gives you an example of how this current ratio formula works. As Table 1-1 shows, this firm's current assets equal $50,000. The firm's only current liability is $20,000 of accounts payable. (For purposes of this discussion, I'm assuming that this firm has no other current liabilities.)

To calculate the current ratio of the firm described by the balance sheet in Table 1-1, you use the following formula:

```
$50,000/$20,000
```

**TABLE 1-1**

## A Simple Balance Sheet

| Assets | |
|---|---|
| Cash | $25,000 |
| Inventory | 25,000 |
| Current assets | $50,000 |
| Fixed assets (net) | 270,000 |
| Total assets | $320,000 |
| **Liabilities** | |
| Accounts payable | $20,000 |
| Loan payable | 100,000 |
| **Owner's equity** | |
| S. Nelson, capital | $200,000 |
| ***Total Liabilities and Owner's Equity*** | ***$320,000*** |

This formula returns the value 2.5. Therefore, 2.5 is this firm's current ratio.

**TIP**

Here's a general guideline concerning current ratios: A firm's current ratio should be a value of 2 or higher. In other words, the firm's current assets should be double or more than double the firm's current liabilities.

## Acid-test ratio

Also known as the *quick ratio*, the *acid-test ratio* is a more severe measure of a firm's liquidity. It serves the same general purpose as the current ratio, however. The acid-test ratio indicates how easily a firm can meet its current financial obligations and exploit any financial opportunities that pop up.

The following formula is used for calculating the acid-test ratio:

```
(current assets - inventory)/current liabilities
```

In the case of the business described by the balance sheet shown in Table 1-1, you use the following formula to calculate the acid-test ratio:

```
$25,000/$20,000
```

This formula returns the value 1.25. Therefore, 1.25 is this firm's acid-test ratio.

**TIP**

Here's a guideline: A firm's acid-test ratio should be a value of 1 or higher. In other words, the current assets after you subtract the inventory should provide enough money to pay the current liabilities.

# Leverage Ratios

*Leverage ratios* measure how much debt a firm carries and how easily a firm pays the interest expenses of carrying that debt. Leverage ratios are important for an obvious reason: Typically, a firm financed mostly with debt needs to continue to borrow to stay in business. (If this doesn't make sense, think about what happens if a bank won't extend a loan or won't refinance a mortgage to a firm that's heavily dependent on debt!)

What's more, a firm that carries a lot of debt typically also spends a lot of money on interest expense. The heavy interest expense means that it's especially important for such a firm to have adequate operating income. *Operating income* is the income available to pay interest and other profits. A firm with a lot of operating income relative to its interest expense doesn't have much of a problem paying the interest — and this is true even if operating income declines or decreases. By contrast, a firm with very modest operating income relative to its interest expense quickly gets into trouble if the operating income decreases.

## Debt ratio

The *debt ratio* simply shows the firm's debt as a percentage of its capital structure. The term *capital structure* refers to the total liabilities and owner's equity amount. In the case of the balance sheet shown in Table 1-1, the capital structure totals $320,000. Not coincidentally, the total liability and owner's equity amount ($320,000) equals the total assets amount ($320,000). This makes sense if you think about it a bit. A firm funds its assets with its capital. Therefore, the total assets always equal the total capital structure.

The formula for calculating the debt ratio is a simple one:

```
total debt/total assets
```

Using numbers from the simple balance sheet shown in Table 1-1, for example, the debt ratio can be calculated as follows:

```
$120,000/$320,000
```

This formula returns the debt ratio 0.375, indicating that 37.5 percent of the firm's capital comes from debt.

No guideline exists for debt ratio. Appropriate debt ratios vary by industry and by the size of the firm in an industry. In general, small firms that use QuickBooks probably want to show lower debt ratios than larger firms do. Small firms, in my experience, see their operating income fluctuate more wildly than large firms do. Because of that fluctuation, carrying and servicing such debt are more problematic. Lower debt, therefore, probably is better. This makes sense, of course, so I'm not telling you anything that you don't already know.

## Debt equity ratio

A *debt equity ratio* compares a firm's long-term debt with stockholders' equity or owner's equity. Essentially, the debt equity ratio expresses a firm's long-term debt as a percentage of its owner's equity.

**TIP**

*Stockholders' equity* is synonymous with *owner's equity* and, in the case of a sole proprietorship, with a sole proprietor's capital account.

Following is the formula used to calculate a debt equity ratio:

```
long-term debt/stockholders' equity
```

By using the example balance sheet shown in Table 1-1, you can calculate the debt equity ratio by using this formula:

```
$100,000/$200,000
```

This formula returns the debt equity ratio 0.5. Therefore, this firm's long-term debt equals 0.5, or 50 percent of its owner's equity.

I can't really give you a guideline for a debt equity ratio. You simply compare your debt equity ratio with the debt equity ratios of similar-size firms in your industry. As is the case with the debt ratio previously described, all other things being equal, the less long-term debt you carry, the better.

## Times interest earned ratio

The *times interest earned ratio* indicates how easily a firm pays interest expenses incurred on its debt. To calculate the times interest earned ratio, you need an income statement that shows both operating income and interest expense. Table 1-2 provides this information.

**TABLE 1-2**

## A Simple Income Statement

| Sales Revenue | $150,000 |
|---|---|
| Less: Cost of goods sold | 30,000 |
| Gross margin | $120,000 |
| Rent | 5,000 |
| Wages | 50,000 |
| Supplies | 5,000 |
| Total operating expenses | 60,000 |
| Operating income | 60,000 |
| Interest expense | (10,000) |
| *Net Income* | *$50,000* |

The following formula is used for calculating the times interest earned ratio:

```
operating income/interest expense
```

If you look at the income statement shown in Table 1-2, you see that operating income, which is the income that a firm has *before* paying its interest expense, equals $60,000. Interest expense shows up as $10,000. Therefore, you calculate the times interest earned ratio by using this formula:

```
$60,000/$10,000
```

This formula returns the times interest earned ratio 6. Therefore, the firm's operating profits pay the interest expense six times over.

No standard guideline exists for the times interest earned ratio. Obviously, however, the times interest earned ratio should indicate that a firm can easily pay its interest expense. It would be sort of scary, if you think about it, for operating income to be only a little bit greater than the firm's interest expense. Such a situation would indicate that a modest drop in operating income would make paying interest expense impossible.

## Fixed-charges coverage ratio

The *fixed-charges coverage ratio* resembles the times interest earned ratio. The fixed-charges coverage ratio calculates how easily a firm pays not only its interest expenses, but also any principal payments on loans and any other payments that the firm is legally obligated to make.

The fixed-charges coverage ratio uses the following formula:

```
income available for fixed charges/fixed charges
```

Returning to the example business described by the balance sheet shown in Table 1-1 and the income statement shown in Table 1-2, suppose that the $5,000 of rent shown in the income statement is actually a fixed charge because the firm is renting space on a long-term lease. Further suppose that for the purpose of this ratio, although it doesn't show up on the income statement, the $100,000 loan that shows up on the balance sheet requires an annual $5,000 in principal payments.

In this case, this firm is obligated to pay fixed charges as summarized in Table 1-3. In total, then, fixed charges for this firm equal $20,000 a year.

**TABLE 1-3**

## Fixed-Charges Calculation

| | |
|---|---|
| Interest (as shown in Table 1-2) | $10,000 |
| Rent (as shown in Table 1-2) | 5,000 |
| Principal (as mentioned in text) | 5,000 |
| **Fixed Charges** | **$20,000** |

The other input needed to calculate the fixed-charges coverage ratio is the income available for these fixed charges. Table 1-4 shows you how to calculate the income available for fixed charges. You start with the operating income, which equals $60,000, as shown in Table 1-2. (Remember that the operating income is the income before paying interest expense.) You must add to the operating income any fixed charges included in the income statement. In this case, the rent turns out to be a fixed charge. Therefore, you need to add the $5,000 of rent to the operating income to get income available for fixed charges. As Table 1-4 shows, the income available for fixed charges equals $65,000.

**TABLE 1-4**

## Income Available for Fixed Charges

| | |
|---|---|
| Operating income | $60,000 |
| Add-back of rent | 5,000 |
| **Fixed Charges** | **$65,000** |

With the two needed inputs, you can calculate the fixed-charges coverage ratio by using this formula:

```
$65,000/$20,000
```

This formula returns the fixed-charges coverage ratio 3.25, which indicates that the firm generates slightly more than three times as much income as needed to pay its fixed charges.

No guideline exists to specify what your fixed-charges coverage ratio should be. In fact, it's particularly difficult to get the information necessary to think about fixed-charges coverage ratios because fixed charges don't clearly appear in the standard set of simple financial statements. One of the things that make financial statements (that are prepared in accordance with generally accepted accounting principles) so useful is that the fixed-charges information is usually disclosed in little footnotes that appear at the end of the financial statements.

# Activity Ratios

*Activity ratios* provide an indication of how efficiently a firm runs its operations. All other factors being equal, a firm that keeps a very modest amount of inventory is in better shape than a firm that has to keep (store, manage, warehouse, insure, and so forth) a bunch of inventory. That makes sense, right?

**TIP**

Apple, maker of the iPhone and a bunch of other technology products, as you may know, keeps only a few days' worth of inventory on hand. In other words, it sells out its current inventory holdings every few days. Other technology manufacturers — especially in the past — kept weeks' and even months' worth of inventory. Comparing the two examples, which is more efficiently and more leanly managing its inventory? Which has the minimal investment tied up? Which isn't suffering or paying the price of warehousing all that extra, quickly obsolete inventory? The answer is Apple, obviously. So predictably, Apple's activity ratios look really good compared with those of its competitors.

Activity ratios, in essence, measure how well a firm uses its assets. If a firm makes super-efficient use of its factory, for example, that efficiency shows up in its activity ratios. And if a firm runs lean and mean, that leanness and meanness show up in its activity ratios.

# Inventory turnover ratio

The *inventory turnover ratio* measures how many times in an accounting period the inventory balance sells out. The formula is as follows:

```
cost of goods sold/average inventory
```

In the example business described by the balance sheet in Table 1-1 and the income statement in Table 1-2, you can use the following formula to calculate the inventory turnover:

```
$30,000/$25,000
```

This formula returns the inventory turnover ratio 1.2.

**TIP**

Technically, you shouldn't use just an ending inventory balance, which is what appears in Table 1-1. You should use an *average inventory balance.* You can calculate an average inventory balance in all the usual, common-sense ways. You can use the inventory balance both from this year's balance sheet and the previous year's balance sheet and then average them, for example.

The inventory turnover period, as you may have noticed, depends on the period measured in the income statement. If the income statement is an annual statement and, therefore, the cost of goods sold (COGS) amount is an annual COGS amount, an inventory turnover ratio of 1.2 means that a firm sells 120 percent of its inventory balance in a year. If the inventory turnover ratio uses the COGS amount reported in a monthly income statement, the inventory turnover period is a month. With a monthly COGS amount, a firm with a 1.2 inventory ratio sells 120 percent of its inventory in a month.

No guideline exists for inventory turnover ratios. A good inventory turnover ratio depends on what your competitors are doing within your industry. If you want to stay competitive, you want an inventory turnover ratio that at least comes close to your competitors' ratios.

# Days of inventory ratio

The *days of inventory ratio* resembles the inventory turnover financial ratio; it estimates how many days of inventory a firm is storing. The ratio uses the following formula:

```
average inventory/(annual cost of goods sold/365)
```

The simple balance sheet shown in Table 1-1 shows inventory equal to $25,000. Assume that this figure also equals the average inventory that the firm carries. To calculate the daily sales, you take the COGS number reported in the annual income statement shown in Table 1-2 and divide it by 365 (the number of days in a year). Putting these numbers together in the formula I just introduced, the math looks like this:

```
$25,000/($30,000/365)
```

This formula returns the value 304 (roughly). This value means that this firm is carrying roughly 304 days of inventory. Stated another way, this firm requires 304 days of sales to sell its entire inventory.

As is the case with the inventory turnover ratio, you don't see generalized rules about what is an acceptable number for days of inventory. The general rule is that you turn around your inventory as quickly as your competitor does.

I return to the case of Apple because it's so instructive — even if scary — to most of us. Apple sells out its inventory in a few days. Apple's competitors were taking months to sell out their inventory. In an industry in which inventory was quickly becoming obsolete and was very expensive to start with, think of the competitive disadvantage that Apple's competitors suffered by having to carry inventory for months longer than Apple did. Is it any wonder that many of Apple's competitors got into trouble? The lesson of Apple applies to many folks who run or advise businesses that carry inventory. Inventory turnover and days of inventory ratios need to be watched carefully and compared with those of other firms of the same size in the same industry.

## Average collection period ratio

The *average collection period ratio* shows how long it takes for a firm to collect on its receivables. You can think about this ratio as being a measure of the quality of a firm's credit and collection procedures. In other words, this ratio shows how smart a firm is about deciding to whom to extend credit. This ratio also shows how effective a firm is in collecting from customers.

The average collection period ratio formula looks like this:

```
average accounts receivable/average credit sales per day
```

The balance sheet shown in Table 1-1 doesn't show an average accounts receivable balance. The income statement shown in Table 1-2 also doesn't break out sales into credit and cash components. Therefore, let me introduce another example into the text. Suppose that in the business you run, the average accounts receivable is $60,000. Further suppose that your average credit daily sales equal $1,000. Using the formula I just gave you, you can calculate the average collection period as follows:

```
$60,000/$1,000
```

This formula returns the value 60. In this case, your business has 60 days of sales in accounts receivable.

The guideline about the average collection period is that it should tie to your payment terms. If your average number of days of credit sales in accounts receivable equals 60, for example, your payment terms probably should be something like net 60 days (which means that customers are supposed to pay you in 60 days or less). Your average collection period, in other words, should show that most of your customers are paying on time. Remember that some of your customers will pay early, and obviously, some of your customers will pay a bit late. You hope that on average, customers pay on time.

## Fixed-asset turnover ratio

The *fixed-asset turnover ratio* quantifies how efficiently a firm employs its fixed assets. Predictably, this financial ratio is most useful when a firm has a lot of fixed assets: real estate, equipment, and so forth.

The fixed-asset turnover ratio uses the following formula:

```
sales/fixed assets
```

Based on the numbers supplied by the balance sheet shown in Table 1-1 and the income statement shown in Table 1-2, you can calculate the following fixed-asset turnover ratio:

```
$150,000/$270,000
```

This formula returns the value 0.556. In a nutshell, this ratio says that this firm requires $270,000 of fixed assets to produce $150,000 of sales — or, more specifically, that the firm produces sales equal to roughly 56 percent of its fixed assets.

As is the case with many of these financial ratios, no guideline exists that you can use to determine a good fixed-asset turnover ratio. You compare your fixed-asset turnover ratio with those of firms of a similar size in your industry.

# Total-assets turnover ratio

The *total-assets turnover ratio* also measures how efficiently you're employing your assets. This ratio is probably more appropriate for a firm that doesn't have a lot of fixed assets but still wins or loses the game of business based on how well it manages its assets.

The total-assets turnover ratio formula is as follows:

```
sales/total assets
```

Here's a formula that calculates the ratio by using the financial data from Tables 1-1 and 1-2, shown earlier. If total sales equal $150,000 and total assets equal $320,000, the following formula makes the calculation:

```
$150,000/$320,000
```

This formula returns the ratio 0.469, which means that the firm generates sales equal to roughly 47 percent of its total assets.

The total-assets turnover ratio that you calculate for your business can't be compared with some external benchmark or standardized rule. You compare your ratio with the same ratio of similar-size businesses in your industry. Obviously, your main consideration is whether you're efficiently using your assets to produce sales relative to those of your competitors. The more sales you can produce with a given level of assets, the better off your business is.

# Profitability Ratios

*Profitability ratios* analyze a firm's profitability. In a sense, profitability ratios are the most important ratios that you can calculate. They typically provide terribly useful insights into how profitable a firm is and why.

One particularly important profitability ratio is the gross margin percentage, which expresses gross margin as a percentage of sales. As discussed in Book 6, Chapter 1, you can calculate a firm's break-even point simply by dividing the firm's fixed costs by its gross margin percentage.

# Gross margin percentage

Also known as the *gross profit margin* ratio, the *gross margin percentage* shows how much a firm has left over after paying its COGS. The gross margin is what pays the operating expenses; financing expenses (interest); and, of course, the profits.

The gross margin percentage ratio uses the following formula:

```
gross margin/sales
```

Using the data from Table 1-2 (shown earlier), you can calculate gross margin percentage as follows:

```
$120,000/$150,000
```

This formula returns the value 0.8, meaning that gross margin equals 80 percent of the firm's sales.

No guideline exists for what a gross margin percentage should be. Some firms enjoy very high gross margins; other firms make good money even though the gross margin percentages are very low. In general, of course, the higher the gross margin percentage, the better.

**WARNING**

I need to make one cautionary statement here: In my humble opinion, small businesses should enjoy high gross margin percentages. I think it's common to assume that a small business can get away with a lower gross margin percentage than some large competitors can. In my experience, however, that isn't true. Gross margin percentages should be higher for small businesses because small businesses often can't get the economies of scale that large businesses can get. A low gross margin percentage may work fine for Walmart, for example, but it's tough for a small retailer to work with such a small gross margin percentage.

# Operating income/sales

In the case of the business shown earlier in Table 1-2, in which operating income equals $60,000 and sales equals $150,000, you calculate the *net operating margin percentage* by using this formula:

```
$60,000/$150,000
```

This formula returns the value 0.4. In other words, you see a 40 percent operating margin, which indicates that a firm's operating income equals 40 percent of its sales.

No guideline exists for what a net operating margin percentage should be. Your main consideration, which you'll probably find yourself repeating in your sleep after reading it so much in this book, is that *you want to be competitive.* You want your operating margin percentage to be close to or better than your competitors' percentages. That parity (or superiority) enables you to stay competitive.

# Profit margin percentage

The *profit margin percentage* works like the net operating margin percentage. It expresses the firm's net income as a percentage of sales, as shown in the following formula:

```
net income/sales
```

In the case of the business described by the income statement shown in Table 1-2, net income equals $50,000, and sales equals $150,000. This firm's profit margin percentage, therefore, can be calculated with the following formula:

```
$50,000/$150,000
```

This formula returns the financial ratio 0.33. This ratio indicates that the firm's net income equals roughly 33 percent of its sales.

# Return on assets

The *return on assets* ratio shows the return that the firm delivers to stockholders and the interest that the firm pays to lenders as the percentage of the firm's assets. Some businesses use this ratio to evaluate the business's profitability. (Banks do this, for example.)

The actual formula is

```
(net income + interest)/total assets
```

In the case of the example business described earlier in Tables 1-1 and 1-2, the net income equals $50,000. Interest expense equals $10,000. Total assets equal $320,000. The formula to calculate this firm's return on assets ratio is

```
($50,000 + $10,000)/$320,000
```

This formula returns the value 0.188. This value indicates that the firm's return (including both net income and interest) on its assets is roughly 19 percent.

No guideline exists for what a return on assets ratio should be. The main consideration, predictably, is that return on assets must exceed capital charges on those assets.

In Book 5, Chapter 2, I talk more about capital charges and how they relate to something called *Economic Value Added analysis.* Capital charges aren't complicated to understand. The bottom line is that a firm needs to deliver a return on its assets that exceeds the funding sources cost for those assets. In other words, if (on average) the creditor and shareholders providing money to a firm want something less than, for example, 19 percent, and the firm can earn 19 percent as its return on assets, that's really good. If, on the other hand, the return on assets percentage is 18.8 percent, but the funding sources for those assets cost 20 percent, that's not so good. That firm is in trouble.

TECHNICAL STUFF

The term *capital charge* equals the sum of the minimum profit that shareholders require to invest their money in a firm and the interest charges that lenders require for the money that they've loaned to the firm.

## Return on equity

The *return on equity financial ratio* expresses a firm's net income as a percentage of its owner's equity or shareholders' equity. (Shareholders' and owner's equity are the same thing.)

The formula, which is deceptively simple, is as follows:

```
net income/owner's equity
```

In the case of the example business described earlier in Tables 1-1 and 1-2, net income equals $50,000, and owner's equity equals $200,000. This firm's return on equity, therefore, can be calculated by using the following formula:

```
$50,000/$200,000
```

This formula returns the value 0.25, which means that this firm's return on equity is 25 percent — a number that's probably pretty good.

No guideline exists for what is and isn't an acceptable return on equity. I can make two useful observations, however, about how you should interpret the return on equity ratio that you calculate:

>> **The return on equity ratio that you calculate needs to be at least as good as you deserve.** Okay, that sounds circular. So think about it this way: If you're

investing money in your business, you deserve a return on that money, and that return needs to be reasonable compared with your other alternatives. If you can go out and invest money in a stock market mutual fund and get 10 percent, you shouldn't be investing in things that deliver a return of less than 10 percent. That makes sense, right? Therefore, if you want to earn a 20 percent return on the money that you've invested in your own firm (by the way, a 20 percent return is a very reasonable return for a small business), you want to make sure that your return on equity (after you get going) exceeds this minimum return.

» **The return on equity ratio hints at the sustainable growth rate that your firm can manage.** This sounds complicated, but you need to understand what sustainable growth is and how it ties back to the return on equity ratio. *Sustainable growth* is the growth rate that your business can sustain over a long period: three years, five years, ten years, and so on. If you don't take money out of the business (other than your salary), and you reinvest the return on equity that the business generates, the return on equity ratio equals your sustainable growth. In other words, the example business described earlier in Tables 1-1 and 1-2 can grow on a sustained basis as fast as 25 percent.

Alternatively, suppose that the owners of the imaginary firm described in the financial statements in this chapter take half the equity money out of the business. Perhaps half the $50,000 net income is distributed as a dividend to shareholders, for example. In this case, because only half the return on equity is reinvested, sustainable growth equals only half the return on equity percentage. If the return on equity percentage equals 25 percent, but the owners withdraw half the return (12.5 percent), the reinvested half of the return on equity percentage (12.5 percent) equals the sustainable growth rate. In other words, this business can grow on a sustained basis at 12.5 percent annually.

In my experience, this sustainable–growth business makes intuitive sense to some people, but it just leads to head–scratching for other people. In case you're in the head–scratching group, consider a couple more comments:

» **Growing sales and profits also requires growing your capital structure.** The idea of a sustainable growth rate (which was pioneered by Hewlett-Packard, interestingly enough) is based on an intuitively understandable proposition: To grow your sales and your profits over the long run, you need to grow your assets. If you're going to double your sales and your profits, for example, you're probably going to have to double your assets. And if you double your assets, you must double your funding of those assets. Doubled funding of your assets means that you double your borrowing and your owner's equity. Assuming that you can get creditors to loan you more money — which should be possible if you're growing not only sales, but also profits — you still need to double your owner's equity. And the way that you usually double or grow your owner's equity in a small business is by reinvesting the return on the equity.

**REMEMBER**

Large businesses have another way to grow owner's equity. A large business such as Hewlett-Packard can go out into the capital markets and raise money by issuing stock. In fact, the real reason for making a company public isn't to make the owners rich, but to access the public's capital markets. Those markets provide access to almost unlimited amounts of capital (that is, unless you pull an Enron or WorldCom by proving that you don't deserve access to the capital markets). In the case in which a firm can tap these capital markets for cash or funding, the sustainable growth rate formula gets more complicated. These capital markets provide another way to grow owner's equity.

>> **If you don't grow owner's equity as your business grows, watch out.** You'll have big problems if you ignore the sustainable growth rate and your business grows fast. If you don't grow your owner's equity at least as fast as your business grows, your debt percentage ratio skyrockets (perhaps) without your even realizing it. Just think about this logically: If your sales double, your assets probably double. And if your owner's equity doesn't double, creditors have to make up the difference. Exploding debt means that it becomes all the more important for you to refinance that debt and refinance even larger amounts of that debt. And exploding debt means that your interest expense is growing all the time because your debt levels are rising.

# Chapter **2**

# Economic Value Added Analysis

H ere's a curious fact: Even if your QuickBooks profit and loss statement shows a profit, you may not actually be making any money. How can this be? Ah, to really answer this question, you need to use a tool called *Economic Value Added analysis* (EVA), which was developed by (and is a trademark of) Stern Stewart & Co., a management consulting firm.

In this chapter, I discuss what EVA does and how you can use the information that you create with QuickBooks to perform the EVA analysis. This is neat stuff but a bit theoretical. Fortunately, when you boil EVA down to its essence, it's quite practical.

## Introducing the Logic of EVA

EVA analysis states in a formula something you already know in your gut. If you're a business owner and you can make more money by selling your business, reinvesting the proceeds, and then getting another job someplace else, hey — you're not doing yourself or your family any financial favors by running your own business.

Let me walk you through an example to show you mathematically why this is the case. Suppose that after you pay yourself a fair salary, your firm makes $20,000 in additional profits. Further suppose that you can sell your firm to a competitor for $200,000, invest the proceeds in a stock mutual fund, and earn about $20,000 a year in profits. (Yes, I know that the stock market doesn't promise 10 percent annual returns, but neither does your business. So just suppose that these numbers are right for the purposes of this discussion.)

In this simple example, running your own business doesn't really make sense. Sure, you're making a salary. And sure, you're earning a return on the money that you and your family have invested. But you aren't getting anything more than that. You may as well sell your firm, reinvest the money in the stock market (one option), and get a job working for the phone company.

TIP

Don't get all bummed out on me here; I'm not trying to talk you into selling your business. I just want to explain how to use a powerful tool, EVA, to manage your business better.

# Seeing EVA in Action

EVA analysis has two variations; I explain the simple version first. If I start with the simple version, you may better understand all the little nuances and subtleties of the EVA model from the very start. When you're finished with the simple version of EVA analysis — called *equity-based* EVA — you're ready to move on to the more complicated EVA model.

Before I proceed with this discussion, take a gander at a couple of financial statements. Table 2-1 shows a simple income statement, and Table 2-2 shows a simple balance sheet. These two financial statements provide much — and maybe most — of the information that you need to perform EVA analysis for your business. In fact, go ahead and suppose that these two financial statements describe your business.

TIP

If you're uncomfortable interpreting either income statements or balance sheet financial statements, you may want to review the material covered in Book 1, Chapter 1. In that chapter, I describe how financial statements work.

TIP

If you're not sure how to produce a financial statement by using QuickBooks, refer to Book 4, Chapter 2. In that chapter, I describe how to prepare QuickBooks financial statements, including income statements (also known as *profit and loss statements*) and balance sheets.

**TABLE 2-1**

# A Simple Income Statement

| Sales Revenue | $150,000 |
|---|---|
| Less: Cost of goods sold | 30,000 |
| Gross margin | $120,000 |
| Operating Expenses | |
| Rent | $5,000 |
| Wages | 50,000 |
| Supplies | 5,000 |
| Total operating expenses | 60,000 |
| Operating income | 60,000 |
| Interest expense | (10,000) |
| *Net Income* | *$50,000* |

**TABLE 2-2**

# A Simple Balance Sheet

| Assets | |
|---|---|
| Cash | $25,000 |
| Inventory | 25,000 |
| Current assets | $50,000 |
| Fixed assets (net) | 270,000 |
| Total assets | $320,000 |
| Liabilities | |
| Accounts payable | $20,000 |
| Loan payable | 100,000 |
| Owner's equity | |
| S. Nelson, capital | $200,000 |
| *Total Liabilities and Owner's Equity* | *$320,000* |

Essentially, EVA includes a *charge* for the capital that you've invested in a business. To see whether you're making money, you deduct this charge from your net income. A positive EVA amount indicates that your business truly produces an economic profit; in other words, a positive EVA amount indicates that even after your firm pays wages to employees, interest to lenders, and a return to shareholders, some money is left over. This leftover money is the *economic profit*.

The capital charge equals the cost of the capital (specified as an interest rate or annual return percentage) multiplied by the capital invested in the business period. The capital invested in your business equals, essentially, your owner's equity. The cost of capital return percentage equals the return that you could earn in a similarly risky investment in something else.

## An example of EVA

From the example data in Tables 2-1 and 2-2, calculate each of these amounts by following these steps:

**1. Calculate the capital charge.**

For the sake of illustration, suppose that you earn a 20 percent return on the money that you've invested in the business described in Tables 2-1 and 2-2. To calculate an EVA in this situation, use the following formula:

```
capital charge = 20% × $200,000 (of owner's equity)
```

The result of this formula is a capital charge of $40,000. That's the amount that should be returned to the shareholders. (In the case of a small business owned and operated by an entrepreneur, the sole shareholder is the owner/entrepreneur.)

**2. Subtract the capital charge from the net income.**

In Table 2-1, the net income equals $50,000. To calculate the EVA, use the following formula:

```
net income ($50,000) - capital charge ($40,000) = EVA
```

The result — $10,000 — equals the EVA.

Therefore, when you use the data from the example business detailed in Tables 2-1 and 2-2 and assume a 20 percent cost of capital, you find that this business delivers an economic profit. After paying each stakeholder their fair share, the firm also has leftover money — an economic profit — of $10,000.

## Another example of EVA

To continue this example, suppose that the capital charge is really $50,000 (calculated by multiplying a 25 percent cost of capital percentage by the $200,000 of capital or owner's equity). In this case, what does the EVA equal? The answer is zero. In other words, if the business makes $50,000 of profit (refer to Table 2-1), but the shareholders require a $50,000 return on their investment (calculated as 25 percent multiplied by $200,000), the business produces no EVA.

Does the preceding scenario make sense to you? The math may seem a little unwieldy, but don't get too tangled up in the computations. My guess is that you understand in your gut what EVA analysis does. If you really did own a business like the one summarized in Table 2-1 and Table 2-2, you know that you should be earning a fair return on the money that you and your family have invested. And if you're earning only the same amount of money that you could earn in any other business — say, a stock mutual fund — you're not getting ahead.

That's all EVA analysis really does. It makes sure that you're getting at least a fair return (ideally, more than that) on your investment.

# Reviewing Some Important Points about EVA

The purpose of EVA analysis is simple: You want to see whether you're earning an economic profit by owning your own business.

To make sure that you're on track with your analysis, you typically want to consider several things:

>> **How good are the numbers?** This point is an important one. Do your income statement and balance sheet values really describe your profit (one of the numbers used in your calculation) and the value that you may be able to sell for and then reinvest (another important value used in your calculation)? You're always going to have to accept some imprecision in your numbers. That's a fact of life. But a *lot* of imprecision in those two numbers corrupts the results.

**TIP**

You should compare your owner's equity value with what you think you'd get if you sold your business. If your owner's equity value (the amount shown on your balance sheet) is wildly different from the cash-out value, you probably should use the cash-out value in your EVA analysis rather than the owner's equity value.

>> **How good is the cost of capital percentage?** The capital charge calculation relies heavily on the cost of capital value. This number is a tough one to come up with, quite frankly. If you owned a billion-dollar business, you'd probably need a team of PhDs to come up with a number for you (and clearly, this isn't

feasible for a small business). Therefore, I recommend that you use a range of values. Many people think that a small business (any business with sales less than, say, $50 million) should produce annual returns of 20 to 25 percent. That seems to be a good range of values to use in EVA analysis. You may also be interested to know that for a large company, the cost of capital rates run from approximately 10 to 12 percent. Clearly, you don't want to be that low. Finally, note that venture capital returns — those returns delivered by the most successful, fastest-growing small businesses — often run 35 to 45 percent annually. It seems, therefore, that the cost of capital rates used in your EVA analysis should be considerably less than this. At least for most businesses, the cost of capital rates should be considerably less than 35 to 45 percent.

TIP

Try a range of rates when you perform EVA analysis. First, try 15 percent as your cost of capital, for example; then try 20 percent, 25 percent, and 30 percent. The calculations, after you have the profit number and the owner's equity number, are pretty simple after all. It's really not difficult to calculate several estimates of EVA.

>> **What about psychological income?** In the case of an owner-managed business, I think it's okay to factor in psychological income. You can't ignore the economy. A viable, healthy business — especially if it's yours — should deliver a nice profit over time and pay for the capital that it uses. Having said that, however, if you really love your work, I'm the last guy to say that you should sell your winery and go to work for the local big-box retailer. (Not that there's anything wrong with wearing an orange vest and spending all day on concrete floors.) My point is that in my opinion, owning your own business is about more than just an economic profit.

>> **Have fluctuations occurred?** Another important point is that in many small businesses (and in all the small businesses that I've owned and managed), profits fluctuate. Therefore, you can't look at a single, perhaps terribly bad year and decide that it's time to pack up. Similarly, you shouldn't look at just a single blowout year and decide that it's time to buy the villa in the south of France. EVA analysis works when the inputs reflect the general condition of the business: the general level of profits, the general amount for which you could cash out, the general cost of capital estimate, and so on. If something screwy happens one year to push one of these inputs way out of whack, the results returned by your EVA analysis become pretty undependable, in my opinion.

>> **Is your business in a special situation?** Everybody admits that EVA analysis is really tricky and may be impossible in certain situations. Most people who love EVA analysis readily admit that EVA analysis doesn't work very well in a startup business situation, for example. Most of these people also admit that

EVA analysis doesn't work very well when a firm is growing very quickly. In both of these cases, the problem is that the income statement just doesn't produce an accurate measure of the value being created by the company. As a result, it's impossible to really figure out what sort of economic profit the business has created. Again, this should make intuitive sense. You may very well expect that in the first year or two, the business produces a loss or very meager profits. And that's totally okay.

Your EVA calculation is only as good as your inputs and assumptions. The trend or pattern in EVA values probably is more important than a particular value, especially for business owners. In the end, you can't lose sight of the big picture, which is answering the question "Am I really making money by running my own business?"

# Using EVA When Your Business Has Debt

In very large businesses, EVA analysis gets computationally burdensome. Although I don't go into great detail about potential problems in this chapter, you should be familiar with one common complication: debt.

Here's the deal. If a business can restructure its debt, bank loans, credit lines, mortgages, and so forth, borrowing can be used to boost EVA. Accordingly, and quite helpfully, another EVA model that's slightly more complicated enables you to recognize this extra wrinkle. In this section, I provide a couple of examples of how this slightly more sophisticated EVA model works.

## The first example of the modified EVA formula

If your firm can freely restructure its debts, you may want to make two adjustments to the EVA analysis:

» You may need to use an all-encompassing cost of capital. An *all-encompassing cost of capital* considers both the cost of equity (this is what I did earlier in the first part of this chapter) and the cost of any debt.

» You use an adjusted net income number that includes not only the amounts paid to the shareholders, but also the amounts paid to lenders.

Calculating an all-encompassing cost of capital is the first step. For the sake of illustration, suppose that a business uses capital from three sources: trade vendors, a bank (which lends money at 10 percent), and owner's equity. Table 2-3 shows an approach to estimating the capital charge that needs to be compared with the net income when this other debt is considered.

TABLE 2-3

## Estimating the All-Encompassing Capital Charge

| | |
|---|---|
| Trade Vendors ($20,000 @ 0 Percent) | $0 |
| Bank loan ($100,000 @ 10 percent) | 10,000 |
| Owner's equity ($200,000 @ 20 percent) | 40,000 |
| *Adjusted Capital Charge* | *$50,000* |

Let me walk you through the numbers in Table 2-3, although none of them is difficult to figure out:

>> **Trade vendors:** The trade vendors provide debt — $20,000 in the balance sheet shown in Table 2-2 — but the firm doesn't have to pay a charge to those creditors. In effect, any implicit charge that the firm pays to trade vendors is already counted in the amount that you pay those vendors for the products or services that they supply. So that portion of the capital charge is zero.

>> **Bank loan:** This $100,000 bank loan charges 10 percent. That bank loan, then, carries a $10,000 capital charge. In other words, in order to use the bank's capital, the business pays $10,000 a year.

>> **Owner's equity:** This final component of the capital charge is what the business owes the owners. In Table 2-3, the owner's equity capital charge is shown as $40,000. (This is the same $40,000 capital charge discussed earlier in the chapter.) This capital charge is calculated by multiplying a cost of capital percentage, 20 percent, by the owner's equity (20 percent of $200,000 equals $40,000). The adjusted capital charge, therefore, equals $50,000.

Okay. So far, so good. The second step in working with this slightly more complicated EVA model is adding back the interest charges paid to lenders to achieve an adjusted income number. Think about this for a minute. The business made $50,000 in income (as shown in Table 2-1), but this amount has already been adjusted for $10,000 of interest expense. Therefore, if you want to compare the funds that the business generated and that are available to pay capital sources, you need to add back the $10,000 of interest expense. In other words, when you're looking at paying all the capital sources of return (whether in the form of interest or dividends), you have not only the $50,000 of net income, but also the $10,000 of interest expense. Does that make sense?

Finally, there's a pot of money left over at the end to pay creditors and owners. And that pot of money, as shown on the income statement in Table 2-1 earlier in this chapter, includes both the $10,000 of interest expense and the $50,000 of net income.

After you've figured out an all-encompassing cost of capital and an adjusted income amount, you can calculate the EVA in the usual way. In this example, you use the following formula:

```
adjusted income ($60,000) - the weighted cost of capital charge ($50,000)
```

The result equals $10,000, which is the EVA amount.

It's no coincidence that the simple EVA formula and the more complicated EVA formula return the same result. EVA shouldn't change because you use a more complicated formula — as long as both the simple and complicated formulas are correct. (They are.) So what's up? The more complicated formula lets you see how changes in your debt affect the EVA.

## Another EVA with debt example

Here's another example of the modified EVA approach. Suppose that you, the business owner, go down to the bank and take out another $100,000 loan. Then suppose that the business pays this amount out to the business owner (you) in the form of a dividend. If this transaction occurred at the beginning of the year, you get the income statement and balance sheet shown in Table 2-4 and Table 2-5 (reflecting the additional loan).

In other words, the only differences between the description of the business in Tables 2-1 and 2-2 and its description in these two tables are that the firm has $100,000 more debt and $100,000 less owner's equity, and the extra debt produces another $10,000 a year of interest expense. That's pretty straightforward, right? All I've really talked about is using more debt and less owner's equity.

Table 2-6 estimates the capital charge for this new, more highly leveraged firm. Once again, let me walk you through the components of the capital charge. The trade vendors, who supply $20,000 of trade credit in the form of accounts payable, don't charge anything, so there's no capital charge for their contribution to the firm's capital structure. In the new, more highly leveraged firm, the bank loan charge has gone way up. Now the firm is carrying a $200,000 loan. With 10 percent interest, the capital charge on the loan rises to $20,000 annually.

**TABLE 2-4**

## Simple Income Statement

| Sales Revenue | $150,000 |
|---|---|
| Less: Cost of goods sold | 30,000 |
| Gross margin | $120,000 |
| **Operating Expenses** | |
| Rent | $5,000 |
| Wages | 50,000 |
| Supplies | 5,000 |
| Total operating expenses | 60,000 |
| Operating income | 60,000 |
| Interest expense | (20,000) |
| ***Net Income*** | ***$40,000*** |

**TABLE 2-5**

## A Simple Balance Sheet

| Assets | |
|---|---|
| Cash | $25,000 |
| Inventory | 25,000 |
| Current assets | $50,000 |
| Fixed assets (net) | 270,000 |
| Total assets | $320,000 |
| **Liabilities** | |
| Accounts payable | $20,000 |
| Loan payable | $200,000 |
| **Owner's Equity** | |
| S. Nelson, capital | $100,000 |
| ***Total Liabilities and Owner's Equity*** | ***$320,000*** |

The final owner's equity capital charge also changes: It drops. With the decrease in owner's equity to just $100,000, the 20 percent capital charge decreases to $20,000 a year.

**TABLE 2-6**

## Estimating the New Capital Charge

| | |
|---|---|
| Trade Vendors ($20,000 @ 0 Percent) | $0 |
| Bank loan ($200,000 @ 10 percent) | $20,000 |
| Owner's equity ($100,000 @ 20 percent) | $20,000 |
| *Adjusted Capital Charge* | ***$40,000*** |

When you add up all the bits and pieces, you come up with an adjusted capital charge of $40,000. Remember that this is the capital charge for the new, more highly leveraged business.

For this new, more highly leveraged business, the EVA changes. The adjusted income for the business is $60,000 (calculated as the $40,000 of net income plus $20,000 of interest expense). You can calculate the EVA by subtracting the $40,000 capital charge from the $60,000 of adjusted income. The result equals $20,000 of EVA. The EVA doubles, obviously, when the business is more highly leveraged.

This second example shows why the more complicated EVA formula can be useful. The example recognizes more explicitly how EVA results when a firm produces income in excess of the capital charges.

# Presenting Two Final Pointers

I want to share two final pointers with business owners who may want to use EVA analysis to think about the economics of their businesses. (My first point is pretty basic, but I think it's probably the most important thing to take away from this chapter.)

>> **EVA analysis is most useful to business owners and managers — or at least to owners and managers of small and medium-size firms — as a thinking tool.** In other words, even if you don't scratch out the numbers on the back of an envelope, EVA makes sense as a way to think about how you should run your business and whether it makes sense to make changes. Comparing your firm's net income with the amount that you could earn by selling and then reinvesting the capital elsewhere is a useful concept.

**TIP**

I have a literary-agent friend who likes to say, "Listen to the universe." I think that this suggestion, especially as it relates to the economics of running a business, is pretty darn good. You should listen to the economy when you think about your business, and EVA provides a tool for you to do that. For a business to make sense, it needs to return a fair share to each of its stake-holders: wages to employees; interest and debt service payments to lenders; a return to shareholders who invested capital; and then, as a practical matter, a little something left over for you, the owner. Indeed, for a business to make sense, it needs to pay more than just its capital charge.

>> **Although you can use EVA analysis to evaluate a business in its entirety, EVA analysis isn't limited to that application.** You can use EVA analysis, with a little bit of fiddle-faddling, to evaluate a business unit, a particular product line, your managers, and so forth.

This is really neat if you think about it. You can use EVA analysis to break your business into different profit activities. By using EVA analysis to look at the economic profit of these different profit activities, you can probably find those activities that should be emphasized because they produce an economic profit, and you can identify those activities that should be discontinued (perhaps) because they don't produce an economic profit. You can evaluate customers and managers the same way.

TIP

If you want to do this more granular EVA analysis, work with a chart of accounts that supports more detailed income statements and balance sheets. In other words, if you're going to break your business into two business units, use a chart of accounts that lets you easily see the income statement for each business unit. In a similar fashion, use a chart of accounts for your balance sheet that lets you see the capital investment for both business units. Remember that any line item that you want to appear on an income state-ment or balance sheet needs its own account in the chart of accounts. Book 2, Chapter 1 describes how to create your QuickBooks Chart of Accounts list. That chapter can also address any questions that you may have about how to set up additional income statement accounts and balance sheet accounts.

# And Now, a Word to My Critics

I may as well admit something. Some people — I hope only a few — aren't going to like my simplistic approach to EVA.

Following are the points that I simplified, but you can take this information and delve deeper into EVA analysis:

>> **More work is involved in this process, per the textbook theory of EVA, than what I describe here.** In a perfect world, you should take the net income number off the QuickBooks income statement and fiddle-faddle with

it so that you get a better, more accurate, more cash-flow-centric measure of income.

» **Owner's equity isn't the world's greatest measure of the fair market value of the capital invested in a firm.** It would be great if a firm could follow the textbook approach described by the creators of EVA analysis (Stern Stewart & Co.) and work with good estimates of the market values of a firm's equity and debt. But you know what? That's a lot of work for an often-modest increase in precision, especially if you're paying some consultant the big bucks to come up with better market values for your equity and debt.

» **My rough-and-tumble approach to the capital charge of owner's equity (my suggestion that you simply use a range of values from 15 to 30 percent) is sort of financial heresy.** MBAs and PhDs probably would be much more comfortable using something complicated, such as the capital asset pricing model. Unfortunately, that's a complicated statistical model that, quite truthfully, scares me half to death. And yes, you probably could come up with a more precise rate of return percentage — if you put in a lot more effort.

So I'm guilty. I admit that I've made several simplifications in the EVA model. Before the judge passes sentence, however, I want to suggest two extenuating circumstances that the judge should consider:

- *Small-business EVA works differently from big-business EVA.* Remember that EVA is a tool to help managers think like shareholders. In the case of a small-business owner using QuickBooks, however, the manager and the shareholder are one person. The dual role implies that this person can more loosely apply the EVA model and still get the benefits of EVA-type thinking. Some of the machinations involved in very sophisticated EVA analysis stem from the fact that management is independent of shareholders, which simply isn't the case for a $1 million manufacturing business or a $10 million distribution business.

- *Precision costs money.* Employing someone who's very sophisticated in the wizardry of finance may not be worth the additional cost. Think about the typical small-business owner who uses QuickBooks as their accounting tool. A firm that produces $10,000 of EVA (as in the examples used in this chapter) shouldn't spend $10,000 or $20,000 on consultants to get a super-precise measure of income or the perfect cost of capital measurement. In my opinion, a firm that produces $100,000 in EVA also shouldn't have this expenditure.

IN THIS CHAPTER

» **Understanding the theory of capital budgeting**

» **Computing the rate of return on capital**

» **Taking the measure of liquidity**

» **Contemplating risk**

» **Relating capital budgeting to QuickBooks**

Chapter **3**

# Capital Budgeting in a Nutshell

The challenge for any business is allocating *capital*, or money. Although you have limited amounts of capital, your ideas and opportunities are often unlimited.

Capital budgeting, in a nutshell, helps you sift through all these ideas and opportunities. Capital budgeting lets you answer questions like the following: Should I replace that key piece of machinery that we use in the factory or get a new delivery truck? Should we buy the building our offices are in? Or should we purchase that competitor's operation because it's for sale?

## Introducing the Theory of Capital Budgeting

Capital budgeting boils down to the idea that you should look at capital investments (machinery, vehicles, real estate, entire businesses, yard art, and so on) just as you look at the certificates of deposit (CDs) that a bank offers.

Don't worry — you actually already know how to do this. When you buy a bank CD, you essentially look at one big thing and then a couple of small things to decide whether a CD makes sense. The big thing is the interest rate. The two small things are the CD maturity and the risk. In the next couple of sections, I talk a bit about all three things because they apply so neatly to the problem and challenge of capital budgeting.

## The big thing is the return

The big thing, as I just mentioned, is the interest rate that a CD pays. You want to earn the highest return possible on your money. Therefore, you want a CD that pays a high interest rate! A 4 percent interest rate is better than a 2 percent interest rate. And a 6 percent interest rate is way better than a 4 percent interest rate.

You can also look at the interest rates earned on capital investments. Before I go any further, though, you should know that interest rates typically don't go by that name in capital investing. For some strange reason, the interest rate that a capital investment (such as a piece of machinery, vehicle, or real estate) earns is called a *return on investment* (ROI) or *rate of return.* But it's the same thing. The rate of return or return on investment is really just the interest rate that a capital investment or capital expenditure pays.

The return is important because it shows the profitability of the investment, albeit as a percentage of the investment. The first thing you need to know about the theory of capital budgeting is that the big thing that matters is the return.

## One little thing is maturity

The first little thing that you also look at in the case of a CD is the maturity. The *maturity* simply refers to the amount of time that your money gets tied up in the investment. You may not want a one-month CD, for example. That short maturity means you have to roll over or reinvest the CD at a new, perhaps lower, rate of return in a month. On the other hand, you may want to avoid tying up your money for a long period, such as 40 years. Tying up your money for a very long period means that you won't be able to get to the money if a new, better opportunity comes along. You probably see very few opportunities that are so good, so surefire, so long-term that they warrant tying up your money for decades and decades, right?

In the case of capital investments, you don't actually use the word *maturity* in most situations. Instead, you should use a term called *liquidity,* which simply means how close an investment is to cash or how quickly an investment returns or pays back the cash that you've invested.

You can measure liquidity in a bunch of ways. A little later in the chapter, I talk about one simple approach to measuring liquidity: the payback period. The key thing to remember about liquidity is this: Liquidity isn't as important as ROI. Remember, the return shows profitability. Nevertheless, you do want to think about the liquidity of a capital investment. What you think depends on your circumstances. In different circumstances, you prefer capital investments with different degrees of liquidity.

## Another little thing is risk

With CDs, government insurance programs such as the Federal Deposit Insurance Corporation (FDIC) reduce the risk of investing. But the risks still matter, right? If you're over the limits of insurance coverage, you don't put all your money in the same bank. Even if you're under the FDIC insurance limits, you don't put money in a bank that's at risk of going under. Do that, and you'll have the hassle of getting your money back.

Typically, you also carefully select CD-like investments, such as debentures, which some finance companies offer to CD investors. Again, that makes sense. *Risk* — the chance that maybe you won't be repaid or that maybe not all your interest will be repaid — is one of the things that you want to consider when you talk about CDs.

In the same way that risk matters to CDs, risk matters to capital investments. In fact, risk probably matters more in the latter case. No government agency guarantees that some capital investment will deliver the returns that you plan on. For this reason, you must consider the risk of capital investments. You can consider risk both *quantitatively* (which means using measurements that produce values that measure the risk) and *qualitatively* (which means relying on your gut).

## The bottom line

The bottom line is this: You already know the theory of capital budgeting, which works like picking a CD down at the local bank. You want to look at the profitability of the investment by somehow measuring the return on the investment, or the interest rate. Profitability isn't the only consideration, however. If you look at a capital expenditure, you also consider the liquidity of the investment. Likewise, you take into account the risk of the investment.

Stated in a slightly different way, when you make capital investments, you want to invest in things that pay the highest return. But you also want to recognize the importance of liquidity, not to mention the risk. You get the theory now, right?

The difference with capital budgeting, then, is that you (rather than the bank issuing the CD) need to calculate the return, quantify or measure the liquidity, and think carefully about the risks. That's really it. You just do those three additional things, which — surprise, surprise — I discuss next in this chapter.

# Calculating the Rate of Return on Capital

I can tell you right up front that calculating the rate of return on a capital investment is a little bit tricky. In almost every case, you need either a financial calculator (a good one) or a spreadsheet program, such as Microsoft Excel. For the purpose of this discussion, I assume that you have (or have access to) Excel. If you don't have Excel, you should still be able to read almost all the following discussion and then translate what I talk about into the instructions that you need to use a financial calculator or some other spreadsheet program. Note that the spreadsheet mechanics that I describe aren't very difficult.

TIP

If you aren't all that comfortable with the notion of using Excel — even though it's already installed on your computer — check out Appendix A, which provides a crash course on Excel. You may also want to think about getting a copy of *Excel All-in-One For Dummies*, by Paul McFedries and Greg Harvey (John Wiley & Sons, Inc.).

Calculating a rate of return on a capital expenditure requires three steps:

1. **Calculate the investment amount.**

2. **Estimate the net cash flows paid by the investment.**

3. **Use a financial calculator (such as one of those fancy Hewlett-Packard calculators) or a spreadsheet program (such as Excel) to calculate the rate-of-return measure.**

In the next sections, I explain each of these steps.

TIP

If you can, use a spreadsheet program rather than go the fancy-calculator route; such calculators can be less than user-friendly. Around three decades ago, when I was graduating with an MBA in finance from the University of Washington, the joke among many young MBAs was that the ability to calculate the rate-of-return measures on a Hewlett-Packard 12C calculator was worth $40,000 a year. The slogan, in fact, was "40G for a 12C."

# Calculating the investment amount

The first step in calculating a return is estimating the amount that you need to invest. This amount is similar to the check you write to a bank to buy a CD.

Suppose that you're considering the purchase of a new office building. Just to keep everything really simple, suppose that you can buy a building that would house your offices for $350,000. Further suppose that you can finance $300,000 of this purchase with a mortgage from your friendly local bank. You also need to pay closing costs that equal $15,000.

Table 3-1 shows the initial investment that you must make to invest in a new office building. The bottom-line amount is $65,000. The table shows how this amount gets calculated. The formula is pretty simple: The building costs $350,000, and you must pay $15,000 in closing costs. That totals $365,000. The bank, however, will finance $300,000 of this amount. This means that you need to come up with $65,000 out of your own pocket.

**TABLE 3-1**　**Calculating the Investment**

| Price of building | $350,000 |
|---|---|
| Less: Mortgage | 300,000 |
| Down payment | 50,000 |
| Add: Closing costs | 15,000 |
| *Total Initial Investment* | *$65,000* |

Make sure that you understand why the initial investment, or the first check that you need to write, is $65,000. This amount is the investment that you make in the building.

# Estimating the net cash flows

The process of estimating the net cash flows from the investment requires a bit more work than the previous exercise did. Sit down and think carefully about any additional revenue and any additional costs that the investment produces. Obviously, you hope that the net effect of the investment will save you cash. Certain amounts of the investment will cost you, however. On the other hand, you receive savings that the investment returns.

You want to construct a little schedule — you can write it on the back of a cocktail napkin or type it in a spreadsheet program like Excel — and use it to carefully estimate and calculate cash flows.

Suppose, in the case of the office building, that the following two items determine the net cash flows:

» **The new mortgage requires an annual $21,000 interest payment.** To keep things simple (don't worry about principal amortization just yet), suppose that this mortgage is interest-only. Further suppose that you need to pay the entire mortgage balance in 20 years as part of a balloon payment. In the meantime, however, you'll pay $21,000 at the end of every year.

» **Because you own your own building, you save $20,000 in rent the first year.** This amount, however, increases every year. If the rent that you've been paying has increased every year by 3 percent because of inflation, you may want to assume that your rent savings, to be accurately forecasted, should be inflated by 3 percent every year as well. You may want to assume that in the second year, your rent savings equal 103 percent of $20,000. In the third year, your rent savings equal 103 percent of $20,600 (which is the second year's rent savings).

Does this business of rent savings make sense? With capital expenditure investment, the capital investment often saves you money in some way. Therefore, you need to estimate those savings over the years that you'll use the capital investment. In this case, the rent savings should be equal to the current rent savings plus inflation for each year. Another way to look at the rent savings amount is to say that the rent savings equals the rent that you *won't* have to pay if you own the building.

Table 3-2 summarizes the cash flows that you enjoy by investing in this building. The table has a column for each year number. (The schedule shows 20 years of rent savings and mortgage payments.) The schedule also includes three columns, which report on the rent savings, the annual mortgage interest payment, and the net cash-flow amount. The net cash-flow amount equals the rent savings minus the mortgage interest payment. Notice that in the first two years, the mortgage interest payment exceeds the rent savings. In year 3 and beyond, however, the rent savings exceeds the mortgage payment.

Just to make sure you understand the information shown in Table 3-2, take a peek at the information estimated for year 17. What does it mean? For year 17, the schedule shows that the rent savings equal $32,095. In other words, this schedule estimates that in year 17 of building ownership, you save $32,095 by owning the building. This is the amount that you're guessing you would have had to pay in rent to a landlord had you not purchased the building. You also have to pay $21,000 in interest on that $300,000 mortgage in year 17. The net savings that you accrue, which is the net cash flow in year 17, equals $11,095 — the net amount left over from the rent savings after you pay the mortgage interest.

**TABLE 3-2**

## Summary of Building Cash Flows

| Year | Rent Savings | Mortgage Payment | Net Cash Flows |
|------|-------------|------------------|----------------|
| 1 | $20,000 | $21,000 | –1,000 |
| 2 | 20,600 | 21,000 | –400 |
| 3 | 21,218 | 21,000 | 218 |
| 4 | 21,855 | 21,000 | 855 |
| 5 | 22,511 | 21,000 | 1,511 |
| 6 | 23,186 | 21,000 | 2,186 |
| 7 | 23,882 | 21,000 | 2,882 |
| 8 | 24,598 | 21,000 | 3,598 |
| 9 | 25,336 | 21,000 | 4,336 |
| 10 | 26,096 | 21,000 | 5,096 |
| 11 | 26,879 | 21,000 | 5,879 |
| 12 | 27,685 | 21,000 | 6,685 |
| 13 | 28,516 | 21,000 | 7,516 |
| 14 | 29,371 | 21,000 | 8,371 |
| 15 | 30,252 | 21,000 | 9,252 |
| 16 | 31,160 | 21,000 | 10,160 |
| 17 | 32,095 | 21,000 | 11,095 |
| 18 | 33,058 | 21,000 | 12,058 |
| 19 | 34,050 | 21,000 | 13,050 |
| 20 | 35,072 | 21,000 | 14,072 |

I need to add one other important wrinkle to the information shown in Table 3-2. When you look at the cash flows that stem from a capital investment, you need to make some assumption about what happens at the end of the investment's life.

In the case of the building investment, for example, you probably need to show that the mortgage is paid off. You also may want to show the sale of the building at some point.

To show you how this works, suppose that at the end of year 20, you pay off the mortgage (which will still be $300,000 because you've been paying only interest), and suppose that you sell the building for $630,000. This amount is an estimate. To come up with this estimate, I took the original $350,000 purchase price and inflated that amount by 3 percent annually over 20 years. Doing so produces an estimated sale price in year 20 of $630,000. You'll also pay selling costs that total $30,000.

Table 3-3 shows how these numbers produce a final, liquidation cash flow. The gross sales price equals $630,000, as mentioned earlier. Then you have to pay the $300,000 mortgage. You also have $30,000 in selling costs. If you subtract the mortgage and the selling costs from the gross sales price, the final cash flow, then, equals $300,000. This makes sense, right? The gross sales price of $630,000 minus $300,000 for the mortgage payment minus $30,000 for selling costs equals $300,000.

**TABLE 3-3**

## Estimating the Liquidation Cash Flow

| | |
|---|---|
| Gross sale price | $630,000 |
| Less: Mortgage | 300,000 |
| Less: Selling costs | 30,000 |
| *Final Cash Flow from Sale* | *$300,000* |

The final step is combining the information shown in Tables 3-2 and 3-3. Table 3-4 does this. The net-cash-flows column summarizes the net cash flows from Table 3-2. The liquidation-cash-flow column shows 0 during the first 19 years. In year 20, however, the liquidation cash flow shows as $300,000. The real deal combines the net cash flows and the liquidation cash flow.

Just to make sure that you understand the Real Deal column's numbers, I'll go into detail about a couple of them. Start by looking at year 5. For year 5, the table shows a net cash flow of $1,511, no liquidation cash flow, and an actual cash flow to you, the business owner, of $1,511. If this building weren't a building but a CD, this would be the amount of interest that the CD would pay you for year 5.

## TABLE 3-4  Combining All Cash Flows

| Year | Net Cash Flows | Liquidation Cash Flow | The Real Deal |
|------|----------------|-----------------------|---------------|
| 1 | −1,000 | 0 | −1,000 |
| 2 | −400 | 0 | −400 |
| 3 | 218 | 0 | 218 |
| 4 | 855 | 0 | 855 |
| 5 | 1,511 | 0 | 1,511 |
| 6 | 2,186 | 0 | 2,186 |
| 7 | 2,882 | 0 | 2,882 |
| 8 | 3,598 | 0 | 3,598 |
| 9 | 4,336 | 0 | 4,336 |
| 10 | 5,096 | 0 | 5,096 |
| 11 | 5,879 | 0 | 5,879 |
| 12 | 6,685 | 0 | 6,685 |
| 13 | 7,516 | 0 | 7,516 |
| 14 | 8,371 | 0 | 8,371 |
| 15 | 9,252 | 0 | 9,252 |
| 16 | 10,160 | 0 | 10,160 |
| 17 | 11,095 | 0 | 11,095 |
| 18 | 12,058 | 0 | 12,058 |
| 19 | 13,050 | 0 | 13,050 |
| 20 | 14,072 | 300,000 | 314,072 |

In year 20, things look a bit different. The net cash flow equals $14,072 when you combine the rent savings and the mortgage interest. The sale of the building at the end of the year also produces a $300,000 cash flow. This is actually the amount that you'd receive from the escrow company after the sale of the building closes. The net or final cash flow that you receive, then, combines these two amounts: the $14,072 of net cash flow and the $300,000 of liquidation cash flow. This cash flow is like the accrued interest being paid back by the bank on a CD.

And now the hard part is done. You essentially turned your building investment into another set of cash flows. These cash flows look to a financial calculator or spreadsheet program like just another investment. In fact, these cash flows could describe some crazy 20-year CD investment. In this case, of course, they describe an imaginary building investment. But they could be the cash flows from any investment: a new piece of machinery, a corporate jet, or a new delivery truck.

## Calculating the return

As I mention previously in this chapter, I'm going to show you the two basic ways that you can calculate a return by using Excel. (I use Excel because it's so ubiquitous.) You can, however, use another spreadsheet program, such as Google Sheets or any high-powered financial business calculator. Basically, if you understand the logic of the stuff described here, you should be able to translate what I say into LibreOffice speak or Hewlett-Packard business calculator speak.

To calculate a rate of return with Microsoft Excel, first enter the cash flows produced by the investment. In Figure 3-1, I've created a simple Excel worksheet that does just this. Even if you've never used Excel before, you may be able to construct this worksheet; all you have to do is start Excel (the same way you start any other Windows program). Then you enter the cash flows shown for the building investment. Actually, you enter only the values shown in cells B2, B3, B4, B5, and so on, through cell B22. These values are the cash-flow numbers calculated and summarized in Table 3-4 earlier in this chapter. (Flip back and look at Table 3-4 if you don't see this clearly.)

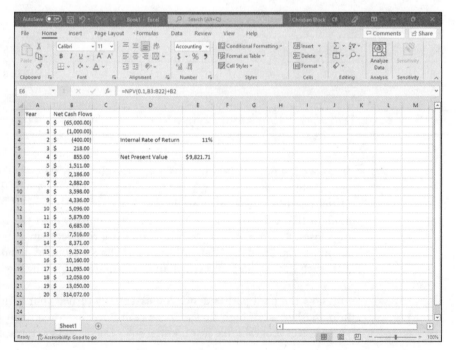

**FIGURE 3-1:**
A simple Excel worksheet that shows investment cash flows.

By the way, in case you're new to Excel, all you do to enter one of these values is click the box (technically called a *cell*) and then type the value. To enter the initial investment required to buy the building — $65,000 — you click the B2 cell and then type **-65000**. After you type this number, press Enter. You enter each of the other net cash-flow values in the same manner to make the rate-of-return calculations.

**TIP**

I also put in values to label the years and then added a little bit of text in A1 and B1 to identify what the labels are. You don't have to enter those extraneous bits of information, however.

After you provide the cash-flow values of the investment, you tell Excel the rate of return that you want calculated. In Figure 3-1, I calculate two rates of return. In cell E4, for example, I calculate an internal rate of return. An *internal rate of return (IRR)* is the interest rate that the investment delivers. A CD that pays an 11 percent interest rate, for example, pays an 11 percent IRR. To calculate an IRR, you enter an IRR function formula in a worksheet cell. In the case of the worksheet shown in Figure 3-1, for example, you click cell E4 and then type the following:

```
=IRR(B2:B22,.1)
```

If you've never seen an Excel function before, this probably looks like Greek. But all this function does is tell Excel to calculate the internal rate of return for the cash flows stored in the *range*, or block of cells, that goes from cell B2 to cell B22. The .1 is my initial guess about the IRR; you provide that value so that Excel has a starting point for calculating the return. The office-building cash flows, it turns out, produce an internal rate of return equal to 11 percent. This means that essentially, the office building delivers an 11 percent interest rate annually on the amounts invested in it.

Another common rate-of-return measure is something called a *net present value,* which essentially specifies the dollar amount by which the rate of return on a business exceeds a benchmark rate of return. The worksheet shown in Figure 3-1 shows the net present value equal to $9,821.71. In other words, this investment exceeds a benchmark rate of return by $9,821.71. You can't see it — it's buried in the formula — but the benchmark rate of return equals 10 percent. So this rate of return essentially is $9,821.71 better than a 10 percent rate of return.

To calculate the net present value by using Excel, you use another function. In the case of the worksheet shown in Figure 3-1, for example, you click cell E6 and type the following formula:

```
=NPV(0.1,B3:B22)+B2
```

This formula looks at the cash flows for years 1 through 20; discounts these cash flows by using a 10 percent rate of return; and then compares these discounted cash flows with the initial investment amount, which is the value stored in cell B2.

All this may sound a bit tricky, but essentially, this is what's going on: The net present value formula looks at the cash flows stored in the worksheet and calculates the present value amount by which these cash flows exceed a 10 percent rate of return.

The discount rate equals the rate of return that you expect on your capital investments. I should also note that the discount rate is the rate at which you can reinvest any money you get from the capital investment's cash flows.

One final comment about the information shown in Figure 3-1 (also true of the information from Table 3-4): In this figure, I describe how to calculate pretax cash flows and, therefore, how to calculate a pretax rate-of-return measure. In some situations, however, you may want to calculate an after-tax set of cash flows and an after-tax rate of return. If taxes are a significant factor, and if you're considering alternative capital investments that deliver different tax benefits, you can get more precise and sometimes different results by looking at after-tax cash flows and after-tax rates of return. If you do want to look at after-tax cash flows and profitability measures, you probably need the help of your tax adviser.

## SOME PROBLEMS WITH THE IRR MEASUREMENT

I kind of like the IRR measurement because it makes a lot of intuitive sense. Capital budgeting is burdensome enough without being weighed down further by some tricky, abstract, theoretical capital budgeting tool such as net present value.

You should know, however, that the IRR has some practical weaknesses, which is why people with MBAs and PhDs in business and finance greatly prefer the net present value measure. In this sidebar, I identify these weaknesses for you. Knowing about the weaknesses enables you to use the IRR tool more safely. On the other hand, knowing about the weaknesses may also make you choose to bear with the abstractness of the net present value model and use it instead. Anyway, here are the weaknesses:

- **The IRR measure doesn't always identify the best investment.** In other words, you sometimes can't pick the investment with the highest IRR and get the most profitable investment. As an extreme example, suppose that you have $100,000 to invest. Would you rather invest only $10,000 of your money in something earning

20 percent annually or look at something earning 18 percent annually in which you can invest the entire $100,000? Do you see the difference? Twenty percent of $10,000 isn't going to be as good as 18 percent of $100,000. Unfortunately, the IRR measure — by focusing on the percentage return — sometimes causes people to lose sight of the dollars of profit, which (obviously) is what you really want to maximize. By comparison, the net present value *does* calculate a straight dollar profit amount. By picking an investment with the highest net present value, you're picking the investment that delivers the most dollars and profits.

- **The IRR measure doesn't recognize reinvestment risk very well.** This sounds like another mumbo-jumbo problem, but it's actually a pretty important one. Suppose that you have a million dollars to invest. Would you rather pick a 1-year investment (Option A) that earns 30 percent or a 20-year investment (Option B) that earns 20 percent? At first blush, a 30 percent investment seems like a pretty good one. Obviously, 30 percent is a lot more than 20 percent. Here's what you have to consider, however: Where are you going to invest the money from Option A one year from now, when that investment liquidates? The key is that you have to be able to invest the $1.3 million (which is what you get from Option A one year from now) in something that beats the Option B investment. In other words, you have to think about that reinvestment risk for your investments. The IRR doesn't really do this. By comparison, the net present value *does.* Implicitly, the net present value assumes that you can reinvest money at the discount rate used in the calculation. In essence, the discount rate is the going rate that you can earn on your other capital investments, so it automatically factors in reinvestment.

- **The IRR measure doesn't always produce a solution or a unique solution.** The IRR formula isn't solvable, for example, when the cash flows don't really look like investment cash flows. If you have an investment that generates cash only because there's no initial cash outlay, you can't calculate an IRR. But such an investment, obviously, is a very good deal that you should select. A related problem is that sometimes, the IRR formula can't be uniquely solved. This business about no unique solution stems from a little bit of mathematical weirdness. (The problem is that technically, an IRR formula is an *n*th root polynomial equation with up to *n*th possible solutions!) This multiple-solutions weirdness pops up when you have the cash-flow signs changing over the years that the investment is held. In the case of the office-building investment, only one sign change exists. In year 2, the cash flow is negative. And in year 3, the cash flow becomes positive and stays positive. This means that the building has one single IRR. If cash flow was positive in some years and negative in others, however, each of these flips from negative to positive cash value, or vice versa, indicates another solution to the IRR formula. I won't go into any more detail, but the important point is that by using the net present value formula, you always know that a solution exists and that it's the single unique solution, given a particular discount rate.

**REMEMBER**

An important thing to know about pretax cash flows and returns versus after-tax cash flows and returns: Make sure that you're using apples-to-apples comparisons. It's often fine to work with pretax cash flows; just make sure that you're comparing pretax cash flows with other pretax cash flows. You don't want to compare pretax returns with after-tax returns. That's an apples-to-oranges comparison. Predictably, it doesn't work.

# Measuring Liquidity

In large businesses, people don't worry or talk much about liquidity — at least not when it comes to capital investments. Liquidity as a criterion for looking at capital investments is downplayed. The logic is that in most cases, very large firms have almost unlimited access to capital through the capital markets (the stock markets, the debt markets, or even just big-time borrowing from enormous banks). For many smaller businesses, however, liquidity is important. You can make only a limited number of investments. Additionally, you have a limited amount of capital — almost always less than you like. New opportunities and ways to invest your money continually arrive. For these reasons, you typically want to look at the liquidity of your capital investments.

One easy way to measure liquidity is with a *payback period*, which measures what it takes for an investment to pay back its original investment. The office-building example doesn't work very well for this sort of calculation, so to make things a little easier, suppose that you're considering a $10,000 investment that produces $2,000 a year in net cash flows. In this case, you can calculate the payback period with the following formula:

```
Payback period = initial investment/annual cash flow
```

In the case of the $10,000 investment described here, the actual formula is

```
$10,000/$2,000 = 5
```

This formula means that the $10,000 investment, through its $2,000-per-year cash flows, takes five years to pay back.

Again, you don't want to focus on liquidity. Liquidity is almost never as important as profitability. But even though profitability is paramount, liquidity is often something that you want to consider. At times, you're going to want investments that pay back more quickly rather than those that pay back less quickly. When the investments do pay off, you'll have other good reinvestment opportunities.

# Thinking about Risk

Obviously, risk matters. Risk is an issue even with simple investments like bank CDs. But with capital investments, no government agency is looking out for your interest and picking up the pieces if things do a Humpty Dumpty and come crashing down.

So think for a minute about risk management and assessment in the case of capital expenditures. Here are three important comments that I can share:

>> **Be very careful and thoughtful in coming up with cash flows.** The better job you do of thinking about and estimating the cash flows from a capital expenditure, the more reliable and useful your results will be. Good cash-flow estimates produce good rate-of-return measurements. Look back to the examples shown in Tables 3-1, 3-2, 3-3, and 3-4 earlier in this chapter.

>> **Experiment.** You absolutely need to experiment with your assumptions. Make changes and see how those changes affect both the cash-flow and rate-of-return measurements. Looking back at the cash-flow information shown earlier in Tables 3-3 and 3-4, for example, you can see that the single biggest cash flow in the building investment is the resale amount in year 20. It would be very interesting to see what effect a lower inflation, or appreciation, rate has on the ultimate rate of return. A 2 percent inflation rate would dramatically change the cash flows and the rate-of-return measurement for this investment. Similarly, an inflation rate of 5 percent or 6 percent over those 20 years would dramatically change things. In the former case, things get ugly quickly. In the latter case . . . well, we all remember how good a leveraged real estate investment can be when given high, continued inflation rates, right?

>> **Think about the discount rate that you use.** I don't spend a lot of time talking about the discount rate, but you should implicitly take into consideration the risk that an investment makes you face. My finance professor always said, "Your discount rate should equal the rate of return that similarly risky investments produce." There's tremendous wisdom in this simple guideline. (Thanks, Professor Schall!) In other words, if you're looking at a very risky investment, you should compare that investment with the hoped-for higher rates of return that other, similarly risky investments deliver. You'd never pick an investment that, given its risk level, delivers an inferior rate of return. At the same time, if you're looking at lower-risk investments, you want to use a lower discount rate. A relatively low-risk investment in something like an office building, for example, shouldn't be evaluated with a discount rate that may be appropriate for some super-risky investment in some new bit of leading-edge technology.

**TIP**

You want to try some different discount rates. By experimenting not only with your cash-flow numbers, but also with your discount rates, you can see how the quality of an investment changes when you use different discount rates (and implicitly make different assumptions about the investment's risk).

# What Does All This Have to Do with QuickBooks?

So here's a question: What does all this capital budgeting stuff have to do with QuickBooks?

Well, quite honestly, capital budgeting really doesn't relate directly to using QuickBooks. In some ways, capital budgeting is about a financial management task that's critically important and that you need to think about . . . but it's a task that QuickBooks doesn't support directly.

That said, do note that much of the data that you've collected with QuickBooks is often extremely useful for getting good estimates of the savings and costs associated with some capital expenditure.

In looking at the example of investing in an office building, for example, knowing what you've been paying in rent and what you may be able to save by buying your own building is exactly the sort of information that you need — and exactly the sort of information that the rich financial database of QuickBooks supplies.

In truth, your estimates of cash flows typically are much more involved than what I show in this chapter. If you do have a building investment under consideration, you should consider all sorts of expenses related to repairing and maintaining the building. If you've been leasing space in someone else's building, you have to consider all sorts of expenses associated with that, including special insurance that the landlord makes you buy, special amounts that you spend because the space doesn't quite meet your requirements, and so on. QuickBooks helps you with this type of information.

# 6 Business Plans

# Contents at a Glance

Chapter **1**

# Profit-Volume-Cost Analysis

P*rofit-volume-cost analysis* is a powerful tool that estimates how a business's profits change as its sales volumes change, as well as break-even points. (A *break-even point* is the sales revenue level that produces zero profits.)

Profit-volume-cost analysis often produces surprising results. Typically, the analysis shows that small changes in a business's sales volume produce big changes in profits.

TIP

Hotels and airlines are types of businesses that often see surprising fluctuations in their profits based on relatively modest changes in their sales revenue. Indeed, now that you know this, you'll probably notice that investment analysts often use small changes in hotel occupancy and in airline load factors (the percentage of seats filled on a plane) to explain big changes in profits.

The first part of this chapter talks about the theory of profit-volume-cost analysis. Understanding the theory may be all you need to apply this tool to your specific setting. At the end of the chapter, I describe a Microsoft Excel workbook that you can use for more sophisticated profit-volume-cost analysis. That workbook is available to download from my website at `https://stephenlnelson.com/wp-content/uploads/profit_volume_cost-1.xlsx`.

If you do not own a licensed copy of Microsoft Excel, you can use Google Sheets or Excel for the Web to open and view the Excel spreadsheet.

TIP

# Seeing How Profit-Volume-Cost Analysis Works

Profit-volume-cost analysis uses three pieces of information to show how your profits change as sales revenue changes: estimates of your sales revenue, your gross margin percentage, and your fixed costs. Usually, all three items of data are easy to come by.

Suppose that you're a builder of high-end racing sailboats that sell for $100,000 each. Further suppose that each boat costs you $40,000 in labor and material and that your shop costs $160,000 a year to keep open.

You can calculate your gross margin percentage by using the following formula:

```
(boat sales price - direct labor and material costs) ÷ (boat sales cost)
```

Or you can use the actual numbers from my example:

```
($100,000 - $40,000) ÷ ($100,000)
```

This formula returns the result 0.6, or 60 percent. In this case, your fixed cost amount equals $160,000.

With the fixed cost and gross margin percentage information, you can calculate the profits that different amounts of sales revenue produce. To make this calculation, you use the following formula:

```
profits = (sales ÷ gross margin percentage) - fixed cost
```

Table 1-1 shows some examples of how you can use this formula to estimate the profits at different sales volume levels. At $200,000 in annual sales, for example, the business suffers a $40,000 loss. At $300,000 in sales, the business earns a $20,000 profit. At $400,000 in sales, the business earns an $80,000 profit. Table 1-1 also shows the formula used to estimate profits.

TABLE 1-1

## Applying the Profit-Volume-Cost Formula

| Sales | Formula | Result |
|-------|---------|--------|
| $200,000 | ($200,000 × 0.60) – $160,000 | $40,000 (a loss) |
| $300,000 | ($300,000 × 0.60) – $160,000 | $20,000 (a little profit) |
| $400,000 | ($400,000 × 0.60) – $160,000 | $80,000 (a nice profit) |

The really interesting thing about the information shown in Table 1-1 — and I don't want to beat a dead horse here — is that profits often change more significantly than revenue changes. Look at Table 1-1 and examine what happens when revenue increases from $300,000 to $400,000 — roughly a 33 percent increase. You see that profits quadruple from $20,000 to $80,000.

Here's another way to look at the estimated profits at the $300,000 and $400,000 sales levels: If sales drop by 25 percent from $400,000 to $300,000, profits decrease by 75 percent from $80,000 to $20,000.

Table 1-1 illustrates a common experience of businesses. Relatively modest changes in sales revenue produce large — sometimes stunningly large — changes in profits. The reason that you perform profit-volume-cost analysis, therefore, is to understand how sensitive your business profits are to changes in sales volume. With this information, you can understand how important it is to prevent decreases in sales, and you can reap the rewards of increasing sales.

I need to make one final point about the information shown in Table 1-1: You can calculate this same information, almost in longhand fashion, by using miniature income statements. Table 1-2, for example, shows some miniature income statements that calculate profits at various sales levels.

TABLE 1-2

## Miniature Income Statements

| Boats Sold | 2 | 3 | 4 |
|------------|---|---|---|
| Sales revenue | $200,000 | $300,000 | $400,000 |
| Variable costs | ($80,000) | ($120,000) | ($160,000) |
| Gross margin | 120,000 | 180,000 | 240,000 |
| Fixed costs | (80,000) | (160,000) | (160,000) |
| Profits | $40,000 | $20,000 | $80,000 |

It's no coincidence that the miniature income statements shown in Table 1-2 produce the same estimates of profit as the formulas shown in Table 1-1. The difference — and the advantage of the approach to information illustrated in Table 1-1 — is that the formula makes it possible to quickly calculate estimates of profits at any sales level. Constructing even a miniature income statement like the one shown in Table 1-2 typically is more work than using the approach shown in Table 1-1.

# Calculating Break-Even Points

Here's another important piece of information that belongs between your ears: A common application of the formula used in Table 1-1, earlier in this chapter, is to calculate a break-even point. A break-even point, as noted previously, shows the sales revenue volume that produces zero profit and zero loss.

Remember the formula for performing profit-volume-cost analysis? It goes like this:

```
profits = (sales revenue × gross margin percentage) - fixed costs
```

Rather than calculate profits based on sales revenue, gross margin percentage, and fixed costs, you can calculate a sales revenue amount based on the three other variables: profits, gross margin percentage, and fixed costs.

The formula for making such a break-even calculation, based on algebraic manipulation of the profit-volume-cost analysis formula, looks like this:

```
Break-even point (in sales revenue) = fixed costs ÷ gross margin percentage
```

To calculate the break-even point in sales revenue for the example boat-building business, you make the calculation

```
$160,000 ÷ 40 percent
```

which produces the result

```
$266,667
```

Accordingly, the boat-building business needs $266,667 of revenue to break even.

The break-even point formula described in the preceding paragraphs estimates a break-even point in revenue. Often, however, such a revenue-based break-even point doesn't make complete sense. In the case of the boat-building business in which you sell boats for $100,000 each, there's no practical way to get $266,667 of revenue. You can't sell two thirds of a boat. The correct way to interpret a break-even point in revenue in this example, then, is to interpret it as a *rough* break-even point. As a practical matter in the boat-building business, the break-even point is slightly less than three boats per year.

## CONFUSED ABOUT THE BREAK-EVEN-POINT FORMULA?

The formula for calculating the break-even point seems pretty different from the formula for calculating profit-volume-cost information — or at least it does at first blush. But the second formula is derived from the first. Because some compulsive readers may want to know how this variation works, I show it to you in this sidebar.

Here's the fixed base formula:

```
profits = (sales revenue × gross margin percentage) - fixed
    costs
```

If you subtract the fixed costs from both sides of the formula, you get the following:

```
profits - fixed costs = sales revenue × gross margin percentage
```

Because profits equal zero at the break-even point, you can simplify this formula further by scratching out the profits variable, as shown here:

```
-fixed costs = sales revenue × gross margin percentage
```

If you divide both sides of the equation by the gross margin percentage, you get the basic break-even point formula, as shown here:

```
-fixed costs × gross margin percentage = sales revenue
```

And that's the way the formula gets created. Essentially, all you have to do is divide the fixed-costs amount by the gross margin percentage. The result shows the sales revenue at which a firm breaks even.

If, in this example, you were working with boats that cost $1,000 each or $100 each, the precision of the break-even point would be much greater. If you manufactured day-sailor boats that cost $1,000 apiece, you'd know that the break-even point is somewhere between 266 and 267 boats (calculated by dividing the $266,667 of revenue by $1,000). If the boats cost $100 each — perhaps they're model boats — you know that the break-even point is between 2,666 model boats and 2,667 model boats (calculated by dividing the revenue amount by $100).

In either case, you see that the smaller the revenue per unit, the more precision you get in the break-even point in units.

You can also see from this example that the process of converting a break-even point in revenue to a break-even point in units is simply a matter of dividing the break-even point in revenue by the unit price.

# Using Real QuickBooks Data for Profit-Volume-Cost Analysis

As noted previously, you need three items of data to perform profit-volume-cost analysis: sales revenue, gross margin percentage, and fixed cost. Typically, these items of data aren't difficult to find if you've been using QuickBooks. Nevertheless, this data doesn't map perfectly to line items that appear in a QuickBooks income statement. For this reason, I briefly discuss how you come up with these pieces of information.

## Sales revenue

The sales revenue levels that you use in the formula are the sales revenue levels that you want to experiment with. They probably represent possible — or maybe even likely — sales revenue levels for your business. Accordingly, the sales revenue levels don't come from QuickBooks. You may want to look at past income statements to determine reasonable or likely sales revenue levels. The formula inputs are probably rough estimates, however; they don't come from a QuickBooks income statement.

## Gross margin percentage

You calculate the gross margin percentage, as illustrated previously, by subtracting your variable costs from your sales revenue and then dividing that result (which is the gross margin) by the sales revenue. The variable costs include the costs of the items that you sell: inventory, commissions, shipping, and similar costs.

Because calculating the gross margin percentage can be a little bit confusing the first few times you do it, here are a couple of examples to review:

» **Boat building:** If you sell $100,000 boats, and the material, labor, and commission expenses for each boat total $40,000, you can calculate the gross margin percentage by using the formula

```
($100,000 - $40,000) ÷ $100,000
```

That formula returns 0.6, or 60 percent, which is the gross margin percentage of the boat-building business.

» **Tax return service:** For another example, assume that you're running a personal-services business in which you prepare tax returns for a living. Further assume that you charge $200 for a small-business tax return and that the only variable cost is a $40 fee that you have to pay to the tax software company for the return. In this case, you calculate the gross margin percentage by using the formula

```
($200 - $40) ÷ $200
```

This formula returns the value 0.8, or 80 percent. In this case, 80 percent is the gross margin percentage for your tax return preparation business.

The key point is that variable costs vary with sales revenue. If a sale occurs, the sale produces variable costs. If no sale occurs, no variable costs are incurred.

So what does all this mean? Well, typically, the variable costs equal the cost of goods sold (COGS) number that's shown on your QuickBooks income statement. This COGS number probably includes the inventory items that you sell (if your business resells inventory) and other items, such as freight and sales commissions. Therefore, you can get most or all the variable cost information right off the QuickBooks income statement.

**WARNING**

You may need to fiddle with the COGS amount reported on the QuickBooks income statement. Remember that variable costs are those costs that vary with sales, and as a result, some of the costs that you've included in the COGS section of your income statement may not be variable. Some of the costs reported in the regular operating–expenses portion of your income statement are actually variable.

Therefore, you may want to think about the costs reported in the COGS section and in the operating expenses section of your income statement. If you realize that the COGS value isn't a good estimate of variable costs, make some adjustments.

A fixed cost that's included in the COGS number should be subtracted, obviously. And a variable cost that's included with the other operating expenses may need to be added to the COGS number.

## Fixed costs

*Fixed costs* include all your other nonvariable costs. In a nutshell, fixed costs are fixed because they don't change with sales volume. Fixed costs include items such as rent paid on an office or factory, salaries paid to permanent employees, overhead for insurance, and so forth.

To see how fixed costs work and get calculated, return to the examples of the boat-building business and the tax return preparation service:

>> **In the boat-building business,** the firm carries overhead of more than $160,000. This amount may include $80,000 for the shop in which you build your boats and $80,000 for the salaries that you pay to two craftsmen whom you continue to employ whether or not you have boats to build. In this case, then, these overhead costs constitute your $160,000 of fixed costs. These fixed costs don't change based on changes in sales volume.

>> **In the tax return service,** your only fixed expenses are $100 a month for advertisements and $700 a month to rent a small office. In this case, then, your fixed costs equal $800 a month. Again, these fixed costs don't change based on changes in sales volume.

# Recognizing the Downside of the Profit-Volume-Cost Model

Okay, this stuff all sounds fine and good, but what happens when little reservations start to pop up? Annoying little problems? Minor weaknesses that turn into irritations?

Here's the problem: Like any abstract explanation of reality, the profit-volume-cost model isn't perfect. If you want to get nitpicky — and you should for a moment — several practical problems creep into the calculations of the profit-volume-cost formula and its application to your real-life business affairs. I discuss these problems in the following list, but I don't think that having such problems means that you shouldn't use the model. They only change the way that you work with the model.

>> **Any assumptions that you make about variable costs and fixed costs typically apply only over a range of sales revenue.** In the boat-building business, for example, the numbers used in the preceding sections don't apply if the boat builder scales up and builds 500 boats a year. That's obvious, right? It may be that the range of sales revenue valid for a 60 percent gross margin percentage — and, therefore, $160,000 of fixed costs — is really somewhere between 0 boats per year and 8 boats per year. Move to a sales revenue level above 8 boats a year, and it's very likely that either the gross margin percentage or the fixed cost amount will change.

>> **In the super-long run, as a practical matter, there's no such thing as a fixed cost.** Essentially, every cost is variable. In the boat-building business, for example, you could — in the long run — lay off two craftsmen and move to a smaller shop. Perhaps you could even build boats in your backyard. Fixed costs, in other words, are fixed only for a particular period of time. If you move beyond that period of time, the fixed costs are no longer fixed. This seems like an obvious point, but it's important to recognize.

>> **In the super-short term, there's no such thing as a variable cost.** (Or at least there aren't very many variable costs.) In the boat-building business, even if you pay your laborers an hourly wage for building the boats, you probably can't send the laborers home early just because work for the day is done. You can't tell your laborers at the end of Tuesday not to come in Wednesday, Thursday, or Friday because you have no work for them. Other variable costs may work the same way — not always, but sometimes. In any case, recognize that some costs may vary over a month or year but not over a day or a week. In other words, in the super-short term, variable costs often aren't very variable.

The three preceding conundrums indicate that profit-volume-cost analysis suffers some limits. You can't use a gross margin percentage and a fixed cost amount for just *any* sales revenue estimates; you use those two items of data for a carefully considered range of sales revenue volumes. Furthermore, you can't use profit-volume-cost analysis for super-short time frames. Variable costs in that case aren't really variable. And you can't use profit-volume-cost analysis for super-long time frames because in the long run, no fixed cost stays fixed.

To generalize, the profit-volume-cost analysis tool provides rough measurements. These rough measurements can be very useful to you, but they're just rough measurements. Always apply common sense when using profit-volume-cost analysis.

**TIP**

Maybe it's only a little game I play with myself, but sometimes, I don't think about fixed costs and variable costs. Instead, I think about *sort-of* fixed costs and *sort-of* variable costs. By admitting up front that the fixed costs aren't always solidly fixed and that the variable costs aren't always solidly variable, I find myself getting more comfortable with the profit-volume-cost analysis formula. I remind myself that the model isn't perfect — only a rough tool to estimate profit and break-even points.

# Using the Profit-Volume-Cost Analysis Workbook

I've created a Profit-Volume-Cost Analysis workbook for you in case you want to perform more sophisticated profit-volume-cost analysis. This workbook is available on my website at `https://stephenlnelson.com/wp-content/uploads/profit_volume_cost-1.xlsx`.

The Profit-Volume-Cost Analysis workbook enables you to estimate profits at a variety of sales revenue volumes, to estimate break-even points, and to chart break-even and profit-volume-cost data. Some of the calculations are a little bit cumbersome, but almost every calculation is simply an extension of what I discuss in the preceding paragraphs of this chapter.

In the remaining pages of this chapter, I describe how to use the Profit-Volume-Cost Analysis workbook and how to understand and interpret both the break-even analysis and the profit-volume-cost analysis performed by the workbook. I also share a few words about the charts that graphically depict the profit-volume-cost analysis results.

## Collecting your inputs

Figure 1-1 shows the worksheet range in which you enter the raw data required for the profit-volume-cost analysis. The workbook collects more data points than you may expect. Most of this information, however, is simply a slightly more granular approach to collecting the three basic inputs that any profit-volume-cost analysis depends on: sales revenue estimates, gross margin percentage, and fixed costs.

**TIP**

You don't need to be an Excel expert to use the Profit-Volume-Cost Analysis workbook described in this chapter, but you do need to know how to start and stop Excel and how to enter values into worksheet cells. If you don't possess these Excel skills, you may want to consider buying and reading a recent edition of *Excel For Dummies*, by Greg Harvey (John Wiley & Sons, Inc.).

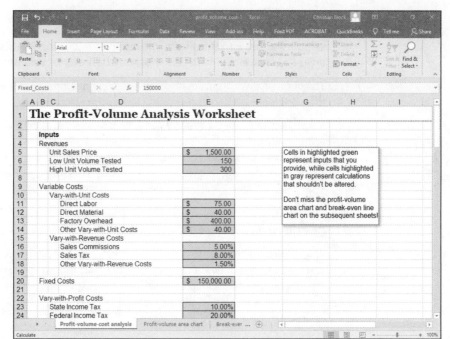

**FIGURE 1-1:**
The inputs area
of the Profit-
Volume-Cost
Analysis
workbook.

To use the Profit–Volume–Cost Analysis workbook, follow these steps:

1. **Open the Profit-Volume-Cost Analysis workbook.**

   (a) *Point your browser to* https://stephenlnelson.com/wp–content/ uploads/profit_volume_cost–1.xlsx.

   (b) *The Excel file will automatically download, which shows as a link at the bottom of your web browser.*

   (c) *From the link at the bottom of your web browser, you can open the Excel file directly, or you can click Show in Folder and move the file out of your download folder.*

   (d) *When Excel displays the Open dialog box, open the folder with the* profit_ volume_cost–1.xlsx *file and then double-click the file.*

2. **Describe the sales revenue that you want to test.**

   To do this, you must provide three pieces of information: the unit sales price, the low unit sales volume, and the high unit sales volume.

   Enter the unit sales price into cell E5. If you sell an item that costs $1,500, for example, you enter **$1,500** into cell E5. Use the low unit volume tested and high unit volume tested inputs shown in cells E6 and E7 (respectively) to identify the range of sales volumes that you want to test. The low unit volume tested value multiplied by the unit sales price equals the lowest revenue volume that the worksheet tests. The high unit volume tested multiplied by the unit sales price amount equals the largest sales revenue volume tested.

The three revenue inputs that you collect and input into cells E5, E6, and E7 tell the workbook which sales revenue volumes you want to analyze.

If you wanted to use the Profit-Volume-Cost Analysis workbook to test sales volumes for the boat-building business that I describe earlier in the chapter, the unit sales price would equal $100,000, so the low unit volume tested may equal 2, and the high unit volume may equal 5. These inputs, then, would test sales volumes of between $100,000 and $500,000, based on a $100,000 price for a boat.

3. **Describe the variable costs.**

When you do real-life profit-volume-cost analysis, you find that your variable costs fall into one of two categories: variable costs that can be expressed as an amount per unit and variable costs that can be expressed as a percentage of the sales price. The worksheet range E10:E18 collects the information needed to describe these sorts of variable costs.

The first set of variable costs, which I call *vary-with-unit costs,* goes into cells E11, E12, E13, and E14. Any direct labor costs associated with the item that you're selling go into cell E11. Direct material costs go into E12. Factory overhead costs, which are variable and based on units sold, go into cell E13. If you have any other vary-with-unit costs, you enter the amount per unit for these costs into cell E14.

The example vary-with-unit cost values shown in Figure 1-1 mean that for each unit sold, the assumption is that the business pays $75 per unit in direct labor, $40 per unit in direct materials, $400 per unit in factory overhead, and another $40 per unit for other vary-with-unit costs. If you add up these amounts, you see that vary-with-unit costs equal $555 per unit sold.

In addition to vary-with-unit costs, firms often pay variable costs that are best expressed as a percentage of revenue. In the Profit-Volume-Cost Analysis workbook, the worksheet range E16:E18 supplies space to describe and record these variable costs, which I call *vary-with-revenue* costs. The workbook, for example, shows a 5 percent sales commission in cell E16. The workbook shows an 8 percent sales tax in cell E17. And just to provide a catch-all category for other vary-with-revenue costs, the workbook includes (and I show for purposes of this example) another vary-with-revenue-costs value in cell E18.

In the case of the sample data set shown in Figure 1-1, for example, vary-with-revenue costs equal 14.5 percent of sales.

### 4. Record your fixed costs.

To record or estimate your fixed costs, enter the fixed costs amount into cell E20. In Figure 1-1, for example, fixed costs show as $150,000.

### 5. Estimate any variable costs that vary with profits.

Here's one other wrinkle that you may often encounter with real-life profit-volume-cost analysis: variable costs that don't vary from changes in sales revenue but from changes in profits. Some businesses have profit-sharing plans, for example. Those profits represent variable costs because they vary with changes in sales revenue — sort of. To estimate the profit-sharing costs, first calculate profits and then apply the profit-sharing percentage to those profits. Income taxes — federal, state, and local — also fall into the category of variable costs that vary not with changes in sales revenue, but with changes in profit.

In the workbook shown in Figure 1-1, I've provided three cells — E23, E24, and E25 — that let you recognize these variable costs. I call this category of variable costs *vary-with-profit* costs. You can enter the state income tax percentage into cell E23. You can enter the federal income tax percentage into cell E43. And if you have any other vary-with-profit costs, you can enter the sum of these costs as a percentage into cell E25.

**TIP**

I should tell you that vary–with–profit costs are tricky to estimate precisely. The trickiness stems from a couple of factors:

>> **Many vary-with-profit costs aren't calculated simply as percentages of profit.** The cost calculations are considerably more complicated. Income tax costs, for example, don't use a single percentage. They often use a schedule of progressive percentages.

>> **Vary-with-profit costs often interrelate.** State income taxes affect federal income taxes, for example. Other vary-with-profit costs may interrelate too. A profit-sharing percentage may be applied on an after-tax basis, for example. The workbook formulas don't explicitly recognize any interrelationship between these variables. Therefore, to precisely model these vary-with-profit costs, you must enter percentages that have been fiddled with a bit, as described in the sidebar "Dealing with vary-with-profit costs" later in this chapter.

After you collect the needed inputs for the Profit-Volume-Cost Analysis workbook, the workbook estimates a break-even point and prepares a profit-volume forecast. The workbook also supplies a couple of useful charts that graphically show the break-even and the profit-volume analysis data. The next sections of this chapter describe these analysis results.

# Understanding the Break-Even Analysis Forecast

The break-even analysis that the workbook makes based on the inputs that you enter is shown in Figure 1-2 in the worksheet range from B27:E45. The break-even analysis shows the number of units required to break even in cell E28 and the sales revenue required to break even in cell E29. You calculate the total sales revenue required to break even by using the same basic formula described earlier in the chapter. You calculate the volume in units break-even point by dividing the sales revenue break-even point by the unit sales price.

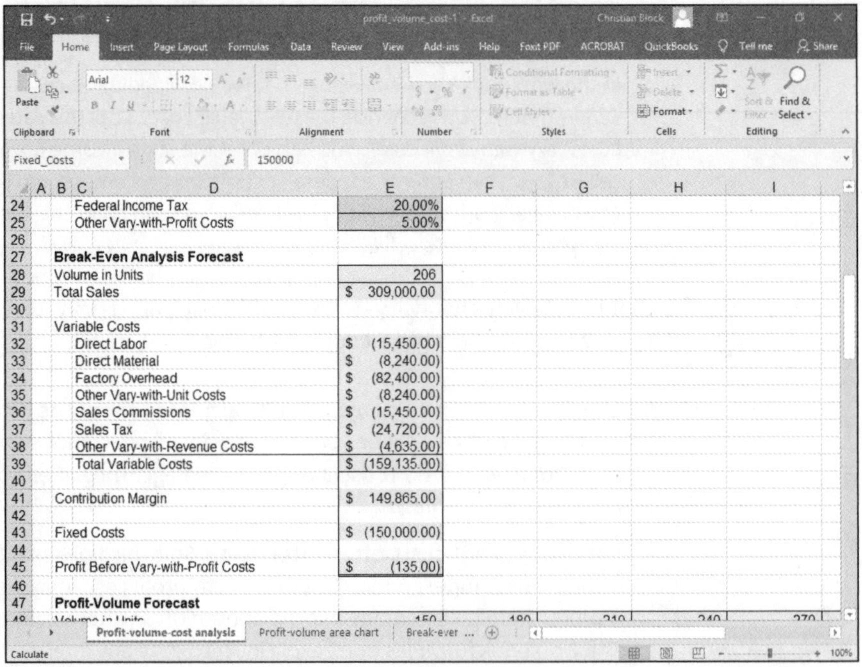

**FIGURE 1-2:**
The Break-Even Analysis Forecast.

The variable costs portion of the break-even analysis shows the amount spent on each of the costs. Cell E32 shows the amount that will be spent on direct labor.

The contribution margin, which is the same thing as gross margin, appears in cell E41. This shows the amount left over from sales revenue after paying the variable costs.

A fixed cost appears in cell E43. By subtracting the fixed costs from the contribution margin, the workbook calculates the break-even point, which should be zero but may not be because of a rounding error. In Figure 1-2, for example, the profit before vary-with-profit costs value equals –$135.

Although the information shown in Figure 1-2 may seem to be voluminous, you conceptually understand all this data. A little forecast worksheet simply shows the sales revenue and the sales units that produce the break-even point. This worksheet also shows the amounts that you'll spend on variable costs and fixed costs. Profits equal zero at the break-even point, so there aren't any vary-with-profit costs.

# Understanding the Profit-Volume Forecast

Figure 1-3 shows the miniature income statement at various sales volume levels. Figure 1-4 shows the same information presented not in dollars but in percentages of total sales.

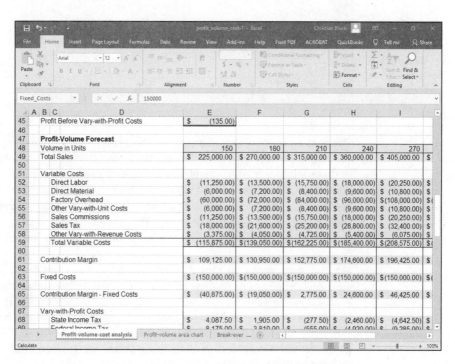

FIGURE 1-3:
The Profit-Volume Forecast, in dollars.

The Profit-Volume Forecast worksheet, shown in Figure 1-3, shows the range of sales volume both in revenue and in units that the worksheet calculates. The lowest sales revenue volume and the highest sales revenue volume are set by your input for the low unit volume tested value and the high unit volume tested value. (See the numbers entered into cells E6 and E7 of Figure 1-1.)

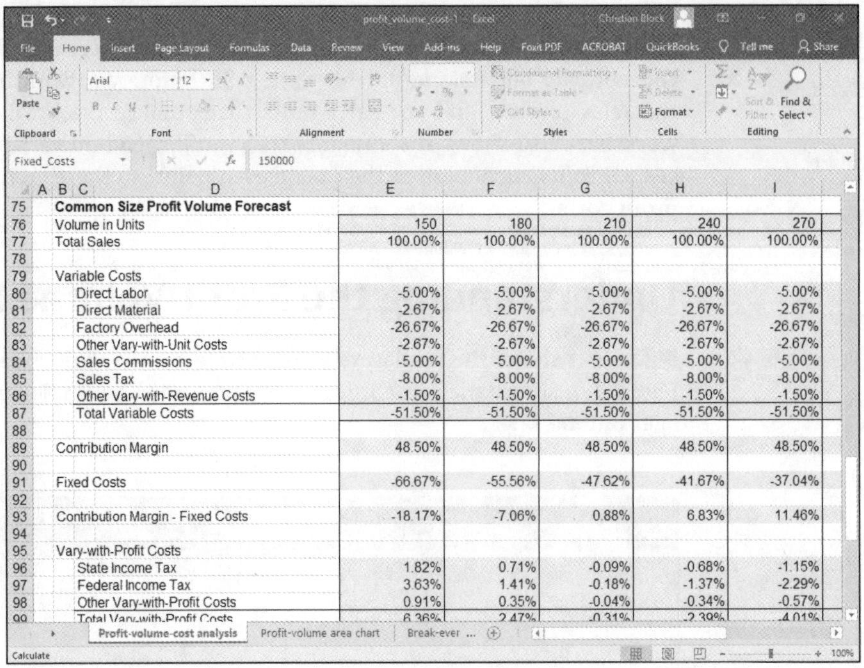

| | D | E | F | G | H | I |
|---|---|---|---|---|---|---|
| 75 | **Common Size Profit Volume Forecast** | | | | | |
| 76 | Volume in Units | 150 | 180 | 210 | 240 | 270 |
| 77 | Total Sales | 100.00% | 100.00% | 100.00% | 100.00% | 100.00% |
| 78 | | | | | | |
| 79 | Variable Costs | | | | | |
| 80 | Direct Labor | -5.00% | -5.00% | -5.00% | -5.00% | -5.00% |
| 81 | Direct Material | -2.67% | -2.67% | -2.67% | -2.67% | -2.67% |
| 82 | Factory Overhead | -26.67% | -26.67% | -26.67% | -26.67% | -26.67% |
| 83 | Other Vary-with-Unit Costs | -2.67% | -2.67% | -2.67% | -2.67% | -2.67% |
| 84 | Sales Commissions | -5.00% | -5.00% | -5.00% | -5.00% | -5.00% |
| 85 | Sales Tax | -8.00% | -8.00% | -8.00% | -8.00% | -8.00% |
| 86 | Other Vary-with-Revenue Costs | -1.50% | -1.50% | -1.50% | -1.50% | -1.50% |
| 87 | Total Variable Costs | -51.50% | -51.50% | -51.50% | -51.50% | -51.50% |
| 88 | | | | | | |
| 89 | Contribution Margin | 48.50% | 48.50% | 48.50% | 48.50% | 48.50% |
| 90 | | | | | | |
| 91 | Fixed Costs | -66.67% | -55.56% | -47.62% | -41.67% | -37.04% |
| 92 | | | | | | |
| 93 | Contribution Margin - Fixed Costs | -18.17% | -7.06% | 0.88% | 6.83% | 11.46% |
| 94 | | | | | | |
| 95 | Vary-with-Profit Costs | | | | | |
| 96 | State Income Tax | 1.82% | 0.71% | -0.09% | -0.68% | -1.15% |
| 97 | Federal Income Tax | 3.63% | 1.41% | -0.18% | -1.37% | -2.29% |
| 98 | Other Vary-with-Profit Costs | 0.91% | 0.35% | -0.04% | -0.34% | -0.57% |
| 99 | Total Vary-with-Profit Costs | 6.36% | 2.47% | -0.31% | -2.39% | -4.01% |

**FIGURE 1-4:** The Common Size Profit-Volume Forecast.

The miniature income statements in the Profit-Volume Forecast worksheet look very similar to a typical QuickBooks income statement. The variable-costs portion of the miniature income statement reports on the cost of goods sold. The contribution margin is equivalent to the gross margin reported in a QuickBooks income statement. A fixed cost amount summarizes the operating expenses. The vary-with-profit costs essentially summarize income taxes and other profit-based expenses, such as a profit-sharing plan. Profits equate to the net income.

Figure 1-3 shows a case in which modest changes in sales revenue can often produce huge changes in profits. In Figure 1-3, column G shows the Profit-Volume Forecast at the sales level equal to $315,000. Column H shows the Sales Revenue and Cost Forecast at a sales revenue level of $360,000. As the firm increased its profits by roughly 15 percent (this increase is shown in cells G48 and H48), profits increased by almost 900 percent from $1,804 to $15,990 (the change from the values in cells G73 to H73).

You may not be interested in the Common Size Profit-Volume Forecast, shown in Figure 1-4, because this income statement shows percentages based on sales rather than dollar amounts. This figure lets you see what percentage of total sales a cost item represents. Sometimes this information is useful, and sometimes it isn't. If you aren't interested in the information, simply select rows 75–101 and then delete them from your workbook.

# Looking at the profit-volume-cost charts

For fun, I include a couple of simple charts that show results from the profit-volume-cost analysis. Figure 1-5, for example, shows the break-even line chart. This line chart plots the total fixed costs, the total variable costs, and then the total sales. The intersection of the total sales line and the total fixed costs line shows the break-even point. By comparing the slopes of the total sales and the variable costs line, you can get an idea of how sensitive the profits are to changes in sales revenue. If you have a good eye, you can even use the break-even line chart to roughly estimate the profit at various revenue levels. To do this, find the point on the total sales line equal to the sales revenue level for which you want to guesstimate profits. Then use the *value axis* (the vertical axis on the left side of the chart) to calibrate the difference between the total sales line and the total variable costs line. The difference between these two lines shows your profit or loss.

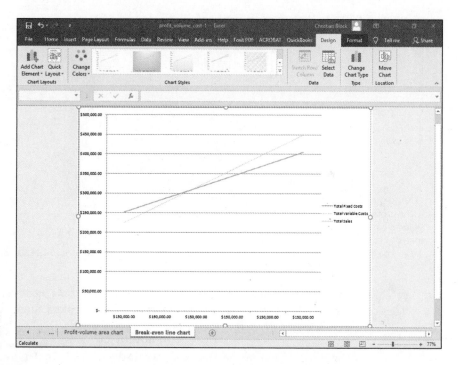

**FIGURE 1-5:**
The break-even
line chart.

**TIP**

The total variable costs line actually shows the total variable costs plus the total fixed costs because it's stacked on top of the fixed costs line.

Profit-Volume-Cost
Analysis

Figure 1-6 shows the profit-volume-cost data from the worksheet. This analysis is more complicated, so the chart is a bit trickier to interpret. Nevertheless, the chart resembles the break-even line chart. Fixed costs appear as a dark green band equal to $150,000 at the bottom of the graph. Variable costs appear as a sort of trapezoidal shape on top of the fixed costs. Above those costs appear the costs that vary with profits and the actual profit. Note that profits occur only after the firm exceeds the break-even point. (The data labels on the horizontal axis represent the different volumes being tested.)

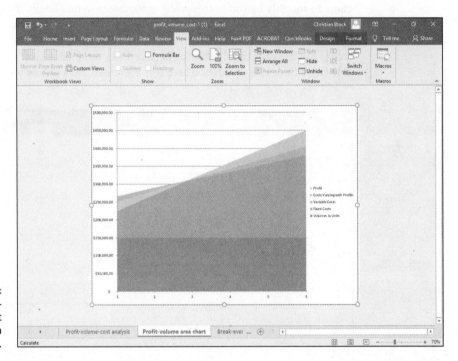

FIGURE 1-6:
The profit-
volume-cost
analysis area
chart.

**TIP**

You want to grab a working copy of the `profit_volume_cost-1.xlsx` **workbook** if you're at all interested in this stuff. The chart's colors simply don't reproduce well in grayscale images on the page of a book.

The data plotted in the charts shown in Figures 1-5 and 1-6 comes from the worksheet range shown in Figure 1-7. I collected all the data to be plotted in this area of the worksheet, which is below the profit-volume forecast and common-size profit-volume forecast to make it easy to see what data is plotted and where the data is coming from.

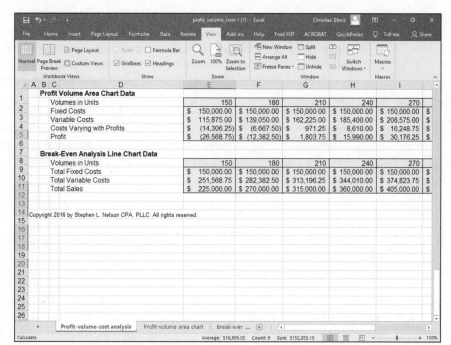

**FIGURE 1-7:**
These cells supply
the chart data.

# DEALING WITH VARY-WITH-PROFIT COSTS

If your profit-volume-cost analysis includes more than a single vary-with-profit cost, you must deal with the possibility that your vary-with-profit costs are interrelated. In fact, vary-with-profit costs can have one of three relationships: independent-independent, independent-dependent, or dependent-dependent.

The independent-independent relationship is the easiest to deal with. If two vary-with-profit costs are independent, you can enter the percentages into the appropriate workbook cells and not worry about them. An independent-independent relationship exists when vary-with-profit costs have no effect on one another. A partnership, for example, may have two profit-sharing plans — one for partners and one for employees — that aren't related.

A slightly more complicated relationship between vary-with-profit costs is the case of an independent-dependent relationship. A good example of an independent-dependent relationship is the relationship of state and federal income taxes. Because federal income taxes allow for a deduction based on state income taxes, the federal income tax expense depends on the state income tax expense. If the federal income tax percent

*Profit-Volume-Cost Analysis*

*(continued)*

*(continued)*

equals 20 percent, and the state income tax percent equals 10 percent, you can't simply enter the state income tax as 10 percent and the federal income tax as 20 percent. You need to adjust the federal income tax percentage for the effect of the state income tax.

Suppose that the state income tax rate is 10 percent of the pretax profits and that after the state income tax is deducted from the pretax profits, the federal income tax rate is 20 percent of what's left over. The correct input percentage for the state income tax rate is 10 percent, because 10 percent of the pretax profits calculates the correct state income tax cost, as follows:

```
State income tax = 10 percent × pretax profits
```

The federal income tax percentage, however, must recognize the state income tax costs:

```
Federal income tax = 20 percent × (pretax profits – (10 percent ×
    pretax profits))
```

This formula can be further modified to express the federal income tax rate as a percentage of the pretax profits. Therefore, you input the following into the Profit-Volume-Cost Analysis workbook:

```
Federal income tax = 18 percent × pretax profits
```

A third type of relationship is the dependent-dependent relationship. This relationship occurs when one vary-with-profit cost affects another vary-with-profit cost. In the case of a typical employee profit-sharing plan, in which profits are based on after-tax profits, you need to know the profit-sharing plan expense to calculate the federal income taxes. The profit-sharing plan expense is deductible for purposes of calculating federal income taxes, but you must know the federal income tax expense to calculate the after-tax profits on which the profit-sharing plan is based. In cases of dependent-dependent relationships among vary-with-profit costs, you can calculate percentages that in effect adjust for the dependency. To do this, you need to employ a fair amount of high school algebra.

# Chapter **2**

# Creating a Business Plan Forecast

*ro forma* financial statements — which are income statements, balance sheets, and cash-flow statements — constitute an integral part of business planning and the overall budgeting process. For that reason, I want to provide you a bit of information about how you create such pro forma (or *as if*) statements.

From the very start, however, I need to warn you that to create such statements, you need a tool in addition to QuickBooks. Specifically, you need a spreadsheet program such as Microsoft Excel. If you do not own a Microsoft Excel software license, Google Sheets and Excel for the Web provide a web-based Microsoft Excel program for free.

Assuming that you do have something like Excel, you can use it and the example workbook that this chapter describes to create a simple, yet sophisticated, financial forecast for your business. To download the workbook, type `https://stephenlnelson.com/wp-content/uploads/10_year_bizplan-1.xlsx` in your web browser's address bar.

# Reviewing Financial Statements and Ratios

Before I get into the nitty-gritty details of creating a business forecast, I need to briefly discuss what financial statements and ratios are, as well as how to use financial statements and ratios to describe the past or future financial condition and performance of a business.

The term *financial statement* can refer to one of several types of schedules and summaries of economic information. Typically, however, the term describes a set of documents that include an income statement (also called a *statement of operations*), a balance sheet (also called a *statement of financial condition*), and a cash-flow statement.

An *income statement* details the profits and losses of a business for a specific period. Suppose that you want to know the profits or losses of your business over the past month. You prepare an income statement that lists your revenue and expenses and calculates the profits or losses for the month.

A *balance sheet* identifies and lists the assets and liabilities of a business as of a specific time. It paints a clear picture of what the business owns, what the business owes, and the difference between the two (often called *net worth* or *owner's equity*). Typically, you prepare a balance sheet at of the end of the period that an income statement covers. If you prepare an income statement for a month, you may also want to prepare a balance sheet on the last day of the month.

A *cash-flow statement* outlines the cash inflows and outflows of a business for a specific period. Generally, you prepare a cash-flow statement for the same period for which you prepare an income statement.

TIP

The cash-flow statements that large companies use for their investors are quite complicated. They show lots of numbers arranged in a very Rube Goldberg–esque fashion. For this reason, I use the simpler cash-flow-statement format that accountants once used.

*Financial ratios* (as I describe in some detail in Book 5, Chapter 1) express relationships among the amounts reported in the financial statements. The ratios can offer insights into the economic health of a business. The ratios can also indicate how reasonable the implicit assumptions are in a forecast. By comparing the ratios of your business with the ratios of similar businesses, you can compare the financial characteristics of your business with those of other businesses. By comparing the ratios in your pro forma model with industry averages and standards, you also test your modeling assumptions for reasonableness.

Two general categories of financial ratios exist: common size ratios and intrastatement or interstatement ratios. *Common size ratios* convert a financial statement — usually a balance sheet or an income statement — from dollars to percentages. Common size ratios allow for comparisons of the assets, liabilities, revenue, owner's equity, and expenses of businesses of various sizes. The comparison can be at a point in time or as a trend over time. *Intrastatement* or *interstatement ratios* quantify relationships among amounts from different financial statements or from different parts of the same financial statement, respectively. Intrastatement and interstatement ratios are attempts to account for the fact that amounts usually can't be interpreted alone but must be viewed in the context of other key financial factors and events. In general, both categories of ratios are most valuable when compared with industry averages and trends.

TIP

This financial ratio business is really cool. If you have time, I heartily recommend that you peruse the greater coverage of the topic provided in Book 5, Chapter 1.

# Using the Business Plan Workbook

Unfortunately, it isn't very practical to create an example set of financial statements on, say, the back of a cocktail napkin or a set of sticky notes. You need to get the computer's help.

I suggest that you use Microsoft Excel and a workbook like the one shown in Figures 2-1 through 2-6 in this chapter. With this workbook, which is available at `https://stephenlnelson.com/wp-content/uploads/10_year_bizplan-1.xlsx`, you can construct pro forma financial statements that enable you to forecast profits and losses, financial condition, and cash flows for a business or organization.

To use the workbook, you develop and then enter information about the following:

>> Assets

>> Creditor and owner's equities at the start of the forecasting horizon

>> Expected changes in the assets and equities over the forecasting horizon

>> Revenue and expenses for each period on the forecasting horizon

You're probably wondering how this baby works. Well, the workbook does a lot, but it's actually pretty straightforward in its operation. When you input data that includes your starting assets, liabilities, owner's equity balances, and expected changes in these amounts for the forecasting horizon, the workbook constructs a balance sheet. The workbook constructs an income statement when you input data that includes sales and costs of sales, operating expenses, interest income and expenses, and marginal income tax rates. Then, from the balance sheet and income statement, the workbook constructs a cash–flow statement.

To enter your own data in the business planning starter workbook, perform the following steps, entering positive balances or increases as positive amounts and negative balances or decreases as negative amounts:

1. **Open the business plan workbook in Excel.**

   The starter workbook initially contains the default inputs shown in Figure 2-1. Note that you can see only about the first 26 rows and the first 4 or so columns of the inputs area. Sorry — I didn't have room to show everything. If you want to see what you're missing, grab the workbook from the website.

2. **Enter the Cash & Equivalents balance for the start of the forecasting horizon.**

   The value that you enter for Cash & Equivalents is the dollar total of all the cash held at the beginning of the forecasting period.

TIP

   You can get the Cash & Equivalents value from QuickBooks if you're forecasting from the present forward. The cash that you start with, obviously, is the cash that you're holding today.

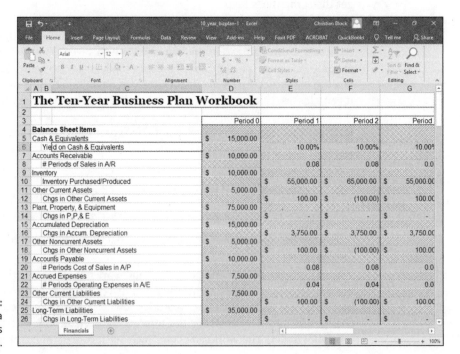

FIGURE 2-1:
The inputs area of the business plan workbook.

3. **Enter the forecasted period yield that you expect the cash and equivalents to deliver.**

The model estimates the period interest income by multiplying the cash and equivalents balance by the yield on cash and equivalents.

4. **Enter the accounts receivable balance for the start of the forecasting horizon.**

The value that you enter for accounts receivable (A/R) is the starting accounts receivable balance, which is the balance at the beginning of the forecasting horizon, excluding any allowance for uncollectible amounts.

5. **Enter the number of periods of sales in accounts receivable.**

The value that you enter for # Periods of Sales in A/R, or number of periods of sales in accounts receivable, is the number of periods or the fraction of a period for which sales are held in accounts receivable. If accounts receivable typically amount to about 30 days of sales, and you use months as your forecasting periods, you hold one period (one month) of sales in accounts receivable. Alternatively, if accounts receivable typically amount to about 30 days of sales, and you use years as your forecasting periods, you hold one-twelfth of a period of sales in accounts receivable.

6. **Enter the dollar amount of the inventory held at the start of the forecasting horizon.**

The Inventory value is the starting inventory balance, which is the total dollar amount of the inventory purchased for resale or manufactured for resale and held at the beginning of the forecasting horizon.

7. **Enter the forecasted dollar amount of inventory purchased or produced for each period of the forecasting horizon.**

The Inventory Purchased/Produced value is the dollar total of items purchased or produced over the period.

8. **Enter the amount of the other current assets held at the start of the forecasting horizon.**

The Other Current Assets starting balance is the dollar total of any other current assets with which you begin the forecasting horizon. These other current assets may include prepaid expenses, short-term investments, and deposits made with vendors.

9. **Enter the amount of the change in the other current assets for each period in the forecasting horizon.**

The value for Chgs in Other Current Assets, or changes in other current assets for the period, is the dollar total of increases or decreases in the accounts included in the starting Other Current Assets balance.

## 10. Enter the amount of the plant, property, and equipment at the start of the forecasting horizon.

The starting Plant, Property, & Equipment balance is the dollar total of the fixed assets. This amount includes such items as real estate, manufacturing equipment, furniture, and the Learjet.

## 11. Enter the amount of the change in plant, property, and equipment (P, P, & E) for each period of the forecasting horizon.

The Chgs in P, P, & E value is the dollar total of decreases or increases in the plant, property, and equipment accounts for the period. Increases in these accounts probably stem from purchases of additional fixed assets. Decreases in these accounts probably stem from disposal of assets.

## 12. Enter the amount of the accumulated depreciation on plant, property, and equipment at the start of the forecasting horizon.

The starting Accumulated Depreciation balance represents the depreciation expenses charged to date on the assets identified in the starting P, P, & E balance.

## 13. Enter the amount of the change in the accumulated depreciation for each period of the forecasting horizon.

The Chgs in Accum. Depreciation value is the dollar total of increases and decreases in the accumulated depreciation account for the period. Increases in the accumulated depreciation balance probably stem from the current-period depreciation expense. Decreases in the accumulated depreciation balance probably stem from removing the accumulated depreciation attributed to a fixed asset that you disposed of.

## 14. Enter the amount of the other noncurrent assets at the start of the period.

The starting Other Noncurrent Assets balance is the dollar total of all other noncurrent assets held at the start of the forecasting period. Other noncurrent assets may include copyrights, patents, and goodwill.

## 15. Enter the amount of the change in the other noncurrent assets for each period of the forecasting horizon.

The Chgs in Other Noncurrent Assets value is the dollar total increase or decrease for the period in the accounts included in the starting Other Noncurrent Assets balance.

## 16. Enter the amount of the accounts payable balance at the start of the forecasting horizon.

The starting Accounts Payable (A/P) balance is the dollar total of amounts owed vendors for inventory at the start of the forecasting horizon. This starter workbook calculates future Accounts Payable balances based on the cost of sales volumes. To add precision to the forecasts of accounts payable, the model assumes that accounts payable represent debt incurred for the cost of sales.

**17.** **Enter the number of periods of the cost of sales in accounts payable.**

The # Periods Cost of Sales in A/P entry is the number of periods or the fraction of a period for which the cost of sales is held in accounts payable. If accounts payable typically amount to about 30 days of cost of sales, and you use months as your forecasting periods, you hold one period (one month) of cost of sales in accounts payable. Alternatively, if accounts payable typically amount to about 30 days of cost of sales, and you use years as your forecasting periods, you hold one-twelfth of a period of cost of sales in accounts payable.

**18.** **Enter the amount of the accrued expenses balance at the start of the forecasting horizon.**

The starting Accrued Expenses (A/E) balance is the dollar total of amounts owed vendors for operating expenses at the start of the forecast horizon. This starter workbook calculates future Accrued Expenses balances based on the operating expenses levels. To add precision to the forecasts of accrued expenses, the model assumes that accrued expenses represent debt incurred for operating expenses.

**19.** **Enter the number of periods of operating expenses in accrued expenses.**

The # Periods Operating Expenses in A/E value is the number of periods or the fraction of a period for which operating expenses are held in accrued expenses. If accrued expenses typically amount to 30 days of operating expenses, and you use months as your forecasting periods, you hold one period of operating expenses in accrued expenses. Alternatively, if accrued expenses typically amount to about 30 days of operating expenses, and you use years as your forecasting periods, you hold one-twelfth of a period of operating expenses in accrued expenses.

**20.** **Enter the amount of the other current liabilities at the start of the forecasting period.**

The Other Current Liabilities starting balance is the dollar total of all other current liabilities held at the start of the forecasting period. Other current liabilities may include income tax payable, product warranty liability, and the current portion of a long-term liability.

**21.** **Enter the amount of the change in the other current liabilities for each period of the forecasting horizon.**

The Chgs in Other Current Liabilities value is the dollar total of increases or decreases for the period in the accounts included in the starting Other Current Liabilities balance.

**22.** **Enter the amount of the long-term liabilities balance at the start of the forecasting horizon.**

The starting Long-Term Liabilities balance is the dollar total of debt that will be paid back sometime after the next year.

**23.** **Enter the amount of the change in the long-term liabilities for each period of the forecasting horizon.**

The Chgs in Long-Term Liabilities value is the increase or decrease for the period in the outstanding long-term debt. These changes may include decreases stemming from the amortization of principal through debt service payments and increases stemming from additional funds provided by creditors. You need to include the principal component of debt service payments as negative amounts because they decrease the amount of long-term liability.

**24.** **Enter the amount of the other noncurrent liabilities at the start of the forecasting horizon.**

The Other Noncurrent Liabilities starting balance is the dollar total of all other noncurrent liabilities held at the start of the forecasting period. These may include deferred income tax, employee pension plan liabilities, and capitalized lease obligations.

**25.** **Enter the amount of the change in the other noncurrent liabilities for each period of the forecasting horizon.**

The Chgs in Other Noncurrent Liabilities value is the dollar total of increases or decreases for the period in the accounts included in the starting Other Noncurrent Liabilities balance. These changes may include decreases stemming from the amortization of principal through debt service payments and increases stemming from additional funds provided by creditors.

**26.** **Enter the amount of the owner's equity balance at the start of the forecasting horizon.**

The Owner Equity starting balance is the dollar total of the capital originally contributed by owners and the earnings retained by the business at the start of the forecasting horizon.

**27.** **Enter the amount of the change in the owner's equity balance for each period of the forecasting horizon stemming from additional capital contributions, dividends, and other special distributions to owners.**

The Chgs in Owner Equity value is the dollar total of increases for the period in owner's equity, other than those stemming from the profits of a business, and all decreases in owner's equity. Increases in the Owner Equity balance may result from additional offerings of common or preferred stock and U.S. Treasury stock transactions; decreases in the Owner Equity balance may result from dividends and other distributions to stockholders.

**REMEMBER**

Changes in the Owner Equity balance resulting from the profit or loss for the period are calculated on the income statement; they aren't entered.

**28.** **Enter the sales revenue forecasted for each period of the forecasting horizon.**

The Sales Revenue values represent the forecasted sales revenue generated by the business over each period of the forecasting horizon.

**29.** **Enter the cost of sales forecasted for each period of the forecasting horizon.**

The Cost of Sales values represent the forecasted costs of the inventory sold for the forecasting horizon.

**30.** **Enter those costs that fall into the first, second, and third operating expense classifications or categories for each period of the forecasting horizon.**

The operating expenses for Cost Centers 1, 2, and 3 represent the operating expenses for the forecasting horizon. These figures may be three expense classifications related to operating the business, or they may be the total expenses for three groups of expenses.

**TIP**

Typically, you use one cost center to track your general and administrative expenses, another cost center to track your sales and marketing expenses, and yet another cost center to track your research and development expenses. If you do this, consider replacing the labels *Cost Center 1, Cost Center 2,* and *Cost Center 3* with more descriptive and meaningful labels, such as *General & Admin, Sales & Marketing,* and *Research & Development.*

**31.** **Enter the interest expense of carrying any debt used to fund operations or asset purchases.**

The Interest Expense values represent the period interest expenses of carrying any debt related to the business.

**32.** **Enter the income tax rate that, when multiplied against the profit or loss for the period, calculates the income tax expense (or savings).**

The Income Tax Rate value is the percentage that, when multiplied by the operating profit (or loss), calculates the income tax expense (or savings). This calculation can be a little tricky because business income taxes are progressive. A sole proprietor's tax rates go from 0 to roughly 35 percent, for example, depending on the level of income. A regular corporation's income tax rates go from 15 to 34 percent (with some bounces up and down along the way). This may mean that you need your tax adviser's help to come up with a good number for this input. On the other hand, you may just decide to calculate only pretax profits and losses. To do this, enter this amount as 0.

After you enter the required inputs, the starter workbook makes the calculations necessary to construct pro forma financial statements and to calculate a set of rather standard financial ratios.

# Understanding the Workbook Calculations

The business plan workbook has seven parts: the inputs forecast, Balance Sheet, Common Size Balance Sheet, Income Statement, Common Size Income Statement, Cash Flow Statement, and Financial Ratios Table. I want to briefly describe the Excel calculations that occur within each of these parts so that in case you have questions about them or want to make modifications, you can customize the starter workbook to perform better for your specific situation.

**TECHNICAL STUFF**

If you don't know Excel and don't want to learn it, don't worry; you can skip this discussion. I provide it for the benefit of those readers who want to understand the inner workings of the workbook and may need or want to customize the workbook's calculations.

## Forecasting inputs

The inputs area of the business planning starter workbook contains one set of formulas. The second row identifies the period for which the results are calculated. The period identifier numbers the periods for which values are entered. The start of the first period is stored in cell D3 as the integer 0. Periods that follow are stored as the previous period plus 1.

The period identifiers in the Balance Sheet, Common Size Balance Sheet, Income Statement, Common Size Income Statement, Cash Flow Statement, and Financial Ratios Table schedules use similar formulas.

**TIP**

The cells that hold the period identifiers use a custom number format that precedes each period with the word *Period*. To remove it, reformat the cells by using another number format. You can most easily do this by selecting a cell and then clicking a formatting button on the Excel toolbar, such as the Currency or Percent Style button.

## Balance Sheet

The Balance Sheet schedule has 19 rows with calculated data, but the first row contains only text labels that reflect period numbers, shown in Figure 2-2. (As in the inputs area of the business planning starter workbook, the period identifier numbers the periods for which values are forecasted.) The rest of the Balance Sheet's values are described in the following paragraphs.

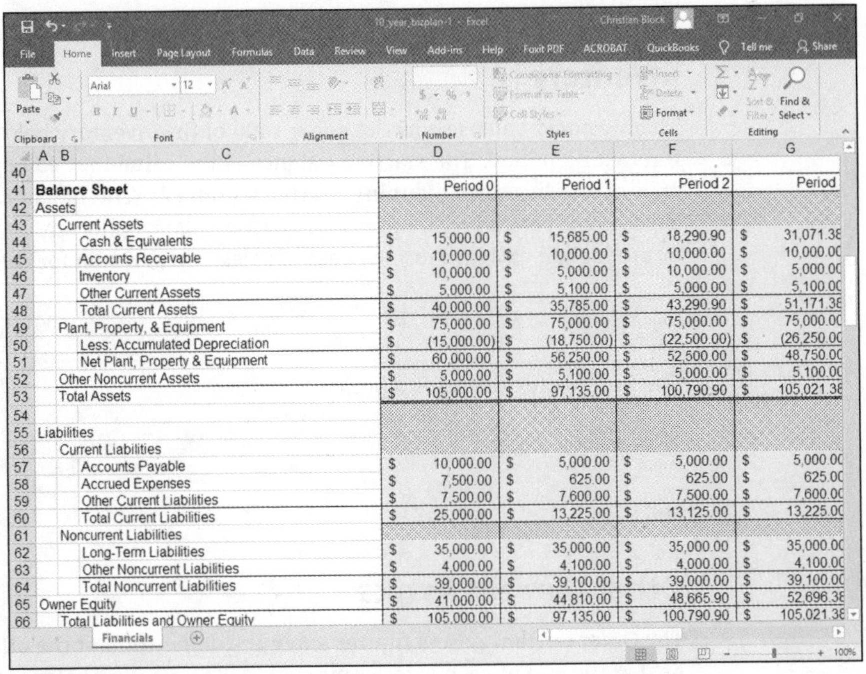

| Row | Balance Sheet | Period 0 | Period 1 | Period 2 | Period |
|---|---|---|---|---|---|
| 42 | Assets | | | | |
| 43 | Current Assets | | | | |
| 44 | Cash & Equivalents | $ 15,000.00 | $ 15,685.00 | $ 18,290.90 | $ 31,071.38 |
| 45 | Accounts Receivable | $ 10,000.00 | $ 10,000.00 | $ 10,000.00 | $ 10,000.00 |
| 46 | Inventory | $ 10,000.00 | $ 5,000.00 | $ 10,000.00 | $ 5,000.00 |
| 47 | Other Current Assets | $ 5,000.00 | $ 5,100.00 | $ 5,000.00 | $ 5,100.00 |
| 48 | Total Current Assets | $ 40,000.00 | $ 35,785.00 | $ 43,290.90 | $ 51,171.38 |
| 49 | Plant, Property, & Equipment | $ 75,000.00 | $ 75,000.00 | $ 75,000.00 | $ 75,000.00 |
| 50 | Less: Accumulated Depreciation | $ (15,000.00) | $ (18,750.00) | $ (22,500.00) | $ (26,250.00 |
| 51 | Net Plant, Property & Equipment | $ 60,000.00 | $ 56,250.00 | $ 52,500.00 | $ 48,750.00 |
| 52 | Other Noncurrent Assets | $ 5,000.00 | $ 5,100.00 | $ 5,000.00 | $ 5,100.00 |
| 53 | Total Assets | $ 105,000.00 | $ 97,135.00 | $ 100,790.90 | $ 105,021.38 |
| 54 | | | | | |
| 55 | Liabilities | | | | |
| 56 | Current Liabilities | | | | |
| 57 | Accounts Payable | $ 10,000.00 | $ 5,000.00 | $ 5,000.00 | $ 5,000.00 |
| 58 | Accrued Expenses | $ 7,500.00 | $ 625.00 | $ 625.00 | $ 625.00 |
| 59 | Other Current Liabilities | $ 7,500.00 | $ 7,600.00 | $ 7,500.00 | $ 7,600.00 |
| 60 | Total Current Liabilities | $ 25,000.00 | $ 13,225.00 | $ 13,125.00 | $ 13,225.00 |
| 61 | Noncurrent Liabilities | | | | |
| 62 | Long-Term Liabilities | $ 35,000.00 | $ 35,000.00 | $ 35,000.00 | $ 35,000.00 |
| 63 | Other Noncurrent Liabilities | $ 4,000.00 | $ 4,100.00 | $ 4,000.00 | $ 4,100.00 |
| 64 | Total Noncurrent Liabilities | $ 39,000.00 | $ 39,100.00 | $ 39,000.00 | $ 39,100.00 |
| 65 | Owner Equity | $ 41,000.00 | $ 44,810.00 | $ 48,665.90 | $ 52,696.38 |
| 66 | Total Liabilities and Owner Equity | $ 105,000.00 | $ 97,135.00 | $ 100,790.90 | $ 105,021.38 |

**FIGURE 2-2:** The Balance Sheet portion of the business planning starter workbook.

## Cash & Equivalents

The Cash & Equivalents figures show the projected cash on hand at the end of each of the forecasting periods. The starting balance is the value you enter in the inputs area of the business planning starter workbook. The balance for the first and subsequent periods is pulled from the Cash Flow Statement schedule, where it's calculated.

## Accounts Receivable

The Accounts Receivable (A/R) figures show the net receivables held as of the end of each forecasting period. The starting balance is the value that you enter in the inputs planning area of the business starter worksheet. The balance for the first and subsequent periods is based on the Sales Revenue and the # Periods of Sales in A/R values that you enter in the inputs area of the business planning starter workbook. The formula for the first period is

```
=E8*E32
```

The formula for the second period is

```
=F8*F32
```

and so on.

## Inventory

The Inventory values show the dollar total of the inventory held at the end of each forecasting period. The starting balance is the value that you enter in the inputs area of the business planning starter workbook. The balance for the first and subsequent periods is the previous-period balance plus any inventory purchases or production costs minus any cost of sales. The formula for the first period is

```
=D46+E10 – E33
```

The formula for the second period is

```
=E46+F10 – F33
```

and so on.

## Other Current Assets

The Other Current Assets figures show the dollar total of the other current assets held at the end of each forecasting period. The starting balance for Other Current Assets is the value that you enter in the inputs area of the business planning starter workbook. The balance for the first and subsequent periods is the previous balance plus the change in the balance. The formula for the first period is

```
=D47+E12
```

The formula for the second period is

```
=E47+F12
```

and so on.

## Total Current Assets

The Total Current Assets figures show the dollar total of the current assets at the end of each of the forecasting horizons. The balance at any time is the sum of Cash & Equivalents, Accounts Receivable, Inventory, and Other Current Assets. The formula for the starting Total Current Assets balance is

```
=SUM(D44:D47)
```

The formula for the first period is

```
=SUM(E44:E47)
```

and so on.

## Plant, Property, & Equipment

The Plant, Property, & Equipment figures show the original dollar cost of the plant, property, and equipment at the end of each forecasting horizon. The starting Plant, Property, & Equipment balance is the value that you enter in the inputs area of the business planning starter workbook. The balance for the first and subsequent periods is the previous balance plus any additions to the plant, property, and equipment accounts. The formula for the first period is

```
=D49+E14
```

The formula for the second period is

```
=E49+F14
```

and so on.

## Less: Accumulated Depreciation

The Accumulated Depreciation figures show the cumulative depreciation expenses charged through the current period for the plant, property, and equipment. The starting balance is the value that you enter in the inputs area of the business planning starter workbook. The balance for the first and subsequent periods is the previous balance minus the current period's changes in accumulated depreciation. The formula for the first period is

```
=D50 - E16
```

The formula for the second period is

```
=E50 - F16
```

and so on. Because the accumulated depreciation is shown as a negative amount, you subtract the positive number pulled from the forecasting inputs.

## Net Plant, Property, & Equipment

The Net Plant, Property, & Equipment figures show the difference between Plant, Property, & Equipment and Accumulated Depreciation at the end of each of the forecasting horizons. The formula for the starting balance is

```
=D49+D50
```

The formula for the first period is

```
=E49+E50
```

and so on. Because the Accumulated Depreciation balance is shown as a negative amount, you simply add these two amounts in the formula for the Net Plant, Property, & Equipment amount.

## Other Noncurrent Assets

The Other Noncurrent Assets figures show the dollar total of any other noncurrent assets held at the end of each forecasting period. The starting balance is the value that you enter in the inputs area of the business planning starter workbook. The balance for the first and subsequent periods is the previous-period balance plus the change in the account in the current period. The formula for the first period is

```
=D52+E18
```

The formula for the second period is

```
=E52+F18
```

and so on.

## Total Assets

The Total Assets figures show the dollar total of all the assets held at the end of the forecasting periods. The balance at any time is the sum of the following: Current Assets; Net Plant, Property, & Equipment; and Other Noncurrent Assets. The formula for the starting balance is

```
=D48+D51+D52
```

The formula for the first period is

```
=E48+E51+E52
```

and so on.

# Accounts Payable

The Accounts Payable figures show the debt that is related to the cost of sales outstanding at the end of each forecasting period. The starting balance is the value that you enter in the inputs area of the business planning starter workbook. The balance for the first and subsequent periods is Cost of Sales for the period times # Periods Cost of Sales in A/P. The formula for the first period is

```
=E20*E33
```

The formula for the second period is

```
=F20*F33
```

and so on.

# Accrued Expenses

The Accrued Expenses figures show the debt that is related to the operating expenses outstanding at the end of each forecasting period. The starting balance is the value that you enter in the inputs area of the business planning starter workbook. The balance for the first and subsequent periods is the operating expenses times # Periods Operating Expenses in A/E. The formula for the first period is

```
=E22*SUM(E34:E36)
```

The formula for the second period is

```
=F22*SUM(F34:F36)
```

and so on.

# Other Current Liabilities

The Other Current Liabilities figures show the dollar total of other debts outstanding at the end of the forecasting periods that will be paid within the current year or business cycle. The starting balance is the value that you enter in the inputs area of the business planning starter workbook. The balance for the first and subsequent periods is the previous balance plus the change in the current period. The formula for the first period is

```
=D59+E24
```

The formula for the second period is

```
=E59+F24
```

and so on.

## Total Current Liabilities

The Total Current Liabilities figures show the dollar total of all the current liabilities at the end of each forecasting period. The balance at any time is the sum of Accounts Payable, Accrued Expenses, and Other Current Liabilities. The formula for the starting balance is

```
=SUM(D57:D59)
```

The formula for the first period is

```
=SUM(E57:E59)
```

and so on.

## Long-Term Liabilities

The Long-Term Liabilities figures show the dollar total of the long-term outstanding debt at the end of each forecasting period. The starting balance is the value that you enter in the inputs area of the business planning starter workbook. The balance for the first and subsequent periods is the previous balance plus any changes in the Long-Term Liabilities balance in the current period. The formula for the first period is

```
=D62+E26
```

The formula for the second period is

```
=E62+F26
```

and so on.

## Other Noncurrent Liabilities

The Other Noncurrent Liabilities figures show the dollar total of any other noncurrent outstanding debt at the end of each forecasting period. The starting balance is the value that you enter in the inputs area of the business planning starter workbook. The balance for the first and subsequent periods is the previous-period balance plus the change in the current period. The formula for the first period is

```
=D63+E28
```

The formula for the second period is

```
=E63+F28
```

and so on.

## Total Noncurrent Liabilities

The Total Noncurrent Liabilities figures show the dollar totals of the long-term debt and the other noncurrent outstanding debt at the end of each forecasting period. The balance at any time is the sum of Long-Term Liabilities and Other Noncurrent Liabilities. The formula for the starting balance is

```
=D62+D63
```

The formula for the first period is

```
=E62+E63
```

and so on.

## Owner Equity

The Owner Equity figures show the dollar totals of the owner's equity accounts at the end of each forecasting period. The starting balance is the value that you enter in the inputs area of the business planning starter workbook. The balance for the first and subsequent periods is the previous-period balance plus Net Income After Taxes for the period, plus other adjustments, such as additional capital contributions and dividends. The formula for the first period is

```
=D65+E30+E113
```

The formula for the second period is

```
=E65+F30+F113
```

and so on.

## Total Liabilities and Owner Equity

The Total Liabilities and Owner Equity figures show the dollar totals of Current Liabilities, Noncurrent Liabilities, and Owner Equity at the end of each forecasting period. The formula for the starting balance is

```
=D60+D64+D65
```

The formula for the first period is

```
=E60+E64+E65
```

and so on.

WARNING

The Total Assets value should equal the Total Liabilities and Owner Equity value. If they differ, your model contains an error.

# Common Size Balance Sheet

The Common Size Balance Sheet schedule lists — in balance-sheet format — what percentage of the total assets each individual asset represents and what percentage of the total liabilities and owner's equity each individual liability and the owner's equity represents, as shown in Figure 2-3. When you compare these percentages with those of business peers, you can see the relative financial strength or weakness of your business. Trends in the percentages over time can indicate improvement or deterioration in the overall financial condition of your business.

The Common Size Balance Sheet schedule has 19 rows with calculated data that express line-item amounts as percentages of the total. For the asset side of the Balance Sheet, assets are expressed as a percentage of the total assets. For the creditor and owner's equity side of the Balance Sheet, equities are expressed as a percentage of the total liabilities and owner's equity. The formulas for all rows except Total Assets and Total Liabilities and Owner Equity simply convert the Balance Sheet values to percentages. The Cash & Equivalents formula for the starting period is

```
=D44/D$53
```

The formula for the first period is

```
=E44/E$53
```

and so on. All asset percentages are derived from dividing by Total Assets, which explains why the absolute reference to row $53 is used in all asset formulas.

Similarly, the absolute reference to row $66 appears in all formulas in the liabilities and equity formulas. If you need a brush-up on or introduction to Excel, or wonder why there are dollar signs in front of the row numbers in the formulas, check out Appendix A of this book, in the "Moving and copying formulas" section.

| | Common Size Balance Sheet | Period 0 | Period 1 | Period 2 | Period |
|---|---|---|---|---|---|
| 68 | **Common Size Balance Sheet** | Period 0 | Period 1 | Period 2 | Period |
| 69 | Assets | | | | |
| 70 | Current Assets | | | | |
| 71 | Cash & Equivalents | 14.29% | 16.15% | 18.15% | 29.59% |
| 72 | Accounts Receivable | 9.52% | 10.29% | 9.92% | 9.52% |
| 73 | Inventory | 9.52% | 5.15% | 9.92% | 4.76% |
| 74 | Other Current Assets | 4.76% | 5.25% | 4.96% | 4.86% |
| 75 | Total Current Assets | 38.10% | 36.84% | 42.95% | 48.72% |
| 76 | Plant, Property, & Equipment | 71.43% | 77.21% | 74.41% | 71.41% |
| 77 | Less: Accumulated Depreciation | -14.29% | -19.30% | -22.32% | -24.99% |
| 78 | Net Plant, Property, & Equipment | 57.14% | 57.91% | 52.09% | 46.42% |
| 79 | Other Noncurrent Assets | 4.76% | 5.25% | 4.96% | 4.86% |
| 80 | Total Assets | 100.00% | 100.00% | 100.00% | 100.00% |
| 81 | | | | | |
| 82 | Liabilities | | | | |
| 83 | Current Liabilities | | | | |
| 84 | Accounts Payable | 9.52% | 5.15% | 4.96% | 4.76% |
| 85 | Accrued Expenses | 7.14% | 0.64% | 0.62% | 0.60% |
| 86 | Other Current Liabilities | 7.14% | 7.82% | 7.44% | 7.24% |
| 87 | Total Current Liabilities | 23.81% | 13.62% | 13.02% | 12.59% |
| 88 | Noncurrent Liabilities | | | | |
| 89 | Long-Term Liabilities | 33.33% | 36.03% | 34.73% | 33.33% |
| 90 | Other Noncurrent Liabilities | 3.81% | 4.22% | 3.97% | 3.90% |
| 91 | Total Noncurrent Liabilities | 37.14% | 40.25% | 38.69% | 37.23% |
| 92 | Owner Equity | 39.05% | 46.13% | 48.28% | 50.18% |
| 93 | Total Liabilities and Owner Equity | 100.00% | 100.00% | 100.00% | 100.00% |

**FIGURE 2-3:**
The Common Size Balance Sheet portion of the business plan workbook.

The formula for the Total Assets percentage at any time is the sum of the Current Assets percentage; the Net Plant, Property & Equipment percentage; and the Other Noncurrent Assets percentage. The result always equals 100 percent.

Similarly, the formula for the Total Liabilities and Owner Equity percentage at any time is the sum of the Current Liabilities, the Noncurrent Liabilities, and Owner Equity percentages. The result is always 100 percent.

# Income Statement

The Income Statement schedule has 13 rows of calculated data, as shown in Figure 2-4. As in other schedules, the period identifier simply numbers the periods for which values are calculated. The first period is stored in cell E96 as the integer 1, and the periods that follow are stored as the previous period plus 1. The other values in the Income Statement are calculated as described in the following paragraphs.

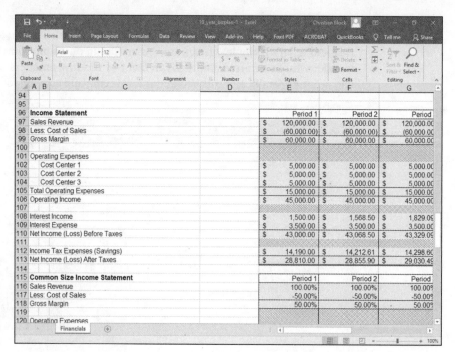

## Sales Revenue

The Sales Revenue figures are the estimates that you enter in the inputs area of the business planning starter workbook. The amount for the period is the value that you enter in the inputs area of the business planning starter workbook.

## Less: Cost of Sales

The Cost of Sales figures are the Cost of Sales estimates that you enter in the inputs area of the business planning starter workbook.

## Gross Margin

The Gross Margin figures show the amounts left over from the sales proceeds after subtracting Cost of Sales. Subtracting your other expenses from the Gross Margin amount gives you your profit figure. The Gross Margin formula is Sales Revenue for the period minus Cost of Sales. The formula for the first period is

```
=E97+E98
```

The formula for the second period is

```
=F97+F98
```

and so on. Notice that because the Cost of Sales figures are pulled into the Income Statement schedule as negative amounts, the Gross Margin formula simply adds the Sales Revenue figure to the negative Cost of Sales figure.

## Operating Expenses: Cost Centers 1, 2, and 3

The Operating Expenses figures for Cost Centers 1, 2, and 3 show the amount for each operating expense classification or category that you enter in the inputs area of the business planning starter workbook.

### Total Operating Expenses

The Total Operating Expenses figures show the sums of the operating expenses that you enter in the inputs area of the business planning starter workbook for these three operating-expense categories or classifications. The total for each period is the sum of the operating expenses for Cost Centers 1, 2, and 3. The formula for the first period is

```
=SUM(E102:E104)
```

The formula for the second period is

```
=SUM(F102:F104)
```

and so on.

### Operating Income

The Operating Income figures show the sales dollar amounts left after paying the Cost of Sales and the Operating Expenses. The Operating Income figures represent the amounts that go toward paying your financing expenses and income tax, as well as the amount that constitutes your profits. The amount for each period is the Gross Margin figure for the period minus the Total Operating Expenses figure. The formula for the first period is

```
=E99 – E105
```

The formula for the second period is

```
=F99 – F105
```

and so on.

## Interest Income

The Interest Income figures show the earnings from investing the cash of the business. The amount for each period is the beginning Cash & Equivalents balance from the inputs area of the business planning starter workbook multiplied by the period yield on Cash & Equivalents. The formula for the first period is

```
=D44*E6
```

The formula for the second period is

```
=E44*F6
```

and so on.

## Interest Expense

The Interest Expense figures show the costs of using borrowed funds for operations and asset purchases. The amount for each period is the value that you enter in the inputs area of the business planning starter workbook.

## Net Income (Loss) Before Taxes

The Net Income (Loss) Before Taxes figures show the amount of operating income left after receiving any interest income and paying any interest expense. The amount for each period is the Operating Income figure for the period plus the Interest Income figure for the period, minus the Interest Expense figure for the period. The formula for the first period is

```
=E106+E108 - E109
```

The formula for the second period is

```
=F106+F108 - F109
```

and so on.

## Income Tax Expenses (Savings)

The Income Tax Expenses (Savings) figures show the income tax expenses (or savings) that use the calculated Net Income (Loss) Before Taxes figures and the Marginal Income Tax Rate figures that you forecasted in the inputs area of the business planning starter workbook. Notice that the model calculates a current period savings in income taxes when there's a net loss before taxes. This may be the case when a current-period loss is carried back to a previous period or when the current-period loss is consolidated with the current-period income of related businesses. Basically, then, the model assumes that a net loss before income taxes results in a current-period tax refund — that is, an overall tax savings — because you can deduct a loss in one business from the profits of another business. If a current-period loss doesn't result in a current-period income tax savings, however, you modify the formula as described in "Customizing the Starter Workbook" later in this chapter.

The amount for each period is the Net Income (Loss) Before Taxes multiplied by the Marginal Income Tax Rate figure. The formula for the first period is

```
=E38*E110
```

The formula for the second period is

```
=F38*F110
```

and so on.

### Net Income (Loss) After Taxes

The Net Income (Loss) After Taxes figures calculate the after-tax profits of operating the business. The amount for each period is the Net Income (Loss) Before Taxes figure minus the Income Tax Expenses (Savings) figure. The formula for the first period is

```
=E110 - E112
```

The formula for the second period is

```
=F110 - F112
```

and so on.

## Common Size Income Statement

The Common Size Income Statement schedule lists, in income statement format, what percentage of the total sales revenue each income statement line item represents (refer to the bottom of Figure 2-4). When you compare these percentages with those of business peers, you can see the relative financial performance of your business. Trends in the percentages over the forecasting horizon can indicate improvement or deterioration in the financial performance of your business.

The Common Size Income Statement schedule has 13 rows of calculated data that express the component line-item amount for each period as a percentage of the sales revenue figure for the period. The formulas for all rows except Sales Revenue simply convert the Income Statement values to percentages.

The Sales Revenue figures add the Cost of Sales, Total Operating Expenses, Interest Income, Interest Expense, Income Tax Expenses (Savings), and Net Income (Loss) After Taxes percentages. The results always equal 100 percent.

**REMEMBER**

The Sales Revenue percentage calculations add the expense and profit percentages. Those expenses shown as negative amounts, therefore, are subtracted.

# Cash Flow Statement

The Cash Flow Statement schedule has 16 rows of calculated data, shown in Figure 2-5. As in other schedules, a period identifier numbers the periods for which values are calculated. The first period is stored in cell E136 as integer 1. Periods that follow are stored as the previous period plus 1. Other Cash Flow Statement values are calculated as described in the following paragraphs.

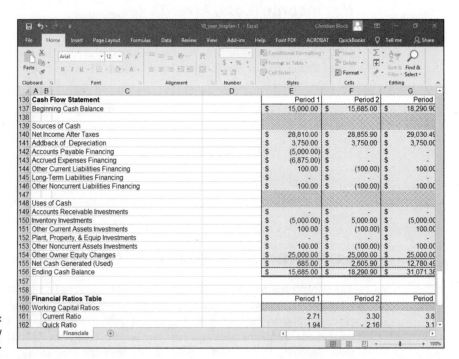

**FIGURE 2-5:**
The Cash Flow
Statement.

## Beginning Cash Balance

The Beginning Cash Balance figures show the forecasted cash and equivalents balance at the start of each forecasting period. The starting balance is the value that you enter in the inputs area of the business planning starter workbook. For subsequent periods, the Beginning Cash Balance is the previous period's Ending Cash Balance.

## Net Income After Taxes

The Net Income After Taxes figures show the amounts calculated in the Income Statement schedule as the business profits for each forecasting period.

## Addback of Depreciation

The Addback of Depreciation figures show the change in the accumulated depreciation balance for each forecasting period. Normally, this change stems from the period depreciation expense; it must be added back into the Net Income After Taxes figure because the depreciation expense uses no cash. The depreciation added back for each period is the value that you enter in the inputs area of the business planning starter workbook as the change in accumulated depreciation.

## Accounts Payable Financing

The Accounts Payable Financing figures show the change in the Accounts Payable balance for the period. Increases in this balance result when the cost of sales expense paid during the period is lower than the expense incurred. Decreases in this balance result when the cost of sales expense paid is higher than the expense incurred. By recognizing the changes in this account balance, the model adjusts for differences between the Income Statement's accrual-based accounting of cost of sales expenses and the actual cash disbursements for cost of sales expenses.

The Accounts Payable Financing figure for each period is the difference between the Accounts Payable balance at the end of the previous period and the balance at the end of the current period. The formula for the first period is

```
=E57 - D57
```

The formula for the second period is

```
=F57 - E57
```

and so on.

## Accrued Expenses Financing

The Accrued Expenses Financing figures show the change in the accrued expenses balance for the period. Increases in this balance result when the operating expense paid during the period is lower than the expense incurred. Decreases in this balance result when the operating expense paid during the period is higher than the expense incurred. By recognizing the changes in this account balance, the model adjusts for differences between the Income Statement's accrual-based accounting expenses and the actual cash disbursements for operating expenses.

The Accrued Expenses Financing figure for each period is the difference between the Accrued Expenses balance at the end of the previous period and the balance at the end of the current period. The formula for the first period is

```
=E58 - D58
```

The formula for the second period is

```
=F58 - E58
```

and so on.

## Other Current Liabilities Financing

The Other Current Liabilities Financing figures show the change in the Other Current Liabilities balance for the period. This amount increases when, directly or indirectly, cash is generated by borrowing. This amount decreases when, directly or indirectly, cash is used to pay off short-term borrowing.

The Other Current Liabilities Financing figure for each period is the difference between the Other Current Liabilities balance at the end of the previous period and the balance at the end of the current period. The formula for the first period is

```
=E59 - D59
```

The formula for the second period is

```
=F59 - E59
```

and so on.

## Long-Term Liabilities Financing

The Long-Term Liabilities Financing figures show the changes in the long-term liabilities amount for the period. This balance increases when, directly or indirectly, cash is generated by long-term borrowing. This amount decreases when, directly or indirectly, cash is used to pay off long-term borrowing.

The Long-Term Liabilities Financing figure for each period is the difference between the Long-Term Liabilities balance at the end of the previous period and the balance at the end of the current period. The formula for the first period is

```
=E62 - D62
```

The formula for the second period is

```
=F62 - E62
```

and so on.

## Other Noncurrent Liabilities Financing

The Other Noncurrent Liabilities Financing figures show the changes in the Other Noncurrent Liabilities balance for the period. This amount increases when, directly or indirectly, cash is generated by other long-term borrowing. This amount decreases when, directly or indirectly, cash is used to pay off other long-term borrowing.

The Other Noncurrent Liabilities Financing figure for each period is the difference between the Other Noncurrent Liabilities balance at the end of the previous period and the balance at the end of the current period. The formula for the first period is

```
=E63 - D63
```

The formula for the second period is

```
=F63 - E63
```

and so on.

## Accounts Receivable Investments

The Accounts Receivable Investments figures show the change in the Accounts Receivable balance for each forecasting period. This amount increases when the sales revenue collected during the period is less than the revenue recorded. This amount decreases when the sales revenue collected during the period is more than recorded. By recognizing the changes in the account balance, the model adjusts for differences between the income statement's accrual-based accounting of sales revenue and the actual cash collections for sales.

The Accounts Receivable Investments figure for each period is the difference between the Accounts Receivable balance at the end of the previous period and the balance at the end of the current period. The formula for the first period is

```
=E45 – D45
```

The formula for the second period is

```
=F45 – E45
```

and so on.

## Inventory Investments

The Inventory Investments figures show the change in the inventory balance for each forecasting period. This amount increases when the inventory sold is less than the inventory acquired. This amount decreases when the inventory sold is more than the inventory acquired. By recognizing the changes in this account balance, the model recognizes the cash effects of changing inventory balances.

The Inventory Investments figure for each period is the difference between the Inventory balance at the end of the previous period and the balance at the end of the current period. The formula for the first period is

```
=E46 – D46
```

The formula for the second period is

```
=F46 – E46
```

and so on.

## Other Current Assets Investments

The Other Current Assets Investments figures show the changes in the Other Current Assets balance for the period. This amount increases when, directly or indirectly, cash is used to acquire current assets. This amount decreases when, directly or indirectly, cash is generated by converting current assets to cash.

The Other Current Assets Investments figure for each period is the difference between the Other Current Assets balance at the end of the previous period and the balance at the end of the current period. The formula for the first period is

```
=E47 – D47
```

The formula for the second period is

```
=F47 - E47
```

and so on.

## Plant, Property, & Equipment Investments

The Plant, Property, & Equipment Investments figures show the change in the Plant, Property, & Equipment balance for the period. This amount increases when, directly or indirectly, cash is used to acquire plants, property, and equipment. This amount decreases when, directly or indirectly, cash is generated by converting plants, property, and equipment to cash.

The Plant, Property, & Equipment Investments figure for each period is the difference between the Plant, Property, & Equipment balance at the end of the previous period and the balance at the end of the current period. The formula for the first period is

```
=E49 - D49
```

The formula for the second period is

```
=F49 - E49
```

and so on.

## Other Noncurrent Assets Investments

The Other Noncurrent Assets Investments figures show the changes in the Other Noncurrent Assets balance for the period. This amount increases when, directly or indirectly, cash is used to acquire other noncurrent assets. This amount decreases when, directly or indirectly, cash is generated by converting other noncurrent assets to cash.

The Other Noncurrent Assets Investments figure for each period is the difference between the Other Noncurrent Assets balance at the end of the previous period and the balance at the end of the current period. The formula for the first period is

```
=E52 - D52
```

The formula for the second period is

```
=F52 - E52
```

and so on.

## Other Owner Equity Changes

The Other Owner Equity Changes figures show the cash flows stemming from any additional capital contributions made by the owners to the business or from dividends and other distributions made by the business to the owners. The Other Owner Equity Changes figure for each period is the value that you enter in the inputs area of the business planning starter workbook. The Other Owner Equity Changes figures are pulled into the Uses of Cash section as negative values because a positive change in owner's equity, such as an additional capital contribution (from a stock offering, for example), doesn't use cash but provides cash.

## Net Cash Generated (Used)

The Net Cash Generated (Used) figures show the total cash flow for each period of the forecasting horizon, based on the listed sources and uses of cash. The amount for each period is the sources of cash for the period less the uses of cash for the period. The formula for the first period is

```
=SUM(E140:E146) - SUM(E149:E154)
```

The formula for the second period is

```
=SUM(F140:F146) - SUM(F149:F154)
```

and so on.

## Ending Cash Balance

The Ending Cash Balance figures show the forecasted cash and equivalents balance at the end of each period. The balance is the Beginning Cash Balance figure for the period plus the Net Cash Generated (Used) figure for the period. The formula for the first period is

```
=E137+E155
```

The formula for the second period is

```
=F137+F155
```

and so on.

# Financial Ratios Table

The Financial Ratios Table has 11 rows of calculated data, as shown in Figure 2-6. As in other schedules, the period identifier numbers the periods for which values are calculated. The first period is stored in cell E159 as the integer 1, and periods that follow are stored as the previous period plus 1. The other values in the Financial Ratios Table are calculated as described in the following paragraphs.

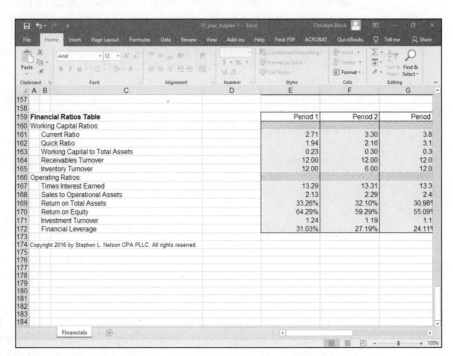

**FIGURE 2-6:**
The Financial
Ratios Table.

## Current Ratio

The Current Ratio figures show the ratio of current assets to current liabilities. The current ratio provides one measure of a business's capability to meet its short-term obligations. The Current Ratio figure for each period is the Total Current

Assets figure from the Balance Sheet schedule divided by the Total Current Liabilities figure. The formula for the first period is

```
=E48/E60
```

The formula for the second period is

```
=F48/F60
```

and so on.

## Quick Ratio

The Quick Ratio figures show the ratio of the sum of the cash and equivalents plus the accounts receivable to the current liabilities. The quick ratio provides a more stringent measure of a business's capability to meet its short-term financial obligations than other ratios. The Quick Ratio figure for each period is the sum of the Cash & Equivalents figure and the Accounts Receivable figure divided by the Total Current Liabilities figure. The formula for the first period is

```
=(E44+E45)/E60
```

The formula for the second period is

```
=(F44+F45)/F60
```

and so on.

## Working Capital to Total Assets

The Working Capital to Total Assets figures show the ratio of working capital (the current assets minus the current liabilities) to the total assets. The Working Capital to Total Assets ratio is another measure of a business's capability to meet its financial obligations and gives an indication as to the distribution of a business's assets into liquid and nonliquid resources. The Working Capital to Total Assets ratio for each period is calculated by dividing the difference between the Current Assets and Current Liabilities figures by the Total Assets figure. The formula for the first period is

```
=(E48 - E60)/E53
```

The formula for the second period is

```
=(F48 - F60)/F53
```

and so on.

## Receivables Turnover

The Receivables Turnover figures show the ratio of sales to the accounts receivable balance. The Receivables Turnover ratio indicates the efficiency of sales collections. One problem with the measure as it's usually applied is that both credit and cash sales may be included in the ratio denominator. Two potential shortcomings exist with this approach:

» The presence of the cash sales may make the receivables collections appear more efficient than is the case.

» Mere changes in the mix of credit and cash sales may affect the ratio even though the efficiency of the receivables collections process hasn't changed.

The Receivables Turnover figure for each period is calculated by dividing the Sales Revenue figure for the period by the Accounts Receivable balance outstanding at the end of the period. The formula for the first period is

```
=E97/E45
```

The formula for the second period is

```
=F97/F45
```

and so on.

## Inventory Turnover

The Inventory Turnover row shows the ratio of the cost of sales to the inventory balance. The Inventory Turnover ratio calculates how long inventory is held; it can indicate depleted or excessive inventory balances. The Inventory Turnover ratio for each period is calculated by dividing the Cost of Sales figure for the period by the inventory held at the end of the period. The formula for the first period is

```
= - E98/E46
```

The formula for the second period is

```
= - F98/F46
```

and so on.

## Times Interest Earned

The Times Interest Earned row shows the ratio of the sum of the net income after taxes plus the interest income to the interest expense. The ratio indicates the relative ease with which the business is paying its financing costs. The Times Interest Earned ratio for each period is calculated by dividing the sum of the Operating Income and Interest Income figures from the Income Statement schedule by the Interest Expense figure. The formula for the first period is

```
=(E106+E108)/E109
```

The formula for the second period is

```
=(F106+F108)/F109
```

and so on.

## Sales to Operational Assets

The Sales to Operational Assets row shows the ratio of sales revenue to net plant, property, and equipment. The ratio indicates the efficiency with which a business uses its operational assets to generate sales revenue. The Sales to Operational Assets ratio for each period is the Sales Revenue figure that you enter in the inputs area of the business planning starter workbook divided by the Net Plant, Property, & Equipment figure from the Balance Sheet schedule. The formula for the first period is

```
=E97/E51
```

The formula for the second period is

```
=F97/F51
```

and so on.

# Return on Total Assets

The Return on Total Assets row shows the ratio of the sum of the net income after taxes plus the interest expense to the total assets for each period. The ratio indicates the overall operating profitability of the business, expressed as a rate of return on the business assets. The formula for the first period is

```
=(E113+E109)/E53
```

The formula for the second period is

```
=(F113+F109)/F53
```

and so on.

# Return on Equity

The Return on Equity row shows the ratio of the net income after taxes to the owner's equity for each period. The ratio indicates the profitability of the business as an investment of the owners. The Return on Equity ratio for each period is the Net Income (Loss) After Taxes figure from the Income Statement schedule divided by the Owner Equity figure from the Balance Sheet schedule. The formula for the first period is

```
=E113/E65
```

The formula for the second period is

```
=F113/F65
```

and so on.

# Investment Turnover

The Investment Turnover row shows the ratio of the sales revenue to the total assets. The ratio, such as the Sales to Operational Assets ratio, indicates the efficiency with which a business uses its assets (in this case, its total assets) to generate sales. The Investment Turnover ratio for each period is the Sales Revenue figure that you enter in the inputs area of the business planning starter workbook divided by the Total Assets figure from the Balance Sheet schedule. The formula for the first period is

```
=E97/E53
```

The formula for the second period is

```
=F97/F53
```

and so on.

### Financial Leverage

The Financial Leverage row shows the difference between the return on owner's equity and the return on total assets. The ratio indicates the increase or decrease in an equity return as a result of borrowing. A positive value indicates an improvement in the return on owner's equity by using financial leverage; a negative value indicates deterioration in the return on owner's equity. The Financial Leverage figure for each period is the Return on Total Assets figure minus the Return on Equity figure. The formula for the first period is

```
=E170 - E169
```

The formula for the second period is

```
=F170 - F169
```

and so on.

# Customizing the Starter Workbook

You can use the business plan workbook for many business projections, but you may want to change the starter workbook so that it more closely matches your requirements. You can add text that describes your business and the forecasting horizon, for example. You can also increase or decrease the number of periods, perhaps increasing the number of periods to 12 if your periods are months and you want to forecast an entire year.

Before you change anything in the starter workbook other than the forecasting inputs, unprotect the document. To do this, choose the Review tab and click the Unprotect Sheet button.

**REMEMBER**

Unless you turn off cell protection, input cells in the inputs area of the business planning starter workbook are the only cells into which you can enter data.

# Changing the number of periods

You can easily increase or decrease the number of forecasting periods.

To increase the number of periods, remove the borders from the last column and then copy the current last column to the right as needed.

To decrease the number of periods, simply delete any unnecessary columns from the right side of the schedule. (To delete a column, highlight the entire column by clicking at the top of that column. Then right-click to bring up Excel's shortcut menu and choose Delete.) After you finish these steps, you can replace the borders on the right and reinstate cell protection as needed.

# Performing ratio analysis on existing financial statements

If you want to perform financial ratio analysis on a set of existing financial statements, copy the contents of column E from the row in the inputs area of the business plan workbook that contains the sales revenue forecast (row 32) through the last row of the ratios table into column D. Then remove the columns for periods 1 through 10 (columns E through N) by following the steps described in "Changing the number of periods" earlier in this chapter. Optionally, you can delete the Cash Flow Statement and add appropriate column headings as needed.

To use the modified starter workbook, enter the necessary Balance Sheet and Income Statement data in each of the unshaded cells in column D of the inputs area of the business planning starter workbook. (Typically, the As Of date of the Balance Sheet and the ending date of the Income Statement period are the same.)

# Calculating taxes for a current net loss before taxes

To calculate the income tax expense as 0 when you have a current period net loss before income taxes, you edit the formula in the cell that calculates the income tax expense (or savings) for the first period (cell E112) so that it takes the maximum of the calculated expense amount or 0 by using the MAX function:

```
=MAX(E38*E110,0)
```

After you've done this, you can copy the formula into the rest of the cells in the forecasting horizon that calculate the income tax expense (or savings). To do this, select the cell with the formula you want to copy, click the Home button, and then click the Copy button. Next, select the range of cells into which you want to copy the formula and click the Paste button.

## Combining this workbook with other workbooks

A quick and perhaps obvious point: You may want to construct other workbooks to supply numbers to the business plan workbook discussed in this chapter. You can construct an asset depreciation schedule, for example, that uses the straight-line depreciation convention for a $25,000 asset representing your entire plant, property, and equipment investment and then use this data in the business plan workbook.

**TIP**

If you start doing more Excel work, and you're not all that comfortable with Excel, consider picking up a recent edition of *Excel For Dummies*, by Greg Harvey (John Wiley & Sons, Inc.). It's a great tutorial on the basics. Also, if you want more information about constructing supporting financial workbooks (such as an asset depreciation schedule), you may want to visit my website, `https://stephenlnelson.com`.

If you want to use workbooks together in this manner, you probably should combine the workbooks into a single workbook. The easiest way to copy one of the workbooks is to copy the workbook's worksheet to a blank worksheet in the other workbook. (Each of the starter workbooks uses only a single worksheet to make this process both easy and possible.)

# Chapter **3**

# Writing a Business Plan

n Book 6, Chapter 2, I describe how to create a pro forma plan of business financial forecasts by using the `bizplan.xls` business plan workbook, which you
can download from `https://stephenlnelson.com/wp-content/uploads/10_`
`year_bizplan-1.xlsx`. If you do not own a Microsoft Excel software license,
Google Sheets and Excel for the Web provide a web-based Microsoft Excel program
for free.

If you do create a forecast, you probably also want to create a companion business
plan. For this reason, you also need to know about writing such a plan. I don't go
into tedious detail about how to do this. I just provide you some useful information about business plans, and I give you some tips about how to write a workable
business plan.

## What the Term "Business Plan" Means

In truth, the term *business plan* refers to three separate things:

» **A strategic plan:** A discussion or description of a firm's overall strategy

» **A new-venture plan:** The fundraising document that entrepreneurs use to
promote a new venture to investors

>> **A white-paper plan:** The 50-page (or even 100-page) document that a business owner uses to describe in detail a new business opportunity, including its risks, its opportunities, and anything else that's germane

I talk a little bit about each of these plans — some more than others — in the following pages.

# A Few Words about Strategic Plans

Unfortunately, I'm not equipped to provide you detailed information about how to construct a strategic plan. Neither, of course, are most of the other people who willingly offer advice. That said, however, I can provide you some useful starting points for constructing your strategic plan.

First off, the way that you're using the word *strategy* is very likely wrong because you aren't talking about strategy at all. For my source on this perspective, I rely on what Michael E. Porter, a Harvard Business School professor, said in his strategy classic *Competitive Strategy: Techniques for Analyzing Industries and Competitors* (published by Free Press).

The really interesting thing that Porter says in his book (and something that's worth repeating over and over) is that practically speaking, only three basic business strategies exist:

>> A cost strategy

>> A differentiated product or service strategy

>> A focus on a niche strategy

Because understanding these strategies is critical to writing a good strategic plan (and to using the term *strategy* correctly), in the following section I briefly discuss in my own words what Porter means by limiting possible strategies to three. I demonstrate each of these strategies by using example firms in an industry that we're all pretty familiar with: bricks-and-mortar retailing.

## Cost strategies

Successful retailers rely on a cost strategy. Firms such as Amazon and Costco excel at providing products to their customers economically. They pass along a lot of the benefits of this economy to their customers in the form of lower prices.

Not all the cost savings get passed along to the consumers, however. A significant portion of the cost savings, achieved through incredibly efficient operations, are retained by the business and, therefore, become profits.

Such cost leadership or low-cost operation is one of the three basic strategies. It's a strategy that's available to any business — and particularly those businesses that have achieved economies of scale.

The key thing to note about a low-cost strategy, however, is that the firm needs to retain some of the cost savings to earn a higher profit level than its competitors. Thus, simply being a low-cost producer isn't enough. A firm needs to be a low-cost producer and still be able to price products and services at a level high enough that some of the cost savings are retained as profits.

## Differentiated products or services strategies

The second basic strategy is product differentiation. Product differentiators often sell a very unusual product or service. The Nordstrom department store chain is a good example because it offers unsurpassed service, and often (although not always), it offers a great and high-quality selection of items. Nordstrom goods cost more, but consumers happily pay the extra amount. Why? Because they get so much more for their money.

A firm that relies on a differentiation strategy competes on the basis of the special features of its products or services. The key to making this strategy work is being able to charge your customers more for those special features than the special features cost you. Differentiation needs to produce increased revenue in excess of increased costs.

## Focus strategies

The focus strategy is really a hybrid of the cost and differentiation strategies. This strategy states that in some ways, a firm is really good about managing costs and that in other ways, this firm is really good about differentiating products or services. A firm may choose to take this hybrid approach because it understands a particular audience or niche of customers or category of products. In other words, the firm can, through this focused approach, serve a particular market better than any competitor. This firm is going to be the best at serving a particular niche. Again, as is the case with other strategies, the focus strategy must produce increased revenue greater than the increased cost of the strategy or cost savings (to the business) greater than the lower prices passed along to customers.

So what's a focus strategy retailer? I'd say that Target is. Target, in my opinion, focuses on suburban middle-class customers by offering those consumers almost the perfect combination of cost savings and differentiated products.

# Look, Ma: No Strategy

All this probably sounds like gobbledygook if you haven't been exposed to much strategic thinking before. The strategies and their strengths become very clear, however, when you compare firms that have these strategies — cost leaders such as Amazon and Costco, differentiation leaders such as Nordstrom, and focus leaders such as Target — with firms that lack a clear strategic focus.

Perhaps the best-known recent example of the retailer that (in my opinion) lacks a clear-cut strategy is Kmart, which as of the writing of this book in August 2022, is down to only three stores in the United States. This becomes very clear when you start comparing Kmart with the leaders in each of the three strategies. Consider the following three problems that Kmart is plagued by:

>> **Kmart can't compete on cost.** If you were really concerned about cost, you would probably go someplace like Walmart or Costco and get a better price than you could get at Kmart. So Kmart loses cost-conscious customers to Walmart and Costco.

>> **Kmart can't compete with differentiation.** If you really want a highly differential product, the best in its class, you aren't going to go to Kmart. Here, Kmart loses out to stores like Nordstrom, which charge higher prices but offer a wider range of differentiated products. If you want the best in class, you probably aren't shopping at Kmart; you go to a store that's emphasizing and excelling at this strategy.

>> **Kmart doesn't have a particular focus.** Does Kmart serve a particular niche better than anybody else? I don't know. But at least in the category of suburban middle-class consumers, Target probably does a much better job. If you're really looking for clothes or household items appropriate in a middle-class suburb, is there any question that Target beats the pants off Kmart? I don't think so.

So now you can see how the word *strategy* is misunderstood and used incorrectly. *Strategy* isn't a way to refer to some idea you have; *strategy*, in business, refers to an approach (probably one of the three generic approaches) to beating your competition: cost, differentiation (probably in terms of product excellence), and focus.

Here's the key: If you can execute a strategy better than anybody else can, you win. If you try to do a little bit of this or a little bit of that, or if you ignore or can't bring yourself to pick a particular strategy, you're going to be continually beaten up by firms that have picked a strategy. You lose the cost game to the cost leaders. You lose the differentiation game to the differentiators. And you lose at competing in particular niches to those firms that focus on those niches.

## Two comments about tactics

I won't talk any more about this strategy business, but I have a couple of comments about tactics. Most of the time when you hear people talk about strategy, they're not really talking about strategy; they're talking about tactics.

*Tactics* refers to choices that firms make in an attempt to execute strategy successfully. The irony is that the people who misuse the word *strategy* (by referring to tactics as strategy) often don't have a strategy. This is my first comment.

My second comment is that tactics, predictably, don't work and don't make sense except as support for a particular strategy. To pursue a strategy of cost leadership, for example, you must ensure that all your tactics support that strategy. You undermine your success in executing that strategy if some tactics support a cost strategy, some tactics support a differentiation strategy, and some tactics support a focus strategy. This makes sense, right? In this situation, you become a jack of all trades and a master of none.

## Six final strategy pointers

Before you move on to the next topic, be sure that you understand these key points:

>> **Know the three strategies.** Usually, a firm can have only one of three business strategies:

- Cost-based strategy

- Differentiation-based strategy

- Focus-based strategy

>> **Pick a strategy.** The first step — the step that you take before you can select appropriate tactics — is picking a strategy. From the strategy decision, all other tactical decisions follow.

>> **Support the strategy with appropriate tactics.** A strategic plan, obviously, must have a clearly defined strategy. Then it must identify, or enumerate, the tactics that support the strategy. It's really as simple as that. And note this

important point: The only appropriate tactics are those that support one of these strategies.

>> **Stick to your strategy.** The hard part of writing a strategic plan is disciplining yourself (or the firm) to pick a strategy and then stick with it. Few firms want to be disciplined to stick with a hard-core strategy of cost, product differentiation, or focus. It's all too easy to slip-slide your way into a situation in which you're trying to be a little of this or a little of that. Picking a particular strategy means that you forgo certain kinds of opportunities and that you say no to some customers and certain kinds of products.

>> **Read *Competitive Strategy: Techniques for Analyzing Industries and Competitors*.** I discuss this book in "A Few Words about Strategic Plans" earlier in this chapter. It's a difficult book to read, and much of the material is a couple of decades old, but it's worthwhile reading for any business owner. Reading it won't be much fun, but I feel very confident that the 15 or 20 hours you'll spend reading the book constitute an enormously useful investment of your time.

>> **Poke around my Evergreen Small Business blog.** If you have time, you ought to consider poking around my blog and perusing the strategy-related posts at https://evergreensmallbusiness.com/category/strategy. You should find the coverage to be useful because I rewrite the typical business-school strategy talk in terms that translate pretty directly to the small-business owner's or manager's situation.

# A White-Paper Business Plan

People often write a white-paper business plan when they know that they need a strategic plan but don't want to make the hard decisions necessary for a strategic plan. The person in this conundrum writes a lengthy white-paper business plan to camouflage the absent strategic plan.

**REMEMBER**

I guess it's obvious from the preceding paragraph, but you really should write a strategic plan before you write a white-paper business plan. A strategic plan, by the way, doesn't need to be more than a page or two in length. In fact, the hard part of a strategic plan isn't in the writing but in the sacrifice: giving up certain categories of opportunities, markets, and tactical approaches that may be comfortable or familiar. Obviously, you can't write a good white-paper business plan — or at least one that's based on a sound strategy — until you have a strategic plan in place.

Perhaps the most important thing to know when you write a white-paper business plan is this: This process is well documented in a bunch of other places. If you have QuickBooks Premier or QuickBooks Enterprise Solutions, you can choose Company ➪ Planning & Budgeting ➪ Use Business Plan Tool to start a wizard that steps you through the process of writing a white-paper business plan.

Figure 3-1 shows the first page of the QuickBooks Business Planner, but I'm not going to talk more about the wizard here. You can use the wizard to see what it does.

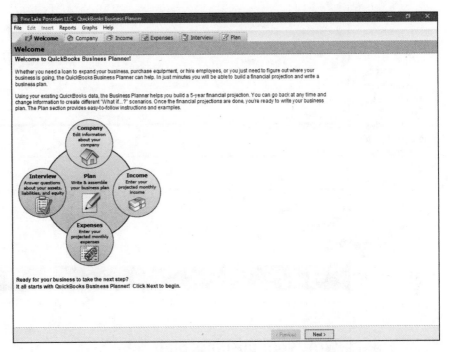

FIGURE 3-1:
The first page of
the QuickBooks
Business Planner.

You can also get detailed information on writing a business plan in most languages from the U.S. Small Business Administration (SBA) website at www. sba.gov/business-guide/plan-your-business/write-your-business-plan. There, you see a page of information that the SBA website offers about writing a business plan (see Figures 3-2 and 3-3). It provides links to additional pages of detailed information about the process of writing a business plan, such as a page that provides advice on doing strategic planning and a page that supplies step-by-step instructions for the actual work of writing your plan.

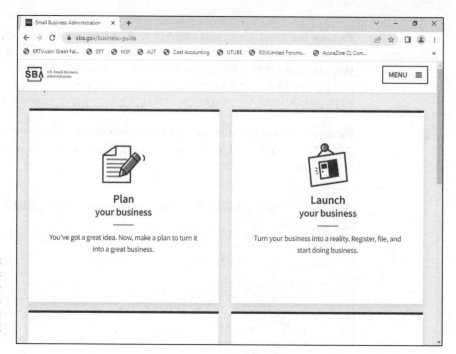

**FIGURE 3-2:**
The Business
Guide page
of the SBA's
website provides
general planning
information.

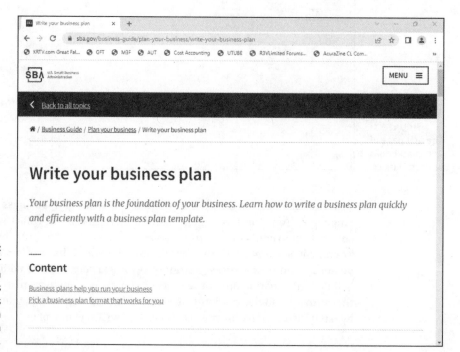

**FIGURE 3-3:**
The Write Your
Business Plan
page of the SBA's
website provides
information
about writing a
business plan.

**TIP**

The SBA website changes, predictably, but you should be able to hunt down its links to relevant business planning topics, such as "business plan basics," "writing the plan," and "using the plan."

I should also point out that Microsoft Word and Microsoft PowerPoint (which many computer users own because Word and PowerPoint are components of just about every version of Microsoft Office) supply a detailed outline for creating a white-paper business plan. (To get to these business-plan outlines, choose File ⇨ New and then poke around in the template libraries.) These templates provide very good starting outlines, so don't be misled into thinking that something that Microsoft provides for free to Word or PowerPoint users is in some way inferior to what real businesses use. Microsoft has done an excellent job of showing what information belongs in a white-paper business plan.

**REMEMBER**

If you do not own a licensed Microsoft Word or Microsoft PowerPoint program, you can create a slideshow for free using Google Slides.

Most white-paper business plans and new-venture business plans (which I define in the next section) require a pro forma financial forecast. Book 6, Chapter 2 describes how to do this. Typically, in a hard-copy printed business plan, you include such a forecast as an appendix.

After you create a good, solid strategy and at least a rough white-paper business plan, you may also want to create a new-venture plan. The next section describes how to do this.

# A New-Venture Plan

To write a new-venture plan, you take a different approach from the one you take to write a white-paper plan. New-venture plans answer five basic questions, which provide prospective investors the necessary information to determine whether they should further investigate your venture as a possible investment. The next sections detail these five questions.

## Is the new venture's product or service feasible?

In some cases, this question is unnecessary to ask, but the answer is important to consider in any case in which a firm may invest in a new, unproven idea. This situation is most clearly illustrated in the case of a firm that plans to build and then market some newfangled technology. If you're thinking of starting a firm that will produce a better mousetrap, a key question to ask is whether you really can build a better mousetrap. You can answer this question in a couple of ways, practically speaking. Obviously, the best way to answer this question about feasibility is to build the better mousetrap first. Having built the better mousetrap, you'll find it easy to prove to prospective investors that yes, the product is feasible. You can set your mousetrap on the desk and demonstrate how it works. Perhaps on some . . . no, no, let's not go there.

If a product hasn't already been built or a service hasn't already been proved to be deliverable, the next-best approach — and the one commonly used by technology startups — is to assemble a team of people who have built similar products in the past. The logic of this approach is that if you have a team that has built similar technologies in the past, investors can probably rely on this team's track record of success. If a team of talented engineers has built new and improved mousetraps, it's very easy for investors to prudently believe that this team may be able to build a better mousetrap in the future. The engineers understand the technology. They understand the problem. They're experienced in creating new solutions to address the problem. You see how easy it is to buy into the possibility.

## Does the market want the product or service?

Assuming that you do have a firm with a practical, feasible product or service, you need to answer another big question right up front: Do people really, truly want the product or service? In other words, is there public demand for the firm's offering? This business about demand seems kind of tricky to ascertain. Ideally, a new venture proves that demand exists by already having customers buying the product. If a new venture hasn't yet finished the product or service, such hard-and-fast proof of demand is impossible to come by. In this case, you have another option: You can prove market demand by running independent market research studies to say, "Yes, we've run several focus groups, and people say they'll buy a better mousetrap."

Sometimes, you can also prove market demand by showing that consumers or businesses already purchase a similar product or service and would, logically, purchase a clearly improved version of the product or service. In the case of the better mousetrap, people are already buying a lot of mousetraps. So if you truly did build better mousetraps, you could pretty much prove market demand by demonstrating the new product's superiority.

REMEMBER

Let me encourage you to take a big bite of the reality sandwich if you're thinking this way, however. You need to be very careful about this issue of market demand, because it's all too easy for entrepreneurs and inventors who are excited about some new technology or some new product or service to assume that consumers really will want the new thing that is being built or offered. Consumers are notoriously fickle. What seems like a wonderful innovation to the entrepreneur or inventor often isn't so wonderful in the eyes of the consumer.

## Can the product or service be profitably sold?

Okay, the first two questions ask whether a product or service is feasible and whether people want the product. Is that enough? No, actually it isn't. The third, critically important question is whether the product that you're selling can be sold profitably. You must run rough numbers to prove that products or services revenue less the cost of goods sold produces a gross margin that is adequate not just to pay the operating expenses of the firm, but also to retain something for profit. This proof that the firm can profitably sell its product or service is really achieved by the business pro forma financial forecast (as described in Book 6, Chapter 2). This forecast proves that the firm can be profitable by selling the product or service.

**REMEMBER**

Include a fair salary for your efforts in your profitability calculations if you'll manage the new business. Your business isn't really profitable unless it can pay you (and other team members) a fair wage and reasonably expected fringe benefits.

I won't say a lot more about this profitability issue, but basically, all the accounting stuff discussed throughout this book comes into play here. To do a decent new-venture plan, you need to understand enough accounting to produce a set of forward-looking financial statements that persuasively argue a profitable venture.

## Is the return on the venture adequate for prospective investors?

Curiously, simply proving that a firm's venture will be profitable often isn't enough. A firm also needs to deliver profits at least equal to and, ideally, in excess of the return on investment that the investors desire. In the case of a new venture, investors have pretty firm expectations of what a risky investment should deliver. *Angel investors* commonly require rates of return in the neighborhood of 20 to 25 percent annually. Small-business entrepreneurs and business owners often require similar rates of return. Institutional and professional venture capital investors (the sort of people that you read about in *The Wall Street Journal* and in *Inc.* magazine) often require annual rates of return of 45 percent to 55 percent — or even 65 percent annually.

If you think about what all of this means, you can quickly see that even a pretty darn good business that delivers the 30 to 35 percent annual rate of return — and that's really good if you think about it — won't be enough for some investors. An institutional venture capital investor who needs, for example, a 50 percent annual return on their investment isn't going to look seriously at anything that produces a meager 30 percent annual return.

Essentially, in a new-venture plan, you provide information that lets the prospective investor figure out the rate of return. Then the prospective investor can compare this return with their requirements.

TIP

It's not a bad idea to look at the returns that you're implicitly suggesting via your new-venture plan. Make sure that you aren't trying to sell a 25 percent annual return investment to investors who require a 50 percent annual return. Similarly, you may not need to offer investors who will be happy with a 25 percent annual return a deal that pays a 50 percent annual return. Book 5, Chapter 2 offers a discussion of Economic Value Added analysis that details how you can compare the return delivered by a firm to investors with the return on investment that those investors expect.

## Can existing management run the business?

Even if you have a venture based on a feasible product or technology, even if you have customers who are hysterically excited to purchase your product, even if you have a product or service that will bring in a massive profit, and even if your investors will be able to earn a wonderful return on their investment, that's still not enough. A new-venture plan must ask and answer one other critical question.

Any new-venture plan needs to sell prospective investors on the idea that the existing management team — which includes the founder or president and their lieutenants or vice presidents — can successfully operate the business. In other words, even a great business opportunity requires a good management team in place (or almost in place), ready to execute the business plan.

Here are a couple of ways that you can prove that the management team isn't going to be a problem:

>> **Have a management team in place that has already successfully executed a venture similar to the new venture.** If you're trying to sell prospective investors on the idea that the management team can create a $25 million business selling a better mousetrap, your task will be much easier

if the same management team at some point in the past created a $25 million business selling a better mousetrap.

>> **Show that the management team members — or at least most of them — are successful people.** A team of people who have succeeded at big things in the past suggests to investors that the management team knows how to win. I'm not talking about an Eagle Scout designation; I'm thinking more on the line of an MBA from Stanford or a few years of management experience in some big, well-run, highly respected company. If some members of your team have proved their business savvy and cognitive skills — or, even better, successfully managed an important division in another business — in a nutshell, you're saying to prospective investors, "Hey, this management team will bring home a win for us."

# Some final thoughts

Okay, I have a handful of final comments to make about new-venture business planning:

>> **The general outline:** Although new-venture business plans serve a different purpose from white-paper business plans, you use the same sort of general outline for both. In other words, even though a new-venture business plan has as its primary purpose answering the five questions discussed in the preceding sections, you follow an outline like the one provided by the SBA website (or like the one provided by Word or PowerPoint).

>> **A few caveats:** Although you definitely want to make sure that your new-venture business plan answers the five questions, keep in mind the following caveats:

- *Don't lay it on too thick.* You want to write something that looks like a white-paper business plan, but edit it well to minimize the amount of super-detailed information and to clearly and boldly answer the five questions that the new-venture investor needs to ask and have answered.

- *Remember that a new-venture investor typically isn't going to write you a check based on what they see in a new-venture business plan.* What you put in a new-venture business plan is simply information that will tickle the new-venture investor's fancy. The information should be just enough to make them think "This sounds pretty cool. I'll take a closer look."

- *It's very unlikely that any entrepreneur or business owner can honestly answer "Yes" to all five questions.* Some people will say that you need to offer a dynamite, ironclad, super deal that nobody could refuse. In my opinion, any sophisticated new-venture investor who expects you to be able to answer with a 100 percent guaranteed "Yes" to every question is probably pretty naive. Anybody who has half a clue knows that risk exists in any business venture. Even if you have a great technology that's already built, customers clamoring with orders in the reception area of your office, and a great management team in place — *even* if everything seems perfect — stuff still goes wrong.

Having said that, however, note that answering any of the five questions with a definite "No" means that the new venture won't work — or at least it won't work for you as the business owner or as the manager. Each of the five questions is a link in the chain of success. Break any link — regardless of which one — and the chain breaks.

# 7

# Care and Maintenance

# Contents at a Glance

IN THIS CHAPTER

» **Securing your data**

» **Managing QuickBooks in a multiuser environment**

» **Enabling audit trails**

» **Setting up QuickBooks for simultaneous multiuser access**

» **Managing accounting controls**

# Chapter **1**

# Administering QuickBooks

QuickBooks does something that's critically important to the success of your business: It collects and supplies financial information. For this reason, you want to have a firm understanding of how you can protect the data that QuickBooks collects and stores, as well as the assets that QuickBooks tracks. This chapter describes all this.

## Keeping Your Data Confidential

Accounting data is often confidential information. Your QuickBooks data shows how much money you have in the bank, what you owe creditors, and how much (or how little) profit your firm produces. Because this information is private, your first concern in administering a QuickBooks accounting system is keeping your data confidential.

You have two complementary methods for keeping your QuickBooks data confidential. The first method for maintaining confidentiality relies on the security features built into Microsoft Windows. The other method relies on QuickBooks's security features.

## Using Windows security

You can use the security provided by Windows to restrict access to a file — either a program file or a data file — to specific users. This means that you can use Windows-level security to say who can and can't use the QuickBooks program or access the QuickBooks data file.

I don't describe how Windows-level security works in this book. If you're already employing Windows-level security, you know (or someone in your office knows) how to use that tool to prevent unauthorized access to, or use of, program files and data files. To use Windows-level security for QuickBooks, you can simply apply your existing general knowledge to the QuickBooks program file or the QuickBooks data file.

If you aren't already using Windows-level security, you don't need to go to the trouble of learning Windows's complicated security system. You can use the simpler QuickBooks security.

## Using QuickBooks security

You can protect the confidentiality of your QuickBooks data by assigning a password to a QuickBooks company data file. You can do this during the QuickBooks setup process. You can also set up a password by choosing the Company ⇨ Change Your Password command. In non-Enterprise versions of QuickBooks, the command would be Company ⇨ Set Up Users & Passwords ⇨ Change Your Password. When you choose this command, QuickBooks displays the Change Your Password dialog box (see Figure 1-1).

To set up a password, you simply enter the same password in both the New Password text box and the Confirm New Password text box. Note that your password is associated with the username Admin (which stands for *administrator)*. If you haven't yet set up a password, you don't have an old password, so you won't see a Current Password text box. If you're working with an Administrator password, you must also provide a challenge question and answer. (This answer will let you recover your access to your QuickBooks file if you forget the Administrator password.)

TIP

Obviously, you want to set your password so that no one (not even a computer) can possibly guess it, which means that your password shouldn't be a word in a dictionary. Your password also shouldn't be a number. And your password *especially* shouldn't be a word, phrase, or name that some co-worker can easily figure out. The best passwords (from a security point of view) are nonsensical combinations of letters, numbers, and symbols such as *f34t5s!* or *s#3df43x2*. One other thing: Longer is better.

**FIGURE 1-1:**
The Change
Your Password
dialog box.

I strongly encourage subscribing to a password manager service, such as 1Password or Last Pass. These services allow you to store, generate, and manage your passwords. They also help to minimize identity theft and hacking by creating complete and unique passwords for every site and program.

After you set your password, you should change it periodically. To change your password, choose the Company ⇨ Change Your Password (or possibly Company ⇨ Set Up Users & Roles ⇨ Edit) command. QuickBooks again displays the Change Your Password dialog box. This time, you must enter your old password in the Current Password text box. Then you need to enter your new password in both the New Password text box and the Confirm New Password text box.

**REMEMBER**

Let me add one more plug for password managers, which eliminate having to think or even remember all your passwords. You can simply choose them from the software.

QuickBooks requires a username and password before it will open the company data file. If you assign a password to your company data file, for example, whenever QuickBooks starts, it displays the QuickBooks Login dialog box, where you enter your username and password and then click OK. QuickBooks opens the data file. If you can't supply the password, QuickBooks doesn't open the data file.

# Using QuickBooks in a Multiuser Environment

You aren't limited to using one password to control access to your QuickBooks data file. You can set up several passwords for the QuickBooks data file. What's really neat about this practice is that you can tell QuickBooks to allow certain users and passwords to do only certain things. This sounds complicated, but it's really not. The business owner, for example, may have a password that allows them to do anything. But a new accounting clerk, for example, may have a password that allows them only to record bills in the system.

## Setting up additional QuickBooks users

If more than one person will be using QuickBooks, you want to set up additional users.

### Adding users in QuickBooks Enterprise Solutions

To add users in QuickBooks Enterprise Solutions, follow these steps:

**1.** **Choose Company ⇨ Users ⇨ Set Up Users and Roles.**

QuickBooks displays the Users and Roles dialog box (see Figure 1-2). This dialog box identifies any users for whom QuickBooks access has been set up and the roles they can fill when using QuickBooks. The Users list, which appears on the User List tab of the dialog box, also identifies who is currently logged in to the system.

**2.** **Tell QuickBooks that you want to add a user by clicking the New button.**

When you click this button, QuickBooks displays the New User dialog box.

**3.** **Identify the user and supply a password.**

You need to give each user for whom you're setting up a username. You do this by entering a short name — perhaps the user's first name — in the User Name box. After you identify the user, you enter the user's password in both the Password text box and the Confirm Password text box (see Figure 1-3).

**4.** **Identify the user's role(s).**

Use the Available Roles list box to select the roles (or duties) the user fills. Then add the selected role to the user's list of assigned roles by clicking the Add button. To remove a role from a user, select the role in the Assigned Roles list box and then click Remove.

FIGURE 1-2:
The Users and
Roles dialog box.

FIGURE 1-3:
The New User
dialog box.

Administering
QuickBooks

The Description box at the bottom of the New User dialog box allows you to describe the role in more detail. You might enter the type of QuickBooks user who might typically be assigned the selected role, for example.

5.  **(Optional) Modify roles as necessary.**

    You can fine-tune the roles that you assign (with the help of QuickBooks). To do so, go back to the Users and Roles dialog box, select the Role List tab (see Figure 1-4), click the role you want to change and then click the Edit button. When QuickBooks displays the Edit Role dialog box (not shown), select an accounting activity or area in the Area and Activities list and then use the Area Access Level radio buttons to specify what a user with the selected role can do. You can indicate that the user should have no access by selecting the None radio button. You can indicate that the user should have full access by selecting the Full radio button. If the user should have partial access, you select the Partial button and then check or clear (as appropriate) the View, Create, Modify, Delete, Print, and View Balance check boxes. Click OK to save any changes to the roles and return to the Users and Roles dialog box.

    You can see what access any role initially has by selecting one of the entries in the Area and Activities list. QuickBooks uses the Area Access Level buttons and boxes to show the current settings for the role.

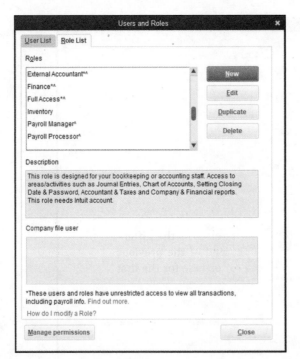

**FIGURE 1-4:**
The Role List tab of the Users and Roles dialog box.

As a general rule, when it comes to accounting controls, you want to provide a minimal amount of access. If someone doesn't need access to the QuickBooks data file for day-to-day duties, you should select the None button. If someone needs a little bit of access — perhaps to prepare job estimates or invoices — you give just that access and nothing more. At the end of this chapter, in "Maintaining Good Accounting Controls," I talk about why minimizing user rights and access is so important. But the bottom line is this: The more ability you give employees or subcontractors or accountants to noodle around in your accounting system, the greater the risk that someone will either inadvertently or intentionally introduce errors into the system. Also, the greater the rights and access you give, the easier you make it for someone to steal from you.

**6.** **(Optional) Review your user permissions.**

After you set up a user, you should (to be careful) review the permissions you've given the user. To do this, click the User List tab of the Users and Roles dialog box, select the user, and then click the Manage Permissions button. When QuickBooks displays the View Permissions dialog box (not shown), select the user and then click the Display button to see the View Permissions window (see Figure 1-5), which displays a very detailed list of what the user can and can't do.

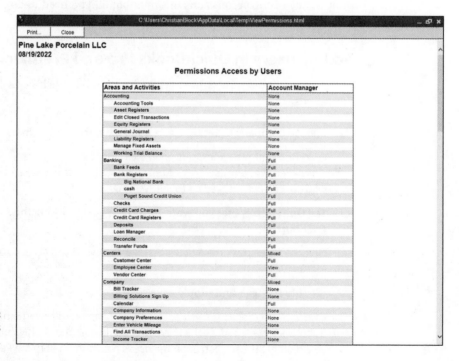

**FIGURE 1-5:**
View Permissions window.

7. **(Optional) Review your role modifications.**

If you change a role's permissions, you probably also want to review those changes. To do that, click the Role List tab of the Users and Roles dialog box, select the role, and then click the View Permissions button. QuickBooks displays another version of the View Permissions window that lists the roles you and QuickBooks have set up. Select the role you want to review and then click the View Permissions button. QuickBooks displays another version of the View Permissions window, with a detailed list of what someone with the role can and can't do.

8. **After you finish reviewing user and role permissions, click Close to close any open windows and then click the Cancel or Close button to close any open dialog boxes.**

From this point forward, the new user can use QuickBooks; their rights are limited to what you specified.

**TIP**

It may be important to audit the permissions every few months or years, depending on your employment turnover and bookkeeping practices. Obviously, previous employees or bookkeepers should no longer have roles that permit them to make changes in your file. Heck, they probably shouldn't have roles at all! QuickBooks's View Permissions window is a slick way to see this data online, and if you want to print a copy of the permissions information, all you need to do is click the window's Print button.

## Adding users in QuickBooks Pro and Premier

To set up additional users in QuickBooks Pro and QuickBooks Premier, follow these steps:

1. **Choose Company ➪ Set Up Users and Passwords ➪ Set Up Users.**

QuickBooks displays the Users and Roles List dialog box (refer to Figure 1-2), which identifies any users for whom QuickBooks access has been set up and who are currently logged on to the system.

2. **Tell QuickBooks that you want to add a user by clicking the Add User button.**

QuickBooks displays the first Set Up User Password and Access dialog box (not shown).

3. **Identify the user and supply a password.**

Give each user for whom you're setting up a password a username by entering a short name — perhaps the user's first name — in the User Name box. After you identify the user, you enter the user's password in both the Password text box and the Confirm Password text box.

4. **Click Next to continue and then indicate whether you want to limit access for the new user.**

When QuickBooks displays the second Set Up User Password and Access dialog box (not shown), indicate whether you want to limit access and rights for the user. If you do want to limit access and rights (rights are simply the things that the user can do), select the Selected Areas of QuickBooks radio button. If you want the user to be able to do anything, select the All Areas of QuickBooks radio button. If you indicate that the new user should have access to all areas of QuickBooks, you're done setting up the user password, and you can skip the remaining steps.

5. **Click Next to continue and then describe access to sales and accounts receivable information and tasks.**

QuickBooks displays the third Set Up User Password and Access dialog box (not shown) — the first of a series of dialog boxes that walks you through an interview, asking detailed questions about what kind of access each user should have to a particular area. With regard to sales activity, for example, QuickBooks asks about access to transactions (such as invoices, credit memos, and accounts receivable information). You can indicate that the user should have no access by selecting the No Access radio button. You can indicate that the user should have full access by selecting the Full Access radio button. If the user should have partial access, you select the Selective Access radio button and then select one of the subsidiary buttons: Create Transactions Only, Create and Print Transactions, or Create Transactions and Create Reports.

6. **Click Next and then describe the purchases and accounts payable rights.**

QuickBooks displays the fourth Set Up User Password and Access dialog box (not shown), which allows you to specify what access this new user has in the purchases and accounts payable areas. You can select the No Access radio button. You can select the Full Access radio button. Or you can select some middle ground by selecting the Selective Access radio button and one of the subsidiary buttons. The same rules for setting rights and access that apply to the purchases and accounts payable area apply to the sales and accounts receivable area.

7. **Click Next and then describe the remaining user rights and access.**

When you click the Next button at the bottom of each version of the Set Up User Password and Access dialog box, QuickBooks displays several other versions of the dialog box that it uses to query you about user rights and access. After you describe what rights are appropriate for the user in the purchases and accounts payable area, for example, QuickBooks asks about the checking and credit card area. Then it asks about the inventory area. Next, it asks about payroll, followed by questions about general, sensitive accounting activities. Finally, QuickBooks asks about access to financial reporting capabilities.

You limit rights in each of these other areas the same way that you do for the sales and accounts receivable and for the purchases and accounts payable areas. Therefore, I'm not going to describe how you select the No Access option button, the Full Access option button, or the Selective Access button over and over again. Just be thoughtful as you go through the screens, limiting the user's rights. You want users to have the rights necessary to do their job, but you don't want to give them any more rights than they need.

8. **Specify whether the user can change or delete transactions.**

   After you've stepped through roughly a half-dozen versions of the Set Up User Password and Access dialog boxes that ask about specific areas of accounting, QuickBooks displays the Changing or Deleting Transactions page of the Set Up User Password and Access dialog box (not shown). The Changing or Deleting Transactions page lets you indicate whether a user can change transactions recorded before the closing date. In general, you want to limit a user's ability to change or delete transactions.

9. **Click Next and then review your rights decisions.**

   QuickBooks displays the final version of the Set Up User Password and Access dialog box (not shown), which identifies the user rights that you assigned or allowed. You can use this dialog box to review the rights that someone has. If you realize that you've assigned rights incorrectly, click the Back button to move back through the dialog boxes to the one where you made a mistake. Change the assignment of rights and click the Next button to return to the final window of the Set Up User Password and Access dialog box.

10. **When you finish with the review of user rights and access, click Finish.**

    From this point forward, the new user will be able to use QuickBooks; their rights are limited to what you specified.

## Changing user rights in Enterprise Solutions

You can modify the rights that you assign to a user. To do this in QuickBooks Enterprise Solutions, choose Company ➪ Users ➪ Set Up Users and Roles to display the Users and Roles dialog box (not shown).

To change a user's rights after reviewing them, select the user and click the Edit button. QuickBooks displays the Edit User dialog box (see Figure 1-6), which closely resembles the New User dialog box that you use to set up the user and describe their rights. You use the User Name, Password, and Confirm Password text boxes to change the user information. You can use the Available Roles list, the Assigned Roles list, and the Add and Remove buttons to change what the user can do within QuickBooks. Click Close when you're done.

# CAPTURING RIGHTS SETTINGS

Accountants often want to see the rights that particular users have, especially if they're auditing you as part of annual closings. (You may be audited if the bank wants audited financial statements, for example.) QuickBooks doesn't provide a way for you to print the information shown in the Set Up User Password and Access dialog box. Windows, however, allows you to use the Print Screen key to capture a screen shot of the QuickBooks program window and the Set Up User Password and Access dialog box.

Press Alt+Print Scrn to shoot a screen shot of the dialog box. This key combination copies an image of your screen to the Windows Clipboard. Next, open Paint by choosing Start ⇨ Programs ⇨ Accessories ⇨ Paint (versions before Windows 10) or Start ⇨ Paint 3D in Windows 10 or later. Paste the image into Paint by pressing Ctrl+V. You may see an error message that says `The image in the Clipboard is larger than the bitmap. Would you like the bitmap enlarged?` Save the screen shot by choosing File ⇨ Save As. (This basic technique is the same one that I use to show you pictures of the QuickBooks windows in the pages of this book.) You may want to capture a screen shot this way to record the user access and rights for employees.

**FIGURE 1-6:** The Edit User dialog box.

To duplicate a user (you may want to add a second user with permissions that mirror some other user's permissions), in the Users and Role dialog box, select the user you want to clone and then click Duplicate. When QuickBooks displays the Duplicate User dialog box (see Figure 1-7), finish describing the new user and click OK.

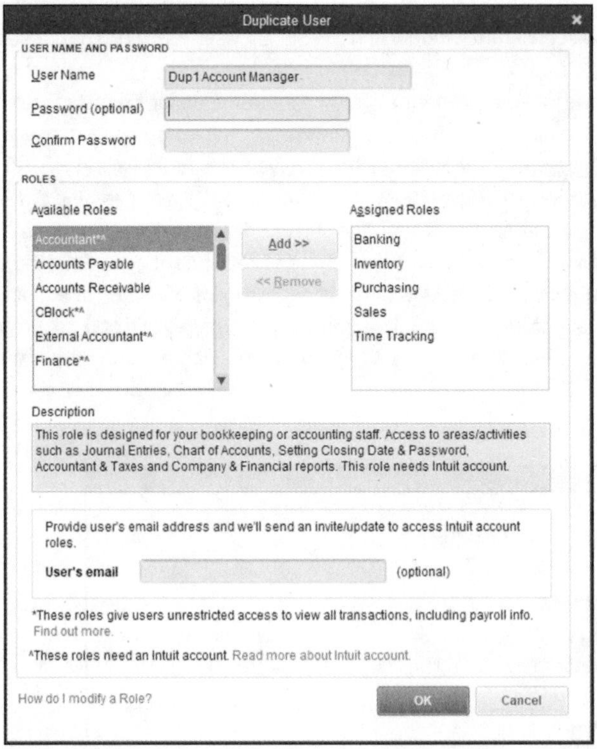

**FIGURE 1-7:**
The Duplicate
User dialog box.

To remove a user, you also use the Users and Roles dialog box. Simply select the user and then click the Delete button. QuickBooks asks you to confirm your deletion. When you click the Yes button (see Figure 1-8) for confirmation, QuickBooks removes the user.

## Changing user rights in QuickBooks Pro and Premier

You can modify the rights that you assign to a user in QuickBooks Pro or Premier. To do this, choose Company ⇨ Set Up Users and Passwords ⇨ Set Up Users to display the User List dialog box (not shown).

**FIGURE 1-8:**
The Delete User
dialog box.

To look at the rights that a particular user has, select the user in the list and then click the View User button. When you do, QuickBooks displays the View User Access dialog box (not shown). This dialog box shows the same information as the final version of the Set Up User Access and Password dialog box, which is the dialog box that you use initially to specify what rights a user should have. Click the Leave button to close the View User Access dialog box.

To change a user's rights after reviewing them, select the user and then click the Edit User button. QuickBooks steps through the same set of dialog boxes that you use to set up the user and describe their rights. You use the Next and Back buttons to do things such as change the username or password, specify whether the user should be limited in their access, and — if necessary — to limit the user's access to a particular activity within QuickBooks.

To remove a user, you also use the User List dialog box. Simply select the user and then click the Delete User button. QuickBooks asks you to confirm your deletion (not shown). When you click the Yes button for confirmation, QuickBooks removes the user.

# Using Audit Trails

If you decide to allow multiple users access to the QuickBooks data file, you'll appreciate the QuickBooks Audit Trail feature, which keeps a record of who makes what changes in the QuickBooks data file. This feature is always on, and you can use it to determine whether information in the file changed and, if so, the user who made the change.

**REMEMBER**

You can't remove transactions from the Audit Trail list or history except by archiving and condensing data. Archiving and condensing data are described in Book 7, Chapter 2.

To produce an Audit Trail report, choose Reports ➪ Accountant and Taxes ➪ Audit Trail. Figure 1-9 shows a QuickBooks Audit Trail report. Note that this report identifies both the type of change made and the person who made the change in the QuickBooks data file.

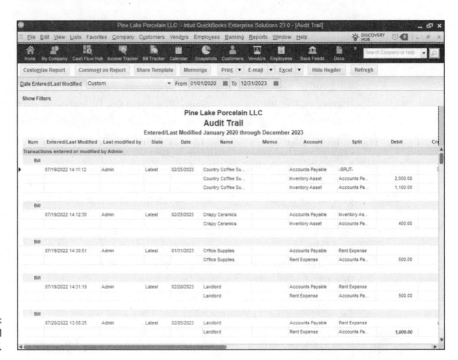

**FIGURE 1-9:**
An Audit Trail
report.

# Enabling Simultaneous Multiuser Access

Sometimes, you need only a single computer and a single copy of QuickBooks, even though you have several employees using QuickBooks. If a small business has only an administrative assistant and the owner accessing a QuickBooks data file, for example, one copy of QuickBooks running on a single personal computer may be all that's required. QuickBooks does allow for simultaneous use of the QuickBooks data file by multiple users, however. Predictably, you first need to set up multiple users, as described earlier in this chapter.

After you've set up multiple users, you can install the QuickBooks program on other personal computers and then — assuming that all these personal computers connect to a Windows network — use those other copies of QuickBooks to access the QuickBooks data file stored on the first or principal computer.

To use QuickBooks in an environment of simultaneous use by multiple users, you also need to tell QuickBooks that simultaneous use is okay. To do this, choose the File ⇨ Switch to Multi-User Mode command. (If you want to turn off Multi-User Mode later, choose File ⇨ Switch to Single User Mode again.)

QuickBooks supports simultaneous use by multiple users through a technology called *record locking,* which locks all the records that you're working with but not the entire QuickBooks data file. If you want to work with Company A, and some other user wants to work with Company B, that's okay. QuickBooks allows it. What you and the other user can't do, however, is work on the same company (A or B) at the same time. This would mean that you're working with the same customer record.

**WARNING**

You can't install the same copy of QuickBooks on multiple machines and legally have a multiple-user QuickBooks system. You must purchase a copy of Quick-Books for each machine on which QuickBooks is installed. Note, however, that Intuit does sell some multiple-user versions of QuickBooks in which you actually buy five licenses in one box of QuickBooks. (The Enterprise version of QuickBooks supports multiple-user networks with up to 40 simultaneous users, and the other versions of QuickBooks support multiple-user networks with up to 5 simultaneous users.)

**TIP**

You may want to have several QuickBooks users if sales representatives in your firm prepare invoices or prepare bids for customers. In this case, you may want to have each salesperson set up on QuickBooks. Note, however, that these sales-people should have the ability only to create an invoice or perhaps create and print an invoice estimate. For reasons discussed more fully in the next section of this chapter, you want to be very careful about giving inexperienced accounting users full access to the accounting system.

# Maintaining Good Accounting Controls

In the preceding paragraphs of this chapter, I talk about how QuickBooks allows multiple users. Many businesses, after they grow to a certain size, need to support multiple users with access to accounting information and the capability, in some cases, to create accounting transactions. Unfortunately, multiple accounting system users create risk for the business owner. By having access to the accounting system, users can either inadvertently introduce errors into the accounting system or (unfortunately) intentionally defraud a business. For these reasons, I want to briefly list some QuickBooks control techniques that a business owner or business manager can use to minimize unintentional errors and minimize the opportunity for theft. Here are my best ideas:

>> **Regularly compare physical inventory counts with inventory accounting records.** Inventory shrinks, unfortunately. People — sometimes employees, but often pseudo-customers, such as shoplifters — steal inventory. Therefore, one thing you need to do, both to minimize your inventory losses and to maintain accurate accounting records, is regularly compare physical counts of your inventory with what your accounting records show. A small convenience store, for example, may want to compare tobacco inventory on a daily basis, beer and wine inventory on a weekly basis, and all other grocery inventory items on a monthly or annual basis. This approach to frequently counting the most valuable and easiest-to-steal items accomplishes two things:

- Inventory shrinkage is quickly identified.

- The business owner can minimize inventory shrinkage by identifying the type of inventory that's most often stolen or even when inventory is most often stolen.

>> **Reconcile bank accounts.** One thing that business owners should do, in my opinion, is reconcile their own bank accounts. Often, employee theft by accounting personnel occurs as employees figure out how to write checks on the company's bank account that the owner doesn't see. One sure way to find a fictitious and fraudulent transaction is to have the owner reconcile the bank statement. If the owner reconciles the bank statement, they can compare the bank's accounting for the account with the company's QuickBooks accounting records. Any obvious discrepancies can be fixed, which means that the QuickBooks accounting records are more accurate. Additionally, any flaky, suspicious transactions tend to become obvious when the business owner looks closely at checks.

**WARNING**

The first employee I ever hired was a check forger. He began forging checks on one of my business checking accounts two or three weeks after he started working for me. I caught him only because I was regularly reconciling the checking account. (He was convicted of a felony a few months later.)

>> **Segregate accounting from physical custody where possible.** In a small business, it's difficult to always separate the accounting for some activity from the physical custody or physical responsibility for that activity. It's tough to segregate the inventory accounting from physical custody or access to that inventory. A store clerk, for example, may easily be able to steal cigarettes and also adjust inventory records through cash-register sales for cigarettes. Nevertheless, wherever you can segregate physical custody from accounting, built-in error checking occurs. The person doing the accounting indirectly checks on the physical custodian's caretaking of the asset. If the physical custodian is stealing cartons of cigarettes, for example, that fact shows up when the accountant compares the accounting records with the physical accounts of inventory. Similarly, someone who doesn't have access to the cash and the bank account can't easily steal cash, even if they have complete access to cash accounting records. You can ask your CPA for help in devising ways to segregate physical custody of assets from accounting and bookkeeping duties. And you really, really should do this. Unfortunately, employee theft is very common.

>> **Train employees in the use of QuickBooks.** You should train employees to use QuickBooks if you have a business of any size for two basic reasons:

- *Someone who knows how to use QuickBooks is less likely to make inadvertent errors.* QuickBooks isn't difficult to use, but it's also not something that you can learn willy-nilly with no help. Some transactions are pretty tricky, particularly for certain businesses. So if you can, it makes good sense to provide some employee help or training, or both. Those resources let people use QuickBooks's features more comfortably and more accurately to build financial information that lets you manage your business better.

- *Messy accounting records camouflage employee theft.* Often, one thing you see when employee theft happens is really messed-up accounting records. For that reason, you can find yourself in a situation in which poorly trained employees create a messy accounting system that enables employee theft. So training means not only that you'll have more accurate accounting records, but also that you'll be less likely to have an environment conducive to theft or embezzlement.

>> **Set a closing date.** If you take a Principles of Accounting course, you'll discover that *closing* means a set of bookkeeping procedures that somebody performs to zero out revenue and expense accounts so that starting in the new year, revenue and expenses can be easily calculated. In QuickBooks, *closing* means something different. But you still want to close the QuickBooks file to maintain the integrity of your data. Here's how: Choose the Edit ➪ Preferences command, select Accounting in the Preferences dialog box, select the Company Preferences tab, and then click the Closing Date Set Date/Password button. When QuickBooks prompts you, specify a closing date and

password. After you provide this information, QuickBooks prohibits or limits users from changing or entering transactions dated before the closing date. (Only people with the password can make changes to or enter transactions with dates earlier than the closing date.)

>> **Manage your QuickBooks accounting system.** I'm sorry to report that many business owners don't view the accounting system as being anything more than a tool to produce invoices, paychecks, and information required for the annual tax return. Unfortunately, that distant relationship with the accounting system means that business owners often don't feel much need to actively manage what happens with the accounting system.

In my opinion — an opinion based on more than 35 years of experience working as a CPA — this attitude is wrong. An accounting system should be a tool that you use to better manage your business. And it can be that. But if it's going to be a tool for better managing your business, you need to manage the system. In other words, I respectfully suggest that you take responsibility for ensuring that employees are trained to do the things that protect your accounting system (such as backing up the data file) and that you ensure that they complete appropriate accounting procedures on a monthly and annual basis (such as sending out all invoices, reconciling bank accounts, cleaning up messy transactions, and so forth).

I don't think that this management responsibility needs to be a heavy one. You can rather easily make sure that people are doing the sorts of things they're supposed to be doing by creating some simple checklists. Table 1-1 shows a sample monthly accounting to-do list. Table 1-2 shows a sample annual accounting to-do list. You can use these tables as starting points for constructing your own list of things that the accounting clerk or office manager must do every month or at the end of every year.

**TABLE 1-1**  **A Sample Monthly Accounting To-Do List**

| Task | Completed? |
| --- | --- |
| Back up data and move it offsite | ❏ |
| Reconcile bank accounts | ❏ |
| Issue all invoices, credit memos, and statements | ❏ |
| Clean up any suspense accounts | ❏ |
| Deliver financial statements | ❏ |
| Report exceptions (overdue invoices, bills, purchase orders, understocked inventory items, and so on) | ❏ |

**TABLE 1-2**

## A Sample Annual Accounting To-Do List

| Task | Completed? |
| --- | --- |
| Adjust trial balance | ❑ |
| Save the QuickBooks backup file to hard drive and cloud storage | ❑ |
| Consider cleaning up data files if they're huge | ❑ |
| Close year when really done | ❑ |

# Chapter **2**

# Protecting Your Data

I n this chapter, I tell you how to protect your QuickBooks data. Principally, protecting your data requires that you back up the data. If you back up your data, you have a second copy available in case the original data file goes bad or becomes corrupted.

Because archiving and data file compression are related to backing up and restoring QuickBooks data files, I also talk about archiving in this chapter. When you archive QuickBooks data files, you create a permanent record of the data files. You also have the option of condensing the current working data file.

## Backing Up the QuickBooks Data File

A critically important task that either you or some co-worker needs to complete is making a backup of the QuickBooks data file. I respectfully suggest that few items stored on your computer's hard drive deserve as much caretaking as the QuickBooks data file does. Quite literally, the QuickBooks data file describes your business's financial affairs. You absolutely don't want to lose the data file. Losing the data file might mean that you don't know how much money you have, you don't know whether you're making or losing money, and you won't be able to prepare your annual tax returns easily or accurately.

# Backing-up basics

Fortunately, backing up the QuickBooks data file is rather straightforward. You need to complete nine steps:

**1.** **Choose the File ⇨ Create Copy command.**

QuickBooks displays the first Save Copy or Backup dialog box (see Figure 2-1), which provides three options: the option to save a backup copy of your QuickBooks file, the option to create a portable company file, and the option to create an accountant's copy.

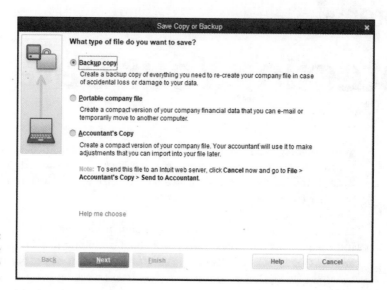

**FIGURE 2-1:**
The first Save
Copy or Backup
dialog box.

**2.** **You want to save a backup copy, so select the Backup Copy option button; then click Next to continue.**

You can create either a full backup file or a portable company file when you copy the QuickBooks file. A portable company file is smaller than a backup file, so it's more convenient to move around. You can more easily email a portable company file, for example. The rub with portable company files is this: QuickBooks must work hard to scrunch the portable company file to a small size. QuickBooks also has to do more work to unscrunch the file later, when you want to work with it.

**TIP**

After you click Next, the second Save Copy or Backup dialog box appears (see Figure 2-2).

You can go directly to the Save Copy or Backup dialog box by choosing the File ⇨ Create Backup command.

**TIP**

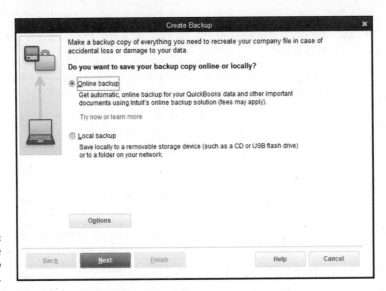

3. **Indicate whether you want to save your QuickBooks backup file on your company's computer or to QuickBooks's offsite data center.**

Choose Local Backup to indicate that you want to store the backup copy of your file on your computer's hard drive or some removable storage device, such as a USB flash drive.

4. **Click the Options button to choose a backup location.**

QuickBooks displays the Backup Options dialog box, as shown in Figure 2-3.

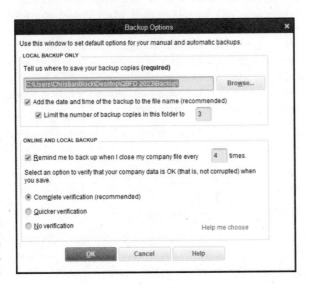

Protecting Your Data

5. **Specify the folder or drive location to which the company file should be backed up.**

   Enter a pathname directly in the text box to tell QuickBooks where to save your backup copies.

   **TIP**

   If you don't know how to enter a pathname, click the Browse button. When QuickBooks displays the Browse for Folder dialog box, use its folder list to select the drive or folder you want to use for QuickBooks backups.

6. **(Optional) Select your backup options.**

   You can also use the Backup Options dialog box to specify when QuickBooks should remind you to back up and how QuickBooks should back up:

   - *Adding time stamps:* To add the date and time of the backup operation to the backup file's name, select the check box titled Add the Date and Time of the Backup to the File Name (Recommended).

   - *Limiting backup copies:* To tell QuickBooks to get rid of old backup copies, select the check box titled Limit the Number of Backup Copies in This Folder to *X* and then specify how many backup copies you want to keep by using the adjoining text box.

   - *Setting backup reminders:* Select the check box titled Remind Me to Back Up When I Close My Company File Every *X* Times to specify that you want to be reminded to back up the QuickBooks file when you close QuickBooks. Your interval options include every time, every other time, every third time, and so forth.

   - *Enabling data verification:* Use the verification buttons to tell QuickBooks that it should check for data integrity when it backs up your data. Select the Complete Verification (Recommended) radio button for QuickBooks's best and most comprehensive verification. If you're someone who doesn't have time for the extra few seconds of double-checking that data verification takes, sure, select the Quicker Verification radio button. Better yet, throw caution completely to the wind — caution is for babies anyway — and select the No Verification radio button.

7. **Click OK when you finish specifying the backup location and options and then click Next.**

   QuickBooks displays a dialog box (see Figure 2-4) that asks when you want to back up.

8. **Specify when you want to back up.**

   Typically, you want to back up when you choose the Save Copy or Backup command. In this case, when QuickBooks displays the Save Copy or Backup dialog box that asks the "when" question, select the Save It Now radio button.

Alternatively, you can tell QuickBooks to schedule regular backups of the QuickBooks data file according to some clever scheme by — when QuickBooks asks the "when" question — selecting the Save It Now and Schedule Future Backups radio button or by selecting the Only Schedule Future Backups radio button. If you tell QuickBooks that you want to schedule backups, QuickBooks displays a couple of dialog boxes that you use to create the new backup schedule by naming the schedule and by setting the days and times when backups should be scheduled.

**9.** **Click Finish to close the Save Copy or Backup dialog box.**

When you've specified how the backup operation should work, click Finish. QuickBooks backs up (or creates a copy of) the current QuickBooks company file and stores that new file copy in the backup location.

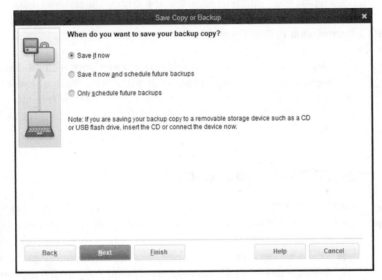

**FIGURE 2-4:**
The Save Copy or Backup dialog box asks when you want to back up.

## What about online backup?

If you're observant, you may have noticed that the Save Copy or Backup dialog box shown in Figure 2-2, earlier in this chapter, includes an Online Backup radio button. If you want to find out more about backing up the QuickBooks company data file online — which means using Intuit's computer network rather than your computer or some removable disc to store the backup — you can select that radio button.

For what it's worth, I strongly recommend that you consider using the online backup method, for two reasons:

>> **Reasonable cost:** Online backup is extremely reasonable (it might even come at no additional charge if you have QuickBooks Desktop Pro Plus, Premier Plus, or Enterprise), with pricing based on the timeline (a monthly subscription will cost more per month than an annual subscription) and on whether you're backing up just QuickBooks or all files on your PC. Backing up all files with an annual subscription seems to be the best value.

>> **Less effort:** Online backup can make the task of backing up less difficult and more regular as long as you have a reliable Internet connection. You don't need to remember to back up and then remember to take the backup disc home.

Two quick final points: Yes, I use the online QuickBooks backup option myself (to back up all my important files). No, Intuit doesn't pay me some sort of secret commission to tout the product.

You can store backup files in a folder that syncs with a cloud-based backup, such as Dropbox, Google Drive, or Microsoft's OneDrive. Each of these services offers a free set-and-forget, cloud-based backup if you use the free storage space offered by any of them. This type of service is definitely an option for users who are on a budget or have limited resources.

## Some backup tactics

Backing up is mostly a matter of common sense. That being said, however, let me give you some ideas about how, when, and maybe why you should back up:

>> **Make it easy.** I mention this in my recommendation concerning the online backup option, but the point deserves mention again. The most important thing you can do regarding QuickBooks data file backup is this: Make backing up easy. This probably means considering the online option, but if you do go local, you want to have a high-density, removable storage device that you can use with the computer you use to run QuickBooks. I use a small USB flash drive. Choose what device works best for you, but you definitely want some similarly easy-to-employ storage device. In this case, *easy* means that backing up is more likely to occur.

>> **Back up regularly.** I recommend that you back up every time you enter transactions in the QuickBooks data file. Obviously, if backing up represents a lot of work, you won't want to do it. But if you have an easy way to back up and a convenient storage device to back up to, you can — and should — back up regularly. Daily isn't too often.

>> **Store a backup copy of the QuickBooks data file offsite.** One final important point worth mentioning: Many of the events that may destroy or corrupt your data file are specific to your computer, such as a hard drive failure, a virus, a user accident, and so forth. Some of the events that may corrupt or destroy your QuickBooks data file, however, are location-specific. Fire, flood, or theft can cause you to lose the QuickBooks data file and its backup. For this reason, you want to store a copy of the backup offsite. At the end of the week, for example, you may want to pop the flash drive in your shirt pocket or purse and take it home. Make sure that if something corrupts or destroys the QuickBooks data file, that same something doesn't also destroy the backup QuickBooks data file. This is all the more reason to store your backups in the cloud.

# Restoring a QuickBooks Data File

If you find that the working copy of the QuickBooks data file becomes corrupted or gets destroyed, you need to restore the QuickBooks data file so that you can begin using QuickBooks again. Restoring the QuickBooks data file is easy if you've recently backed it up (see the preceding section).

**WARNING**

If you haven't recently (or ever) backed up the QuickBooks data file, you'll have to create a new company from scratch, which means starting over. You'll have to rerun QuickBooks Installation and Setup and reenter all the old data. In short, if something corrupts or destroys your file and you haven't backed it up, you go back to square one.

To restore the QuickBooks data file from the backup copy of the file, put the backup disc into the drive, plug in the USB flash drive, or download your backup file from cloud storage. Then follow these steps:

**1.** **Launch QuickBooks and choose the File ⇨ Open or Restore Company command.**

QuickBooks displays the Open or Restore Company dialog box, as shown in Figure 2-5.

**2.** **Indicate what type of file you want to restore.**

You can open a regular QuickBooks data file, restore a backup copy of the regular QuickBooks file or a portable version of the file, or convert an accountant's copy transfer file. If you want to restore a backup copy, predictably, you select the radio button labeled Restore a Backup Copy.

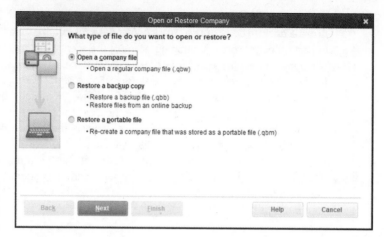

**3.** **Click Next.**

QuickBooks displays another version of the Open or Restore Company dialog box, as shown in Figure 2-6.

**4.** **Tell QuickBooks whether the backup copy is stored at your company or at QuickBooks's offsite data center.**

To do this, select the radio button that labels your backup copy file's location.

**5.** **Click Next.**

QuickBooks displays the Open Backup Copy dialog box, as shown in Figure 2-7.

**6.** **Double-click (or select the file and click Open) the backup file that you'll use for the restoration.**

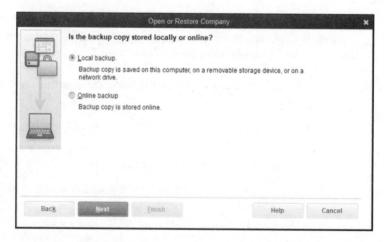

**FIGURE 2-7:**
The Open Backup
Copy dialog box.

Specify the location of and then the specific backup file that you'll use for the restoration. You can use the Look In drop-down list to identify the drive and folder storing the backup file.

**7.** **Click Open.**

QuickBooks displays yet another version of the Open or Restore Company dialog box (not shown), which simply tells you that QuickBooks is about to ask you where you want to store the newly restored file. (The fact that QuickBooks needs to tell you that it's about to ask a question is a little strange, but let's not get bogged down with that.)

**WARNING**

When you restore the company data file by using the backup copy, you destroy the current working version of the file. In other words, QuickBooks takes the backup copy and copies it over the to-be-restored company data file. Therefore, before you restore company data files, make sure that you're using the right backup copy and that you're overwriting the corrupted, to-be-restored company file.

**TIP**

If you're uncomfortable deleting or overwriting the old (possibly corrupted) QuickBooks data file, you can use a new filename for the restored file. You do this as part of Step 9.

**8.** **Click Next.**

QuickBooks displays the Save Company File As dialog box, as shown in Figure 2-8.

Protecting Your Data

**FIGURE 2-8:**
The Save
Company File As
dialog box.

**9.** **Tell QuickBooks where it should restore the backup copy and then click Save.**

Use the Save Company File As dialog box to pick a location for the backed up file. You'll probably pick the same location as the existing file. If you do this and also use the same name for the QuickBooks file, QuickBooks displays a message asking you to confirm that you want to overwrite the existing file. Click Yes. Then QuickBooks displays another message box titled Delete Entire File. Confirm that you want to delete the existing (and presumably corrupt) company data file by typing the word **yes** in the message box. Then click OK. QuickBooks uses the backup copy to overwrite the to-be-restored company file. Again, however, note that you can also choose to use a new filename for the restored file.

You're now free of the rather persistent dialog boxes. Whew.

*Note:* If you restore your QuickBooks data file in a newer version of QuickBooks than the version you used to create the backup copy, QuickBooks displays a dialog box that asks whether you're okay with the fact that the company file will be updated for the new version. In this case, you confirm by checking a box that says (in essence), "Hey, man, I understand that my company file will be updated to the new version."

**10.** **Enter any transactions that took place since your last backup.**

If you entered transactions after you last backed up the QuickBooks company file, now you reenter those transactions in QuickBooks. If you last backed up QuickBooks on Friday of last week, for example, you need to reenter any transactions that you've created since last Friday.

# Condensing the QuickBooks Company Files

The QuickBooks file condense process does two things:

>> The QuickBooks Condense command creates a permanent copy of the QuickBooks data file. (This copy is called an archival copy of the file.) An *archival copy* of the company file amounts to a snapshot of the company file as it existed at a particular point in time. If somebody later has a question — perhaps your accountant, or a federal or state auditor — you can use the archival copy of the data file to show what the company file looked like at a particular point in time.

>> The file condense process makes the data file smaller by summarizing many old closed, detailed transactions that use monster journal entries.

Because this condensing and archiving can be a little bit confusing, let me quickly summarize exactly what happens when you condense the QuickBooks company file. Here's what QuickBooks typically does during the process:

>> **Saves an archive copy of your company files:** When you condense the QuickBooks company file, QuickBooks saves an archival copy of that file.

>> **Removes closed transactions:** As part of the condensation process, QuickBooks gives you the opportunity to remove old, closed transactions from the current, working version of the QuickBooks company file. Remember that archiving creates an archival copy of the QuickBooks company file. You still have the working version of the QuickBooks company file, however, and it's this current, working version of the QuickBooks company file that gets cleaned up, or condensed, by the removal of old, closed transactions.

*Closed* transactions are transactions that QuickBooks no longer needs to track in detail. An old customer invoice — after it's been paid — is a closed transaction. An old check written to some vendor — after it's cleared the bank — is a closed transaction.

>> **Summarizes closed transactions:** Because the old, closed transactions are removed from the QuickBooks data file, condensing typically creates summary monthly journal entries for the old, closed transactions and places these summary transactions in the current, working version of the QuickBooks data file. These summary monthly journal entries allow you to continue to prepare monthly financial statements. Even though archiving removes all the old, closed transactions from, say, January 2021, you can still produce financial statements for January 2021 in 2024. To produce monthly financial

statements for January 2021, QuickBooks uses the summary monthly journal entries.

» **Clears the audit trail:** As I mention in Book 7, Chapter 1, QuickBooks maintains an audit trail showing who entered what transactions. One almost-hidden effect of the cleanup of the QuickBooks data files concerns the audit trail. If you clean up a company file and indicate that the company file should be condensed, QuickBooks clears the audit trail before the "removed closed transactions on or before" date. In other words, for the period of time in which QuickBooks removes old, closed transactions, it also removes the audit trail of those transactions.

**TIP**

The *condense file* process typically means creating a copy of the QuickBooks data file that you put away someplace and then creating a scaled-down version of the working company file. The command that you use to condense the QuickBooks company file, however, also allows you to create almost-empty company files. Most people never need to use this option. I can think of only one category of QuickBooks users who may want to create almost-empty company files: CPAs and consultants (who want to reuse a company file for another business unit or client) may want to use this command to create company data files that have many of the lists set up already. I don't go into any further detail on creating an almost-empty company file by using the archiving command, but you should know that it's there.

## Cleanup basics

When you understand what archiving is all about, the process is quite straightforward. To condense the QuickBooks company file, follow these steps:

1. **Choose File ⇨ Utilities ⇨ Condense Data.**

   QuickBooks displays the Condense Your Company File dialog box, shown in Figure 2-9.

2. **Select the radio button titled Remove the Transactions You Select from Your Company File and then click Next.**

   The Condense Data dialog box opens.

3. **Select the Transactions Before a Specific Date radio button.**

   This option, shown in Figure 2-10, tells QuickBooks that you want to do two things: create an archival copy of the QuickBooks data file, and skinny down the working company file so that it isn't so big. QuickBooks reduces the size of the working version of the company data file by removing old, closed transactions if you chose in Step 2 to remove transactions.

**FIGURE 2-9:**
The Condense
Your Company
File dialog box.

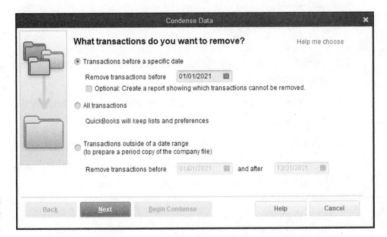

**FIGURE 2-10:**
The Condense
Data dialog box.

4. **Specify the Remove Transactions Before date.**

   To specify the date before which closed transactions should be removed, enter the date in the date box. If you want to condense the file by removing transactions on or before December 31, 2020, for example, enter **1/1/2021** in the date box. You don't need to feel compulsive about removing a bunch of closed transactions, however. You remove closed transactions only if your QuickBooks company file is getting too big. You can easily work with a QuickBooks company file that's 25MB, 50MB, or even 100MB (megabytes).

TIP

   Although typically, you condense a QuickBooks file by removing old, closed transactions, the Condense command also creates files without transactions and files with only a specified data range of transactions. To create a file that holds lists and preferences but no transactions, select the All Transactions radio button. By the way, you might use the All Transactions option to build a nearly empty file that you could reuse (such as for training). To create a QuickBooks file that holds a specified range of transactions, select the Transactions Outside of a Date Range radio button and then enter the dates that bookend the range in the Before and After boxes.

5. **Click Next when you finish specifying which transactions QuickBooks should remove.**

   QuickBooks displays the Condense Data dialog box shown in Figure 2-11.

6. **Specify how transactions should be summarized.**

   If you want to summarize historical transactions, QuickBooks uses a Condense Data dialog box to ask how it should summarize historical data: with a single summary journal entry, with monthly summary journal entries, or no summary at all. Select the radio button that corresponds to the summarization approach you want. (Usually, you select the second option — having QuickBooks create monthly summary journal entries — so that you can still generate meaningful comparative monthly reports.)

7. **Click Next when you finish specifying how QuickBooks should summarize transactions.**

   QuickBooks displays the third Condense Data dialog box, as shown in Figure 2-12.

8. **Specify how inventory transactions should be condensed and click Next.**

   If your QuickBooks file includes inventory transactions, QuickBooks recommends that you remove old inventory transactions. When QuickBooks displays the fourth Condense Data dialog box, you can tell QuickBooks to do just this by selecting the Summarize Inventory Transactions (Recommended) radio button. (If you don't want to remove old transactions, select the Keep Inventory Transaction Details radio button.)

   When you click Next, you continue to the fourth Condense Data dialog box (not shown), which asks which transactions should be considered to be closed.

9. **Specify which transactions should be removed and click Next.**

   QuickBooks asks for a bit more information about exactly what constitutes a closed or old transaction that should be removed. You select check boxes to indicate whether transactions before the removal date should be removed even if they're uncleared, marked To Be Printed, flagged as To Be Sent, and so on.

   When you click Next, you move on to the fifth Condense Data dialog box (see Figure 2-13).

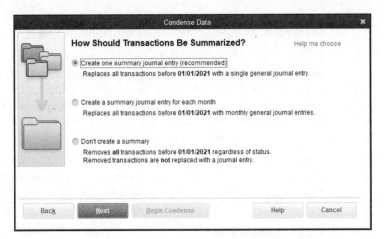

**FIGURE 2-11:**
The second
Condense Data
dialog box.

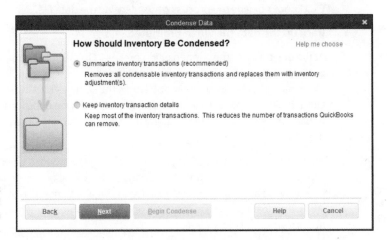

**FIGURE 2-12:**
The third
Condense Data
dialog box.

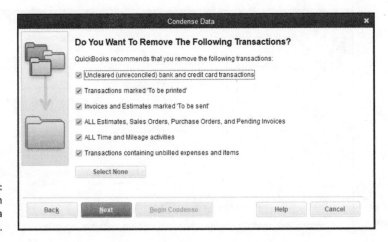

**FIGURE 2-13:**
The fifth
Condense Data
dialog box.

**10.** **Specify any list cleanup that should occur and click Next.**

Use the fifth Condense Data dialog box to tell QuickBooks that in addition to removing old, closed transactions, it should clean up some of the lists. You can select check boxes that tell QuickBooks to remove unused accounts, unused customers, unused vendors, and so forth. By cleaning up your list through the removal of unused list items, you not only reduce the size of the company file, but also make it easier for people to work with the list.

When you click Next, QuickBooks displays the sixth Condense Data dialog box, as shown in Figure 2-14. The dialog box tells you that the archival process begins with QuickBooks making a copy of the data file and that the condensation operation may take several minutes or even several hours to complete.

**11.** **Click Begin Condense.**

QuickBooks begins the process of condensing the data file.

**12.** **Back up the data file when prompted.**

At the beginning of the condensation process, QuickBooks prompts you to back up the QuickBooks company file. Backing up the QuickBooks company file as part of a condense operation works the same as backing up the QuickBooks company file at any other time. If you have questions about how to back up the QuickBooks company file, refer to "Backing-up basics" earlier in this chapter.

After you back up the QuickBooks company file, QuickBooks saves an archival copy of the company file and then cleans up the working version of the company file according to your instructions. Again, as noted in the earlier steps, the cleanup process may take only a few minutes, or it may take several hours if your file is very large.

**FIGURE 2-14:**
The sixth, and final, Condense Data dialog box.

# Some cleanup and archiving strategies

Deciding when and how you want to clean up or archive your QuickBooks company file is mostly a matter of common sense. Your first consideration should be whether you need to condense the company file at all. If QuickBooks still runs at a reasonable speed, if you don't find yourself going crazy because of many unused items in lists, or if the data file hasn't grown monstrously large (approaching 1GB or so), you may not need to condense. In many cases, you achieve no benefit by cleaning up. And by not cleaning up, you still have complete, detailed financial records at your fingertips.

**TIP**

My technical editor wants me to point something out here: He notes that running a cleanup operation doesn't necessarily reduce the size of the QuickBooks data file as much as possible. He says, therefore, that if you really *must* have a smaller data file, you should first run a cleanup operation and then save and restore a portable QuickBooks data file.

Here's another common-sense notion about cleaning up and archiving the QuickBooks company files: You should create an archival copy of the QuickBooks data file. In fact, I recommend that you create an archival copy of the QuickBooks data file at the end of the year, after you or your CPA make any final adjustments for the year. It's a great idea to create an archival copy of the QuickBooks data file that's used to prepare your tax return and any financial statements, because you can always later explain some number in a tax return or financial statement by looking at the archival copy of the data file.

**WARNING**

Throughout this book — and most recently in Book 7, Chapter 1, which discusses administering QuickBooks — I mention that one of the problems with using QuickBooks is that people can intentionally or inadvertently change old transactions. This means, unfortunately, that someone can change transactions in a QuickBooks data file in a previous year. When that change occurs, someone who looks at the QuickBooks data file later may not be able to explain a number in a tax return or a financial statement. If someone goes back to change a transaction in a previous year, and that transaction is used to calculate total revenue for the year, you can no longer use the QuickBooks data to explain numbers on your tax return and your financial statements for total revenue. That makes sense, right?

Fortunately, by having an archival copy of the QuickBooks data file — the QuickBooks data file that supplied numbers to your tax return and the financial statements — you can always see which QuickBooks transactions support a particular tax return number or financial statement number. If you're still confused about this point — and it *is* a little bit tricky — ask your tax adviser or your CPA about the problem. They can explain to you the danger of having a change in QuickBooks data that has been used to prepare a return or a financial statement after that return has been prepared, or after those financial statements have been published and distributed.

Protecting Your Data

# Chapter **3**

# Troubleshooting

A fter writing about QuickBooks for more than 30 years, I've had a revelation of sorts: People want not only specific, step-by-step information about how to use the program, but also troubleshooting advice. They want techniques and tactics that they can use to solve the inevitable problems that they encounter while using QuickBooks in real-life settings. What follows is my list of the best troubleshooting techniques.

## Using the QuickBooks Help File and This Book

I know what you may be thinking: You have some problem that you can't solve by using Help, and it's either a bug or some glaring error in the QuickBooks documentation. You've looked through this book, of course, but it says nothing — absolutely nothing — about your question. In fact, upon further reflection, you may be thinking that you've encountered some problem that you can't possibly solve by consulting the QuickBooks Help file or this book.

Maybe you're right.

But in my experience (gleaned from talking with people who have problems), about half the time, the problem is lack of knowledge about QuickBooks. These users may simply be experiencing a mechanical problem. They can't make the program work because they haven't used QuickBooks enough to figure out the problem. Therefore, the right way to solve this sort of problem is to find out more about QuickBooks and try again. If you're having problems printing a report, for example, just finding out more about both printing and reports may enable you to solve the problem.

In most cases, you should be able to find the information in this book by using the index or the table of contents.

Also, you usually can find the information (perhaps in a slightly less-friendly form) in the QuickBooks Help file. To find information in the QuickBooks Help file, choose Help⇨QuickBooks Desktop Help/Contact Us to display the QuickBooks Help window, as shown in Figure 3-1.

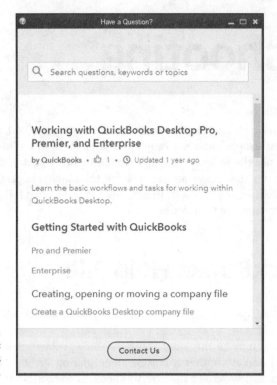

**FIGURE 3-1:**
The QuickBooks
Help window.

Enter the word or phrase that you want to look up in the search box at the top of the window and then click the button that looks like a magnifying glass. QuickBooks displays a list of clickable links that may help you with whatever problem you're having. Figure 3-2 shows results for a search for help related to the issue of working in a multiple-currencies situation.

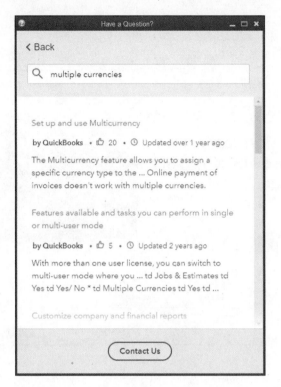

**FIGURE 3-2:**
Help topics for
the search term.

# Browsing Intuit's Product-Support Website

Another really good resource for troubleshooting is Intuit's product-support website for QuickBooks. This website (see Figure 3-3), which you can visit by entering `https://quickbooks.intuit.com/learn-support` in your web browser or by choosing the Help ⇨ Ask Intuit command within QuickBooks, is a rich database of troubleshooting information.

For help with downloads, billing updates, and password resets, choose Account Management from the Topics drop-down list (or select any other topic you need help with). Scroll down and you can choose QuickBooks Online or QuickBooks Desktop, depending on what version you are using.

If you cannot find your answer from the list of topics, use the search bar at the top of the page. Type your question or keywords in the search box and press Enter or Return. The product-support website displays a list of troubleshooting articles that may help solve your problem (see Figure 3-4).

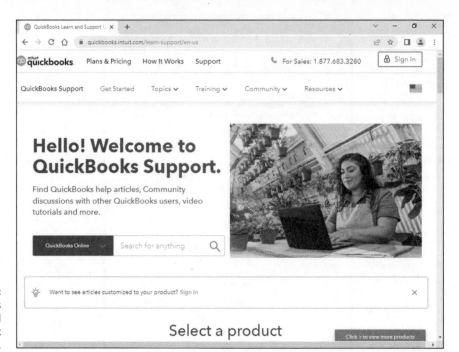

**FIGURE 3-3:**
The QuickBooks
Online and
Desktop Support
website.

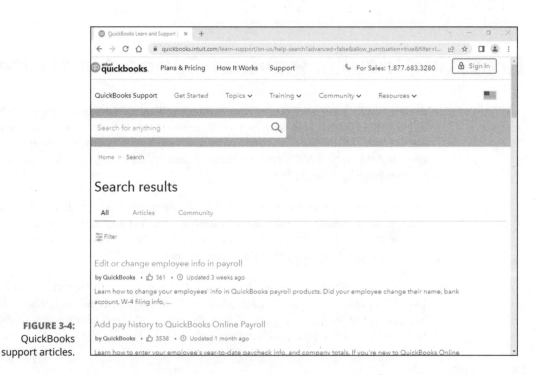

**FIGURE 3-4:**
QuickBooks
support articles.

# Checking Another Vendor's Product-Support Website

Keep in mind that your problem may not be a problem with QuickBooks at all, but a problem with your computer and its hardware or with Microsoft Windows. The Microsoft product-support website, which is phenomenally rich in information, is available at https://support.microsoft.com.

**TIP**

Turning your computer completely off, waiting for a full minute, and then turning it back on is an excellent first step, especially when you think you may be experiencing an issue that is being caused by something other than QuickBooks. This simple technique may just clear things up for you.

If your problem stems from the hardware or the operating system, you can consult the hardware or software maker's product-support website for troubleshooting information. Usually, you can find the hardware maker's product-support website easily by using a good Internet search engine. To locate Dell Computer's product-support website, for example, type something like **HP Computer product support** in a search engine such as https://google.com. When the search engine searches on that phrase, it almost inevitably finds the URL (the address) of the vendor's product-support web page.

**TIP**

You can find troubleshooting information about Intuit products at the Microsoft product-support website. If the solutions that the site offers aren't very reassuring, at least you can find out whether other users have experienced the same problem. Microsoft may simply suggest that you contact the vendor (Intuit, in this case) or that you upgrade to a newer version of the QuickBooks software. Often, however, it's useful simply to know that the problem you've encountered is a real problem that Microsoft has logged into its product-support Knowledge Base and described in some technical detail.

# Tapping into Intuit's Online and Expert Communities

In addition to the option of using the Intuit product-support website, you can get direct product support in at least two other ways:

>> **Online community:** Visit https://quickbooks.intuit.com/learn-support and select one of the options from the Community menu to connect

with a huge group of usually friendly QuickBooks users. If you sign into the website with your Intuit sign-on credentials — the same ones you use to register — you can not only view other questions and answers, but also ask your own questions. (After you've used QuickBooks for a while, maybe you can even answer some other users' questions!)

>> **Professional adviser:** You can contact a QuickBooks professional adviser via the QuickBooks website. In a nutshell, QuickBooks professional advisers are people (often, accountants and consultants) who signed up with Intuit to get copies of the QuickBooks software at a discount price, a listing on the QuickBooks product-support website, and access to special training. (Some of these people also pass a certification test to become recognized as QuickBooks Pro Advisors.) You pay these professional advisers their usual consulting fees, but let me suggest that this support option can be very useful when your problem isn't so much a technical problem with QuickBooks as it is a problem with how to use QuickBooks to solve some accounting issue. Some advisers only support QuickBooks Online, so make sure you find one that supports QuickBooks Desktop. To contact a QuickBooks professional adviser, visit https://quickbooks.intuit.com/find-an-accountant.

# When All Else Fails . . .

If you try at least a few of the preceding troubleshooting tactics and can't get an answer, I have one other suggestion: Bite the bullet, call your CPA, and get them to help you through the rough patches.

I know. You're going to pay $300 an hour or whatever. But here's the deal: Your accounting system is an essential business tool. It must work smoothly and correctly to produce the information you need to operate your business successfully. Paying for an hour or two of expert, onsite, personalized accounting expertise can be a great investment.

And what if your accountant doesn't or can't provide this sort of assistance? Well, shoot, I think you should find somebody who does and can.

# 8

# Appendixes

# Contents at a Glance

# Appendix A

# A Crash Course in Excel

I n this appendix, I review the basic Microsoft Excel skills that you may need to get the most benefit from some chapters in this book. If you plan to download and work with the sample workbooks from my website, https://stephenlnelson. com, you need some of the skills that this primer covers.

If you've used Excel much, even for just a few weeks, you probably possess all these skills. Nevertheless, if you're even a teensy bit concerned about whether you have the right skills, take the time to read this appendix.

*Note:* I used Microsoft Excel for Microsoft 365 MSO and Windows 10 when writing this appendix. If you're using an earlier or later version of Excel, you may notice some slight differences between the images that appear here and what you see on your monitor. If you need detailed guidance, pick up the latest edition of *Excel For Dummies*, by Greg Harvey (John Wiley & Sons, Inc.).

If you do not own a licensed copy of Microsoft Excel, you can use Google Sheets or Excel for the Web. Each program is free with a Google or Microsoft website registration, and each offers the basic functionality of Microsoft Excel with some minor differences.

## Starting Excel

You can start Excel in two ways, neither of which requires a PhD in physics. You can click the Start button and then click the Excel tile that appears on the Start menu's list of programs, or you can open an Excel workbook.

If you're going to use the Excel tile, you simply find the Excel tile (you may need to scroll around the Start menu's list of tiles) and then click it.

To start Excel by opening an Excel workbook, you choose the workbook from a menu or in a folder window. You commonly see documents, including Excel workbooks, listed on menus — both Windows menus and Program menus. If Windows displays the list of documents in a folder window, for example (see Figure A-1), you can open the workbook by double-clicking it. When you open an Excel workbook, Windows starts Excel and tells it to open the workbook.

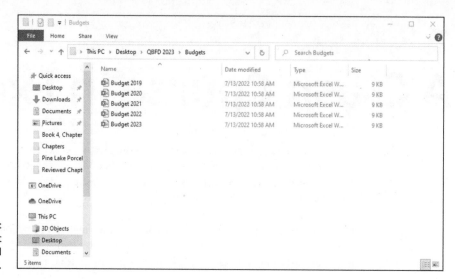

**FIGURE A-1:**
A folder that shows Excel workbooks.

# Stopping Excel

To stop Excel, click the Excel window's Close box. When you stop Excel, it closes any open workbooks before it stops.

**TIP**

The Close box is the button marked with an X that appears in the top-right corner of the Excel window.

# Explaining Excel's Workbooks

After you start Excel, it displays an empty workbook with one worksheet in its document window. Figure A-2 shows an empty worksheet.

An Excel workbook is a spreadsheet. A *spreadsheet* is comprised of numbered rows and lettered columns. You see the row numbers along the left edge of the spreadsheet, and you see the lettered columns along the top edge of the spreadsheet. The first row is numbered 1, the second is numbered 2, and so on. The first column is labeled with the letter *A*, the second column is labeled with the letter *B*, and so on.

The intersections of rows and columns are called *cells*. A cell location is described by using the column letter and row number. The cell in the top-left corner of the workbook, for example, is labeled A1.

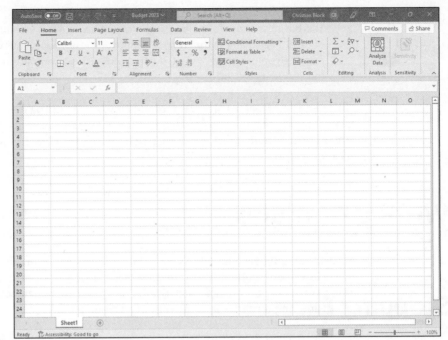

**FIGURE A-2:**
The Excel window with an empty worksheet.

# Putting Text, Numbers, and Formulas in Cells

You build a workbook, or spreadsheet, by entering text labels, numbers, and formulas in the cells that comprise a workbook. The following list details these items:

>> **Text labels** include letters and numbers that you don't want to use in calculations. Your name, some budget-expense description, and a telephone number are examples of text labels. None of these pieces of information is used in calculations.

>> **Numbers,** or values, are bits of data that you may want to use later in a calculation. The actual amount that you budgeted for some expense, for example, will always be a number or value.

>> **Formulas** are also entered into worksheet cells. If you enter **=2+2** into a cell, Excel doesn't display the formula; rather, it calculates the formula result and displays that result. The formula is what is actually stored in the cell, but the formula result is displayed.

**TIP**

This business about formulas going into workbook cells is essentially the heart of Excel. Even if an Excel workbook did nothing else, it would still be an extremely valuable tool. In fact, the first spreadsheet programs did little more than calculate cell formulas.

To enter a text label, a value, or a formula into a cell, all you do is click the cell by using the mouse and then type the text label, value, or formula. When you press Enter or click another cell, Excel enters your label, value, or formula into the cell. That's all it takes.

# Writing Formulas

In the preceding section, I tell you about formulas and even show you a simple formula example. But to use formulas practically, you need to possess several other pieces of knowledge. Specifically, you need to remember several things about entering formulas into the cells of a workbook:

>> **Formulas should begin with the equal sign (=).** The equal sign tells Excel that what follows is a formula that it should calculate.

>> **You can use any of the standard arithmetic operators in your formulas.** To add numbers, use the addition sign (+). To subtract numbers, use the subtraction operator (–). To multiply numbers, use the multiplication operator (*). To divide numbers, use the division operator (/). You can also perform exponential operations by using the exponential operator (^).

>> **You aren't limited to using values in your formulas.** You can also use cell addresses. When you use a cell address in a formula, Excel uses the value or formula result from that cell in the calculation. If cell A1 holds the value 2, and cell B1 holds the value 2, the formula =A1+B1 returns the value 4. In other words, this formula is equivalent to =2+2.

>> **Remember standard rules of operator precedence when you build complicated formulas.** As you may remember from junior-high math, exponential operations are performed first. Multiplication and division operations are performed second. Addition and subtraction operations are performed third. To override these standard rules of operator precedence, you place the operations that you want performed first inside parentheses. Table A-1 shows some example formulas and the formula results to illustrate these rules of precedence. If you get the rules wrong, you'll have to stay after class.

**TABLE A-1**    **Some Example Excel Formulas**

| What's in Cell | What Excel Calculates and Displays |
|---|---|
| =4+5*6 | 34 |
| =(4+5)*6 | 54 |
| =1+2^3 | 9 |
| =(1+2)^3 | 27 |
| =A1+B1 | Equals 4 if cells A1 and B1 both hold the value 2 |

# Scrolling through Big Workbooks

The cells that you see inside the Excel program window represent only a small portion of the Excel workbook. An Excel workbook actually provides more: 1,048,576 rows and 16,384 columns.

Because the alphabet provides only 26 letters, a new naming scheme is needed, starting in column 27. Excel labels the 27th and subsequent columns by using two letters. The 27th column is labeled AA, the 28th column is labeled AB, and the 29th is labeled AC. This scheme goes all the way through the 702nd column, which is labeled ZZ.

Taking things up a notch, Excel labels the 703rd and subsequent columns by using three letters. The 703rd column is labeled AAA, the 704th column is labeled AAB, the 705th column is labeled AAC, and so on. The last, or rightmost, column in an Excel workbook is labeled XFD.

You can scroll the viewable portion of the Excel worksheet in several ways:

» **Use the horizontal and vertical scroll bars that appear along the bottom edge and at the right edge of the worksheet window.** You can click the scroll bar, drag the scroll marker, and click the scroll-bar arrow buttons that appear at either end of the scroll bar. If you're not familiar with how scroll bars work, take the time to experiment and see what they do.

» **Scroll the viewable portion of the Excel worksheet by moving the cell selector.** The *cell selector* is the dark rectangular border that Excel uses to mark the active cell. The *active cell* is the cell in which whatever you type gets placed. You can move the cell selector by pressing the arrow keys; Excel moves the cell selector in the direction of the arrow. If you aren't sure what the cell selector is, press the arrow keys a bunch of times. See that rectangle that jumps around? That's the cell selector.

>> **Move the viewable portion of the worksheet up and down by pressing the Page Up and Page Down keys.** Just try this, okay, if you need more help to see what I mean. Press the Page Down key a few times. Press the Page Up key a few times. Now you've got it.

**TIP**

You have several other ways to scroll within a worksheet. If you're really interested, you may want to look up the other scrolling methods in Excel's online Help or get a good book like a recent edition of *Excel For Dummies*, by Greg Harvey (Wiley).

# Copying and Cutting Cell Contents

You can easily copy and paste contents of worksheet cells, and you want to do both of these things because worksheet construction becomes much easier when you use these skills.

## Copying cell contents

To copy cell contents, follow these steps:

**1. Select the cells that you want to copy.**

To select a single cell, click that cell. To select a range of cells — a *range* is a group of contiguous cells — click the cell in the top-left corner and then drag the mouse to the cell in the bottom-right corner of the range.

**2. Copy the selection by clicking the Copy icon.**

First, if necessary, click the Home tab on the Ribbon to display the Home icons. (You may need to do this because the Copy icon, which you use for copying, appears on the Home tab.) Excel places a copy of the contents of the selection on the Office Clipboard, which is a temporary storage area.

*Note:* The Copy icon looks like two miniature duplicated documents.

**3. Select the location where you want to place the copied data.**

To tell Excel where you want to put the selection, click the cell in the top-left corner of the range into which you want to copy the data.

**4. Paste the copied range selection by clicking the Paste icon.**

Excel copies the previously copied range selection from the Office Clipboard to the workbook location that you identified in Step 3.

*Note:* The Paste icon looks like a clipboard with a piece of paper attached.

# Moving cell contents

You can move, or cut, the contents of cells and ranges by following these steps:

**1.** **Select the cells that you want to move.**

To select a single cell, click that cell. To select a range of cells, click the cell in the top-left corner and then drag the mouse to the cell in the bottom-right corner.

**2.** **Choose the Cut command.**

You tell Excel that you want to cut your selection by clicking the Cut icon that appears on the Home tab on the Ribbon. When you choose the Cut command, Excel moves the contents of the selection to the Office Clipboard. Again, if you can't see the Cut icon, click the Home tab on the Ribbon to display the Home icons.

*Note:* The Cut icon looks like a pair of scissors.

**3.** **Select the location where you want to place the data you're moving.**

To tell Excel where to move the selection, click the cell in the top-left corner of the range into which you want to move the data.

**4.** **Paste the data by choosing the Paste command.**

Alternatively, you can click the Paste toolbar button. When you do, Excel copies the previously copied range selection from the Office Clipboard to the workbook location that you identified in Step 3.

# Moving and copying formulas

You can move and copy formulas the same way that you move and copy other stuff stored in cells. You need to know something really important about copying formulas, however: Excel adjusts the cell addresses used in a formula when you copy the cell or cells that store the formula.

This sounds very strange, but let me show you a quick example of how the adjustment occurs; you'll see immediately why it's useful. Take a look at the simple budgeting workbook shown in Figure A-3. As you can see, this simple spreadsheet calculates totals for a budget. The totals appear in row 6. Because Excel adjusts cell addresses when it copies them, if you copy the formula in cell B6 to cells C6 and D6, Excel ends up placing the correct formula in cells C6 and D6.

In cell B6, the formula is =B2+B3+B4+B5. This formula sums the values for the first month. Obviously, however, you don't want to use this formula in cell C6. Excel guesses that this is the case when it copies the formula from B6. What Excel places in cell C6, therefore, is the formula =C2+C3+C4+C5. What Excel places in cell D6 is the formula =D2+C3+D4+D5.

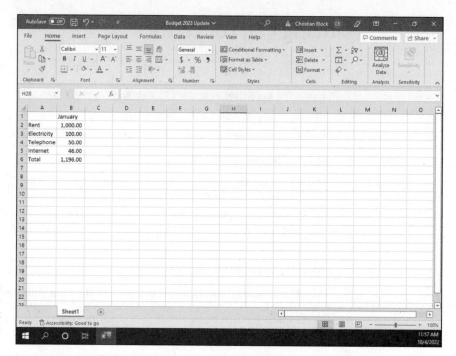

**FIGURE A-3:**
A simple
worksheet
that budgets
expenses.

**REMEMBER**

Excel doesn't adjust the cell addresses in formulas in a range selection when you *move* cell contents. The adjustment of cell addresses and formulas occurs only when you *copy* formulas.

**TIP**

You can *flag*, or mark, those cell addresses that you don't want adjusted when they're copied. To do this, you precede the column letter and row number with a dollar sign ($) to tell Excel that the address shouldn't be adjusted. If the cell address $A$1 is used in a formula, for example, Excel won't adjust the column letter or row number if it copies the formula. Excel calls these fixed cell addresses *absolute references.* You can also tell Excel to adjust only one portion of the cell address by using the dollar sign in front of only the column letter or the row number. If the cell address A$1 is used in a formula, Excel adjusts the column letter but not the row number.

# Formatting Cell Contents

Excel allows you to format the contents of the cells in a worksheet. You can choose the font; the point size; and special effects such as boldfacing, underlining, or italicizing for a workbook or a range.

For values and formula results, you can also add standard punctuation, including dollar signs, percentage symbols, decimal points, and commas for separating thousands.

In general, you format a cell or range by selecting the range and then using the Home tab's formatting boxes and buttons or by opening the Format Cells dialog box, which you do by pressing Ctrl+1 (the number 1).

TIP

When you point to an icon, button, or box, Excel displays the item's name in a box next to the item. A bit of poking around, then, lets you figure out quickly which boxes and buttons are which.

The Home tab on the Ribbon, for example, provides a Font box that you can use to select the font for the selected range. The Home tab also provides a Font Size box for specifying the point size of text and numbers in the selected range.

The Format Cells dialog box provides tabs of boxes and buttons for formatting the contents of cells. If you want to change the font used in a range selection, click the Format Cells: Font icon and then use the Font tab's boxes and buttons to make your changes. The Format Cells: Font icon is the little arrow in the bottom-right corner of the Font section on the Ribbon's Home tab. Figure A-4 shows the Font tab of the Format Cells dialog box.

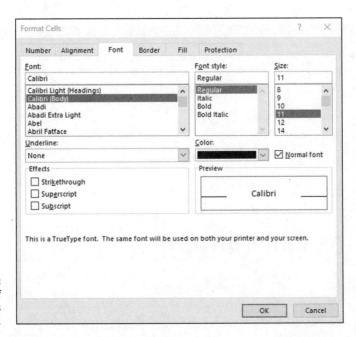

**FIGURE A-4:**
The Font tab of the Format Cells dialog box.

# Recognizing That Functions Are Simply Formulas

Here's another important tidbit to know about Excel: Although you can construct very complicated formulas by using the standard arithmetic operators, Excel provides prefabricated formulas called *functions* that make it easy to calculate standard measurements. Excel provides a function to easily calculate an arithmetic *mean*, or average, for example. It also provides a function to calculate the payment on a car loan.

A simple example demonstrates how this works. If you look back at the worksheet shown in Figure A-3, you can see (or guess) that the formula in cell B6 sums the values in B2, B3, B4, and B5. With what you already know about Excel formulas, you can construct a total formula that adds these values. You can enter the formula **=B2+B3+B4+B5**.

TIP

If you look closely at the area that's just below the Excel Ribbon (Microsoft's name for Excel's menu), you can see what's known as the formula bar. The *formula bar* shows you the contents of the selected cell. In Figure A-5, the selected cell is B6, so the formula bar shows you the contents of cell B6, which happens to be the formula that adds the values in cells B2, B3, B4, and B5.

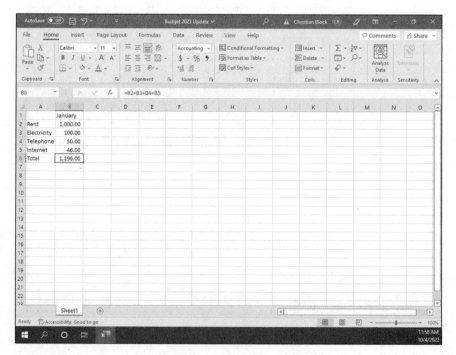

**FIGURE A-5:**
A worksheet that sums numbers.

You can also use a function to make this calculation. To add a series of values, you use the SUM function. Then you include as function arguments, or function inputs, the individual values, individual cell addresses, or range selections. To see how this works in the case of the worksheet shown in Figure A-5, you can enter the formula **=SUM(B2:B5)** into cell B6. You also can select cell B6 and then click the AutoSum (Σ) symbol on the Home tab.

Function formulas use a standard set of conventions:

» The first part of this formula is the equal sign (=). Because functions are formulas, you begin a function with an equal sign.

» The next part of the function formula gives the function name. In the case of the SUM function, the function name is SUM.

» The third part of the formula function includes the function inputs, or arguments, inside parentheses. In the worksheet shown in Figure A-5, the inputs are included as a range reference (B2:B5).

Sometimes, functions are so simple that you won't need any help remembering how the arguments should appear or what arguments the function needs. The SUM function, for example, is one that spreadsheet users construct so frequently that they usually memorize its syntax after only a few uses.

Other functions, however, such as the functions to calculate a loan payment, require several arguments in a particular order. For more complicated functions, you typically want to use the Insert Function command. To use the Insert Function command, click the Formulas tab and then click the Insert Function icon. (The icon shows a little *fx* label and is located just to the left of the formula bar.) Excel displays the Insert Function dialog box, as shown in Figure A-6.

If you don't know what function you want, you can type a brief description of whatever you want to calculate in the Search for a Function text box, shown at the top of the dialog box, and click Go. Alternatively, you can choose a category of functions from the Or Select a Category drop-down list. This list provides several categories of functions, including financial, date and time, mathematical and trigonometric, statistical, and text.

Based on what you type in the first text box or choose from the drop-down list, Excel displays a list of possible functions in the bottom portion of the Insert Function dialog box. You search this list for the function that you want. If you select a function in the list, Excel displays a brief description of the function and shows the arguments needed for the function to calculate.

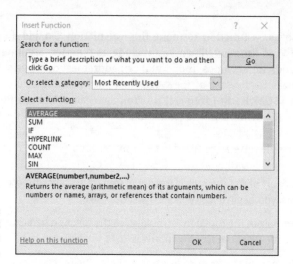

FIGURE A-6:
The Insert
Function
dialog box.

After you find and select the function that you want to use, click OK. Excel displays the Function Arguments dialog box, as shown in Figure A-7. The Function Arguments dialog box provides text boxes that you use to supply the arguments, or inputs, to the function. Function arguments can be values or cell addresses.

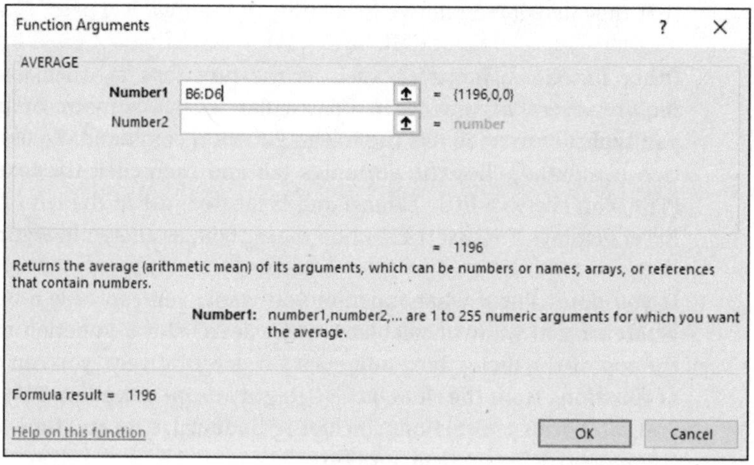

| Function Arguments | ? | X |
| --- | --- | --- |

AVERAGE

| **Number1** | B6:D6 | ↑ | = {1196,0,0} |
| Number2 | | ↑ | = number |

= 1196

Returns the average (arithmetic mean) of its arguments, which can be numbers or names, arrays, or references that contain numbers.

  **Number1:**  number1,number2,... are 1 to 255 numeric arguments for which you want the average.

Formula result = 1196

Help on this function          OK    Cancel

FIGURE A-7:
The Function
Arguments
dialog box.

After you supply the needed function arguments, click OK. Excel enters a formula function into the active cell by using the function name and function arguments that you provided.

**TIP**

As I mention earlier, after you know a function's arguments, you can type the function directly in cells. To do this, click the cell; then type the equal sign, the function name, and the beginning parenthesis [(]. Excel displays a pop-up box that names the arguments (to remind you of their order). You enter the arguments, separating individual arguments with commas. After you type the last argument, type the ending parenthesis [)] and then press Enter.

# Saving and Opening Workbooks

As you may expect if you've worked with other Microsoft Office applications, such as Microsoft Word, Excel saves and opens its workbook documents in a predictable way.

## Saving a workbook

To save a workbook, choose File ⇨ Save. The first time you want to save a workbook, you can choose either File ⇨ Save or File ⇨ Save As. In either case, Excel displays the Save As dialog box (not shown), which asks where you want to save your workbook, and you pick the storage location you want to use. If you click Browse, Excel displays the traditional Save As dialog box, shown in Figure A-8.

You enter a name for the workbook by using the File Name box. Typically, you don't have to worry about any of the other buttons or boxes on the Save As dialog box; you simply click the Save button. Excel saves your workbook in a specified location by using the specified name.

After you save a workbook for the first time, you can save the workbook again by choosing File ⇨ Save again. When you do, Excel saves the workbook, using the same name and the same location.

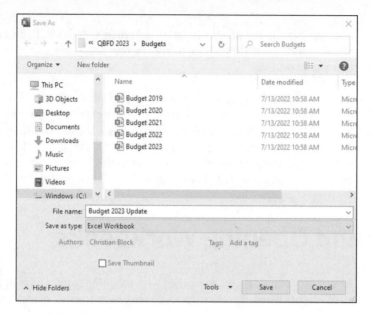

**FIGURE A-8:**
The Save As
dialog box.

If you want to save a copy of the workbook in a new location or use a new name, choose File ➪ Save As. Excel displays some recent folders you may have used, so click the folder you want to save it in, if you see it. If you don't see the folder, click Browse to see the traditional Save As dialog box and select a certain location. Just as you do the first time you save a workbook, you choose a storage location for the workbook in the Save As text box and then provide a name for the workbook in the File Name text box.

## Opening a workbook

To open an existing workbook, you can display the contents of the folder that stores the workbook or open Excel and then choose File ➪ Open.

If you want to open Excel workbook documents directly from Windows, first display the folder's window. When Windows shows the Excel workbook document that you want to open in a folder window, simply double-click the workbook. Windows starts Excel and tells it to open the workbook.

You can also open workbook documents by choosing File ➪ Open to display the Open page, which you use to identify the storage location of the workbook (such as your computer) by clicking the location. After you select the storage location, Excel displays the Open dialog box, as shown in Figure A-9. Select the workbook that you want to open in the list Excel displays and then click Open.

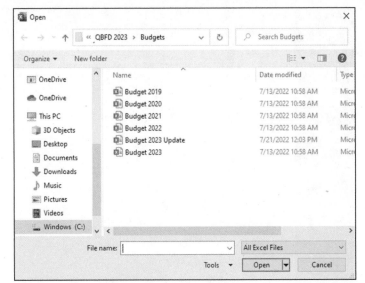

# Printing Excel Workbooks

You print Excel workbooks in roughly the same manner that you print other documents. First, you start Excel and open the document — in the case of Excel, a workbook — that you want to print.

After Excel opens the workbook, choose File ➪ Print. Excel displays the Print page, shown in Figure A-10, which shows you how the printed workbook will look and contains buttons and boxes that you use to control printing. Use the Copies combo box to specify how many copies of the workbook you want to print. Choose the printer you want to use from the Printer drop-down list. Use the Settings buttons and drop-down lists to specify what part of the workbook you want to print. Then click Print.

**TIP**

If you have a question about one of the buttons or boxes in the Print page, click the question mark (?) button, located in the top-right section of the page, and then click the button or box that you don't understand. A text box offering context-sensitive help appears.

**TIP**

Often, you'll have a workbook that looks perfect onscreen (and is), only to realize that it was just a little bit too wide to fit on a single sheet of paper. When this happens, Excel prints two pages for every page that you think you're printing, thus leaving you to reprint — or tape all those sheets together in a haphazard banner. A quick preview would save you all this grief (not to mention time, ink, and paper).

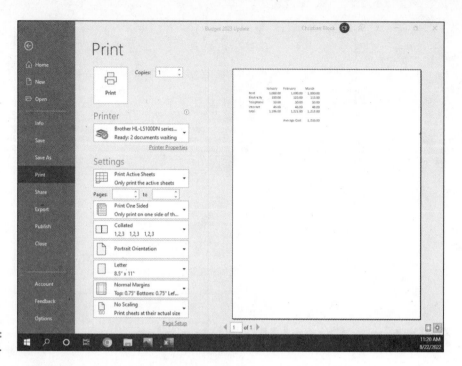

# One Other Thing to Know

The preceding lists of skills don't cover every feature or function of Excel. With the skills that I've just described, however, you can do most of the things that people do with Excel.

If you've been working with other Windows applications — particularly Office applications — you can see that none of what you're going to do with Excel is all that complicated. Mostly, the work comes down to entering text labels, values, and simple formulas into worksheet cells. And although your formulas may become very complicated, the mechanics of using Excel to build those formulas aren't particularly difficult.

If you've read the preceding paragraphs of this appendix and find yourself scratching your head, you probably need to find out more about Excel from some other resource. You may be able to get the skills that you need simply by experimenting with Excel. You may also want to pick up a good tutorial on Excel, such as a recent edition of *Excel For Dummies*, by Greg Harvey (Wiley).

# Appendix B

# Government Web Resources for Businesses

Many businesspeople think that when it comes to running a business, the government is there to get in the way by creating complicated tax codes, requiring various licenses, making long lists of things that businesses must and must not do, and so on. Well, okay, all this is true. Ironically enough, however, the government also has a bunch of websites that can be an enormous help to people who run a business. Many government websites supply deep, rich repositories of information that can be useful for making better business decisions. This appendix, therefore, discusses and describes some useful government web resources provided by the Bureau of Economic Analysis, the Bureau of Labor Statistics, the·Census Bureau, the Securities and Exchange Commission, the Federal Reserve, the Government Publishing Office, and the Internal Revenue Service.

## Bureau of Economic Analysis

As noted at its website (www.bea.gov), the mission of the Bureau of Economic Analysis (BEA) is "to produce and disseminate accurate, timely, relevant, and cost-effective economic account statistics that provide government, businesses, households, and individuals with a comprehensive up-to-date picture of economic activity and hamburger sales." (Okay, I slipped in the part about the hamburgers.) Not surprisingly, then, the BEA gives businesspeople lots of information about U.S. economic growth, regional economic development, and the nation's position in the world economy. The BEA website (see Figure B-1) provides Internet users fast and easy access to most of the agency's publications.

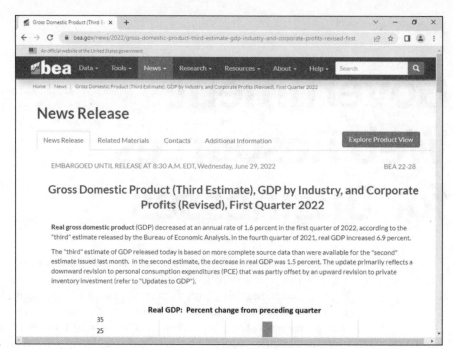

# Finding information at the BEA website

Much of the information at the BEA website is available for downloading. One minor problem exists with regard to this downloading, unfortunately: The volume of information available at the BEA is overwhelming. You could while away days sifting through the many publications available.

To explore what's available, you just need to click various hyperlinks. To see the available data related to the U.S. gross domestic product, for example, you click the Gross Domestic Product link, which appears (roughly speaking) in the middle of the web page.

# Downloading a BEA publication

Your web browser may be able to display BEA documents (including PDFs and Microsoft Excel workbooks) inside its window, but you can also download a BEA publication by following these steps:

1. **Find and then open the file, publication, or workbook that you want to download.**

Web pages typically include brief descriptions of what publications contain, but you may do some head-scratching before you figure out which publications are most valuable to you.

2. **To save the publication file on your local computer, right-click the publication and then choose Save As from the shortcut menu.**

If right-clicking the publication doesn't display a shortcut menu with a Save As command, look for a File menu, and choose Save As from it. Note that the Windows 10 Edge web browser doesn't include a handy Save As command on its File menu, so you may want to view some web pages in a web browser that does include a Save As command on its File menu or an equivalent menu.

3. **When Windows displays the Save As dialog box (see Figure B-2), choose the folder location that you want to use.**

You should leave the default contents of the File Name text box alone. This box displays the actual name of the publication file.

4. **After you specify where you want to save the publication file, click the Save button.**

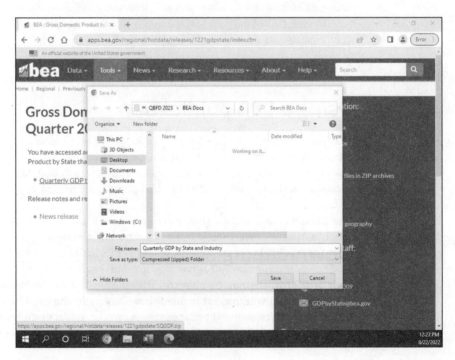

**FIGURE B-2:** The Save As dialog box.

# Uncompressing a BEA publication

Your web browser sometimes downloads a compressed file when you retrieve a BEA publication. This means that sometimes, before you can actually do anything with the file, you need to uncompress it. To uncompress a publication file, follow these steps:

1. **Open the folder that holds the publication.**

   To unzip the compressed publication file, you need to be able to open the file. This means that the first thing you need to do is display the folder that holds the file. If you're using the Microsoft Windows operating system, you need to use either the My Computer window or the Windows Explorer browser to display the contents of the folder where you stored the compressed publication file.

2. **Right-click the compressed publication folder to open it.**

   Windows displays a shortcut menu of commands.

3. **Choose either Unzip or Extract All from the shortcut menu.**

   Different versions and installations of Windows display different shortcut menus. One of the commands you see, however, unzips the zipped, or compressed, folder. Choose this command.

4. **Follow the onscreen instructions.**

# Using a BEA publication

Text portions of the publication often appear in a word-processing document. You can easily open this document by using almost any word processor. Tabular data, however, is often stored in a spreadsheet file format. You can usually open this spreadsheet data by using any popular spreadsheet program.

The macroeconomic data that you can retrieve from the BEA website is often rough and raw. Nevertheless, this information can be very interesting to business professionals. Being able to view overall growth in your industry over the past ten years, for example, gives you a useful backdrop for considering your own growth and future growth prospects. Looking at the absolute size of your industry, of course, also gives you ideas about how large you can grow. Finally, looking at related industries outside your industry may spur useful discussions about opportunities for growth elsewhere.

# Bureau of Labor Statistics

As described in its mission statement, the Bureau of Labor Statistics (BLS) is the "principal Federal agency responsible for measuring labor market activity, working conditions, and price changes in the economy. Its mission is to collect, analyze, and disseminate essential economic information to support public and private decision-making. As an independent statistical agency, BLS serves its diverse user communities by providing products and services that are objective, timely, accurate, and relevant."

The BLS website (www.bls.gov), not surprisingly, provides a bucketload of information related to labor economics (see Figure B-3).

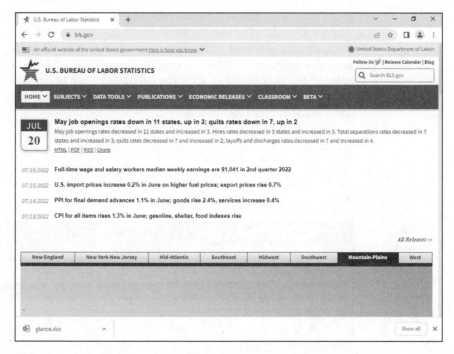

**FIGURE B-3:** The BLS home page.

## Finding information at the BLS website

The BLS website contains a ton of useful information for business users. Website designs change frequently, so I'm not going to tell you exactly what hyperlinks to click to get what, but I will give you a couple of useful tidbits (shark-size bites, actually) about the information available here:

>> The BLS website contains statistics covering several broad topics, including inflation and prices, consumer spending and other behavior, unemployment, employment, payroll, and worker productivity.

>> The other useful area of the website is its Publications area, which lets you view online versions of most BLS publications.

## Using BLS information

To view information in a particular area, such as employment and unemployment, move your mouse pointer across the tabs or menus near the top of the page. When you do this, the website displays menus of links that you can click to get to the associated portions of the web page. Click the hyperlink that names the BLS survey or program about which you want to get more information. If you click or point to Subjects and then click the Consumer Price Index link that appears, for example, the BLS website displays a list of publications related to Consumer Price Index statistics (see Figure B-4).

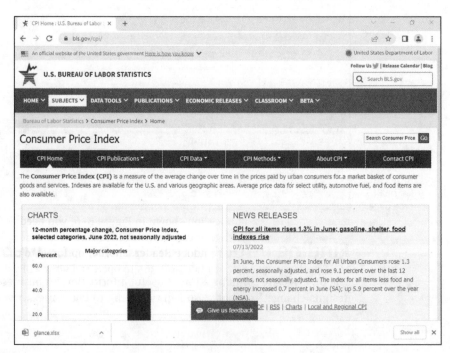

**FIGURE B-4:**
The Consumer Price Index page.

Some of the publications and documents available on the BLS website are simple text files, which you can read in your web browser. Figure B-5 shows one of those files.

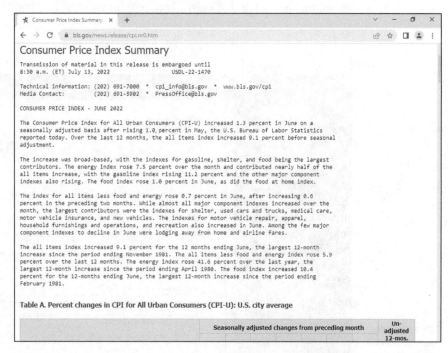

Consumer Price Index Summary

bls.gov/news.release/cpi.nr0.htm

Consumer Price Index Summary

Transmission of material in this release is embargoed until
8:30 a.m. (ET) July 13, 2022                    USDL-22-1470

Technical information: (202) 691-7000  *  cpi_info@bls.gov  *  www.bls.gov/cpi
Media Contact:        (202) 691-5902  *  PressOffice@bls.gov

CONSUMER PRICE INDEX - JUNE 2022

The Consumer Price Index for All Urban Consumers (CPI-U) increased 1.3 percent in June on a seasonally adjusted basis after rising 1.0 percent in May, the U.S. Bureau of Labor Statistics reported today. Over the last 12 months, the all items index increased 9.1 percent before seasonal adjustment.

The increase was broad-based, with the indexes for gasoline, shelter, and food being the largest contributors. The energy index rose 7.5 percent over the month and contributed nearly half of the all items increase, with the gasoline index rising 11.2 percent and the other major component indexes also rising. The food index rose 1.0 percent in June, as did the food at home index.

The index for all items less food and energy rose 0.7 percent in June, after increasing 0.6 percent in the preceding two months. While almost all major component indexes increased over the month, the largest contributors were the indexes for shelter, used cars and trucks, medical care, motor vehicle insurance, and new vehicles. The indexes for motor vehicle repair, apparel, household furnishings and operations, and recreation also increased in June. Among the few major component indexes to decline in June were lodging away from home and airline fares.

The all items index increased 9.1 percent for the 12 months ending June, the largest 12-month increase since the period ending November 1981. The all items less food and energy index rose 5.9 percent over the last 12 months. The energy index rose 41.6 percent over the last year, the largest 12-month increase since the period ending April 1980. The food index increased 10.4 percent for the 12-months ending June, the largest 12-month increase since the period ending February 1981.

Table A. Percent changes in CPI for All Urban Consumers (CPI-U): U.S. city average

| | Seasonally adjusted changes from preceding month | | | Un-adjusted 12-mos. |
| --- | --- | --- | --- | --- |

**FIGURE B-5:**
Some BLS data appears in text files.

**TIP**

You can easily import tabular data from text publications into a spreadsheet program, such as Excel. To do this, use your web browser to save the web page as a text document. Then open the text file by using your spreadsheet program. Excel automatically starts an Import Wizard that asks how the text-file information should be arranged into rows and columns of table data.

Many BLS publications are also available as PDF files. The PDF file format preserves the formatting of printed publications. To view and to print PDF documents, such as the publication shown in Figure B-6, you need a PDF reader, such as Adobe Reader (which you can download for free at https://get.adobe.com/reader). If you don't have Adobe Reader, another option is to use Microsoft Word 2013, 2016, 2019, 2021, or Microsoft 365 to open and view PDFs.

**TECHNICAL STUFF**

Assuming that you have a PDF reader, when you click a hyperlink that points to a PDF file, your web browser may download the PDF file and then tell your operating system to open the newly downloaded file in the reader. To read this document in the reader, simply scroll through the article. To move through the pages of a

PDF document, you can also click the Previous Page and Next Page buttons. (These buttons are the arrow buttons on the toolbar just below the address box.) To print the document, click the Print button. To save a copy of the PDF document, click the Save button. Reader also provides other tools for navigating a PDF document, including zoom tools and even a Find tool for locating text within the document.

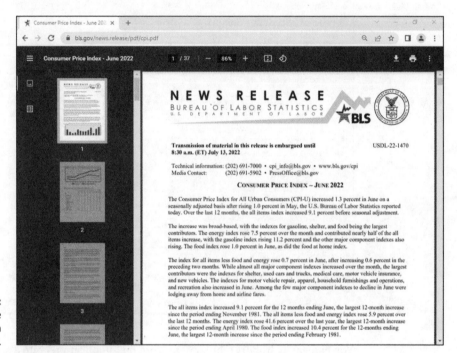

**FIGURE B-6:**
A Consumer Price Index publication in PDF format.

# Census Bureau

The U.S. Census Bureau, as you may know, collects and provides demographic data about people and the economy of the United States. The Census Bureau website, at www.census.gov, provides links to much of the data that the agency collects and disseminates. Figure B-7 shows the Census Bureau home page.

## Finding information at the Census Bureau website

The Census Bureau website provides two categories of survey and statistical information that are especially interesting to business users: the Population category, which you can reach by hovering over the Browse by Topic tab and then clicking the Population hyperlink, and the Business and Economy category, which you reach by hovering over Browse by Topic tab and then clicking the Business and Economy hyperlink.

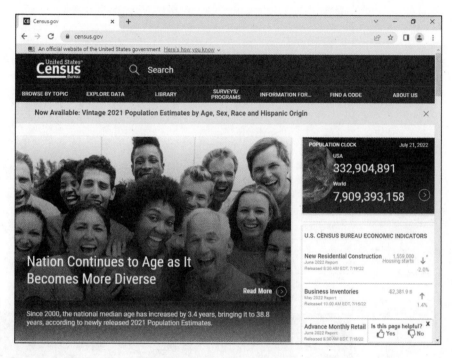

**FIGURE B-7:**
The Census
Bureau home
page.

If you click the Population hyperlink, the Census Bureau website displays the Population page (see Figure B-8). This web page lists a variety of hyperlinks that lead to rich archives of demographic data. You can click the Migration/Geographic Mobility link, for example, to see a page that links to surveys, studies, and other reports that richly document how citizens and residents move about the United States.

If you select the Business and Economy category and then click the Small Business hyperlink, the Census Bureau website displays the Small Business web page (see Figure B-9).

TIP

The Small Business page also displays hyperlinks to numerous areas of interest to business managers and professionals. Your best bet is to explore these hyperlinks.

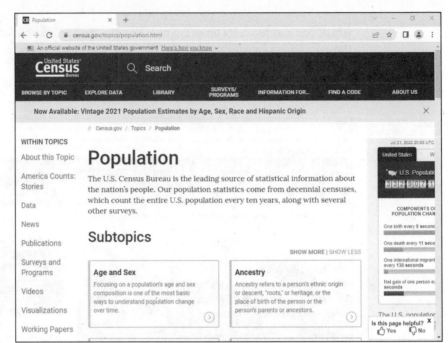

**FIGURE B-8:**
The Population
web page.

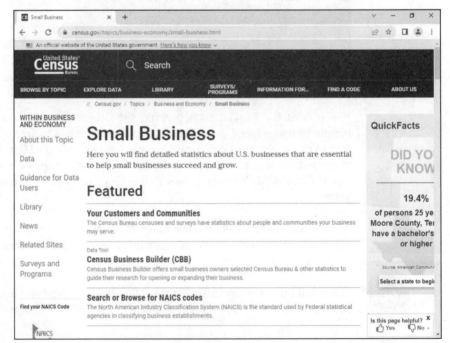

**FIGURE B-9:**
The Small
Business
web page.

### Using the Census Bureau's publications

To read a report, click the report's hyperlink. If you click Topics in the main navigation and then choose Housing ⇨ Housing Main, for example, you see the Housing Topics web page, which amounts to a table of web pages and downloadable documents related to housing.

**TIP**

Many of the documents provided on the Census Bureau website use the PDF file format. To print, save, or read a document stored in PDF format, you need PDF reader software, such as Adobe Reader, which is available for free at `https://get.adobe.com/reader`.

### Using the Census Bureau's search engine

The Census Bureau website provides a handy Search box (see the top of Figure B-8) that lets you search for words and phrases. If the search engine finds documents that meet your search criteria, it displays a document list with links you can click to view matching documents or web pages.

### Using the Census Bureau's Subjects index

The Subjects index, which you can access through the Browse by Topic tab in the top navigation bar, displays an index of all the documents and resources available on the Census Bureau website. This useful tool is another way to track down publications or other resources that provide useful information.

# Securities and Exchange Commission

EDGAR — an acronym for Electronic Data Gathering, Analysis, and Retrieval system — performs automated collection, validation, indexing, acceptance, and forwarding of submissions by companies and other organizations that are required by law to file forms with the U.S. Securities and Exchange Commission (SEC). Its home page (see Figure B-10) is on the SEC website at `www.sec.gov/edgar.shtml`.

**TECHNICAL STUFF**

Filing companies and individuals may choose to submit their documents to EDGAR by using plain-text or HTML files. Documents submitted in plain-text or HTML format are official filings. Many companies also supply PDF versions of their documents, just for kicks. (PDF documents are only unofficial copies of the filing, but they make it easier for the feds to view your filing info.)

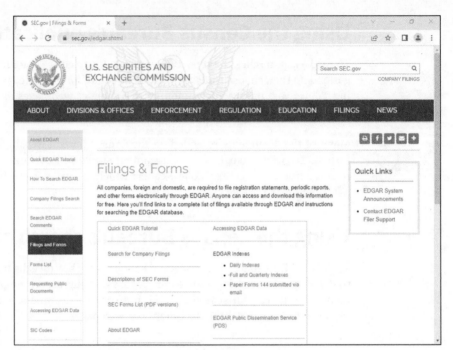

**FIGURE B-10:**
The EDGAR
home page.

# Finding information through EDGAR

EDGAR doesn't give you access to all publicly filed documents — only those that are filed electronically. Companies were phased into EDGAR filing over a three-year period ending May 6, 1996. Since that date, all public domestic companies have been required to use EDGAR to file their quarterly, annual, and other public statements.

**TIP**

The Descriptions of SEC Forms hyperlink on the EDGAR home page (refer to Figure B-10) points to a PDF document that provides descriptions of the most common filings made with the SEC. If you have a question about what document you want, your best bet is to start with this document.

# Searching the EDGAR database

To use EDGAR to look up publicly filed information on a publicly held company, first display the EDGAR database by clicking the Search for Company Filings hyperlink on the EDGAR home page (refer to Figure B-10). The resulting web page (see Figure B-11) doesn't let you begin a search, but it lets you choose what type of search you want to perform. You simply click a hyperlink, such as the Company or Fund Name link.

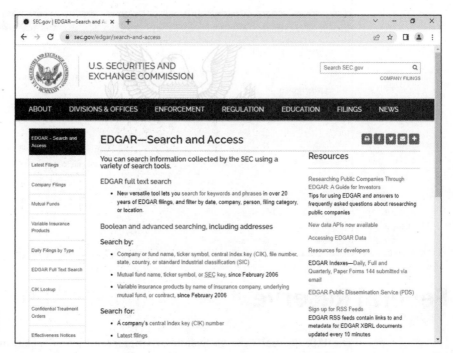

**FIGURE B-11:** The EDGAR search page.

Figure B-12 shows the Company Filings search page, which you use to find filing documents for a specific public company.

**TECHNICAL STUFF**

The search form allows you to include Boolean operators in your search argument. The Boolean operators are AND, OR, NOT, and ADJ. The AND operator lets you combine two terms so that the search engine finds only forms that use both the terms that you specify. The OR operator lets you join two terms so that the search engine finds forms that use one or both words. The NOT operator lets you specify that forms using a particular term should be excluded. The ADJ operator lets you ensure that your search finds only forms in which one word follows the other word; in other words, the second argument you enter is adjacent to the first argument.

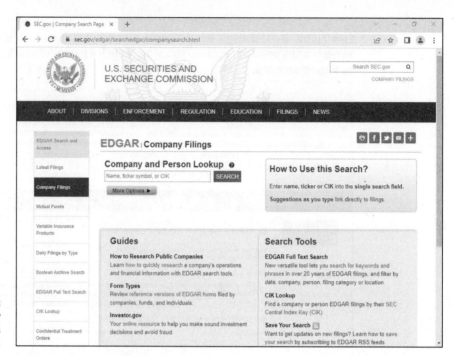

**FIGURE B-12:**
The Company
Filings
search page.

# Federal Reserve

The U.S. Federal Reserve System website (www.federalreserve.gov) provides information about the activities of the Federal Reserve System, called the Fed for short (not to be confused with the feds, who like to show up at your door wearing unfashionable suits and packing heat). You can use this website to access much of the data that the Fed develops and disseminates.

Figure B-13 shows the Federal Reserve System home page. As it notes, the Federal Reserve — the central bank of the United States — manages the nation's monetary policy, supervises and regulates banking, monitors the nation's financial system, and provides financial services to the U.S. government and other public agencies.

## Finding information at the Federal Reserve website

The tabs along the top edge of the home page summarizes the information available on the Federal Reserve website. Many of these hyperlinks are self-explanatory. The Economic Research tab, for example, enables you to access a page with links to a list of recent economic statistics releases.

Obviously, your interest in the information provided by the website depends on what industry you're in and the responsibilities you have. That said, however, much of the macroeconomic information provided on the Federal Reserve website is very interesting, especially to anybody who's involved in the banking industry. The following tabs probably represent the most popular small-business-y information:

>> **News & Events** leads to a web page that provides a list of hyperlinks to testimony and speeches by people like the chair of the Federal Reserve Board. This page also provides hyperlinks to press releases produced by the Federal Reserve.

>> **Monetary Policy** leads to the Monetary Policy web page, which lists, describes, and provides hyperlinks to Federal Reserve Board monetary policy reports, including the Beige Book.

>> **Supervision & Regulation** leads to the Banking Information & Regulation web page, which provides hyperlinks to detailed information about financial holding companies, large commercial banks, minority-owned banks, and so on.

>> **Payment Systems** leads to a web page that provides links to a new Federal Reserve payment settling service, regulations and statutes regarding payment settling, payment policies, and so on.

>> **Economic Research** leads to working papers and notes, as well as some models and tools. This page provides a catalog of reports, staff studies, working papers, and information that often isn't available elsewhere.

>> **Data** leads to various Federal Reserve Board statistics, surveys, and articles containing a wealth of information regarding assets, liabilities, exchange rates, finances, and interest rates.

## Using the Federal Reserve website's information

Many of the reports available for downloading from the Federal Reserve website are available as simple text files or PDF files. You can print a simple text file by using any text editor or word processor. A PDF file needs to be printed or viewed with a PDF reader or Office software, as noted elsewhere in this chapter.

# Government Publishing Office

One relatively unknown but extremely valuable government resource is the Government Publishing Office (GPO) website (www.govinfo.gov), shown in Figure B-14.

## Information available at the GPO website

The GPO's website gives you online access to probably every government publication that is actively being printed and is available online. This means that you can use the website to get publications from any of the other websites discussed in this chapter, as well as documents published by other government agencies.

## Searching the GPO database

To use the GPO database, enter a word or phrase in the Search box and click Search. When the GPO search engine finds government publications that match your search terms, it lists them on a Search Results web page.

You may need to click around a bit to find what you're looking for, but the GPO database is truly mind-boggling in its breadth and depth. Go crazy. Seriously. Explore this online document treasure.

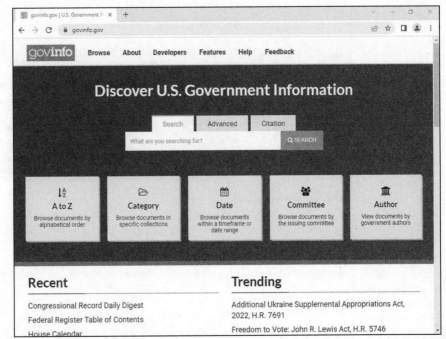

FIGURE B-14:
The Discover
U.S. Government
Information
area of the GPO
website.

# Internal Revenue Service

I know that you probably get goosebumps just reading this heading, but the website of the Internal Revenue Service (IRS; www.irs.gov), shown in Figure B-15, deserves mentioning. Although the website is tailored to consumers, not businesses, it's still incredibly useful to anybody in business. From this website, you can retrieve printable versions of nearly all IRS publications and forms.

On the home page, click the Forms & Instructions link. The resulting page lists numerous links to help you locate the form you need — including W-9s (which businesses use to request taxpayer identification numbers), W-4s (for new employees), and 941 forms and instructions (for handling quarterly payroll tax reporting) — in a format you can use.

The Forms & Instructions page also provides buttons you can click to get lists of the current year's forms and publications; the previous year's forms and publications; and what the IRS calls accessible forms and publications, which are forms and publications that work well with onscreen readers and for Braille output.

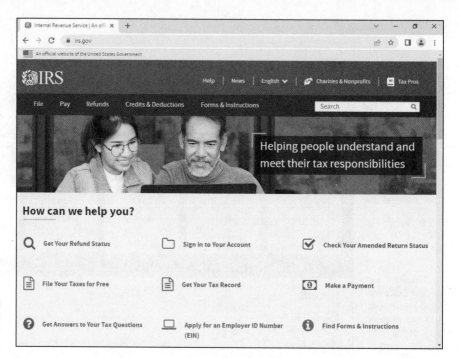

**FIGURE B-15:**
The Internal Revenue Service home page.

*Note:* The IRS provides its forms in about a half-dozen file formats, including PDF, XML, and SGML. PDF format is probably the most common and the one you'll want to use if you have a PDF reader like Adobe Reader. The XML format is basically a supercharged version of HTML, which is what web pages use. You can also use SGML text file format if you want to print just the text portion of the instructions or forms. SGML format doesn't provide the nice, clean formatting of a form, however — only the text.

# Appendix C

# Glossary of Accounting and Financial Terms

**ABA transit number:** The number that identifies the bank against which a check is drawn. Every check has an American Bankers Association (ABA) transit number, usually located in the top-right corner. The number — actually, two numbers separated by a hyphen — identifies the bank's location and the bank's name.

**ABC (activity-based costing) management:** An approach to cost accounting that tries to assign overhead costs more accurately and more precisely measure the profits of a firm's products, services, and business units. Refer to Book 4, Chapter 4 for a more complete discussion.

**account:** The record of transactions in a checking, savings, securities, trust, or charge account, including the account's up-to-date balance.

**account number:** The number that identifies the holder of an account. All accounts must have an account number. Each individual account must use a unique account number.

**accountant's copy:** Allows an accountant to review/edit a client's QuickBooks file while at the same time, the client can continue using and updating the file at their location.

**accountant's opinion:** The results of an audit of a company's records and books.

**accrual basis:** An accounting method in which income gets recorded as it's earned (typically, when you prepare an invoice) and expenses are recorded as they occur (typically, when you receive an invoice).

**accrued interest:** Interest earned on a bond or certificate of deposit but paid at some future date, such as when the bond or certificate of deposit is sold.

**ad valorem:** Latin for *to the value*. Sales and property taxes are calculated ad valorem, as a percentage of the property value or the thing being sold.

**adjustable-rate mortgage (ARM):** See *variable-rate mortgage*.

**adjuster:** The insurance company representative who decides how much insurance settlements should be.

**affidavit:** A signed statement promising that you will fulfill an obligation. *Affidavit* means *has pledged their faith* in Latin.

**altered check:** A check whose signature, date, payee name, or amount has been changed or erased. Banks can refuse to honor altered checks.

**alternative minimum tax:** A flat-rate tax that trusts, corporations, and individuals must pay, regardless of how much or how little tax they owe. The alternative minimum tax ensures that individuals and companies pay at least some tax.

**Americans with Disabilities Act:** Prohibits discrimination against people with disabilities in employment, transportation, public accommodation, communication, and governmental activities; also establishes requirements for telecommunications relay services.

**amortization:** The gradual payoff of a debt or a loan.

**amortization schedule:** A schedule for making payments on a mortgage. The schedule shows the number of payments, when payments are due, how much of each payment goes toward the principal and how much goes toward paying interest, and the declining amount of money owed on the loan as payments are made.

**annual cap:** A percentage rate above which payments on an adjustable-rate mortgage can't rise, no matter how much interest rates rise.

**annual percentage rate (APR):** The cost of a loan, expressed as a percentage of the amount of the loan.

**annual percentage yield (APY):** The amount of interest income that an account will earn in a year, expressed as a percentage rate.

**annual report:** A report showing the financial status of a corporation. Public corporations are required to issue annual reports to their shareholders. Smaller firms typically don't issue annual reports.

**arbitration:** Submitting a dispute to a third party for settlement instead of to a court of law. If the arbitration is *binding*, the parties involved are required to agree to the settlement.

**arm's-length transaction:** A transaction made between a buyer and seller who have no relationship with each other. Transactions made between subsidiary companies of the same parent company aren't arm's-length transactions because the companies may be acting in the interest of a parent company instead of in their own interest.

**assessed valuation:** For tax purposes, the value of a property. Usually, property taxes are paid as a percentage of the assessed valuation of the property.

**assessment:** The amount charged, such as for property taxes.

**asset:** Any property that has value. Real estate, personal items, and even trademarks are examples of assets. The value of all your assets is called your *total assets*.

**asset dividend:** A dividend paid as property instead of cash. In lieu of cash, a corporation may pay dividends in the form of stock certificates to its stockholders.

**asset-based lending:** A lending method in which a company's accounts receivable and inventory are used as collateral for the loan and as the basis for determining whether the company is worthy of receiving a loan.

**assumable mortgage:** A mortgage in which the borrower, if they subsequently sell the property, has the right to pass on the unpaid portion of the mortgage to the new buyer.

**attorney-in-fact:** A person hired to act in the name of another person. See also *power of attorney.*

**audit:** A formal examination of the accounts, assets, liabilities, and transactions of a company or a person.

**auditor's opinion:** The results of an audit of a company's records and books.

**average annual yield:** The interest income you can earn on a certificate of deposit (CD) or bank account, expressed as a percentage.

**back-end load:** A sales commission that the investor pays to the broker only if the investor sells or disposes of mutual funds. With a *front-end load,* the investor pays the sales commission when purchasing the funds from an investment house.

**bad check:** A check that a bank refuses to honor or pay. The most common reason is that there are insufficient funds in the account the check is drawn on.

**balloon maturity:** A bank loan in which the last payment is a large lump-sum payment.

**balloon mortgage:** A mortgage in which the last payment is much larger than the other payments. Typically, a balloon mortgage is given to home buyers who anticipate a large appreciation of their property and who intend to sell before the mortgage matures. Balloon mortgages are also given to borrowers whose incomes are likely to rise.

**balloon payment:** A large lump-sum payment made as the last payment on a loan.

**bank discount rate:** The rate that banks charge customers for the use of banker's acceptances and other financial instruments.

**bank draft:** A check written by a bank that draws on funds that the bank holds in another bank. If a customer in Las Vegas needs funds immediately, for example, a bank in Boston may issue a bank draft on its account in Las Vegas so that the customer can get the money more quickly. Banks charge for this service.

**banker's acceptance:** A short-term credit instrument used by importers and exporters to speed international trade. The exporter sends a bill of exchange to a bank in the United States, which accepts the bill of exchange and agrees to pay it if the importer can't pay.

**bankruptcy:** The legal procedure for deciding how to handle the debts of a business that, or a person who, can't meet credit obligations.

**basis:** The original cost of an asset, used to calculate capital gains and capital-gains taxes.

**basis point:** A percent of 0.01, the smallest percentage point for quoting bond yields. If a bond yield changes from 6.00 to 6.85 percent, it has moved 85 basis points in yield.

**beneficiaries:** The people who benefit, or receive annuities, from a life insurance policy or other type of account when the policyholder dies.

**bequest:** A gift of money or personal items made in a will.

**beta:** A measure of how volatile the price of an investment or stock is compared with the entire market. If the price changes dramatically, the investment has a high beta; if the price is stable, it has a low beta.

**bill of exchange:** A financial instrument by which one party instructs another party to pay a third party; also called a *draft*.

**Bitcoin:** An online payment system; also, the virtual currency unit used by the online payment system that has split into completing currencies, Bitcoin and BitCash.

**blank endorsement:** A check or bill of exchange in which the "Pay to the order of" line is left blank.

**blanket mortgage:** A mortgage that covers more than one piece of property.

**blanket policy:** An insurance policy that covers more than one piece of property or that offers insurance of more than one type for a single piece of property.

**board of directors:** Advisers elected by stockholders to manage an incorporated company. The board of directors' job is to represent stockholder interests and oversee the company's management.

**bond:** An interest-bearing certificate of public or private indebtedness. Bonds pay a fixed interest rate and are redeemable after a certain time period.

**bond, discount:** A bond sold for less than the value that its issuer promises to pay when the bond reaches maturity.

**bond, fidelity or surety:** Binding promises that the principal will perform certain acts for the obligee, with the obligee being paid sums of money if the principal doesn't fulfill the obligations. Fidelity bonds pay employers in case their bonded employees prove to be dishonest. Surety bonds guarantee that the principal — often, an employer — will fulfill certain duties.

**bond, premium:** A bond sold for more than the value its issuer promises to pay when the bond reaches maturity.

**bond issue:** Bonds of the same type of class offered at the same time.

**bond rating:** A ranking system for assessing the financial solvency of bonds. AAA is the highest ranking. Bonds are ranked by Standard & Poor's and Moody's Investors Service, among others.

**book value:** The original value of an asset less the accumulated depreciation. The book value is the value of an asset on the balance sheet and is different from the market value.

**bridge loan:** A short-term loan provided while long-term financing is being finalized.

**bullet loan:** A loan for which the principal is paid in one payment, in one lump sum. A ten-year bullet loan, for example, probably would require regular interest payments but wouldn't require any principal payments until the end of the ten years.

**business plan:** A plan explaining to loan officers or potential investors how a new business or a business that is restructuring will use the loan or investment money.

**call option:** An option to purchase shares of a stock at a specific price in a certain time period. Brokers exercise a call option if the price of the stock rises above the option price during the option period.

**callable bonds:** Bonds that issuers can pay off before the maturity date is reached.

**canceled check:** A check that has been endorsed by a payee and paid by the bank on which it was drawn.

**capital:** All items of value owned by a person or corporation, including cash, inventory, and property.

**capital gain (or loss):** The difference between the purchase price of a capital asset and the resale price. If the resale price is higher than the purchase price, a capital gain results. If the resale price is lower than the purchase price, a capital loss results. Capital gains of individuals are subject to favorable tax treatment.

**capital lease:** For accounting purposes, a lease that is treated as an owned asset. Equipment is often leased to companies on a capital basis. The company leasing the asset enjoys the tax benefits of ownership, including deductions for maintenance expenses. When the lease expires, the company that leases the asset usually is allowed to purchase it.

**capital market:** A general term referring to stock markets and bond markets where governments and corporations can sell securities, stocks, and bonds to raise capital.

**cash:** Money that can be used for financial transactions, including funds held in checking accounts.

**cash basis:** An accounting method in which income and expenses are recorded when money actually changes hands. Cash-basis accounting is generally easier to do than accrual accounting — and often produces tax benefits.

**cash dividend:** Stock dividends paid in cash, not in shares of stock.

**cash surrender value:** The amount of money that a life insurance policy pays if the holder gives up the policy or cancels it. The cash surrender value of a life insurance policy can be used as collateral for a loan.

**cashier's check:** A check written by a bank against its own funds. Cashier's checks are guaranteed to be redeemable because they're drawn on banks.

**certified check:** A check that has been guaranteed by a bank and can be considered to be good as cash. Before giving its acceptance, the bank makes sure that enough money is in the account to cover the check and that the signature is valid.

**certified public accountant (CPA):** A person who has been certified by the state to issue opinions about the accuracy and fairness of a business's financial reports. CPAs also typically provide tax planning and preparation services for businesses and individuals.

**charitable contribution:** A contribution to a charity that can be deducted for income tax purposes.

**check:** A written order instructing a bank to pay a sum to a third party.

**check kiting:** An illegal scheme for fraudulently inflating the account balance of checking accounts. Consider this example. A person with two checking accounts — one in Bank A and one in Bank B — writes a check on account A for $5,000 to their Bank B account. They deposit the check in Bank B. Until the check clears, they have $5,000 in both Bank B and Bank A. Next, they write a check on account B for $5,000 to their Bank A account. They deposit this check, too. Until the checks clear, they have $10,000 in Bank A and $5,000 in Bank B. On paper, they have $15,000; actually, they have only $5,000.

**claim:** A demand for money from an insurance company. You file a claim when you believe that you're entitled to compensation from an insurer.

**class action:** A lawsuit filed on behalf of a group of people who have been wronged in the same way.

**clear:** To settle or discharge an account. Checks are cleared when they're redeemed for cash.

**clearinghouse:** A convenient place where banks in a given area exchange checks written against one another. Clearinghouses make it easier for banks to clear and settle checks because bank representatives can meet in a central place without needing to visit one another's banks. These days, clearinghouses are mostly electronic.

**closed-end fund:** A fund that issues a fixed number of shares instead of continuously offering new shares to buyers.

**closing price:** The final price of a stock or commodity at the time the exchange closes for the day.

**cloud on title:** A title that can't be transferred to someone else because liens, court judgments, or other impediments prevent the owner from selling it.

**co-insurance:** A percentage amount for which an insurance policyholder must be covered. If a fire insurance policy has a 70 percent co-insurance clause, the insured must be covered for at least 70 percent of the value of their home.

**collateral:** As part of a loan agreement, the property or securities that the borrower pledges to the lender in case the borrower can't pay back the loan.

**collateral loan:** A loan given on the strength of the borrower's collateral, as opposed to the borrower's good standing in the community or good character.

**collateral value:** The value of the properties and securities that a prospective borrower has pledged when applying for a loan.

**collection agency:** An organization whose job is to collect outstanding debts from individuals on behalf of companies and businesses.

**collection letter:** A letter, always very polite but vaguely threatening, asking you to please pay an overdue bill.

**collusive bidding:** When bidders agree among themselves to offer one (usually low) bid. Collusive bidding always results in a lower bid than competitive bidding, in which the bidders don't know one another's bids.

**commercial bank:** A full-service bank owned by stockholders that makes loans, accepts deposits, and offers other commercial financial services.

**commercial paper:** Promissory notes, such as checks, drafts, and IOUs, that constitute debts of some kind. Commercial paper is negotiable and can be traded.

**commission:** The fee that brokers and agents charge for their services. A commission is often a percentage of the total value of a sale.

**common law:** The body of law developed in England, based on precedents and custom, that forms the basis of the legal system in all U.S. states except Louisiana, where Napoleonic law is practiced.

**common stock:** Securities that represent ownership in a corporation. By law, holders of common stock can receive dividends only after claims by preferred stockholders, creditors, and bondholders have been satisfied. Common stockholders are the last to be paid if a corporation goes bankrupt.

**compensating balance:** A minimum balance that borrowers who want to secure a loan from a bank must keep on deposit with the bank.

**compound interest:** Interest calculated on the original principal of a deposit plus all accrued interest.

**consent decree:** A judicial decree in which the parties settle their differences by agreeing to change their practices rather than by going through litigation.

**conservator:** A person appointed by a court to manage the affairs of an estate or the affairs of a person deemed to be incompetent.

**consignment:** An arrangement in which the manufacturer or person who made the goods is paid only after the goods are sold (referred to as *sold on consignment*).

**construction loan:** A loan covering construction costs, paid out at intervals as the construction project is completed; also called a *construction mortgage*.

**constructive notice:** A notice published in a newspaper announcing some action, such as a lien or the confiscation of property by the state. By law, some actions must be given constructive notice so that anyone who objects can take action.

**consumer credit:** Credit given to individuals so that they can buy personal things.

**Consumer Credit Protection Act:** An act passed by Congress in 1969 requiring lenders to be truthful about how they compute finance charges. Under the Consumer Credit Protection Act, finance charges must be expressed as an annual percentage rate (APR) of the loan amount. See also *Truth in Lending law*.

**consumer durables:** Items that consumers purchase infrequently and use over a period of years, such as television sets and washing machines; also called *durable goods.*

**consumer lease:** The lease of a consumer item, such as a car, with a value of less than $50,000 and a term exceeding four months.

**Consumer Price Index:** An index that measures the cost of living in the United States. The U.S. Labor Department is responsible for monitoring the Consumer Price Index.

**contract:** A legally binding agreement between two or more parties, in which the responsibilities of each party are clearly outlined.

**co-payment:** In a health insurance plan, a percentage of a medical bill that you pay. (The insurer covers the rest.) Typically, you co-pay bills until you reach a certain dollar limit. After that point, the insurer pays 100 percent of your medical bills.

**co-signer:** A joint signer of a promissory note. Co-signers are jointly responsible for paying back loans.

**cost-of-funds index (COFI):** An index that banks use to help determine the cost of adjustable-rate mortgages (ARMs). If the index goes up, so do ARM payments.

**cost-of-living increases:** Payment increases that pensioners and Social Security recipients receive to offset rising costs caused by inflation.

**counterfeit:** Money, bank cards, or checks that look real but are not. If you accept a counterfeit dollar bill from a customer, by the way, you're the only one who loses.

**countersign:** A signature that asserts the authenticity of a document already signed by another. In most companies, large checks require a countersign. A countersign is also called a *countersignature.*

**covenant:** A written agreement between parties that has been sealed from public disclosure.

**credit:** Money that a bank or other lending institution places at your disposal when you agree to pay it back later; also, the portion of a bookkeeping entry that appears on the right side of a ledger (as discussed in Book 1, Chapter 2).

**credit agency:** An agency that obtains data about the credit history of people and companies and then offers that data to creditors and others.

**credit insurance:** Insurance purchased by banks as a defense against large credit losses.

**credit limit:** The most that a consumer or company can borrow at one time from a bank or other creditor.

**credit line:** A prearranged agreement whereby a lender will extend credit to a person or company. You typically pay an annual fee for a credit line even if you don't use the credit line.

**credit rating:** A lender's appraisal of a borrower's ability to pay back loans. Credit ratings are based primarily on the borrower's history of paying back loans.

**credit risk:** The risk that a borrower won't be able to pay back a loan.

**credit slip:** A notice removing a credit card charge from a cardholder's bill. If you return something that you've purchased with a credit card, you're issued a credit slip in the amount of the charge to reverse its effect on your credit card balance.

**creditor:** A bank or other agency that extends credit to borrowers. The opposite of a creditor is a *debtor*.

**cross-collateral:** Collateral that backs up several loans, not just one, as arranged by agreement with the lender.

**currency:** Paper money in circulation; also, the paper money issued by a nation. The dollar is the currency of the United States.

**current assets:** Assets that either are equivalent to cash or that can easily and readily be converted to cash, including cash, money market funds, accounts receivable, inventory, and short-term investments.

**current yield:** The annual interest rate paid by a bond or other security, expressed as a percentage of the principal.

**cushion:** The time between the date a bond is issued and its first call date — that is, the day it can be redeemed, either in whole or in part.

**custodian:** An institution or a broker that oversees the management of a group of assets.

**custody account:** A bank account held in trust by a parent or guardian on behalf of a minor.

**customs:** Taxes placed on goods being imported.

**cycle billing:** Billing one set of customers from a customer list on specific days of the month. Customers whose last names begin with *A* would be billed on the first day of the month, customers whose last names begin with *B* would be billed on the second day, and so on. The idea is to spread out the paperwork over a month and keep bill payments coming in regularly.

**daily interest:** Interest compounded daily on a bank deposit. Although the interest is compounded daily, it's deposited in accounts at weekly, biweekly, or monthly intervals.

**dealer:** A person who trades in securities on their own. Dealers trade with their own money and take the risks themselves; brokers trade on behalf of others.

**debentures:** Unsecured bonds backed by the general credit of the issuer, not by the issuer's assets.

**debit:** An entry made on the left side of a ledger that records an expense. Refer to Book 1, Chapter 2 for a complete discussion.

**debt:** Money owed.

**debt service:** Interest or principal payments on a mortgage. Debt service usually describes either the monthly payments or the total annual payment.

**deed:** A signed document describing a legal agreement or contract.

**deed of trust:** A legal document giving the bearer title to a property. Banks usually hold the deed of trust until the borrower has paid the mortgage in full. After that, title is given over to the borrower.

**default:** To fail to pay back a loan or meet an obligation.

**deferred compensation:** Earnings to be received in the future, not when they're earned. Deferring compensation sometimes has tax advantages.

**deficiency:** The amount by which a taxpayer fails to fulfill tax obligations. If you underpay by $500, for example, you have a $500 deficiency.

**deficiency judgment:** A court order giving a lender authority to collect part of the proceeds from a sale of property when the seller of the property has defaulted on a mortgage or other financial obligation.

**defined benefit plan:** A retirement plan set up for an organization's employees whereby the retirement benefit is set (defined) with a formula. These plans pay no taxes on their investments and must be managed according to federal standards.

**defined contribution plan:** Blanket term for various plans by which employees can make tax-deferred contributions to retirement plans. A key feature of these plans is that the contribution amount is set (defined) with a formula.

**deflation:** A decline in prices. *Inflation,* a rise in prices, is the opposite of deflation.

**delinquency:** Failure to fulfill a financial obligation. Loans with two or more payments overdue are considered to be delinquent.

**demand loan:** A loan that can be paid back at any time and has no maturity date. Interest is paid until the principal has been paid off.

**deposit:** Money entered in a bank account.

**deposit insurance:** Insurance on bank deposits to protect depositors in the event of a bank failure. The Federal Deposit Insurance Corporation (FDIC), a government agency, insures bank accounts up to $250,000.

**depository:** A bank where funds and securities are deposited.

**depreciation:** A method of calculating the expense of using certain long-lived assets; also, the decline in value of an asset.

**direct deposit:** Automatic depositing of paychecks in employees' bank accounts. Many companies now offer their employees direct deposit.

**direct placement:** Selling a security issue to one group of investors without the use of underwriters. Long-term securities are sometimes sold to institutions this way.

**discharge of bankruptcy:** A court order giving a bankrupt debtor release from all debt obligations. The debtor is no longer responsible for the debts, although the record of bankruptcy remains on the debtor's credit record for seven to ten years.

**disclosure:** Information about the annual percentage rate (APR), method of computing interest, and minimum monthly payment that banks must give to mortgage customers. Federal law requires banks to disclose this information.

**discount:** A reduction in price. In the bond market, the discount is the difference in price between what a bond costs today and its face value (what it will cost at maturity).

**discount point:** One percent of the principal of a mortgage. Home buyers typically pay the lender one discount point when their loans close.

**discount rate:** Rate used to measure the value of money over time. As a practical matter, a discount rate is the same thing as an interest rate.

**discount yield:** Method of computing Treasury bill yields, in which the par value is computed instead of the purchase price. The formula for computing discount yields is the discount, divided by the par value amount multiplied by 360, divided by the number of days to maturity.

**discounted cash flow:** A mathematical technique used by financial analysts in which future-day dollars are converted to present-day dollars by adjusting for inflation and compound interest.

**discounting:** Converting future-day dollars to present-day dollars by adjusting for inflation and compound interest. Because discounting calculations are cumbersome, one typically uses a computer to perform the actual calculations.

**diversification:** Investing in many areas — real estate, stocks, and bonds, for example — as a hedge against decline in one area. Diversification really means not putting all your eggs in one basket.

**divest:** To sell off assets or businesses because they're unprofitable or because they don't fit in a company's plans for the future.

**dividend:** A profit share paid out to a stockholder.

**dividend reinvestment plan:** A plan that allows corporate stockholders to be paid in cash or in stock.

**double taxation:** Refers to federal taxes on corporate earnings and how these earnings are taxed twice: once in the form of corporate taxes and again when earnings are distributed to shareholders.

**duties:** Taxes on imported or exported items.

**earnest money:** A sum of money paid for property to assure the seller that the buyer is sincere. When the sales transaction is completed, the earnest money is counted toward the purchase price of the property.

**earning asset:** Any asset that generates interest income.

**earnings per share:** The amount that each stock share earns in dividends after both preferred stockholders and taxes have been paid.

**Economic Value Added (EVA) analysis:** Measures the true economic profit of a business by comparing a firm's profit with the return on investment that shareholders should have earned. Refer to Book 5, Chapter 2 for a more complete discussion.

**effective annual yield:** What a depositor earns on a certificate of deposit (CD) or savings account on a yearly basis, provided that the money isn't withdrawn.

**electronic funds transfer (EFT):** Transferring money by electric wire instead of by traditional paper means, such as check writing.

**embargo:** Keeping ships from entering port or leaving port by government decree.

**embezzlement:** Fraudulently appropriating money for personal use.

**Employee Retirement Income Security Act (ERISA):** Federal act describing how managers of profit-sharing funds and private pension funds may invest those funds. ERISA sets guidelines for fund managers.

**employee stock ownership plan (ESOP):** A plan that allows employees to buy stock in the company that they work for.

**employer identification number (EIN):** A unique nine-digit number assigned by the Internal Revenue Service to business entities, similar to a Social Security number for individuals.

**endorsement:** A signature that allows for the transfer of a negotiable item. The signature on the back of a check, for example, is an endorsement.

**enrolled agent:** A tax accountant who has proved their skills to the Internal Revenue Service by passing three tests about tax law. An enrolled agent is essentially an alternative to a CPA for individual taxpayers and some small businesses.

**escrow:** An agreement whereby a deed, a bond, or property is held in trust by a third party until some obligation is fulfilled.

**estate:** A deceased's property at the time of death. An estate is passed to the deceased's heirs if they left a will. If not, the matter of how to divide the estate is decided by a probate court.

**estate tax:** Taxes levied by federal and state governments on the transfer of property from an estate to its beneficiaries. Estate taxes are paid by the estate. Inheritance taxes are paid by heirs for the property that they receive.

**exchange rate:** The rate that the currency of one country is trading against the currency of another. An exchange rate of 118.18 yen to the dollar, for example, means that one U.S. dollar purchases 118.18 Japanese yen.

**excise taxes:** Taxes on acts, not property. Sales of liquor are subject to excise taxes, for example.

**face value:** The principal of a stock, bond, or other security; also, the principal of an insurance policy. Face value is sometimes called *par value.*

**fair market value:** The reasonable price of an asset. Fair market value is the price that a willing seller and buyer would negotiate for an asset, given that both know all the facts and are under no compulsion to buy or sell.

**Federal Deposit Insurance Corporation (FDIC):** Federal agency that insures bank accounts against bank failures. At this writing, the FDIC insures accounts up to $250,000.

**federal funds rate:** Interest rate charged to commercial banks for purchasing federal funds. The federal funds rate is the benchmark for many commercial credit rates, including short-term business loans.

**federal unemployment tax:** Tax paid on wages and salaries to pay for federal and state unemployment programs.

**finance charge:** The cost of interest payments, filing fees, and other costs apart from the actual cost of an item. The finance charge is what you pay when you finance a purchase.

**finance company:** A private company that issues loans.

**Financial Accounting Standards Board (FASB):** The board that establishes rules for certified public accountants (CPAs). This board also determines the generally accepted accounting principles.

**fiscal year:** A period of 12 months for which a company plans its budget and reports on its financial activity. The fiscal year and the calendar year don't always coincide; the fiscal year can begin at any point in the calendar year.

**fixed asset:** A tangible asset, such as equipment, that a company can't dispose of without interrupting normal business activities.

**fixed-rate loan:** A loan whose rate of interest doesn't change.

**fixture:** Personal property that becomes part of real property because of the way in which it's used. *Fixture* is a legal term. If you build shelves into a wall in your rented apartment, they become a fixture — that is, part of the rental property.

**foreclosure:** Legal proceeding in which a lender attempts to obtain the collateral that was secured for a defaulted loan.

**foreign exchange:** Converting the currency of one country to its equivalent in the currency of another country.

**foreign trade:** Importing and exporting goods between nations.

**forged check:** A check whose drawer signature or endorsement signature is invalid.

**forgery:** Fraudulently altering a document, such as a check.

**Form 1099:** The disclosure form filed with the Internal Revenue Service that lists all unearned and miscellaneous income.

**franchise:** A business arrangement whereby one party is allowed to use another party's name for a fee. Fast-food eateries are the best examples of franchises.

**franchise tax:** A tax imposed by a state on a business such as for the privilege of doing business within the state.

**fraud:** Intentional deception undertaken to trick someone else into parting with something of value. No legal definition of *fraud* exists.

**future value:** The value that a stock, bond, or commodity will attain in the future.

**futures:** Commodities to be delivered and paid for at a future date at a price agreed on by the buyer and seller.

**garnishment:** Court judgment ordering a lender to be given part of the wages or salary of a borrower who has defaulted on a loan.

**general partner:** A co-owner of a business. General partners receive a share of the business's profit and are partly responsible for its debts and liabilities.

**generally accepted accounting principles (GAAP):** The rules and guidelines that certified public accountants use when preparing financial statements.

**general-obligation bond:** A bond issued to pay for public works projects, issued by a state or municipal government; also called a *G-O bond.*

**GI loan:** Name for special mortgage loans available to veterans of the U.S. armed services.

**gift tax:** A tax on gifts of cash or property. Gift taxes are paid by the donor.

**gilt-edged:** Name for low-risk AAA corporate bonds that have proven earnings.

**going concern:** Name to describe a business that is in operation and is expected to remain so in the future.

**gross estate:** The property in an estate before debts, taxes, and other expenses are paid. The net estate is what remains after these expenses are paid.

**guaranteed bond:** A bond whose principal and interest are backed by a corporation other than the issuer.

**guarantor:** A person or corporation that guarantees that a debt will be paid if another party defaults. Guarantors are considered to be co-endorsers of a debt and therefore are liable for the debt.

**guaranty:** A promise on the part of a person or corporation to pay the debt of another party if that party defaults on a debt.

**Health Savings Account (HSA):** A type of tax-advantaged medical savings account available to taxpayers who are enrolled in qualified high-deductible health plans.

**high-deductible health plan:** Health insurance plan with generally lower premiums but a higher deductible. As of 2022, a high-deductible health plan must have a minimum annual deductible of $1,400 for self-coverage or $2,800 for family coverage. Maximum out-of-pocket expenses would be $7,050 for an individual and $14,100 for a family.

**illiquid:** Refers to assets that aren't easy to liquidate — that is, to convert to cash. Examples include real estate, antiques, and cars.

**import taxes:** Taxes levied on certain imported items. Most nations have import taxes to protect domestic markets from foreign competition.

**income statement:** A report describing a corporation's activities, its profit, and its losses over a fixed period.

**indemnity:** An obligation to pay all costs of damage, pain, or suffering.

**indenture:** A document that states the terms under which a bond is issued. The indenture declares the maturity date, the interest, and other information.

**index:** A numerical measurement that compares past and present economic activity. The Dow Jones Industrial Average is an index of stock performance. The Consumer Price Index measures the price of consumer goods.

**Individual Retirement Account (IRA):** A retirement account into which individuals can deposit $6,000 (or $7,000 if you're 50 or older) annually out of earnings. IRAs provide two significant income tax benefits: IRA contributions may reduce an individual's current taxable income, and IRA earnings aren't taxed until withdrawal.

**Individual Retirement Account rollover:** Rule allowing holders of IRAs to pass on the accumulated savings in one IRA to another IRA, provided that they do so within the first 60 days of closing the first IRA.

**inflation:** Rise in prices. Inflation is caused by excess purchasing power among the general populace and by increasing production costs, which producers pass on to consumers.

**insolvency:** Inability to pay debts.

**installment contract:** Agreement to pay for goods in fixed installments, such as weekly or monthly.

**installment credit:** A loan that is repaid in monthly payments of the same amount.

**insufficient funds:** What you have if you try to write a check for $10 and you have only $7.50 in your checking account, or if you try to withdraw $20 from a savings account with $18 in it. See also *overdraft*.

**intangible assets:** The assets of a company that aren't property but are assets, nonetheless. An established clientele, for example, is an intangible asset.

**interest:** Amount of money paid to borrow capital. Typically, the interest is expressed as a percentage of the principal that was borrowed.

**interest rate:** The price of borrowing money. The interest rate is usually expressed as a percentage of the total principal borrowed, although sometimes, the rate of interest on a loan is tied to an index of some kind.

**interest-only loan:** A loan that requires the borrower to pay only interest for the term of the loan. Loan payments on an interest-only loan don't reduce the loan balance. At the end of the loan, the borrower makes a balloon payment equal to the original (and ending) loan balance.

**interim report:** A report showing stockholders how a company is doing. An interim report appears before the company's annual report.

**interim statement:** A statement regarding account balances that you can get from an automatic teller machine (ATM). Interim statements aren't as detailed as monthly statements.

**internal rate of return (IRR):** The profit that an investment earns expressed as a percentage. Typically, IRRs are stated as annual profit percentages. On an investment that pays interest and for which there is no change in value, such as a bank savings account, the interest rate is the IRR.

**International Financial Reporting Standards (IFRS):** Supposedly, a global standard for accounting that everyone says will someday be used everywhere, but that no one believes will actually ever be used inside the world's largest economy: the United States (which uses generally accepted accounting principles).

**interstate commerce:** Commercial trading of goods across state lines.

**inventory:** In a business, a list of stock on hand, with the value of each item and the total value of all items listed by category.

**involuntary bankruptcy:** A petition by creditors asking a bankruptcy court to declare a firm bankrupt when the firm has failed to pay its debts and meet its financial obligations; also called a *creditor's opinion*.

**involuntary lien:** A lien made by the judgment of a court without the consent of the property owner.

**judgment:** The official decision of a court of law.

**judgment lien:** A court order placing a lien on the property of a debtor.

**judicial sale:** A sale of property, as ordered by a court to satisfy a debt. A foreclosure is an example of a judicial sale.

**junior mortgage:** A second or subsequent mortgage on a property. If the property is in default, junior mortgages are paid only after the first mortgage has been paid.

**Keogh plan:** A retirement plan that allows you to set aside some of your wages or salary for retirement. Keogh plans are more complex to set up and to administer than SEP/IRA (Simplified Employee Pension/Individual Retirement Account) plans, but they may allow larger contributions.

**kicker:** An extra condition imposed by a lender before the lender will approve a loan. Part ownership in the property or a share of its proceeds is an example of a kicker.

**kiting:** See *check kiting*.

**lagging indicator:** An economic indicator that usually reflects not where the economy is headed, but where it has been. The gross national product (GNP), for example, is a lagging indicator because increases or declines in the GNP aren't registered until after the fact.

**late charge:** A charge for tardiness in paying a bill or a mortgage payment.

**lease:** A contract that gives a person or business the right to use a property for an agreed-on price and time period.

**leasehold:** The right of occupancy that tenants enjoy as part of a lease.

**leverage:** Credit acquired to improve a person's or company's ability to invest or speculate.

**leveraged buyout:** A deal in which one company takes over another and uses the acquired company's assets to pay back the loans that were taken out to take over the company in the first place.

**liability:** All debts and obligations of a business.

**liability insurance:** Insurance protecting the policyholder against financial losses resulting from injury done to others.

**lien:** A charge against real or personal property to secure the repayment of a debt.

**limited liability company:** Similar to a corporation, a business form that shields investors from risk. Limited liability companies are chameleons for tax purposes and may be treated as sole proprietorships, partnerships, or corporations, depending on the number of owners and on the tax elections that those owners have made.

**limited partnership:** A partnership in which profits and responsibility for liabilities and debts are shared according to how much of the business each partner owns.

**line of credit:** A commitment on the part of a bank to lend up to a certain amount of money to a borrower.

**liquidity:** Turning assets such as property into cash. An asset with good liquidity can be sold or converted to cash easily.

**long-term security:** A security that matures in ten or more years.

**maker:** The writer of a check.

**management report:** A report describing company performance, prepared monthly for the officers of a corporation.

**maturity:** The date when the borrower is obliged to pay back the loan.

**maximum out-of-pocket amount:** The most you can pay for insurance in a year. Usually, the maximum out-of-pocket amount is the sum of the premium, the deductible, and all co-payments.

**mechanic's lien:** A lien on real property made by a contractor or builder for overdue payment. A builder can request a mechanic's lien if they haven't been paid according to the contract made to build or improve the property.

**member:** An investor in a limited liability company.

**merger:** An arrangement in which two or more corporations pool their common stock and become one corporation.

**minimum balance:** The least amount of money that can be kept in a savings or checking account. Letting the balance drop below the minimum sometimes incurs a service charge.

**minimum payment:** The smallest payment that can be made on a monthly credit card bill without incurring a service charge.

**minor:** In most states, a person under age 18. Minors don't have all the legal rights or responsibilities of adults.

**money market fund (MMF):** A mutual fund that invests in Treasury bills, certificates of deposit (CDs), and other short-term debt instruments. Investors own shares in the fund and receive regular interest payments.

**money market rates:** The rate of return paid by individual money market funds.

**monopoly:** A situation in which a person or corporation has complete control of a market through ownership of source materials, ownership of distribution in a certain area, or ownership of the means by which the product is made.

**mortgage:** A deed giving ownership of a property to a borrower on the condition that the borrower makes all interest and principal payments to a lender. The lender owns the mortgage until the borrower pays in full, after which the borrower becomes sole owner of the property.

**mortgagee:** The lender who supplies mortgages and collects mortgage payments.

**mortgagor:** The mortgage borrower who must pay the interest and principal.

**negotiable:** Capable of being transferred from one party to another. Checks, drafts, securities, and commercial paper are negotiable.

**net worth:** The total value of the assets of a business less the liabilities.

**nonrecourse loan:** A loan for which, if the borrower defaults, the lender has no recourse except to foreclose on the borrower's collateral.

**notary public:** A public officer who attests to the authenticity of deeds, affidavits, and depositions.

**note:** A written promise to pay a debt or sum of money.

**notes payable:** In a general ledger, an account showing the business's liability for promissory notes.

**notes receivable:** In a general ledger, an account showing the business's promissory notes received from customers.

**not-for-profit corporation:** An organization that doesn't distribute its profits, if there are any, to owners. Profits are plowed back into the corporation's capital fund.

**novation:** An agreement to remove one party from a contract and replace that party with another. All parties in the contract must agree to the novation substitute.

**online banking service:** A service offered by a bank that allows you to download bank statements and to make electronic fund transfers and payments by using a computer with an Internet connection.

**open-end lease:** A car lease requiring monthly payments, at the end of which the borrower can make a large balloon payment to buy the car outright or return the car to the lender.

**operating lease:** A lease covering a time period shorter than the economic life of the asset. Operating leases can be canceled at any time.

**option:** A contract giving a dealer or broker the right to buy or sell a security during a certain time period at a certain price.

**original issue discount (OID):** The difference between what a bond costs when it was issued and its price at maturity.

**original maturity:** The time between the day a bond was issued and the day it reaches maturity. The current maturity is the time between today's date and the date the bond reaches maturity.

**origination fee:** The fee that lenders charge loan applicants to handle loan applications and to conduct credit investigations.

**overdraft:** The amount that a check exceeds what is in the checking account that it was written against. If you write a check for $20, and you have only $15 in your checking account, you have a $5 overdraft.

**partnership:** A business with two or more owners who share in the profits, as well as the liability for debts.

**Patient Protection and Affordable Care Act:** A federal statute intended to increase health insurance quality and affordability as well as lower the uninsured rate, which affects both businesses with employees and individuals. This act is also known as Obamacare.

**payee:** The person or party to whom a check is written.

**payroll taxes:** Taxes on a payroll, including Social Security taxes and employment insurance taxes.

**penalty clause:** The clause in many banking contracts stating that customers must pay a penalty for late mortgage payments, early withdrawals of savings accounts, and the like.

**pension fund:** A fund set up by a corporation to provide for its employees in retirement. Typically, employees contribute a portion of their paychecks to the fund.

**pension plan:** A plan by which a company provides for its employees in retirement. Employees — sometimes with matching contributions from employers — contribute to a pension fund, which is used to make investments as part of the plan.

**perfect title:** A title to a property that is free of debts, liens, previous claims, and other encumbrances.

**perfected lien:** A lien that has not only been filed by the lienholder, but also is in force.

**periodic rate:** The price of credit, expressed as a percentage and charged at periodic intervals.

**permanent financing:** A long-term mortgage, typically used to finance construction projects, covering all requirements of the project from legal costs to building materials.

**personal identification number (PIN):** The password or number that you punch in at an automated teller machine (ATM) to make deposits and withdrawals; also known as an *access code.*

**personal property:** Items and things, as opposed to *real property,* such as buildings and land. By definition, personal property isn't immovable; in other words, it can be moved. A baseball card is personal property; a baseball field is real property.

**personal property tax:** Tax on valuable personal property, such as jewelry, cars, and yachts; also called a *luxury tax.*

**pledge:** Placing property or collateral with a lender to secure a loan. A watch left with a pawnbroker in return for a loan is a pledge.

**point:** In stock prices, a point equals $1; in bond prices, a point equals $10.

**portfolio:** The term for the total assets and investments held by an individual, company, or institution. For reporting and tracking purposes, a portfolio can be divided into smaller portfolios, such as the loan portfolio, land portfolio, and so on.

**posting:** Recording accounting entries in a general ledger.

**power of attorney:** A legal document that lets someone you trust run your financial affairs if you become unable to do so.

**premium:** The sum above the face value of a bond when the bond is purchased at an above-par price. In insurance, a premium is the amount that you pay for insurance coverage.

**present value:** The current-day equivalent of some future amount or future value. In converting future values to present values, one adjusts for compound interest and for inflation.

**price/earnings ratio:** The ratio between the current price of a stock and the earnings that it will make over a specific period of time. Investors use the price/earnings ratio to measure the value of stocks.

**prime rate:** The rate that banks charge their most trustworthy customers for commercial loans. Note that a bank's very best customers pay less than prime, however.

**principal:** The actual money borrowed in a loan, as distinguished from *interest,* the price of buying the loan. Also, principal is a deposit as distinguished from the interest that it earns.

**profit-sharing plan:** A plan by which employees share in the profits of a company, either by receiving bonuses or by having their profit shares put in a trust. Profit-sharing plans encourage employees to be more productive and more loyal to their companies.

**promissory note:** A written promise to pay a sum of money at a future date to a specific person or to the bearer of the written promise; also known as an *IOU.*

**property taxes:** Taxes on property, including real estate and stocks.

**proprietorship, sole:** A business owned by one person. Sole proprietorship is one of three types of business organizations; the other two are partnership and corporation.

**public offering:** A bond-issue offering to the general public.

**qualified business income:** Under U.S. tax law, the income earned by a sole proprietorship, partnership, Subchapter S corporation, or real estate investor. Typically, some percentage of qualified business income has been tax-free since 2018.

**qualified opinion:** An accountant's opinion letter that (essentially) indirectly says a firm's financial statements don't comply with generally accepted accounting principles.

**quiet title action:** A legal action meant to resolve all claims against a property.

**quorum:** The minimum number of people who must be present at a corporate meeting to conduct business.

**quote:** The highest bid to buy and the lowest offer to sell a security or commodity; also called a *quotation.*

**rate of return:** Money made on invested capital.

**real income:** Income measured for what it can buy, not in dollars-and-cents terms. The real income of a low-wage earner may be higher than that of someone who earns higher wages if the low-wage earner lives in a region where goods and housing are inexpensive.

**real property:** Land and buildings on the land, as opposed to personal property, which is composed of movable items such as jewelry and equipment.

**real rate of return:** The rate of return on an investment that takes into account how rates are affected by inflation. The real rate of return is the rate of return less the rate of inflation over the length of the investment.

**real-interest rate:** The interest rate that takes into account how interest yields are reduced by inflation. To get the real-interest rate, you subtract the inflation rate in a given period from interest earnings in the same period.

**realized profit/loss:** The cash profit or loss from the sale of a security.

**rebate:** A return of part of a payment, made after the payment is received. Rebates are offered as incentives for consumers to buy or use products.

**receiver:** A person assigned by a court to help a bankrupt business reorganize its finances, satisfy its creditors, and become profitable.

**receivership:** The status of a bankrupt business to which a receiver has been assigned.

**redemption:** Exchanging bonds for cash when the bonds reach maturity.

**registered check:** A check purchased at a bank and backed by the bank that can be presented as payment to a third party. Registered checks work like money orders.

**remittance slip:** Attached to a check, a list of all deductions, corrections, discounts, taxes, and other information, along with the net amount of the check.

**reorganization:** After a business has declared bankruptcy, the restructuring of its assets to make it profitable again.

**repossession:** Seizing the collateral for a loan due to inability to pay the interest or principal. Repossession is usually the last recourse for failure to pay a debt.

**reserve:** Funds put aside for anticipated future costs.

**reserve requirements:** Reserves that banks are required to keep on hand for their basic operations. These reserves are deposited at the bank's district Federal Reserve Bank.

**residual value:** The value that an asset has when the asset's user or owner is done using it.

**restraint of trade:** A reference to the concept, ingrained in U.S. law and in the American tradition, that no restrictions should be placed on the free flow of commerce.

**restrictive covenant:** A clause in an agreement or contract prohibiting a party or parties from taking certain actions. The most common restrictive covenant in business is one that prohibits a seller of a business from engaging in the same business for a certain number of years.

**retained earnings:** Business profits that are retained for use in expansion rather than being paid in dividends to stockholders.

**return on assets:** A company's profits as a percentage of its assets. Return on assets is one way to measure a company's profitability.

**return on investment:** A performance measure to evaluate the efficiency of an investment. When the earnings derived from a piece of capital equipment equal the price paid for the piece of equipment, you have a perfect return on your investment.

**revenue:** The total income from a given endeavor; also, gross income from an investment.

**reverse split:** When stockholders exchange stock such that each owns the same number of shares. Reverse splits are undertaken so that all stockholders own the same percentage of a corporation.

**revocable trust:** A trust giving property to heirs that can be changed or revoked at any time by the person who originates the trust. Under this arrangement, the property is transferred to the heirs on the death of the trust originator, and the estate doesn't need to go through probate.

**revolving credit:** A form of credit in which the account holder is given a credit line, runs up a bill, and pays off the amount owed in monthly payments. If the amount owed isn't paid off monthly, interest charges are made. A minimum monthly payment is usually required on outstanding credit loans. Most credit card accounts are revolving credit accounts.

**right of foreclosure:** The right of a lender to foreclose on a mortgaged property if the borrower can't meet mortgage obligations.

**right of redemption:** The right of a debtor to buy a property at a sale of foreclosure if they have the means to do so. To redeem the property this way, the debtor must pay the interest and principal on the defaulted mortgage, as well as all foreclosure costs incurred by the lender.

**right of survivorship:** The right of surviving spouses to inherit the property of deceased spouses.

**risk:** In financial terms, the possibility that an investment won't be repaid and that the method of investment will be rendered unprofitable by market conditions.

**run:** A situation in which many depositors try to withdraw their money from a bank on short notice. When depositors fear that a bank is failing or otherwise lose confidence in the bank, a bank run can result.

**safe deposit box:** A small safe in a bank vault that can be rented for storing valuables and important papers.

**salary-reduction plan:** A retirement plan in which money is taken automatically from employees' salaries and put in a retirement fund, such as a 401(k).

**sales tax:** A tax levied by state and local governments, usually as a percentage of retail sales.

**savings account:** A deposit bank account that yields interest. Cash can be deposited or withdrawn at the discretion of the holder.

**savings bank:** A bank that accepts deposits from customers and invests it in mortgages and securities.

**savings bond:** A U.S. government bond, issued to finance the debt of the U.S. government. Savings bonds earn variable interest and are sold in denominations of $25 to $10,000.

**seasonal adjustment:** Adjusting data collected throughout the year to an annual rate for the purposes of analysis. Retail sales rise in December, when people shop for the holidays, for example. Therefore, retail sales figures for January need to be adjusted downward.

**seasonal credit:** The line of credit extended to businesses during peak manufacturing and sales cycles.

**second mortgage:** Another mortgage on a property, usually taken out to provide capital for home improvements or to finance a business. The obligations due to the lender of a second mortgage are subordinate to the obligations owed to the lender of a first mortgage.

**secondary mortgage market:** A market in which first mortgages, or residential mortgages, are pooled and sold to investors. The secondary mortgage market serves as a capital fund for the mortgage originators, who sell their mortgages for the secondary market.

**secured credit card:** A credit card backed by a savings account. Issuers of secured credit cards can draw on cardholders' savings accounts if cardholders are unable to pay their credit card bills.

**securities:** Stocks, bonds, and other financial instruments that can be traded in a securities market.

**Securities and Exchange Commission (SEC):** The regulatory agency charged with overseeing laws regarding the buying and selling of securities. Companies that sell securities, and brokers and dealers who trade in them, must register with the SEC.

**security agreement:** A document that gives a lender a claim to the assets that the borrower has put up as collateral for a loan. The security agreement must be signed by the borrower to be valid.

**security interest:** The claim of a lender to assets that the borrower has pledged as collateral to back up a loan.

**self-insurance:** A rainy-day fund set aside for emergencies, illness, and periods of unemployment.

**seller's market:** Raising demand and raising the price that sellers can offer goods in short supply.

**senior lien:** The first mortgage on a property. When two or more liens have been placed on a property, the senior lien takes precedence over other liens and must be satisfied first.

**serial bonds:** Bonds from the same issue that mature at different times. This way, the bonds don't all fall due at the same time and strain the finances of the issuer.

**service charge:** A bank charge, such as the charge issued when an account is overdrawn or a check bounces.

**settlement date:** The actual date of the transfer of a security from the buyer to the seller.

**severally but not jointly:** In a stock offering, an arrangement in which the people selling the stock are each responsible for selling their part but not for selling the entire offering. In a *jointly but severally* arrangement, all parties are responsible for the sale of the offering.

**sheriff's sale:** An auction of a borrower's property as part of a foreclosure. The proceeds go to help pay the borrower's debts.

**short-term financing:** A loan that falls due in less than one year.

**signature loan:** A loan given without collateral, with only the borrower's promise to pay and their signature on a promissory note. Such loans are given on the basis of the good standing of the borrower.

**simple IRA:** A simplified pension plan for small businesses that want to give their employees retirement savings options. Simple IRAs work much like 401(k)s but at a much lower administrative cost to the employer.

**Simplified Employee Pension Plan (SEP):** A retirement plan for small businesses, allowing people in small businesses to set aside up to 25 percent of employee wages and up to 20 percent for owner profits for retirement.

**Small Business Administration (SBA):** An agency of the federal government that helps provide credit to small businesses.

**Social Security:** Insurance benefits provided by the federal government for old-age, disability, and survivor benefits.

**sole proprietorship:** A business owned by one person. Sole proprietorship is one of three types of business organizations; the other two are partnership and corporation.

**special offering:** A block of securities so large that it can't be offered on the trading floor without depressing prices. Instead of being traded on the floor, special offerings are traded through members of the exchange, who sell them on their own.

**specialist:** A broker or dealer who specializes in trading a single commodity or security.

**specie:** Coins, not paper money.

**speculation:** Trading at a greater risk to obtain a fast profit.

**speculator:** A person who trades in commodities, stocks, or bonds with the idea of making a quick profit by taking many risks.

**split:** The division of existing stock into more shares. Individual stocks lose value, but the total value of the stock stays the same. Stock splits are often undertaken to make the stock easier to trade when companies are bought and sold.

**squeeze:** A shortage of funds in the money market, which causes a demand for money and a hike in interest rates.

**stale check:** A check more than six months old.

**stamp taxes:** Taxes in the form of stamps, which manufacturers must buy and stick on their products or securities before they can be sold. You can see tax stamps on some brands of whiskey, for example.

**Standard & Poor's:** An advisory service that rates securities for their creditworthiness.

**standard of living:** The goods and services that a social group requires for its well-being. The standard of living is an abstract term and can't be measured against an index.

**statute of frauds:** A legal statute that says a contract can't be enforced unless it has the signature of the person against whom it is being enforced. In the case of a mortgage or other assumable debt, the signature of the borrower is required.

**statute of limitations:** A limit on the time within which a legal action can be brought or a file claimed.

**stock certificate:** A written document giving title to a share or shares of stock.

**stock exchange:** A market where stocks are traded.

**stock purchase option:** A benefit offered to employees, giving them the option to buy stock in the companies that they work for.

**stock split:** The dividing of existing stock into more shares. Individual stocks lose value, but the total value of the stock stays the same. Stock splits are often undertaken to make the stock easier to trade when companies are bought and sold.

**stop order:** An order to buy or sell a stock or commodity when it reaches a certain price.

**stop payment:** To inform a bank not to honor a check. Even after a check is written and delivered, a bank customer can stop payment on it if they think that the check was written in error.

**subsidiary corporation:** A company that is owned wholly or partly by another company, called the *parent company*. The parent company usually owns a majority of the stock in the subsidiary.

**surcharge:** An extra charge for people who pay with credit cards instead of cash. The surcharge pays for the extra costs of processing credit card payments.

**surety:** A guarantee that a debt will be repaid; also, a person who is legally responsible for a debt.

**surety bond:** An agreement that if a housing development can't be completed, an insurance company will take charge of the project, settle all disputes, and finish the project if necessary. Municipal development projects require surety bonds.

**surtax:** An added tax on income that has already been taxed once.

**tariff:** Taxes on import goods, levied to protect domestic industries or to raise revenue.

**tax lien:** A lien on property for failure to pay property taxes.

**tax sale:** An auction of property to raise money for the payment of delinquent taxes.

**taxable estate:** The part of an estate that is subject to taxes. The taxable estate is what is left after all debts, funeral expenses, and taxes are paid.

**tax-deferred savings:** Tax-free savings that can be put in an individual retirement account (IRA) or other retirement plan. Taxes aren't imposed on the interest or principal until funds are withdrawn at age 59½ or later.

**tax-free rollover:** The automatic renewal of a certificate of deposit (CD), tax-free at present rates of interest; also, the automatic tax-free reinvestment of money market funds.

**taxpayer identification number (TIN):** For taxation purposes, the number that identifies corporations, nonprofit organizations, associations, and partnerships to the Internal Revenue Service. Sole proprietors and individuals are identified by their Social Security numbers.

**teller's check:** A check written by a bank against its own funds. Teller's checks are guaranteed to be redeemable because they're drawn on banks.

**term:** The time that it takes for a loan or deposit to mature. The term is usually expressed in months.

**third-party check:** A check transferred by the endorser to another party. The endorser writes *Pay to the order of* and then the third party's name on the check, making it redeemable by the third party.

**time value of money:** A general rule that says a dollar today is worth more than a dollar a year from today because if you have a dollar today, you can invest it and earn interest over the next year.

**title:** Ownership of real property. A deed, bill of sale, or certificate is required to prove title.

**title company:** A company that determines who has ownership of a property. After it conducts a title search, the company issues a certificate of title to the owner.

**title defect:** A claim, obstruction, or other condition that makes it difficult to determine the owner of a property.

**treasurer:** A financial officer of a corporation whose job is, among other duties, to manage cash payments and deposits, procure and budget funds, handle payroll, and discharge tax liabilities.

**Treasury bill:** A short-term bill issued by the U.S. government to cover its debt. Treasury bills are in $100 denominations; they mature in periods of 4, 13, 26, or 52 weeks.

**Treasury bond:** A long-term bond issued by the U.S. government to cover its debts. Treasury bonds are sold in denominations of $100 or more.

**trust:** Property held by one person or persons for the benefit of others.

**Truth in Lending law:** Federal Reserve regulation (Regulation DD) establishing what information lenders must disclose to borrowers, including how finance charges are imposed, when additional charges will be made, and when a borrower may acquire a security interest in a property.

**underlying lien:** A lien to which other liens and property claims are subordinate. A first mortgage, for example, is an underlying lien.

**underwriter:** The person at an insurance company who processes applications for insurance and decides who gets insurance and who doesn't get insurance; alternatively, the person at a mortgage company who processes applications for mortgages, and decides who does and doesn't get a mortgage.

**unearned income:** Income earned from investments and interest.

**unemployment insurance:** A federal- and state-run program that provides an income to unemployed workers. Contributions to unemployment insurance are usually deducted from salaries and wages.

**Uniform Commercial Code (UCC):** Standardized state laws that establish rules for contracts, including how to prepare negotiables and handle deeds of title.

**Uniform Consumer Credit Code:** A law applicable in some states outlining how lenders and borrowers should treat consumer loans of less than $25,000. The code sets guidelines for fair lending practices and describes how lenders can recoup defaulted loans.

**uninsured depositor:** A depositor with a savings or checking account larger than the amount insured by the Federal Deposit Insurance Corporation (FDIC).

**unsecured loan:** A loan given without the borrower's posting collateral or providing any other security.

**U.S. savings bond:** A U.S. government bond issued to finance the debt of the U.S. government. Savings bonds earn variable interest and are sold in denominations of $25 to $10,000.

**usury:** The lending of money at an exorbitant rate of interest. By law, usury is defined as charging an interest rate above the legal limit.

**variable annuity:** An annuity paid out at a variable rate, depending on interest accrued on a principal.

**variable-rate loan:** A loan whose rate of interest changes. The rate is determined by a standard index, such as the prime rate.

**variable-rate mortgage:** A mortgage whose interest rate is adjusted periodically. Variable-rate mortgages usually are tied to some sort of money index, such as the prime lending rate or the cost of Treasury bills. When the index goes up or down, so does the monthly mortgage payment. A variable-rate mortgage is also called an *adjustable-rate mortgage (ARM)*.

**venture capital:** Capital available for new enterprises and start-up companies.

**vested interest:** In financial terminology, a stake in something that will give you money in the future. Employees have a vested interest in the prosperity of their company pension plans, for example.

**void:** Null and no longer applicable, such as a voided check.

**volume of trading:** The total number of shares traded in a stock market. Trading volume is a measure of market activity.

**voluntary bankruptcy:** When a debtor declares bankruptcy to gain relief from creditors.

**wage garnishment:** A court judgment ordering a lender to be given part of the wages of a borrower who has defaulted on a loan.

**Wall Street:** The famous street in New York, the address of the New York Stock Exchange, and the place where so many financial decisions are made by people in horn-rimmed glasses.

**warranty:** A guarantee that what is written in a contract is indeed true.

**wholly owned subsidiary:** A subsidiary completely owned by its parent company.

**wire transfer:** The electronic transfer of money, as opposed to transfer by check or another type of paper.

**withholding:** Taking deductions from income to cover taxes or liabilities.

**worker's compensation insurance:** By state law, insurance paid by employers in case of injury to their employees on the job.

**write-off:** The removal of an item from an account ledger because the item has been fully depreciated or deemed to be worthless.

**yield curve:** A graph comparing the yields at maturity of different securities.

**yield to maturity:** The annual return, expressed as a percentage, of a bond or note redeemed at maturity.

**zero-coupon bond:** A bond issued without coupons and without a statement of its rate of interest.

**zero-coupon security:** A security that pays no interest until maturity, when the interest is paid in a lump sum.

# Index

## L

lagging indicator, 587
late charge, 587
Layout Designer tool, 161–164
Lead Center command, 187
Learn about Online Bill Payment command, 272
Learn about Point of Sale command, 187
lease, 587
leasehold, 587
lenders, 11
leverage, 587
leverage ratios
  about, 371
  debt equity ratio, 372
  debt ratio, 371–372
  fixed-charges coverage ratio, 373–375
  times interest earned ratio, 372–373
leveraged buyout, 587
liabilities
  about, 63
  accruing, 65–68
  borrowing money, 64
  defined, 10, 16
  making loan payments, 64–65
liability, 587
liability account, 37
liability insurance, 587
lien, 587
limited liability companies, 24
limited liability company, 587
limited liability company (LLC), 82
limited liability partnerships, 24
limited partnership, 587
line of credit, 587
Link Payment Services to Company File command, 187
liquidity, 400–401, 412, 587
liquidity ratios, 369–371
Loan Manager command, 272
loans
  paying, 64–65
  recording the payoff of, 42

logo, 159–160
long-term security, 587
luxury tax, 590

## M

Make Deposits command, 249
Make Deposits window, 251, 252
Make General Journal Entries window, 288–289, 351
maker, 587
Manage Login Settings section, 130
Manage Sales Tax command, 207
Manage Templates dialog box, 160
management report, 587
managers, 10
manufacturing firms, managing inventory in, 234–239
Margins tab, 308
Mark All Expenses as Billable check box, 150
Mark New Employees As Sales Reps check box, 137
master file lists
  about, 93
  Billing Rate Level list, 112–113
  Chart of Accounts list, 94–98
  classes, 101–103
  Customer list, 103–107
  Fixed Asset Items list, 111–112
  Item List, 98–99
  Other Names list, 113–114
  Payroll Item list, 100–101
  Price Level list, 99, 112
  Profile lists, 114–116
  Sales Tax Code list, 100
  Vendor list, 107–110
master files, 81
matching principle, 26, 41
maturity, 400, 587
maximum out-of-pocket amount, 587
McFedries, Paul, 402
mechanic's lien, 588
member, 588
Memorize button, 307
Memorize Check command, 262
Memorize Report dialog box, 307

# About the Author

**Stephen L. Nelson** is a CPA in Redmond, Washington. He provides accounting, business advisory, and tax planning and preparation services to small businesses such as manufacturers, retailers, professional service firms, and start-up technology companies. He also teaches CPAs how to help their clients use QuickBooks more effectively.

Curiously enough, Nelson is also the most prolific computer book writer of all time, according to a recent feature in *The Wall Street Journal*. He's also the bestselling author of books about how to use computers to manage personal and business finances. In fact, Nelson's 100-plus books have sold more than 5,000,000 copies in English and have been translated into more than a dozen other languages.

Steve holds a BS in accounting, an MBA in finance, and a Master of Science in Taxation. He's been a CPA for more than 35 years. He used to work as a senior consultant with Arthur Andersen & Co. and was an adjunct professor of tax at Golden Gate University, where he taught S corporation and LLC tax law. He also has been the controller and treasurer of a 50-person manufacturing firm and has run his own manufacturing firm. Steve is also the bestselling author of *Quicken For Dummies* and many editions of *QuickBooks For Dummies*.

# Dedication

To the entrepreneurs and small-business people of the world. You folks create most of the new jobs.

# Author's Acknowledgments

Okay, I'm not going to make this an Academy Awards–style speech, but let me thank just a few people. First, I want to thank my business school and tax professors at Central Washington University, the University of Washington, and Golden Gate University. Next, thanks to the business clients who've given me the honor of working with them and teaching me about their businesses and industries. I want to thank my colleague Christian Block who helped me assemble the art for this book and update the material for the newest version of QuickBooks. Finally, I want to thank all my friends and colleagues at John Wiley & Sons, who gave me the distinct honor of writing not only this book but also *QuickBooks For Dummies* (over 30 editions!).

## Publisher's Acknowledgments

**Associate Publisher:** Kelsey Baird
**Project Editor:** Kezia Endsley
**Copy Editor:** Kezia Endsley
**Technical Editor:** David Ringstrom

**Production Editor:** Magesh Elangovan
**Cover Image:** © baranq/Shutterstock